STAFFING
ORGANIZATIONS

Herbert G. Heneman III
University of Wisconsin–Madison

Timothy A. Judge
University of Florida

Mendota House
Middleton, WI

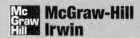 McGraw-Hill
Irwin

Boston   Burr Ridge, IL   Dubuque, IA   Madison, WI   New York   San Francisco   St. Louis
Bangkok   Bogotá   Caracas   Kuala Lumpur   Lisbon   London   Madrid   Mexico City
Milan   Montreal   New Dehli   Santiago   Seoul   Singapore   Sydney   Taipei   Toronto

McGraw-Hill Higher Education

A Division of The McGraw-Hill Companies

STAFFING ORGANIZATIONS

This book is printed on acid-free paper.

This publication is designed to provide accurate and authoritative information in regard to the subject matter covered. It is sold with the understanding that the publisher is not engaged in rendering legal, accounting, or other professional services. If legal advice or other expert assistance is required, the services of a competent professional should be sought. (FROM A DECLARATION OF PRINCIPLES JOINTLY ADOPTED BY A COMMITTEE OF THE AMERICAN BAR ASSOCIATION AND A COMMITTEE OF PUBLISHERS.)

domestic   2 3 4 5 6 7 9 0 DOC/DOC 0 9 8 7 6 5 4 3 2
international   1 2 3 4 5 6 7 9 0 DOC/DOC 0 9 8 7 6 5 4 3 2

ISBN 0-07-248259-1

Publisher: *John E. Biernat*
Executive editor: *John Weimeister*
Editorial coordinator: *Trina Hauger*
Senior marketing manager: *Ellen Cleary*
Project manager: *Destiny Rynne*
Senior production supervisor: *Michael R. McCormick*
Coordinator freelance design: *Mary L. Christianson*
Supplement producer: *Joyce J. Chappetto*
Senior digital content specialist: *Brian Nacik*
Typeface: *11/12.5 Times Roman*
Compositor: *Impressions Book and Journal Services, Inc.*
Printer: *R. R. Donnelley & Sons Company*

Address orders and customer service questions to: *Address editorial correspondence to:*
McGraw-Hill Higher Education   *Herbert G. Heneman III, President*
1333 Burr Ridge Parkway   *Mendota House, Inc.*
Burr Ridge, IL 60527   *5621 Mendota Drive*
1-800-338-3987   *Middleton, WI 53562*
        (608) 233-4417

Library of Congress Control Number   2002107965

www.mhhe.com

Dedication
To Susan and Jill

AUTHOR PROFILES

Herbert G. Heneman III is the Dickson-Bascom Professor (Emeritus) in the School of Business, Management and Human Resources Department, at the University of Wisconsin–Madison. He also serves as a senior research associate in the Wisconsin Center for Education Research. Herb has been a visiting faculty member at the University of Washington and the University of Florida and was University Distinguished Visiting Professor at The Ohio State University. His research is in the areas of staffing, performance appraisal, union membership growth, work motivation, and compensation systems. He currently is investigating the design and effectiveness of compensation, evaluation, and staffing systems for school teachers. He is also currently on the Board of Directors of the Society for Human Resource Management Foundation and serves as its vice president for research. Herb is the senior author of three prior textbooks: *Managing Personnel and Human Resources: Strategies and Programs* (1981), *Perspectives on Personnel/Human Resource Management*, 3/e (1986), and *Personnel/Human Resource Management*, 4/e (1989). Herb is a fellow of the Academy of Management and former chair of its Human Resources Division, which honored him with its Career Achievement Award. He also is a member of the American Psychological Association, the Society for Industrial and Organizational Psychology, the Industrial Relations Research Association, the American Educational Research Association, the Society for Human Resource Management, the International Personnel Management Association, and the World at Work.

Timothy A. Judge is the Matherly-McKethan Eminent Scholar, Department of Management, Warrington College of Business, University of Florida. Prior to receiving his Ph.D. at the University of Illinois, Tim was a manager for Kohl's Department Stores. Tim also has served on the faculties of Cornell University and the University of Iowa.

Tim's primary research and teaching interests are in the areas of personality assessment, leadership, and staffing. He has published numerous articles on these topics and sits on the editorial review boards of six journals, including *Personnel Psychology* and *Journal of Applied Psychology*. Tim is chair of the Human Resources Division of the Academy of Management. He also is chair of the Scientific Affairs Committee for the Society of Industrial and Organizational Psychology.

Note to the Instructor:

Mendota House and McGraw-Hill/Irwin have combined their respective skills to bring *Staffing Organizations* to your classroom. This text is marketed and distributed by McGraw-Hill/Irwin. For assistance in obtaining information or supplementary material, please contact your McGraw-Hill/Irwin sales representative or the customer services division of McGraw-Hill/Irwin at 800-338-3987.

PREFACE

Designing and managing successful staffing processes are major challenges for an organization. These processes require multiple tools, techniques, activities, and participants. They must occur within a complex set of external influences beyond organizational control such as laws and regulations and labor markets. Science, past experience, and instinct must carefully blend together to create a process that maximizes the likelihood of effective staffing levels and successful person/job matches, both of which are important drivers of organizational effectiveness. This book seeks to both describe and prescribe staffing activities that can be undertaken to meet the staffing challenges.

The fourth edition of *Staffing Organizations* contains substantial changes that reflect the rapidly evolving terrain of strategic, technological, legal, and practical issues confronting organizations and their staffing systems. To reflect this evolution, we now define *staffing* as "the process of acquiring, deploying, and retaining a workforce of sufficient quantity and quality to create positive impacts on the organization's effectiveness." This definition emphasizes the strategic nature and importance of staffing, and it recognizes that both staffing levels and staffing quality (person/job and person/organization matches) must be reckoned with throughout the staffing process. A revision of the staffing organizations model reflects this new definition and guides the structural changes in the revision.

The first chapter, "Staffing Models and Strategy," has been substantially rewritten and expanded to elaborate on the new staffing definition and revised staffing organizations model and to emphasize strategic elements of staffing. Staffing's importance to organizational effectiveness is illustrated through quotes from organization leaders, survey results, organization's experiences, and emerging research findings. In addition, a series of strategic staffing decisions about staffing levels and quality are identified and explained. These decisions are amplified on throughout the book.

The last chapter, "Retention Management," is new. It reflects a recognition that although some loss of employees is inevitable, the organization should actively manage and minimize how many employees it loses as well as the types and quality of its employee losses. Strategic costs and benefits of turnover are discussed in detail to guide the development of explicit retention strategies and practices. The chapter also provides thorough analysis and guidelines for successfully managing retention in the context of both voluntary and involuntary (discharge, downsizing) turnover.

We have eliminated the chapter on economic conditions, labor markets, and labor unions and incorporated that material, in reduced form, in the chapter on staffing planning. We have also eliminated the appendices of federal regulations. The regulations are now readily accessible online, and Web addresses for them are provided. Summaries of the regulations, however, are given in the text. Though not eliminated, the chapter on measurement has been moved to become the lead chapter in Part Four, "Staffing Activities: Selection."

The new edition also reflects substantial technological and legal changes in staffing. Recruitment, selection, and staffing system management activities continue to incorporate technology in many ways that we explain. We also treat how applicants, employees, and staffing and line managers are affected by these new technologies. On the legal front, numerous new federal regulations have emerged that we cover, most notably the new Affirmative Action Programs regulations that replace Revised Order No. 4. We also incorporate Supreme Court decisions into the legal materials, though, as before, not by case name.

The new chapter structure of the book, and specific topical additions and updates for each chapter, are as follows:

Chapter One: Staffing Models and Strategy

- Definition of staffing
- Staffing levels model
- Staffing organizations model
- Importance to organizational effectiveness
- Strategic decisions—staffing levels and staffing quality
- Staffing system example—telephone company

Chapter Two: Legal Compliance

- EEO laws—state governments; personal liability for managers; U.S. citizens as overseas employees
- Consent decree example
- Definition of a disability
- Affirmative Action Program regulations
- Temporary foreign workers

Chapter Three: Planning

- External influences—economic conditions, labor markets, and labor unions
- Affirmative Action Program regulations

Chapter Four: Job Analysis

- Extrinsic rewards
- Intrinsic rewards

Chapter Five: External Recruitment

- Recruitment alliances
- Recruiter training
- Recruitment sources
- Online recruiting
- Recruitment communication
- Organization Web sites
- Affirmative Action Program regulations

Chapter Six: Internal Recruitment

- Targeted recruitment
- Job postings
- Employee referrals
- Glass ceiling
- Affirmative Action Program regulations

Chapter Seven: Measurement

- Testing procedures
- Applicant reactions
- Acquisition of tests and test manuals
- Professional standards

Chapter Eight: External Selection I

- Résumés
- Application blanks
- Educational requirements
- Reference reports
- Background checks

Chapter Nine: External Selection II

- Personality tests
- Situational judgment tests
- Structured interviews
- Drug testing
- Medical exams

Chapter Ten: Internal Selection

- Performance ratings
- Assessment centers

Chapter Eleven: Decision Making

- Face validity
- Weighting and combining scores
- Adverse impact

Chapter Twelve: Final Match

- Unfulfilled promises
- Differential starting pay
- Variable pay—short term and long term
- Hot skills premiums
- Severance packages
- Online salary information
- Reneging

Chapter Thirteen: Staffing System Management

- Job descriptions for staffing jobs
- Information systems and software
- Outsourcing
- Staffing metrics
- Staffing costs
- Affirmative Action Program regulations
- Arbitration

Chapter Fourteen: Retention Management

- All new material

Applications (cases and exercises) at the end of each chapter are an important part of the book. The revision contains seven new ones:

1. "Staffing Strategy for a New Plant" (Chapter One)
2. "Internet Recruiting" (Chapter Five)
3. "Reference Reports and Initial Assessment in a Start-Up Organization" (Chapter Eight)
4. "Promotion From Within at Citrus Glen" (Chapter Ten)
5. "Evaluating a Hiring and Variable Pay Program" (Chapter Twelve)
6. "Managerial Turnover: A Problem" (Chapter Fourteen)
7. "Retention: Deciding to Act" (Chapter Fourteen)

Finally, we thank our many colleagues at the University of Wisconsin–Madison, University of Florida, and elsewhere for their inputs and assistance. Their advice has been very helpful. We also thank Donna Wallace of the University of Wisconsin–Madison, the McGraw-Hill/Irwin publishing team, and Impressions Book and Journal Services, Inc., for their dedicated work in this collaborative undertaking.

CONTENTS

The Staffing Organizations Model

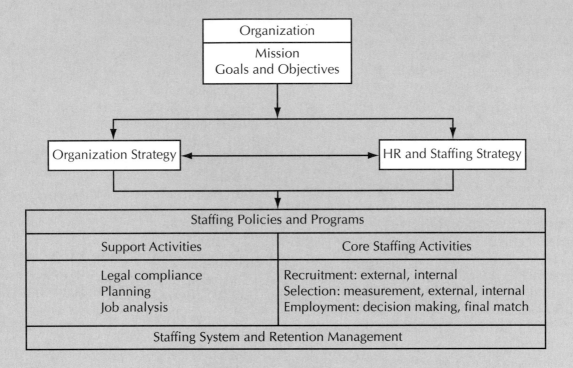

PART ONE

The Nature of Staffing

CHAPTER ONE
Staffing Models and Strategy

CHAPTER ONE

Staffing Models and Strategy

The Nature of Staffing
Definition of Staffing
Implications of Definition
Importance to Organizational Effectiveness

Staffing Models
Staffing Quantity: Levels
Staffing Quality: Person/Job Match
Staffing Quality: Person/Organization Match
Staffing System Components
Staffing Organizations

Staffing Strategy
Staffing Levels
Staffing Quality

Staffing System Examples
Police Department
Automobile Plant
Theme Park
Telephone Company

Plan for the Book

Summary

Discussion Questions

Applications

S taffing is a critical organizational function concerned with the acquisition, deployment, and retention of the organization's workforce. This chapter begins with a formal definition of staffing, followed by a detailed examination of the implications of the definition for helping us understand staffing systems. Staffing is also looked at from the perspective of the numerous ways staffing is important for organizational effectiveness.

Five models are then presented to elaborate on and illustrate various facets of staffing. The first model shows how projected workforce head-count requirements and availabilities are compared to determine the appropriate staffing level for the organization. The next two models illustrate staffing quality, which refers to matching a person's qualifications relative to the requirements of the job or organization. The person/job match model is the foundation of all staffing activities; the person/organization match model shows how person/job matching could extend to how well the person will also fit with the organization. The core staffing components model identifies recruitment, selection, and employment as the three key staffing activities, and it shows that both the organization and job applicant interact in these activities. The final model, staffing organizations, provides the entire framework for staffing and the structure of this book. It shows that organizations, human resources (HR), and staffing strategy interact to guide the conduct of staffing support activities (legal compliance, planning, job analysis) and core staffing activities (recruitment, selection, employment); employee retention and staffing system management are shown to cut across both types of activities.

Staffing strategy is then explored in detail by identifying and describing a set of 12 strategic staffing decisions that any organization is confronted with. Several of the decisions pertain to staffing levels, and the remainder to staffing quality.

Descriptions of several staffing systems are then given. The systems involve a police department, an automobile manufacturing plant, a theme park, and a telephone company. Though their staffing systems are very different in some respects, they share the components shown in the staffing organizations model.

Finally, the plan for the remainder of the book is presented. The overall structure of the book is shown, along with key features of each chapter.

THE NATURE OF STAFFING

Definition of Staffing

The following definition of staffing is offered and will be used throughout this book:

> Staffing is the process of acquiring, deploying, and retaining a workforce of sufficient quantity and quality to create positive impacts on the organization's effectiveness.

This straightforward definition contains several implications, which are identified and explained next.

Implications of Definition

Acquire, Deploy, Retain

Any organization must have staffing systems that guide the acquisition, deployment, and retention of its workforce. Acquisition activities involve external staffing systems that govern the initial intake of applicants into the organization. It involves planning for the numbers and types of people needed, establishing job requirements in the form of the qualifications or KSAOs (knowledge, skill, ability, and other characteristics) needed to perform the job effectively, establishing the types of rewards the job will provide, conducting external recruitment campaigns, using selection tools to evaluate the KSAOs that applicants possess, deciding which applicants are the most qualified and will receive job offers, and putting together job offers that applicants will hopefully accept.

Deployment refers to the placement of new hires on the actual job they will hold, something that may not be entirely clear at the time of hire, such as the specific work unit or geographic location. Deployment also encompasses guiding the movement of current employees throughout the organization through internal staffing systems that handle promotions, transfers, and new project assignments for employees. Internal staffing systems mimic external staffing systems in many respects, such as planning for promotion and transfer vacancies, establishing job requirements and job rewards, recruiting employees for the promotion or transfer opportunities, evaluating employees' qualifications, and making them job offers for the new position.

Retention systems seek to manage the inevitable flow of employees out of the organization. Sometimes these outflows are involuntary on the part of the employee, such as through layoffs or the sale of a business unit to another organization. Other outflows are voluntary in that they are initiated by the employee, such as leaving the organization to take another job (a potentially avoidable turnover by the organization) or leaving the organization to follow one's spouse or partner to a new geographic location (a potentially unavoidable turnover by the organization). Of course, no organization can or should seek to completely eliminate employee outflows, but the organization should try to minimize the types of turnover in which valued employees leave for "greener pastures" elsewhere—namely, voluntary-avoidable turnover. Such turnover can be very costly to the organization. So can turnover due to employee discharges and downsizing. Through various retention strategies and tactics, the organization can combat these types of turnover, seeking to retain those employees it thinks it cannot afford to lose.

Staffing as a Process or System

Staffing is not an event, such as "we hired two people today." Rather, staffing is a process that establishes and governs the flow of people into the organization, within the organization, and out of the organization. There are multiple, interconnected systems that organizations use to manage the people flows. These include planning, recruitment, selection, decision making, job offer, and retention systems. Occurrences or actions in one system inevitably affect other systems. If planning activities show a forecasted increase in vacancies relative to historical standards, for example, the recruitment system will need to gear up for generating more applicants than previously, the selection system will have to handle the increased volume of applicants needing to be evaluated in terms of their KSAOs, decisions about job offer receivers may have to be speeded up, and the job offer packages may have to be "sweetened" in order to entice the necessary numbers of needed new hires. Further, steps will have to be taken to try to retain the new hires in order to avoid having to repeat the above experiences in the next staffing cycle.

Quantity and Quality

Staffing the organization requires attention to both the numbers (quantity) and types (quality) of people brought into, moved within, and retained by the organization. The quantity element basically refers to having enough headcount to conduct business, and the quality element entails having people with the requisite KSAOs so that jobs are performed effectively. It is important to recognize that it is the combination of sufficient quantity and quality of labor that creates a maximally effective staffing system.

Organization Effectiveness

Staffing systems exist, and should be used, to contribute to the attainment of organizational goals such as survival, profitability, and growth. A macro view of staffing like this is often lost or ignored because most of the day-to-day operations of staffing systems involve micro activities that are procedural, transactional, and routine in nature. While these micro activities are essential for staffing systems, they must be viewed within the broader macro context of the positive impacts staffing can have on organization effectiveness. There are many indications of this critical role of staffing, as explained below.

Importance to Organizational Effectiveness

Specific recognition and indications of staffing's importance to organizational effectiveness abound. The primary sources to illustrate this importance are quotes for organization leaders, survey results, organization experiences, and research findings.

Quotes from Organization Leaders

Interviews with key organization leaders about their strategies for organization success clearly show a recognition of the importance of staffing to them.

Rajat Dupta, the managing director of McKinsey and Company, a global consulting firm with 84 offices worldwide, described a key strategic thrust for the firm as follows:[1] "The new economy, very much the Internet and the entrepreneurial opportunities it created, intensified the competition for outstanding people. And we started to grow to a size and scope where it was important for us not only to get outstanding people but also to get them in significant numbers. So the emphasis shifted towards making to people value propositions that were the absolute best they could be."

Meg Whitman, the chief executive officer (CEO) of Ebay, showed staffing to be important to her when she was asked about her priorities:[2] "Getting the organizational design right, hiring fabulous people, and making sure we are putting as much effort into training development and mentoring as we should be."

Jeff Bezos, the CEO of Amazon.com, recognized that hiring decisions not only by him, but by other managers, are critical:[3] "I think about this in hiring, because our business all comes down to people. . . . In fact, when I'm interviewing a senior job candidate, my biggest worry is how good they are at hiring. I spend at least half the interview on that."

Finally, Steve Case is the CEO of AOL Time Warner, a media, film, publishing and Internet giant created by a merger of AOL (which he headed) and Time Warner. He described his success in the merger and subsequent growth of the new company as follows:[4] "As we built AOL 10 years ago we had 150 employees or something like that. Now AOL Time Warner has 90,000 employees. The only way to be successful, particularly in a rapidly growing, rapidly changing market is to hire terrific people and point them generally in the right direction. And let them go. I think almost everything comes down to people."

Survey Results

Survey results of executives regarding what they view as important issues also demonstrate the critical role of staffing. A survey of 1,969 executives from four levels of management in organizations across the country asked them to rate (on a 1–7 scale) how pressing each of 46 problems was for them in their role.[5] For the executives overall, the top five problems were:

1. attracting, developing, and keeping good people (mean = 6.18)
2. thinking and planning strategically (mean = 6.00)

3. maintaining a high performance climate (mean = 5.95)
4. improving customer satisfaction (mean = 5.85)
5. managing time and stress (mean = 5.83)

The problem "attracting, developing, and keeping good people" was in the top four problems for executives in all functional areas and was first for those in production and operations, human resources, research and development, general management, finance and accounting, and engineering.

Within the scope of just human resource issues and problems, a survey of 525 HR professionals and general managers found that recruiting/retention was the most important workplace issue for both groups, followed by compensation/benefits, legal compliance, managing change, and employee/labor relations to round out the top five.[6] While the above two surveys were conducted during a time of very low unemployment and resulting labor shortages, the results convincingly show that staffing issues indeed can rise to the top of concerns for organizations.

Organizations' Experiences

Leadership talent is at a premium, with very large stakes associated with the new leader acquisition. Sometimes new leadership talent is bought and brought from the outside to hopefully execute a reversal of fortunes for the organization or a business unit within it. The U.S. automobile manufacturers, for example, have sought new leaders to halt the continuing decline in their market share (GM has gone from 50% to 37% market share), prop up stock prices, and design new automobiles that are technologically sophisticated and can compete with foreign autos, particularly European and Japanese models.[7] Other organizations acquire new leaders to start new business units or ventures that will feed organization growth. The flip side to leadership acquisition is leadership retention. A looming fear for organizations is the unexpected loss of a key leader, particularly to a competitor. The exiting leader carries a wealth of knowledge and skill out of the organization and leaves a hole that may be hard to fill, especially with someone of equal or higher leadership stature. The leader may also take other key employees along, thus increasing the exit impact.

Organizations also recognize that talent hunts and loading up on talent are ways to expand organization value and provide protection from competitors. Such a strategy is particularly effective if the talent is unique and rare in the marketplace, valuable in the anticipated contributions to be made (such as new product creations or design innovations), and difficult for competitors to imitate (such as through training current employees). Talent of this sort can serve as a source of competitive advantage for the organization, hopefully for an extended time period.[8]

Talent acquisition is essential for growth even when it does not have such competitive advantage characteristics. Information technology companies, for example, cannot thrive without talent infusions via staffing. An Internet start-up called edocs, inc., sold Internet bill presentment and payment software. It doubled its employee ranks to over 100 in five months and sought to double that number in another five months. The CEO said this was necessary or "we won't have the resources we need to keep up the growth and go public. You grow fast or you die."[9]

Finally, quantity or quality labor shortages can mean lost business opportunities, scaled-back expansion plans, inability to provide critical consumer goods and services, and even threats to organization survival. Examples abound. Regional airlines are facing a halt to growth due to raiding of their pilots by larger airlines and expensive training for replacements—they must rent simulators at $400/hour (it would cost $10–12 million to build their own) and incur training costs of $60,000 per pilot. Large airlines also have problems. Air Canada was besieged by customer complaints about long lines and lost baggage and decided to spend $300 million to add 2,000 jobs to customer service and computer operations (the CEO said "staffing is key to our ability to improve customer service and relieve congestion").[10] In the energy industry, sudden upsurges in the demand for coal cannot be met because of shortages of qualified coal miners—the result of a decades-long decline in the industry as demand for coal waned. Shortages also confront the oil industry. Growth plans and new drilling are being put on hold due to shortages of petroleum engineers, geophysicists and geologists.[11] The childcare industry has faced chronic labor shortages and these are intensifying as workplaces increasingly move to 24/7/365 operations, which child-care providers must match to meet the needs of their customers. Acquiring a high quality, around-the-clock child-care workforce is proving very elusive.[12]

Finally, for individual managers, having sufficient numbers and types of employees on board is necessary for the smooth, efficient operation of their work unit. Employee shortages often require disruptive adjustments, such as job reassignments or overtime for current employees. Underqualified employees present special challenges to the manager, such as a need for close supervision and training. Failure of the underqualified to achieve acceptable performance may require termination of employees, a difficult decision to make and implement.

In short, organizations experience and respond to staffing forces and recognize how critical these forces can be to organizational effectiveness. The forces manifest themselves in numerous ways: acquisition of new leaders to change the organization's direction and effectiveness; prevention of key leader losses; usage of talent as a source of growth; and competitive advantage; shortages of labor—both quantity and quality—that threaten growth and even survival; and the ability of individual managers to effectively run their work units.

Research Findings

Research findings constantly emerge to shed light on how staffing affects organizational and individual performance. Some of the most recent findings indicate an important impact of staffing on organizational performance. For example, one major study compared the staffing practices (among others) of 15 organizations that went from "good to great" results in terms of cumulative stock returns to a set of organizations in the same industries that simply produced average stock returns. It was found that relative to the comparison organizations, the "good to great" ones first hired key top managers and then developed a strategy for the organization, rather than the other way around. As the researchers put it, "The main point is to *first* get the right people on the bus (and the wrong people off the bus) *before* you figure out where to drive it."[13]

Another study compared 50 higher and lower performing organizations, where performance was measured in a success index of revenue growth, productivity, profitability, and market value. Both leaders and associates of the organizations were surveyed about the quality of their staffing practices (among others). It was found that perceptions of the accuracy of employee selection and placement decisions were significantly related to the success index. It was concluded that "When the right leaders were in the right positions, organizations performed better. Also, when new hires were carefully selected to make sure they have the right skills for job success, organizations scored higher on the success index."[14] Other studies have also found that the degree of selectivity in hiring is related to organizational performance.[15]

Another study examined the impact of countercyclical hiring and organization performance. Countercyclical hiring occurs when an organization does selective hiring during downturns or recessions that occur prior to a clear upturn in economic strategy. The strategic rationale for such hiring is that there is a greater, higher quality number of key managerial and professional individuals available to acquire during downturns (relative to demand), and that they might be hired at comparatively low salaries and other compensation components. Countercyclical hiring thus permits the organization to invest in the stockpiling of key talent and have it in place for the next business upturn, giving the organization a competitive edge. Results of the research indicated that countercyclical hiring was associated with organizations' subsequent financial performance two years after the downturn.[16]

Another excellent illustration of the impact of staffing involves an executive selection system used by a Fortune 500 organization to assess the general competencies of managers being considered for promotion to heads of divisions with between $125–775 million annual revenues. Prior to promotion, a very thorough competency assessment was made on several competencies: understanding business, short-term execution, climate setting and communication, customer interaction, staffing, financial analysis, strategic planning, product planning, organizational acumen, and overall competence. The ratings were correlated with various performance indicators of the executives after they were promoted. Some of the ratings were found to significantly predict annual sales and profitability levels of the division, and other ratings—including staffing—predicted division growth in sales and profitability. Use of the selection system resulted in $3 million more profit each year for each candidate selected. In short, the selection system had a direct impact on organizational effectiveness, and furthermore, it showed that executives' own staffing competence was an important predictor of how successful they were in financially growing their divisions.[17]

Finally, research shows, for example, that certain selection techniques are more valid than others for identifying which applicants will turn out to be the most effective employees on the job. Research also shows how to calculate the performance implications of using more valid selection techniques, such as improvements in productivity or sales revenue generated by employees. As another example, research procedures exist for calculating the cost of employee turnover and for estimating the cost savings that accrue from an employee retention program. Specific examples of such research will be shown and used throughout the book.[18]

In short, research results demonstrate that staffing is an effective HR strategy and tool. Sound staffing impacts on, and improves, both organization and employee performance.

STAFFING MODELS

Several models depict various elements of staffing. Each of these is presented and described to more fully convey the nature and richness of staffing the organization.

Staffing Quantity: Levels

The quantity or head-count portion of the staffing definition means organizations must be concerned about staffing levels and their adequacy. Exhibit 1.1 shows the basic model. The organization as a whole, as well as for each of its units, forecasts workforce quantity requirements—the needed head count—and then compares these to forecasted workforce availabilities—the likely employee head count—to determine its likely staffing level position. If head-count requirements match availabilities, the projection is that the organization will be fully staffed. If requirements exceed availabilities, the organization will be understaffed, and if availabilities exceed requirements, the organization will be overstaffed.

Making such forecasts to determine like staffing levels and then developing specific plans on how to cope with them are the essence of planning. Being understaffed means the organization will have to gear up its staffing efforts, starting with accelerated recruitment and carrying on through the rest of the staffing system. It may also require development of retention programs that will slow the outflow of people, thus avoiding costly "turnstile" or "revolving door" staffing. Overstaffing projections signal the need to slow down or even halt recruitment,

EXHIBIT 1.1   Staffing Quantity

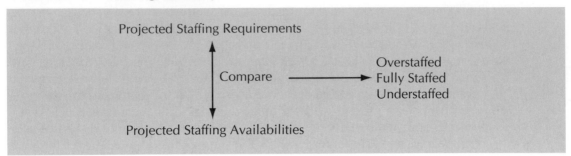

as well as to take steps that will actually reduce head count, such as through reduced workweeks, early retirement plans, or layoffs.

Staffing Quality: Person/Job Match

The person/job match seeks to align characteristics of individuals and jobs in ways that will result in desired HR outcomes. Casual comments made about applicants often reflect awareness of the importance of the person/job match. "Clark just doesn't have the interpersonal skills that it takes to be a good customer service representative." "Mary has exactly the kinds of budgeting experience this job calls for; if we hire her, there won't be any downtime while she learns our systems." "Gary says he was attracted to apply for this job because of its sales commission plan; he says he likes jobs where his pay depends on how well he performs." "Diane was impressed by the amount of challenge and autonomy she will have." "Jack turned down our offer; we gave him our best shot, but he just didn't feel he could handle the long hours and amount of travel the job calls for."

Comments like these raise four important points about the person/job match. First, jobs are characterized by their requirements (e.g., interpersonal skills, previous budgeting experiences) and embedded rewards (e.g., commission sales plan, challenge and autonomy). Second, individuals are characterized by their level of qualification (e.g., few interpersonal skills, extensive budgeting experience) and motivation (e.g., need for pay to depend on performance, need for challenge and autonomy). Third, in each of the previous examples the issue was one of the likely degree of fit or match between the characteristics of the job and the person. Fourth, there are implied consequences for every match. For example, Clark may not perform very well in his interactions with customers; retention might quickly become an issue with Jack.

These points and concepts are shown more formally through the person/job match model in Exhibit 1.2. In this model, the job has certain requirements and rewards associated with it. The person has certain qualifications, referred to as KSAOs (knowledges, skills, abilities, and other characteristics), and motivations. There is a need for a match between the person and the job. To the extent that the match is good, it will likely have positive impacts on HR outcomes, particularly attraction of job applicants, job performance, retention, attendance, and satisfaction.

There is actually a need for a dual match to occur: job requirements to KSAOs, and job rewards to individual motivation. In and through staffing activities, there are attempts to ensure both of these. Such attempts collectively involve what will be referred to throughout this book as the matching process.

Several points pertaining to staffing need to be made about the person/job matching model. First, the concepts shown in the model are not new.[19] They have been used for decades as the dominant way of thinking about how individuals successfully adapt to their work environments. The view is that the positive interaction of individual and job characteristics creates the most successful matches. Thus, a person with a given "package" of KSAOs is not equally suited to all jobs, because jobs vary in the KSAOs required. Likewise, an individual with a given

EXHIBIT 1.2   Person/Job Match

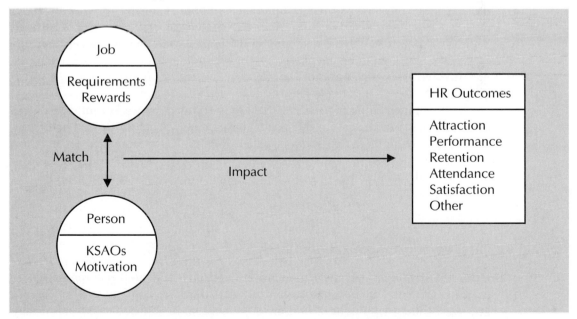

set of needs or motivations will not be satisfied with all jobs, because jobs differ in the rewards they offer. Thus, in staffing, each individual must be assessed relative to the requirements and rewards of the job being filled.

Second, the model emphasizes that the matching process involves a dual match of KSAOs to requirements and motivation to rewards. Both matches require attention in staffing. For example, a staffing system may be designed to focus on the KSAOs/requirements match by carefully identifying job requirements and then thoroughly assessing applicants relative to these requirements. While such a staffing system may be one that will accurately identify the probable high performers, problems may arise with it. By ignoring or downplaying the motivation/rewards portion of the match, the organization may have difficulty getting people to accept job offers (an attraction outcome) or having new hires remain with the organization for any length of time (a retention outcome). It does little good to be able to identify the likely high performers if they cannot be induced to accept job offers or to remain with the organization.

Third, job requirements should usually be expressed in terms of both the tasks involved and the KSAOs thought necessary for performance of those tasks. Most of the time, it is difficult to establish meaningful KSAOs for a job without having first identified the job's tasks. KSAOs usually must be derived or inferred from knowledge of the tasks. An exception to this involves very basic or generic KSAOs, such as literacy and oral communication skills, that are reasonably deemed necessary for most jobs.

Fourth, job requirements often extend beyond task and KSAO requirements. For example, the job may have requirements about reporting to work on time, attendance, safety toward fellow employees and customers, and needs for travel. With such requirements, the matching of the person to them must also be considered when staffing the organization. Travel requirements of the job, for example, may involve assessing applicants' availability for, and willingness to accept, travel assignments.

Finally, the matching process can yield only so much by way of impacts on the HR outcomes. The reason for this is that these outcomes are influenced by factors outside the realm of the person/job match. Retention, for example, depends not only on how close a match there is between job rewards and individual motivation but also on the availability of suitable job opportunities in other organizations and labor markets.

Staffing Quality: Person/Organization Match

Often the organization seeks to determine not only how well the person fits or matches the job but also the organization. Likewise, applicants often assess how they think they might fit into the organization, in addition to how well they match the specific job's requirements and rewards. For both the organization and the applicant, therefore, there may be a concern with a person/organization match.[20]

Exhibit 1.3 shows this expanded view of the match. The focal point of staffing is the person/job match, and the job is like the bull's-eye of the matching target. Four other matching concerns, however, involving the broader organization, also arise in staffing. These concerns involve organizational values, new job duties, multiple jobs, and future jobs.

Organizational values are norms of desirable attitudes and behaviors for the organization's employees. Examples include honesty and integrity, achievement and hard work, fairness, and concern for fellow employees and customers. Though such values may never appear in writing, such as in a job description, the likely match of the applicant to them is judged during staffing.

EXHIBIT 1.3   Person/Organization Match

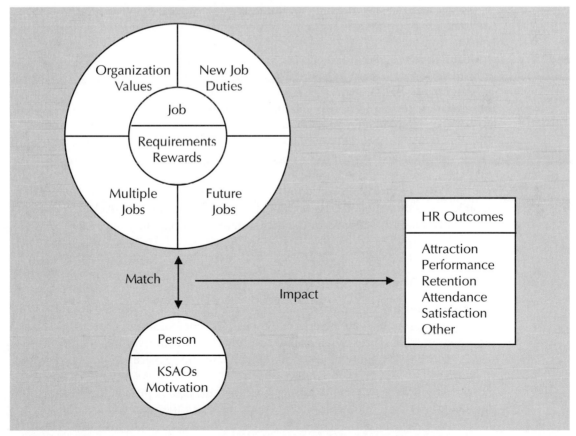

New job duties represent tasks that may be added to the target job over time. Organizations desire new hires who will be able to successfully perform these new duties as they are added. In recognition of this, job descriptions often contain the catchall phrase "and other duties as assigned." These other duties are usually vague at the time of hire, and they may never materialize. Nonetheless, the organization would like to hire persons it thinks could perform these new duties. Having such people will provide the organization a degree of flexibility in getting new tasks done without having to hire additional employees to do them.

Flexibility concerns also enter into the staffing picture in terms of hiring persons who could perform multiple jobs. Small businesses, for example, often desire new hires who can wear multiple hats, functioning as "jacks-of-all-trades"; or, organizations experiencing rapid growth may require new employees who can handle several different job assignments, splitting their time between them on an "as-needed" basis. Such expectations obviously require assessments of person/organization fit.

Future jobs represent forward thinking by the organization and person as to what job assignments the person might assume beyond the initial job. Here the applicant and the organization are thinking of long-term matches over the course of transfers and promotions as the employee becomes increasingly "seasoned" for the long run.

In each of the above four cases, the matching process is expanded to include consideration of requirements and rewards beyond those of the target job as it currently exists. Though the dividing line between person/job and person/organization matching is fuzzy, both types of matches are frequently of concern in staffing. Ideally, the organization's staffing systems focus first and foremost on the person/job match. This will allow the nature of the employment relationship to be specified and agreed to in concrete terms. Once these terms have been established, person/organization match possibilities can be explored during the staffing process. In this book for simplicity's sake we will use the term "person/job match" broadly to encompass both types of matches, though most of the time the usage will be in the context of the actual person/job match.

Staffing System Components

As noted, staffing encompasses managing the flows of people into and within the organization, as well as retaining them. The core staffing process has several components that represent steps and activities that occur over the course of these flows. Exhibit 1.4 shows these components and the general sequence in which they occur.

As shown in the exhibit, staffing begins with a joint interaction between the applicant and the organization. The applicant seeks the organization and job op-

EXHIBIT 1.4   Staffing System Components

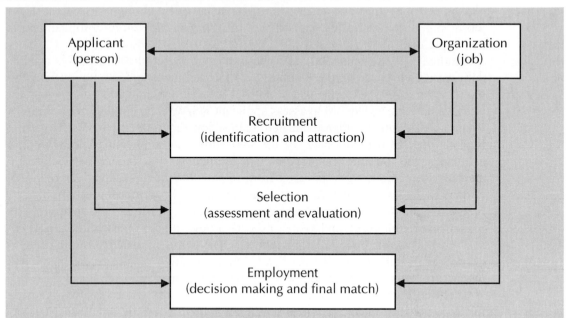

portunities within it, and the organization seeks applicants for job vacancies it has or anticipates having. Both the applicant and the organization are thus involved as "players" in the staffing process from the very beginning, and they remain joint participants throughout the process.

At times, the organization may be the dominant player, such as in aggressive and targeted recruiting for certain types of applicants. At other times, the applicant may be the aggressor, such as when the applicant desperately seeks employment with a particular organization and will go to almost any length to land a job with it. Most of the time, staffing involves a more balanced and natural interplay between the applicant and the organization, which occurs over the course of the staffing process.

The initial stage in staffing is recruitment, which involves identification and attraction activities by both the organization and the applicant. The organization seeks to identify and attract individuals so that they become job applicants. Activities such as advertising, job fairs, use of recruiters, preparation and distribution of informational brochures, and "putting out the word" about vacancies among its own employees are undertaken. The applicant attempts to identify organizations with job opportunities through activities such as reading advertisements, contacting an employment agency, mass mailing résumés to employers, and so forth. These activities are accompanied by attempts to make one's qualifications (KSAOs and motivation) attractive to organizations, such as by applying in person for a job or preparing a carefully constructed résumé that highlights significant skills and experiences.

Gradually, recruitment activities phase into the selection stage and its accompanying activities. Now, the emphasis is on assessment and evaluation. For the organization, this means the use of various selection techniques (interviews, application blanks, and so on) to assess applicant KSAOs and motivation. Data from these assessments are then evaluated against job requirements to determine the likely degree of person/job fit. At the same time, the applicant is assessing and evaluating the job and organization. The applicant's assessment and evaluation are based on information gathered from organizational representatives (e.g., recruiter, manager with the vacancy, other employees); written information (e.g., brochures, employee handbook); informal sources (e.g., friends and relatives who are current employees); and visual inspection (e.g., a video presentation, a worksite tour). This information, along with a self-assessment of KSAOs and motivation, is evaluated against the applicant's understanding of job requirements and rewards to determine if a good person/job match is likely.

The next core component of staffing is employment, which involves decision making and final match activities by the organization and the applicant. The organization must decide which applicants to reject from further consideration and which to allow to continue in the process. This may involve multiple decisions over successive selection steps or hurdles. Some applicants ultimately become finalists for the job. At that point, the organization must decide to whom it will make the job offer, what the content of the offer will be, and how it will be drawn up and presented to the applicant. Upon the applicant's acceptance of the offer, the final match is complete, and the employment relationship is formally established.

For the applicant, the employment stage involves self-selection, a term that refers to decisions about whether to continue in or drop out of the staffing process. These decisions may occur anywhere along the selection process, up to and including the moment of the job offer. If the applicant continues as part of the process through the final match, the applicant has decided to be a finalist. The individual's attention now turns to a possible job offer, possible input and negotiation on its content, and making a final decision about the offer. The applicant's final decision is based on overall judgment about the likely suitability of the person/job match.

It should be noted that the above staffing components apply to both external and internal staffing. Though this may seem obvious in the case of external staffing, a brief elaboration may be necessary for internal staffing. In internal staffing, the applicant is a current employee, and the organization is the current employer. Job opportunities (vacancies) exist within the organization and are filled through the activities of the internal labor market. Those activities involve recruitment, selection, and employment, with the employer and employee as joint participants. For example, the employer may recruit through use of an internal job posting system. Employees who apply may be assessed and evaluated on the basis of supervisory recommendation, a formal promotability rating, and previous job assignments for the employer. Decisions are made by both the employer and the employees who are applicants. Ultimately, the position will be offered to one of the applicants and, hopefully, accepted. When this happens, the final match has occurred, and a new employment relationship has been established.

Staffing Organizations

The overall staffing organizations model, which forms the framework for this book, is shown in Exhibit 1.5. It depicts that the organization's mission and goals and objectives drive both organization and HR and staffing strategy, which interact

---

EXHIBIT 1.5   Staffing Organizations Model

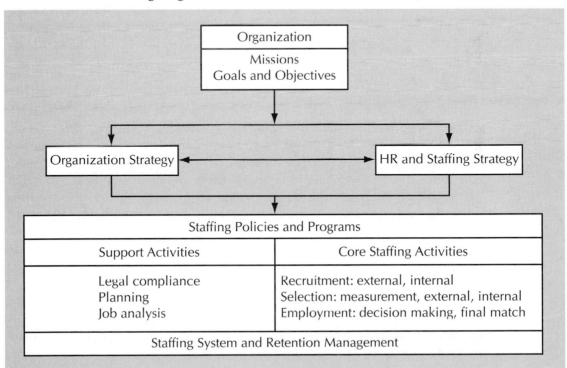

with each other when they are being formulated. Staffing policies and programs result from such interaction and serve as an overlay to both support activities and core staffing activities. Employee retention and staffing system management concerns cut across these support and core staffing activities. Finally, though not shown in the model, it should be remembered that staffing levels and staffing quality are the key focal points of staffing strategy, policy, and programs. A more thorough examination of the model follows next.

Organization, HR, and Staffing Strategy

Organizations formulate strategy to express an overall purpose or mission and to establish broad goals and objectives that will guide the organization toward fulfillment of its mission. For example, a newly formed software development organization may have a mission to "help individuals and families manage all of their personal finances and records through electronic means." Based on this mission statement, the organization might then develop goals and objectives pertaining to product development, sales growth, and competitive differentiation through superior product quality and customer service.

Underlying these objectives are certain assumptions about the size and types of workforces that will need to be acquired, trained, managed, rewarded, and retained. HR strategy represents the key decisions about how these workforce assumptions will be handled. Such HR strategy may not only flow from the organization strategy but also may actually contribute directly to the formulation of the organization's strategy.

Consider again the software development organization and its objective pertaining to new product development. Being able to develop new products assumes that sufficient, qualified product-development team members are available internally and externally, and assurances from the HR department about availability may have been critical in helping the organization to decide on its product-development goals. From this general assumption, HR strategy may suggest (a) obtaining new, experienced employees from other software companies, rather than going after newly minted college and graduate school graduates; (b) building a new facility for software development employees in a geographic area that will be an attractive place to work, raise families, and pursue leisure activities; (c) developing relocation assistance packages and family-friendly benefits; (d) offering wages and salaries above the market average, plus using hiring bonuses to help lure new employees away from their current employers; (e) creating special training budgets for each employee to use at his or her own discretion for skills enhancement; and (f) putting in place a promotion system that is fast-track and allows employees to rise upward in either their professional specialty or the managerial ranks. In all of these ways, HR strategy seeks to align acquisition and management of the workforce with organization strategy.

Staffing strategy is an outgrowth of the interplay between organization and HR strategy described above. It deals directly with key decisions regarding the acquisition, deployment, and retention of the organization's workforces. Such decisions guide the development of recruitment, selection, and employment programs. In the software development example discussed above, the strategic decision to acquire new employees from the ranks of experienced people at other organizations may lead the organization to develop very active, personalized, and secret recruiting activities for luring these people away. It may also lead to the development of special selection techniques for assessing job experiences and accomplishments. In such ways, strategic staffing decisions shape the staffing process.

Support Activities

Support activities serve as the foundation and necessary ingredients for the conduct of core staffing activities. Legal compliance represents knowledge of the myriad laws and regulations, especially equal employment opportunity and affirmative action (EEO/AA), and incorporation of their requirements into all phases of the core staffing activities. Planning serves as a tool for first becoming aware of key external influences on staffing, particularly economic conditions, labor markets, and labor unions. Such awareness shapes the formulation of staffing levels— both requirements and availabilities—the results of which drive staffing planning for the core staffing activities. Job analysis represents the key mechanism by which the organization identifies and establishes the KSAO requirements for jobs, as well as the rewards jobs will provide, both first steps toward seeking to begin filling projected vacancies through core staffing activities.

Returning to the software development organization, if it meets various size thresholds for coverage (usually 15 or more employees), it must ensure that the staffing systems to be developed will comply with all applicable federal, state, and local laws and regulations. Planning activities will revolve around first determining the major types of jobs that will be necessary for the new product development venture, such as computer programmers, Internet specialists, and project managers. For each job, a forecast must be made about the number of employees that will be needed and the likely availability of individuals both externally and internally for the job. Results of such forecasts serve as the key input to the development of detailed staffing plans for the core staffing activities. Finally, job analysis will be needed to specify for each job exactly what KSAOs and rewards will be necessary for these sought-after new employees. Once all of these support activities are in place, the core staffing activities can begin.

Core Staffing Activities

Core staffing activities focus on recruitment, selection, and employment of the workforce. Since staffing levels have already been established as part of staffing planning, emphasis shifts to staffing quality to ensure that successful person/job and person/ organization matches will be made. Accomplishment of this end result will require multiple plans, decisions, and activities, ranging from recruitment methods to use, communication with potential applicants with a special recruitment message, recruitment media, types of selection tools, deciding which applicants will receive job offers, and job offer packages. Both staffing experts and the hiring manager will be involved in these core staffing activities. Moreover, it is likely that the activities will have to be developed and tailor-made for each type of job.

Consider the job of computer programmer in our software development example. It will be necessary to decide and develop specific plans for such issues as: Will we recruit only online, or will we use other methods such as newspaper ads or job fairs (recruitment methods)? What exactly will we tell applicants about the job and our company (recruitment message) and how will we deliver the message, such as on our Web site or a recruitment brochure (recruitment media)? What specific selection tools, such as interviews, assessments of experience, work samples, and background checks, will we use to assess and evaluate the applicants' KSAOs (selection techniques)? How will we combine and evaluate all of the information we gather on applicants with these selection tools and then decide which applicants will receive job offers (decision making)? What exactly will we put in the job offer, and will we be willing to negotiate on the offer (employment)?

Staffing and Retention System Management

The various support and core staffing activities are quite complex, and they must be guided, coordinated, controlled, and evaluated. Such is the role of staffing system management. In our new product development example, what will be the role of the HR department, and what types of people will it need to develop and manage the new staffing systems (administration of staffing systems)? How will we evaluate the results of these systems—will we collect and look at cost-per-hire and time-to-hire data (evaluation of staffing systems)? Data such as these are key effective indicators that both general and staffing managers are attuned to.

Finally, voluntary employee departure from the organization is usually costly and disruptive, and it can involve the loss of critical talent that is difficult to replace. Discharges too can be disruptive. Unless the organization is downsizing, however, replacements must be found in order to maintain desired staffing levels. The burden for such replacement staffing can be substantial, particularly when the turnover was unanticipated and unplanned. Other things equal, greater employee retention means less staffing, so that effective retention programs complement staffing programs.

In our software development organization example, the primary focus will likely be on "staffing up" in order to keep producing existing products and developing new ones. Unless attention is also paid to employee retention, however, maintaining adequate staffing levels and quality may become problematic. Hence, the organization will need to monitor the amount and quality of employees who are leaving and the reasons they are leaving in order to learn how much of the turnover is voluntary and avoidable; monitoring discharges will also be necessary. Based on these data, specific and tailor-made retention strategies and programs to better meet employees' needs can be developed. If effective, strains on the staffing system will be lessened.

The remainder of the book is structured around and built on the staffing organizations model shown in Exhibit 1.5.

STAFFING STRATEGY

As noted, staffing strategy requires making key decisions about the acquisition, deployment, and retention of the organization's workforce. Thirteen such decisions are identified and discussed below. Some decisions pertain primarily to staffing levels and others primarily to staffing quality. A summary of the decisions is shown in Exhibit 1.6. While each decision is shown as an "either-or" one, each is more appropriately thought of as lying on a continuum anchored at either end by these either-or extremes. When discussing the decisions, continued reference is made to the software development organization involved in developing personal finances software.

EXHIBIT 1.6   Strategic Staffing Decisions

Staffing Levels
- Acquire or Develop Talent
- Lag or Lead System
- External or Internal Hiring
- Core or Flexible Workforce
- Hire or Retain
- National or Global
- Attract or Relocate
- Overstaff or Understaff
- Hire or Acquire

Staffing Quality
- Person/Job or Person/Organization Match
- Specific or General KSAOs
- Exceptional or Acceptable Workforce Quality
- Active or Passive Diversity

Staffing Levels

Acquire or Develop Talent

To fulfill its staffing needs, a pure acquisition staffing strategy would have an organization concentrate on acquiring new employees who can "hit the ground running" and be at peak performance the moment they arrive. These employees would bring their talents with them to the job, with little or no need for training or development. A pure development strategy would lead to acquisition of just about anyone, as long as they were willing and able to learn the KSAOs required by the job. Staffing strategy must position the organization appropriately along this "buy or make" your talent continuum. For critical positions and newly created ones, such as might occur in the software company example, the emphasis would likely be on acquiring talent because of the urgency of developing new products. There may be no time to train, nor may qualified internal candidates be available.

Lag or Lead System

The organization's staffing systems may develop in response to organization and HR strategy (lag system), or staffing considerations may serve as key inputs to organization and HR strategy (lead system). With staffing as a lag system, strategic organization objectives and plans are developed first, and staffing systems are then developed to deliver the numbers and types of employees needed. Using staffing as a lead system involves the acquisition of people and their accompanying skills without a formal blueprint for how many are needed or when. Such people are acquired to come into the organization and "make things happen," so that organization strategy becomes a reflection of newly acquired employees' talents and ideas. In the software organization illustration, it may decide to use a lead system approach to "staff up" on good programmers whenever they can be found, regardless of whether specific, defined jobs exist for them at the moment.

External or Internal Hiring

When job vacancies occur or new jobs are created, should the organization seek to fill them from the external or internal labor market? While some mixture of external and internal hiring will be necessary in most situations, the relative blend could vary substantially. To the extent that the organization wants to cultivate a stable, committed workforce, it will probably need to emphasize internal hiring. This will allow employees to use the internal labor market as a springboard for launching long-term careers within the organization. External hiring might then be restricted to specific entry-level jobs, as well as newly created ones for which there are no acceptable internal applicants. External hiring might also be necessary when there is rapid organization growth, such that the number of new jobs created outstrips internal supply.

Core or Flexible Workforce

The organization's core workforce is made up of individuals who are viewed (and view themselves) as regular employees of the organization, either full-time or part-time. They are central to the core goods and services delivered by the organization.

The flexible workforce is composed of more peripheral workers who are used on an as-needed, just-in-time basis. They are not viewed (nor do they view themselves) as "regular"; and legally, most of them are not even employees of the organization. Rather, they are employees of an alternative organization, such as a staffing firm (temporary help agency) or independent contractor, that provides these workers to the organization. Strategically, the organization must decide whether it wishes to use both core and flexible workforces, what the mixture of core versus flexible workers will be, and in what jobs and units of the organization these mixtures will be deployed. Within the software development organization, programmers might be considered as part of its core workforce, but ancillary workers (e.g., clerical) may be part of the flexible workforce, particularly since the need for them will depend on the speed and success of new product development.

Hire or Retain

There are trade-offs between hiring and retention strategies for staffing. At one extreme the organization can accept whatever level of turnover occurs and simply hire replacements to fill the vacancies. Alternatively, the organization can seek to minimize turnover so that the need for replacement staffing is held to a minimum. Since both strategies have costs and benefits associated with them, the organization could conduct analysis to determine these and then strive for an optimal mix of hiring and retention. In this way the organization could control its inflow needs (replacement staffing) by controlling its outflow (retention).

National or Global

An organization can choose to staff itself with people from within its borders, or it can supplement or replace such recruitment with employees recruited from other countries. As trading restrictions and immigration barriers are lessened, global staffing becomes a more distinct possibility.[21] The organization may seek to overcome quantity or quality labor shortages, or excessive labor costs, by staffing with foreign workers. The software development organization might seek some technology employees from India, for example, because of the large number of technology workers being trained in that country. It seems likely that global staffing will intensify within the United States, based on projections for long-term labor shortages in many occupations.

Attract or Relocate

Typical staffing strategy is based on the premise that the organization can induce sufficient numbers of qualified people to come to it for employment. Another version of this premise is that it is better (and cheaper) to bring labor to the organization than to bring the organization to labor. Some organizations, both established and new ones, challenge this premise and decide to go to locations where there are ample labor supplies. The shift of lumber mills and automobile manufacturing plants to the southern United States reflects such a strategy. Likewise, the growth of high technology pockets such as Silicon Valley reflects establishment or movement of organizations to geographic areas where there is ready access to highly skilled labor and where employees would like to live, usually locations with research universities nearby to provide the needed graduates for jobs. The software development organization might find locating in such an area very desirable.

Overstaff or Understaff

While most organizations seek to be reasonably fully staffed, some opt for or are forced away from this posture to being over- or understaffed. Overstaffing may occur when there are dips in demand for the organization's products or services that the organization chooses to "ride out." Organizations may also overstaff in order to stockpile talent, recognizing that the staffing spigot cannot be easily turned on or off. Understaffing may occur when the organization is confronted with chronic labor shortages, such as is the case for nurses in health care facilities. Also, prediction of an economic downturn may lead the organization to understaff in order to avoid future layoffs. Finally, the organization may decide to understaff and adjust staffing level demand spikes by increasing employee overtime or using flexible staffing arrangement such as temporary employees. The software development organization might choose to overstaff in order to retain key employees and to be poised to meet the hopeful surges in demand as its new products are released.

Hire or Acquire

Rather than hire new talent through normal staffing systems, it might be possible to acquire it en masse through a merger or an acquisition.[22] This acquisition strategy has the potential to quickly deliver large numbers of qualified people, allowing the organization to grow through new or better projects and business units. The downsides to such a strategy are numerous. Staffing costs are greater since the acquired employees may have to be provided special compensation incentives to join the organization. Care will be required during the predeal and due diligence stages of the merger or acquisition to insure accurate KSAO assessments of the to-be-acquired employees. Finally, retention will become an issue, with some individuals refusing to join, some being laid off, and others leaving soon after the acquisition, due to a poor person/job or person/organization fit. Seeking a merger or acquisition for staffing purposes would likely not happen with our software development company, at least in its early growth stages.

Staffing Quality

Person/Job or Person/Organization Match

When acquiring and deploying people, should the organization opt for a person/ job or person/organization match? This is a complex decision. In part a person/ job match will have to be assessed any time a person is being hired to perform a finite set of tasks. In our software development example, programmers might be hired to do programming in a specific language such as Java, and most certainly the organization would want to assess whether applicants meet this specific job requirement. On the other hand, jobs may be poorly defined and fluid, making a person/job match infeasible and requiring a person/organization match instead. Such jobs are often found in technology and software development organizations.

Specific or General KSAOs

Should the organization acquire people with specific KSAOs or more general ones? The former means focusing on job-specific competencies, often of the job knowledge and technical skill variety. The latter requires a focus on KSAOs that will be applicable across a variety of jobs, both current and future. Examples of such KSAOs include flexibility and adaptability, ability to learn, written and oral communication skills, and algebra/statistics skills. An organization expecting rapid changes in job content and new job creation, such as in the software development example, might position itself closer to the general competencies end of the continuum.

Exceptional or Acceptable Workforce Quality

Strategically, the organization could seek to acquire a workforce that was preeminent KSAO-wise (exceptional quality) or one that was a more "ballpark" variety KSAO-wise (acceptable quality). Pursuit of the exceptional strategy would allow the organization to stock up on the "best and the brightest" with the hope that this exceptional talent pool would deliver truly superior performance. The acceptable strategy means pursuit of a less high powered workforce and probably a less expensive one as well. Owners of professional sports teams confront this choice and make their decisions accordingly. For the software development organization, if it is trying to create clearly innovative and superior products, it will likely opt for the exceptional workforce quality end of the continuum.

Active or Passive Diversity

The labor force is becoming increasingly diverse in terms of demographics, values, and languages. Does the organization want to actively pursue this diversity in the labor market so that its own workforce mirrors it, or does the organization want to more passively let diversity of its workforce happen to it? Advocates of an active diversity strategy argue that it is not only legally and morally appropriate but also that a diverse workforce allows the organization to be more attuned to the diverse needs of the customers it serves. Those favoring a more passive strategy suggest that diversification of the workforce takes time because it requires substantial planning and assimilation activity. In the software development illustration, an active diversity strategy might be pursued as a way of acquiring workers who can help identify a diverse array of software products that might be received favorably by various segments of the marketplace.

STAFFING SYSTEM EXAMPLES

Any organization with more than one member has some sort of staffing system. These systems elude easy characterization because they are tailored to suit the unique needs of each organization, its applicants, and its external influences. Despite these differences, all staffing systems share in common the elements shown in the staffing organizations model. Described below are four staffing systems that illustrate the diversity within the confines of these shared elements.

Police Department

The Madison, Wisconsin, police department staffs its entry-level police officer jobs periodically, under the direction of the public Police and Fire Commission (PFC). In one instance, vacancies for 30 positions were publicly announced and widely advertised in order to attract an applicant pool that was diverse with respect to gender and minority group membership. Police officers themselves served as active, outreaching recruiters throughout the total staffing process. This recruitment yielded 1,284 applicants. After ascertaining possession of key KSAOs (e.g., high school graduate, driver's license, no felony conviction record, vision correctable to 20/20), applicants took a written test of reading comprehension and vocabulary.

For the 900 who passed the test, written application materials were reviewed by a four-person panel of police force members. The 200 survivors then took a physical ability test (sit-ups, lifting, running, and trigger pull), which 68 passed. These persons were then given a panel (group) interview, followed by a thorough background check. The 40 finalists were then individually interviewed by the Chief of Police. Those offered and accepting a job were required to pass a medical exam before being placed into an eight-month training program, followed by a regular job assignment.[23]

Automobile Plant

Toyota's automobile assembly plant in Georgetown, Kentucky, has received more than 200,000 applications for 7,500 assembly job vacancies since it opened in

1986. Its selection system seeks to identify applicants with the right mix of physical dexterity, teamwork skills, and problem-solving ability, which are the critical KSAO requirements for assembly team jobs. After completing and passing the initial application process, applicants report to the Toyota Assessment Center for participation in a simulated day at work. They spend four hours on a simulated assembly line, screwing and unscrewing nuts, bolts, and metal plates. Additional time is spent inspecting parts for defects, participating in group problem-solving sessions, and taking written tests. Some applicants self-select out of further consideration once they have experienced this realistic job preview. Those who remain must be assessed further through a job interview. Successful applicants receive a preliminary job offer, followed by a physical exam. Final job offers are made to those deemed fit after a discussion with the applicant about the most appropriate job placement.[24]

Theme Park

At Walt Disney World there is a 42,000-employee workforce, with many working part-time. Employees are referred to as cast members in keeping with the company's culture of wanting to provide a flawless show for guests. Applicants come to the Casting Center (employment office), which is decorated with Disney characters in murals to convey the Disney culture immediately to cast members. These potential hires first view a 10-minute video that discusses pay, transportation to work, working hours, appearance requirements, and benefits (on-site credit union, gas station, two daycare centers, a hair salon, and a company store). The video also shows Disney's customer-focused work environment and what is expected from cast members to function successfully within it. About 10 to 15% of the applicants self-select out of the hiring process after seeing the video. Those who remain in the process are subject to two interviews. The first is a phone interview, with the applicant having the option of being interviewed in English, Spanish, or Creole. The second interview is face-to-face with a Disney HR representative. For the affiliated Epcot center—which has as a theme the sampling of many international cultures—about 1,000 international students are recruited each year, with recruiters visiting the countries featured in Epcot twice each year. Since 25% of its guests are from foreign countries, such recruitment helps ensure that its cast members are reflective of the guest population.[25]

Telephone Company

Bell Atlantic is a large telephone company in 13 eastern states. It fills between 18,000–19,000 nonmanagement job requisitions per year through external and internal hires. To manage the staffing process, Bell Atlantic entered into an agreement with the staffing firm vendor ASI Solutions, Inc. ASI and Bell Atlantic use a projection of staffing needs to create pools of available applicants, a process of "steady-state" recruiting. Applicants may call an 800 phone number and follow an interactive voice response system to learn about job openings and schedule testing. A three-hour selection test is administered to candidates initially to assess for behavior and skill competency, using computer-based, keyboarding, paper-and-pencil, and telephone assessment techniques, prior to a personal interview. The staffing system has reduced hiring cycle time from over 70 days to 30 days, resulting in quicker revenue generation by the new hire and reduced staffing costs. In addition, the testing process has a close fidelity to the jobs being filled so that applicants may learn what the job is like and self-select out of being a candidate at that point, thus reducing likely turnover later on. The Bell Atlantic vice president in charge of HR concludes that "it's critical that the level of customer service we provide is top notch, and that goes back to the hiring process."[26]

PLAN FOR THE BOOK

The book is divided into six parts:

1. The Nature of Staffing
2. Support Activities
3. Staffing Activities: Recruitment
4. Staffing Activities: Selection
5. Staffing Activities: Employment
6. Staffing System and Retention Management

Each chapter in these six parts begins with a brief topical outline to help the reader quickly discern its general contents. The "meat" of the chapter comes next. A chapter summary then reviews and highlights points from the chapter. A set of discussion questions, applications (cases and exercises), and detailed endnotes complete the chapter.

The importance of laws and regulations is such that they are considered first in Chapter 2 (Legal Compliance). The laws and regulations, in particular, have become so pervasive that they require special treatment. To do this, Chapter 2 reviews the basic laws affecting staffing, with an emphasis on the major federal laws and regulations pertaining to EEO/AA matters generally. Specific provisions relevant to staffing are covered in depth. Each subsequent chapter then has a separate section at its end labeled "Legal Issues" in which specific legal topics relevant to the chapter's content are discussed. This allows for a more focused discussion of legal issues while not diverting attention from the major thrust of the book.

The endnotes at the end of each chapter are quite extensive. They are drawn from academic, practitioner, and legal sources with the goal of providing a balanced selection of references from each of these sources. Emphasis is on inclusion of recent references of high quality and easy accessibility. Too lengthy a list of references to each specific topic is avoided; instead, a sampling of only the best available is included.

The applications at the end of each chapter are of two varieties. First are cases that describe a particular situation and require analysis and response. The response may be written or oral (such as in class discussion or a group presentation). Second are exercises that entail small projects and require active practice of a particular task. Through these cases and exercises the reader becomes an active participant in the learning process and is able to apply the concepts provided in each chapter.

SUMMARY

Staffing is defined as "the process of acquiring, deploying, and retaining a workforce of sufficient quantity and quality to create positive impacts on the organization's effectiveness." The definition emphasizes that both staffing levels and labor quality contribute to organization effectiveness, and that a concerted set of labor acquisition, deployment, and retention actions guide the flow of people into, within, and out of the organization.

Several models illustrate various elements of staffing. The staffing level model shows how projected labor requirements and availabilities are compared to derive staffing levels that represent being overstaffed, fully staffed, or understaffed. The next two models illustrate staffing quality via the person/job and person/organization match. The former indicates there is a need to match (a) the person's KSAOs to job requirements and (b) the person's motivation to the job's rewards. In the person/organization match, the person's characteristics are matched to additional factors beyond the target job, namely, organizational values, new job duties for the target job, multiple jobs, and future jobs. Managing the matching process effectively results in positive impacts on HR outcomes such as attraction, performance, and retention. The core staffing components model shows that there are three basic activities in staffing. Those activities and their fundamental purposes are recruitment (identification and attraction of applicants), selection (assessment and evaluation of applicants), and employment (decision making and final match). The staffing organizations model shows that organization, HR, and staffing strategies are formulated and shape staffing policies and programs. In turn, these meld into a set of staffing support activities (legal compliance, planning and job analysis), as well as the core activities (recruitment, selection, and employment). Retention and staffing system management activities cut across both support and core activities.

Staffing strategy is both an outgrowth of and contributor to HR and organization strategy. Thirteen important strategic staffing decisions loom for any organization. Some pertain to staffing level choices, and others deal with staffing quality choices.

Staffing systems, though diverse in many respects, share the elements of the staffing organizations model. Examples of these systems are provided for a police department, an automobile plant, a theme park, and a telephone company.

The staffing organizations model serves as the structural framework for the book. The first part treats staffing models and strategy. The second part treats the support activities of legal compliance, planning, and job analysis. The next three parts treat the core staffing activities of recruitment, selection, and employment. The last section addresses staffing systems and employee retention management. Each chapter has a separate section labeled "Legal Issues," as well as discussion questions, applications, and endnotes (references).

DISCUSSION QUESTIONS

1. What would be potential problems with having a staffing process in which vacancies were filled (a) on a lottery basis from among job applicants, or (b) on a first come–first hired basis among job applicants?

2. Why is it important for the organization to view all components of staffing (recruitment, selection, employment) from the perspective of the job applicant?

3. Would it be desirable to hire people only according to the person/organization match, ignoring the person/job match?

4. What are examples of how staffing activities are influenced by training activities? Compensation activities?

5. Are some of the thirteen strategic staffing decisions more important than others? Which ones? Why?

APPLICATIONS

Staffing for Your Own Job

Instructions
Consider a job you previously held or your current job. Use the staffing components model to help you think through and describe the staffing process that led to your getting hired for the job. Trace and describe the process (a) from your own perspective as a job applicant, and (b) from the organization's perspective. Listed below are some questions to jog your memory. Write your responses to these questions and be prepared to discuss them.

Applicant Perspective
Recruitment:

1. Why did you identify and seek out the job with this organization?
2. How did you try to make yourself attractive to the organization?

Selection:

1. How did you gather information about the job's requirements and rewards?
2. How did you judge your own KSAOs and needs relative to these requirements and rewards?

Employment:

1. Why did you decide to continue on in the staffing process, rather than drop out of it?
2. Why did you decide to accept the job offer; what were the pluses and minuses of the job?

Organization Perspective

Even if you do not know, or are unsure of, the answers to these questions, try to answer them or guess at them.

Recruitment:

1. How did the organization identify you as a job applicant?
2. How did the organization make the job attractive to you?

Selection:

1. What techniques (application blank, interview, etc.) did the organization use to gather KSAO information about you?
2. How did the organization evaluate this information; what did it see as your strong and weak points KSAO-wise?

Employment:

1. Why did the organization decide to continue pursuing you as an applicant, rather than reject you from further consideration?
2. What was the job offer process like? Did you receive a verbal or written (or both) offer? Who gave you the offer? What was the content of the offer?

Reactions to the Staffing Process

Now that you have described the staffing process, what are your reactions to it?

1. What were the strong points or positive features of the process?
2. What were the weak points and negative features of the process?
3. What changes would you like to see made in the process, and why?

Staffing Strategy for a New Plant

Household Consumer Enterprises, Inc. (HCE) has its corporate headquarters in downtown Chicago, with manufacturing and warehouse/distribution facilities throughout the north-central region of the United States. It specializes in the design and production of nondisposable household products such as brooms, brushes, rakes, kitchen utensils, and garden tools. The company has recently changed its mission from "providing households with safe and sturdy utensils" to "providing households with visually appealing utensils that are safe and sturdy." The new emphasis on "visually appealing" will necessitate new strategies for designing and producing new products that have design flair and imagination built into them. One strategy under consideration is to target various demographic groups with different utensil designs. One group is 25–40-year-old professional and managerial people, whom it is thought would want such utensils for both their visual and conversation-piece appeal.

A tentative strategy is to build and staff a new plant that will have free reign in the design and production of utensils for this 25–40 age group. To start, the plant will focus on producing a set of closely related (designwise) plastic products: dishwashing pans, outdoor wastebaskets, outdoor plant holders, and watering cans. These items can be produced without too large a capital and facilities investment, can be marketed as a group, and can be on stores' shelves and on HCE's store Web site in time for Christmas sales.

The facilities design and engineering team has initially decided that each of the four products will be produced on a separate assembly line, though the lines will share common technology and require roughly similar assembly jobs. Based on advice from the HR vice president, Jarimir Zwitski, it is decided the key jobs in the plant for staffing purposes will be plant manager, product designer (computer-assisted design), assemblers, and packers/warehouse workers. The initial staffing level for the plant will be 150 employees. Because of the riskiness of the venture and the low margins that are planned initially on the four products due to high start-up costs, the plant will be run on a continuous basis six days per week (i.e., a 24/6 schedule), with the remaining day reserved for cleaning and maintenance. It is planned for pay levels to be at the low end of the market, except for product designers, who will be paid above market. There will be limited benefits for all employees, namely, health insurance with a 30% employee copay after one year of continuous employment, no pension plan, and an earned time-off bank (for holidays, sickness, and vacation) of 160 hours per year.

The head of the design team, Maria Dos Santos, and Mr. Zwitski, wish to come to you, the corporate manager of staffing, to share their preliminary thinking with you and ask you some questions, knowing that staffing issues loom large for this new venture. They ask you to discuss the following questions with them and send them to you in advance so you can prepare for the meeting. Your task is to write out a tentative response to each question that will be the basis for your discussion at the meeting. The questions are:

1. What geographic location might be best for the plant in terms of attracting sufficient quantity and quality of labor, especially for the key jobs?

2. Should the plant manager come from inside the current managerial ranks or be sought from the outside?

3. Should staffing be based on just the person/job match or also the person/organization match?

4. Would it make sense to staff the plant initially with a flexible workforce by using temporary employees and then shift over to a core workforce if it looks like the plant will be successful?

5. In the early stages should the plant be fully staffed, understaffed, or over-staffed?

6. Will employee retention likely be a problem, and if so, how would this affect the viability of the new plant?

ENDNOTES

1. J. V. Singh, "McKinsey's Managing Director Rajat Gupta on Leading a Knowledge-Based Global Consulting Organization," *Academy of Management Executive,* 2001, 15(2), p. 35.

2. A. Hanft, "The Best CEOs," *Worth,* May 2001, p. 87.

3. G. Anders, "Taming the Out-of-Control In-Box," *Wall Street Journal,* Feb. 4, 2000, p. B1.

4. J. Angwin and M. Peers, "The Re-Emergence of Steve Case," *Wall Street Journal,* Jan. 17, 2002, p. B1.

5. University of Michigan Business School, "Innovative Solutions to the Pressing Problems of Business" (Ann Arbor: author, 2000).

6. Society for Human Resource Management, "Human Resources Strategy Study" (Alexandria, VA: author, 2001).

7. D. Welch, "Can Lutz Help Steer GM Out of Its Slide?," *Business Week,* Aug. 27, 2001, p. 54.

8. J. B. Barney and P. M. Wright, "On Becoming a Strategic Partner: The Role of Human Resources in Gaining Competitive Advantage," *Human Resource Management,* 1998, 37(1), pp. 31–46; C. G. Brush, P. G. Greene, and M. M. Hart, "From Initial Idea to Unique Advantage: The Entrepreneurial Challenge of Constructing a Resource Base," *Academy of Management Executive,* 2001, 15(1), pp. 64–80.

9. J. S. Lublin, "An E-Company CEO Is Also Recruiter-in-Chief," *Wall Street Journal,* Nov. 9, 1999, p. B1.

10. D. Field, "Smaller Airlines Struggle to Train Pilots," *USA Today,* July 27, 2000, p. 1B; M. Stinson, "Air Canada Beefs Up Staffing," *Report on Business,* Aug. 4, 2000, p. B1.

11. N. Banerjee, "A Second Oil Shortage: Experienced Workers," *New York Times,* July 1, 2000, p. BU3.

12. B. Carton, "In 24-Hour Workplace, Day Care Is Moving to the Night Shift," *Wall Street Journal,* July 6, 2000, p. A1; R. G. Matthews, "It's Boom Time for Coal, but Now the Industry Can't Dig Up Miners," *Wall Street Journal,* May 1, 1991, p. A1.

13. J. Collins, *Good to Great* (New York: Harper Collins, 2001), p. 44.

14. P. R. Bernthal, S. M. Rioux, and R. Wellins, *The Leadership Forecast: A Benchmarking Study* (Pittsburgh: Developmental Dimensions, Inc., 2001), p. 27.

15. M. A. Youndt, S. A. Snell, J. W. Dean Jr., and D. P. Lepak, "Human Resource Management, Manufacturing Strategy, and Firm Performance," *Academy of Management Journal,* 1996, 39, pp. 836–866; J. T. Delaney and M. A. Huselid, "The Impact of Human Resource Management Practices on Perceptions of Organizational Performance," *Academy of Management Journal,* 1996, 39, pp. 949–969.

16. C. R. Greer, T. C. Ireland, and J. R. Wingender, "Contrarian Human Resource Investments and Financial Performance After Economic Downturns," *Journal of Business Research,* 2001, 52, pp. 249–261.

17. C. J. Russell, "A Longitudinal Study of Top-Level Executive Performance," *Journal of Applied Psychology,* 2001, 86, pp. 560–573.

18. W. F. Cascio, *Costing Human Resources,* fourth ed. (Cincinnati, OH: Southwestern, 2000); R. W. Griffeth and P. W. Hom, *Retaining Valued Employees* (Thousand Oaks, CA: Sage, 2001).

19. D. F. Caldwell and C. A. O'Reilly III, "Measuring Person-Job Fit with a Profile-Comparison Process," *Journal of Applied Psychology,* 1990, 75, pp. 648–657; R. V. Dawis, "Person-Environment Fit and Job Satisfaction," in C. J. Cranny, P. C. Smith, and E. F. Stone, *Job Satisfaction* (New York: Lexington, 1992), pp. 69–88; R. V. Dawis, L. H. Lofquist, and D. J. Weiss, *A Theory of Work Adjustment (A Revision)* (Minneapolis: Industrial Relations Center, University of Minnesota, 1968).

20. D. E. Bowen, G. E. Ledford Jr., and B. R. Nathan, "Hiring for the Organization and Not the Job," *Academy of Management Executive,* 1991, 5(4), pp. 35–51; T. A. Judge and R. D. Bretz Jr., "Effects of Work Values on Job Choice Decisions," *Journal of Applied Psychology,* 1992, 77, pp. 1–11; C. A. O'Reilly III, J. Chatman, and D. F. Caldwell, "People and Organizational Culture: A Profile Comparison Approach to Assessing Person-Organization Fit," *Academy of Management Journal,* 1991, 34, pp. 487–516; R. J. Karren and L. M. Graves, "Assessing Person-Organization Fit in Personnel Selection: Guidelines for Future Research," *International Journal of Selection and Placement,* 1994, 3, pp. 146–156; A. L. Kristof, "Person-Organization Fit: An Intergrative Review of its Conceptualizations, Measurement, and Implications," *Personnel Psychology,* 1996, 49, pp. 1–50; D. M. Cable and T. A. Judge, "Interviewers' Perceptions of Person-Organization Fit and Organizational Selection Decisions," *Journal of Applied Psychology,* 1997, 82, pp. 546–561; A. L. Kristof-Brown, "Perceived Applicant Fit: Distinguishing Between Recruiters' Perceptions of Person-Job and Person-Organization Fit," *Personnel Psychology,* 2000, 53, pp. 643–671; A. F. Miller Jr. and M. Hanson, "Mismatches," *Across the Board,* June 2000, pp. 25–29; M. C. McCulloch and D. B. Turban, "Using Person-Organization Fit to Predict Job Departure in Call Centers," paper presented at the annual meeting of Society for Industrial-Organization Psychology, April 2001, San Diego.

21. Society for Human Resource Management, "The Labor Shortage," *Workplace Visions,* 2000; Society for Human Resource Management, "Globalization and the HR Profession," *Workplace Visions,* 2000.

22. M. L. Marke and P. H. Mirvis, "Making Mergers and Acquisitions Work," *Academy of Management Executive,* 2001, 15(2), pp. 80–94; E. R. Silverman, "Supply for Demand," *Human Resource Executive,* May 15, 2000, pp. 76–77; J. A. Schmidt (ed.), *Making Mergers Work: The Strategic Importance of People* (Alexandria, VA: Society for Human Resource Management, 2001).

23. J. Richgels, "Future Cops Face Grueling Obstacles," *The Madison (Wis.) Capital Times,* Dec. 29, 1993, p. A1.

24. M. Maynard, "Toyota Devises Grueling Workout for Job Seekers," *USA Today,* Aug. 11, 1997, p. 3B.

25. V. C. Smith, "Spreading the Magic," *Human Resource Executive,* Dec. 1996, pp. 28–31.

26. J. S. Arthur, "Screen Test," *Human Resource Executive,* Oct. 18, 1999, pp. 40–41.

The Staffing Organizations Model

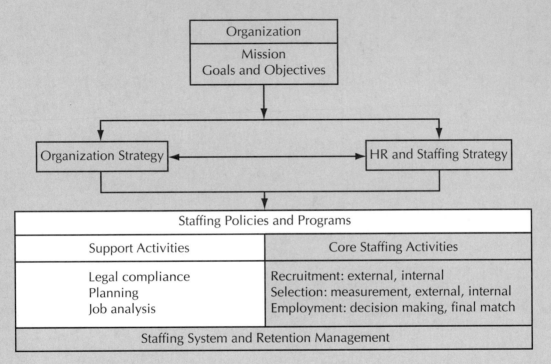

PART TWO

Support Activities

CHAPTER TWO

Legal Compliance

The Employment Relationship
Employer–Employee
Independent Contractors
Temporary Employees

Laws and Regulations
Need for Laws and Regulations
Sources of Laws and Regulations

EEO/AA: Preliminary Issues
EEO, AA, and Quotas
Disparate Treatment and Disparate Impact

EEO/AA Laws: General Provisions and Enforcement
General Provisions
Enforcement: EEOC
Enforcement: OFCCP

EEO/AA Laws: Specific Staffing Provisions
Civil Rights Acts (1964, 1991)
Age Discrimination in Employment Act (1967)
Americans With Disabilities Act (1990)
Rehabilitation Act (1973)
Executive Order 11246 (1965)

EEO/AA: Regulations and Information
Regulations and Guidelines
Information Sources

EEO/AA: Best Practices
Best Practice Criteria
Best Practice Examples

Other Staffing Laws
Federal Laws
State and Local Laws
Civil Service Laws and Regulations

Laws and regulations have assumed an importance of major proportions in the process of staffing organizations. Virtually all aspects of staffing are subject to their influence. No organization can or should ignore provisions of the law; in this case, ignorance truly is not bliss.

This chapter begins by discussing the formation of the employment relationships from a legal perspective. It first defines what an employer is, along with the rights and obligations of being an employer. The employer may acquire people to work for it in the form of employees, independent contractors, and temporary employees. Legal meanings and implications for each of these terms is provided.

For many reasons, the employment relationship has become increasingly regulated. Reasons for the myriad laws and regulations affecting the employment relationship are suggested. Then, the major sources of the laws and regulations controlling the employment relationship are indicated.

Equal employment opportunity and affirmative action (EEO/AA) laws and regulations have become paramount in the eyes of many who are concerned with staffing organizations. This dominance is illustrated first by a general discussion of EEO, AA, and quotas, as well as the two approaches for bringing forth and resolving discrimination charges. Following that, the general provisions of five major EEO/AA laws are summarized, along with indications of how these laws are administered and enforced.

For these same five laws, their specific (and numerous) provisions regarding staffing are then presented in detail. Within this presentation the true scope, complexity, and impact of the laws regarding staffing become known.

Numerous regulations and guidelines have been issued to assist in interpretation, implementation, and enforcement of these five laws. The most prominent are the Uniform Guidelines on Employee Selection Procedures, Affirmative Action Programs regulations, and the Employment Regulations of the Americans With Disabilities Act. Each of these is introduced. Also, numerous information sources about EEO/AA laws and regulations are presented.

Compliance with the various laws and regulations requires comprehensive and integrated EEO programs. Criteria for, and examples of, best practices by organizations in recruiting, hiring, promotion, and career advancement to achieve EEO objectives are described.

Attention then turns to other staffing laws and regulations. These involve myriad federal laws, state and local laws, and civil service laws and regulations. These laws, like federal EEO/AA ones, have major impacts on staffing activities.

Finally, the chapter concludes with an indication that each of the chapters that follows has a separate section, "Legal Issues," at the end of it. In these sections, specific topics and applications of the law are presented. Their intent is to provide guidance and examples (not legal advice per se) regarding staffing practices that are permissible, impermissible, and required.

THE EMPLOYMENT RELATIONSHIP

From a legal perspective the term "staffing" refers to formation of the employment relationship. That relationship involves several different types of arrangements between the organization and those who provide work for it. These arrangements have special and reasonably separate legal meaning. This section explores those arrangements: employer–employee, independent contractor, and temporary employee.[1]

Employer–Employee

By far the most prevalent form of the employment relationship is that of employer–employee. This arrangement is the result of the organization's usual staffing activities—a culmination of the person/job matching process. As shown in Exhibit 2.1, the employer and employee negotiate and agree on the terms and conditions that will define and govern their relationship. The formal agreement represents an employment contract, the terms and conditions of which represent the promises

EXHIBIT 2.1   Matching Process, Employment Contract, and Employment Relationships

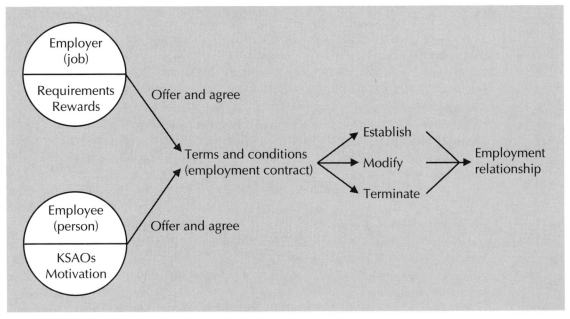

and expectations of the parties (job requirements and rewards, and KSAOs and motivation). Over time, the initial contract may be modified due to changes in requirements or rewards of the current job, or employee transfer or promotion. The contract may also be terminated by either party, thus ending the employment relationship.

Employment contracts come in a variety of styles. They may be written or oral (both types are legally enforceable), and their specificity may vary from extensive to bare bones. In some instances, where the contract is written, terms and conditions are described in great detail. Examples of such contracts are collective bargaining agreements and contracts for professional athletes, entertainers, and upper-level executives. At the other extreme, the contract may be little more than some simple oral promises about the job, such as promises about wages and hours, agreed to on the basis of a handshake.

From a legal perspective, an employer is an entity that employs others (employees or independent contractors) to do its work or work on its behalf. When these "others" are employees, the employer has the right to specify both the work output (results) expected and the work methods to be followed by its employees. In exchange for this right to control employees, the employer incurs certain legal responsibilities and liabilities. Specifically, the employer becomes (a) required to withhold employee payroll taxes (income, Social Security), (b) required to pay taxes (unemployment compensation, employer's share of Social Security and Medicare), (c) covered under the myriad laws and regulations governing the employment relationship, and (d) liable for the acts of its employees during employment.

When and how the employment relationship may end is a matter of great importance to the employer and the employee. For the employer, it bears on the degree of staffing flexibility possible to quickly terminate employees without constraint. For employees, the issue is the degree of continued employment and job security that will be expected. Under the common-law principle of employment-at-will, in the absence of any contract language to the contrary, the employment relationship is strictly an at-will one, meaning that either the employer or the employee may terminate the employment relationship at any time, for any reason, without prior notification.

Restrictions on the employment-at-will right are usually established as part of the employment contract. For example, a set-term contract specifies a definite duration and ending date; normally it will (or should) have a clause stating that it may not be terminated during that period without showing "just cause" or "failure to perform." As another example, labor union contracts usually contain a provision stating that an employee can be terminated only for "just cause." As another example, a letter of appointment to a new hire may contain a clause saying it is the policy of the organization to terminate its employees only "for cause." For an organization wishing to avoid such restrictions and to be governed by employment-at-will, it must take care to ensure that its employment contracts explicitly state that there will be an employment-at-will relationship and that the contracts contain no language providing restrictions on such a relationship.

There are numerous exceptions to employment-at-will, outside of specific contract language restrictions, that limit the right of the employer to terminate the employment relationship at will.[2] These include prohibitions of discharge on the basis of legally protected characteristics (e.g., age, sex, race), for exercising rights guaranteed by law (e.g., filing a discrimination charge against the employer), for refusing to engage in illegal acts for the employer, or when there is an implied set-term or just-cause contract. Specific prohibitions vary among the 50 states.

Independent Contractors

The employer may also hire independent contractors.[3] An independent contractor is not legally considered an employee, however; because of this the rights and responsibilities the employer has toward the independent contractor are different than those for its employees. Classifying and using a person as an independent contractor frees the employer of the tax withholding and tax payment obligations it has for employees. It may also reduce employer exposure under laws and regulations governing the employment relationship. For example, nondiscrimination laws (e.g., Civil Rights Act) apply to the employer and its employees, but not to its independent contractors.

In exchange for these advantages of using independent contractors, the employer substantially loses the right to control the contractor. In particular, while the employer can still control expected results, the employer cannot dictate where, when, or how work is to be done. Thus, the employer loses control over the means (work processes, tools, equipment, work schedules, and so forth) by which the work is performed.

Beyond this crucial distinction, the line of demarcation between what constitutes an employee and what constitutes an independent contractor is often fuzzy. Numerous other factors come into play. For example, a person is more likely to be considered an independent contractor than an employee when

- working in a distinct occupation or business
- working without supervision or oversight from the employer
- paying one's own business and travel expenses
- setting one's own hours of work
- possessing a high degree of skill
- using one's own tools, materials, office
- working on a project with a definite completion date
- working on relatively short projects
- being paid by the project or commission, rather than by the time spent

The above examples are based on common-law interpretations, and on a list of 20 criteria used by the Internal Revenue Service to determine the appropriate classification of people as employees or independent contractors. Misclassification of people as independent contractors can result in substantial tax liabilities and fines for the employer.

Temporary Employees

Temporary employees do not have special legal stature. They are considered employees of the temporary help agency that obtained them through its own staffing process. Temporary employees are then given job assignments with other employers (clients) by the agency. During these assignments the temporary employee remains on the payroll of the agency, and the client employer simply reimburses the agency for its wage and other costs. The client employer must recognize that it has a severely limited right to control temporary employees that it utilizes because they are not its employees but employees of the agency.

Use of temporary employees often raises issues of coemployment, in which the client employer and the temporary agency share the traditional role of employer.[4] Because both function as employers to an extent, there is a need to sort out their obligations and liabilities under various laws. Depending on the specific issue and law involved, both the client employer and agency may be legally considered the employer. Employment discrimination laws such as the Civil Rights Act, for example, apply to both the client employer and the agency. Thus, usage of temporary employees by a client employer should be preceded by a thorough review of the coemployment legal ramifications.

The demarcation between an employee and a temporary employee becomes increasingly blurred when an employer uses a set of temporary employees from an agency on a long-term basis, resulting in so-called permatemps. Nationally, 29% of such employees work for the same client employer for a year or more, so they appear more like employees of the client than of the temporary agency. Which are they, and what factors might determine this? Several court cases suggest that these individuals are in fact employees of the client employer rather than of the temporary agency, particularly because of the strong degree of control the client employer typically exercises over those people. Hence, to help ensure that permatemps will not be legally considered the client's employees, the client must give up, or never exercise, direct control over these people and treat them as truly separate from regular employees. This may require, for example, not training or supervising them, not listing them in the phone directory, or not allowing them to use the organization's stationery. Clearly, therefore, organizations must examine all policies and practices regarding the acquisition and management of temporary employees to ensure that they are being appropriately treated and classified as such.[5]

LAWS AND REGULATIONS

Establishment and maintenance of the employment relationship involves exercising discretion on the part of both the employer and the employee. Broadly speaking, laws affecting the employment relationship spring from a need to define the scope of permissible discretion and place limits on it. Specific factors contributing to the need for laws and regulations and the sources of laws and regulations are explored below.

Need for Laws and Regulations

Balance of Power

Entering into and maintaining the employment relationship involve negotiating issues of power.[6] The employer has something desirable to offer the employee (a job with certain requirements and rewards), and the employee has something to offer the employer (KSAOs and motivation). Usually, the employer has the upper hand in this power relationship because the employer has more to offer, and more control over what to offer, than does the employee. It is the employer who controls the creation of jobs; the definition of jobs in terms of requirements and rewards; access to those jobs via staffing systems; movement of employees among jobs over time; and ultimately, the retention or termination of employees. While employees participate in these processes and decisions to varying degrees, it is seldom as an equal or a partner of the employer. Employment laws and regulations thus exist, in part, to reduce or limit the employer's power in the employment relationship. Laws pertaining to wages, hours, equal employment opportunity, and so forth, all seek to limit employer discretion in the establishment of the terms and conditions of employment.

Protection of Employees

Laws and regulations seek to provide specific protections to employees that they could conceivably, though improbably, acquire individually in an employment contract.[7] These protections pertain to employment standards, individual workplace rights, and consistency of treatment. Employment standards usually represent minimum acceptable terms and conditions of employment. Examples include minimum wage, nondiscrimination, overtime pay, and safety and health standards. Laws and regulations also provide employees with individual rights that they could not acquire alone in a contract with their employers. Examples of these are organizing and collective bargaining rights, civil rights protections, and constraints that place limits on the right of the employer to unilaterally terminate the employment relationship. Finally, laws and regulations, in effect, provide guarantees of consistency of treatment among employees. They constitute a constraint on the employer to treat employees differently from one another in terms and conditions of employment and afford employees some measure of procedural justice, or fairness in the process whereby decisions are made about them. Hiring and promotion decisions, for example, cannot be made on the basis of protected employee characteristics (e.g., race, sex).

Protection of Employers

Employers also gain protections from laws and regulations. First, they provide guidance to employers as to what are permissible practices as well as impermissible practices. The Civil Rights Act, for example, not only forbids certain types of discrimination on the basis of race, color, religion, sex, and national origin but also specifically mentions employment practices that are permitted. One of those practices is the use of professionally developed ability tests, a practice that has major implications for external and internal selection. Second, questions about the meaning of the law are clarified through many avenues—court decisions, policy statements from government agencies, informal guidance from enforcement officials, and networking with other employers. The result is increasing convergence on what is required to comply with the laws. This allows the employer to implement needed changes, which then become standard operating procedure in staffing systems. In this manner, for example, affirmative action programs have developed and been incorporated into the administrative mainstream for many employers.

Sources of Laws and Regulations

There are numerous sources of laws and regulation that govern the employment relationship. Exhibit 2.2 provides examples of these as they pertain to staffing. Each of these is commented on next.

Common Law

Common law, which has its origins in England, is court-made law, as opposed to law from other sources such as the state. It consists of the case-by-case decisions of the court, which determine over time permissible and impermissible practices, as well as their remedies. There is a heavy reliance in common law on the precedence established in previous court decisions. Each state develops and administers its own common law. Employment-at-will and workplace tort cases, for example, are treated at the state level. As noted, employment-at-will involves the rights of employer and employee to terminate the employment relationship at will. A tort is a civil wrong that occurs when the employer violates a duty owed to its employees or customers that leads to harm or damages suffered by them. Staffing tort examples include negligent hiring of unsafe or dangerous employees, fraud and misrepresentation regarding employment terms and conditions, defamation of former employees, and invasion of privacy.[8]

EXHIBIT 2.2   Sources of Laws and Regulations

SOURCE	EXAMPLES
Common law	Employment-at-will Workplace torts
Constitutional	Fifth Amendment Fourteenth Amendment
Statutory	Civil Rights Act Age Discrimination in Employment Act Americans With Disabilities Act Rehabilitation Act Immigration Reform and Control Act Fair Credit Reporting Act Employee Polygraph Protection Act State and local laws Civil service laws
Executive order	11246 (nondiscrimination under federal contracts)
Agencies	Equal Employment Opportunity Commission (EEOC) Department of Labor (DOL) Office of Federal Contract Compliance Programs (OFCCP) State Fair Employment Practice (FEP) agencies

Constitutional Law

Constitutional law is derived from the U.S. Constitution and its amendments. It supersedes any other source of law or regulation. Its major application is in the area of the rights of public employees, particularly their due process rights.

Statutory Law

Statutory law is derived from written statutes that are passed by legislative bodies. These bodies are federal (Congress), state (legislatures and assemblies), and local (municipal boards and councils). Legislative bodies may create, amend, and eliminate laws and regulations. They may also create agencies to administer and enforce the law.

Agencies

Agencies exist at the federal, state, and local level. Their basic charge is to interpret, administer, and enforce the law. At the federal level, the two major agencies of concern to staffing are the Department of Labor (DOL) and the Equal Employment Opportunity Commission (EEOC). Housed within DOL are several separate units for administration of employment law, notably the Office of Federal Contract Compliance Programs (OFCCP).

Agencies rely heavily on written documents to perform their functions. These documents are variously referred to as rules, regulations, guidelines, and policy statements. Rules, regulations, and guidelines are published in the *Federal Register,* as well as incorporated into the Code of Federal Regulations (CFR), and have the weight of law. Policy statements are somewhat more benign in that they do not have the force of law. They do, however, represent the agency's official position on a point or question.

EEO/AA: PRELIMINARY ISSUES

The numerous and complex equal employment opportunity and affirmative action (EEO/AA) laws and regulations are major sources of influence on staffing. Understanding them requires familiarity first with some preliminary issues that set the context for the specifics of the laws and regulations.

EEO, AA, and Quotas

The terms equal employment opportunity (EEO), affirmative action (AA), and quotas are encountered frequently and often lead to confusion. There are conceptual, semantic, and practical differences among these three terms as they apply to staffing.[9] What follows is a brief overview of the distinctions to help clarify their meaning and usage.

EEO
As applied to staffing, EEO refers to practices that are designed and used in a "facially neutral" manner, meaning that all applicants and employees are treated similarly without regard to protected characteristics such as race and sex. Consistent application of and adherence to these practices is thought to create an equal opportunity for everyone to obtain a job or promotion.

To illustrate, consider a simple example where an organization is filling a vacant position and uses both a written job knowledge test and an interview in assessing job applicants. Anyone is free to apply for the position, and all that do so will be given both the test and the interview. How well each performs on the test and in the interview determines who is hired. Thus, all applicants have an equal chance or opportunity to be considered for the job, and which applicant receives the job offer depends on an unbiased assessment of applicants' job qualifications.

AA
AA requirements in staffing must be placed in the context of past practices that were discriminatory against minorities and women, as well as other groups. Through

changing existing staffing practices and adding new ones, AA seeks to rectify the discriminatory effects of these past practices. In this sense, AA is less than completely facially neutral. AA may be voluntarily undertaken by an employer, without anyone "pointing a finger" at specific actions. AA may also be court-ordered, or agreed to, as a remedy for past actions that indeed were discriminatory.

Consider again the preceding staffing example, and assume that the staffing system has operated the same way for many years. Several features of the system may have created potentially unequal employment opportunities for women and minorities, resulting in their being numerically underrepresented relative to their availability and qualifications in the labor market. For example, there may have been an outright refusal to recruit women and minorities, or the recruitment methods used—referrals from current, mostly male, employees—may have greatly favored male applicants. As another example, women and minorities may have scored poorly on the job knowledge test because of lack of access to the types of training and/or job experience necessary to acquire that knowledge. Special affirmative actions, voluntary or court-imposed, seek to enhance the employment of women and minorities and help deal with these sorts of historical problems.[10]

What might these actions entail? The organization might undertake special recruiting methods, other than just current employees' referral, to identify and attract women and minority applicants. Management might establish specific hiring goals and timetables for achieving those goals for women and minorities. The organization would make good faith efforts to meet the hiring goals and timetables. Also, the organization could place less weight on the job knowledge test when making hiring decisions and create a training program for new job entrants to provide them the types of job knowledge they need in order to perform effectively on the job.

Quotas

Quotas represent more rigid hiring and promotion requirements that must be adhered to. Quotas do not leave staffing to the somewhat ill-defined concept of affirmative action; quotas focus on and demand staffing results. If a quota staffing system were applied in the previous example, a hiring formula would be established that specifies the number or percentage of women and minorities to be hired so that their numerical representation in the workplace reflects the percentage of potentially qualified women and minorities in the population. Quota staffing systems of this kind are legally permissible as a judicial remedy for past discrimination, though there are limitations on their usage and features.[11] AA quotas have raised substantial legal turmoil, as well as more practical questions as to whether they have in fact worked effectively to advance the hiring and promotion of minorities and women. Of utmost concern are issues of "reverse discrimination" or special racial or gender preferences that weigh too heavily into hiring and promotion decisions, relative to the qualifications of candidates for the job.[12] The permissibility and legal status of AA and quotas are explained in detail in Chapter 3, along with a description of AA plan requirements and the content of AA programs.

Disparate Treatment and Disparate Impact

Claims of discrimination in staffing ultimately require evidence and proof, particularly as these charges pertain to the staffing system itself and its specific characteristics as it has operated in practice. Toward this end, there are two different avenues or paths to follow—disparate treatment and disparate impact.[13] While both paths may be followed for Title VII of the Civil Rights Act and Americans With Disabilities Act claims, the courts vary on whether a disparate impact path may be followed for an Age Discrimination in Employment Act claim.

Disparate Treatment

Claims of disparate treatment involve allegations of intentional discrimination where it is alleged that the employer knowingly and deliberately discriminated against people on the basis of specific characteristics such as race or sex. Evidence for such claims may be of several sorts.

First, the evidence may be direct. It might, for example, involve reference to an explicit, written policy of the organization such as one stating that "women are not to be hired for the following jobs."

The situation may not involve such blatant action, however, but may consist of what is referred to as a mixed motive. Here, both a prohibited characteristic (e.g., sex) and a legitimate reason (e.g., job qualifications) are mixed together to contribute to a negative decision about a person, such as a failure to hire or promote. If an unlawful motive, such as sex, plays any part in the decision, it is illegal, despite the presence of a lawful motive as well.

Finally, the discrimination may be such that evidence of a failure to hire or promote because of a protected characteristic must be inferred from several situational factors. Here, the evidence involves four factors:

1. The person belongs to a protected class.
2. The person applied for, and was qualified for, a job the employer was trying to fill.
3. The person was rejected despite being qualified.
4. The position remained open and the employer continued to seek applicants as qualified as the person rejected.

Most disparate treatment cases involve and require the use of these four factors to initially prove a charge of discrimination.

Disparate Impact

Disparate impact is also known as adverse impact and focuses on the effect of employment practices, rather than on the motive or intent underlying them. Accordingly, the emphasis here is on the need for direct evidence that, as a result of a protected characteristic, people are being adversely affected by a practice. Statistical evidence must be presented to support a claim of adverse impact.[14] Three types of statistical evidence may be used, and these are shown in Exhibit 2.3.

Shown first in the exhibit are applicant flow statistics, which look at differences in selection rates (proportion of applicants hired) among different groups for a particular job. If the differences are large enough, this suggests that the effect of the selection system is discriminatory. In the example, the selection rate for men is .50 (or 50%) and for women it is .11 (or 11%), suggesting the possibility of discrimination.

A second type of statistical evidence, shown next in the exhibit, involves the use of stock statistics. Here, the percentage of women or minorities actually employed in a job category is compared with their availability in the relevant population. Relevant is defined in terms of such things as "qualified," "interested," or "geographic." In the example shown, there is a disparity in the percentage of minorities employed (10%) compared with their availability (30%), which suggests their underutilization.

The third type of evidence involves use of concentration statistics. Here, the percentages of women or minorities in various job categories are compared to see if women are concentrated in certain workforce categories. In the example shown, there is a concentration of women in clerical jobs (97%), a concentration of men in production (85%) and managerial (95%) jobs, and roughly equal concentrations of men and women in sales jobs (45% and 55%, respectively).

EEO/AA LAWS: GENERAL PROVISIONS AND ENFORCEMENT

In this section, the major federal EEO/AA laws are summarized in terms of their general provisions. Mechanisms for enforcement of the laws are also discussed.[15]

General Provisions

The federal EEO/AA laws that are major follow:

1. Title VII of the Civil Rights Acts (1964, 1991)
2. Age Discrimination in Employment Act (1967)
3. Americans With Disabilities Act (1990)
4. Rehabilitation Act (1973)
5. Executive Order 11246 (1965)

Exhibit 2.4 contains a summary of the basic provisions of these laws, pertaining to coverage, prohibited discrimination, enforcement agency, and important rules, regulations, and guidelines.

Inspection of Exhibit 2.4 suggests that these laws are appropriately labeled "major" for several reasons. First, the laws are very broad in their coverage of

EXHIBIT 2.3   Types of Disparate Impact Statistics

A. FLOW STATISTICS

Definition:

Significant differences in selection rates between groups

Example

Job Category: Customer Service Representative

No. of Applicants		No. Hired		Selection Rate (%)	
Men	**Women**	**Men**	**Women**	**Men**	**Women**
50	45	25	5	50%	11%

B. STOCK STATISTICS

Definition:

Underutilization of women or minorities relative to their availability in the relevant population

Example

Job Category: Management Trainee

Current Trainees (%)		Availability (%)	
Nonminority	**Minority**	**Nonminority**	**Minority**
90%	10%	70%	30%

C. CONCENTRATION STATISTICS

Definition:

Concentration of women or minorities in certain job categories

Example

	Job Category			
	Clerical	**Production**	**Sales**	**Managers**
% Men	3%	85%	45%	95%
% Women	97%	15%	55%	5%

employers. Second, they specifically prohibit discrimination on the basis of several individual characteristics (race, color, religion, sex, national origin, age, disability, handicap). Third, separate agencies have been created for their administration and enforcement. Finally, these agencies have issued numerous rules, regulations, and guidelines to assist in interpreting, implementing, and enforcing the law.

For the Civil Rights Act, Age Discrimination in Employment Act (ADEA), and Americans With Disabilities Act (ADA), Exhibit 2.4 shows that whether the organization is covered depends on its number of employees. To count employees, the EEOC has issued guidance indicating that the organization should include any employee with whom the organization had an "employment relationship" in each of 20 or more calendar weeks during the current or preceding year. In essence, this means that full-time and part-time employees—and possibly temporary employees if there is true coemployment—should be included in the employee count.[16]

EXHIBIT 2.4   Major Federal EEO/AA Laws: General Provisions

Law or Executive Order	Coverage	Prohibited Discrimination	Enforcement Agency	Important Rules, Regulations, and Guidelines
Civil Rights Act (1964, 1991)	Private employers with 15 or more employees Federal, state, and local governments Educational institutions Employment agencies Labor unions	Race, color, religion, national origin, sex	EEOC	Uniform Guidelines on Employee Selection Procedures Sex Discrimination Guidelines Religious Discrimination Guidelines National Origin Discrimination Guidelines
Age Discrimination in Employment Act (1967)	Private employers with 20 or more employees State, and local governments Employment agencies Labor unions	Age (40 or over)	EEOC	Interpretations of the Age Discrimination in Employment Act
Americans With Disabilities Act (1990)	Private employers with 15 or more employees State and local governments	Qualified individual with a disability	EEOC	ADA—Employment Regulations Definition of the Term Disability Pre-Employment Disability-Related Questions and Medical Examinations
Rehabilitation Act (1973)	Federal contractors with contracts in excess of $2,500	Individual with a handicap	DOL (OFCCP)	Affirmative Action Regulations on Handicapped Workers
Executive Order 11246 (1965)	Federal contractors with contracts in excess of $10,000	Race, color, religion, national origin, sex	DOL (OFCCP)	Sex Discrimination Guidelines Affirmative Action Programs regulations

NOTE: Full text of the laws and Executive Order, as well as the important rules, regulations, and guidelines, may be found in the Bureau of National Affairs publication, *Fair Employment Practices*, Volume 1 (Washington, DC: author, periodically up-dated).

It should also be noted that employees are protected from retaliation by the organization for engaging in activities protected by the laws shown in Exhibit 2.4. In the case of the Civil Rights Act, ADEA, and ADA, the EEOC has issued specific guidance protecting employees who oppose any organizational practices that may be illegal and who file a charge, testify, or participate in an investigation under these laws. The guidance also discusses what constitutes evidence of retaliation, as well as special remedies for retaliatory actions by the employer.[17]

Three other general features of the EEO laws, as interpreted by the EEOC and the courts, should be noted.[18] First, state (but not local) government employers are immune from lawsuits by employees who allege violation of the ADA or ADEA. State employees must thus pursue age and disability discrimination claims under applicable state laws. Second, company officials and individual managers cannot be held personally liable for discrimination under the Civil Rights Act, the ADA, or the ADEA. They might be liable, however, under state law. Third, the ADA, the Civil Rights Act, and the ADEA extend to U.S. citizens employed overseas by American employers. Also, a foreign company that is owned or controlled by an American employer and is doing business overseas generally also must comply with the Civil Rights Act, the ADA, and the ADEA.

Enforcement: EEOC

As shown in Exhibit 2.4, the EEOC has responsibility for enforcing the Civil Rights Act, ADEA, and ADA. Though each law requires separate enforcement mechanisms, some generalizations about their collective enforcement are possible.[19]

Initial Charge and Conciliation

Enforcement proceedings begin when a charge is filed by an employee or job applicant (the EEOC itself may also file a charge). In states where there is an EEOC-approved fair enforcement practice (FEP) law, the charge is initially deferred to the state. An investigation of the charge occurs to determine if there is "reasonable cause" to assume discrimination has occurred. If reasonable cause is not found, the charge is dropped. If reasonable cause is found, however, the EEOC attempts conciliation of the charge. Conciliation is a voluntary settlement process that seeks agreement by the employer to stop the practice(s) in question and abide by proposed remedies. This is the EEOC's preferred method of settlement. Whenever the EEOC decides not to pursue a claim further, it will issue a "right to sue" letter to the complaining party, allowing a private suit to be started against the employer.

Complementing conciliation is the use of mediation. With mediation, a neutral, third-party mediator is used to mediate the dispute between the employer and the EEOC and to obtain an agreement between them that resolves the dispute. Participation in mediation is voluntary, and either party may opt out of it for any reason. Mediation proceedings are confidential. Any agreement reached between the parties is legally enforceable.[20]

EXHIBIT 2.5   Basic Litigation Process: EEOC

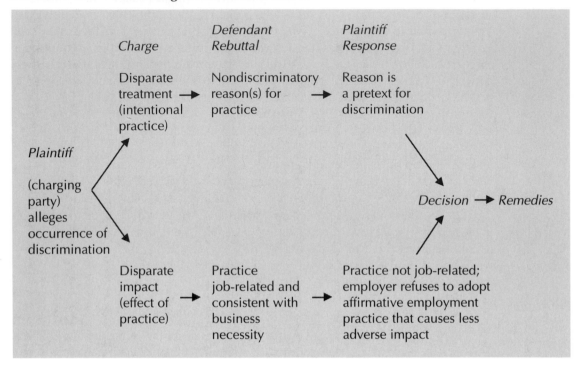

Litigation and Remedies

Should conciliation fail, suit is filed in federal court. The ensuing litigation process is shown in Exhibit 2.5. As can be seen, the charge of the plaintiff (charging party) will follow either a disparate treatment or disparate impact route.[21] In either event, the plaintiff has the initial burden of proof. Such a burden requires the plaintiff to establish a prima facie case that demonstrates reasonable cause to assume discrimination has occurred. Assuming this case is successfully presented, the defendant must rebut the charge and accompanying evidence.

In disparate treatment cases, the defendant must provide nondiscriminatory reasons during rebuttal for the practice(s) in question. In disparate impact cases, the employer must demonstrate that the practices in question are job-related and consistent with business necessity.

Following rebuttal, the plaintiff may respond to the defense provided by the defendant. In disparate treatment cases, that response hinges on a demonstration that the defendant's reasons for a practice are a pretext, or smoke screen, for the practice. In disparate impact cases, the plaintiff's response will focus on showing that the defendant has not shown its practices to be job-related and/or that the employer refuses to adopt a practice that causes less adverse impact.

Who bears the final, or ultimate, burden of proof? In disparate treatment cases, the plaintiff must ultimately prove that the defendant's practices are discriminatory. For disparate impact cases, on the other hand, the burden is on the defendant. That is, it is the defendant who must prove that its practices are not discriminatory.

The plaintiff and defendant have an opportunity to end their dispute through a consent decree. This is a voluntary, court-approved agreement between the two parties. The consent decree may contain not only an agreement to halt certain practices but also an agreement to implement certain remedies, such as various forms of monetary relief and AA programs.

An example of a consent decree is the $8.5 million agreement between the EEOC and Eagle Global Logistics, an airfreight company.[22] Among its many provisions, the agreement represents back pay and damages for African-American, Hispanic, and female employees and job applicants who allegedly experienced discrimination in external staffing and promotions across several job categories, as well as a fund to establish a corporate leadership development program to train women and minorities for leadership roles. Eagle denied the allegations but said it was in the best interests of the company to settle the dispute.

In the absence of a consent decree, the court will fashion its own remedies from those permitted under the law. There are several remedies available. First, the court may enjoin certain practices, which means requiring the defendant to halt the practices. Second, the court may order the hiring or reinstatement of individuals. Third, the court may fashion various forms of monetary relief, such as back pay, front pay, attorney's fees, and compensatory and punitive damages. Compensatory and punitive damages may be applied only in cases involving disparate treatment, and there is a cap of $300,000 on them; front pay and back pay are excluded from the cap. Finally, under the Civil Rights Act and ADA, the court may order "such affirmative action as may be appropriate," as well as "any other equitable relief" that the court deems appropriate. Through these provisions, the court has considerable latitude in the remedies it imposes. Note that this court's prerogative includes imposition of AA plans, as well as hiring and promotion quota systems.

Enforcement: OFCCP

Enforcement mechanisms used by the OFCCP are very different from those used by the EEOC.[23] Most covered employers are required to develop and implement written AA plans for women and minorities. Specific AA plan requirements for employers under EO 11246 are spelled out in Affirmative Action Programs regulations.

To enforce these requirements, the OFCCP conducts off-site desk audits and reviews of employers' records and affirmative action plans and on-site visits and compliance reviews of employers' AA plans. It also investigates complaints charging noncompliance. Employers found to be in noncompliance are urged to change their practices through a conciliation process. Summaries of conciliation agree-

---

EXHIBIT 2.6   Summaries of Three Conciliation Agreements

Three employers—Goodyear Tire and Rubber Company in Houston, the University of California at San Diego, and American of Martinsville in Va.—will pay more than $1.25 million in back pay and salary adjustments to resolve alleged federal equal employment opportunity law violations, Secretary of Labor Robert B. Reich announced today.

"These settlements clearly demonstrate our strong commitment to ensure that our nation's workers are protected and have access to equal employment opportunity in the workplace," Reich said. "Employers must understand that we take our mandate to enforce the law in a fair and responsible manner very seriously and will take necessary action to ensure compliance."

The conciliation agreements resolve alleged discrimination based on race and gender and other faulty personnel practices identified in compliance reviews conducted by the department's Office of Federal Contract Compliance Programs (OFCCP). OFCCP monitors federal contractors and subcontractors to ensure they are in compliance with federal antidiscrimination laws.

Details of the conciliation agreements follow:

—The University of California at San Diego has agreed to pay $608,403 in back pay to 28 individuals. The university will pay $600,000 to 27 women and minorities who were denied jobs or promotions although they were fully qualified. An additional $8,403 will be paid a current employee who was given a retroactive promotion to July 1992.

—American of Martinsville, Martinsville, Va., a furniture manufacturer, has agreed to pay $417,000 to resolve alleged discriminatory employment practices. About $217,123 in back pay is to be paid to nearly 200 minorities and women. Back pay, based on length of service from one to 48 years, ranges from $100 to $2,700 per individual. The company also has agreed to pay about $200,000 in front pay. Front pay is the difference between the new and old pay systems, which will be paid retroactively from the period July 1 to January 1995 when the new system is fully operational. In addition, the company will spend approximately $200,000 to design and implement a completely revised blue-collar pay system to be in place no later than Jan. 1, 1995.

—Goodyear Tire and Rubber Company in Houston has agreed to pay $229,361 in back wages to 42 employees and applicants who were alleged victims of racial discrimination. The settlement resolves discriminatory hiring and personnel practices identified in a combined compliance review and a class action complaint investigation. OFCCP identified 33 victims of discrimination due to Goodyear's promotion policies and practices; seven minorities were paid unequal wages compared to nonminority workers, and two applicants were denied employment because of their ethnic identification.

Source: U.S. Department of Labor, OFCCP, *News* (Washington, DC: author, 10/28/95).

ments for three organizations are shown in Exhibit 2.6. Should conciliation not be successful, employers are subject to various penalties that affect their status as a federal contractor. These include cancellation of contracts and debarment from bidding on future contracts.

EEO/AA LAWS: SPECIFIC STAFFING PROVISIONS

Each of the major laws covered in the previous section contains specific provisions pertaining to staffing practices by organizations. This section summarizes those specific provisions, including agencies and courts' interpretations of them.[24] Phrases in quotation marks are direct quotations from the laws themselves. Applications of these provisions to staffing policies, practices, and actions occur throughout the remainder of the book.

Civil Rights Acts (1964, 1991)

The provisions of the Civil Rights Acts of 1964 and 1991 are combined for discussion purposes here. The 1991 law is basically a series of amendments to the 1964 law, though it does contain some provisions unique to it.

Unlawful Employment Practices
This section of the law contains a comprehensive statement regarding unlawful employment practices. Specifically, it is unlawful for an employer

1. "to fail or refuse to hire or to discharge any individual, or otherwise discriminate against any individual with respect to his compensation, terms, conditions, or privileges of employment, because of such individual's race, color, religion, sex, or national origin"; or
2. "to limit, segregate, or classify his employees or applicants for employment in any way which would deprive or tend to deprive any individual of employment opportunities or otherwise adversely affect his status as an employee because of such individual's race, color, religion, sex, or national origin."

These two statements are the foundation of civil rights law. They are very broad and inclusive, applying to virtually all staffing practices by an organization. There are also separate statements for employment agencies and labor unions.

Establishment of Disparate Impact
As discussed previously, a claim of discrimination may be pursued via a disparate impact or disparate treatment approach. The law makes several points regarding the former approach.

First, staffing practices that do not cause adverse impact are not illegal (assuming, of course, that no intention to discriminate underlies them). Thus, while certain practices may somehow seem unfair, outrageous, or of dubious value to the employer, they are a matter of legal concern only if their usage causes disparate impact.

Second, staffing practices that the plaintiff initially alleges to have caused adverse impact are unlawful unless the employer can successfully rebut the charges. To do this, the employer must show that the practices are "job-related for the position in question and consistent with business necessity." Practices that fail to meet this standard are unlawful.

Third, the plaintiff must show adverse impact for each specific staffing practice or component. For example, if an employer has a simple selection system in which applicants first take a written test and those who pass it are interviewed, the plaintiff must show adverse impact separately for the test and the interview, rather than for the two components combined.

Disparate Treatment

Intentional discrimination with staffing practices is prohibited, and the employer may not use a claim of business necessity to justify intentional use of a discriminatory practice.

Mixed Motives

An employer may not defend an action by claiming that while a prohibited factor, such as sex, entered into a staffing decision, other factors, such as job qualifications, did also. Such "mixed motive" defenses are not permitted.

Bona Fide Occupational Qualification (BFOQ)

An employer may attempt to justify use of a protected characteristic, such as national origin, as being a bona fide occupational qualification, or BFOQ. The law permits such claims, but only for sex, religion, and national origin—not race or color. The employer must be able to demonstrate that such discrimination is "a bona fide occupational qualification reasonably necessary to the normal operation of that particular business or enterprise." Thus, a maximum security prison with mostly male inmates might hire only male prison guards on the grounds that by doing so it ensures the safety, security, and privacy of inmates. However, it must be able to show that doing so is a business necessity.

Testing

The law explicitly permits the use of tests in staffing. The employer may "give and act upon the results of any professionally developed ability test, provided that such test, its administration, or action upon the basis of results is not designed, intended, or used to discriminate because of race, color, religion, sex, or national origin."

Interpretation of this provision has been difficult. What exactly is a "professionally developed ability test"? How does an employer use a test to discriminate? Not discriminate? The need for answers to such questions gave rise to the Uniform Guidelines on Employee Selection Procedures (UGESP).

Test Score Adjustments

Test scores are not to be altered or changed to somehow make them more fair; test scores should speak for themselves. Specifically, it is an unlawful employment practice "to adjust the scores of, use different cutoff scores for, or otherwise alter the results of employment related tests on the basis of race, color, religion, sex, or national origin." This provision bans so-called race norming in which people's scores are compared only to members of their own racial group and separate cutoff or passing scores are set for each group.

Seniority or Merit Systems

The law explicitly permits the use of seniority and merit systems as a basis for applying different terms and conditions to employees. However, the seniority or merit system must be "bona fide," and it may not be the result of an intention to discriminate.

This provision has particular relevance to internal staffing systems. It in essence allows the employer to take into account seniority (experience) and merit (e.g., KSAOs, promotion potential assessments) when making internal staffing decisions.

Employment Advertising

Discrimination in employment advertising is prohibited. Specifically, the employer may not indicate "any preference, limitation, specification, or discrimination based on race, color, religion, sex, or national origin." An exception to this is if sex, religion, or national origin is a BFOQ.

Preferential Treatment and Quotas

The law does not require preferential treatment or quotas. Thus, the employer is not required to have a balanced workforce, meaning one whose demographic composition matches or mirrors the demographic makeup of the surrounding population from which it draws its employees.

Note that the law does not prohibit preferential treatment, AA, and quotas. It merely says they are not required. Thus, they may be used in certain instances, such as a voluntary AA plan or a court-imposed remedy.

Age Discrimination in Employment Act (1967)

Prohibited Age Discrimination

The law explicitly and inclusively prohibits discrimination against those age 40 and older. It is unlawful for an employer

1. "to fail or refuse to hire or to discharge any individual or otherwise discriminate against any individual with respect to his compensation, terms, conditions or privileges of employment, because of such individual's age"; and

2. "to limit, segregate, or classify his employees in any way which would deprive or tend to deprive any individual of employment opportunities or otherwise adversely affect his status as an employee, because of such individual's age."

Bona Fide Occupational Qualification (BFOQ)

Like the Civil Rights Act, this law contains a BFOQ provision. Thus, it is not unlawful for an employer to differentiate among applicants or employees on the basis of their age "where age is a bona fide occupational qualification reasonably necessary to the normal operation of the particular business."

Factors Other Than Age

The employer may use "reasonable factors other than age" in making employment decisions. Such factors must be applied equally to all applicants, cannot include age in any way, must be job-related, and cannot result in discrimination on the basis of age. Factors that are correlated with age, such as job experience, may be used.

Seniority Systems

The law permits the use of seniority systems (merit systems are not mentioned). Thus, the employer is permitted "to observe the terms of a bona fide seniority system that is not intended to evade the purposes" of the act.

Employment Advertising

Age discrimination in employment advertising is prohibited. Ads may not indicate "any preference, limitation, specification, or discrimination based on age."

Americans With Disabilities Act (1990)

The ADA is a new and sweeping piece of legislation whose application to employment did not occur until mid-1992. Its basic purpose is to prohibit discrimination against qualified individuals with disabilities and to require the employer to make reasonable accommodation for such individuals unless that would cause undue hardship for the employer.

Prohibited Discrimination

The law contains a broad prohibition against disability discrimination. It specifically says that an employer may not "discriminate against an individual with a disability because of the disability of such individual in regard to job application procedures, the hiring, advancement or discharge of employees, employee compensation, job training, and other terms, conditions, and privileges of employment."

The law does not apply to all disabled people, only those who are "otherwise qualified." It therefore does not require the hiring, promotion, or retention of unqualified people. There is thus an important emphasis on the determination of qualifications for decision-making purposes. This emphasis is very consistent with the person/job matching model.

Definition of Disability

Disability refers to both physical and mental impairments that substantially limit a major life activity of the person (e.g., breathing, walking, working). It also refers to persons who have a record of such impairment in the past or are regarded by others as having such an impairment. Determination of whether a person has a disability should take into account measures that mitigate or correct the impairment, such as eyeglasses or medication, so that the impairment is assessed in its mitigated or corrected state.

Disability refers not only to obvious impairments, such as blindness, but also to many others—for example, cancer, AIDS, and many mental illnesses. Current users of illegal drugs are excluded from coverage. Recovering former drug users, though, are covered, as are both practicing and recovering alcoholics.

The EEOC has provided written clarification of the meaning of the term "disability." First, the EEOC defines an impairment as "a physiological disorder affecting one or more of a number of body systems or a mental or psychological disorder." Excluded from this definition are (a) environmental, cultural, and economic disadvantages, (b) homosexuality and bisexuality, (c) pregnancy, (d) physical characteristics, (e) common personality traits, and (f) normal deviations in height, weight, or strength. Second, the EEOC expanded major life activities to include "sitting, standing, lifting, and mental and emotional processes such as thinking, concentrating, and interacting with others." Third, whether an impairment is substantially limiting depends on its nature and severity, duration or expected duration, and its permanency or long-term impact. For example, a broken arm or leg would generally not be considered a disability. Fourth, to be substantially limiting the impairment must prevent or significantly restrict the individual from performing a class of jobs or a broad range of jobs in various classes. For example, an impairment that prevented the individual from performing only a single job likely would not be considered a disability.[25]

Additional guidance from the EEOC pertains to persons with psychiatric disabilities as mental impairments.[26] A mental impairment includes mental or emotional illness, examples of which are major depression, bipolar disorder, anxiety disorders (including panic disorder, obsessive-compulsive disorder, and post-traumatic stress disorder), schizophrenia, and personality disorders. To count as a disability, the mental impairment must substantially limit one or more of the major life activities as defined above.

Qualified Individual with a Disability

A qualified individual with a disability is "an individual with a disability who, with or without reasonable accommodation, can perform the essential functions of the employment position that such individual holds or desires."

Essential Job Functions

The law provides little guidance as to what are essential job functions. It would seem that they are the major, nontrivial tasks required of an employee. The employer has great discretion in such a determination. Specifically, "consideration shall be given to the employer's judgment as to what functions of a job are essential, and if an employer has prepared a written description before advertising or interviewing applicants for the job, this description shall be considered evidence of the essential functions of the job." Subsequent regulations amplify on what are essential job functions; these are explored in Chapter 4.

Reasonable Accommodation and Undue Hardship

Unless it would pose an "undue hardship" on the employer, the employer must make "reasonable accommodation" to the "known physical or mental impairments of an otherwise qualified, disabled job applicant or employee." The law provides actual examples of such accommodation. They include changes in facilities (e.g., installing wheelchair ramps); job restructuring; changes in work schedules; employee reassignment to a vacant position; purchase of adaptive devices; provision of qualified readers and interpreters; and adjustments in testing and training material. For mental impairment and psychiatric disabilities, EEOC guidance indicates several types of reasonable accommodations: leaves of absence and other work schedule changes, physical changes in the workplace, modifications to company policy, adjusting supervisory methods, medication monitoring, and reassignment to a vacant position.[27] In general, only accommodations that would require significant difficulty or expense are considered to create an undue hardship.

Selection of Employees

The law deals directly with discrimination in the selection of employees. Prohibited discrimination includes

1. "using qualification standards, employment tests or other selection criteria that screen out or tend to screen out an individual with a disability or a class of individuals with disabilities unless the standard, test, or other selection criteria, as used by the covered entity, is shown to be job related for the position in question and is consistent with business necessity"; and
2. "failing to select and administer tests concerning employment in the most effective manner to ensure that, when such a test is administered to a job applicant or employee who has a disability that impairs sensory, manual, or speaking skills, such results accurately reflect the skills, aptitude or whatever

other factor of such applicant or employee that such test purports to measure, rather than reflecting the impaired sensory, manual, or speaking skills of such employee or applicant (except where such skills are the factors that the test purports to measure)."

These provisions seem to make two basic requirements of staffing systems. First, if selection procedures cause disparate impact against people with disabilities, the employer must show that the procedures are job-related and consistent with business necessity. The requirement is similar to that for selection procedures under the Civil Rights Act. Second, the employer must ensure that employment tests are accurate indicators of the KSAOs they attempt to measure.

Medical Exams for Job Applicants and Employees

Prior to making a job offer, the employer may not conduct medical exams of job applicants, inquire whether or how severely a person is disabled, or inquire whether the applicant has received treatment for a mental or emotional condition. Specific inquiries about a person's ability to perform essential job functions, however, are permitted.

After a job offer has been made, the employer may require the applicant to take a medical exam, including a psychiatric exam. The job offer may be contingent on the applicant successfully passing the exam. Care should be taken to ensure that all applicants are required to take and pass the same exam. Medical records should be confidential and maintained in a separate file.

For employees, medical exams must be job-related and consistent with business necessity. Exam results are confidential.

Affirmative Action

There are no affirmative action requirements for employers.

Rehabilitation Act (1973)

This law has many similarities to the ADA. Indeed, the ADA draws heavily on it and complements it in providing similar coverage to employers who are not federal contractors. Hence, its provisions are mentioned only briefly.

Prohibited Discrimination

According to the law, "no otherwise qualified individual with handicaps . . . shall, solely by reason of his handicaps, be excluded from participation in, or denied the benefits of, or be subjected to discrimination under any program or activity receiving federal assistance." The term "handicaps" is used in a similar fashion and with similar meaning to the term "disability" under the ADA. There are other similarities between the two laws as well. Both, for example, use the terms "otherwise qualified," "essential job functions," and "reasonable accommodation."

Affirmative Action

The law explicitly requires employers to undertake affirmative action. It says that the federal contractor "shall take affirmative action to employ and advance in employment qualified individuals with handicaps."

Executive Order 11246 (1965)

Prohibited Discrimination

The federal contractor is prohibited from discrimination on the basis of race, color, religion, sex, and national origin. (A similar prohibition against age discrimination by federal contractors is contained in Executive Order 11141.)

Affirmative Action

The order plainly requires affirmative action. It says specifically that "the contractor will take affirmative action to ensure that applicants are employed, and that employees are treated during employment, without regard to their race, color, religion, sex, or national origin. Such actions shall include, but not be limited to the following: employment, upgrading, demotion, or transfer; recruitment or recruitment advertising; layoff or termination; rates of pay or other forms of compensation; and selection for training, including apprenticeship." (Executive Order 11141 does not require affirmative action.) Regulations for these affirmative action requirements are discussed below.

EEO/AA: REGULATIONS AND INFORMATION

As noted previously and in Exhibit 2.4, numerous regulations and guidelines have been issued to further implement the enforcement of the EEO/AA law. Three major sets of these, with particular relevance to staffing, are briefly mentioned in the following sections. Also briefly mentioned are various information sources that are useful to consult regarding EEO/AA regulations and guidelines.

Regulations and Guidelines

Staffing policies and practices are most directly affected by the Uniform Guidelines on Employee Selection Procedures (UGESP), Affirmative Action Programs regulations, and Employment Regulations for the Americans With Disabilities Act. The general content of each of these is indicated next.

UGESP

The UGESP deals with adverse impact issues, requiring the organization to keep detailed records about the demographics of its applicants and new hires and to use these data to generate applicant flow statistics (selection rates). If significant differences in selection rates between protected groups are found—that is, there is adverse impact—the UGESP requires the organization to take steps to eliminate it, to use alternative selection procedures that have less adverse impact, or to justify it through the conduct of validation studies. Detailed technical standards for these studies are provided. The UGESP also indicates the relationship between its requirements and AA obligations of the organization. The UGESP may be found at *www.eeoc.gov/regs*.

Affirmative Action Programs Regulations

Enforced by the OFCCP, the regulations replace a previous set of regulations known as Revised Order No. 4. They apply to federal contractors and subcontractors. The first portion (Part 60–1) indicates general obligations of contractors, compliance evaluations, and complaint procedures. The second portion (Part 60–2) contains the specific Affirmative Action Programs (AAP) regulations. The AAP regulations require the contractor to develop an organizational profile that depicts its external and internal staffing patterns. Also required is a job group analysis that shows wage rates, and the percentages of women and minorities employed, in each job group. The percentages of women and minorities available, according to external and internal standards, must then be determined in each job group. The percentages of women and minorities employed must then be compared to the percentages available. Where the percentages employed are less than what would reasonably be expected given the availability for the job group, placement (hiring and promotion) goals must be set. The goals may not be rigid and inflexible quotas. To attempt to achieve the goals, the contractor must (1) designate a person responsible for implementation of the affirmative action program, (2) perform an in-depth analysis of its total employment process to determine whether and where there are impediments to equal employment opportunity, (3) develop and implement action-oriented programs to correct problem areas and meet the goals, and (4) develop and implement an internal auditing system that measures the effectiveness of the total affirmative action program. The contractor must also prepare and file, if chosen by the OFCCP, an equal opportunity survey. Finally, the contractor must conduct a special corporate management compliance evaluation to assess problems of advancement into and through the management ranks for women and minorities (i.e., the glass ceiling). The regulations may be found at *www.dol.gov/dol/esa/public/regs/fedregs/final.*

Employment Regulations for ADA

These regulations seek to clarify the meanings of terms used in the ADA, such as "disability," "qualified individual with a disability," and "reasonable accommodation." There are several sections explicitly dealing with selection of new employees. These pertain to the use and administration of tests and other selection procedures, as well as hiring standards. Medical examinations also receive detailed treatment. Employer defenses to discrimination charges, both disparate treatment and disparate impact, are specified. Finally, the regulations contain a lengthy appendix providing additional interpretive guidance. These and other regulations may be found at *www.eeoc.gov/regs.*

Information Sources

The sheer volume and complexity of EEO/AA laws and regulations is staggering. Several key information sources are available that collect, categorize, and summarize the information in very understandable, user-friendly ways. Each of these sources is described next, and the reader is well advised to become familiar with these sources and consult them for assistance.

Enforcement Agencies

The enforcement agencies have considerable online information available, including compliance manuals, regulations, and policy guidance. Consult the EEOC (*www.eeoc.gov*), the DOL (*www.dol.gov*), and the OFCCP (*www.dol.gov/dol/esa/public/ofcp*) Web sites.

Information Services

Two major fee-based information services organizations are the Bureau of National Affairs (BNA) and the Commerce Clearing House (CCH). The BNA (*www.bna.com*) offers numerous products in print, on CD-ROM, and on the Web. These include a policy and practice series on fair employment practices; official government compliance manuals for equal employment opportunity, affirmative action, and disability compliance; fair employment practice cases; individual employment rights cases; and an employment discrimination report. The CCH (*www.cch.com*) likewise offers several products in print, CD-ROM, and online format. Examples include the employment practices guide; official government compliance manuals for equal employment opportunity and affirmative action; an employment law manual for supervisors and managers; and an employment practices newsletter.

Compliance Manuals

Various compliance manuals are published that provide very practical, hands-on suggestions and guidance for employers' compliance attempts. The Bureau of National Affairs publishes the *EEOC Compliance Manual,* covering the Civil Rights Acts, the Age Discrimination in Employment Act, and the Americans With Disabilities Act; and the *Affirmative Action Compliance Manual for Federal Contractors,* covering Executive Order 11246 and the Rehabilitation Act. The Equal Employment Opportunity Commission publishes the *Technical Assistance Manual,* covering the Americans With Disabilities Act.[28]

Reference Books

There are certain books that review and summarize permissible and impermissible practices, as well as court cases pertaining to them. Examples include *Federal Law of Employment Discrimination, Employment Discrimination Law, Employment Law Manual,* and *Fair Employment Practices.*[29] These books contain a wealth of summarized and condensed material.

Professional Associations and Web Sites

Most professional associations provide informational services to their members. For example, the Society for Human Resource Management publishes *HR Magazine,* a monthly journal frequently containing staffing and EEO/AA articles (*www.shrm.org*). The society also puts out a monthly newsletter and a quarterly legal report, which often contain EEO/AA material. Likewise, the International Personnel Management Association publishes *Public Personnel Management* and a monthly newsletter, both containing EEO/AA material (*www.ipma-hr.org*). Two employment law Web sites are the employment law practice center (*www.law.com*) and hr comply (*www.hrcomply.com*).

EEO/AA BEST PRACTICES

Although organizations must comply with all of the specific EEO laws and regulations, they must also develop and implement comprehensive and integrated programs to not only foster technical compliance but also reflect an overall organization commitment to basic EEO principles. In this regard, an EEOC task force sought to establish "best practice" criteria for such overall programs and to study large organizations' actual EEO and diversity programs to identify specific examples of best practices that other organizations might seek to emulate.[30]

Best Practice Criteria

The task force specified several criteria that contribute to the concept of best practices. According to these criteria, a best practice:

- complies with the law
- promotes EEO and addresses one or more barriers that adversely affect EEO
- manifests management commitment and accountability
- ensures management and employee communication
- produces noteworthy results
- does not cause or result in unfairness

The task force elaborated at length on each of these criteria.

Best Practice Examples

After extensive study of organizations' practices, as well as input from various associations and groups, the task force identified best practice ideas applicable to all EEO areas and to several specific areas, including recruitment/hiring and promotion/career advancement.

The general set of best practices correspond to the acronym SPLENDID. This acronym refers to the following key elements for a successful EEO program:

- Study—know the laws and standards, remove barriers to EEO, identify technical assistance prospects
- Plan—formulate strategies for successful EEO results
- Lead—have senior, middle, and lower management champion the cause and provide actual leadership for implementation
- Encourage—identify and reward proper actions by managers, supervisors, and employees
- Notice—take notice of the impact of your practices, monitor and assess progress, ensure that unfairness does not occur
- Discussion—communicate and reinforce the EEO message
- Inclusion—bring all employees and groups into the process
- Dedication—assign needed resources, do not be afraid of bumps on the road

As the SPLENDID suggestions indicate, successful EEO programs are planned, integrated, coordinated, and well funded. These programs include employees at all levels, and they provide constant communication and reinforcement of desired practices.

The broad suggestions can guide more specific actions and programs by the organization. The task force identified such best practice ideas in the areas of recruitment/hiring and promotion/career advancement. It then developed summary descriptions of organizations' practices that exemplified actions consistent with the best practice ideas. Descriptions for several of the organizations studied are shown in Exhibit 2.7.

OTHER STAFFING LAWS

In addition to the EEO/AA laws, there are a variety of other laws and regulations affecting staffing. At the federal level are the Immigration Reform and Control Act, the Employee Polygraph Protection Act, and the Fair Credit Reporting Act. At the state and local level are a wide array of laws pertaining to EEO, as well as a host of other areas. Finally, there are civil service laws and regulations that pertain to staffing practices for federal, state, and local government employers.

Federal Laws

Immigration Reform and Control Act (1986)

The purpose of this law and its amendments is to prohibit the employment of unauthorized aliens and to provide civil and criminal penalties for violations of this law.

EXHIBIT 2.7   Examples of EEO Program Best Practices

A. Recruitment and Hiring

GTE Telephone Operations	Professional Recruitment Strategy, a comprehensive multi-faceted plan. Needs Assessment done annually.
	Specific recruiting activities carefully planned, i.e., career fairs, open houses, targeting where diversity of student population is key factor. Major professional associations are targeted.
	In-house contract and full-time experienced recruiters and researchers are dedicated to researching and sourcing world class candidates. Attend career fairs. Visit military bases.
	Monthly reports made of progress and results. Bonuses paid for successful referrals that result in hire.
Price Waterhouse LLP	Recruits women and people of color from approximately 250 colleges and universities throughout the country.
	Formed partnerships with national organizations.
	Among its many internship programs, almost 20 of its practice offices participate in INROADS internship program.
	Has long been a sponsor of A Better Chance, a national program supporting gifted students of color, and recently became a partner in helping prepare participating students and alumni for entry into the business world.
	Member of Project Equality, which is committed to maintaining policies and practices that affirmatively promote EEO for people of color, women, persons with disabilities, and others who encounter discrimination.
Turner Construction	Puts effort into developing a future recruitment resource pool through its YouthForce 2000 activity, which includes a Mentor/Prodigy Program, strong relationships with Junior and High School Guidance Counselors, a Summer Internship Program, and a Turner Speakers Bureau.
	Company offers summer scholarships through INROADS to women and minority youths.
	Turner Construction Management Training Program has trained 5,000 minority and women business representatives; and more than half go to work with Turner.
	Recruits annually at predominantly black and minority colleges.

(continued)

EXHIBIT 2.7   Continued

B. Promotion and Career Advancement

Baltimore Gas and Electric	Company has a "promote from within" tradition; revised its Job Posting Policy to state clearly that diversity is a corporate value and consideration in filling jobs; added diversity as an important tiebreaker, rather than seniority, in workforce selection.
	Uses three strategies to eliminate barriers: mentoring, supervisor goals, and succession planning.
	Emphasizes importance of including women and/or minorities in supervisory roles, and links incentive pay to progress.
	Has used Human Resources/Succession Planning for years; now encourages leaders of the company, in completing profiles of employees and in selecting replacement candidates for their own positions, to include women and minorities in these pools.
Fannie Mae	Career Development Plan Program helps each employee reach his or her full career potential.
	Corporate Mentor Program includes the Speaker Series, the Mentor/Protégé Matching Program, and the Peer Mentor or Fannie Buddy Program.
	Training and Development Program includes Computer and Information Systems Education, and Industry Training.
	Employee Development Program covers executive training, diversity training, management development courses, team building, and conflict resolution classes.
PPG Industries, Inc.	Individual Development Plan. Management Development Program. Executive Development Process.
	Top level management replacement program attempts to include a minority and/or a woman to be among the nominees for every job opening that occurs above middle-level management; posted jobs; Human Resources monitors hires and placements and provides feedback to business units for developmental activities. Mentoring teams.

Source: Equal Employment Opportunity Commission, *Best Equal Employment Opportunity Policies, Programs, and Practices in the Private Sector* (Washington, DC: author, 1998), pp. 77–127.

Prohibited Discrimination   The law prohibits the initial or continuing employment of unauthorized aliens. Specifically,

> 1. "it is unlawful for a person or other entity to have, or to recruit or refer for a fee, for employment in the United States an alien knowing the alien is an unauthorized alien with respect to such employment"; and

2. "it is unlawful for a person or other entity, after hiring an alien for employment . . . to continue to employ the alien in the United States knowing the alien is (or has become) an unauthorized alien with respect to such employment." (This does not apply to the continuing employment of aliens hired before November 6, 1986.)

The law also prohibits employment discrimination on the basis of national origin or citizenship status. The purpose of this provision is to discourage employers from attempting to comply with the prohibition against hiring unauthorized aliens by simply refusing to hire applicants who are foreign-looking in appearance or have foreign-sounding accents.

Employment Verification System   The employer must verify that the individual is not an unauthorized alien and is legally eligible for employment. To do this, the individual seeking employment must offer proof of identity and eligibility for work. Documents that will establish proof are shown on the back of the I-9 form that must be signed by the employer and the employee. To prevent illegal discrimination, the organization should not ask for these documents until after the individual is actually hired, and the new employee is entitled to three days to produce the documents. Only documents shown on the I-9 form may be requested. The I-9 information should be kept separate from the employee's personnel file.

Temporary Foreign Workers   Employers may apply for temporary (up to six years) H-1B visas for foreign workers. There is a cap of 195,000 workers per year who may obtain such visas. Universities and nonprofit and government research entities are exempt from the cap. The position the foreign national is being hired for must require a minimum of a bachelor's degree in a "specialty occupation" (mostly in computer programming, engineering, and physical therapy), and the person being hired must posses the bachelor's degree or its equivalent. The employer must pay the employee the prevailing wage for employees working in a similar position for the employer and attest that the employee will not displace any other U.S. employees. H-1B visa holders may change jobs as soon as their employer files an approval petition and they are not restricted to their current geographic area.

Enforcement   The law is enforced by the Department of Justice. Noncompliance may result in fines of up to $10,000 for each unauthorized alien employed, as well as imprisonment for up to six months for a pattern or practice of violations. Federal contractors may be barred from federal contracts for one year.

Employee Polygraph Protection Act (1988)

The purpose of this law is to prevent most private employers from using the polygraph or lie detector on job applicants or employees. The law does not apply to other types of "honesty tests," such as paper-and-pencil ones.

Prohibited Practices   The law prohibits most private employers (public employers are exempted) from (a) requiring applicants or employees to take a polygraph test, (b) using the results of a polygraph test for employment decisions, and (c) discharging or disciplining individuals for refusal to take a polygraph test.

There are three explicit instances in which the polygraph may be used. First, it may be used by employers who manufacture, distribute, or dispense controlled substances, such as drugs. Second, the polygraph may be used by private security firms that provide services to businesses affecting public safety or security, such as nuclear power plants or armored vehicles. Third, the polygraph may be used in an investigation of theft, embezzlement, or sabotage that caused economic loss to the employer.

Enforcement   The law is enforced by the Department of Labor. Penalties for noncompliance are fines of up to $10,000 per individual violation. Also, individuals may sue the employer, seeking employment, reinstatement, promotion, and back pay.

Fair Credit Reporting Act (1970)

The Fair Credit Reporting Act, as amended, regulates the organization's acquisition and use of consumer reports on job applicants.[31] A consumer report is virtually any information on an applicant that is compiled from a database by a consumer reporting agency and provided to the organization. The information may be not only credit characteristics but also employment history, income, driving record, arrests and convictions, and lifestyle; medical information may not be sought or provided without prior approval of the applicant.

Required Compliance   Several steps must be followed. Before obtaining a consumer report, the organization must (a) give the applicant clear notice in writing that a report may be obtained, and (b) obtain written authorization to do so from the applicant. The consumer reporting agency may not furnish a consumer report to the organization unless the organization certifies to the agency that it has given the required notice and received authorization. Before taking any "adverse action," such as denial of employment, based in whole or part on the report received, the organization must provide the applicant a copy of the report and a written description of their consumer rights put forth by the Federal Trade Commission. After taking an adverse action, the organization must (a) notify (written, oral, electronic) the applicant of the adverse action, (b) provide the name, address, and phone number of the consumer reporting agency to the applicant, and (c) provide notice of the applicant's rights to obtain a free copy of the report from the agency and to dispute the accuracy and completeness of the reports. The organization is not required to inform the applicant which information in the report led to the adverse action, but it must inform the applicant that the agency had no part in the decision.

A second type of consumer report is investigative. It is prepared on the basis of personal interviews with other individuals, rather than through search of a database. There are separate compliance steps for this type of report.

Enforcement   The law is enforced by the Federal Trade Commission. Penalties for willful or negligent noncompliance go up to $1,000.

State and Local Laws

The emphasis in this book is on federal laws and regulations. It should be remembered, however, that an organization is subject to law at the state and local level as well. This greatly increases the array of applicable laws to which the organization must attend.

EEO/AA Laws

These laws are often patterned after federal law. Their basic provisions, however, vary substantially from state to state. Compliance with federal EEO/AA law does not ensure compliance with state and local EEO/AA law, and vice versa. Thus, it is the responsibility of the organization to be explicitly knowledgeable of the laws and regulations that apply to it.

Of special note is the fact that state and local EEO/AA laws and regulations often provide protections beyond those contained in the federal laws and regulations. State laws, for example, may apply to employers with fewer than 15 employees, which is the cutoff for coverage under the Civil Rights Act. State laws may also prohibit certain kinds of discrimination not prohibited under federal law, for example, sexual preference. The law for the District of Columbia prohibits 13 kinds of discrimination, including sexual orientation, physical appearance, matriculation, and political affiliation. Finally, state law may deviate from federal law with regard to enforcement mechanisms and penalties for noncompliance.

Other State Laws

Earlier reference was made to employment-at-will and workplace torts as matters of common law, which, in turn, are governed at the level of state law. Statutory state laws applicable to staffing, in addition to EEO/AA laws, are also plentiful. Examples of areas covered in addition to EEO/AA include criminal record inquiries by the employer, polygraph and "honesty testing," drug testing, AIDS testing, and employee access to personnel records.

Civil Service Laws and Regulations

Federal, state, and local government employers are governed by special statutory laws and regulations collectively referred to as civil service. Civil service is guided by so-called merit principles that serve as the guide to staffing practices. Following these merit principles results in notable differences between public and private employers in their staffing practices.

Merit Principles and Staffing Practices

The essence of merit principles relevant to staffing is fourfold:

1. to recruit, select, and promote employees on the basis of their KSAOs
2. to provide for fair treatment of applicants and employees without regard to political affiliation, race, color, national origin, sex, religion, age, or handicap
3. to protect the privacy and constitutional rights of applicants and employees as citizens
4. to protect employees against coercion for partisan political purposes[32]

Merit principles are codified in civil service laws and regulations.

Comparisons with Private Sector

The merit principles and civil service laws and regulations combine to shape the nature of staffing practices in the public sector. This leads to some notable differences between the public and private sectors. Examples of public sector staffing practices are:

1. open announcement of all vacancies, along with the content of the selection process that will be followed
2. very large numbers of applicants due to applications being open to all persons
3. legal mandate to test applicants only for KSAOs that are directly job-related
4. limits on discretion in the final hiring process, such as number of finalists, ordering of finalists, and affirmative action considerations
5. rights of applicants to appeal the hiring decision, testing process, or actual test content and method[33]

These examples are unlikely to be encountered in the private sector. Moreover, they are only illustrative of the many differences in staffing practices and context between the private and public sectors.

LEGAL ISSUES IN REMAINDER OF BOOK

The laws and regulations applicable to staffing practices by organizations are multiple in number and complexity. The emphasis in this chapter has been on an understanding of the need for law, the sources of law, general provisions of the law, and a detailed presentation of specific provisions that pertain to staffing activities. Little has been said about practical implications and applications.

In the remaining chapters of the book, the focus shifts to the practical, with guidance and suggestions on how to align staffing practices with legal requirements. The last section of each remaining chapter is devoted to "Legal Issues" and discusses major issues from a compliance perspective. The issues so addressed, and the chapter in which they occur, are shown in Exhibit 2.8. Inspection of the exhibit should reinforce the importance accorded laws and regulations as an external influence on staffing activities.

It should be emphasized that there is a selective presentation of the issues in Exhibit 2.8. Only certain issues have been chosen for inclusion, and only a summary of their compliance implications is presented. It should also be emphasized that the discussion of these issues does not constitute professional legal advice.

SUMMARY

Staffing involves the formation of the employment relationship. That relationship involves the employer acquiring individuals to perform work for it as employees, independent contractors, and temporary employees. The specific legal meanings and obligations associated with these various arrangements were provided.

Myriad laws and regulations have come forth from several sources to place constraints on the contractual relationship between employer and employee. These constraints seek to ensure a balance of power in the relationship, as well as provide protections to both the employee and employer.

Statutory federal laws pertaining to EEO/AA prohibit discrimination on the basis of race, color, religion, sex, national origin, age, and disability. This prohibition applies to staffing practices intentionally used to discriminate (disparate treatment), as well as to staffing practices that have a discriminatory effect (disparate or adverse impact). Equal employment opportunity, affirmative action, and quotas are general attempts to bring staffing practices into compliance with these legal requirements.

Such attempts must occur within the specific provisions of the laws pertaining to staffing, which specify both prohibited and permissible practices. In both instances, the emphasis is on use of staffing practices that are job-related and focus on the person/job match.

Interpretation and implementation of the major EEO/AA laws occur through federal guidelines and regulations. The most prominent of these regarding staffing are the Uniform Guidelines on Employee Selection Procedures, Affirmative Action Programs regulations, and the Employment Regulations for the ADA.

In addition to compliance with specific laws and regulations, organizations must also develop overall, comprehensive EEO programs. An EEOC task force has identified best practice criteria for such programs and also indicated specific examples of these best practice programs in larger organizations.

EXHIBIT 2.8   Legal Issues Covered in Other Chapters

Chapter Title and Number	Topic
Planning (3)	Affirmative Action Programs regulations
	Legality of affirmative action plans (AAPs)
	Diversity of programs
	EEO and temporary employment agencies
Job Analysis (4)	Job-relatedness and court cases
	Job analysis and selection
	Essential job functions
External Recruitment (5)	Definition of job applicant
	Targeted recruitment
	Electronic recruitment
	Job advertisements
	Fraud and misrepresentation
Internal Recruitment (6)	Affirmative Action Programs regulations
	Bona fide seniority system
	Glass ceiling
Measurement (7)	Disparate impact statistics
	Standardization and validation
External Selection I (8)	Disclaimers
	Reference checks
	Preemployment inquiries
	Bona fide occupational qualifications (BFOQs)
External Selection II (9)	Uniform Guidelines on Employee Selection Procedures (UGESP)
	Selection under the ADA
	Drug testing
Internal Selection (10)	UGESP
	Glass ceiling
Decision Making (11)	UGESP
	Choices among finalists
Final Match (12)	Authorization to work
	Negligent hiring
	Employment-at-will
Staffing System Management (13)	Record keeping and reports
	Audits
	Managing legal compliance
Retention Management (14)	Separation laws and regulations
	Performance appraisal

Other laws and regulations also affect staffing practices. At the federal level, there is a prohibition on the employment of unauthorized aliens and on the use of the polygraph (lie detector), as well as constraints on the use of credit reports on job applicants. State and local EEO/AA laws supplement those found at the federal level. Many other staffing practices are also addressed by state and local law. Finally, civil service laws and regulations govern staffing practices in the public sector. Their provisions create marked differences in certain staffing practices between public and private employers.

Legal issues will continue to be addressed throughout the remainder of this book. The emphasis will be on explanation and application of the laws' provisions to staffing practices.

DISCUSSION QUESTIONS

1. Do you agree that "the employer usually has the upper hand" when it comes to establishing the employment relationship? When might the employee have maximum power over the employer?
2. What is the nature of the distinction between AA and quotas?
3. What are the limitations of disparate impact statistics as indicators of potential staffing discrimination?
4. Why is each of the four situational factors necessary to establishing a claim of disparate treatment?
5. What factors would lead an organization to enter into a consent agreement rather than continue pursuing a suit in court?
6. What are the differences between staffing in the private and public sectors? Why would private employers probably resist adopting many of the characteristics of public staffing systems?

APPLICATIONS

Age Discrimination in a Promotion?

The Best Protection Insurance Company (BPIC) handled a massive volume of claims each year in the corporate claims function, as well as its four regional claims centers. Corporate claims was headed by the Senior Vice President of Corporate Claims (SVPCC); reporting to the SVPCC were two managers of corporate claims (MCC-Life and MCC-Residential) and a highly skilled corporate claims specialist (CCS). Each regional office was headed by a regional center manager (RCM); the RCM was responsible for both supervisors and claims specialists within the regional office. The RCMs reported to the Vice President of Regional Claims (VPRC). Here is the structure before reorganization:

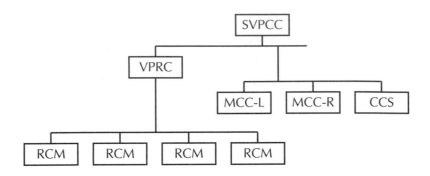

BPIC decided to reorganize its claims function by eliminating the four regional offices (and the RCM position) and establishing numerous small field offices throughout the country. The other part of the reorganization involved creating five new CCS positions. The CCS job itself was to be redesigned and upgraded in terms of knowledge and skill requirements. It was planned to staff these new CCS positions through internal promotions from within the claims function.

The plaintiff in the case was Gus Tavus, a 52-year-old RCM. Since his job was being eliminated, Gus was asked by the SVPCC to apply for one of the new CCS positions, as were the other RCMs, all of whom were over 40 years of age. Neither Gus nor the other RCMs were promoted to the CCS positions. Other candidates were also bypassed, and some of them were also over 40. The promotions went to five claims specialists and supervisors from within the former regional offices, all of whom were under age 40. Two of these newly promoted employees had worked for, and reported to, Gus as RCM.

Upon learning of his failure to be promoted, Gus sought to determine why he was not promoted. What he learned (described below) led him to feel he had been discriminated against because of his age. He then retained legal counsel, attorney Bruce Davis. Bruce met informally with the SVPCC to try to determine what had happened in the promotion process and why his client Gus had not been promoted. He was told that there were a large number of candidates who were better qualified than Gus and that Gus lacked adequate technical and communication skills for the new job of CCS. The SVPCC refused to reconsider Gus for the job and said that all decisions were "etched in stone." Gus and Bruce then filed suit in federal district court, claiming a violation of the Age Discrimination in Employment Act. They also subpoenaed numerous BPIC documents, including the personnel files of all applicants for the CCS positions.

Based on these documents, and discussions with Gus, the following information emerged about the promotion process actually used by BPIC. The SVPCC and the two MCCs conducted the total process; they received no input from the VPRC or the HR department. There was no formal, written job description for the new CCS position, nor was there a formal internal job posting as required by company policy. The SVPCC and the MCCs developed a list of employees they thought might be interested in the job, including Gus, and then met to consider the list of candidates. At that meeting, the personnel files and previous performance appraisals of the candidates were not consulted. After deciding on the five candidates who would be offered the promotion (all five accepted), the VPCC and MCCs did scan the personnel files and appraisals of these five (only) to check for any disconfirming information about the employees. None was found. Inspection of all the files by Bruce Davis revealed no written comments suggesting age bias in past performance appraisals for any of the candidates, including Gus. Also, there was no indication that Gus lacked technical and communication skills. All of Gus's previous appraisal ratings were above average, and there was no evidence of decline in the favorability of the ratings recently. Finally, an interview with the VPRC (Gus's boss) revealed that he had not been consulted at all during the promotion process, that he was "shocked beyond belief" that Gus had not been promoted, and that there was "no question" but that Gus was qualified in all respects for the CCS job.

1. Based on the above facts, prepare a written report that presents a convincing disparate treatment claim that Gus had been intentionally discriminated against on the basis of his age. Do not address the claim as a disparate impact one.
2. Present a convincing rebuttal, from the viewpoint of BPIC, to this disparate treatment claim.

Disparate Impact: What Do the Statistics Mean?

Claims of discrimination can be pursued under an allegation of disparate impact. According to this approach, the effect or impact of staffing practices can be discriminatory and thus in violation of the Civil Rights Act. Such an impact could occur even though there may be no underlying intention to discriminate against members of a protected group or class (e.g., women or minorities). Pursuit of a disparate impact claim requires the use of various statistics to show that, in effect, women or minorities are being treated differently than men or nonminorities under the law.

Exhibit 2.3 shows three types of disparate impact statistics: flow statistics, stock statistics, and concentration statistics. Also shown is a statistical example of disparate impact for each type. For each of these three types of statistics, prepare a report in which you discuss the following:

1. How could an organization go about collecting and reporting these statistics in the form shown in Exhibit 2.3?
2. What "rule of thumb" or guidelines would you recommend for deciding whether statistical differences between men and women, or nonminorities and minorities, reflect discrimination occurring through its staffing system?

3. What types of staffing activities (recruitment, selection, employment) might be causing the statistical differences? For example, in Exhibit 2.3 the selection rate for men is 50% and for women is 11%. How would the organization collect the data necessary to compute these selection rates, how would you decide if the difference in selection rates (50% vs. 11%) is big enough to indicate possible discrimination, and what sorts of practices might be causing the difference in selection rates?

ENDNOTES

1. M. W. Bennett, D. J. Polden, and H. S. Rubin, *Employment Relationships: Law and Practice* (Frederick, MD: Aspen, 2001), pp. 1-1 to 3-39.

2. C. J. Muhl, "The Employment-At-Will Doctrine: Three Major Exceptions," *Monthly Labor Review,* Jan. 2001, pp. 3–11.

3. M. W. Bennett, D. J. Polden and H. S. Rubin, *Employment Relationships: Law and Practice,* pp. 1-4 to 1-7; S. Bates, "A Tough Target: Employee or Independent Contractor?," *HR Magazine,* July 2001, pp. 69–74; K. M. Willner, *Managing the Alternative Workforce* (Alexandria, VA: International Personnel Management Association,1999).

4. D. C. Feldman and B. S. Klaas, "Temporary Workers: Employee Rights and Employer Responsibilities," *Employee Rights and Responsibilities Journal,* 1996 (1), pp. 1–21; J. W. Tansky and P. A. Veglahn, "Legal Issues in Co-Employment," *Labor Law Journal,* 1995, 46, pp. 293–300.

5. A. Bernstein, "When Is a Temp Not a Temp?," *Business Week,* Dec. 7, 1998, pp. 90–92; "Microsoft Changes Policy on Use of Temporary Employees," *Daily Labor Report,* Feb. 23, 2000, p. A-7.

6. A. G. Feliu, *Primer on Individual Employee Rights,* second ed. (Washington, DC: Bureau of National Affairs, 1996), pp. 1–5.

7. A. G. Feliu, *Primer on Individual Employee Rights,* pp. 1–5.

8. R. M. Green and R. J. Reibstein, *Employer's Guide to Workplace Torts* (Washington, DC: Bureau of National Affairs, 1992); M. W. Bennet, D. J. Polden, and H. S. Rubin, *Employment Relationships: Law and Practice,* pp. 8-1 to 8-56; M. W. Finkin, *Privacy in Employment Law* (Washington, DC: Bureau of National Affairs, 1998).

9. Bureau of National Affairs, *Fair Employment Practices,* vols. 1 and 2 (Washington, DC: author, periodically updated); Commerce Clearing House, *1991 Guidebook to Fair Employment Practices* (Chicago: author, 1991), pp. 15–73, 153–162; B. S. Gamble (ed.), *Sex Discrimination Handbook* (Washington, DC: Bureau of National Affairs, 1992), pp. 149–174; M. A. Player, *Federal Law of Employment Discrimination* (St. Paul, MN: West, 1992), pp. 47–49, 59–66, 217–225.

10. Bureau of National Affairs, *Fair Employment Practices,* vols. 1 and 2; Commerce Clearing House, *1991 Guidebook to Fair Employment Practices,* pp. 15–73, 153–162; B. S. Gamble (ed.), *Sex Discrimination Handbook,* pp. 149–174; M. A. Player, *Federal Law of Employment Discrimination,* pp. 47–49, 59–66, 217–225.

11. Bureau of National Affairs, *Fair Employment Practices,* vol. 1, pp. 431:363–374; T. Johnson, "The Legal Use of Racial Quotas and Gender Preference by Private and Public Employers," *Labor Law Journal,* 1989, 40, pp. 419–425.

12. S. Meisinger, "Affirmative Action Comes Under Review by States, Nation—An Analysis of the Issue," *Society for Human Resource Management Mosaics,* April 1995; R. K. Robinson, J. Seydel, and H. J. Sloan, "Reverse Discrimination Employment Litigation: Defining the Limits of Preferential Promotion," *Labor Law Journal,* 1995, 46, pp. 131–141.

13. Bureau of National Affairs, *Fair Employment Practices,* vol. 1, pp. 431:225–250; M. W. Bennett, D. J. Holden, and H. S. Rubin, *Employment Relationships: Law and Practice,* pp. 4-75 to 4-82.

14. R. D. Arvey and R. H. Faley, *Fairness in Selecting Employees,* second ed. (Reading, MA: Addison-Wesley, 1988), pp. 73–80; J. Cook, "Preparing for Statistical Battles Under the Civil Rights Act," *HR Focus,* May 1992, pp. 12–13; W. M. Howard, "The Decline and Fall of Statistical Evidence as Proof of Employment Discrimination," *Labor Law Journal,* 1994, 45, pp. 208–220.

15. Bureau of National Affairs, *Fair Employment Practices,* vol. 1, pp. 401:1–4241; R. C. West (ed.), *U.S. Labor and Employment Laws* (Washington, DC: author, 1991).

16. Equal Employment Opportunity Commission, *EEOC Enforcement Guidance on How to Count Employees When Determining Coverage Under Title VII, the ADA, and the ADEA* (Washington, DC: author, 1997).

17. Equal Employment Opportunity Commission, *EEOC Guidance on Investigating, Analyzing Retaliation Claims* (Washington, DC: author, 1998).

18. W. A. Carmell, "Application of U.S. Antidiscrimination Laws to Multinational Employers," *Legal Report,* Society for Human Resource Management, May/June 2001; W. Bliss, "The Wheel of Misfortune," *HR Magazine,* May 2000, pp. 207–218; S. Lash, "Supreme Court Disables State Employees," *HR News,* April 2001, p. 6.

19. Bureau of National Affairs, *Fair Employment Practices,* vol. 1, pp. 431:1–55, 151–170, 301–375; P. E. Varca and P. Pattison, "Evidentiary Standards in Employment Discrimination: A View Toward the Future," *Personnel Psychology,* 1993, 40, pp. 239–258.

20. Equal Employment Opportunity Commission, *EEOC Policy Statement on Alternative Dispute Resolution* (Washington, DC: author, 1995); Bureau of National Affairs, "EEOC's Nationwide Mediation Plan Offers Informal Settlement Option," *Daily Labor Report,* Feb. 12, 1999, p. 1.

21. M. W. Bennett, D. J. Polden, and H. S. Rubin, *Employment Relationships: Law and Practice,* pp. 4-75 to 4-82; T. S. Bland, "Anatomy of an Employment Lawsuit," *HR Magazine,* March 2001, pp. 145–151.

22. "Eagle Logistics Will Pay $9 Million to Settle EEOC Claims on Behalf of Minorities, Women," *Daily Labor Report,* Oct. 3, 2001, p. A-13.

23. Bureau of National Affairs, *Fair Employment Practices,* vol. 1, pp. 431:55–64, 481–490.

24. Bureau of National Affairs, *Fair Employment Practices,* vol. 1, pp. 401:1–4241; R. C. West, (ed.), *U.S. Labor and Employment Laws.*

25. Equal Employment Opportunity Commission, "Definition of the Term Disability," *Compliance Manual Section 902* (Washington, DC: author, 1995).

26. Equal Employment Opportunity Commission, *EEOC Enforcement Guidance on the Americans With Disabilities Act and Psychiatric Disabilities* (Washington, DC: author, 1997).

27. Equal Employment Opportunity Commission, *EEOC Enforcement Guidance on the Americans With Disabilities Act and Psychiatric Disabilities.*

28. Bureau of National Affairs, *EEOC Compliance Manual* and *Affirmative Action Compliance Manual for Federal Contractors* (Washington, DC: author, periodically updated); Equal Employment Opportunity Commission, *Technical Assistance Manual of the Employment Provisions of the Americans With Disabilities Act* (Washington, DC: author, periodically updated).

29. Commerce Clearing House, *1994 Guidebook to Fair Employment Practices* (Chicago: author, 1994); G. P. Panaro, *Employment Law Manual,* second ed. (Boston: Warren Gorham Lamont, 1993); M. A. Player, *Federal Law of Employment Discrimination;* B. L. Schlei and P. Grossman, *Employment Discrimination Law* (Washington, DC: Bureau of National Affairs, 1987).

30. Equal Employment Opportunity Commission, *Best Equal Employment Opportunity Policies, Programs, and Practices in the Private Sector* (Washington, DC: author, 1998).

31. A. H. Weitzman, "Fair Credit Reporting Act Amendments," *Society for Human Resource Management Legal Report,* Fall 1997, pp. 5–7.

32. J. P. Wiesen, N. Abrams, and S. A. McAttee, *Employment Testing: A Public Sector Viewpoint* (Alexandria, VA: International Personnel Management Association Assessment Council, 1990), pp. 2–3.

33. J. P. Wiesen, N. Abrams, and S. A. McAttee, *Employment Testing: A Public Sector Viewpoint,* pp. 3–7.

CHAPTER THREE

Planning

External Influences
  Economic Conditions
  Labor Markets
  Labor Unions

Human Resource Planning
  Process and Example
  Initial Decisions
  Forecasting HR Requirements
  Forecasting HR Availabilities
  External and Internal Environmental Scanning
  Reconciliation and Gaps
  Action Planning

Staffing Planning
  Staffing Planning Process
  Core Workforce
  Flexible Workforce

Legal Issues
  Affirmative Action Plans (AAPs)
  Legality of AAPs
  Diversity Programs
  EEO and Temporary Workers

Summary

Discussion Questions

Applications

H R planning is the process of forecasting the organization's future employment needs and then developing action staffing plans and programs for fulfilling these needs in ways that are in alignment with the strategy. It is important to recognize and consider the impact of external influences on HR planning and the resultant staffing planning. Three major external influences are economic conditions, labor markets, and labor unions. The nature, and examples, of these forces is described first. Attention then turns to HR planning, staffing planning, and legal issues.

The HR planning process involves several components, simplified examples of which are presented for the sales and customer service unit of an organization. Then, each of these components is described in detail. These components consist of making initial planning decisions, forecasting HR requirements, forecasting HR availabilities, scanning the external and internal environments, determining employee shortages and surpluses, and developing action plans. For each of these components specific examples are provided, drawing from the initial example of the sales and customer service unit.

Staffing planning is shown to be a logical outgrowth of HR planning. It generally involves setting staffing objectives, generating alternative staffing activities, and assessing and choosing from among these activities. Guided by staffing strategy, one of the key staffing planning areas involves planning for the core (regular employees) and flexible (temporary employees and independent contractors) workforces. The unique nature and requirements for planning each type of workforce is indicated.

The major legal issue for HR staffing planning is that of affirmative action plans (AAPs). The basic components of an AAP are provided, along with the AAP requirements for federal contractors. A summary of the legality of AAPs is then presented. Diversity programs represent a natural extension of AAPs. They seek to prepare organizational members for a diverse workforce and to develop HR programs that will foster successfully acquiring, managing, and retaining a diverse workforce. A different legal issue, that of EEO coverage for temporary employees and their agencies, is also discussed.

EXTERNAL INFLUENCES

There are three major sources of external influence on HR and staffing planning, namely, economic conditions, labor markets, and labor unions. Exhibit 3.1 provides specific examples of these influences, which are discussed next.

Economic Conditions

Numerous macro forces operate to determine the overall economic climate in which the organization functions. These include product and labor market com-

EXHIBIT 3.1   Examples of External Influences on Staffing

ECONOMIC CONDITIONS

- Economic expansion and contraction
- Job growth and job opportunities
- Internal labor market mobility
- Turnover rates

LABOR MARKETS

- Labor demand: employment patterns, KSAOs sought
- Labor supply: labor force, demographic trends, KSAOs available
- Labor shortages and surpluses
- Employment arrangements

LABOR UNIONS

- Negotiations
- Labor contracts: staffing levels, staffing quality, internal movement
- Grievance systems

petition (both national and global), inflation, interest rates, currency exchange rates, and government fiscal and monetary policy. Resulting from such forces is the degree of overall economic expansion or contraction.

A direct derivative of expansion and contraction forces is the amount of job creation and growth, both positive and negative. Positive job growth means expanding job opportunities for individuals, while slowdowns or contractions in job growth yield dwindling job opportunities. Organizations move people into (new hires), within (internal labor markets) and out of (turnover) the organization in varying rates, depending on the amount of job growth. Job growth thus functions like a spigot governing the movement of people.

Consider the case of job expansion. When new jobs are created, new hire rates begin to increase for both entry-level and higher-level jobs. These new hires are either new entrants into the labor force (e.g., recent college graduates) or current members of the labor force, both unemployed and employed. There will also be increased movement within organizations' internal labor markets through the operation of their promotion and transfer systems. This movement will be necessitated by a combination of new jobs being created that will be filled internally and the exit of current employees from the organization. Most likely, the departure of employees will be due to their leaving the organization to take new jobs at other organizations. Some, however, may be temporarily unemployed (while they look for new job opportunities), and others may leave the labor force entirely.

Consider the airline industry and the job of airplane pilot. Fueled by very favorable economic conditions and rising consumer demand for both pleasure and business travel, job expansion in the pilot ranks is high. Airlines need substantial numbers of both additional pilots (incremental staffing) and replacement pilots for the record number of pilots retiring (replacement staffing). The major airlines have stepped up recruitment efforts at universities with pilot training programs and expanded their "raiding" of pilots from commuter airlines and the military. Accompanying these efforts have been sizable boosts in pilots' pay and some reductions in required qualifications, such as the number of flying hours' experience required. The boom creates high turnover and shortages of pilots in the commuter airlines and the military, which in turn fashion their own responses to the overall job expansion in the industry. The U.S. Air Force, for example, sought to retain more of its pilots by increasing its retention bonus from $60,000 to $110,000 for pilots who would stay an additional five years beyond their required stint.[1]

With lesser rates of job growth or actual job contraction, the movement flows are lessened. Organizations will be hiring fewer people, and job seekers will have longer job searches and few job opportunities to choose from. Promotion and transfer opportunities for current employees will dry up, and many employees may even experience termination through involuntary layoff or a voluntary early retirement program.

Labor Markets

In and through labor markets, organizations express specific labor preferences and requirements (labor demand) and persons express their own job preferences and requirements (labor supply). Ultimately, person/job matches occur from the interaction of the demand and supply forces. Both labor demand and supply contain quantity and quality components, as described below. Labor shortages and surpluses are possible, as are a variety of possible employment arrangements that are also discussed.

Labor Demand: Employment Patterns

Labor demand is a derived demand, meaning it is a result of consumer demands for the organization's products and services. The organization acquires and deploys its workforce in ways that will allow it to be responsive to consumer demand in a competitive manner.

To learn about labor demand, national employment statistics are collected and analyzed. They provide data about employment patterns and projections for industries, occupations, and organization size.

Projections to year 2008 indicate that most job growth will occur in the services sector, led by the computer and data-processing services industry, followed by health care services, and numerous business and professional services. Manufacturing employment will remain steady, and declines will occur in mining, agriculture, and the federal government.[2]

Employment growth to 2008 will vary across occupations.[3] Examples of growth "winners" include financial managers (44%), medical and health services managers (33%), computer systems analysts and engineers (93%), special education teachers (34%), physician assistants (48%), surgical technologists (42%), securities and financial sales agents (41%), parking attendants (31%), and telephone and cable TV installers (30%). Examples of "losers" include machine tool cutting operators (−19%), sewing machine operators (−30%), photoengravers (−51%), computer operators (−26%), statement clerks (−22%), and private household workers (−19%).

Labor Demand: KSAOs Sought

KSAO requirements or preferences of employers are not widely measured, except for education requirements. Projecting to 2008, occupations requiring an associate (two-plus years post–high school) degree or more education will account for 40% of the job growth, and occupations requiring no education beyond high school will account for 57% of the job growth. A very small proportion of jobs (3.5%) will require more than a bachelor's degree.[4]

Surveys of employers regarding labor quality preferences and perceived deficiencies in labor quality provide a glimpse of patterns in this area.

A survey of employers in many different types of businesses and geographic locations (most with between 100 and 1,000 employees) sought opinions on the skill deficiencies they felt were present in their current and prospective employees. Results are shown in Exhibit 3.2. As can be seen, there are critical skill needs reported in all seven skills areas surveyed, starting with basic computer and interpersonal and written communication skills. These are closely followed by organizational, customer service, cross-cultural communication, and basic math skills. More than 50% of the companies reported a critical skill deficiency in each of these skills. The skill deficiencies varied by type of employee; for example, basic math skills are a major deficiency for blue-collar employees, and interpersonal communication skills are the biggest deficiency for professional/technical employees.

In the manufacturing sector, a national survey of employers provided opinions about skill deficiencies in their current workforces. The most frequently cited deficiency (63%) is basic job skills (arriving on time, calling in sick, staying at work all day). Other deficiencies are basic math skills (60%), basic written language and comprehension skills (55%), ability to read and translate drawings and flowcharts (48%), technical skills (44%), verbal communication (40%), computer skills (30%), and teamwork skills (28%).[5]

At the managerial level, rather than assessing current deficiencies, an interesting attempt was made to have experts forecast the most critical skills that managers

EXHIBIT 3.2   Employer Opinions About Needed Skills Enhancement

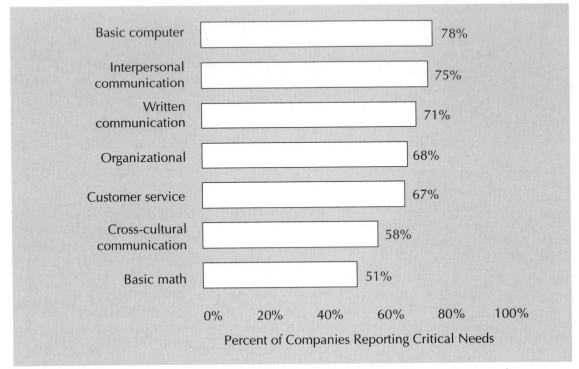

Source: Olsten Corporation, Westbury, NY. *Olstem Forum™ on Human Resource Issues and Trends, Skills for Success: Training and Developing the Work Force of the 1990s,* p. 5. Reprinted with permission.

will need for the future. The six identified skills are rapid response, sharp focus, stress busting, strategic empowerment, juggling, and team building.[6]

The above survey results show that employers have multiple general KSAO requirements that accompany their quantitative labor requirements. Naturally, the more specific requirements vary according to type of employer and type of job. It also appears that employers have identified general future KSAO needs for their workforces on the basis of skill gaps in their current workforces and, in the case of managers, what their projected critical KSAO requirements will be.

Labor Supply: The Labor Force and Its Trends

Quantity of labor supplied is measured and reported periodically by the Bureau of Labor Statistics in the U.S. Department of Labor. An example of basic results for September 2000 and 2001 is given in Exhibit 3.3. It shows that the labor force

EXHIBIT 3.3   Labor Force Statistics

	September 2000	September 2001
Civilian noninstitutional population	210,161,000	212,357,000
Civilian labor force	140,847,000	142,190,000
Employed	135,310,000	135,181,000
Unemployed	5,537,000	7,009,000
Not in labor force	69,314,000	70,167,000
Labor force participation rate (%)	67.0%	67.0%
Unemployment rate (%)	3.9%	4.9%

Source: U.S. Department of Labor, "The Employment Situation: September 2001," *News,* Oct. 5, 2001.

reached about 142 million individuals (employed + unemployed), and that unemployment rose from a very low 3.9% to 4.9%.

Data reveal several labor force trends that have particular relevance for staffing organizations. Labor force growth is slowing, going from an annual growth rate of around 2% in the early 1990s to a projected rate of 1.1% by the year 2006. There are increasingly fewer new entrants to the labor force. This trend, coupled with the severe KSAO deficiencies that many of the new entrants will have, creates major adaptation problems for organizations.

Demographically, the labor force has become more diverse, and this trend will continue. If current demographic levels are extrapolated to the year 2006, it can be seen that the composition of the labor force will include (a) fewer men and more women; (b) fewer whites; (c) more blacks, Asians, and Hispanics; (d) fewer younger (age 16–24) workers; and (e) more older (age 55+) workers.

Other, more subtle labor force trends are also under way. There has been a slight upward movement overall in the average number of hours that people work and a strong rise in the proportion of employees who work very long hours in certain occupations, such as managers and professionals. Relatedly, there is an increase in multiple job holding, with 6.2% of employed people holding more than one job. There are a growing number of immigrants in the population; nearly 1 in 10 people is foreign born, the highest rate in more than 50 years. New federal and state policies are increasingly pushing welfare recipients into the labor force, and they are mostly employed in low-wage jobs with low educational requirements. People historically out of the labor force mainstream—such as those with disabilities and the growing number of retirees—may assume a greater presence in the labor force.[7]

Labor Supply: KSAOs Available
Data on KSAOs available in the labor force are very sparse. A labor force survey showed that about 28% of the population age 25 or older had attained a college

degree or higher, whereas 16% had less than a high school diploma; the remainder had education attainment levels within this band.[8]

A more focused survey found that 38% of the job applicants tested by organizations lacked the necessary reading, writing, and math skills to do the jobs they sought. This number is up from 23% in 1997.[9] Another study found 33 + % of new labor force entrants fit into the bottom two categories of literacy levels. Here, literacy was measured in terms of prose, reading tables and charts, and quantitative data manipulation.[10] Data such as these suggest serious KSAO deficiencies in at least some portions of the labor force.

Labor Shortages and Surpluses

When labor demand exceeds labor supply for a given pay rate, the labor market is said to be "tight" and labor shortages are experienced by the organization. Shortages tend to be job- or occupation-specific. The past several years saw very low unemployment rates overall, surges in labor demand in certain occupations, and skill deficiencies, all fueling both labor quantity and labor quality shortages for many organizations. The shortages caused numerous responses, such as:

- Increased pay and benefit packages
- Hiring bonuses and stock options
- Use of nontraditional labor (e.g., retirees, people with disabilities)
- Use of temporary employees
- Recruitment of immigrants
- Lower hiring standards
- Partnerships with high schools, technical schools, and colleges
- Increased mandatory overtime work
- Reduced hours of operation

Employment Arrangements

Though labor market forces bring organizations and job seekers together, the specific nature of the employment arrangement can assume many forms. One form is whether the person will be employed on a full-time or a part-time basis. Data show that about 82% of people work full-time and 18% work part-time.[11]

A second arrangement involves the issue of regular or shift work. About 82% of employees work a regular schedule, while 18% perform shift work. The latter, in turn, have a variety of different shift arrangements possible, such as evening, night, split, and rotating shifts.[12]

Two other types of arrangements, often considered in combination, are various "alternative" arrangements to the traditional employer–employee one, and the use of contingent employees. Alternative arrangements include the organization filling its staffing needs through use of independent contractors, on-call workers and day laborers, temporary help agency employees, and employees provided by a contract firm that provides a specific service (e.g., accounting). Contingent employees do not have an explicit or implicit contract for long-term employment; they expect their employment to be temporary rather than long-term. Contingent employees may occur in combination with any of the four alternatives given above.

National data on the use of alternative employment arrangements and contingent employees are shown in Exhibit 3.4. It can be seen that 90% of surveyed individuals worked in a traditional employer–employee arrangement, and the vast majority of these (97.1%) considered themselves noncontingent. The most prevalent alternative was to work as an independent contractor (6.2%), followed by on-call employees and day laborers (1.5%), temporary help agency employees (.9%), and employees provided by a contract firm (.4%). The percentage of contingent employees in these alternative arrangements ranged from 4.1% (independent contractors) to 55.4% (temporary help employees).

The above survey also found that a smaller percentage of contingent employees than noncontingent employees receive employer-provided health insurance (20% versus 55%) and pensions (10% versus 47%).

Labor Unions

Labor unions are legally protected entities that organize employees and bargain with management to establish terms and conditions of employment via a labor contract. About 15% of the labor force is unionized, with about 10% unionization in the private sector and 40% in the public sector.[13]

EXHIBIT 3.4 **Usage of Alternative Employment Arrangements and Contingent Workers**

Arrangement	Total (millions)	Percent	Percent Contingent	Percent Noncontingent
Alternative Arrangements				
Independent contractor	8.6	6.2%	4.1%	95.9%
On-call workers and day laborers	2.1	1.5%	24.6%	75.4%
Temporary help agency workers	1.2	.9%	55.4%	44.6%
Workers provided by contract firm	.6	.4%	17.1%	82.9%
Traditional Arrangements	121.9	90.0%	2.9%	97.1%
	134.4	100%		

Source: U.S. Department of Labor, Bureau of Labor Statistics, *Contingent and Alternative Employment Arrangements,* February, 2001.

Labor and management are required to bargain in good faith to try to reach agreement on the contract. Many staffing issues may be bargained, including staffing levels, location of facilities, overtime and work schedules, job description and classifications, seniority provisions, promotion and transfers, layoffs and terminations, hiring pools, KSAO requirements, grievance procedures, alternative dispute resolution procedures, employment discrimination protections, and very important, pay and benefits. Virtually all aspects of the staffing process are thus affected by negotiations and the resultant labor agreement.

Once a contract is agreed to, it standardizes the terms and conditions of employment, making them uniform for all covered employees. The contract cannot be replaced or supplemented by individual agreements with employees, as would be the case in a nonunion setting. Moreover, the terms in the contract are binding and cannot be unilaterally changed by management, thus "locking in" everything agreed to.

Labor unions thus have direct and powerful impacts on staffing and other HR systems. Even in nonunion situations the union influence can be felt through "spillover effects" in which management tries to emulate the pay and benefits, as well as staffing practices, found in unionized settings.

HUMAN RESOURCE PLANNING

Human resource planning (HRP) is a process and set of activities undertaken to forecast an organization's labor demand (requirements) and internal labor supply (availabilities), to compare these projections to determine employment gaps, and to develop action plans for addressing these gaps. Action plans include staffing planning to arrive at desired staffing levels and staffing quality.

A general model depicting the process of HRP is presented first, followed by an operational example of HRP. Detailed discussions of the major components of HRP are then given.[14]

Process and Example

The basic elements of virtually any organization's HRP are shown in Exhibit 3.5. As can be seen, the HRP process involves five sequential steps:

1. determine future human resource requirements
2. determine future human resource availabilities
3. conduct external and internal environmental scanning
4. reconcile requirements and availabilities—that is, determine gaps (shortages and surpluses) between the two
5. develop action plans to close the projected gaps

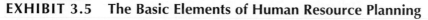

EXHIBIT 3.5   The Basic Elements of Human Resource Planning

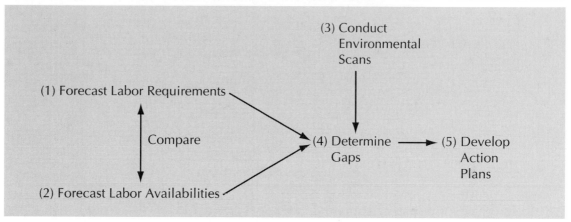

An example of HRP, including results from forecasting requirements and availabilities, is shown in Exhibit 3.6. The exhibit shows a partial HRP being conducted by an organization for a specific unit (sales and customer service). It involves only two job categories (A or sales, and B or customer service) and two hierarchical levels for each category (1 or entry level, and 2 or manager level). All of the HRP steps are confined to this particular organizational unit and its job categories/levels, as shown.

The current workforce size (number of employees) is given for each job category/level. Requirements and availabilities are forecast for a one-year time frame, and the results are shown in the relevant columns. After the reconciliation process, final gap figures are agreed on and entered into the gap column. It can be seen that in total there is an estimated shortage of 145 employees. This overall shortage is very unevenly distributed across the four job categories/levels. In three of these, there are shortages projected (39, 110, and 3), and in the remaining one, there is a projected surplus (7).

These gap data serve as the basic input to action planning. Because the gaps show both shortages and a surplus, and because the gaps vary in severity relative to the current workforce, a specific action plan will probably have to be developed and implemented for each job category/level. The resultant four staffing (and other) plans hopefully will bring staffing into an orderly balance of requirements and availabilities over the course of the planning period.

The above process and example identify and illustrate the rudiments of HRP. Within them are several distinct HRP components that require elaboration. We turn now to these components, emphasizing that each component represents a factor that must be considered in HRP and that there are specific choices to be made regarding the operational details for each component.

EXHIBIT 3.6 Operational Format and Example for Human Resource Planning (HRP)

Organizational Unit: Sales and Customer Service

Job Category and Level	Current Workforce	Forecast for Workforce— One Year		Reconciliation and Gaps	Action Planning
		Requirements	Availabilities		
A1 (Sales)	100	110	71	−39 (shortage)	Staffing activities Recruitment
A2 (Sales manager)	20	15	22	+7 (surplus)	Selection Employment
B1 (Customer service representative)	200	250	140	−110 (shortage)	Other HR activities Compensation
B2 (Customer service manager)	15	25	22	−3 (shortage)	Training and development
	335	400	255	−145 (shortage)	

Initial Decisions

Before HRP per se can be undertaken, there are several critical decisions that must be made. These decisions will shape the nature of the resultant HRP process, and they will influence the output of the process, namely, the gap estimates. The quality and potential effectiveness of the action plans developed from the gap estimates are thus at stake when these initial decisions are confronted and made.

Comprehensiveness of Planning

Often, HRP takes place as an integral part of an organization's business planning process; this is referred to as plan-based HRP. This is a logical approach because most organizations do business planning, and these plans almost always have HR implications. It is always a good idea to have a close, reciprocal linkage between business and HR plans.

Not all important business developments are captured in formal business plans, however, particularly if they occur rapidly or unexpectedly. Sudden changes in consumer preferences or legal requirements, for example, can wreak havoc on business plans. Organizational responses to these changes often occur in the form of special projects, rather than in changes in the total business plan. Part of each response requires consideration of HR implications, however, resulting in what is called project-based HRP. This type of planning helps ensure that the necessary creation of new jobs, changes in requirements and rewards for existing jobs, and employee job changes are undertaken systematically and without undue interruption.

In addition, many organizations do HRP outside the formal planning cycle for critical groups of employees on a regular basis. This often occurs for jobs in which there are perennial shortages of employees, both externally and internally. Examples here include nurses in health care organizations, faculty in certain specialized areas at colleges and universities, and teachers in elementary and secondary schools. Planning focused on a specific employee group is referred to as population-based HRP.

Planning Time Frame

Since planning involves looking into the future, the logical question for an organization to ask is, How far into the future should our planning extend? Typically, plans are divided into long-term (three years and more), intermediate (one to three years), and short-term (one year or less). Organizations vary in their planning time frame, often depending on which of the three types of HRP is being undertaken.

For plan-based HRP, the time frame will be the same as that of the business plan. In most organizations, this is between three and five years for so-called strategic planning and something less than three years for operational planning. Planning horizons for project-based HRP vary depending on the nature of the projects involved. Solving a temporary shortage of, say, salespeople for the introduction of a new product might involve planning for only a few months, whereas planning for the start-up of a new facility could involve a lead time of two or more years. Population-based HRP will have varying time frames, depending on the time necessary for labor supply (internal as well as external) to become available. As an example, for top-level executives in an organization, the planning time frame will be lengthy.

Job Categories and Levels

The unit of HRP and analysis is comprised of job categories and hierarchical levels among jobs. These job category/level combinations, and the types and paths of employee movement among them, form the structure of an internal labor market. Management must choose which job categories and which hierarchical levels to use for HRP. In Exhibit 3.6, for example, the choice involves two jobs (sales and customer service) and two levels (entry and manager) for a particular organizational unit.

Job categories are created and used on the basis of the unit of analysis for which projected shortages and surpluses are being investigated. These categories should be consistent with results of the job analysis. Major attention should also be paid to EEO/AA activities and commitments.

Hierarchical levels should be chosen so that they are consistent with or identical to the formal organizational hierarchy. The reason for this is that these formal levels define employee promotions (up levels), transfers (across levels), and demotions (down levels). Having gap information by level facilitates planning of internal movement programs within the internal labor market. For example, it is difficult to have a systematic promotion-from-within program without knowing probable numbers of vacancies and gaps at various organizational levels.

Head Count (Current Workforce)

Exactly how does an organization count or tally the number of people in its current workforce for forecasting and planning purposes? Simply counting the number of employees on the payroll at the beginning of the planning period may be adequate for intended purposes. It ignores two important distinctions, however.

First, it ignores the amount of scheduled time worked by each employee relative to a full workweek. For example, it treats full-time employees as synonymous with part-time employees. To rectify this, an employee head count may be made and stated in terms of full-time equivalents, or "FTEs." To do this, simply define what constitutes full-time work in terms of hours per week (or other time unit), and count each employee in terms of scheduled hours worked relative to a full workweek. If full-time is defined as 40 hours per week, a person who normally works 20 hours per week is counted as a .50 FTE, a person normally working 30 hours per week is a .75 FTE, and so on.

A second problem with current payroll head count is that it ignores vacancies that exist at the time of the count. Since most of such vacancies are probably so-called authorized ones, derived from previous HRP, they are better added into any head-count tallies for the current workforce.

Roles and Responsibilities

Both line managers and staff specialists (usually from the HR department) become involved in HRP, so the roles and responsibilities of each must be determined as part of HRP. Most organizations take the position that line managers are ultimately responsible for the completion and quality of HRP. But the usual practice is to have HR staff assist with the process.

Initially, the HR staff take the lead in proposing which types of HRP will be undertaken and when and in making suggestions with regard to comprehensiveness, planning time frame, job categories and levels, and head counts. Final decisions on these matters are usually the prerogative of line management. Once an approach has been decided on, task forces of both line managers and HR staff people are assembled to design an appropriate forecasting and action planning process and to do any other preliminary work.

Once these processes are in place, the HR staff typically assumes responsibility for collecting, manipulating, and presenting the necessary data to line management and for laying out alternative action plans (including staffing plans). Action planning usually becomes a joint venture between line managers and HR staff, particularly as they gain experience with, and trust for, each other.

Forecasting HR Requirements

Forecasting HR requirements is a direct derivative of business and organizational planning. As such, it becomes a reflection of projections about a variety of factors, such as sales, production, technological change, productivity improvement, and the regulatory environment. Many specific techniques may be used to forecast HR requirements; these are either statistical or judgmental in nature, and are usually tailor-made by the organization.

Statistical Techniques

A wide array of statistical techniques is available for use in HR forecasting. Prominent among these are regression analysis, ratio analysis, time series analysis, and stochastic analysis. Brief descriptions of two of these techniques, regression analysis and ratio analysis, are given in Exhibit 3.7.

We will not elaborate on these techniques for several reasons. First, their very complexity would lead away from a staffing focus. Second, all of these techniques are designed simply to project the past into the future. These techniques thus have limited applicability in organizations whose immediate past and/or future forecast are characterized by significant alterations in products and services, technologies, or organizational structures. (Obviously, this includes a large percentage of or-

---

EXHIBIT 3.7   Examples of Statistical Techniques to Forecast HR Requirements

(A)   Ratio Analysis

1. Examine historical ratios involving workforce size

Example: $\dfrac{\$\text{ sales}}{1.0\text{ FTE}} = ?$ $\dfrac{\text{No. of new customers}}{1.0\text{ FTE}} = ?$

2. Assume ratio will be true in future
3. Use ratio to predict future HR requirements

Example: (a) $\dfrac{\$4{,}000\text{ sales}}{1.0\text{ FTE}}$ is past ratio

(b) Sales forecast is $4,000,000
(c) HR requirements = 100 FTEs

(B)   Regression Analysis

1. Statistically identify historical predictors of workforce size

Example: FTEs = $a + b_1$ sales $+ b_2$ new customers

2. Only use equations with predictors found to be statistically significant
3. Predict future HR requirements, using equation

Example: (a) FTEs = 7 + .0004 sales + .02 new customers
(b) Projected sales = $1,000,000
Projected new customers = 300
(c) HR requirements = 7 + 400 + 6 = 413

---

ganizations of varying size today.) Third, as they are dependent on the discovery of historical relationships between certain so-called leading indicators (e.g., sales or production volume) and head count, often these relationships are difficult to find; if found, they may not hold up in the future.

Judgmental Techniques

Judgmental techniques represent human decision-making models that are used for forecasting HR requirements. Unlike statistical techniques, it is the decision maker who collects and weighs the information subjectively and then turns it into forecasts of HR requirements. The decision maker's forecasts may or may not agree very closely with those derived from statistical techniques.

Implementation of judgmental forecasting can proceed from either a "top-down" or "bottom-up" approach. In the former case, top managers of the organization, organizational units, or functions rely on their knowledge of business and organizational plans to make predictions about what future head counts will be. At times, these projections may, in fact, be dictates rather than estimates, necessitated by strict adherence to the business plan. Such dictates are common in organizations undergoing significant change, such as restructuring, mergers, and cost-cutting actions.

In the bottom-up approach, lower-level managers make initial estimates for their unit (e.g., department, office, or plant) based on what they have been told or presume are the business and organizational plans. These estimates are then consolidated and aggregated upward through successively higher levels of management. Then, top management establishes the HR requirements in terms of numbers.

Forecasting HR Availabilities

In Exhibit 3.6 head count data are given for the current workforce and their availability as forecast, in each job category/level. These forecast figures take into account movement into each job category/level, movement out of each job category/level, and exit from the organizational unit or the organization. Exhibit 3.8 shows this.

Numerous techniques could have been used, alone or in combination, to generate the availabilities forecast from the current workforce figures shown in Exhibit 3.6. As with HR requirements, these techniques can be classified as statistical or judgmental.[15]

Statistical Techniques

Statistical techniques seek to predict availabilities on the basis of historical patterns of job stability and movement among employees. Referring again to Exhibit 3.8, note that between any two time periods, the following possibilities exist for each employee in the internal labor market:

1. job stability (remain in A1, A2, B1, B2)
2. promotion (move to a higher level: A1 to A2, A1 to B2, B1 to B2, B1 to A2)
3. transfer (move at the same level: A1 to B1, B1 to A1, A2 to B2, B2 to A2)
4. demotion (move to a lower level: A2 to A1, A2 to B1, B2 to B1, B2 to A1)
5. exit (move to another organizational unit or leave the organization)

These possibilities may be thought of in terms of flows and rates of flow or movement rates. Past flows and rates may be measured and then used to forecast the future availability of current employees, based on assumptions about the extent to which past rates will continue unchanged in the future. For example, if it is known that the historical promotion rate from A1 to A2 is .10 (10% of A1 employees are promoted to A2), we might predict that A1 will experience a 10% loss of employees due to promotion to A2 over the relevant time period.

EXHIBIT 3.8   A Forecast of Future Human Resource Availabilities

Job Category and Level	Current Workforce	Movement In			Movement Out			Exit	
		Promotion	Transfer	Demotion	Promotion	Transfer	Demotion	Unit	Org. Availability
A1	100				[specific cell entries not shown]				71
A2	20								22
B1	200								140
B2	15								22
	335								255

To be beneficial, the study and use of flows and rates must capture all of them simultaneously within the internal labor market. That is, we must know all of the job stability, promotion, transfer, demotion, and exit rates for an internal labor market before we can forecast future availabilities. Markov Analysis is a statistical technique that accomplishes this; it is discussed next. Other possible techniques, not discussed here, include renewal and goal programming models.

Markov Analysis   The elements of Markov Analysis are shown in Exhibit 3.9 for the organizational unit originally presented in Exhibit 3.6. Refer first to part A of the exhibit. There are four job category/level combinations for which movement rates are calculated between two time periods (T and T + 1). This is accomplished as follows. For each job category/level, take the number of employees who were in it at T, and use that number as the denominator for calculating job stability and movement rates. Then, for each of those employees determine which job category/level they were employed in at T + 1. Then, sum up the number of employees in each job category/level at T + 1, and use these as the numerators for calculating stability and movement rates. Finally, divide each numerator separately by the denominator. The result is the stability and movement rates expressed as proportions, also known as transition probabilities. The rates for any row (job category/level) must add up to 1.0.

For example, consider job category/level A1. Assume that at time T in the past there were a total of 400 people in it. Further assume that at T + 1, 240 of these

EXHIBIT 3.9   Use of Markov Analysis to Forecast Availabilities

A. Transition Probability Matrix Job Category and Level		A1	A2	T + 1 B1	B2	Exit
	A1	.60	.10	.20	.00	.10
T	A2	.05	.60	.00	.00	.35
	B1	.05	.00	.60	.05	.30
	B2	.00	.00	.00	.80	.20

B. Forecast of Availablities	Current Workforce				
A1	100	60	10	20	0
A2	20	1	12	0	0
B1	200	10	0	120	10
B2	15	0	0	0	12
		71	22	140	22

employees were still in A1, 40 had been promoted to A2, 80 had been transferred to B1, 0 had been promoted to B2, and 40 had exited the organizational unit or the organization. The resulting transition probabilities, shown in the row for A1, are .60, .10, .20, .00, and .10. Note that these rates sum to 1.00.

By referring to these figures, and the remainder of the transition probabilities in the matrix, an organization can begin to understand the workings of the unit's internal labor market. For example, it becomes clear that 60–80% of employees experienced job stability and that exit rates varied considerably, ranging from 10% to 35%. Promotions occurred only within job categories (A1 to A2, B1 to B2), not between job categories (A1 to B2, B1 to A2). Transfers were confined to the lower of the two levels (A1 to B1, B1 to A1). Only occasionally did demotions occur, and only within a job category (A2 to A1). Presumably, these stability and movement rates are a reflection of specific staffing policies and procedures that were in place between T and T + 1.

With these historical transitional probabilities, it becomes possible to forecast the future availability of the current workforce over the same time interval, T and T + 1, assuming that the historical rates will be repeated over the time interval and that staffing policies and procedures will not change. Refer now to part B of Exhibit 3.9. To forecast availabilities, simply take the current workforce column and multiply it by the transition probability matrix shown in part A. The resulting availability figures (note these are the same as those shown in Exhibits 3.6 and 3.8) appear at the bottom of the columns: A1 = 71, A2 = 22, B1 = 140, B2 = 22. The remainder of the current workforce (80) are forecast to exit and will not be available at T + 1.

Limitations of Markov Analysis   Markov Analysis is an extremely useful way to capture the underlying workings of an internal labor market and then use the results to forecast future HR availabilities. Markov Analysis, however, is subject to some limitations that must be kept in mind.[16]

The first and most fundamental limitation is that of sample size, or the number of current workforce employees in each job category/level. As a rule, it is desirable to have 20 or more employees in each job category/level. Since this number serves as the denominator in the calculation of transition probabilities, with small sample sizes there can be substantial differences in the values of transition probabilities, even though the numerators used in their calculation are not that different (e.g., 2/10 = .20 and 4/10 = .40). Thus, transition probabilities based on small samples yield unstable estimates of future availabilities.

A second limitation of Markov Analysis is that it does not detect multiple moves by employees between T and T + 1; it only classifies employees and counts their movement according to their beginning (T) and ending (T + 1) job category/level, ignoring any intermittent moves. To minimize the number of undetected multiple moves, therefore, it is necessary to keep the time interval relatively short, probably no more than two years.

A third limitation pertains to the job category/level combinations created to serve as the unit of analysis. These must be meaningful to the organization for the HRP purposes of both forecasting and action planning. Thus, extremely broad categories (e.g., managers, clericals) and categories without any level designations should be avoided. It should be noted that this recommendation may conflict somewhat with HRP for affirmative action purposes, as discussed later.

Finally, the transition probabilities reflect only gross, average employee movement, and not the underlying causes of the movement. Stated differently, all employees in a job category/level are assumed to have an equal probability of movement. This is unrealistic because organizations take many factors into account (e.g., seniority, performance appraisal results, and KSAOs) when making movement decisions about employees. Because of these factors, the probabilities of movement may vary among specific employees.

Judgmental Techniques

There are three judgmental techniques for forecasting availabilities that enjoy widespread acceptance: executive reviews, succession planning, and vacancy analysis. In this context, the main difference between statistical and judgmental techniques is that the former treat employees as numbers and forecast their movements based on probabilities. The latter treat them as individuals and forecast their movements person by person.

Executive Reviews   Executive reviews focus on small and unique groups of employees, most commonly top executives and other managers and professionals judged to have the potential to be top executives. Thus, executive reviews are a form of population-based HRP. The actual reviews are carried out through a series of meetings at which the top executives in a given unit consider anticipated HR requirements and then thoroughly discuss each person under review to determine who is likely to be, or should be, promoted, reassigned, developed for future assignments, or dismissed from the organization. Determinations are made based on judgments about performance, promotability, and potential, taking into account the long-term career interests of the employee being considered. The process produces a clear indication of where the organization can expect to have managerial shortages or surpluses. It also provides career and development plans for individuals.

Succession Planning   This planning is often an adjunct to executive reviews. It helps identify backup candidates who are, or soon will be, qualified to replace current executives or upper-level managers. Succession planning results are typically summarized on charts such as the one shown in Exhibit 3.10. These greatly facilitate the planning of likely retirements, terminations, promotions, and transfers within and across organizational units. These charts also show which managers are in need of further development to become ready to fill job(s) for which they are (or might be) considered as replacements.

EXHIBIT 3.10   Employee Replacement Chart for Succession Planning

Organizational Unit _____

Date _____

Position		Position	
Incumbent _____	Current job: years: ___ Total service: years: ___	Incumbent _____	Current job: years: ___ Total service: years: ___
Promote to _____	Date ready: _____	Promote to _____	Date ready: _____
Replacement (1) _____	Current job: years: ___ Total service: years: ___	Replacement (1) _____	Current job: years: ___ Total service: years: ___
Present position _____	Date promotable: _____	Present position _____	Date promotable: _____
Replacement (2) _____	Current job: years: ___ Total service: years: ___	Replacement (2) _____	Current job: years: ___ Total service: years: ___
Present position _____	Date promotable: _____	Present position _____	Date promotable: _____

Position		Position	
Incumbent _____	Current job: years: ___ Total service: years: ___	Incumbent _____	Current job: years: ___ Total service: years: ___
Promote to _____	Date ready: _____	Promote to _____	Date ready: _____
Replacement (1) _____	Current job: years: ___ Total service: years: ___	Replacement (1) _____	Current job: years: ___ Total service: years: ___
Present position _____	Date promotable: _____	Present position _____	Date promotable: _____
Replacement (2) _____	Current job: years: ___ Total service: years: ___	Replacement (2) _____	Current job: years: ___ Total service: years: ___
Present position _____	Date promotable: _____	Present position _____	Date promotable: _____

Vacancy Analysis   In vacancy analysis, judgments are made about likely employee movement on an individual basis, as in executive reviews and succession planning. Because large numbers of employees are usually involved, the results may be aggregated and summarized statistically. Vacancy analysis is akin to judgmental Markov Analysis; employee movement is "guesstimated" through managerial judgment rather than estimated statistically through calculation and use of transition probabilities.

Exhibit 3.11 shows a vacancy analysis, using the same four job categories/levels, current workforce numbers, and forecast of requirements as previously. Vacancy analysis begins with a forecast about numbers of exits from each job category/level. This yields an effective internal labor supply, which can then be compared to a forecast of demand to arrive at a gross shortage or surplus number for each job category/level. These numbers are then adjusted for likely movement into and out of the job category/levels, resulting in final gap figures. These gaps serve as the input to action planning. Since both shortages and surpluses were forecast in Exhibit 3.6, these plans are likely to involve both accessions (internal and external) and workforce reductions in head count and/or hours of work.

It should be noted that the data in Exhibit 3.11 were constructed to yield the same availability results and employment gaps as shown in Exhibits 3.6 and 3.8. Referring to Exhibit 3.11, note that A1 may be calculated as $(90 + 11 - 30 = 71)$, A2 as $(13 + 10 - 1 = 22)$, B1 as $(160 + 0 - 20 = 140)$, and B2 as $(12 + 10 - 0 = 22)$. In essence, the results of judgmental forecasting have been "rigged" to yield the same results as statistical forecasting. In actual practice, such a result is extremely unlikely. But our example does illustrate that if decision makers are knowledgeable about their internal labor markets, their judgments may yield results similar to those that would have been obtained from statistical forecasting, such as Markov Analysis.

External and Internal Environmental Scanning

External Scanning

This is the term applied to the process of tracking trends and developments in the outside world, documenting their implications for the management of human resources, and ensuring that these implications receive attention in the HRP process. Many large corporations maintain fairly elaborate networks of line managers, technical specialists, and human resource specialists, who monitor large numbers of publications, broadcast media, futurist think tanks, and conferences for relevant data. Periodically, these data are assembled and trend reports are prepared and made available to those responsible for HRP. These reports usually include a summary of the major environmental trends and their implications for human resource management. Exhibit 3.12 shows an example of an environmental scan regarding the employment outlook.

EXHIBIT 3.11   Vacancy Analysis for Sales and Customer Service Unit

Job Category and Level	Current Workforce	Exit Forecast Org.	Exit Forecast Unit	Effective Supply	Forecast of Demand	(Shortages) or Surpluses	Movements Within Unit Into	Movements Within Unit Out	Gap/Net Shortages or Surplus	Accessions From Other Units	Accessions External New Hires	Accessions Reductions
A1	100	8	2	90	110	(20)	11	30	(39)			
A2	20	4	3	13	15	(2)	10	1	7	Action planning		
B1	200	25	15	160	250	(90)	0	20	(110)			
B2	15	2	1	12	25	(13)	10	0	(3)			

Of the various areas monitored through external scanning, the labor market is most directly relevant to staffing planning. For a start-up organization in genetic engineering, for example, the future availability of geneticists, biologists, and other types of scientists and engineers is an important strategic contingency. If tight labor markets for these skills are expected, the organization must plan to put considerable time and money into attracting and retaining the needed talent (for example, by raising salaries or offering child care programs) or into developing alternative means of accomplishing its key research and development work (for instance, by using technicians wherever possible, thus reducing the need for scientists and engineers).

Clearly, then, an organization's grasp of impending developments in the outside world is very helpful to HR planners. It puts them in an excellent position to influence the nature of business plans (and thus the nature of future HR requirements) and to ensure that planned HR activities are both realistic and supportive of these business plans.

Internal Scanning

Also important is a firm grasp of an organization's internal environment. Thus, planners must be out and about in their organizations, taking advantage of opportunities to learn what is going on. Informal discussions with key managers can help, as can employee attitude surveys, special surveys, and the monitoring of key indicators such as employee performance, absenteeism, turnover, and accident rates. Of special interest is the identification of nagging personnel problems, as well as prevailing managerial attitudes concerning HR.

EXHIBIT 3.12   Example of Environmental Scan for Employment Outlook

- The labor force will grow at a slightly lower rate between 2000 and 2008.
- The use of contingent workers will grow, and wage disparities with noncontingent workers may lead to new legislative protections, such as with health insurance and pensions.
- Company shareholders may become more active "watchdogs" on employment issues that can lead to costly litigation.
- New reward systems will need to replace loss of promotion opportunities due to flattened organization hierarchies.
- Telecommuting will rise in popularity.
- Students preparing for high-demand jobs may opt out of school without graduating.
- Real wages and salaries will be flat, due to restraints caused by use of offshore labor and new immigrants.
- Employees may favor pay for experience, responsibility, and seniority over pay for performance.
- Employers will cooperate more with one another in the recruitment and selection process.

Source: Adapted from Society for Human Resource Management, *Environmental Scan 2000* (Alexandria, VA: author, 2000).

Nagging personnel problems refer to recurring difficulties that threaten to interfere with the attainment of future business plans or other important organizational goals. High turnover in a sales organization, for example, is likely to threaten the viability of a business plan that calls for increased sales quotas or the rapid introduction of several new products.

The values and attitudes of managers, especially top managers, toward HR are also important to HRP. Trouble brews when these are inconsistent with the organization's business plans. For example, a mid-sized accounting firm may have formulated a business plan calling for very rapid growth through aggressive marketing and selected acquisitions of smaller firms, but existing management talent may be inadequate to the task of operating a larger, more complex organization. Moreover, there may be a prevailing attitude among the top management against investing much money in management development and against bringing in talent from outside the firm. This attitude conflicts with the business plan, requiring a change in either the business plan or attitudes.

Reconciliation and Gaps

The reconciliation and gap determination process is best examined by means of an example. Exhibit 3.13 presents intact the example in Exhibit 3.6. Attention is now directed to the reconciliation and gaps column. It represents the results of bringing together requirements and availability forecasts with the results of external and internal environmental scanning. Gap figures must be decided on and entered into the column, and the likely reasons for the gaps need to be identified.

Consider first job category/level A1. A relatively large shortage is projected due to a mild expansion in requirements coupled with a substantial drop in availabilities. This drop is not due to an excessive exit rate but to losses through promotions and job transfers (refer back to the availability forecasts in Exhibits 3.9 and 3.11).

For A2, decreased requirements coupled with increased availabilities lead to a projected surplus. Clearly, changes in current staffing policies and procedures will have to be made to stem the availability tide, such as a slowdown in the promotion rate into A2 from A1 or an acceleration in the exit rate, through an early retirement program.

Turning to B1, note that a huge shortage is forecast. This is due to a major surge in requirements and a substantial reduction in availabilities. To meet the shortage, the organization could increase the transfer of employees from A1. While this would worsen the already projected shortage in A1, it might be cost-effective to do this and would beef up the external staffing for A1 to cover the exacerbated shortage. Alternately, a massive external staffing program could be developed and undertaken for B1 alone. Or, a combination of internal transfers and external staffing for both A1 and B1 could be attempted. To the extent that external staffing

EXHIBIT 3.13 Operational Format and Example for Human Resource Planning (HRP)

Organizational Unit: Sales and Customer Service

| Job Category and Level | Current Workforce | Forecast for Workforce— One Year | | Reconciliation and Gaps | Action Planning |
		Requirements	Availabilities		
A1 (Sales)	100	110	71	−39 (shortage)	Staffing activities Recruitment Selection Employment
A2 (Sales manager)	20	15	22	+7 (surplus)	
B1 (Customer service representative)	200	250	140	−110 (shortage)	Other HR activities Compensation Training and development
B2 (Customer service manager)	15	25	22	−3 (shortage)	
	335	400	255	−145 (shortage)	

becomes a candidate for consideration, this will naturally spill over into other HR activities, such as establishing starting pay levels for A1 and B1.

Finally, for B2 there is a small projected shortage. This gap is so small, however, that for all practical purposes it can be ignored. The HRP process is too imprecise to warrant concern over such small gap figures.

In short, the reconciliation and gap phase of HRP involves coming to grips with projected gaps and likely reasons for them. Quite naturally, thoughts about future implications begin to creep into the process. Even in the simple example shown, it can be seen that considerable action will have to be contemplated and undertaken to respond to the forecasting results for the organizational unit. That will involve mixtures of external and internal staffing, with compensation as another likely HR ingredient. Through action planning these possibilities become real.

Action Planning

Action planning involves four basic sequential steps: set objectives, generate alternative activities, assess alternative activities, and choose alternative activities. Movement through these steps is a logical outgrowth of HRP and is greatly enhanced by its occurrence. Indeed, without HRP the organization rarely has the luxury of doing action planning. Instead, reaction becomes the mode of operation, leading to crash or crisis activities and programs.

These general statements apply to virtually all HR activities that are in any way dependent on the existence of employment gaps and the need to close them. The focus in this chapter is on staffing planning as a specific form of action planning.

STAFFING PLANNING

The four stages of action planning translate directly into a general staffing planning process. After discussing this general process, staffing planning is divided into planning for the core and the flexible workforces.

Staffing Planning Process

Staffing Objectives

Staffing objectives are derived from identified gaps between requirements and availabilities. As such, they involve objectives responding to both shortages and surpluses. They may require the establishment of quantitative and qualitative targets.

Quantitative targets should be expressed in head count or FTE form for each job category/level and will be very close in magnitude to the identified gaps. Indeed, to the extent that the organization believes in the gaps as forecast, the objectives will be identical to the gap figures. A forecast shortage of 39 employees in A1, for example, should be transformed into a staffing objective of 39 accessions (or something close to it) to be achieved by the end of the forecasting time interval. Exhibit 3.14 provides an illustration of these points regarding quantitative staffing objectives.

Qualitative staffing objectives refer to the types or qualities of people in KSAO-type terms. For external staffing objectives, these may be stated in terms of averages, such as average education level for new hires and average scores on ability tests. Internal staffing objectives of a qualitative nature may also be established. These may reflect desired KSAOs in terms of seniority, performance appraisal record over a period of years, types of on- and off-the-job training, and so forth.

Qualitative (KSAO) staffing concerns are usually not part of the previously described forecast process. Gaps are thus not likely to be identified or expressed in qualitative terms. Hence, establishment of qualitative staffing objectives involves considerable judgment on the part of the organization. Ideally, the organization will have conducted job analysis and have available formal job specifications that it can use to guide it in establishing qualitative objectives.

Generating Alternative Staffing Activities

With quantitative and, possibly, qualitative objectives established, it is necessary to begin identifying possible ways of achieving them. This requires an identification of the fullest possible range of alternative activities, which, if pursued, might lead to achievement of the objectives. At the beginning stages of generating alternatives, it is wise to not prematurely close the door on any alternatives. Exhibit 3.15 provides an excellent list of the full range of options available for initial consideration in dealing with employee shortages and surpluses.

EXHIBIT 3.14   Setting Numerical Staffing Objectives

Job Category and Level	Gap	Objectives					Total
		New Hires	Promotions	Transfers	Demotions	Exits	
A1	−39						+39
A2	+7	For each cell, enter a positive number for head count					−7
B1	−110	additions and a negative number for head count					+110
B2	−3	subtractions.					+3
Total							

Note: Assumes objective is to close each gap exactly.

Since the focus of this book is on acquisition of a workforce, our concern is with the employee shortage options. As shown in Exhibit 3.15, both short- and long-term options for shortages, involving a combination of staffing and workload management, are possible. Short-term options include better utilization of current employees (through more overtime, productivity increases, buybacks of vacation and holidays), outsourcing work to other organizations (subcontracts, transfer work out), and acquiring additional employees on a short-term basis (temporary hires and assignments). Long-term options include staffing up with additional employees (recall former employees, transfer in employees from other work units, new permanent hires), skill enhancement (retrain), and pushing work on to other organizations (transfer work out).

Assessing and Choosing Alternatives

As should be apparent, there is a veritable smorgasbord of alternative staffing activities available to address staffing gaps. Each of these alternatives needs to be assessed systematically to help decision makers choose from among the alternatives.

The goal of such assessment is to identify one or more preferred activities. A preferred activity is one offering the highest likelihood of attaining the staffing objective, within the time limit established, at the least cost or tolerable cost, and with the fewest negative side effects. There are no standard or agreed on programs or formats for conducting these assessments. Thus, the organization will need to develop its own internal mechanisms for assessment. Whatever overall mechanism is developed, it should ensure that two things occur. First, a common set of assessment criteria (e.g., time for completion, cost, probability of success) should be identified and agreed on. Second, each alternative should be assessed according to each of these criteria. In this way, all alternatives will receive equal treatment, and tendencies to jump at an initial alternative will be minimized.

For the decade of the 1990s, organizations generally were confronted with a set of favorable economic conditions, which led to substantial job expansion, low unemployment, and high employee turnover. The result was tightening labor markets, persistent employee shortages, and constant understaffing relative to workload needs. Results of a national survey of organizations' experiences with and responses to this staffing dilemma are very instructive. Almost 50% of the organizations reported that they were understaffed, with the range being 80% among high-tech organizations to 40% in insurance and retail organizations. Understaffing was reported to cause numerous problems, among them increased employee stress levels, difficulties in expanding business operations, and decreased quality of customer service. Almost 70% of these organizations reported that finding skilled applicants was their primary staffing challenge. To address these staffing shortfalls, the organizations reported using a number of alternatives, as shown in Exhibit 3.16. These alternatives involved a combination of staffing and workload shifting that encompassed both the core and flexible workforces.

EXHIBIT 3.15   **Staffing Alternatives to Deal with Employee Shortages and Surpluses**

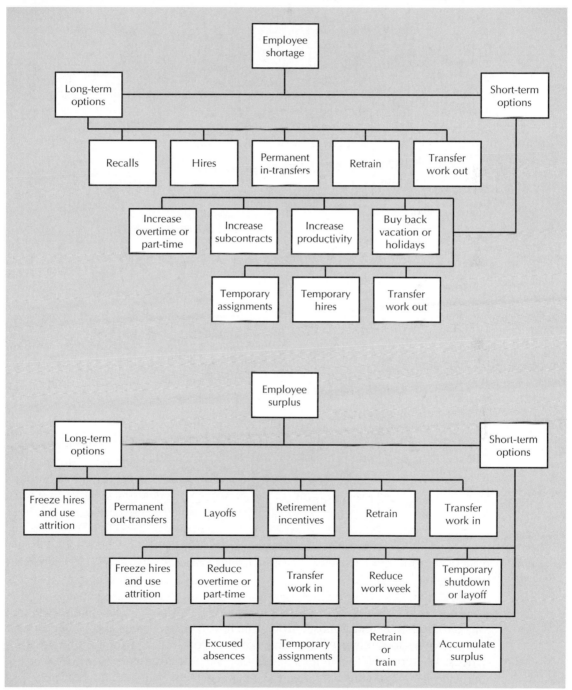

EXHIBIT 3.16 **Organizations' Responses to Staffing Strategies Survey**

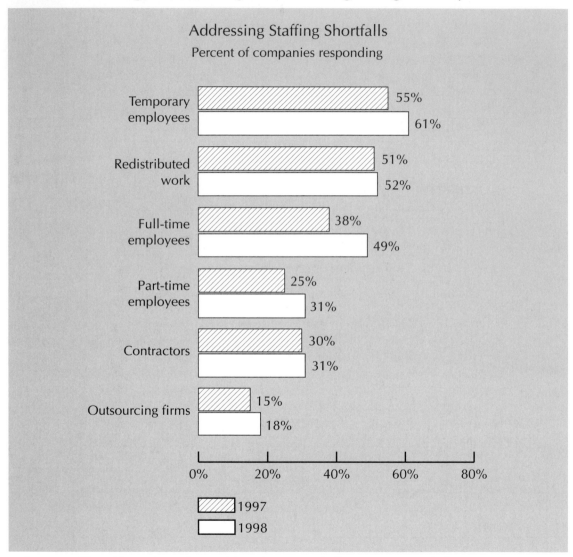

Addressing Staffing Shortfalls
Percent of companies responding

Temporary employees — 1997: 55%, 1998: 61%
Redistributed work — 1997: 51%, 1998: 52%
Full-time employees — 1997: 38%, 1998: 49%
Part-time employees — 1997: 25%, 1998: 31%
Contractors — 1997: 30%, 1998: 31%
Outsourcing firms — 1997: 15%, 1998: 18%

0%   20%   40%   60%   80%

1997
1998

Source: William Olsten Center for Workforce Strategies, *Staffing Strategies* (Melville, NY: 1998), p. 5. Used with permission.

Thus, organizations have many alternatives for meeting employment gaps that need to be assessed and chosen from. The key to wise choices is considering what the appropriate mixture of core and flexible workforces is for fulfilling staffing needs. We turn now to a more detailed treatment of both types of workforces and indicate factors to consider when creating an effective "blended workforce."

Core Workforce

A core workforce, defined as regular full-time and part-time employees of the organization, forms the bulk of most organizations' workforces. The key advantages of a core workforce are stability, continuity, and predictability. The organization can depend on its core workforce and build strategic plans based on it. Several other advantages also accrue to the organization from using a core workforce. The regularity of the employment relationship fosters a sense of commitment and shared purpose toward the organization's mission. Also, the organization maintains the legal right to control employees working on its behalf, both in terms of work process and expected results, rather than having to divide or share that right with organizations providing a flexible workforce, such as temporary employment agencies. Finally, the organization can directly control how it acquires its workforce and the qualifications of those it employs through the management of its own staffing systems. By doing so, the organization may build not only a highly qualified workforce but also one more likely to be retained, thus lessening pressure to continually restaff the organization.

Several disadvantages of a core workforce also exist. The implied permanence of the employment relationship "locks in" the organization's workforce, with a potential loss of staffing flexibility to rapidly increase, reduce, or redeploy its workforce in response to changing market conditions and project life cycles. Reductions of the core workforce, in particular, can be very costly in terms of severance pay packages, low morale, and damage to the organization's reputation as a good employer. Additionally, the labor costs of the core workforce may be greater than that of the flexible workforce due to (a) higher wages, salaries, and benefits for the core workforce; and (b) the fixed nature of these labor costs, relative to the more variable costs associated with a flexible workforce. By using a core workforce, the organization incurs numerous legal obligations—particularly taxation and employment law compliance—that could be fully or partially avoided through use of flexible workforce providers, who would be the actual employer. Finally, use of a core workforce may deprive the organization of new technical and administrative knowledge that could be infused into it by use of flexible workers, such as programmers and consultants.

Consideration of these numerous advantages and disadvantages needs to occur separately for various jobs and organizational units covered by the human resource plan. In this way, usage of a core workforce proceeds along selective, strategic lines. Referring back to the original example in Exhibit 3.6, for example, staffing planners should do a unique core workforce analysis for the sales and customer service unit, and within that unit, for both sales and customer service jobs at the entry and managerial levels. The analysis may result in a decision to use only full-time core workers for the managerial jobs, both full-time and part-time core workers for sales jobs, and a combination of full-time core customer service representatives augmented by both full-time and part-time temporary customer service representatives during peak sales periods. Once the job and work unit locations of the core workers have been determined, specific staffing planning for effective acquisition must occur. This involves planning of recruitment, selection, and employment activities; these topics will be covered in subsequent chapters. However, two overarching issues need to be addressed very early on because of their pervasive implications for all of these staffing activities. The issues are staffing philosophy and staffing flows.

Staffing Philosophy

In conjunction with the staffing planning process, the organization's staffing philosophy should be reviewed. Weighed in conjunction with the organization's staffing strategies, results of this review help shape the direction and character of the specific staffing systems implemented. The review should focus on the following issues: internal versus external staffing, EEO/AA practices, and applicant reactions.

The relative importance to the organization of external or internal staffing is a critical matter because it directly shapes the nature of the staffing system, as well as sends signals to applicants and employees alike about the organization as an employer. For example, at the extreme, an exclusively external focus will require the organization to devote considerable resources to looking outward in order to identify applicant pools to activate and process. For potential applicants, this external focus will likely cause them to perceive any job as fair game, and it will enhance the external reputation of the organization as a desirable place to seek employment at any level. Current employees, however, will perceive a lack of internal mobility possibilities; this may cause such reactions as high turnover and negative feelings toward new external hires. Exhibit 3.17 highlights the advantages and disadvantages of external and internal staffing.

In terms of EEO/AA, the organization must be sure to consider or develop a sense of importance attached to being an EEO/AA-conscious employer, and the commitment it is willing to make in incorporating EEO/AA elements into all phases of the staffing system. Attitudes toward EEO/AA can range all the way from outright hostility and disregard to benign neglect to aggressive commitment and support. As should be obvious, the stance that the organization adopts will have major effects on its operational staffing system, as well as on job applicants and employees.

As a final point about staffing philosophy, planners must continue to bear in mind that staffing is an interaction involving both the organization and job applicants as participants. Just as organizations recruit and select applicants, so, too, do applicants recruit and select organizations (and job offers). Through their job search strategies and activities, applicants exert major influence on their own staffing destinies. Once the applicant has decided to opt into the organization's staffing

---

EXHIBIT 3.17   Staffing Philosophy: Internal versus External Staffing

	Advantages	Disadvantages
Internal	• Positive employee reactions to promotion from within • Quick method to identify job applicants • Less expensive • Little orientation time required	• No new KSAOs into the organization • May perpetuate current underrepresentation of minorities and women • Small labor market to recruit from • Employees may require more training time
External	• Brings employees in with new KSAOs • Larger number of minorities and women to draw from • Large labor market to draw from • Employees may require less training time	• Negative reaction by internal applicants • Time consuming to identify applicants • Expensive to search external labor market • New employees require more orientation time

process, the applicant is confronted with numerous decisions about whether to continue on in the staffing process or withdraw from further consideration. This process of self-selection is inherent to any staffing system. During staffing planning, those within the organization must constantly consider how the applicant will react to the staffing system and its components, and whether they want to encourage or discourage applicant self-selection.

Staffing Flows

Staffing an organization requires not only decisions about discrete staffing system characteristics (for example, which recruitment sources to use and what type of interviews to conduct) but also decisions about the overall flow of events that comprise a staffing system. This flow may be described in general terms or in specific terms. Organizations may use flowcharts to plan and designate the precise nature of the staffing system.

An example of a staffing flowchart is shown in Exhibit 3.18. It is a flowchart that depicts the staffing system of a medium-sized (580 employees) high-tech printing and lithography company. It shows the actual flow of staffing activities, and both organization and applicant decision points, from the time a vacancy occurs until the time it is filled with a new hire.

A detailed inspection of the chart reveals the following sorts of information about the company's staffing system:

1. It is a generic system used for both entry-level and higher-level jobs.

2. For higher-level jobs, vacancies are first posted internally (thus showing a recruitment philosophy emphasizing a commitment to promotion from within). Entry-level jobs are filled externally.

3. External recruitment sources (colleges, newspaper ads, employment agencies) are used only if the current applicant file yields no qualified applicants.

4. Initial assessments are made using biographical information (application blanks, résumés), and results of these assessments determine who will be interviewed.

5. Substantive assessments are made through the interview(s) conducted by the HR manager and the hiring supervisor, and results of these assessments determine who receives the job offer.

6. The applicant may counteroffer, and acceptance by the applicant of the final offer is conditional on passing drug/alcohol and physical tests.

7. The new hire undergoes a six-month probationary employment period before becoming a so-called permanent employee.

If the organization does not have a staffing flowchart for each of its staffing systems, these charts should be developed. The charts can then be used to refresh memories and encourage assessment of current staffing systems in terms of cost, speed and timeliness, and legality. The flowchart may also be used to examine the staffing system from the applicants' perspective, identifying features that might be changed or added to make the system more user-friendly. For example, frequent and informative contact will prevent the applicant from feeling a callous indifference by the organization.

EXHIBIT 3.18   Staffing Flowchart for Medium-Sized Printing Company: Company Perspective

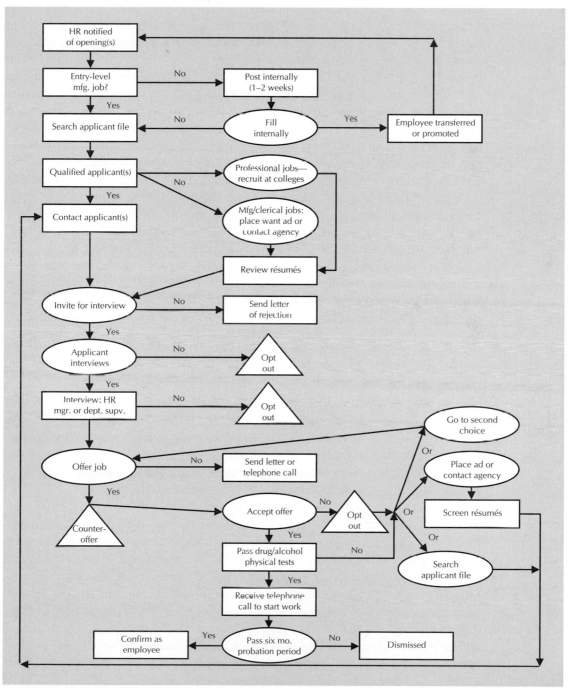

Flexible Workforce

The two major components of the flexible workforce will be temporary employees provided by a staffing firm and independent contractors. Planning for usage of the flexible workforce must occur in tandem with core workforce planning; hence, it should begin with a review of the advantages and disadvantages of a flexible workforce.[17] The key advantage is staffing flexibility. The flexible workforce may be used for adjusting staffing levels quickly in response to changing technological or consumer demand conditions and to ebbs and flows of orders for products and services. Other flexibility advantages are the ability to quickly staff new areas or projects and the ability to fill in for core workers absent due to illness, vacations, and holidays. Relative to the core workforce, the flexible workforce may also present labor cost advantages in the form of lower pay and benefits, more variable labor costs, and reduced training costs. It should be noted, however, that the temporary workforce provider shoulders many of these costs and simply passes them on to the organization through the fees it charges for its services. Another advantage is possibly being relieved of many tax and employment law obligations, since flexible workers are often times not considered employees of the organization. For temporary employees, however, the organization may be considered a coemployer subject to some legal obligations, especially pertaining to equal employment opportunity. An emerging advantage is that the flexible workforce, especially in the professional and technical ranks, may be an important source of new knowledge about organizational best practices and new skills not present in the core workforce, especially "hot skills" in high market demand. Finally, usage of a flexible workforce relieves the organization of the need to design and manage its own staffing systems, since this is done by the flexible workforce provider. An added advantage here is that the organization might use flexible workers on a "try out" basis, much like a probationary period, and then hire into its core workforce those who turn out to be a solid person/job match. Many temporary workers, for example, are "temp-to-perm," meaning that the organization will hire them permanently if they perform successfully in the temporary role. Such an arrangement usually is negotiated up front with the staffing services company.

These numerous advantages must be weighed against several potential disadvantages. Most important is the legal loss of control over flexible workers because they are not employees of the organization. Thus, although the organization has great flexibility in initial job assignments for flexible workers, it is very limited in the amount of supervision and performance management it can conduct for them. Exacerbating the situation is that frictions between core and flexible workers may also arise. Core workers, for example, may feel that flexible workers lack knowledge and experience, are just "putting in time," receive the easy job assignments, and do not act like committed "team players." Also, flexible workers may lack familiarity with equipment, policies, procedures, and important customers; such deficiencies may be compounded by a lack of training in specific job requirements. Finally, it should be remembered that the quality of the flexible workforce will depend heavily on the quality of the staffing and training systems used by the provider of the flexible workers. The organization may end up with flexible but poorly qualified workers.

If the review of advantages and disadvantages of flexible workers confirms the strategic choice to use them in staffing, plans must be developed for the organization units and jobs in which they will be used, and for how they will be acquired. Acquisition plans normally involve the use of staffing firms and independent contractors, both of which perform the traditional staffing activities for the organization. Hence, in contrast to the substantial and sustained staff planning that must occur for the core workforce, planning for the flexible workforce is primarily a matter of becoming knowledgeable about these potential sources and "lining them up" in advance of when they are actually needed.

Staffing Firms

Recall that staffing firms (also called temporary help agencies) are the legal employers of the workers being supplied, though there may also be matters of coemployment that may arise. Hence, the firm conducts recruitment, selection, training, compensation, performance appraisal, and retention activities for the flexible workers. The firm also is responsible for their on-site supervision and management, as well as all payrolling and the payment of legally required insurance premiums. For such services the firm charges the organization a general fee for its labor costs (wages and benefits) plus a "markup" percentage of labor costs (usually 40–50%) to cover these services' costs plus provide a profit. There may be additional charges for specially provided services, such as extra testing or background checks, or skill training. Temp-to-perm temporary workers may be hired away from the firm (with its permission and for a special fee) by the organization to become regular employees in the core workforce. For larger clients the firm may provide an on-site manager to help the organization plan its specific staffing needs, supervise and appraise the performance of the temporary workers, handle discipline and complaints, and facilitate firm–organization relations. With such additional staffing services the firm functions increasingly like a staffing partner, rather than just a staffing supplier.[18]

Planning for use of temporary help firms requires advance planning, rather than a panicky phone call to a firm at the moment of staffing need. In addition to becoming aware of firms that might be accessed, it is wise to become familiar with their characteristics and services. Shown in Exhibit 3.19 are descriptions of the various factors and issues to become knowledgeable about for any firm.

When a firm is actually chosen for use, a formal written agreement should be entered into by both parties. That agreement should cover such matters as specific services to be provided, costs, steps to ensure that the flexible workers are employees of the firm (such as having an on-site manager for them), and the process

EXHIBIT 3.19   Factors to Consider When Choosing a Staffing Firm

Factor	Issues
Agency and Its Reputation	How long in business; location; references from clients available.
Types of Workers Provided	What occupation and KSAO levels; how many available.
Planning and Leadtime	Does agency help client plan staffing levels and needs; how quickly can workers be provided.
Services Provided	
Recruitment	What methods are used; how targeted and truthful is recruitment process.
Selection	What selection techniques are used to assess KSAOs.
Training	What types of training, if any, provided before workers placed with client.
Wages and Benefits	How are wages determined; what benefits are provided.
Orientation	How does the agency prepare workers for assignment with client; does agency have an employee handbook for its workers.
Supervision	How does agency supervise its workers on site of client; does agency provide on-site manager.
Temp-to-Perm	Does agency allow client to hire its temporary workers as permanent employees.
Client Satisfaction	How does agency attempt to gauge client satisfaction with services, workers, costs.
Worker Effectiveness	
Punctuality and Attendance	Does the agency monitor these; what is their record with previous clients.
Job Performance	Is it evaluated; how are the results used.
Retention	How long do workers remain on an assignment voluntarily; how are workers discharged by the agency.
Cost	
Markup	What is the % over base wage charged to client (often it is 50% to cover benefits, overhead, profit margin).
For Special Services	What services cost extra beyond the markup (e.g., temp-to-perm), and what are those costs.

for terminating the firm–organization relationship. It is best to have the agreement prepared/reviewed by legal counsel.

Occasionally the organization may decide to establish its own in-house staffing firm. When this is done, the employees of the firm may even be employees of the organization. Managers thus have readily available flexible workers to whom they can turn, without having to go through all the planning steps mentioned above.

At AT&T, for example, both white-collar and blue-collar staffing firms (pools) were established. Employees in both firms were full-time employees of AT&T, receiving full pay and benefits. The white-collar firm, named Resource Link, had more than 500 managerial, professional, and technical employees available for assignment throughout AT&T's 28 business units. These employees were carefully recruited internally, often from the ranks of employees who had been displaced during a reorganization. The employees were also carefully screened in terms of specific skills, adaptability, flexibility, and customer focus. Their assignments usually lasted between 3 and 18 months. The blue-collar firm, named the Skills Match Center Administrative Intern Program, was run for general secretaries, advanced software specialists, administrative assistants, and word processors. Employees in these jobs were also carefully recruited and screened.[19]

Independent Contractors

An independent contractor (IC) provides specific task and project assistance to the organization, such as maintenance, bookkeeping, advertising, programming, and consulting. The IC can be a single individual (self-employed, freelancer) or an employer with its own employees. Neither the IC nor its employees are intended to be employees of the organization utilizing their services, and care should be taken to ensure that the IC is not treated as an employee (see Chapter 2).[20]

As with staffing firms, the organization must take the initiative to identify and check out ICs for possible use in advance of when they are actually needed. It is desirable to solicit and examine references from past or current clients of the IC. Also, as much as possible the organization should seek to determine how the IC staffs, trains, and compensates its employees. This could occur during a preliminary, get-together meeting with the IC. In these ways, the organization will have cultivated and screened ICs prior to when they are actually needed.

It is recommended that the IC and the organization prepare and enter into a written agreement between them. In general, the agreement should clarify the nature and scope of the project and contain language that reinforces the intent to have the IC function as such, rather than as an employee. For example, the agreement should refer to the parties as "firm" and "contractor," describe the specific work to be completed, specify that payment will be for completion of the project (rather than time worked), make the IC responsible for providing all equipment and supplies, exclude the IC from any of the organization's benefits, and ensure that the IC is responsible for paying all legally required taxes. Preparation of such an agreement might require the assistance of legal counsel.

LEGAL ISSUES

The major legal issue in HR and staffing planning is that of affirmative action plans and programs (AAPs). AAPs originate from many different sources—voluntary employer efforts, court-imposed remedies for discriminatory practices, conciliation or consent agreement, and requirements as a federal contractor. Regardless of source, all AAPs seek to rectify the effects of past employment discrimination by increasing the representation of certain groups (minorities, women, disabled) in the organization's workforce. This is to be achieved through establishing and actively pursuing hiring and promotion goals and adhering to timetables for achieving those goals.

This section describes the general content of AAPs, discusses the affirmative action requirements for federal contractors under Affirmative Action Programs regulations, and provides some general indications as to the legality of AAPs. Also, brief presentations are made of so-called diversity programs and of EEOC guidance on use of temporary workers.

Affirmative Action Plans (AAPs)

AAPs are organization-specific plans, and thus their content varies across organizations. Nonetheless, all AAPs share three general components, namely, quantitative analysis, placement goals, and action plans.

An example of a partial AAP with these three general components is shown in Exhibit 3.20. The example draws from the general HR planning example in Exhibit 3.6. The AAP shown is for only one job category (sales), now called a job group, and for only one group (women).

Inspection of the exhibit reveals that the organization has a current sales force of 100, of whom 10 (10%) are women. A utilization analysis with accompanying stock statistics (see Chapter 2) shows that the current percentage of female salespeople (10%) is less than their estimated availability (20%), based on consideration of availability factors. A comparison of these two percentages suggests that there is underutilization of women in the sales job group.

Based on the identified underutilization, the organization sets an affirmative action placement goal of 20% utilization, with a timetable of one year to achieve that goal. Action plans are now developed for achieving this goal. These involve staffing plans and other HR plans.

In terms of staffing plans, the organization first considers the results of its general HR forecast for the next year, which had predicted a shortage of 39 salespeople. New hires may be obtained from external and internal sources, consistent with past staffing practices. Based on its placement goal, the organization sets a staffing target of 24 men and 15 women, for a total of 39 new salespeople. If, in fact, these targets are met, the organization will come close to its goal of 20%

EXHIBIT 3.20   **Example of Affirmative Action Plan (AAP): Essential Components**

Job Group: Sales
Affirmative Action Plan: Women

Current Workforce		Utilization Analysis		Placement Goal				Action Plan (one year)		
		Avail-ability*		Under-utilization (?)	Goal	Timetable	Forecast of Gap	External Staffing		Other Plans
%M	%F	%M	%F		%F	%F		M F		
90	10	80	20	Yes	20	1 year	−39 (shortage)	24 15		accelerated training program
Total 100										child care program

* Availability determined on the basis of both internal (current employees) and external (labor force) factors.

women in the sales job category (the 15 new saleswomen plus whatever number of the 10 current saleswomen who remain in the job group, out of the total of 112 that were forecast in Exhibit 3.6).

Armed with this numerical staffing target, the organization can develop specific plans for pursuing it. This involves development of detailed staffing plans, as discussed earlier in this chapter. It also involves consideration of other action plans to support the staffing plan. As shown in Exhibit 3.20, the development of an accelerated training program and the development of a child care program have been identified as two possible support plans.

This example illustrates the basics of an affirmative action plan. It is, however, a very simplified version of an AAP. It involves only one job group, one group (women), and a one-year time frame. Specifics of the utilization analysis, and action plans, are ignored. AAPs are, in reality, much more complex than this example suggests. A consideration of the actual AAP requirements for federal contractors under Affirmative Action Programs regulations shows the complexities involved in AAPs.

Affirmative Action Programs Regulations

These regulations spell out in detail the requirements a federal contractor must adhere to as it develops, implements, and administers an AAP. These requirements are summarized below (for full text of the regulations see *www.dol.gov/dol/esa/public/regs/fedregs/final*). It should be noted that the contractor generally must develop a separate AAP, as described below, for each of its establishments.

Organizational Profile   An organization profile is a depiction of the staffing pattern within an establishment. It provides a profile of the workforce at the establishment, and it assists in identifying units in which women or minorities are underrepresented. The profile may be done through either an organizational display or a workforce analysis. The latter requires a showing of job titles, which the former does not. Key elements in both approaches are a showing of organizational structure of lines of progression (promotion) among jobs, or organization units, the total number of job incumbents, the total number of male and female incumbents, and the total number of male and female minority incumbents in each of the following groups: Blacks, Hispanics, Asians/Pacific Islanders, and American Indians/Alaskan Natives.

Job Group Analysis   Jobs with similar content, wage rates, and opportunities (e.g., promotion, training) must be combined into job groups; each group must include a list of job titles. Small (less than 150 employees) establishments may use as job groups the nine categories on the EEO-1 Form: officials and managers, professionals, technicians, sales, office and clerical, craft workers (skilled), operatives (semiskilled), laborers (unskilled), and service workers. The percentage of minorities and the percentage of women (determined in the previous step) employed in each job group must be indicated.

Availability Determination The availability of women and of minorities must be determined separately for each job group. At least the following two factors should be considered when determining availability:

1. the percentage of minorities or women with requisite skills in the reasonable recruitment area,
2. the percentage of minorities or women among those promotable, transferable, and training with the organization.

Current census data (2000), job service data, or other data should be consulted to determine availability. When there are multiple job titles in a job group, with different availability rates, a composite availability figure for the group must be calculated. This requires summing weighted availability estimates for the job titles.

Comparison of Incumbency to Availability For each job group, the percentages of women and minority incumbents must be compared to their availability. When the percentage employed is less than would reasonably be expected by the availability percentage, a placement goal must be established.

Placement Goals If called for, an annual placement goal at least equal to the availability percentage for women or minorities must be established for the job group. Placement goals may not be rigid or inflexible quotas; quotas are expressly forbidden. Placement goals do not require hiring a person who lacks the qualifications to perform the job successfully, or hiring a less-qualified person in preference to a more-qualified one.

Designation of Responsibility An official of the organization must be designated as responsible for the implementation of the affirmative action program.

Identification of Problem Areas The organization must evaluate:

1. if there are problems of minority or female utilization or distribution in each job group,
2. personnel activity (applicant flow, hires, terminations, promotions) and other personnel actions for possible selection disparities,
3. compensation systems for possible gender-, race-, ethnicity-based disparities,
4. selection, recruitment, referral, and other procedures to see if they result in disparities in employment or advancement of minorities or women.

Action-Oriented Programs Where problem areas have been identified, the organization must develop and execute action-oriented programs to correct problem areas and attain placement goals. (No specific guidance as to the nature of these programs is provided—suggestions are provided in Chapters 5, 6, 8, 9, and 10.) A good faith effort to do this must be demonstrated.

Internal Audit and Reporting An auditing system must be developed that periodically measures the effectiveness of the total affirmative action program.

It should be apparent that required affirmative action plans are complex undertakings that must be an integral part of overall staffing planning. Also, it should be remembered that the OFCCP monitors organizations for compliance with the Affirmative Action Programs regulations. Research by the OFCCP indicates several specific reasons why contractors may have their compliance status questioned. These are (a) lack of commitment and EEO/AA accountability by top management; (b) failure to conduct self-audits; (c) absence of consistent personnel policies; (d) faulty job application procedures; (e) lack of proactive recruitment, mentoring, and race and sexual harassment programs; (f) lack of participation of an EEO knowledgeable person in selection decisions; and (g) failure to develop and listen to internal support groups.[21]

Legality of AAPs

AAPs have been controversial since their inception, and there have been many challenges to their legality. Questions of legality are difficult to answer or provide guidance on because of complexities in the interpretations of the relevant laws, as well as complexities in the nature of AAPs themselves as adopted by organizations. Despite these problems, it is possible to provide several conclusions and recommendations regarding AAPs.

AAPs in general are legal in the eyes of the Supreme Court. However, to be acceptable, an AAP should be based on the following guidelines:[22]

1. The plan should have as its purpose the remedying of specific and identifiable effects of past discrimination.
2. There should be definite underutilization of women and/or minorities currently in the organization.
3. Regarding nonminority and male employees, the plan should not unsettle their legitimate expectations, not result in their discharge and replacement with minority or women employees, and not create an absolute bar to their promotion.
4. The plan should be temporary, and eliminated once affirmative action goals have been achieved (this occurred, for example, to the AAP for police officers in the city of Detroit).[23]

5. All candidates for positions should be qualified for those positions.
6. The plan should include organizational enforcement mechanisms, as well as a grievance procedure.

Recent court rulings on the constitutionality of federal and state government AAPs suggest that even more strict guidelines than those above may be necessary. Insofar as these programs are concerned, racial preferences are subject to strict constitutional scrutiny. They may be used only when there has been specific evidence of identified discrimination, the remedy has been narrowly tailored to only the identified discrimination, only those who have suffered discrimination may benefit from the remedy, and other individuals will not carry an undue burden, such as job displacement, from the remedy. Lesser scrutiny standards may apply for gender preferences.[24]

There is substantial debate over affirmative action and its role as a legitimate tool for addressing discrimination. Much of the debate centers around questions of whether affirmative action involves quota hiring and promotion, giving rise to reverse discrimination. Possible outcomes of the debate range from no change in present laws and practices all the way to amending the Civil Rights Act to prohibit affirmative action and preferential treatment and to scrapping EO 11246 and Revised Order No. 4 for federal contractors.[25]

AAPs are not separate staffing systems but integral parts of general staffing systems. As such, AAPs should be incorporated into more general HR and staffing planning. In this way, there is a single, unified staffing system to serve both broad organizational goals and more specific affirmative action ones.

Diversity Programs

Much of staffing focuses on the initial acquisition of people and creation of the initial person/job match. AAPs and organization diversity programs likewise have this focus. Once the initial match has occurred, however, the organization must be concerned about employee adaptation to the job, upward job mobility, and maintenance of the employment relationship over time. Without such a concern, the effectiveness of AAPs can be severely undercut. In particular, satisfaction and retention problems for those acquired through the AAP can arise, and these problems in turn will thwart any meaningful, permanent change in the diversity of the organization's workforce.

Recently, organizations have begun experimenting with diversity programs. These programs arise out of a recognition that the labor force, and thus the organization's workforce, is becoming more demographically and culturally diverse. The focus of diversity programs is on the assimilation and adaptation of a diverse workforce once it has been acquired. Diversity programs thus pick up where AAPs leave off and indeed may be viewed as a logical continuation of them.[26]

A diverse workforce is heterogeneous in terms of individuals' KSAOs and motivation. Such individual diversity requires a diversity in programs designed to facilitate an effective, long-term person/job match. Examples of the types of content found in diversity programs include flexible work schedules, telecommuting, training programs to heighten employee awareness and acceptance of diversity, mentoring relationships, special career- and credential-building assignments, child care, and team building. Other, more traditional HR programs, especially performance management and career development ones, may also be included in an organization's diversity initiative.

Though in their infancy and without any specific legal basis or requirement, diversity programs can be of assistance to organization AAPs in two major ways. First, having a diversity program may aid in the recruitment and attraction of a diverse workforce, thus contributing directly to the achievement of affirmative action goals and timetables, as well as organizational effectiveness. Second, with a diversity program, the organization may increase the retention rates of those acquired through the AAP. As a consequence, underutilization of underrepresented groups will lessen over time and, ideally, lead to the elimination of the need for an AAP at all.

EEO and Temporary Workers

The EEOC has provided guidance on coverage and responsibility requirements for temporary employment agencies (and other types of staffing firms) and their client organizations.[27] When both the agency and the client exercise control over the temporary employee and both have the requisite number of employees, they are considered employers and jointly liable under the Civil Rights Act, Age Discrimination in Employment Act, Americans With Disabilities Act, and the Equal Pay Act. It should be noted that these laws also apply to individuals placed with organizations through welfare-to-work programs. The agency is obligated to make referrals and job assignments in a nondiscriminating manner, and the client may not set discriminatory job referral and job assignment criteria. The client must treat the temporary employees in a nondiscriminatory manner; if the agency knows this is not happening, the agency must take any corrective actions within its control. There are substantial penalties for noncompliance (e.g., back pay, front pay, compensatory damages) that may be obtained from either the agency and the client, or both. There is special guidance for ADA-related issues.

SUMMARY

External forces shape the conduct and outcomes of human resource planning (HRP). The key forces and trends that emerge from them are economic conditions, labor markets, and labor unions.

Human resource planning is described as a process and set of activities under-taken to forecast future HR requirements and availabilities, resulting in the iden-tification of likely employment gaps (shortages and surpluses). Action plans are then developed for addressing the gaps. Before HRP begins, initial decisions must be made about its comprehensiveness, planning time frame, job categories and levels to be included, how to "count heads," and the roles and responsibilities of line and staff (including HR) managers.

A variety of statistical and judgmental techniques may be used in forecasting. Those used in forecasting requirements are typically used in conjunction with business and organization planning. For forecasting availabilities, techniques must be used that take into account the movements of people into, within, and out of the organization, on a job-by-job basis. Here, Markov Analysis is suggested as particularly useful in jobs with relatively large numbers of employees. For other situations, executive reviews, succession planning, and vacancy analysis may be more useful.

External and internal environmental scanning occur after forecasting. Their results temper, and aid in interpretation of, identified employment gaps. Analysis of gaps requires determining probable reasons for them. Such reasons can serve as stimuli for and inputs into action planning.

Staffing planning is a form of action planning. It is shown to generally require setting staffing objectives, generating alternative staffing activities, and assessing and choosing from among those alternatives. A fundamental alternative involves use of core or flexible workforces, as identified in staffing strategy. Plans must be developed for acquiring both types of workforces. Advantages and disadvantages of each type are provided; these should first be reviewed to reaffirm strategic choices about their use. Following that, planning can begin. For the core work-force, this first involves matters of staffing philosophy and staffing flowcharts; these will guide the planning of recruitment, selection, and employment activities. For the flexible workforce, the organization should establish early contact with the providers of the flexible workers (i.e., staffing firms and independent contrac-tors). In general, it is recommended that the organization also enter into written agreements with these providers. Numerous issues need to be addressed in such agreements.

Affirmative action plans (AAPs) are an extension and application of general HR and staffing planning. AAPs have several components. The Affirmative Action Programs regulations, which apply to federal contractors, specify requirements for these components. The legality of AAPs has been clearly established, but the courts have fashioned limits to their content and scope. Diversity programs are organizational initiatives to help effectively manage a diverse workforce. Such programs have the potential for successfully working in tandem with AAPs by contributing to the attraction and retention of AAP-targeted people. To clarify how EEO laws apply to temporary employees and agencies, the EEOC has issued specific guidance.

DISCUSSION QUESTIONS

1. What are ways that the organization can ensure that KSAO deficiencies do not occur in its workforce?

2. What are the types of experiences, especially staffing-related ones, that an organization will be likely to have if it does not engage in HR and staffing planning?

3. Why are decisions about job categories and levels so critical to the conduct and results of HRP?

4. What are the differences between statistical and judgmental techniques for forecasting future availabilities?

5. What is meant by reconciliation, and why can it be useful as an input to staffing planning?

6. What criteria would you suggest using for assessing the staffing alternatives shown in Exhibit 3.15?

7. Some people object to staffing flowcharts as making the staffing process too mechanical, impersonal, and cold. Do you agree? Why?

8. What problems might an organization encounter in creating an AAP that it might not encounter in regular staffing planning?

APPLICATIONS

Markov Analysis and Forecasting

The Doortodoor Sports Equipment Company sells sports clothing and equipment for amateur, light sport (running, tennis, walking, swimming, badminton, golf) enthusiasts. It is the only company in the nation that does this on a door-to-door basis, seeking to bypass the retail sporting goods store and sell directly to the customer. Its salespeople have sales kits that include both sample products and a full-line catalog it can use to show and discuss with customers. The sales function is composed of full-time and part-time salespeople (level 1), assistant sales managers (level 2), and regional sales managers (level 3).

The company has decided to study the internal movement patterns of people in the sales function, as well as to forecast their likely availabilities in future time periods. Results will be used to help identify staffing gaps (surpluses and shortages) and to develop staffing strategy and plans for future growth.

To do this, the HR department first collected data for 1997 and 1998 to construct a transition probability matrix, as well as the number of employees for 1999 in each job category. It then wanted to use the matrix to forecast availabilities for 2000. The following data were gathered:

Job Category	Level	Transition Probabilities (1997–98)					Current (1999) No. Employees
		SF	SP	ASM	RSM	Exit	
Sales, Full-time (SF)	1	.50	.10	.05	.00	.35	500
Sales, Part-time (SP)	1	.05	.60	.10	.00	.25	150
Ass't. Sales Mgr. (ASM)	2	.05	.00	.80	.10	.05	50
Region. Sales Mgr. (RSM)	3	.00	.00	.00	.70	.30	30

Based on the above data:

1. Describe the internal labor market of the company in terms of job stability (staying on same job), promotion paths and rates, transfer paths and rates, demotion paths and rates, and turnover (exit) rates.
2. Forecast the numbers available in each job category in 2000.
3. Indicate potential limitations to your forecasts.

Deciding Whether to Use Flexible Staffing

The Kaiser Manufacturing Company (KMC) has been in existence for over 50 years. Its main products are specialty implements for use in both the crop and dairy herd sides of the agricultural business. Products include special attachments to tractors, combines, discers, and so on, and add-on devices for milking and feeding equipment that enhance the performance and safety of the equipment.

KMC has a small corporate office plus four manufacturing plants (two in the midwest and two in the south). It has a core workforce of 725 production workers, 30 clericals, 32 professional and engineering workers, and 41 managers. All employees are full-time, and KMC has never used either part-time or temporary workers. It feels very strongly that its staffing strategy of using only a core workforce has paid big dividends over the years in attracting and retaining a committed and highly productive workforce.

Sales have been virtually flat at $175 million annually since 1990. At the same time KMC has begun to experience more erratic placement of orders for its products, making sales less predictable. This appears to be a reflection of more turbulent weather patterns, large swings in interest rates, new entrants into the specialty markets, and general uncertainty about the future direction and growth in the agricultural industry. Increased unpredictability in sales has been accompanied by steadily rising labor costs. This has been due to KMC's increasingly older workforce, as well as shortages of all types of workers (particularly production workers) in the immediate labor markets surrounding the plants.

Assume you are the HR manager responsible for staffing and training at KMC. You have just been contacted by a representative of the Flexible Staffing Services

(FSS) Company, Mr. Tom Jacoby. Mr. Jacoby has proposed meeting with you and the president of KMC, Mr. Herman Kaiser, to talk about FSS and how it might be of service to KMC. You and Mr. Kaiser agree to meet with Mr. Jacoby. At that meeting, Mr. Jacoby makes a formal presentation to you in which he describes the services, operation, and fees of FSS and highlights the advantages of using a more flexible workforce. During that meeting, you learn the following from Mr. Jacoby.

FSS is a recent entrant into what is called the staffing industry. Its general purpose is to furnish qualified employees to companies (customers) on an as-needed basis, thus helping the customer implement a flexible staffing strategy. It furnishes employees in four major groups: production, clerical, technical, and professional/managerial. Both full-time and part-time employees are available in each of these groups. Employees may be furnished to the customer on a strictly temporary basis ("temps") or on a "temp-to-perm" basis in which the employees convert from being a temporary employee of FSS to being a permanent employee of the customer after a 90-day probationary period.

For both the temp and temp-to-perm arrangements, FSS offers the following services. In each of the four employee groups it will recruit, select, and hire people to work for FSS, which will in turn lease them to the customer. FSS performs all recruitment, selection, and employment activities. It has a standard selection system used for all applicants, composed of an application blank, reference checks, drug testing, and a medical exam (given after making a job offer). It also offers customized selection plans in which the customer chooses from among a set of special skill tests, a personality test, an honesty test, and background investigations. Based on the standard and/or custom assessments, FSS refers to the customer what it views as the top candidates. FSS tries to furnish two people for every vacancy, and the customer chooses from between the two.

New hires at FSS receive a base wage that is similar to the market wage, as well as close to the wage of the customer's employees with whom they will be directly working. In addition, new hires receive a paid vacation (one week for every six months of employment, up to four weeks), health insurance (with a 25% employee co-pay), and optional participation in a 401(k) plan. FSS performs and pays for all payroll functions and deductions. It also pays the premiums for workers' compensation and unemployment compensation.

The fees charged by FSS to the customer are as follows. There is a standard fee per employee furnished of $1.55 \times$ base wage $\times$ hours worked per week. The 1.55 is labeled "markup"; it covers all of FSS's costs (staffing, insurance, benefits, administration) plus a profit margin. On top of the standard fee is an additional fee for customized selection services. This fee ranges from .50 to .90 $\times$ base wage $\times$ hours worked per week. Finally, there is a special one-time fee for temp-to-perm employees (a one-month pay finder's fee) payable after the employee has successfully completed the 90-day probationary period and transferred to being an employee of the customer.

Mr. Jacoby concludes his presentation by stressing three advantages of flexible staffing as provided by FSS. First, use of FSS employees on an as-needed basis will give KMC greater flexibility in its staffing to match fluctuating product demand, as well as movement from completely fixed labor costs to more variable labor costs. Second, FSS provides considerable administrative convenience, relieving KMC of most of the burden of recruitment, selection, and payrolling. Finally, KMC will experience considerable freedom from litigation (workers' comp, EEO, torts) since FSS and not KMC will be the employer.

After Mr. Jacoby's presentation, Mr. Kaiser tells you he is favorably impressed, but that they clearly need to do some more thinking before they embark on the path of flexible staffing and use of FSS as its provider. He asks you to prepare a brief, preliminary report including:

1. a summary of the possible advantages and disadvantages of flexible staffing
2. a summary of the advantages and disadvantages of using FSS as a service provider
3. a summary of the type of additional information you recommend gathering and using as part of the decision-making process.

ENDNOTES

1. S. Carey, "Demand for Pilots Is Soaring as Old-Timers Take Off," *Wall Street Journal,* June 7, 1998, p. B1.

2. A. Thompson, "Industry Output and Employment Projections to 2008," *Monthly Labor Review,* 1999, 122(11), pp. 33–50.

3. D. Bradock, "Occupational Employment Projects to 2008," *Monthly Labor Review,* 1999, 122(11), pp. 51–77.

4. D. Bradock, "Occupational Employment Projects to 2008."

5. Bureau of National Affairs, "Results of the NAM/Grant Thornton Survey," *Daily Labor Report,* Nov. 17, 1997, p. E1.

6. Society for Human Resource Management, "Management Skills for the Future," *Issues in HR,* March/April 1995, p. 5.

7. Howard N. Fullerton Jr., "Labor Force 2006: Slowing Down and Changing Composition," *Monthly Labor Review,* 1997, 120(11), pp. 23–37; P. L. Rones, R. E. Ilg, and J. M. Garner, "Trends in Hours of Work since the Mid-1970s," *Monthly Labor Review,* 1997, 120(4), pp. 3–14; Society for Human Resource Management, "Workplace Visions," Sept./Oct. 1996, pp. 3–4; J. F. Stinson Jr., "New Data on Multiple Job Holding Available from the CPS," *Monthly Labor Review,* 1997, 120(3), pp. 3–8.

8. D. Bradock, "Occupational Employment Project to 2008."

9. American Management Association, "2000 AMA Survey on Basic Skills Training and Testing" (New York: author, 2000).

10. A. Packer, "Skill Deficiencies: Problems, Policies and Prospects," *Journal of Labor Research,* 1993, 14, pp. 227–247.

11. U.S. Department of Labor, *News,* Oct. 5, 2001, p. 8.

12. U.S. Department of Labor, *News,* Aug. 14, 1992, p. 5.

13. U.S. Department of Labor, *News,* Jan. 18, 2001, p. 1.

14. J. P. Begin, *Strategic Employment Policy* (Englewood Cliffs, NJ: Prentice-Hall, 1991); J. E. Butler, G. R. Ferris, and N. K. Napier, *Strategy and Human Resource Management;* L. Dyer (ed.), *Human Resource Planning: A Case Study Reference Guide to the Tested Practices of Five Major U.S. and Canadian Companies* (New York: Random House, 1986); D. W. Jarrell, *Human Resource Planning* (Englewood Cliffs, NJ: Prentice-Hall, 1993); S. E. Jackson and R. S. Schuler, "Human Resource Planning: Challenges for Industrial/Organizational Psychologists," *American Psychologist,* 1990, 45, pp. 223–239; J. W. Walker, *Human Resource Strategy* (New York: McGraw-Hill, 1992).

15. Jarrell, *Human Resource Planning,* pp. 256–281; L. T. Pinfield and M. Morishima, "Taking the Measure of Human Resource Management Flows," *Public Personnel Management,* 1991, 20, pp. 299–318.

16. H. G. Heneman III and M. H. Sandver, "Markov Analysis in Human Resource Administration: Applications and Limitations," *Academy of Management Review,* 1977, 2, pp. 535–542.

17. D. C. Feldman, H. I. Doerphinghaus, and W. H. Turnley, "Managing Temporary Workers: A Permanent HRM Challenge," *Organizational Dynamics,* 1994, 23(2), pp. 49–63; C. V. von Hippel, S. L. Mangum, D. B. Greenberger, R. L. Heneman, and J. D. Skoglind, "Temporary Employment: Can Organizations and Employees Both Win?," *Academy of Management Executive,* 1997, 11, pp. 93–104; S. F. Matusik and C. W. L. Hill, "The Utilization of Contingent Work, Knowledge Creation, and Competitive Advantage," *Academy of Management Review,* 1998, 23, pp. 680–697; Society for Human Resource Management, *Alternative Staffing Survey* (Alexandria, VA: author, 2000); S. N. Houseman, "Why Employers Use Flexible Staffing Arrangements: Evidence from an Establishment Survey," *Industrial and Labor Relations Review,* 2001, 55, pp. 149–170.

18. V. Zinno, "New Terms for Temps," *Human Resource Executive,* Sept. 1994, pp. 43–45.

19. V. C. Smith, "Temping the AT & T Way," *Human Resource Executive,* Sept. 1994, pp. 52–53.

20. D. P. O'Meara, "Question the Legal Status of Independent Contractors," *HR Magazine,* 1994, 39(8), pp. 33–39; T. Stalnaker, *Using Independent Contractors* (Washington, DC: Bureau of National Affairs, 1993).

21. Bureau of National Affairs, "Regional OFCCP Directors Describe Top Ten Reasons Contractors Get in Trouble," *Daily Labor Report,* Aug. 21, 1998, p. C-2.

22. T. Johnson, "Affirmative Action as a Title VII Remedy: Recent U.S. Supreme Court Decisions, Racial Quotas and Preferences," *Labor Law Journal,* 1987, 38, pp. 574–581; T. Johnson, "The Legal Use of Racial Quotas and Gender Preferences by Public and Private Employers," *Labor Law Journal,* 1989, 40, pp. 419–425; D. D. Bennett-Alexander and L. B. Pincus, *Employment Law for Business,* second ed. (Burr-Ridge, IL: Irwin McGraw-Hill, 1998), p. 139; C. R.Gullett, "Reverse Discrimination and Remedial Affirmative Action in Employment," *Public Personnel Management,* 2000, 29(1), pp. 107–118.

23. International Personnel Management Association, "Court Ends Affirmative Action Plan," *IPMA News,* June 1993, pp. 19–20.

24. R. T. Seymour and B. B. Brown, *Equal Employment Law Update* (Washington, DC: Bureau of National Affairs, 1997), pp. 23-553 to 23-558.

25. F. Bloch, "Affirmative Action Hasn't Helped Blacks," *Wall Street Journal,* March 1, 1995, p. A16; Bureau of National Affairs, "Affirmative Action After Adarand: A Legal, Regulatory,

Legislative Outlook," *Daily Labor Report,* March 23, 1995, pp. S-1 to S-98; Bureau of National Affairs, "Draft Report on Reverse Discrimination Commissioned by Labor Department," *Daily Labor Report,* March 23, 1995, pp. E-1 to E-6; Bureau of National Affairs, "OFCCP Notice Reaffirming Affirmative Action Goals in Light of Adarand Decision, Administration Review," *Daily Labor Report,* Aug. 11, 1995, pp. E-1 to E-2.

26. D. D. Bennett-Alexander and L. B. Pincus, *Employment Law for Business,* pp. 136–140; Society for Human Resource Management, "Impact of Diversity Initiatives on the Bottom Line" (Alexandria, VA: author, 2001); O. C. Richard, "Racial Diversity, Business Strategy, and Firm Performance: A Resource-Based View," *Academy of Management Journal,* 2000, 43, pp. 164–177; E. Raimy, "Dynamic Diversity," *Human Resource Executive,* Oct. 2001, pp. 26–32; V. J. Weaver, "Diversity: One Size Doesn't Fit All," *SHRM Mosaics,* May/June 2000, pp. 1–7.

27. Equal Employment Opportunity Commission, *EEOC Policy Guidance on Temporary Workers* (Washington, DC: author, 1997); Equal Employment Opportunity Commission, *Enforcement Guidance: Application of the ADA to Contingent Workers Placed By Temporary Agencies and Other Staffing Firms* (Washington, DC: author, 2000).

CHAPTER FOUR

Job Analysis

T his chapter begins with a description of several types of jobs: traditional, evolving, flexible, idiosyncratic, team-based, and telework. These types of jobs may be analyzed and described in terms of specific job requirements (tasks, KSAOs, job context), competency requirements (general and job-spanning KSAOs), and job rewards (extrinsic and intrinsic). Job analysis is the general process of studying and describing these requirements and rewards. Separate approaches are needed for job requirements, competency requirements, and job rewards.

Job requirements job analysis is discussed first. It is guided by the job requirements matrix, which contains the three basic components (tasks, KSAOs, job context) that must be considered during the job analysis. Detailed descriptions of each component are provided. Also described are job analysis methods, sources, and processes for collecting the job requirements information.

Competency-based job analysis is described next. It is very new on the job requirements scene. It seeks to identify more general KSAO requirements, such as KSAOs necessary for all jobs to meet the organization's mission and goals and KSAOs that cut across interdependent jobs, such as with work teams. These competencies are presumed to provide a foundation for more flexible staffing in initial job assignments for new hires and in job and project assignments for current employees.

Attention then shifts to the job rewards approach, which is guided by the job rewards matrix. It contains information about the extrinsic and intrinsic rewards of a job, along with indications about their amount, differentials among employees, and stability. Methods, sources, and processes for collecting this information are described.

Finally, three legal issues pertaining to job analysis are treated. All three issues involve the job requirements approach to job analysis as it applies to EEO/AA under the Civil Rights Act and the Americans With Disabilities Act.

TYPES OF JOBS

Jobs are the building blocks of an organization, in terms of both job content and the hierarchical relationships that emerge among them.[1] They are explicitly designed and aligned in ways that enhance the production of the organization's goods and services. Job analysis thus must be considered within the broader framework of the design of jobs, for through their design jobs acquire their requirements and rewards in the first place. Several different types of jobs may be designed by the organization. These include traditional, evolving, flexible, idiosyncratic, team-based, and telework jobs.

Traditional

The traditional way of designing a job is to identify and define its elements and tasks precisely, and then incorporate them into a job description. This task core includes virtually all tasks associated with the job, and from it a fairly inclusive list of KSAOs will flow. Thus defined, there are clear lines of demarcation between jobs in terms of both tasks and KSAOs, and there is little overlap between jobs on either basis. Each job also has its own set of extrinsic and intrinsic rewards. Such job design is marked by formal organization charts, clear and precise job descriptions and specifications, and well-defined relationships between jobs in terms of mobility (promotion and transfer) paths. Also, traditional jobs are very static, with little or no change occurring in tasks or KSAOs.

Certain terms are used frequently in discussions of traditional jobs. Definitions of some of the key terms, and examples of them, are provided in Exhibit 4.1. Note that the terms are presented in a logically descending hierarchy, starting with job category or family, and proceeding downward through job, position, task dimension, task, and element.

Evolving

Traditionally designed and administered jobs may gradually change or evolve over time, yielding an evolving job. These changes are not radical, are usually intentional, and are often due to technological and workload changes. An excellent example of such an evolving job is that of "secretary."[2] Traditional or core tasks associated

---

EXHIBIT 4.1   Terminology Commonly Used in Describing Jobs

TERM	DEFINITION
Job family	A grouping of jobs, usually according to function (e.g., production, finance, human resources, marketing)
Job category	A grouping of jobs according to generic job title or occupation (e.g., managerial, sales, clerical, maintenance), within or across job families
Job	A grouping of positions that are similar in their tasks and task dimensions
Position	A grouping of tasks/dimensions that constitute the total work assignment of a single employee; there are as many positions as there are employees
Task dimension	A grouping of similar types of tasks: sometimes called "duty," "area of responsibility," or "key results area"
Task	A grouping of elements to form an identifiable work activity that is a logical and necessary step in the performance of a job
Element	The smallest unit into which work can be divided without analyzing separate motions, movements, and mental processes

with the job include typing, filing, taking dictation, and answering phones. However, in many organizations the job has evolved to include new tasks such as word processing, managing multiple projects, creating spreadsheets, purchasing supplies and office technology, and gathering information on the Internet. These task changes lead to new KSAO requirements, such as planning and coordination skills and knowledge of spreadsheet software. Accompanying these changes is a change in job title to that of "administrative assistant." It should be noted that jobs may evolve due to changing organization and technology requirements, as well as to employee-initiated changes through a process of job crafting.

Flexible

Flexible jobs have frequently changing task and KSAO requirements. Sometimes these changes are initiated by the job incumbent who constantly adds and drops (or passes off) new assignments or projects in order to work toward moving targets of opportunity. Other times the task changes may be dictated by changes in production schedules or client demands. Many small business owners, general managers of start-up strategic business units, and top management members perform such flexible jobs. These jobs are "loose cannon" ones, characterized by broad job titles (e.g., administrator, general manager, director, scientist) and job descriptions with only cursory statements about tasks and duties (e.g., "manages budget planning, human resources, and marketing processes"). Within this elastic job title-tasks combination the employee is free to rattle and roll around.

Another example of flexible jobs is project jobs. Here, specific projects are undertaken (e.g., designing an advertising campaign) and when they are completed, new projects emerge. Managing and working on project-based jobs requires task and KSAO flexibility across projects.

Idiosyncratic

Idiosyncratic jobs are unique and created in response to the known (or anticipated) availability of a specific person with highly valued skills.[3] The person may be a current employee or an outsider to the organization. The person for whom the position is created may in fact even be the instigator of its creation. He or she may approach the organization and explicitly communicate availability and the type of position (both requirements and rewards) desired. Former politicians and high-level government employees are often hired into such idiosyncratically designed jobs.

Team-Based

Team-based jobs occur within work teams.[4] A work team is an interdependent collection of employees who share responsibility for achieving a specific goal.

Examples of such goals include developing a product, delivering a service, winning a game, conducting a process, developing a plan, or making a joint decision.

Teams, and thus team-based jobs, occur in multiple forms. One classification of such forms is as follows:[5]

1. Advice/involvement teams—such as quality control circles, special committees, and advisory boards
2. Production/service teams—such as assembly, data processing, and client service teams
3. Project/development teams—such as research and development, project management, brand management, engineering, and task force teams
4. Action/negotiation teams—such as sports, collective bargaining, surgery, and flight crew teams

Each of these teams is composed of two or more employees, and there is an identifiable collection of tasks that the team is to perform. Usually, these tasks will be grouped into specific clusters and each cluster constitutes a position or job. A project management team, for example, may have separate jobs and job titles for budget specialists, technical specialists, coordinators, and field staff. Each of these jobs may be traditional, evolving, flexible, or idiosyncratic.

While teams differ in many respects, two differences are very important in terms of their staffing implications. The first difference is in the extent to which each team member performs only one job, as opposed to multiple jobs. When members each perform only a single job, staffing each job requires a focus on recruitment and selection for only job-specific KSAOs. To the extent that members must perform multiple jobs, however, staffing must emphasize recruitment and selection for both job-specific KSAOs and job-spanning KSAOs. Another term used to connote job-spanning KSAOs is competencies. Many of these job-spanning KSAOs will involve flexibility, adaptability, and rapid learning skills that will facilitate performing, and switching between, multiple jobs.

As examples of the above points, a product development team may include mechanical engineers, computer-assisted design specialists, product safety experts, and marketing specialists. Each team member will likely perform only one of these jobs, and thus staffing these jobs will be targeted toward job-specific KSAOs. As a different example, a team responsible for assembly of lawn mower engines may require different members to perform different jobs at any particular moment, but it may also require each member to be (or become) proficient in all phases of engine assembly. Staffing this team will require acquisition of team members that have both job-specific and job-spanning KSAOs.

The second important difference between teams regarding staffing is the degree of task interdependence among team members. The greater the task interdependence, the greater the importance of KSAOs pertaining to interpersonal qualities (e.g., communicating, collaborating, and resolving conflicts) and team self-management qualities (e.g., setting group goals, inspecting each other's work). Thus, task interdependence brings behaviorally oriented KSAOs to the forefront of job requirements for team-based jobs.

Telework

Telework is a work arrangement in which the employee works away from the employer's work location using telecommunications technology (e.g., personal computer, e-mail, fax, cellular phone) to accomplish work. It may be done at home, on the road, or at special satellite locations established by the employer. Also, telework may involve either full-time or part-time work, with either fixed or flexible work hours. Telework is applicable to many different functional work areas such as marketing, sales, technical writing, financial analysis, and programming.[6]

NATURE OF JOB ANALYSIS

Job analysis may be defined as the process of studying jobs in order to gather, analyze, synthesize, and report information about job requirements and rewards. Note in this definition that job analysis is an overall process as opposed to a specific method or technique. Also note that in job analysis information is sought about both job requirements and job rewards.

There are three different types of job analysis; each focuses on the different types of information being sought. As shown in Exhibit 4.2, a job requirements job analysis seeks to identify and describe the specific tasks, KSAOs, and job context for a particular job. This type of job analysis is the most thoroughly developed and commonly used by organizations. The second type of job analysis, competency-based, attempts to identify and describe job requirements in the form of general KSAOs required across a range of jobs; task and work context require-

---

EXHIBIT 4.2   Types of Job Analysis and Information Gathered

	Job Requirements	Competency-Based	Job Rewards
Information Gathered	• Specific tasks for job • Specific KSAOs for job • Job context	• General KSAOs • Job-spanning KSAOs	• Extrinsic rewards • Intrinsic rewards

ments are of little concern. Interpersonal skills, for example, might be identified as a competency for sales and customer service jobs; leadership is a likely competency requirement for managerial jobs. Competency-based job analysis is very recent in origin, though it has some similarities to job requirements job analysis. Job rewards job analysis is the third type, and it focuses on describing the extrinsic and intrinsic rewards that employees receive and experience on their jobs. This form of job analysis is also in its early stages of development, though organizations have always done some description of job rewards and communicated that information to job applicants as a part of their staffing activities.

Since the different job analysis methods seek different types of information, they have differing degrees of relevance to the various staffing activities. Job requirements job analysis yields information helpful in the recruitment, selection, and employment domains in such activities as communicating job requirements to job applicants, developing selection plans for KSAOs to focus on when staffing a job, identifying appropriate assessment methods to gauge applicants' KSAOs, establishing hiring qualifications, and complying with relevant laws and regulations. Competency-based job analysis results will be helpful primarily in identifying a common set of general KSAOs in which all applicants must be proficient, regardless of the specific job for which they are applying. Finally, job rewards job analysis is most beneficial in recruitment activities such as identifying the types of applicants most likely to seek the types of rewards being offered, using recruitment methods that will best convey job rewards information to applicants, and creating effective recruitment advertising and communication programs.

Effective staffing requires job requirements and job rewards information for each of the types of jobs described above. Traditional and evolving jobs readily lend themselves to this. Their requirements and rewards are generally well known and unlikely to change except gradually. For idiosyncratic, flexible, team-based, and telework jobs, job analysis is more difficult and problematic. The requirements and rewards for these jobs may frequently be changing, difficult to pinpoint, and even unknown because they depend heavily on how the job incumbent defines them. Despite the often ambiguous and fluid nature of these jobs, attempts must be made to identify their requirements and rewards through job analysis. Failure to do so invites the occurrence of person/job mismatches.

Job analysis and the information it provides thus serve as basic input to the totality of staffing activities for an organization. In this sense, job analysis is a support activity to the various functional staffing activities. Indeed, without thorough and accurate information about job requirements and rewards, the organization is greatly hampered in its attempts to acquire a workforce that will be effective in terms of HR outcomes such as performance, satisfaction, and retention. Job analysis thus is the foundation upon which successful staffing systems are constructed. Each of the three types of job analysis is discussed in detail subsequently.

JOB REQUIREMENTS JOB ANALYSIS

Overview

A framework depicting job requirements job analysis is shown in Exhibit 4.3. As can be seen, the job analysis begins by identifying the specific tasks and the job context for a particular job.[7] After these have been identified, the KSAOs necessary for performing these tasks within the work context are inferred. For example, after identifying for a sales manager's job, the task of "developing and writing monthly sales and marketing plans," the job analysis would proceed by inferring what specific KSAOs are necessary for performance of this task. The task might require knowledge of intended customers, arithmetic skills, creative ability, and willingness and availability to travel frequently to various organizational units. No particular job context factors, such as physical demands, may be relevant to performance of this task or to its required KSAOs. The task and job context information are recorded

---

EXHIBIT 4.3 Job Requirements Approach to Job Analysis

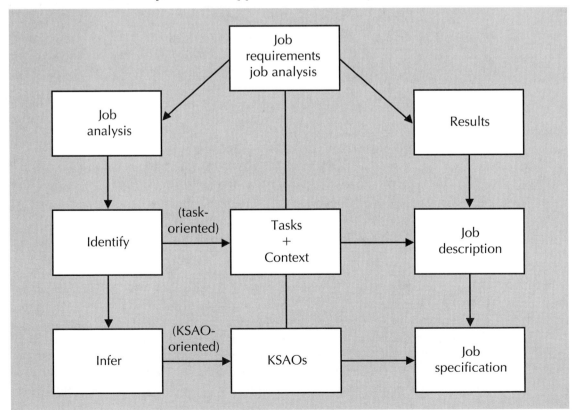

in a job description, whereas the KSAO requirements are placed into a job specification. In practice, these are often contained within a single document.

Job Requirements Matrix

The job requirements matrix shows the key components of job requirements job analysis, each of which must be explicitly considered for inclusion in any job requirements job analysis. Completion of the cell entries in the matrix represents the information that must be gathered, analyzed, synthesized, and expressed in usable written form.

A completed job requirements matrix, a portion of which is shown in Exibit 4.4 for the job of administrative assistant, serves as the basic informational source or document for any job in terms of its job requirements. The resultant information serves as a basic input and guide to all subsequent staffing activities.

Referring to Exhibit 4.4, five specific tasks identified via job analysis are listed. Note that only a portion of the total tasks for the job are shown. In turn, these have been categorized into two general task dimensions—supervision and word processing. An indication of their importance to the overall job is the percent time spent on each, specifically 30% and 20%, respectively. For each task dimension and its specific tasks, several KSAOs have been inferred to be necessary for performance. The nature of these KSAOs is presented, along with a rating (1–5 scale) of how important each KSAO is for performance of the task dimension. At the bottom of the matrix are indications of job context factors pertaining to work setting (indoors), privacy of work area (cubicle), attire (business clothes), body positioning (mostly sitting and standing), and physical work conditions (no environmental or job hazards).

We now turn to a thorough discussion for each of the components of the job requirements matrix: tasks, task dimensions and their importance, KSAOs and their importance, and job context. Discussed are specific definitions, techniques, and taxonomies useful for successfully gathering and recording the information needed in a job requirements matrix. After that, the actual process of collecting job information and conducting the job analysis is discussed.

Task Statements

Job analysis begins with the development of task statements, whose objective is to identify and record a set of tasks that both includes all of the job's major tasks and excludes nonrelevant or trivial tasks.[8] The resultant task statements serve as the building blocks for the remainder of the job requirements job analysis.

Identification and recording of tasks begins with the construction of task statements. These statements are objectively written descriptions of the behaviors or work activities engaged in by employees in order to perform the job. The statements are made in simple declarative sentences.

EXHIBIT 4.4 Portion of Job Requirements Matrix for Job of Administrative Assistant

Tasks			KSAOs	
Specific Tasks	Task Dimensions	Importance (% time spent)	Nature	Importance to Tasks (1–5 rating)
1. Arrange schedules with office assistant/volunteers to ensure that office will be staffed during prescribed hours	A. Supervision	30%	1. Knowledge of office operations and policies	4.9
2. Assign office tasks to office assistant/volunteers to ensure coordination of activities	A. Supervision		2. Ability to match people to tasks according to their skills and hours of availability	4.6
			3. Skill in interaction with diverse people	2.9
			4. Skill in determining types and priorities of tasks	4.0
3. Type/transcribe letters, memos, and reports from handwritten material or dictated copy to produce final copy, using word processor	B. Word processing	20%	1. Knowledge of typing formats	3.1
			2. Knowledge of spelling and punctuation	5.0
			3. Knowledge of graphics display software	2.0
4. Prepare graphs and other visual material to supplement reports, using word processor	B. Word processing		4. Ability to proofread and correct work	5.0
5. Proofread typed copy and correct spelling, punctuation, and typographical errors in order to produce high-quality materials	B. Word processing		5. Skill in use of WordPerfect (most current version)	4.3
			6. Skill in creating visually appealing and understandable graphs	3.4

Job Context: Indoors, cubicle, business clothes, mostly sitting and standing, no environmental or job hazards.

Ideally, each task statement will show several things. These are

1. what the employee does, using a specific action verb at the start of the task statement
2. to whom or what the employee does what he or she does, stating the object of the verb
3. what is produced, indicating the expected output of the verb
4. what materials, tools, procedures, or equipment are used

Use of the sentence analysis technique is very helpful for writing task statements that conform to these four requirements. An example of the technique is shown in Exhibit 4.5 for several tasks from very different jobs.

In addition to meeting the preceding four requirements, there are several other suggestions for effectively writing task statements. First, use specific action verbs that have only one meaning. Examples of verbs that do not conform to this suggestion include "supports," "assists," and "handles."

Second, focus on recording tasks, as opposed to specific elements that comprise a task. This requires use of considerable judgment because the distinction between a task and an element is relative and often fuzzy. A useful rule to keep in mind here is that most jobs can be adequately described within a range of 15–25 task statements. A task statement list exceeding this range is a warning that it may be too narrow in terms of activities defined.

Third, do not include minor or trivial activities in task statements; focus only on major tasks and activities. An exception to this recommendation occurs when a so-called minor task is judged to have great importance to the job (see the following discussion).

Fourth, take steps to ensure that the list of task statements is content valid and reliable.[9] The basic way to conform to this suggestion is to have two or more people ("analysts") independently evaluate the task statement list in terms of (a) inclusiveness, and (b) clarity. Close agreement between people signifies high reliability and content validity, meaning that job content is consistently described in ways not deficient or contaminated. Should disagreements between people be discovered, the nature of the disagreements can be discussed and appropriate modifications to the task statements made.

Fifth, have at least the manager and a job incumbent serve as the analysts, providing the content validity and reliability checks. It is important to have the manager participate in this process in order to verify that the task statements are inclusive and accurate. For the job incumbent, the concern is not only that of verification but also acceptance of the task statements as adequate representations that will guide incumbents' performance of the job. Ideally, there should be multiple managers and job incumbents, along with a representative of the HR department, serving as analysts. This would expand the scope of input and allow for more precise content validity and reliability checks.

EXHIBIT 4.5   Use of the Sentence Analysis Technique for Task Statements

Sentence Analysis Technique			
What does the worker do?		Why does the worker do it? What gets done?	What is the final result or technological objective?
Worker action		Purpose of the worker actions	Materials, products, subject matter, and/or services
(Worker function)	(Work devices, people, or information)	(Work field)	(MPSMS)
Verb	Direct object	Infinitive phrase	
		Infinitive	Object of the infinitive
Sets up *(setting up)*	various types of metal-working machines *(work device)*	to machine *(machining)*	metal aircraft parts. *(material)*
Persuades *(persuading)*	customers *(people)*	to buy *(merchandising)*	automobiles. *(product)*
Interviews *(analyzing)*	clients *(people)*	to assess *(advising–counseling)*	skills and abilities. *(subject matter)*
Drives *(driving–operating)*	bus *(work device)*	to transport *(transporting)*	passengers. *(service)*

Source: Vocational Rehabilitation Institute, *A Guide to Job Analysis* (Menominee, WI: University of Wisconsin-Stout, 1982), p. 8.

Finally, recognize that the accuracy or validity of task statements cannot be evaluated against any external criterion because there is no external criterion available for use. Task descriptions are accurate and meaningful only to the extent that people agree on them. Because of this, the preceding recommendation regarding checks on content validity and reliability takes on added importance.

Task Dimensions

Task statement lists may be maintained in list form and subsequently incorporated into the job description. Often, however, it is useful to group sets of task statements into task dimensions, and then attach a name to each such dimension. Other terms for task dimensions are "duties," "accountability areas," "responsibilities," and "performance dimensions."

A useful way to facilitate the grouping process is to create a task dimension matrix. Each column in the matrix represents a potential task dimension, and a label is tentatively attached to it. Each row in the matrix represents a particular task statement. Cell entries in the matrix represent the assignment of task statements to task dimensions (the grouping of tasks). The goal is to have each task statement assigned to only one task dimension. The process is complicated by the fact that the dimensions and labels must be created prior to grouping; the dimensions and labels may have to be changed or rearranged to make task statements fit as one progresses through the assignment of task statements to dimensions.

Several things should be kept in mind about task dimensions. First, their creation is optional and should occur only if they will be useful. Second, there are many different grouping procedures, ranging from straightforward judgmental ones to highly sophisticated statistical ones.[10] For most purposes, a simple judgmental process is sufficient, such as having the people who participated in the creation of the task statements also create the groupings as part of the same exercise. As a rule, there should be four to eight dimensions, depending on the number of task statements, regardless of the specific grouping procedure used. Third, it is important that the grouping procedure yield a reliable set of task dimensions acceptable to managers, job incumbents, and other organizational members. Finally, as with task statements, it is not possible to empirically validate task dimensions against some external criterion; for both task statements and dimensions, their validity is in the eyes of the definers and beholders.

Importance of Tasks/Dimensions

Rarely are all tasks/dimensions of a job thought to be of equal weight or importance. In some general sense, it is thus felt that these differences must be captured, expressed, and incorporated into job information, especially the job description. Normally, assessments of importance are made just for task dimensions, though it is certainly possible to make them for individual tasks as well.

Before actual weighting can occur, two decisions must be made. First, the specific attribute to be assessed in terms of importance must be decided (e.g., time spent on the task/dimension). Second, a decision is required regarding whether the attribute will be measured in categorical (e.g., essential or nonessential) or continuous (e.g., percent of time spent, 1–5 rating of importance) terms. Exhibit 4.6 shows examples of the results of these two decisions in terms of commonly used importance attributes and their measurement.

Once these decisions are made, it is possible to proceed with the actual process of assessing or weighting the tasks/dimensions in terms of importance. It should be noted here that if the tasks/dimensions are not explicitly assessed in such a manner, all tasks/dimensions end up being weighted equally by default.

If possible, it is desirable for the assessments to be done initially by independent analysts (e.g., incumbents and managers). In this way, it will be possible to check for the degree of reliability among raters. Where differences are found, they can

---

EXHIBIT 4.6   Examples of Ways to Assess Task/Dimension Importance

A.   Relative Time Spent

For each task/dimension, rate the amount of time you spend on it, relative to all other tasks/dimensions of your job.

1	2	3	4	5
Very small amount		Average amount		Very large amount

B.   Percentage (%) Time Spent

For each task/dimension, indicate the percentage (%) of time you spend on it (percentages must total to 100%).

Dimension _____   % Time spent _____

C.   Importance to Overall Performance

For each task/dimension, rate its importance to your overall job performance.

1	2	3	4	5
Minor importance		Average importance		Major importance

D.   Need for New Employee Training

Do new employees receive a standard, planned course of training for performance of this task, other than a customary job orientation?

_____ Yes

_____ No

be discussed and resolved. Just as it is desirable to have high reliability in the identification of tasks and dimensions, it is desirable to have high reliability in judgments of their importance.[11]

KSAOs

KSAOs are inferred or derived from knowledge of the tasks and task dimensions themselves. The inference process requires that the analysts explicitly think in specific cause-and-effect terms. For each task or dimension, the analyst must in essence ask, "Exactly what KSAOs do I think will be necessary for (will cause) performance on this task or dimension?" Then the analyst should ask "Why do I think this?" in order to think through the soundness of the inferential logic. Discussions among analysts about these questions are encouraged.

When asking and answering these questions, it is useful to keep in mind what is meant by the terms "knowledge," "skill," "ability," and "other characteristics." It is also very helpful to refer to research results that help us better understand the nature and complexity of these concepts. As described below, these results have been synthesized to create the Occupational Information Network or O*NET (see *www.onetcenter.org*).

Knowledge Knowledge is a body of information (conceptual, factual, procedural) that can be applied directly to the performance of tasks. It tends to be quite focused or specific in terms of job, organization, or occupation. Assistance to the analyst in identifying and writing statements of knowledge requirements is available from the O*NET. It provides definitions of 33 knowledges that might generally be necessary, in varying levels, in occupations. Exhibit 4.7 provides a listing of those knowledges. Definitions of the knowledges are also provided by O*NET, in print and online. For example, "sales and marketing" knowledge is defined as "knowledge of principles and methods involved in showing, promoting, and selling products or services; this includes marketing strategies and tactics, product demonstration and sales techniques, and sales control systems."[12] Use of O*NET knowledges and their definitions is a helpful starting point in preparing knowledge statements. As the knowledges are intended for general occupations, they will probably have to be supplemented with more job-specific statements crafted by the job analyst. When doing so, analysts should be particularly wary of using global or shorthand terms such as "knowledge of accounting principles." Here, it would be better to indicate which accounting principles are being utilized, and why each is necessary for task performance.

Skill Skill refers to an observable competence for working with or applying knowledge to perform a particular task or closely related set of tasks. A skill is not an enduring characteristic of the person; it depends on experience and practice. Skill requirements are directly inferred from observation or knowledge of tasks performed.

EXHIBIT 4.7   Knowledges Contained in O*NET

Knowledge Areas

- Business and management
  Administration and management
  Clerical
  Economics and accounting
  Sales and marketing
  Customer and personal service
  Personnel and human resources
- Manufacturing and production
  Production and processing
  Food production
- Engineering and technology
  Computers and electronics
  Engineering and technology
  Design
  Building and construction
  Mechanical
- Mathematics and science
  Mathematics
  Physics
  Chemistry
  Biology
  Psychology
  Sociology and anthropology
  Geography

- Health services
  Medicine and dentistry
  Therapy and counseling
- Education and training
  Education and training
- Arts and humanities
  English language
  Foreign language
  Fine arts
  History and archaeology
  Philosophy and theology
- Law and public safety
  Public safety and security
  Law, government, and jurisprudence
- Communications
  Telecommunications
  Communications and media
- Transportation
  Transportation

Source: Adapted from N. G. Peterson, M. D. Mumford, W. C. Borman, P. R. Jeanneret, E. A. Fleishman, and K. Y. Levin, *O*NET Final Technical Report, Vol. 1* (Salt Lake City: Utah Department of Workforce Services, 1997), pp. 4-1 to 4-26. ©Utah Department of Workforce Services on behalf of U.S. Department of Labor.

Considerable research has been devoted to identifying particular job-related skills and to organizing them into taxonomies. Job analysts should begin the skills inference process by referring to the results of this research.

An excellent example of such useful research is found in the O*NET.[13] O*NET identifies and defines 46 skills applicable across the occupational spectrum. The first 10 of these are basic skills involving acquiring and conveying information; the remaining 36 are cross-functional skills used to facilitate task performance. Exhibit 4.8 provides a listing of all these skills. Definitions are also provided by O*NET, in print and online. For example, the basic skill "reading comprehension" is defined as "understanding written sentences and paragraphs in work-related documents"; the cross-functional skill "negotiation" is defined as "bringing others

EXHIBIT 4.8   Skills Contained in O*NET

Basic Skills

- Content
    Reading comprehension
    Active listening
    Writing
    Speaking
    Mathematics
    Science

- Process
    Critical thinking
    Active learning
    Learning strategies
    Monitoring

Cross-Functional Skills

- Social skills
    Social perceptiveness
    Coordination
    Persuasion
    Negotiation
    Instructing
    Service orientation
- Complex problem-solving skills
    Problem identification
    Information gathering
    Information organization
    Synthesis/reorganization
    Idea generation
    Idea evaluation
    Implementation planning
    Solution appraisal
- Resource management skills
    Time management
    Management of financial resources
    Management of material resources
    Management of personnel resources

- Technical skills
    Operations analysis
    Technology design
    Equipment selection
    Installation
    Programming
    Equipment maintenance
    Troubleshooting
    Repairing
    Testing
    Operation monitoring
    Operation and control
    Product inspection
- Systems skills
    Visioning
    Systems perception
    Identification of downstream
        consequences
    Identification of key causes
    Judgment and decision making
    Systems evaluation

Source: Adapted from N. G. Peterson, M. D. Mumford, W. C. Borman, P. R. Jeanneret, E. A. Fleishman, and K. Y. Levin, *O*NET Final Technical Report, Vol. 1* (Salt Lake City: Utah Department of Workforce Services, 1997), pp. 3-1 to 3-36. ©Utah Department of Workforce Services on behalf of U.S. Department of Labor.

together and trying to reconcile differences.'' Reference to these 46 skills is a good starting point for the job analyst. More specific skills may need to be identified and described for the particular job being analyzed.

Ability   An ability is an underlying, enduring trait of the person useful for performing a range of different tasks. It differs from a skill in that it is less likely to change over time and is applicable across a wide set of tasks encountered on many

EXHIBIT 4.9   Abilities Contained in O*NET

Cognitive Abilities
- Verbal abilities
   - Oral comprehension
   - Written comprehension
   - Oral expression
   - Written expression
- Idea generation and reasoning abilities
   - Fluency of ideas
   - Originality
   - Problem sensitivity
   - Deductive reasoning
   - Inductive reasoning
   - Information ordering
   - Category flexibility
- Quantitative abilities
   - Mathematical reasoning
   - Number facility
- Memory
   - Memorization
- Perceptual abilities
   - Speed of closure
   - Flexibility of closure
   - Perceptual speed
- Spatial abilities
   - Spatial organization
   - Visualization
- Attentiveness
   - Selective attention
   - Time sharing

Psychomotor Abilities
- Fine manipulative abilities
   - Arm-hand steadiness
   - Manual dexterity
   - Finger dexterity
- Control movement abilities
   - Control precision
   - Multilimb coordination
   - Response orientation
   - Rate control

- Reaction time and speed abilities
   - Reaction time
   - Wrist-finger dexterity
   - Speed of limb movement

Physical Abilities
- Physical strength abilities
   - Static strength
   - Explosive strength
   - Dynamic strength
   - Trunk strength
- Endurance
   - Stamina
- Flexibility, balance, and coordination
   - Extent flexibility
   - Dynamic flexibility
   - Gross body coordination
   - Gross body equilibrium

Sensory Abilities
- Visual abilities
   - Near vision
   - Far vision
   - Visual color discrimination
   - Night vision
   - Peripheral vision
   - Depth perception
   - Glare sensitivity
- Auditory and speech abilities
   - Hearing sensitivity
   - Auditory attention
   - Sound localization
   - Speech recognition
   - Speech clarity

Source: Adapted from N. G. Peterson, M. D. Mumford, W. C. Borman, P. R. Jeanneret, E. A. Fleishman, and K. Y. Levin, *O*NET Final Technical Report, Vol. 2* (Salt Lake City: Utah Department of Workforce Services, 1997), pp. 9-1 to 9-26. ©Utah Department of Workforce Services on behalf of U.S. Department of Labor.

different jobs. Four general categories of abilities are commonly recognized: cognitive, psychomotor, physical, and sensory abilities. O*NET contains a complete taxonomy of these four categories; they are shown in Exhibit 4.9. Definitions (not shown) accompany the abilities in print and online. The ability "oral expression," for example, is defined as "the ability to communicate information and ideas in speaking so others will understand." As another example, "dynamic flexibility" is "the ability to quickly and repeatedly bend, stretch, twist, or reach out with the body, arms and/or legs."[14]

Other Characteristics   This is a catchall category for factors that do not fit neatly into the K, S, and A categories. Despite the catchall nature of these requirements, they are very important for even being able to enter the employment relationship (legal requirements), being present to perform the job (availability requirements), and having values consistent with organizational culture and values (character requirements). Numerous examples of these factors are shown in Exhibit 4.10. Care should be taken to ensure that these factors truly are job requirements, as opposed to whimsical and ill-defined preferences of the organization.

KSAO Importance
As suggested in the job requirements matrix the KSAOs of a job may differ in their weight or contribution to task performance. Hence, their relative importance must

---

EXHIBIT 4.10   Examples of Other Job Requirements

Legal Requirements
Possession of license (occupational, drivers, etc.)
Citizen or legal alien?
Geographic residency (e.g., within city limits for public employees)
Security clearance

Availability Requirements
Starting date
Worksite locations
Hours and days of week
Travel
Attendance and tardiness

Character Requirements
Moral
Work ethic
Background
Conscientiousness
Honesty and integrity

be explicitly considered, defined, and indicated. Failure to do so means that all KSAOs will be assumed to be of equal importance by default.

As with task importance, deriving KSAO importance requires two decisions. First, what will be the specific attribute(s) on which importance is judged? Second, will the measurement of each attribute be categorical (e.g., required-preferred) or continuous (e.g., 1–5 rating scale)? Examples of formats for indicating KSAO importance are shown in Exhibit 4.11. The O*NET uses a 1–5 rating scale format and also provides actual importance ratings for many jobs.

Job Context

As shown in the job requirements matrix, tasks and KSAOs occur within a broader job context. A job requirements job analysis should include consideration of the job context and the factors that are important in defining it. Such consideration is necessary because these factors may have an influence on tasks and KSAOs; further, information about the factors may be used in the recruitment and selection of job applicants. For example, the information may be given to job applicants to provide them a realistic job preview during recruitment, and consideration of job context factors may be helpful in assessing likely person/organization fit during selection.

O*NET contains a wide array of job and work context factors useful for characterizing occupations.[15] The most relevant for specific job analysis purposes are the physical work conditions: setting, attire, body positioning, environmental conditions, and job hazards. Within each of these categories are numerous specific facets; these are shown in Exhibit 4.12. The job analyst should use a listing such

---

EXHIBIT 4.11   Examples of Ways to Assess KSAO Importance

A.   Importance to (acceptable) (superior) task performance
1 = minimal importance
2 = some importance
3 = average importance
4 = considerable importance
5 = extensive importance

B.   Should the KSAO be assessed during recruitment/selection?
☐ Yes
☐ No

C.   Is the KSAO required, preferred, or not required for recruitment/selection?
☐ Required
☐ Preferred
☐ Not required (obtain on job and/or in training)

EXHIBIT 4.12 Job Context (Physical Work Conditions) Contained in O*NET

Work Setting
- How frequently does this job require the worker to work:
    Indoors, environmentally controlled
    Indoors, not environmentally controlled
    Outdoors, exposed to all weather conditions
    Outdoors, under cover
    In an open vehicle or operating open equipment
    In an enclosed vehicle or operating enclosed equipment
- Privacy of work area
- Physical proximity

Work Attire
- How often does the worker wear:
    Business clothes
    A special uniform
    Work clothing
    Common protective or safety attire
    Specialized protective or safety attire

Body Positioning
- How much time in a usual work period does the worker spend:
    Sitting?
    Standing?
    Climbing ladders, scaffolds, poles, and so on?
    Walking or running?
    Kneeling, stooping, crouching, or crawling?
    Keeping or regaining balance?
    Using hands to handle, control, or feel objects, tools, or controls?
    Bending or twisting the body?
    Making repetitive motions?

Environmental Conditions
- How often during a usual work period is the worker exposed to the following conditions:
    Sounds and noise levels that are distracting and uncomfortable?
    Very hot or very cold temperatures?
    Extremely bright or inadequate lighting conditions?
    Contaminants?
    Cramped work space that requires getting into awkward positions?
    Whole body vibration?

Job Hazards
- How often does this job require the worker to be exposed to the following hazards:
    Radiation
    Diseases/infections
    High places
    Hazardous conditions
    Hazardous equipment
    Hazardous situation involving likely cuts, bites, stings, or minor burns

Source: Adapted from N. G. Peterson, M. D. Mumford, W. C. Borman, P. R. Jeanneret, E. A. Fleishman, and K. Y. Levin, *O*NET Final Technical Report, Vol. 2* (Salt Lake City: Utah Department of Workforce Services, 1997), pp. 7-1 to 7-35. © Utah Department of Workforce Services on behalf of U.S. Department of Labor.

as this to identify the relevant job context factors and include them in the job requirements matrix.

The O*NET also contains work context factors pertaining to interpersonal relationships (communication, types of role relationships, responsibility for others and conflictual contact with others) and to structural job characteristics (criticality of position, routine versus challenging work, pace and scheduling). These factors might also be considered in the job analysis.

Job Descriptions and Job Specifications

As previously noted, it is common practice to express the results of job requirements job analysis in written job descriptions and job specifications. Referring back to the job requirements matrix, note that its sections pertaining to tasks and job context are similar to a job description, and the section dealing with KSAOs is similar to a job specification.

There are no standard formats or other requirements for either job descriptions or job specifications. In terms of content, however, a job description should usually include the following: job family, job title, job summary, task statements and dimensions, importance indicators, job context indicators, and date job analysis conducted. A job specification should usually include job family, job title, job summary, KSAOs (separate section for each), importance indicators, and date conducted. An example of a combined job description/specification is shown in Exhibit 4.13.

Collecting Job Requirements Information

Job analysis involves not only consideration of the types of information (tasks, KSAOs, and job context) to be collected but also the methods, sources, and processes to be used for such collection. These issues are discussed next, and as will be seen, there are many alternatives to choose from for purposes of developing an overall job analysis system for any particular situation. Potential inaccuracies and other limitations in the alternatives will also be pointed out.[16]

Methods

Job analysis methods represent procedures or techniques for collecting job information. There have been many specific techniques and systems developed and named (e.g., Functional Job Analysis, Position Analysis Questionnaire). Rather than discuss each of the many techniques separately, we will concentrate on the major generic methods that underlie all specific techniques and applications. There are many excellent descriptions and discussions of the specific techniques available.[17]

Prior Information   For any job, there is usually some prior information available about it that could and should be consulted. Indeed, this information should routinely be searched for and used as a starting point for a job analysis.

EXHIBIT 4.13   Example of Combined Job Description/Specification

FUNCTIONAL UNIT: CHILDREN'S REHABILITATION
JOB TITLE: REHABILITATION SPECIALIST
DATE: 12/5/01

JOB SUMMARY

   Works with disabled small children and their families to identify developmental strengths and weaknesses, develop rehabilitation plans, deliver and coordinate rehabilitation activities, and evaluate effectiveness of those plans and activities.

PERFORMANCE DIMENSIONS AND TASKS   **Time Spent (%)**

1. Assessment   **10%**

   Administer formal and informal motor screening and evaluation instruments to conduct assessments. Perform assessments to identify areas of strengths and need.

2. Planning   **25%**

   Collaborate with parents and other providers to directly develop the individualized family service plan. Use direct and consultative models of service in developing plans.

3. Delivery   **50%**

   Carry out individual and small group motor development activities with children and families. Provide service coordination to designated families. Work with family care and child care providers to provide total services. Collaborate with other staff members and professionals from community agencies to obtain resources and specialized assistance.

4. Evaluation   **15%**

   Observe, interpret, and report on client to monitor individual progress. Assist in collecting and reporting intervention data in order to prepare formal program evaluation reports. Write evaluation reports to assist in developing new treatment strategies and programs.

JOB SPECIFICATIONS

1. License: License to practice physical therapy in the state

2. Education: B.S. in physical or occupational therapy required; M.S. preferred

3. Experience: Prefer (not required) one year experience working with children with disabilities and their families

4. Skills: Listening to and interacting with others (children, family members, coworkers)
Developing treatment plans
Organizing and writing reports using Microsoft Word

JOB CONTEXT: indoors, office, business clothes, no environmental or job hazards.

There are many possible organizational sources of job information available, including current job descriptions and specifications, job-specific policies and procedures, training manuals, and performance appraisals. Externally, job information may be available from other employers, as well as trade and professional associations. Both the Society for Human Resource Management (SHRM) (*www.shrm.org*) and the International Personnel Management Association (IPMA) (*www.ipma-hr.org*) provide sample job descriptions online. Also, job information is available commercially on the Web (e.g., *www.jobdescription.com*) and in software packages such as Descriptions Now! For Windows.[18]

An important source of public information is the *Dictionary of Occupational Titles* (DOT) provided by the Department of Labor.[19] It contains task statements and other information for over 20,000 separate job titles. The DOT is being replaced by the previously mentioned O*NET, also provided by the Department of Labor (*www.onetcenter.org*). O*NET contains extensive, research-based taxonomies in several categories: occupational tasks, knowledges, skills, abilities, education and experience/training, work context, organizational context, occupational interests and values, and work styles.[20] Additionally, O*NET contains ratings of the specific factors within each category for 80 occupations; ratings for additional occupations are constantly being added. For example, occupational and importance ratings of the specific knowledges, skills, and abilities shown in Exhibits 4.7, 4.8, and 4.9 are provided. The job analyst could use these ratings as benchmarks against which to compare specific importance ratings the analyst determined for a specific job. For example, if the analyst was developing importance ratings for these knowledges, skills, and abilities for the job of registered nurse in a particular hospital, the compiled ratings could be compared to the ratings in O*NET for the same occupation. Reasonable similarity between the two sets of ratings would serve as a source of confirmation of the analyst's accuracy.

The ready availability of prior job information needs to be balanced with some possible limitations. First, there is the general issue of completeness. Usually, prior information will be deficient in some important areas of job requirements, as in evolving or nontraditional types of jobs. Sole reliance on prior information thus should be avoided. A second limitation is that there will be little indication of exactly how the information was collected and, relatedly, how accurate it is. These limitations suggest that while prior information should be the starting point for job analysis, it should not be the stopping point.

Observation   Simply observing job incumbents performing the job is obviously an excellent way to learn about tasks, KSAOs, and context. It provides a thoroughness and richness of information unmatched by any other method. It is also the most direct form of gathering information because it does not rely on intermediary information sources, as would be the case with other methods (e.g., interviewing job incumbents and supervisors).

The following potential limitations to observation should be kept in mind. First, it is most appropriate for jobs with physical (as opposed to mental) components and ones with relatively short job cycles (i.e., amount of time required to complete job tasks before repeating them). Second, the method may involve substantial time and cost. Third, the ability of the observer to do a thorough and accurate analysis is open to question; it may be necessary to train observers prior to the job analysis. Fourth, the method will require coordination with, and approval from, many people (e.g., supervisors and incumbents). Finally, the incumbents being observed may distort their behavior during observation in self-serving ways, such as making tasks appear more difficult or time-consuming than they really are.

Interviews   Interviewing job incumbents and others, such as their managers, has many potential advantages. It respects the interviewee's vast source of information about the job. The interview format also allows the interviewer to explain the purpose of the job analysis, how the results will be used, and so forth, thus enhancing likely acceptance of the process by the interviewees. It can be structured in format to ensure standardization of collected information.

As with any job analysis method, the interview is not without potential limitations. It is time-consuming and costly, and this may cause the organization to skimp on it in ways that jeopardize the reliability and content validity of the information gathered. The interview, not providing anonymity, may lead to suspicion and distrust on the part of interviewees. The quality of the information obtained, as well as interviewee acceptance, depends on the skill of the interviewer. Careful selection, and possible training, of interviewers should definitely be considered when the interview is the method chosen for collecting job information. Finally, the success of the interview also depends on the skill and abilities of the interviewee, such as verbal communication skills and ability to recall tasks performed.

Task Questionnaire   A typical task questionnaire contains a lengthy list of task statements that cut across many different job titles and is administered to incumbents (all or samples of them) in these job titles. For each task statement, the respondent is asked to indicate (a) whether or not the task applies to the respondent's job (respondents should always be given a DNA—does not apply—option), and (b) task importance (e.g., a 1–5 scale rating difficulty or time spent).

The advantages of task questionnaires are numerous. They are standardized in content and format, thus yielding a standardized method of information gathering. They can obtain considerable information from large numbers of people. They are economical to administer and score, and the availability of scores creates the opportunity for subsequent statistical analysis. Finally, task questionnaires are (and should be) completed anonymously, thus enhancing respondent participation, honesty, and acceptance.

A task questionnaire is potentially limited in certain ways. The most important limitation pertains to task statement content. Care must be taken to ensure that the questionnaire contains task statements of sufficient content relevance, representativeness, and specificity. This suggests that if a tailor-made questionnaire is to be used, considerable time and resources must be devoted to its development to ensure accurate inclusion of task statements. If a preexisting questionnaire (e.g., the Position Analysis Questionnaire) is considered, its task statement content should be assessed relative to the task content of the jobs to be analyzed prior to any decision to use the questionnaire.

A second limitation of task questionnaires pertains to potential respondent reactions. Respondents may react negatively if they feel the questionnaire does not contain task statements covering important aspects of their jobs. Respondents may also find completion of the questionnaire to be tedious and boring; this may cause them to commit rating errors. Interpretation and understanding of the task statements may be problematic for some respondents who have reading and comprehension skill deficiencies.

Finally, it should be remembered that a typical task questionnaire focuses on tasks. Other job requirement components, particularly KSAOs and those related to job context, may be ignored or downplayed if the task questionnaire is relied on as the method of job information collection.

Combined Methods   Only in rare instances does a job analysis involve use of only a single method. Much more likely is a "mix-and-match," eclectic approach using multiple methods. This makes job analysis a more complicated process to design and administer than implied by a description of each of the methods alone.

Criteria for Choice of Methods   Some explicit choices regarding methods of job analysis need to be made. One set of choices involves decisions to use or not use a particular method of information collection. An organization must decide, for example, whether to use an "off-the-shelf" method or its own particular method that is suited to its own needs and circumstances. A second set of choices involves how to blend together a set of methods that will all be used, in varying ways and degrees, in the actual job analysis. Some criteria for guidance in such decisions are shown in Exhibit 4.14.

Sources to Be Used

Choosing sources of information involves considering who will be used to provide the information sought. While this matter is not entirely independent of job analysis methods (e.g., use of a task questionnaire normally requires use of job incumbents as the source), it is treated as such in the sections that follow.

Job Analyst   A job analyst is someone who, by virtue of job title and training, is available and suited to conduct job analyses and to guide the job analysis process. The job analyst is also "out of the loop," being neither manager nor incumbent of the jobs analyzed. As such, the job analyst brings a combination of expertise and neutrality to the work.

EXHIBIT 4.14   Criteria for Guiding Choice of Job Analysis Methods

1. Degree of suitability/versatility for use across different types of jobs
2. Degree of standardization in the process and in the reporting of results
3. Acceptability of process and results to those who will serve as sources and/or users
4. Degree to which method is operational and may be used off-the-shelf without modification, as opposed to method requiring tailor-made development and application
5. Amount of training required for sources and users of job information
6. Costs of the job analysis, in terms of both direct administrative costs and opportunity costs of time involvement by people
7. Quality of resultant information in terms of reliability and content validity
8. Usability of results in recruitment, selection, and employment activities

Source: Adapted from E. L. Levine, R. A. Ash, H. Hall, and F. Sistrunk, "Evaluation of Job Analysis Methods by Experienced Job Analysts," *Academy of Management Journal*, 1983, 26, pp. 339–348.

Despite such advantages and appeals, reliance on a job analyst as the job information source is not without potential limitations. First, the analyst may be perceived as an outsider by incumbents and supervisors, a perception that may result in questioning the analyst's job knowledge and expertise, as well as trustworthiness. Second, the job analyst may, in fact, lack detailed knowledge of the jobs to be analyzed, especially in an organization with many different job titles. Lack of knowledge may cause the analyst to bring inaccurate job stereotypes to the analysis process. Finally, having specially designated job analysts (either employees or outside consultants) tends to be expensive.

Job Incumbents   Job incumbents seem like a natural source of information to be used in job analysis, and indeed they are relied on in most job analysis systems. The major advantage to working with incumbents is their familiarity with tasks, KSAOs, and job context. In addition, job incumbents may become more accepting of the job analysis process and its results through their participation in it.

Some skepticism should be maintained about job incumbents as a source of workplace data, as is true for any source. They may lack the knowledge or insights necessary to provide inclusive information, especially if they are probationary or part-time employees. Some employees may also have difficulty in describing the tasks involved in their job or in being able to infer and articulate the underlying KSAOs necessary for the job. Another potential limitation of job incumbents as an information source pertains to their motivation to be a willing and accurate source. Feelings of distrust and suspicion may greatly hamper employees' willingness to function capably as sources. For example, incumbents may intentionally fail to report certain tasks as part of their job so that those tasks are not incorporated into the formal job description. Or, incumbents may deliberately inflate the importance ratings of tasks in order to make the job appear more difficult than it actually is.

Supervisors   Supervisors could and should be considered excellent sources for use in job analysis. They not only supervise employees performing the job to be analyzed but also have played a major role in defining it and later in adding/ deleting job tasks (as in evolving and flexible jobs). Moreover, supervisors ultimately have to accept the resulting descriptions and specifications for jobs they supervise; inclusion of them as a source seems a way to ensure such acceptance.

Subject Matter Experts   Often, the sources previously mentioned are called subject matter experts or SMEs. Individuals other than those mentioned may also be used as SMEs. These people bring particular expertise to the job analysis process, an expertise thought not to be available through standard sources. Though the exact qualifications for being designated an SME are far from clear, examples of sources so designated are available. These include previous jobholders (e.g., recently promoted employees), private consultants, customer/clients, and citizens-at-large for some public sector jobs, such as superintendent of schools for a school district. Whatever the sources of SMEs, a common requirement for them is that they have recent, firsthand knowledge of the job being analyzed.[21]

Combined Sources   Combinations of sources, like combinations of methods, are most likely to be used in a typical job analysis. This is not only likely but also desirable. As noted previously, each source has some potentially unique insight to contribute to job analysis, as well as some limitations. Through a pooling of such sources and the information they provide, an accurate and acceptable job analysis is most likely to result.

Job Analysis Process

Collecting job information through job analysis requires development and use of an overall process for doing so. Unfortunately, there is no set or best process to be followed; the process has to be tailor-made to suit the specifics of the situation in which it occurs. There are, however, many key issues to be dealt with in the construction and operation of the process.[22] Each of these is briefly commented on next.

Purpose   The purpose(s) of job analysis should be clearly identified and agreed on. Since job analysis is a process designed to yield job information, the organization should ask exactly what job information is desired and why. Here, it is useful to refer back to the job requirements matrix to review the types of information that can be sought and obtained in a job requirements job analysis. Management must decide exactly what types of information are desired (task statements, task dimensions, and so forth) and in what format. Once the desired output and results of job analysis have been determined, the organization can then plan a process that will yield the desired results.

Scope   The issue of scope involves which job(s) to include in the job analysis. Decisions about actual scope should be based on consideration of (a) the importance of the job to the functioning of the organization, (b) the number of job applicants and incumbents, (c) whether the job is entry-level and thus subject to constant staffing activity, (d) the frequency with which job requirements (both tasks and KSAOs) change, and (e) the amount of time lapsed since the previous job analysis.

Internal Staff or Consultant   The organization may conduct the job analysis using its own staff, or it may procure external consultants. This is a difficult decision to make because it involves not only the obvious consideration of cost but also many other considerations. Exhibit 4.15 highlights some of these concerns and the trade-offs involved.

Organization and Coordination   Any job analysis project, whether conducted by internal staff or external consultants, requires careful organization and coordination. There are two key steps to take to help ensure that this is achieved. First, an organizational member should be appointed to function as a project manager for the total process (if consultants are used, they should report to this project manager). The project manager should be assigned overall responsibility for the total project, including its organization and control. Second, the roles and relationships for the various people involved in the project—HR staff, project staff, line managers, and job incumbents—must be clearly established.

Communication   Clear and open communication with all concerned facilitates the job analysis process. Job analysis will be thought of by some employees as analogous to an invasive, exploratory surgical procedure, which, in turn, naturally raises questions in their minds about its purpose, process, and results. These questions and concerns need to be anticipated and addressed forthrightly.

Work Flow and Time Frame   Job analysis involves a mixture of people and paper in a process in which they can become entangled very quickly. The project manager should develop and adhere to a work flowchart that shows the sequential ordering of steps to be followed in the conduct of the job analysis. This should be accompanied by a time frame showing critical completion dates for project phases, as well as a final deadline.

Analysis, Synthesis, and Documentation   Once collected, job information must be analyzed and synthesized through use of various procedural and statistical

EXHIBIT 4.15   **Factors to Consider in Choosing Between Internal Staff or Consultants for Job Analysis**

Internal Staff	Consultant
Cost of technical or procedural failure is low	Cost of technical or procedural failure is high
Project scope is limited	Project scope is comprehensive and/or large
Need for job data ongoing	Need for job data is a one-time, isolated event
There is a desire to develop internal staff skills in job analysis	There is a need for assured availability of each type and level of job analysis skill
Strong management controls are in place to control project costs	Predictability of project cost can depend on adhering to work plan
Knowledge of organization's norms, "culture," and jargon are critical	Technical innovativeness and quality are critical
Technical credibility of internal staff is high	Leverage of external "expert" status is needed to execute project
Process and products of the project are unlikely to be challenged	Process and products of the project are likely to be legally, technically, or politically scrutinized
Rational or narrative job analysis methods are desired	Commercial or proprietary job analysis methods are desired
Data collected are qualitative	Data collection methods are structured, standardized, and/or quantitative

Source: D. M. Van De Vort and B. V. Stalder, "Organizing for Job Analysis," in S. Gael (ed.), *The Job Analysis Handbook for Business, Industry and Government.* Copyright © 1988 by John Wiley & Sons, Inc. Reprinted by permission of John Wiley & Sons, Inc.

means. These should be planned in advance and incorporated into the work-flow and time-frame requirements. Likewise, provisions need to be made for preparation of written documents, especially job descriptions and job specifications, and their incorporation into relevant policy and procedure manuals.

Maintenance of the System   Job analysis does not end with completion of the project. Rather, mechanisms must be developed and put into place to maintain the job analysis and information system over time. This is critical because the system will be exposed to numerous influences requiring response and adaptation. Examples of these influences include (a) changes in job tasks and KSAOs—additions, deletions, and modifications; (b) job redesign, restructuring, and realignment; and

(c) creation of new jobs. In short, job analysis must be thought of and administered as an ongoing organizational process.

Example of Job Analysis Process Because of the many factors involved, there is no best or required job analysis process. Rather, the process must be designed to fit each particular situation. Exhibit 4.16 shows an example of the job analysis process with a narrow scope, namely, for a single job—that of administrative assistant (secretary). This is a specially conducted job analysis that uses multiple methods (prior information, observation, interviews) and multiple sources (job analyst, job incumbents, supervisors). It was conducted by a previous holder of the job (subject matter expert), and it took the person about 20 hours over a 30-day period to conduct and prepare a written job description as the output of the process.

COMPETENCY-BASED JOB ANALYSIS

A recently emerging view of job requirements comes from the concepts of competency and competency models. These concepts are closely akin to KSAOs in some respects and are a substantial extension of KSAOs in other respects. They are an innovative and potentially fruitful approach to the identification, definition, and establishment of job requirements. Discussed below are the nature of competencies and the collection of competency information.

Nature of Competencies

A competency is an underlying characteristic of an individual that contributes to job or role performance and to organizational success.[23] Competencies specific to a particular job are the familiar KSAO requirements established through job requirements job analysis. Competency requirements may extend beyond job-specific ones to those of multiple jobs, general job categories, or the entire organization. These competencies are much more general or generic KSAOs, such as "technical expertise" or "adaptability." A competency model is a combination of the several competencies deemed necessary for a particular job or role. Usage of competencies and competency models in staffing reflects a desire to (a) connote job requirements in ways that extend beyond the specific job itself; (b) describe and measure the organization's workforce in more general, competency terms; and (c) design and implement staffing programs focused around competencies (rather than just specific jobs) as a way of increasing staffing flexibility in job assignments.

Despite the strong similarities between competencies and KSAOs, there are two notable differences. First, competencies may be job-spanning, meaning that they contribute to success on multiple jobs. Members of a work team, for example, may each hold specific jobs within the team, but may be subject to job-spanning

EXHIBIT 4.16   Example of Job Requirements Job Analysis

1. Meet with manager of the job, discuss project →
2. Gather existing job information from *Dictionary of Occupational Titles*, current job description, observation of incumbents →
3. Prepare tentative set of task statements →

4. Review task statements with incumbents and managers; add, delete, rewrite statements →
5. Finalize task statements, get approval from incumbents and managers →
6. Formulate task dimensions, assign tasks to dimension, determine % time spent (importance) for each dimension →

7. Infer necessary KSAOs, develop tentative list →
8. Review KSAOs with incumbents and managers; add, delete, and rewrite KSAOs →
9. Finalize KSAOs, get approval from incumbents and manager →

10. Develop job requirements matrix and/or job description in usable format →
11. Provide matrix or job description to parties (e.g., incumbents, manager, HR department) →
12. Use matrix or job description in staffing activities, such as communicating with recruits and recruiters, developing the selection plan →

competency requirements, such as adaptability and teamwork orientation. Such requirements ensure that team members will interact successfully with each other and even perform portions or all of each others' jobs if necessary. As another example, competency requirements may span jobs within the same category, such as sales jobs or managerial jobs. All sales jobs may have as a competency requirement "product knowledge," and all managerial jobs may require "planning and results orientation." Such requirements allow for greater flexibility in job placements and job assignments within the category.

Second, competencies can contribute not only to job performance but also to organizational success. These are very general competencies applicable to, and required for, all jobs. They serve to align requirements for all jobs with the mission and goals of the organization. A restaurant, for example, may have "customer focus" as a competency requirement for all jobs as a way of indicating that servicing the needs of its customers is a key component of all jobs.

Competency Example

An illustration of the competency approach to job requirements is shown in Exhibit 4.17. The Green Care Corporation produces several lawn maintenance products: gas and electric lawn mowers, gas and electric "weed whackers," manual lawn edgers, and electric hedge trimmers. The company is in a highly competitive industry. To survive and grow, the company's core mission is product innovation and product reliability; its goals are to achieve annual 10% growth in revenues and 2% growth in market share. To help fulfill its mission and goals the company has established four general (strategic) workforce competencies—creativity/innovation, technical expertise, customer focus, and results orientation. These requirements are part of every job in the company. At the business unit (gas lawn mowers) level, the company has also established job-specific and job-spanning requirements. Some jobs, such as design engineer, are traditional or slowly evolving jobs and as such have only job-specific KSAO or competency requirements. Because the products are assembled via team assembly processes, jobs within the assembly team (such as engine assembler, final assembler) have both job-specific and job-spanning competency requirements. The job-spanning competencies—team orientation, adaptability, communication—are general and behavioral. They are necessary because of task interdependence between engine and final assembly jobs and because employees may be shifted between the two jobs in order to cover sudden employee shortages due to unscheduled absences and to maintain smooth production flows. Each job in the business unit thus has four general competency requirements, multiple job-specific competency requirements, and, where appropriate, job-spanning competency requirements.

Organization Usage

Organizations are beginning to experiment with the development of competencies and competency models and to use them as the underpinnings of several HR

EXHIBIT 4.17 **Examples of Competencies**

Company: Green Care Corporation
Products: Gas and electric lawn mowers, gas and electric weed whackers, manual lawn edgers, electric hedge trimmers.

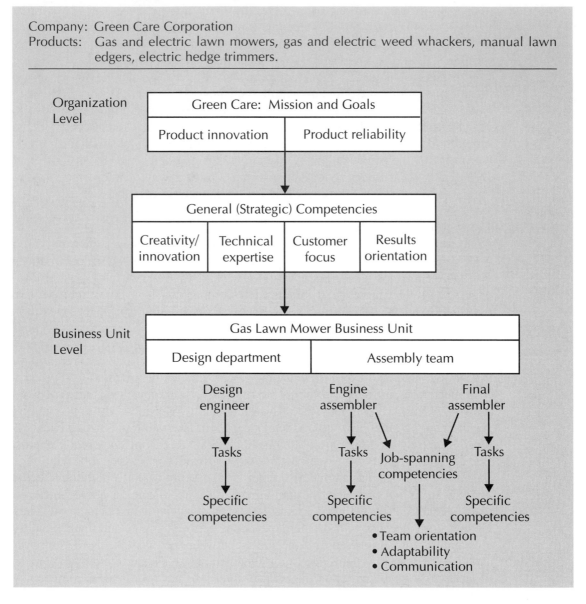

applications.[24] Research indicates that the experimentation is occurring in organizations of all sizes, but especially in large ones. The three key strategic HR reasons for doing competency modeling are to (a) create awareness and understanding of the need for change in business, (b) enhance the skill levels in the workforce, and (c) improve teamwork and coordination. Most of the emphasis has been on establishing general competencies such as:[25]

- customer focus
- communication
- team orientation
- technical expertise
- results orientation
- adaptability
- innovation

Competency models are being used for many HR applications, especially staffing, career development, performance management, and compensation. Pertaining to staffing, one important application is in HR and staffing planning. Here, workforce requirements are specified in competency terms and compared to current workforce competency levels to identify competency gaps. Another important staffing application is in external and internal selection, where applicants are assessed not only for job-specific competencies but also for general competencies. For external hiring, competency-based interviews with applicants are conducted to gauge general competencies as a key factor in selection decisions and then in job placement decisions for those hired. For promotion decisions, competency-based interviews are used in conjunction with supervisory assessments of promotability.[26]

Collecting Competency Information

Techniques and processes for collecting competency information are still in their infancy.[27] An exception, of course, is job requirements job analysis for job-specific competencies. For more general competencies, much less is known about the best ways to identify and define competencies. General competencies at the organization (strategic) level are likely to be established by top management, with guidance from strategic HR managers. At a minimum, effective establishment of general competency requirements would seem to demand the following. First, it is crucial that the organization establish its mission and goals prior to determination of competency requirements; this will help ensure that general competencies are derived from knowledge of mission and goals, much as job-specific competencies are derived from previously identified job tasks. Second, the general competencies should be truly important at all job levels, so that usage of the competencies as job requirements will focus and align all jobs with the organization's mission and goals. This principle also holds in the case where, instead of general competency requirements at the organization level, there are general competency requirements at the strategic business unit or subunit level. Third, all general competencies should have specific, behavioral definitions, not just labels. These definitions provide substance, meaning, and guidance to all concerned.

For job-spanning competencies, these definitions will necessarily be more task-specific. To ensure effective identification and definition, several tasks should be undertaken. First, it is crucial to know the major tasks for which the competencies are to be established, meaning that some form of job analysis should occur first. For now, that process will have to be crafted by the organization, since we lack prototypes or best practice examples as guidance. Second, SMEs familiar with all the jobs or roles to which the competencies will apply should be part of the process. Third, careful definition of the competencies will be necessary. Acquiring definitions from other organizations, consultants, or O*NET will be useful steps here.

A final cautionary note is that the collection and usage of competencies beyond job-specific ones will occur in uncharted legal waters. Recalling the legal standard of job-relatedness for staffing practices that cause adverse impact, will staffing practices and decisions based on general competencies be construed as job-related? Will it be a defensible argument to say that although a particular competency requirement may not have a strong contribution to job success, it is necessary for organizational success? Such questions will inevitably arise; to be able to address them, the organization should conduct a thorough process for establishing competency requirements using the suggestions above as a starting point.

JOB REWARDS JOB ANALYSIS

Overview

Broadly speaking, every job has an array of associated rewards. Some of these rewards are external to the job itself and the tasks that comprise the job. Examples of such rewards include pay, benefits, and promotion opportunities. Collectively, these are referred to as extrinsic rewards. Other rewards, however, are internal to the job itself. They are usually a direct outgrowth of the tasks themselves and the feelings that an employee experiences while performing and completing the tasks. Feelings of autonomy and utilization of skills are examples of these types of rewards. The label generally attached to these is intrinsic rewards.

The job rewards approach to job analysis focuses on both extrinsic and intrinsic rewards, as shown in Exhibit 4.18. As can be seen, the first purpose of job analysis is to identify the extrinsic rewards associated with the job. Usually this is a straightforward process because the extrinsic rewards have already been established by the organization as part of regular HR activities. As an example, the pay is specified as part of the organization's compensation activities, which detail starting pay and pay range. These terms are recorded and reported in a variety of ways,

EXHIBIT 4.18   Job Rewards Approach to Job Analysis

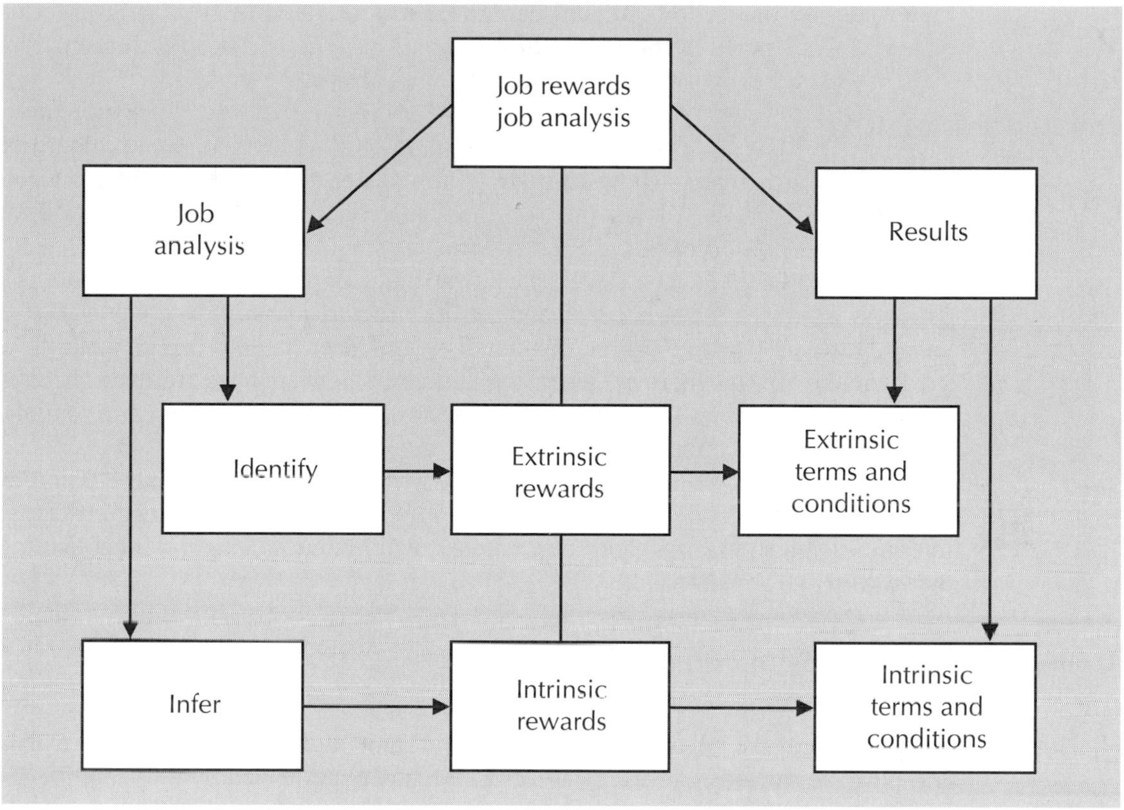

such as HR policy manuals, employee handbooks, labor contracts, and recruitment literature. The result of this job analysis is specification of extrinsic terms and conditions of employment.

A second form of analysis is concerned with inferring the intrinsic rewards associated with the job, as seen in Exhibit 4.18. These inferences are made by studying the tasks identified during the job analysis; for example, the extent of repetitive tasks in a job says something about how challenging it is. Results of analysis of intrinsic rewards are communicated as intrinsic terms and conditions of employment.

Before proceeding, it should be noted that the treatment of job rewards job analysis will be relatively brief. This brevity is the result of two related factors. First, organizations typically pay little or no formal attention to this type of job analysis; whatever energy and resources are devoted to job analysis are usually given to the job requirements variety. Second, the research and knowledge base from which to draw our discussion of job rewards job analysis is quite recent and limited. Hopefully, these circumstances will change in the future. In the meantime, the discussion that follows should be viewed as tentative but promising in terms of job analysis practice and research.

Job Rewards Matrix

The job rewards matrix shows the key components to be addressed by the job analysis and the type of information that must be collected and reported. An example of a portion of the job rewards matrix for the job of administrative assistant is shown in Exhibit 4.19. The reward and dimension columns contain a listing of all of the job's extrinsic and intrinsic rewards—only two (pay and skill variety) are shown. Then three characteristics of each reward are shown—how much of the reward there is generally (amount), how much difference there is between employees in the amount of the reward they get and why (differential), and how often the amount of the reward changes (stability).

Keeping the job rewards matrix in mind, we now turn to a brief discussion of its components. Blended into this discussion are ideas regarding methods (e.g., interviews, questionnaires) and sources (e.g., incumbents, managers) for collecting the rewards information.

Collecting Job Rewards Information

Rewards
This portion of the job analysis requires development of inclusive sets of extrinsic and intrinsic rewards that are a part of the job and experienced by job incumbents. Based on research and organization practices, a suggested set of extrinsic rewards is shown in Exhibit 4.20.[28] It indicates six major dimensions of extrinsic rewards (direct compensation—base pay; direct compensation—variable pay; indirect compensation—benefits; hours of work; career advancement; and job security) and more specific rewards within each category.

Shown in Exhibit 4.21 is a set of seven suggested intrinsic rewards: skill variety, task identity, task significance, autonomy, feedback from job, feedback from agents, and dealing with others. This set of intrinsic rewards is based on considerable research and a resultant measure known as the Job Diagnostic Survey (JDS).[29]

Reward sets such as those shown in Exhibits 4.20 and 4.21 are a useful starting point for any job rewards job analysis. The sets could be amended by inclusion of additional rewards not covered but clearly associated with the job. Such modifications could come about through consultation with various SMEs (e.g., incumbents, supervisors, HR staff representatives), using a variety of methods (e.g., interviews, questionnaires, observation). The desired end product of this part of the job analysis is a set of rewards that are agreed on by all sources and methods as inclusive in scope and acceptable for purposes of capturing the reward domain of jobs.

EXHIBIT 4.19   Portion of Job Rewards Matrix for Job of Administrative Assistant

Reward	Dimension	Amount	Reward Characteristics	
			Differential	Stability
1. Starting pay	A. Base pay (extrinsic)	$2,000/month minimum	May exceed minimum, depending on KSAOs	Changes according to market conditions
2. Pay raises	A. Base pay (extrinsic)	Typically 2–3%	Across the board (same % for all)	Range from 0% to 10%, annually
3. Bonuses	A. Variable pay (extrinsic)	2.5% average	Range from 0% to 10%, depending on performance	Will vary each year, depending on size of bonus pool
4. Doing different tasks	B. Skill variety (intrinsic)	above average	average	Frequent change
5. Using complex skills	B. Skill variety (intrinsic)	average	above average	No recent changes; none anticipated

EXHIBIT 4.20 Extrinsic Rewards

Reward	Explanation
Direct Compensation—Base Pay	
Starting	Beginning wage or salary
Range	Minimum and maximum pay for job
Raises	Increases in base pay
Direct Compensation—Variable Pay	
Short-term incentives (one year or less)	Usually one time cash bonus for performance to individual, team, or operating unit
Long-term incentives (more than one year)	Usually stock options, restricted stock plan, or performance plan tied to long term performance growth or targets
Indirect Compensation—Benefits	
Health insurance	Employer-sponsored health care insurance
Retirement	Defined benefit, defined contribution, or cash balance plan for retirement pay
Work life	Examples include childcare, parenting programs, lactation rooms, concierge services, financial services, employee assistance programs, home computer
Perks	Examples include cell phones, recreation facilities, subsidized cafeteria, free snacks, hair and manicure salon, car wash, student loan payoffs
Other	Examples include vacation, paid holidays, sick pay, life and disability insurance
Hours of Work	
Full- or Part-time	Typical number of hours per week; more than 40 usually considered full-time
Shift	Day, swing, or night work hours; premium pay above base pay for swing or night shift
Flextime	Nonstandard starting and ending daily times
Overtime	Hours beyond normal; voluntary or mandatory; premium pay above base pay
Career Advancement	
Training and development	Opportunities for KSAO and competency improvement, mentoring
Job changes	Opportunities for promotion and transfer
Location Changes	Opportunities or requirements for relocation
Job Security	
Job security enhancements	Fixed-term contracts Performance management Progressive discipline
Termination process	Procedures for terminating an employee
Severance package	Pay, benefits, and assistance provided to a terminated employee

EXHIBIT 4.21   Intrinsic Rewards

Reward	Explanation
Skill variety	Use of complex skills to perform different tasks
Task identity	Complete a whole piece of work, rather than just a part of it
Task significance	Results of your work affect lives of others
Autonomy	Freedom to decide how to do your job
Feedback from job	Job itself gives you information about how well you are performing your job
Feedback from agents	Manager or coworkers give you information about how well you are performing your job
Dealing with others	Job requires you to work closely with others, such as coworkers or clients

Note: Based on the Job Diagnostic Survey.

Reward Dimensions

Once a reward set has been identified, the resulting list of rewards must either stand alone or somehow be collapsed into a set of more general reward dimensions. Either choice is acceptable, and the decision should be based on the ease with which the rewards are likely to be classified, as well as the usefulness of having rewards so cast. It is probably useful, and relatively easy, to distinguish rewards as either "extrinsic" or "intrinsic," as shown in Exhibit 4.19. More detailed dimensions such as those shown in Exhibits 4.20 and 4.21 could also be done. Any such classification is possible; the key consideration is whether it meets the tests of ease and usefulness mentioned earlier.

Reward Characteristics

In the job rewards matrix it is suggested that the organization analyze and record three particular characteristics of rewards: amount, differential, and stability. Each of these characteristics is considered next.

Amount of Reward   Clearly, any analysis of job rewards seeks to provide some indication about their amount or level. For external rewards, this is a relatively straightforward process because the reward amounts are externally defined and specified (e.g., starting pay, hours of work, number of vacation days). Intrinsic reward amounts, by their very nature, are not as easily analyzed and specified. They are not externally established, and there are no objective measures of their amount (e.g., how does one objectively measure amount of task challenge?). The amount of an intrinsic reward thus must be inferred from what various sources (e.g., incumbents, supervisors) tell about it.

The most straightforward procedure to use is for the primary job analyst to classify each intrinsic reward as "above average," "average," or "below average" in amount (or "high," "medium," or low"), as shown in Exhibit 4.19. Such admittedly subjective judgments could be supported by using a trained analyst familiar with the job and by seeking input from job incumbents and supervisors as to the appropriate amount.

Another procedure would be to construct a survey in which job incumbents are asked to rate the amount of each reward on a 1–5 or 1–7 rating scale. The JDS could be used. A set of its items are shown in Exhibit 4.22. The average rating for each reward would then be calculated and it would serve as the indicator of reward amount. While this procedure will yield more precise estimates of reward amount, it is a more cumbersome process to use. Unless the organization uses the JDS to measure intrinsic reward amounts, it must develop its own measure. If this is done, considerable care and caution should be exercised regarding the measure's development, reliability, and validity.

Reward Differential This characteristic refers to the relative differences in reward amount that may be received or experienced by job incumbents. Do all have the same salary? Do all experience the same amount of skill variety? Such questions are at the heart of the reward differential issue.

Analyzing extrinsic job rewards in terms of their differential is quite straightforward. The analyst simply consults the relevant HR policies and activities to determine whether there are reward differentials or not, and if so, how many and how much. Consider the case of wage or salary. The analyst can look at the compensation policies for a job and determine whether all employees receive the same rate of pay, and if they do not, the range of pay rates (minimum and maximum) that are possible.

Analyzing intrinsic reward differentials is more difficult. Even though all employees on a given job may perform roughly the same tasks, they differ in how they perceive or experience the intrinsic rewards that flow from these tasks. The job analysis must be prepared to capture these differentials among employees for each intrinsic reward.

Measurement of differentials for intrinsic rewards could use parallel procedures to those used for reward amounts. The analyst could classify the differential for each reward as "above average," "average," or "below average" (or "high," "medium," or "low"). If a survey is used, the standard deviation of the ratings for each reward is calculated, and it represents the degree of differential present (the larger the standard deviation, the greater the differential). Again, the survey approach will yield more precise estimates but be more cumbersome.

Reward Stability Does the amount of a reward remain stable over time, or does it change? This is the matter of reward stability. For extrinsic rewards, assessment of stability is made by inspection of HR policies and activities that are explicitly

EXHIBIT 4.22 Set of Items from the Job Diagnostic Survey

1. To what extent does your job require you to *work closely with other people* (either "clients" or people in related jobs in your own organization)?

1	2	3	4	5	6	7
Very little; dealing with other people is not at all necessary in doing the job.			Moderately; some dealing with others is necessary.			Very much; dealing with other people is an absolutely essential and crucial part of doing the job.

2. How much *autonomy* is there in your job? That is, to what extent does your job permit you to decide *on your own* how to go about doing the work?

1	2	3	4	5	6	7
Very little; the job gives me almost no personal say about how and when the work is done.			Moderate autonomy; many things are standardized and not under my control, but I can make some decisions about the work.			Very much; the job gives me almost complete responsibility for deciding how and when the work is done.

3. To what extent does your job involve doing a *whole and identifiable piece of work?* That is, is the job a complete piece of work that has an obvious beginning and end? Or is it only a small *part* of the overall piece of work, which is finished by other people or by automatic machines?

1	2	3	4	5	6	7
My job is only a tiny part of the overall piece of work; the results of my activities cannot be seen in the final product or service.			My job is a moderate-sized chunk of the overall piece of work; my own contribution can be seen in the final outcome.			My job involves doing the whole piece of work, from start to finish; the results of my activities are easily seen in the final product or service.

4. How much *variety* is there in your job? That is, to what extent does the job require you to do many different things at work, using a variety of your skills and talents?

1	2	3	4	5	6	7
Very little; the job requires me to do the same routine things over and over again.			Moderate variety.			Very much; the job requires me to do many different things, using a number of different skills and talents.

(continued)

EXHIBIT 4.22   Continued

5. In general, how *significant or important* is your job? That is, are the results of your work likely to significantly affect the lives or well-being of other people?

1	2	3	4	5	6	7
	Not very significant; the outcomes of my work are *not* likely to have important effects on other people.		Moderately significant.			Highly significant; the outcomes of my work can affect other people in very important ways.

6. To what extent do *managers or co-workers* let you know how well you are doing on your job?

1	2	3	4	5	6	7
	Very little; people almost never let me know how well I am doing.		Moderately; sometimes people may give me feedback; other times they may not.			Very much; managers or co-workers provide me with almost constant feedback about how well I am doing.

7. To what extent does *doing the job itself* provide you with information about your work performance? That is, does the actual *work itself* provide clues about how well you are doing aside from any feedback coworkers or supervisors may provide?

1	2	3	4	5	6	7
	Very little; the job itself is set up so I could work forever without finding out how well I am doing.		Moderately; sometimes doing the job provides feedback to me; sometimes it does not.			Very much; the job is set up so that I get almost constant feedback as I work about how well I am doing.

designed to create stability or instability. Consider the extrinsic reward "pay raise." Analysis of the organization's pay raise policies will show whether or not pay raises are given, and if so, how frequently.

Assessing intrinsic reward stability will require gauging employees' perceptions of, or experiences with, these types of rewards over time. Perceptions of skill variety, for example, may change due to changes in actual task content, as occurs in evolving and flexible jobs.[30] Or, changes in employees themselves (e.g., KSAO changes due to new training and/or educational experiences) may lead them to perceive their intrinsic rewards differently over time.

Capturing the effects of these types of changes on employees and their perceptions of rewards may require a substantial commitment from the organization. For example, it may mean establishing and maintaining an intrinsic reward tracking system for employees in each particular job. This might require, for example, periodic (annual) administrations of the JDS to employees, followed by the necessary statistical analysis and interpretation of results as they pertain to trends in perceptions of rewards. Alternately, in a more casual mode, summary written statements about stability may be made (and changed when necessary), as was done in Exhibit 4.19.

Results of Job Rewards Job Analysis

The job analysis produces a thorough description of the structure and pattern of rewards for a particular job. It is a description of the extrinsic and intrinsic terms and conditions of the job. The organization will thus have identified and defined such features as (a) the domain of relevant rewards; (b) broader groupings or dimensions of rewards, both extrinsic and intrinsic; (c) indications about the amount of each reward present; (d) how much difference there is among employees in the amounts of rewards they receive and experience; and (e) how stable or fluctuating are the rewards that employees receive.

Unfortunately, this wealth of job reward information may be difficult to translate into a directly usable form. There are no standard procedures or formats for expressing the information. The job rewards matrix, however, is a good starting point for recording and communicating the job reward information that has been collected.

In addition, the organization can use its own creativity to develop its own unique and useful ways of putting the information into usable formats and then incorporating it into policy manuals, employee handbooks, recruitment literature, college relations programs, and the like. As will be discussed, having and using job rewards information in these ways may play a key role in the multitude of recruitment, selection, and employment activities.

LEGAL ISSUES

This chapter has emphasized the crucial role that job analysis plays in establishing the foundations for staffing activities. That crucial role continues from a legal perspective. Job analysis becomes intimately involved in court cases involving the job relatedness of staffing activities. It also occupies a prominent position in the Uniform Guidelines on Employee Selection Procedures (UGESP). Finally, the Americans With Disabilities Act requires that the organization determine the essential functions of each job, and job analysis can play a pivotal role in that process. As these issues are discussed in the following sections, note the direct relevance of the job requirements matrix and its development to them.

Job Relatedness and Court Cases

In EEO/AA court cases, the organization is confronted with the need to justify its challenged staffing practices as being job-related. Common sense suggests that this requires first and foremost that the organization conduct some type of job analysis to identify job requirements and rewards. In addition, it also is the case that specific features or characteristics of the job analysis make a difference in the organization's defense. Specifically, an examination of court cases indicates that for purposes of legal defensibility the organization should conform to the following recommendations:

1. "Job analysis must be performed and must be for the job for which the selection instrument is to be utilized.
2. Analysis of the job should be in writing.
3. Job analysts should describe in detail the procedure used.
4. Job data should be collected from a variety of current sources by knowledgeable job analysts.
5. Sample size should be large and representative of the jobs for which the selection instrument is used.
6. Tasks, duties, and activities should be included in the analysis.
7. The most important tasks should be represented in the selection device.
8. Competency levels of job performance for entry-level jobs should be specified.
9. Knowledge, skills, and abilities should be specified, particularly if a content validation model is followed."[31]

These recommendations are very consistent with our more general discussion of job analysis as an important tool and basic foundation for staffing activities. Moreover, even though these recommendations were made several years ago, there is little reason to doubt or modify any of them on the basis of more recent court cases.

Job Analysis and Selection

The UGESP places great emphasis on job analysis in the conduct of validation studies. In general, these guidelines indicate that any validation study should begin with a job analysis. More specifically, here is their exact language regarding job analysis for criterion-related and content validation studies:

1. Criterion-related validation: "Validity studies should be based on review of information about the job for which the selection procedure is to be used. The review should include a job analysis except as provided in section 14B(3) below with respect to criterion-related validity. Any method of job analysis may be used if it provides the information required for the specific validation strategy used.

"There should be a review of job information to determine measures of work behavior(s) or performance that are relevant to the job or group of jobs in question. These measures or criteria are relevant to the extent that they represent critical or important job duties, work behaviors, or work outcomes as developed from the review of job information."

2. Content validation: "There should be a job analysis which includes an analysis of the important work behavior(s) required for successful performance and their relative importance and, if the behavior results in work product(s), an analysis of the work product(s). Any job analysis should focus on the work behavior(s) and the tasks associated with them. If work behaviors are not observable, the job analysis should identify and analyze those aspects of the behavior(s) that can be observed and the observed work products. The work behavior(s) selected for measurement should be critical work behavior(s) and/or important work behavior(s) constituting most of the job.

"For any selection procedure measuring a knowledge, skill or ability the user should show that (a) the selection procedure measures and is a representative sample of that knowledge, skill or ability and (b) that knowledge, skill or ability is used in and is a necessary prerequisite to critical or important work behavior(s)."

Reflection on these statements reveals the crucial role accorded to job analysis in the conduct of validation studies. It is essential for derivation of the content of both criterion and predictor measures and for establishment of links between tasks and KSAOs.

Essential Job Functions

Recall that under the Americans With Disabilities Act (ADA), the organization must not discriminate against a qualified individual with a disability who can perform the "essential functions" of the job, with or without reasonable accommodation. This requirement raises three questions: What are essential functions? What is evidence of essential functions? What is the role of job analysis?

What Are Essential Functions?
The ADA employment regulations provide the following statements about essential functions:

1. "The term essential functions refers to the fundamental job duties of the employment position the individual with a disability holds or desires. The term essential function does not include the marginal functions of the position; and

2. A job function may be considered essential for any of several reasons, including but not limited to the following:

   • The function may be essential because the reason the position exists is to perform the function;

   • The function may be essential because of the limited number of employees available among whom the performance of that job function can be distributed; and/or

   • The function may be highly specialized so that the incumbent in the position is hired for his or her expertise or ability to perform the particular function."

Evidence of Essential Functions

The employment regulations go on to indicate what constitutes evidence that any particular function is in fact an essential one. That evidence includes, but is not limited to,

1. the employer's judgment as to which functions are essential
2. written job descriptions, prepared before advertising or interviewing applicants for the job
3. the amount of time spent on the job performing the function
4. the consequences of not requiring the incumbent to perform the function
5. the terms of a collective bargaining agreement
6. the work experience of past incumbents in the job
7. the current work experience of incumbents in similar jobs

Role of Job Analysis

What role(s) might job analysis play in identifying essential functions and establishing evidence of their being essential? The employment regulations are silent on this question. However, the EEOC has provided substantial and detailed assistance to organizations to deal with this and many other issues under the ADA.[32] The specific statements regarding job analysis and essential functions of the job are shown in Exhibit 4.23.

Examination of the statements in Exhibit 4.23 suggests the following. First, while job analysis is not required by law as a means of establishing essential

EXHIBIT 4.23   Job Analysis and Essential Functions of the Job

Job Analysis and the Essential Functions of a Job

The ADA does not require that an employer conduct a job analysis or any particular form of job analysis to identify the essential functions of a job. The information provided by a job analysis may or may not be helpful in properly identifying essential job functions, depending on how it is conducted.

The term "job analysis" generally is used to describe a formal process in which information about a specific job or occupation is collected and analyzed. Formal job analysis may be conducted by a number of different methods. These methods obtain different kinds of information that is used for different purposes. Some of these methods will not provide information sufficient to determine if an individual with a disability is qualified to perform "essential" job functions.

For example: One kind of formal job analysis looks at specific job tasks and classifies jobs according to how these tasks deal with data, people, and objects. This type of job analysis is used to set wage rates for various jobs; however, it may not be adequate to identify the essential functions of a *particular* job, as required by the ADA. Another kind of job analysis looks at the kinds of knowledge, skills, and abilities that are necessary to perform a job. This type of job analysis is used to develop selection criteria for various jobs. The information from this type of analysis sometimes helps to measure the importance of certain skills, knowledge and abilities, but it does not take into account the fact that people with disabilities often can perform essential functions using other skills and abilities.

Some job analysis methods ask current employees and their supervisors to rate the importance of general characteristics necessary to perform a job, such as "strength," "endurance," or "intelligence," without linking these characteristics to *specific* job functions or specific tasks that are part of a function. Such general information may not identify, for example, whether upper body or lower body strength is required, or whether muscular endurance or cardiovascular endurance is needed to perform a particular job function. Such information, by itself, would not be sufficient to determine whether an individual who has particular limitations can perform an essential function with or without an accommodation.

As already stated, the ADA does not require a formal job analysis or any particular method of analysis to identify the essential functions of a job. A small employer may wish to conduct an informal analysis by observing and consulting with people who perform the job, or have previously performed it, and their supervisors. If possible, it is advisable to observe and consult with several workers under a range of conditions, to get a better idea of all job functions and the different ways they

(continued)

EXHIBIT 4.23   Continued

may be performed. Production records and workloads also may be relevant factors to consider.

To identify essential job functions under the ADA, a job analysis should focus on the purpose of the job and the importance of actual job functions in achieving this purpose. Evaluating importance may include consideration of the frequency with which a function is performed, the amount of time spent on the function, and the consequences if the function is not performed. The analysis may include information on the work environment (such as unusual heat, cold, humidity, dust, toxic substances, or stress factors). The job analysis may contain information on the manner in which a job currently is performed, but should not conclude that ability to perform the job in that manner is an essential function, unless there is no other way to perform the function without causing undue hardship. A job analysis will be most helpful for purposes of the ADA if it focuses on the results or outcome of a function, not solely on the way it customarily is performed.

For example:

- An essential function of a computer programmer job might be described as "ability to develop programs that accomplish necessary objectives," rather than "ability to manually write programs." Although a person currently performing the job may write these programs by hand, that is not the essential function, because programs can be developed directly on the computer.

- If a job requires mastery of information contained in technical manuals, this essential function would be "ability to learn technical material," rather than "ability to read technical manuals." People with visual and other reading impairments could perform this function using other means, such as audiotapes.

- A job that requires objects to be moved from one place to another should state this essential function. The analysis may note that the person in the job "lifts 50-pound cartons to a height of 3 or 4 feet and loads them into truck-trailers 5 hours daily," but should not identify the "ability to *manually* lift and load 50-pound cartons" as an essential function unless this is the only method by which the function can be performed without causing an undue hardship.

A job analysis that is focused on outcomes or results also will be helpful in establishing appropriate qualification standards, developing job descriptions, conducting interviews, and selecting people in accordance with ADA requirements. It will be particularly helpful in identifying accommodations that will enable an individual with specific functional abilities and limitations to perform the job.

Source: Equal Employment Opportunity Commission, *Technical Assistance Manual for the Employment Provisions (Title I) of the Americans With Disabilities Act* (Washington, DC: author, 1992), pp. II-18 to II-20.

functions of a job, it is strongly recommended. Second, the job analysis should focus on tasks associated with the job. Where KSAOs are also studied or specified, they should be derived from an explicit consideration of their probable links to the essential tasks. Third, with regard to tasks, the focus should be on the tasks themselves and the outcome or results of the tasks, rather than the methods by which they are performed. Finally, the job analysis should be useful in identifying potential reasonable accommodations.[33]

SUMMARY

Organizations design and use various types of jobs—traditional, evolving, flexible, idiosyncratic, team-based, and telework. These design approaches all result in job content in the form of job requirements and rewards. Job analysis is described as the process used to gather, analyze, synthesize, and report information about job content. The job requirements approach to job analysis focuses on job-specific tasks, KSAOs, and job context. Competency-based job analysis seeks to identify more general KSAOs that apply across jobs and roles. The job rewards approach is concerned with extrinsic and intrinsic job rewards and various characteristics of them.

The job requirements approach is guided by the job requirements matrix. The matrix calls for information about tasks and task dimensions, as well as their importance. In a parallel fashion, it requires information about KSAOs required for the tasks, plus indications about the importance of those KSAOs. The final component of the matrix deals with numerous elements of the job context.

When gathering the information called for by the job requirements matrix, the organization is confronted with a multitude of choices. Those choices are shown to revolve around various job analysis methods, sources, and processes. The organization must pick and choose from among these; all have advantages and disadvantages associated with them. The choices should be guided by a concern for the accuracy and acceptability of the information that is being gathered.

A very new approach to identifying job requirements is competency-based job analysis. This form of job analysis seeks to identify general competencies (KSAOs) necessary for all jobs because the competencies support the organization's mission and goals. Within work units, other general competencies (job-spanning KSAOs) may also be established that cut across multiple jobs. Potential techniques and processes for collecting competency information are suggested.

The job rewards matrix is suggested for use in a job rewards job analysis. The matrix indicates a need to identify the extrinsic and intrinsic rewards offered by the job. It also requires indication of the rewards' amounts, differences among employees, and stability. Instruments and processes for collecting the necessary information are still in their infancy, as is the formal incorporation and use of the information in staffing activities.

From a legal perspective, job analysis is shown to assume major importance in creating staffing systems and practices that are in compliance with EEO/AA laws and regulations. The employer must ensure (or be able to show) that its practices are job-related. This requires not only having conducted a job requirements job analysis but also using a process that itself has defensible characteristics. The UGESP clearly accords job analysis a prominent place in the conduct of validation studies. Indeed, it is required as an initial step in both criterion-related and content validation. Under the ADA, the organization must identify the essential functions of the job. Though this does not require a job analysis, the organization should strongly consider it as one of the tools to be used. Over time, we will learn more about how job analysis is treated under the ADA.

DISCUSSION QUESTIONS

1. Identify a team-based job situation. What are examples of job-spanning KSAOs required in that situation?
2. How should task statements be written, and what sorts of problems might you encounter in asking a job incumbent to write these statements?
3. Would it be better to first identify task dimensions and then create specific task statements for each dimension, or should task statements be identified first and then used to create task dimensions?
4. What would you consider when trying to decide what criteria (e.g., percent time spent) to use for gathering indications about task importance?
5. What are the advantages and disadvantages to using multiple methods of job analysis for a particular job? Multiple sources?
6. What are the advantages and disadvantages of identifying and using general competencies to guide staffing activities?
7. Why might an organization resist doing a job rewards job analysis and using the results in staffing activities?

APPLICATIONS

Conducting a Job Requirements or Job Rewards Job Analysis

Job analysis is defined as "the process of studying jobs in order to gather, synthesize, and report information about job content." Based on the person/job match model, job content consists of job requirements (tasks and KSAOs) and job rewards (extrinsic and intrinsic). There are thus two forms of job analysis: job requirements and job rewards. The goal of the job requirements job analysis is to produce the job requirements matrix. The goal of the job rewards job analysis is to produce the job rewards matrix.

Your assignment is to conduct either a job requirements or job rewards job analysis. In this assignment you will choose a job you want to study, conduct either a job requirements or job rewards job analysis of that job, and prepare a written report of your project.

Your report should include the following sections:

1. The Job—What job (job title) did you choose to study and why?
2. The Form of Job Analysis—Did you choose the job requirements or job rewards form, and why?
3. The Methods Used—What methods did you use (prior information, observation, interviews, task questionnaires, combinations of these), and exactly how did you use them?
4. The Sources Used—What sources did you use (job analyst, job incumbent, supervisor, subject matter experts, combinations of these), and exactly how did you use them?
5. The Process Used—How did you go about gathering, synthesizing, and reporting the information? Refer back to Exhibit 4.16 for an example.
6. The Matrix—Present the actual job requirements or job rewards matrix.

Maintaining Job Descriptions

The InAndOut, Inc., company provides warehousing and fulfillment (order receiving and filling) services to small publishers of books with small print runs (number of copies of a book printed). After the books are printed and bound at a printing facility, they are shipped to InAndOut for handling. Books are received initially by handlers who unload the books off trucks, place them on pallets, and move them via forklifts and conveyors to their assigned storage space in the warehouse. The handlers also retrieve books and bring them to the shipping area when orders are received. The books are then packaged, placed in cartons, and loaded on delivery trucks (to take to air or ground transportation providers) by shippers. Book orders are taken by customer service representatives via written, phone, or electronic (e-mail, fax) forms. New accounts are generated by marketing representatives, who also service existing accounts. Order clerks handle all the internal paperwork. All of these employees report to either the supervisor–operations or supervisor–customer service, who in turn reports to the general manager.

The owner and president of InAndOut, Inc., Alta Fossom, is independently wealthy and delegates all day-to-day management matters to the general manager, Marvin Olson. Alta requires, however, that Marvin clear any new ideas or initiatives with her prior to taking action. The company is growing and changing rapidly. Many new accounts, often larger than the past norm, are opening. Publishers are demanding more services and faster order fulfillment. Information technology is constantly being upgraded, and new machinery (forklifts, computer-assisted conveyor system) is being utilized. And the workforce is growing in size to meet the business growth. There are now 37 employees, and Marvin expects to hire another 15–20 new employees within the next year.

Job descriptions for the company were originally written by a consultant about eight years ago. They have never been revised and are hopelessly outdated. For the job of marketing representative there is no job description at all because the job was created only five years ago. As general manager, Marvin is responsible for all HR management matters, but he has little time to devote to them. To help him get a better grip on his HR responsibilities, Marvin has hired you as a part-time HR intern. He has a "gut feeling" that the job descriptions need to be updated or written for the first time and has assigned you that project. Since Marvin has to clear new projects with Alta, he wants you to prepare a brief proposal that he can use to approach her for seeking approval. In that proposal he wants to be able to suggest to Alta

1. reasons why it is important to update and write new job descriptions

2. an outline of a process that might be followed for doing this that will yield a set of thorough, current job descriptions

3. a process to be used in the future for periodically reviewing and updating these new job descriptions

Marvin wants to meet with you and discuss each of these points. He wants very specific suggestions and ideas from you that he can use to prepare his proposal. What exactly would you suggest to Marvin?

ENDNOTES

1. D. R. Ilgen and J. R. Hollenbeck, "The Structure of Work: Job Design and Roles," in M. D. Dunnette and L. M. Hough (eds.), *Handbook of Industrial and Organizational Psychology,* Vol. 2 (Palo Alto, CA: Consulting Psychologists Press, 1991), pp. 165–207.

2. E. R. Silverman, "You've Come a Long Way . . . ," *Human Resource Executive,* Feb. 2000, pp. 64–68; A. Wrzesniewski and J. E. Dutton, "Crafting a Job: Revisioning Employees as Active Crafters of their Work," *Academy of Management Review,* 2001, 26, pp. 179–201.

3. A. S. Miner, "Idiosyncratic Jobs in Formalized Organizations," *Administrative Science Quarterly,* 1987, 32, pp. 327–351.

4. W. Bridges, "The End of the Job," *Fortune,* Sept. 19, 1994, pp. 62–74; B. Dumaine, "The Trouble with Teams," *Fortune,* Sept. 5, 1994, pp. 86–92; R. J. Klimoski and R. G. Jones, "Staffing for Effective Group Decision Making: Key Issues in Matching People and Teams," in R. A. Guzzo, E. Salas, and Associates, *Team Effectiveness and Decision Making in Organizations* (San Francisco: Jossey-Bass, 1995), pp. 291–332; M. J. Stevens and M. A. Campion, "The Knowledge, Skill, and Ability Requirements for Teamwork: Implications for Human Resource Management,"*Journal of Management,* 1994, 20, pp. 503–530; R. S. Wellins, W. C. Byham, and G. R. Dixon, *Inside Teams* (San Francisco: Jossey-Bass, 1994).

5. E. Sundstrom, K. P. DeMeuse, and D. Futrell, "Work Teams: Applications and Effectiveness," *American Psychologist,* 1990, 45, pp. 120–133.

6. D. C. Feldman and T. W. Gainey, "Patterns of Telecommuting and Their Consequences: Framing the Research Agenda," *Human Resource Management Review,* 1997, 7, pp. 369–388; J. A. Segal, "Home Sweet Office," *HR Magazine,* April, 1998, pp. 119–129; W. F. Cascio, "Managing a Virtual Workplace," *Academy of Management Executive,* 2000, 14(3), pp. 81–90.

7. For excellent overviews and reviews, see S. Gael (ed.), *The Job Analysis Handbook for Business, Industry and Government,* Vols. 1 and 2 (New York: Wiley, 1988); J. V. Ghorpade, *Job Analysis* (Englewood Cliffs, NJ: 1988); R. J. Harvey, "Job Analysis," in Dunnette and Hough, *Handbook of Industrial and Organizational Psychology,* pp. 71–163; M. A. Campion, "Ability Requirement Implications of Job Design: An Interdisciplinary Perspective," *Personnel Psychology,* 1989, 42, pp. 1–24; R. D. Gatewood and H. S. Feild, *Human Resource Selection,* fifth ed. (Orlando, FL: Harcourt, 2001), pp. 267–363.

8. U.S. Department of Labor, *Revised Handbook for Analyzing Jobs* (Washington, DC: author, 1991), pp. 13-1 to 13-13.

9. E. T. Cornelius III, "Practical Findings from Job Analysis Research," in Gael, *The Job Analysis Handbook for Business, Industry and Government,* Vol. 1, pp. 48–70.

10. C. J. Cranny and M. E. Doherty, "Importance Ratings in Job Analysis: Note on the Misinterpretation of Factor Analysis," *Journal of Applied Psychology,* 1988, 73, 320–322.

11. Gatewood and Feild, *Human Resource Selection,* pp. 295–298; Harvey, "Job Analysis," in Dunnette and Hough, pp. 75–79; M. A. Wilson, "The Validity of Task Coverage Ratings by Incumbents and Supervisors: Bad News," *Journal of Business and Psychology,* 1997, 12, pp. 85–95.

12. D. P. Costanza, E. A. Fleishman, and J. C. Marshall-Mies, "Knowledges: Evidence for the Reliability and Validity of the Measures" in N. G. Peterson, M. D. Mumford, W. C. Borman, P. R. Jeannerert, E. A. Fleishman, and K. Y. Levin, *O*NET Final Technical Report Vol. 1* (Salt Lake City: Utah Department of Workforce Services, 1997), pp. 4-1 to 4-26.

13. M. C. Mumford, N. G. Peterson, and R. A. Childs, "Basic and Cross-Functional Skills: Evidence for Reliability and Validity of the Measures" in N. G. Peterson et al., *O*NET Final Technical Report Vol. 1,* pp. 3-1 to 3-36.

14. E. A. Fleishman, D. P. Costanza, and J. C. Marshall-Mies, "Abilities: Evidence for the Reliability and Validity of the Measures" in N. G. Peterson, et al., *O*NET Final Technical Report Vol. 2,* pp. 9-1 to 9-26.

15. M. H. Strong, P. R. Jeanneret, S. M. McPhail, and B. R. Blakley, "Work Context: Evidence for the Reliability and Validity of the Measures," in N. G. Peterson, et al., *O*NET Final Technical Report Vol. 2,* pp. 7-1 to 7-35.

16. F. P. Morgeson and M. A. Campion, "Social and Cognitive Sources of Potential Inaccuracy in Job Analysis," *Journal of Applied Psychology,* 1997, 82, pp. 627–655.

17. For detailed treatments, see Gael, *The Job Analysis Handbook for Business, Industry and Government,* pp. 315–468; Harvey, "Job Analysis," in Dunnette and Hough; E. Levine, *Everything You Always Wanted to Know About Job Analysis but Were Afraid to Ask* (Tampa, FL: Mariner, 1983); Gatewood and Feild, *Human Resource Selection,* pp. 267–363.

18. A. Clardy, review of "Descriptions Now! For Windows," *Personal Psychology,* 1996, 49, pp. 537–539.

19. U.S. Department of Labor, *Dictionary of Occupational Titles,* fourth ed. (Washington, DC: author, 1991).

20. N. G. Peterson, et al., *O*NET Final Technical Report Vols. 1, 2, 3;* N. G. Peterson, M. D. Mumford, W. C. Borman, P. R. Jeanneret, E. A. Fleishman, K. Y. Levin, M. A. Campion, M. S. Mayfield, F. S. Morgeson, K. Pearlman, M. K. Gowing, A. R. Lancaster, M. B. Silver, and D. M. Dye, "Understanding Work Using the Occupational Information Network: Implications for Research and Practice," *Personnel Psychology,* 2001, 54 pp. 451–492.

21. F. J. Landy and J. Vasey, "Job Analysis: The Composition of SME Samples," *Personnel Psychology,* 1991, 44, pp. 27–50; R. G. Jones, J. I. Sanchez, G. Parameswaran, J. Phelps, C. Shoptaugh, M. Williams, and S. White, "Selection or Training? A Two-fold Test of the Validity of Job-Analytic Ratings of Trainability," *Journal of Business and Psychology,* 2001, 15, pp. 363–389.

22. See Gael, *The Job Analysis Handbook for Business, Industry and Government*, pp. 315–390; Gatewood and Feild, *Human Resource Selection,* pp. 267–363.

23. American Compensation Association, *Raising the Bar: Using Competencies to Enhance Employee Performance* (Scottsdale, AZ: author, 1996); M. Harris, "Competency Modeling: Viagraized Job Analysis or Impotent Imposter?," *The Industrial-Organizational Psychologist,* 1998, 36(2), pp. 37–41; R. L. Heneman and G. E. Ledford Jr., "Competency Pay for Professionals and Managers in Business: A Review and Implications for Teachers," *Journal of Personnel Evaluation in Education,* 1998, 12, pp. 103–122; L. M. Spenser and S. M. Spencer, *Competence at Work* (New York: Wiley, 1993); J. S. Shipmann, R. A. Ash, M. Battista, L. Carr, L. D. Eyde, B. Hesketh, J. Kehoe, K. Pearlman, E. P. Prien, and J. I. Sanchez, "The Practice of Competency Modeling," *Personnel Psychology,* 2000, 53, pp. 703–740.

24. American Compensation Association, *Raising the Bar,* pp. 7–15.

25. P. K. Zingheim, G. E. Ledford Jr., and J. R. Schuster, "Competencies and Competency Models: Does One Size Fit All?," *ACA Journal,* Spring 1996, pp. 56–65.

26. American Compensation Association, *Raising the Bar,* pp. 35–36.

27. J. S. Shipman et. al., "The Practice of Competency Modeling."

28. F. H. Borgen, "Occupational Reinforcer Patterns," in Gael, *The Job Analysis Handbook for Business, Industry and Government,* Vol. 2, pp. 902–916; R. V. Dawis, "Person-Environment Fit and Job Satisfaction," in C. J. Cranny, P. C. Smith, and E. F. Stone (eds.), *Job Satisfaction* (New York: Lexington, 1992); C. T. Kulik and G. R. Oldham, "Job Diagnostic Survey," in Gael, *Handbook for Analyzing Jobs in Business, Industry and Government,* Vol. 2, pp. 936–959; G. Ledford, P. Mulvey, and P. LeBlanc, *The Rewards of Work* (Scottsdale, AZ: WorldatWork/Sibson, 2000).

29. Kulick and Oldham, "Job Diagnostic Survey."

30. Campion, "Ability Requirement Implications of Job Design: An Interdisciplinary Perspective."

31. D. E. Thompson and T. A. Thompson, "Court Standards for Job Analysis in Test Validation," *Personnel Psychology,* 1982, 35, pp. 865–874.

32. Equal Employment Opportunity Commission, *Technical Assistance Manual on the Employment Provisions (Title 1) of the Americans With Disabilities Act* (Washington, DC: author, 1992), pp. II-19 to II-21.

33. K. E. Mitchell, G. M. Alliger, and R. Morgfopoulos, "Toward an ADA-Appropriate Job Analysis," *Human Resource Management Review,* 1997, 7, pp. 5–26.

The Staffing Organizations Model

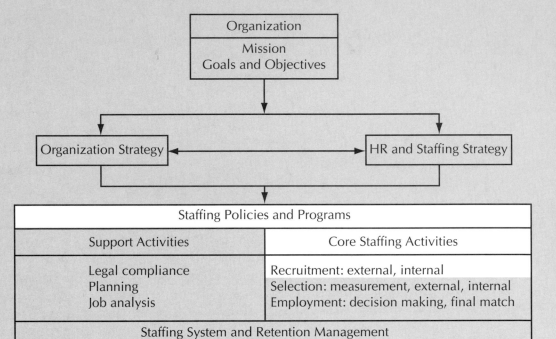

PART THREE

Staffing Activities: Recruitment

CHAPTER FIVE
External Recruitment

CHAPTER SIX
Internal Recruitment

CHAPTER FIVE

External Recruitment

Recruitment Planning
Organizational Issues
Administrative Issues

Strategy Development
Open versus Targeted Recruitment
Recruitment Sources
Choice of Sources
When to Look

Searching
Communication Message
Communication Medium

Applicant Reactions
Reactions to Recruiters
Reactions to the Recruitment Process

Transition to Selection

Legal Issues
Definition of Job Applicant
Affirmative Action Programs
Electronic Recruitment
Job Advertisements
Fraud and Misrepresentation

Summary

Discussion Questions

Applications

T he objective of the external recruitment process is to identify and attract job applicants from outside the organization. From among these applicants hiring decisions are to be made.

The recruitment process begins with a planning phase during which both organizational and administrative issues regarding the identification and attraction of applicants are addressed. Organizational issues include in-house versus external recruitment locations, individual versus cooperative recruitment alliances, and centralized versus decentralized recruitment functions. Administrative issues include requisitions; number and types of contracts; the recruitment budget; development of a recruitment guide; and the selection, training, and rewarding of recruiters.

Next, a recruitment strategy is formed in order to know where, how, and when to look for qualified applicants. Knowing where to look requires an understanding of open and targeted recruitment strategies. Knowing how to look requires an understanding of recruitment sources. Knowing when to look requires an understanding of lead time concerns and time sequence concerns.

Following the formation of strategy, the message to be communicated to job applicants is established, and it is decided which communication medium should be used to communicate the message. The message may be traditional, realistic, attractive, or targeted. It may be communicated with recruitment brochures or videos, advertisements, voice messages, videoconferencing, and online.

Special consideration must be given to applicant reactions to recruiters and the recruitment process in undertaking each of these phases of the external recruitment process. Close attention must also be given to legal issues. This includes consideration of the definition of job applicant, disclaimers, targeted recruitment, electronic recruitment, job advertisements, and fraud and misrepresentation.

RECRUITMENT PLANNING

Before actually identifying and attracting applicants to the organization, two issues must be resolved. First, organizational plans must be made to coordinate the identification and attraction of applicants. Second, administrative issues, such as the number of contacts to be made, recruiters to be used, and the budget to be spent, need to be considered to ensure that there are adequate resources to conduct a successful recruitment campaign.

Organizational Issues

The recruitment process in an organization can be organized in a variety of ways. It can be coordinated in-house or by an external recruitment agency. An organization can do its own recruiting or cooperate with other organizations in a recruitment alliance. Authority to recruit may be centralized or decentralized in the organization.

In-House versus External Recruitment Agency

Most organizational recruiting is done in-house. Smaller organizations may rely on external recruitment agencies rather than an in-house function to coordinate their recruitment efforts, as smaller organizations may not have the staff or budget to run their own recruitment functions. Organizations with low turnover rates may also prefer to use external recruitment agencies because they recruit so infrequently that it would not make sense to have a recruitment function of their own.

External recruitment agencies are growing in number. Some agencies, such as Elaine R. Shepherd Company, provide full-scale recruitment services ranging from identifying recruitment needs to advertising for applicants and checking references. Others, such as National Advertising Services, Inc., simply perform one recruitment activity. Although these services are expensive, the costs may be justified for organizations without a recruitment function or for employers with infrequent vacancies.

Large organizations and ones with frequent recruitment needs should have their own in-house recruitment function. An in-house function is needed to ensure that recruitment costs are minimized, recruitment searches are consistent from opening to opening, and the specific needs of the organization are being met.

Individual versus Cooperative Recruitment Alliances

Most organizations, especially ones that compete with one another in the same product and labor markets, do not cooperate with one another when recruiting. They do not cooperate because one organization's gain (a well-qualified hire) is another organization's loss (loss of a well-qualified candidate). Instead, they conduct their own recruitment programs to maintain a competitive advantage.

There are times, however, when even competitors may enter into cooperative recruitment alliances where arrangements are made to share recruitment resources. Smaller organizations may gain from cooperating with one another in order to minimize recruitment costs. If there is an abundance of applicants in the labor market, with enough good applicants to go around, it may also make sense to cooperate. For example, a group called Hospital Personnel Exchange in Melbourne, Florida, temporarily transfers personnel among hospitals to eliminate the problems of seasonal over- and understaffing for hospitals.

Recruitment alliances take many forms. One major form is government–employer partnership. Such partnerships can involve states or local communities. At the state level, Nebraska discovered that its residents were fleeing to California more than to any other state. In response, Nebraska ran ads at football games, on television, and in print, extolling the state's low cost of living and quality of life. Other states (Michigan, Maryland) have formed similar economic development initiatives to help employers lure qualified applicants to their locations. Even school districts have formed partnerships with local companies to facilitate the hiring of district high school graduates. Another form of partnership involves organizational alliances. The Atlanta Chamber of Commerce, for example, has developed a campaign to lure high-tech talent to the metro area. Syracuse, New York, employers formed a partnership to promote the area as a place to live and work. The goal is to transform Syracuse's permafrost image to a vibrant high-tech center.[1]

Even in a tight market it may make sense to cooperate when it comes to the spouses of job applicants. For example, the Personnel Association of Central Ohio (PACO) has a "trailing spouse network," where employers have a common pool of résumés from spouses following their partners' career move to central Ohio. All PACO members take from and contribute to the résumé pool. By doing so, they are able to hire those job applicants who are unable to relocate unless their spouses find a job in the same area.

Centralized versus Decentralized Recruitment

The recruitment of external job applicants can be centralized or decentralized by an organization. A centralized recruitment function is one for which recruitment activities are coordinated by a central group, usually HR professionals in the corporate offices. A decentralized recruitment system is one where recruitment activities are coordinated by individual business units or individual managers. In most larger organizations, the recruitment function is centralized. Although the ultimate hiring decision resides in the business unit, most organizations centralize the administrative activities associated with recruiting and screening applicants.

One advantage to a centralized recruitment function is that duplications of effort are eliminated. For example, when recruiting at a school, only one advertisement is placed rather than multiple ads for multiple business units. Another advantage to a centralized approach is that it ensures that policy is being interpreted consistently across business units. Along the same lines, a centralized function helps ensure compliance with relevant laws and regulations.

Some organizations do have decentralized recruitment functions. One advantage to decentralized recruitment is that recruitment efforts may be undertaken in a more timely manner when there are fewer people to recruit than when a centralized approach is used. Also, the recruitment search may be more responsive to the business unit's specific needs because those involved with recruitment may be closer to the day-to-day operations of the business unit than their corporate counterparts.

Administrative Issues

In the planning stage of recruitment, attention must be given to administrative as well as organizational issues.

Requisitions

A requisition is a formal document that authorizes the filling of a job opening indicated by the signatures of top management. Supervisors are not given discretion to authorize the filling of job openings. Top managers, rather than supervisors, are more likely to be familiar with staffing planning information for the entire organization, and their approval is needed instead to ensure that recruitment activities are coordinated with staffing planning activities.

An example of a requisition is shown in Exhibit 5.1. A well-developed requisition will specify clearly both the quantity and the quality (KSAOs) of labor to be hired. Hence, each requisition will list the number of openings per job and the minimum qualifications an applicant must have. Qualifications should be based on the job requirements matrix.

Many smaller organizations do not have requisitions. They should, however, for two reasons. First, the procedure ensures that staffing activities are consistent with the business plan of the organization. Second, it ensures that the qualifications of the job are clearly detailed so that a good person/job match is made.

Number of Contacts

The pool of applicants to be selected almost always needs to be larger than the number of applicants that will be hired eventually. Some applicants who are contacted may not be interested in the position, and others may not be qualified.

It is very difficult to identify the exact number of contacts needed to fill a particular vacant position. However, historical data is very useful in establishing the targeted number of contacts. If careful records are kept, then yield ratios can be calculated to summarize the historical data and to guide decisions about the number of contacts to make. A yield ratio expresses the relationship of applicant inputs to outputs at various decision points. For example, if 90 people were contacted (as identified by the number of résumés submitted) to fill one position, then the yield ratio would be 90:1. To fill two identical positions, it would be necessary to contact 180 applicants, based on the historical yield ratio of 90:1.

Types of Contacts

The types of contacts to be made depend on two factors. First, it is essential that the qualifications needed to perform the job are clearly established. This is done through the process of job analysis, which results in the job requirements matrix. The more clearly these requirements are specified, the fewer the number of applicants who must be contacted to yield a successful candidate, and the narrower the recruitment search can be.

Second, consideration must be given to the job search and choice process used by applicants. That is, the organization must be aware of where likely applicants search for employment opportunities and what it will take to attract them to the organization. One consistent finding in the research is that job seekers are more likely to find out about jobs through friends and family than they are through

EXHIBIT 5.1   Personnel Requisition

Position title	Division	Department	Department #
Salary/grade level	Work hours	Location	Reports to

Position eligible for the following incentive programs	
☐ Sales commission ☐ Key contributor ☐ Production incentive ☐ Other (specify) ☐ Management incentive ☐___ _____	Budgeted ☐ Replacement for: _____ ☐ Yes Transfer/term date_____ ☐ No ☐ Addition to staff

POSITION OVERVIEW

Instructions: (1) Complete Parts I, II, and III. (2) Attach position description questionnaire (if available) or complete reverse side.

I. POSITION PURPOSE: Briefly state in one or two sentences the primary purpose of this position.

II. POSITION QUALIFICATIONS: Lists the *minimum* education, formal training, and experience required to perform this position.

III. SPECIAL SKILLS: Lists the specialized clerical, administrative technical, or managerial skills needed to perform this position.

Do current or previous incumbents possess these qualifications and skills? If no, please describe the reason for these requirements when hiring for this position.

APPROVALS	**FOR HUMAN RESOURCES USE ONLY**
Party responsible for conducting second interview _____ Hiring supervisor/manager Date _____ Next approval level Date _____ Human resources approval Date	Posting date_____ Advertising date _____ Req number _____ Job number _____ Acceptance date _____Start date _____ New employee_____ Source _____

Source: Reprinted with permission from United Health Care Corporation.

employment agencies. Another consistent finding in the research is that job seekers rely heavily upon advertisements.[2]

How proactive the organization should be in soliciting applicants is a policy issue that arises when deciding on the types of contacts the organization will make.[3] Some organizations spend very few resources identifying contacts and actively soliciting applicants from these sources. For example, many times grocery stores simply post a job opening in their store window to fill a vacancy. Other organizations, however, are very proactive in making their presence known in the community. For example, Spartan Stores in Michigan has formed a partnership with a local high school so that they will have higher-quality applicants for entry-level positions in their grocery stores.[4] Many organizations are becoming involved with educational institutions through scholarships, adopt-a-school programs, mentorships, equipment grants, internships, and career planning services. NASA has programs to help educate teachers, students, and administrators on the application of science and math.[5] These approaches are likely to build goodwill toward an organization in the community and, as a result, foster greater informal contacts with job applicants.

Research has shown that greater employer involvement with prospective applicants is likely to improve the image of the organization. In turn, a better image of the organization is likely to result in prospective applicants pursuing contact with the organization.[6]

Recruitment Budget

The recruitment process is a very expensive component of organizational staffing. The average cost per hire is $8,924 for exempt employees and $865 for nonexempt employees (see Chapter 13). As a result of these high costs, many organizations are currently using cost containment programs in their recruitment efforts. Examples include the elimination of display advertising, greater reliance on state employment agencies, and the reduction of on-campus visits for college recruitment.[7] An example of a recruitment budget is shown in Exhibit 5.2.

The high costs of recruitment also point to the importance of establishing a well-developed recruitment budget. Two issues need to be addressed in establishing a recruitment budget. First, a top-down or a bottom-up procedure can be used to gather the information needed to formulate the budget. With a top-down approach, the budget for recruitment activities is set by top management on the basis of the business plan for the organization and on the basis of projected revenues. With a bottom-up approach, the budget for recruitment activities is set up on the basis of the specific needs of each business unit. The former approach works well when the emphasis is on controlling costs. The latter approach works better when commitment to the budget by business unit heads is the goal. A cumbersome, yet useful, method is to combine these two approaches into program-oriented budgeting in which there is heavy involvement in the budgeting process by both top management and business unit leaders.

EXHIBIT 5.2   Example of a Recruitment Budget for 500 New Hires

Administrative Expenses	
Staff	32,000
Supplies	45,000
Equipment	10,000
	$87,000

Recruiter Expenses	
Salaries	240,000
Benefits	96,000
Expenses	150,000
	$486,000

Candidate Expenses	
Travel	320,000
Lodging	295,000
Fees	50,000
Relocation	150,000
	$815,000

Total Recruitment Expenses
87,000 + 486,000 + 815,000 = $1,388,000

Total Cost per Hire
$1,388,000/500 new hires = $2,776

A second issue that needs to be addressed in establishing a well-developed recruitment budget is to decide whether to charge recruitment costs to business unit users. That is, should recruitment expenses be charged to HR or to the business unit using HR services? Most organizations charge the HR department for the costs of recruitment rather than the business unit users of recruitment activities. Perhaps this is done to encourage each business unit to use the recruitment services of the HR group. However, it should be recognized that this practice of not charging the business unit may result in the business unit users not being concerned about minimizing recruitment costs.

Development of a Recruitment Guide

A recruitment guide is a formal document that details the process to be followed to attract applicants to a job. It should be based on the organization's staffing flowcharts, if available. Included in the guide are details such as the time, money, and staff required to fill the job as well as the steps to be taken to do so. An example of a recruitment guide is shown in Exhibit 5.3.

Although a recruitment guide takes time to produce—time that may be difficult

---

EXHIBIT 5.3   Recruitment Guide for Director of Claims

Position: Director, Claims Processing

Reports to: Senior Director, Claims Processing

Qualifications: 4-year degree in business;
8 years experience in health care, including 5 in claims, 3 of
which should be in management

Relevant labor market: Regional midwest

Timeline: week of 1/17:   Conduct interviews with qualified applicants
2/1/01:   Targeted hire date

Activities to undertake to source well-qualified candidates:

Regional newspaper advertising

Request employee referrals

Contact regional health and life insurance associations

Call HR departments of regional health and life insurance companies to see if any
are outplacing any middle managers

Contact, if necessary, executive recruiter to further source candidates

Staff members involved:

HR Recruiting Manager
Sr. Director, Claims Processing
V.P. Human Resources
Potential peers and direct reports

Budget:

$3,000–$5,000

---

to find in the face of an urgent requisition to be filled—it is an essential document. It clarifies expectations for both the recruiter and the requesting department as to what will be accomplished, what the costs are, and who will be held accountable for the results. It also clarifies the steps that need to be taken to ensure that they are all followed in a consistent fashion and in accordance with organization policy as well as relevant laws and regulations. In short, a recruitment guide safeguards the interests of the employer, applicant, and recruiter.

Selecting Recruiters

Many studies have been conducted to assess desirable characteristics of recruiters. Reviews of these studies indicate that an ideal recruiter would possess the following characteristics:[8] strong interpersonal skills; knowledge about the organization, jobs, and career-related issues; technology skills (e.g., knowing how to mine databases, Internet recruiting); and enthusiasm about the organization and job candidates. These characteristics represent a start on developing a set of KSAOs to select recruiters.

Actual recruiters used by organizations come from a variety of sources, including HR professionals, line managers, and employees. Each of these sources generally has some distinct advantages and disadvantages relative to the list of desirable characteristics for recruiters. HR professionals may be very knowledgeable about career development issues and enthusiastic about the organization, but lack detailed knowledge regarding specific job responsibilities. Line managers may have detailed knowledge about the company and jobs that they supervise, but not be particularly knowledgeable about career development opportunities. Similarly, employees may have an in-depth understanding of their own jobs, but not have much knowledge of the larger organization. As a result of these tradeoffs, there is no single ideal source to draw recruiters from, and all recruiters need training to compensate for inevitable shortcomings.

Training Recruiters

Many recruiters who come from areas outside HR do not have any specialized training in HR. Hence, the training of recruiters is essential. Unfortunately, very few recruiters ever receive any training. Based on current organizational practices, recruiters should receive training in the following areas:[9] interviewing skills, job analysis, interpersonal aspects of recruiting, laws and regulations, forms and reports, company and job characteristics, and recruitment targets. Beyond these traditional areas, it is critical that recruiters receive training in some "nontraditional" areas: technology skills, marketing skills, working with other departments, and ethics.

First, in terms of technology skills, though access to large recruiting Web sites like *Monster.com* is to be expected, it must be recognized that many recruiters are mining these sites. Thus, recruiters must be instructed on accessing "niche" sites that specialize in a particular candidate cohort (e.g., *CFO.com* for finance executives), or personal Web pages, or even infiltrate corporate Web sites. In surfing the Internet, there are strategies to be learned, including "flipping" (finding résumés with links to a particular company), "peeling" (finding links to staff directories in URLs), and "x-raying" (identifying key employees by accessing those places on a company's Web site not directly accessible via links on the main Web page).

Second, recruiters must be trained in marketing and sales techniques. Some of these techniques are very simple, such as surfing résumé sites at night to get a leg up on the competition. Recruiters also need to be trained on how to be more creative in identifying candidates. For example, in tight labor markets, some recruiters are creative enough to stake out airports, temples and churches, and health clubs. One recruiter even flies from airport to airport just to "raid" the airport clubs for potential recruits. More generally, recruiters need instruction on how to sell their jobs to candidates. For example, recruiters can be trained on how to do market research, where job candidates are the market, to identify what they want. Related in developing their marketing skills, recruiters can be shown how to link up with other departments, such as marketing and public relations. For example, recruiters may be able to collaborate with marketing efforts to achieve a brand image that not only sells products to customers but sells the organization to prospective hires as well.

Finally, in their efforts to recruit more creatively, recruiters need training on ethical issues in recruitment. Is it ethical for a recruiter to recruit at a competitor's place of business? In parking lots? At weddings or funerals? Some recruiters will even lie to applicants in an effort to lure them. Some might even argue that the Internet strategies of "peeling," "flipping," and "x-raying" cross the ethical line. To ensure that recruiters behave ethically, standards should be developed and recruiters trained on these standards.[10]

Rewarding Recruiters

To reinforce effective recruitment practices, it is essential that recruiter performance—both effective recruitment behaviors and end results—be monitored and rewarded. Measures of performance commonly used include being on time for appointments, favorable comments from students, meeting affirmative action goals, and feedback from line managers. Unfortunately, very few organizations collect the data needed to make an objective assessment of these factors.

Rewards can be coupled with performance standards. For example, in one interesting study, it was shown that the efforts of U.S. Navy recruiters were substantially heightened when there was the promise of a monetary reward for meeting their recruitment quotas.[11] In addition to rewarding recruiters for the successful completion of results, rewards should also be provided for the demonstration of critical behaviors. For example, although good public relations activities may not result in more hires, they may result in more customer satisfaction, which is a major goal of most business organizations today. Accordingly, both the successful attraction of candidates and successful publicity concerning the organization should be rewarded.

Process Flow and Record Keeping

Prior to deciding where and how to look for applicants, it is essential that the organization prepare for the high volume of data entry and correspondence that accompanies the filling of vacancies. This high volume of correspondence and data entry results from the use of multiple sources to identify candidates (e.g., advertisements, walk-ins, employment agencies), the need to circulate the applicant's credentials to multiple parties (e.g., hiring managers, human resources), and the need to communicate with candidates regarding the status of their application.

If process flow and record keeping issues are not addressed before the recruitment search, then the organization may become overwhelmed with correspondence that is not dealt with in a timely and professional manner; in turn, the organization may lose well-qualified applicants.

To manage the process flow and record keeping requirements, an information system must be created for recruitment efforts. An effective information system for recruitment purposes allows the candidate, hiring manager, and HR representatives to know the status of a candidate's application file at any point in time. The information system "tracks" the status of the applicant's file as it flows through the recruitment process in the organization. The information system can also periodically issue reports on the timeliness and accuracy with which applicant information is being processed.

The point of entry for most applicants is the presentation of a résumé and/or application to the organization. Upon receipt of these materials, a file is created by the organization for each applicant. Once a file has been created, many steps must be taken to process this file. These steps include the coding (manually or with an optical scanner) of the applicant's credentials, the recording of EEO data to be reported to the federal government, the coding of the source from which the applicant came (e.g., advertisement, school, employment agency) in order to evaluate the effectiveness of each source, the routing (manually or by computer) of the file to hiring managers, and the sending of a letter to the applicant acknowledging receipt of their materials.

As the applicant progresses through the hiring process, additional record keeping is required. Information needs to be kept as to who has reviewed the file, how long each has had the file to be reviewed, what decision has been reached (e.g., reject, invite for a visit, conduct a second interview), and what step needs to be taken next (e.g., arrange for a flight and accommodations, schedule an interview). Throughout the process, communications with the applicant must also be tracked to ensure that applicants know when and if their credentials will receive further review and also to know what other steps, if any, they need to take to secure employment.

Even when an applicant is rejected for a position, there are record-keeping responsibilities. The applicant's file should be stored in the event that another search arises that requires someone with the applicant's qualifications. Such storage should be for a maximum of one year (see Legal Issues, below).

STRATEGY DEVELOPMENT

Once the recruitment planning phase is complete, the next phase is the development of a strategy. In essence, strategy development helps assess those issues fundamental to the organization: open versus targeted recruitment, recruitment sources, choice of sources, and when to look. Each of these issues will be addressed in turn.

Open versus Targeted Recruitment

Once a requisition has been received, one of the most difficult aspects of recruitment is knowing where to look for applicants. In theory, the pool of potential job applicants is the eligible labor force (employed, unemployed, discouraged workers, new labor force entrants, and labor force reentrants). In practice, the organization must narrow down this vast pool into segments or strata of workers believed to be the most desirable applicants for the organization. To do so, organizations can use open or targeted recruitment methods.

Open Recruitment

With an open recruitment approach, organizations cast a wide net to identify potential applicants for specific job openings. Very little effort is made in segmenting the market into applicants with the most desirable KSAOs. This approach is very passive in that anyone can apply for an opening. All who apply for a position are considered regardless of their qualifications. This approach is sometimes taken by public sector organizations, which typically have a high volume of applicants for positions. The advantage to an open recruitment method is that it is often seen as being "fair" by applicants in that everyone has the opportunity to apply. The disadvantage to this approach is that qualified applicants may be overlooked as no concerted effort is made to identify those markets with the most qualified applicants.

Targeted Recruitment

A targeted recruitment approach is one whereby the organization identifies those segments of the labor market where qualified candidates are likely to be. In doing so, qualified candidates are less likely to be overlooked. Also, this system may be seen as less fair because not all applicants are targeted. Yet, the system may be actually more fair in that people with special availabilities (e.g., teenagers, older workers, people with disabilities), who are sometimes unaware of positions with open recruitment systems, can be targeted for recruitment efforts. To target the labor market for applicants, consideration should be given to the job requirements matrix, demographics, geographic areas, recruitment sources, applicant interests, and special availabilities.

Job Requirements Matrix   As with all aspects of staffing, the starting point for targeted recruitment is the job requirements matrix. By knowing the KSAOs needed to perform the job, the applicant pool is narrowed. For example, the fact that a college degree is required to perform the job eliminates those candidates with a high school degree only. The fact that a major in statistics is required eliminates from the sample the nonstatistics majors with a college degree. This iterative process is followed for all the KSAOs specified in the job requirements matrix.

Demographics   Demographics can also be used to target the applicant pools. Older workers are often a particularly attractive group of potential recruits. Accordingly, employers need to recruit in locations frequented by older workers, such as senior centers or in newspapers (older individuals are more likely to read newspapers). Care must be taken not to use demographics to systematically exclude women and minorities from the applicant pool. Job-related demographics, as shown in the job requirements matrix, can and should be used. For example, some positions may require a certain number of years of experience.

Geographic Area   In targeting the applicant pool, one can look on a local, county, regional, state, national, or international basis. In general, the lower the skill levels required to perform the job, the more employers narrow the pool down to close geographic proximity to the organization. This is done to minimize recruitment and selection costs. Chances are that with low-skill jobs, the availability of those people will be high in the local labor market. Hence, an employer will not have to pay for ads in national magazines, relocation costs, and so forth.

On the other hand, for high-skill jobs, the employer is more likely to broaden the search. Although more costly, this is done to locate people who have the requisite high level of KSAOs needed to perform the job.

Recruitment Sources   A critical factor in narrowing down the applicant pool is an organization's previous successes and failures with alternative recruitment sources. Through previous searches, for example, an organization may find that the yield of high-quality candidates is best when applicants from professional societies, rather than applicants from placement agencies, are attracted.

Tradition   Some organizations have a rich history of successful recruitment with various segments of the population. Through their affirmative action efforts, for example, some organizations have hired many successful minority individuals from schools with large minority enrollments. In turn, these schools provide excellent services to these companies for the placement of their students. As a result, there is a tradition of certain schools placing students with certain employers.

Former Employees   It is typical for organizations to treat employees who quit as "traitors"—where the relationship ends once the employee clears his or her desk. It is becoming clear that this is a mistake. Many organizations have put in place programs to recruit, when the need and opportunity arises, former employees. There are several advantages in recruiting former employees, including reduced recruiting costs, a known track record, and pride in enticing former employees back into the fold. Some considerations to keep in mind in instituting these "boomerang" programs are: (1) create "alumni" programs where former employees may be kept in the loop about company news and developments so as to maintain close ties; (2) give employees "get out of jail free" cards where they could be rehired without all of the typical bureaucratic hiring hassles; (3) restore employees to their seniority and benefit levels prior to their leaving; (4) put former employees on external job posting lists; (5) at the time the employee resigns, show regret and tell them you'd like to have them back.[12]

Passive Job Seekers   Most individuals are not actively seeking jobs, including those whom a company might like to hire and who might be enticed to join the company. Thus, special effort must be exerted to recruit these so-called "passive job seekers." These passive job seekers may be of several types. Some are so-called discouraged workers who are no longer part of the labor force. Others are gainfully employed and very happy to remain with a current employer. Another segment may be unwilling to relocate to a different geographic area. Many people, for example, have family constraints that prevent them from moving. The location of these various types of passive job seekers, and what may attract them to the employer, is likely to be different. Thus, recruiting tactics will have to vary.

The Military   For many positions, the military is an excellent source for recruiting talented workers. Most individuals who leave the military are relatively young, diverse, and often highly trained and well disciplined. Where can organizations recruit these individuals? One option is to hire placement firms who already have made inroads into the military. Another option is to advertise in periodicals like the *Navy Times*. Yet another option is to use the Internet. Indeed, there are Web sites such as *Vetjobs* that offer job posting capability and résumé searching. The U.S. Army has even developed a program, the Partnership for Youth Success (PaYS), that links a soldier and prospective employer well before the soldier's enlistment ends.[13]

Special Availabilities   Employers traditionally have limited themselves to applicants who are members of the labor force and are between the ages 18 and 65. This traditional approach has excluded many potential applicants who are fully capable of performing the job even though they do not fit this traditional description. Many organizations have been forced to break away from this traditional view in order to adequately fill jobs when there is a shortage of entry-level employees. Examples of such potential applicants include teenagers, older workers, welfare recipients, people with disabilities, the homeless, and homemakers.

Although they may not be able to work as many hours as more senior employees, teenagers may be less costly to hire. And their initial employment experiences, if favorable, may lead them to pursue other jobs in the organization as they acquire additional skills and education.

Older people who have withdrawn from the labor force represent another group with special availabilities. The number of older workers in the labor force continues to grow at a rapid pace. The older worker may be inclined to return to the workforce to enhance retirement funds or to meet social needs by working with others. As a result of welfare reform passed during the Clinton administration, millions of individuals formerly on welfare support now are vying for work. It is estimated that in this country the number of people with disabilities is about 36 million. People with disabilities include not only those needing wheelchairs but also those with AIDS, lower-back pain, mental illness, and a host of other physically challenging conditions. Many organizations have taken advantage of this large population to fill vacant jobs on an ongoing basis. For example, DuPont Merck has entered into a partnership with the Association for the Rights of Citizens with Mental Retardation to fill permanent jobs with individuals who have developmental disabilities. Homeless people do not have normal access to the labor market. Through rehabilitation centers, churches, and shelters they may receive the training and assistance needed to hold a job. Days Inn, for example, has hired the homeless since 1988, and about half of those employed have turned out to be successful by company standards.[14] Many women are forced to enter the labor force because of the death of a spouse, a divorce, or an abusive home situation. Many of their skills as homemakers are transferable to jobs in the labor force. A group that helps them meet their needs, including employment, is the Displaced Homemakers Network in Washington, DC.

Key Shortages   At times, key shortages absolutely demand targeted recruitment. For example, a brief perusal of the "help wanted" section of your local newspaper will attest to the growing disparity between the demand for high-technology employees and the availability of such employees. One recent study suggested that there is a labor shortage of nearly 200,000 jobs in the information technology area alone. One of the authors currently has five different advertisements for conferences promising the "inside scoop" for how to recruit high-tech employees. The fees for such conferences, which usually last two days, typically cost $1,500 to $2,500. Finally, here are some additional tips regarding how employers can remedy their shortage of high-technology employees:[15]

1. *Incentives.* Monetary incentives, such as signing bonuses, are becoming increasingly common with high-tech employees. Thus, it may take financial incentives to lure high-tech employees. However, employers should remember to promote other aspects of the job that high-tech employees may find attractive, such as flexible working hours, casual dress, and job autonomy.

Because high-tech employees may be more attracted to these attributes than the average employee, wherever possible, these attributes should be advertised and promoted.

2. *Consider the source.* Naturally, high-tech employees are more likely to be connected to the tools of their trade (the computer), so employers should consider posting their positions on their Web site. Some companies have found that buying banner ads on the Internet, where people can click on a banner to go to the company's Web page and complete an application, have resulted in an increase in applications. Other companies have even gone overseas to countries such as India to seek out workers in high-demand jobs.

3. *Research.* One high-tech headhunter buys names of high-tech employees from a research company for $40 a name, and then hires college students at $15–20 per hour to make initial contact with the names. Once contact is made, the headhunter becomes personally involved in trying to lure the person to join a client organization.

4. *Temporary employees.* If the organization has a temporary problem (e.g., maintenance of a mainframe computer until employees transition to a new system), employers can use temporary employment firms such as Manpower to tap certain skills that are needed for certain projects.

5. *Training.* Employers often overestimate the technical expertise needed to solve many computer problems. With a few weeks of training, many current employees are able to provide important assistance to employees with common problems such as printing to a new network printer. Thus, employers should consider training current employees to manage ordinary computer problems.

Recruitment Sources

Fortunately for employers, when conducting a search for applicants, they do not have to identify each possible job applicant. Instead, there are institutions in our economy where job seekers congregate. Moreover, these institutions often act as intermediaries between the applicant and employer to ensure that a match takes place. These institutions are called recruitment sources or methods in staffing. Some are very conventional and have been around for a long time. Others are more innovative and have less of a track record.

Unsolicited

It is a common practice for employers to accept applications from job applicants who physically walk into the organization to apply for a job or who send in résumés. The usual point of contact for unsolicited walk-ins or résumé senders is the receptionist in smaller organizations and the employment office in larger organizations.

Organizations that rely on unsolicited walk-ins and résumé senders must be prepared to deal with the physical demands created by this process. In order for walk-ins not to disrupt the normal work flow in an organization, a contact person who is responsible for processing such applicants needs to be assigned. Space needs to be created for walk-ins to complete application blanks and preemployment tests. Hours need to be established when applicants can apply for jobs. Procedures must be in place to ensure that data from walk-ins and résumé senders are entered into the applicant flow process. If these steps are not taken, not only may the organizational work flow be disrupted but the image of the organization may be tarnished as well. If walk-ins or résumé senders are treated as being unexpected intruders, they may communicate a very negative image about the organization in the community. In turn, this negative image may have a chilling effect on other recruitment efforts by the organization (e.g., advertising). Similarly, unsolicited résumés should immediately be acknowledged by sending the applicants a card or letter to let them know that their résumé has been received and how it will be processed.

Employee Referrals and Networks

Employees currently working for an employer are a valuable source for finding job applicants. The vast majority of organizations accept referrals, though only about half have formal programs. SRA International has recruited nearly half of its employees through referrals. The employees can refer people they know to their employer for consideration. In some organizations, a cash bonus is given to employees who refer job candidates who prove to be successful on the job for a given period of time. To ensure that there are adequate returns on bonuses for employee referrals, it is essential that there be a good performance appraisal system in place to measure the performance of the referred new hire. There also needs to be a good applicant tracking system to ensure that new hire performance is maintained over time before a bonus is offered. Other organizations use more creative incentives. Lands' End, based in Dodgeville, Wisconsin, offers a drawing for each employee referral. The winner receives a free trip to a Green Bay Packers football game. Most bonuses range from a few hundred dollars to $1,000.

Referral programs have many potential advantages, including low cost/hire, high-quality hires, decreased hiring time, and an opportunity to strengthen the bond with current employees. Employee referral programs sometimes fail to work because current employees lack the motivation or ability to make referrals. Employees sometimes don't realize the importance of recruitment to the organization. As a result, the organization may need to encourage employee participation by providing special rewards and public recognition along with bonuses for successful referrals. Employees may not be able to match people with jobs because they do not know about open vacancies or the requirements needed to fill them. Hence, communications regarding job vacancies and the requirements needed to fill these vacancies need to be constantly provided to employees.

Though not a formal referral program, many organizations use networks to identify potential hires. These networks can be one's own network of personal contacts, or they can be formal programs that keep an active database of professional contacts.

Advertisements

A convenient way to attract job applicants is to write an ad that can be placed in newspapers, trade journals, and the like. Advertisements can also be recorded and placed on radio or television. Cable television channels, for example, sometimes have "job shows." Advertisements can be very costly and need to be monitored closely for yield. Advertisements in some periodicals may yield more and better-qualified candidates than others. By carefully monitoring the results of each ad, the organization can then make a more informed decision as to which ads should be run next time a position is vacant. To track ads, each ad should be coded to assess the yield. Then, as résumés come into the organization in response to the ad, they can be recorded, and the yield for that ad can be calculated.

Coding an ad is a very straightforward process. For example, in advertising for a vice president of HR, ads may be placed in a variety of HR periodicals, such as *HR Magazine,* and business publications, such as the *Wall Street Journal.* To track responses sent, applicants for the vacant position are asked to respond to Employment Department A for *HR Magazine* and Employment Department B for the *Wall Street Journal.* (The other part of the return address is, of course, the same for each periodical.) As résumés arrive, those that are addressed to Department A are coded as responses from the *HR Magazine*, and those addressed to Department B are coded as responses from the *Wall Street Journal.*

Recruiting Online

Recent surveys indicate that 85% of recruiters utilize the Internet to source job candidates. Likewise, most applicants for professional jobs now include the Internet in their job search repertoire. Millions of job seekers submit their résumés on the Web every year, and there are tens of thousands of job sites online. More than half of the résumés Microsoft receives are over the Internet. One difficulty in use of the Internet in recruiting is that many sites specifically designed for recruitment become defunct. Conversely, new recruitment Web sites come online on nearly a daily basis. Thus, one cannot assume that the recruiting sites used in the past will be the best ones in the future, or that they even will exist.

There are four primary ways companies use the Web for recruiting: job postings on job boards, searching Web-based applicant databases, job postings on an organization's own Web site, and mining databases. Each of these is described below.

Job Postings on Internet Job Boards One central means of recruiting on the Internet is through online job boards. For example, *Monster.com,* perhaps the largest recruiting site, allows access to both applicants, who can search for positions by location and job category, and recruiters, who can search among applicants by a wide array of search factors. Most of these boards are collection nodes for job postings, listing the jobs from many different companies that applicants can assess. Other systems focus on résumé screening and applicant management. Still other systems are a combination of the two. For example, *webhire.com* allows organizations to search a private candidate pool as well as a large résumé database, create and approve job requisitions online, manage recruiting tasks, track the progress of open positions and candidates, and report on recruiting metrics (time-to-hire, cost per hire, EEO). Organizations need to ensure that they not only post jobs on the large boards such as *Monster.com,* but also smaller boards that may be targeted by occupation (there are job boards for jobs ranging from nurses to geologists to metal workers), by industry (sports, chemicals), or by location (cities, states, or regions often have their own sites).

Searching Web-Based Databases   As opposed to actively posting jobs online, another (but not mutually exclusive) means of recruiting on the Web is to search for applicants without ever having posted a position. Under this process, applicants submit their résumés online, which are then forwarded to employers when they meet the employer's criteria. Such systems allow searching the databases according to various search criteria, such as job skills, years of work experience, education, major, grade-point average, and so forth. It costs applicants anywhere from nothing to $200 or more to post their résumé or other information on the databases. For organizations, there is always a cost. The exact nature of the cost depends both on the database(s) to which the organization subscribes, and on the services requested. More databases allow organizations to search according to Boolean logic. For example, a recruiter interested in locating résumés of prospective human resource managers for a Miami-based manufacturing facility might type "human resources + Miami + manufacturing."

Exhibit 5.4 provides a listing of some Web-based systems that employers can use. Many of these combine the features of Internet job boards and Web-based databases so that employers can post jobs and search existing résumés at the same time. For example, though not listed in the exhibit, many Web browsers contain multipurpose databases. Yahoo! (*www.yahoo.com*) maintains a career center that contains more than 2.5 million résumés and allows employers to post jobs, which then are fed into a database of thousands of jobs posted weekly.

Job Postings on Organization's Web Site   Most large companies have a special section on their Web site that describes employment opportunities in the organization and often provides formal job postings. Many of these Web sites allow applicants to apply online. Despite the widespread use of job postings on an organization's Web site, many of these Web sites do not live up to potential. Many have been likened to little more than post-office boxes where applicants can send

EXHIBIT 5.4 **List of Recruiting Web Sites**

www.careershop.com
Presents job posting, job distribution, résumé collection and management, and candidate searching and tracking. Applicants can post résumés and search for positions.

www.careerbuilder.com
Gives job seekers access to more than 70 sources of print and online want ads. Search over 100,000 new listings per week. Employers can post jobs and search the database. Site includes data on "passive" job candidates.

www.hotjobs.com
Offers job seekers a place to post résumés and organizations a place to post job openings. Provides job tips and career advice. Includes Resumix Internet recruiter that allows employers to post jobs that will be referred to job posting sites viewed by job seekers.

www.flipdog.com
Mines the sites of more than 50,000 employers and gathers open positions in one source. Allows job seekers to post résumés and search for positions by location. When a match is found, candidates receive e-mail notification.

www.monster.com
Allows job seekers to post their résumés and search the database of roughly half a million job postings. Also contains a career center that includes more than 1,700 pages of career advice. Employer section allows recruiters to search database.

www.webhire.com
Searches the Internet, as well as job boards and career databases, to locate candidates. Ranks résumés according to organizational specifications and automatically sends personalized e-mails to selected candidates.

www.headhunter.net
Allows job seekers to search database of over 250,000 jobs by 13 criteria. Allows applicants to post résumés. Includes career resource center. For employers, site contains over 2 million résumés.

www.brassring.com
Applicants can create their own customized account where they can post their résumé or tailor their search from the more than 60,000 jobs in the database.

their résumés. A study of the best practices of the Web sites of 140 high-profile organizations indicates seven features for high-impact Web sites:

1. A site layout that is easily navigated and provides information about the organization's culture.
2. "Job cart" function that allows prospective applicants to search and apply for multiple positions within the organization.
3. Résumé builders where applicants can easily submit their education, background, and experience.

4. Detailed information on career opportunities.
5. Clear graphics.
6. Personal search engines that allow applicants to create profiles in the organization's database and update the data later.
7. Self-assessment inventories to help steer college graduates toward appealing career paths.

We have more to say on organizational Web sites in the Communication Medium section of this chapter.

Mining Databases   Though controversial, as noted earlier, many recruiters use various ploys ("flipping," "peeling") to mine organizational and other databases to obtain intelligence on passive candidates. The power of this strategy is that it allows organizations to identify passive candidates, who may be the best qualified but otherwise might not surface. The disadvantage is that many of these passive candidates may not be interested, and there are ethical issues to consider as well (how would you feel about a competitor "x-raying" your Web site for information you never intended for them to have?).

Web-based recruiting offers many advantages to employers. There is no other method of reaching as many people with a job posting. This advantage is particularly important when filling large numbers of positions, when the labor market is national or international, or when the unique nature of the necessary qualifications require casting a wide net. Furthermore, Web-based recruiting provides faster access to candidates. Most systems have résumés in system within 24 hours of receipt (many nearly instantaneously), and their searchable databases facilitate access to candidates with desired qualifications. It is commonly argued that Internet recruiting presents cost advantages, and if one is comparing the cost of an ad in the *Los Angeles Times* with the price for access to an online database, this is no doubt true. For a small organization seeking to hire a small number of applicants or for low-skilled positions, however, they likely can find a qualified applicant with less expense. Finally, there is administrative convenience (many individuals in the same organization can access the database, it eliminates much "paper pushing").

Some of the past limitations of Web-based recruiting—specifically, that the vast majority of applicants are in the technology area and that most Web users are white males—seem to be improving. On the other hand, recruiting on the Web is not a magical solution for matching applicants to employers. Despite some claims to the contrary, decision makers need to be involved in the process. In fact, some large organizations have created new positions for individuals to manage the Internet sites and databases. It is important to remember that no matter what lofty promises a system makes for screening out undesirable applicants, the system is only as good as the search criteria, which generally make fairly rough cuts (e.g., based on years of experience, educational background, broad areas of expertise, etc.). Like all sources, the Web must be evaluated against other alternatives to

ensure that it is delivering on its considerable promise, and employers must remember that, for the time being, it is unlikely that the Web can be a sole source
for recruiting applicants. The costs of Internet recruiting must be weighed against
the benefits, including the number of qualified applicants, the relative quality of
these applicants, and other criteria such as offer acceptance rates, turnover, and so
forth.[16]

Colleges and Placement Offices

Colleges are a source of people with specialized skills for professional positions.
Most colleges have a placement office or officer who is in charge of ensuring that
a match is made between the employer's interests and the graduating student's
interests. Recruitment at colleges is usually performed at no cost to the employer.

In most cases, the placement office is the point of contact with colleges. It
should be noted, however, that not all students use the services of the placement
office. Students sometimes avoid placement offices because they believe they will
be competing against the very best students and will be unlikely to receive a job
offer. Additional points of contact for students at colleges include individual professors, department heads, professional fraternities, honor societies, recognition
societies, and national professional societies. Sometimes small colleges are overlooked as a recruitment source by organizations because the small number of
students does not make it seem worth the effort to visit. In order to present a larger
number of students to choose from, some small colleges band together in consortia.
For example, the Oregon Liberal Arts Placement Consortia provide a centralized
recruitment source for eight public and private small colleges and universities. It
is essential that appropriate colleges and universities be selected for a visit. Fortunately, many sound guidelines have been written on how to select campuses to
visit.[17] A summary of the recommended factors to consider in selecting campuses
follows:

1. It is essential that schools have degree programs in the areas where job
   openings exist in the organization. To make the match between the curriculum and organizational needs, there must be careful assessment of the job
   requirements matrix as it relates to the specific classes offered on campus.
   Conversation with faculty members is often required to make this match, as
   the description of courses in a course bulletin may be out of date.

2. Many surveys have been conducted on the quality of the educational setting.
   Each year, *Business Week* reports the results of a survey on top MBA programs in the country, and *Peterson's Guide* reports on the quality of undergraduate programs. Care must be exercised in reviewing these reports.
   Though helpful in establishing school reputation, they may fail to consider
   important criteria to judge reputation. For example, to ensure that students
   are being provided with state-of-the-art information, attention should be paid

to the research quality of the faculty. Unfortunately, few surveys use faculty research quality as a criterion in the assessments.

3. The closer the school is to the organization, the less the transportation cost involved in recruitment may be. Many organizations have found that turnover rates are decreased by recruiting locally. Job applicants already have a realistic idea of what it is like to live in the area.

4. The quality of applicants, as measured by both the performance of students while on campus and their subsequent performance on the job, must also be assessed. Hence, one should monitor student GPAs, work experience levels, and other KSAOs while on campus. Also, one should monitor the performance and turnover levels of new hires from various campuses.

5. Previous success at attracting applicants on various campuses should be considered. Indicators to pay attention to here include overall yield ratios, as well as specific ones for women and minorities.

After selecting schools to visit, attention must be devoted to developing a college recruitment program for each school. A uniform college recruitment program is destined to fail. Schools vary considerably on the criteria just reviewed as well as on other characteristics. Consequently, the organization must target its efforts to the specific characteristics of each school. With large schools, the organization may need to target its efforts at the program level as well. Issues to consider in targeting a college recruitment program are life cycle, quality, and structure.

The relationship between college or university placement offices and organizations follows a life cycle. Just as individuals are born, grow, mature, and decline over time, so do relationships between placement offices and hiring organizations. Steps taken by hiring organizations need to be different depending on the stage of the relationship. For example, as an organization enters into a recruitment arrangement with a school or program for the first time, it is unlikely to recruit very many students because the new recruits are a somewhat unknown commodity. As a result, the organization is unlikely to offer scholarships to students at that school or program.

As its relationship to the school grows and matures, however, the organization is likely to recruit more candidates and offer scholarships. More candidates are recruited because they are now a proven commodity, and scholarships are offered to maintain a steady flow of well-qualified candidates into the organization. Other recruitment activities, such as internships and advertising, also need to be considered in relation to the life cycle.

There are several ways an organization can establish a high-quality relationship on campus. A critical task is to establish a good relationship with the placement director. Although most placement directors are eager to make the organization's recruitment process productive and pleasant, there also are many aspects where they exert additional influence over the success of the organization's recruitment of high-quality graduates (e.g., informal discussions with students about good employers, alerting recruiters to impressive candidates). Another way to establish a high-quality relationship with a school is to maintain a presence. This presence can take various forms, and increasingly organizations are becoming more creative and aggressive in establishing relationships with universities and their students. Some investment banks, consulting firms, and other companies shell out $500,000 and more per school to fund career seminars, gifts for students, and fancy dinners. Ernst R Young has built a study room at Columbia University, and GE has sponsored an e-commerce lab at the University of Connecticut.[18]

Of course, relationship building is not just about doling out money, and smaller organizations are not likely to have the resources. Beyond building a good relationship with the placement director and providing financial support, recruiters should build relationships with other key people (associate dean, other placement office staff, key faculty, members of student organizations). It also is important to remember to keep in touch with these people beyond the day or week the recruiter visits campus. Finally, care must be taken to obtain permission for all activities. One dot-com company was banned from a high-prestige MBA program for offering students BMW signing bonuses, among other nonconventional ploys, without alerting career services of their plans.[19]

In terms of structure, a college recruitment program can but does not have to be housed in a single location. A college recruitment program may have multiple structures depending on the stage of its relationship with colleges and depending on the requirements of the organization and program. For example, recruiters may work out of a central office on a full-time basis. They travel to schools to recruit and may recruit by region, size of school, program, or special characteristics of the school. Alternatively, managers can be assigned schools within their geographic area, where they recruit on a part-time basis.

Employment Agencies

A source of nonexempt employees and lower-level exempt employees is employment agencies. These agencies contact, screen, and present applicants to employers for a fee. The fee is contingent on successful placement of a candidate with an employer and is a percentage (around 25%) of the candidate's starting salary. During difficult economic periods, employers cut back on the use of these agencies and/or attempt to negotiate lower fees in order to contain costs.

Care must be exercised in selecting an employment agency. It is a good idea to check the references of employment agencies with other organizations that have already used their services. Allegations abound regarding the shoddy practices of some of these agencies. They may, for example, flood the organization with résumés. Unfortunately, this flood may include both qualified and unqualified applicants. A good agency will screen out unqualified applicants and not attempt to dazzle the organization with a large volume of résumés. Poor agencies may misrepresent the organization to the candidate and the candidate to the organization. Misrepresentation may take place when the agency is only concerned about a quick placement (and fee) without regard to the costs of poor future relationships with clients. A good agency will be in business for the long run and not misrepresent information and invite turnover. Poor agencies may pressure managers to make decisions when they are uncertain or do not want to do so. Also, they may "go around" the HR staff in the organization to negotiate "special deals" with individual managers. Special deals may result in paying higher fees than agreed on with HR and overlooking qualified minorities and women. A good agency will not pressure managers, make special deals, or avoid the HR staff. Finally, it is important to have a signed contract in place where mutual rights and responsibilities are laid out.

Executive Search Firms

For higher-level professional positions or jobs with salaries of $100,000 and higher, executive search firms, or "headhunters," may be used. Like employment agencies, these firms contact, screen, and present résumés to employers. The difference between employment agencies and search firms lies in two primary areas. First, search firms typically deal with higher-level positions than employment agencies. Second, search firms are more likely to operate on the basis of a retainer rather than a contingency. Search firms that operate on a retainer are paid regardless of whether a successful placement is made. The advantage of operating this way, from the hiring organization's standpoint, is that it aligns the interests of the search firm with those of the organization. Thus, search firms operating on retainer do not feel compelled to put forward candidates just so their contingency fee can be paid. Moreover, a search firm on retainer may be less likely to give up if the job is not filled in a few weeks.

The other side of retainer fees, particularly when the economy is growing and good candidates are hard to find, is completing the search. According to some sources, completion rates (percentage of searches that end with the position being filled) are at an all-time low. Whether contracting with a search firm on a contingency or retainer basis, companies cannot take a completely hands-off approach to the recruitment process; they need to keep tabs on the progress of the search and, if necessary, "light a fire" under search firms. To expedite the search process, some companies are going online. *Monster.com*'s Web site has an area that caters to executives. Other executive-oriented Web sites where employers can post positions are *6figurejobs.com* and *ExecuNet.com*. A disadvantage of most online databases is that they do not include passive candidates—executives who may be highly qualified for the position but who are not actively looking. Some companies, such as Direct Search of the United States, sell internal corporate telephone directories to organizations and search firms looking for executives. This practice is, of course, controversial, but it appears to be legal as a copyright on a directory generally only covers artwork and unique design features. For more information about executive recruiters, see *www.kennedypub.com*. This publication lists over 8,000 recruiters along with their specialty.

Professional Associations and Meetings

Many technical and professional organizations have annual meetings around the country at least once a year. Many of these groups run a placement service for their members. There may be a fee to recruit at these meetings. This source represents a way to attract applicants with specialized skills or professional credentials. Also, some meetings represent a way to attract women and minorities. For example, the National Council of Black Engineers and Scientists holds an annual meeting.[20] In addition to having placement activities at annual conventions, professional associations also may have a placement function throughout the year. For example, it is a common practice in professional association newsletters to advertise both positions available and interested applicants. Others may also have a computerized job and applicant bank.

State Employment Services

All states have an employment or job service. These services are funded by employer-paid payroll taxes.[21] This service is provided by the states to help secure employment for those seeking it, particularly those currently unemployed. Typically, these services refer low- to middle-level employees to employers. For jobs to be filled properly, the hiring organization must maintain a close relationship with the employment service. Job qualifications need to be communicated clearly to ensure that proper screening takes place by the agency. Positions that have been filled must be reported promptly to the agency so that résumés are not sent for closed positions. The state employment services are now all networked together through the Interstate Job Bank Center, which has an online job search service to match organizations and job seekers. Organizations no longer need to separately contact each state employment service.[22]

The U.S. Department of Labor has provided the funding for states to develop one-step career centers that will provide workers with various programs, benefits, and opportunities related to finding jobs. The centers' emphasis is on providing customer-friendly services that reach large segments of the population and are fully integrated with state employment services. The state of Illinois provides customized applicant screening and referral to employers so efficiently that some employers, like Jewel Companies, a grocery store chain, use the service as an extension of its HR department.[23]

Outplacement Services

Some organizations retain an outplacement firm to provide assistance to employees who are losing their jobs. Outplacement firms usually offer job seekers assistance in the form of counseling and training to help facilitate a good person/job match. Most large outplacement firms have job banks, which are computerized listings of applicants and their qualifications. Registration by employers to use these job banks is usually free.

Larger organizations experiencing a downsizing may have their own internal outplacement function and perform the activities traditionally found in external outplacement agencies. They may also hold in-house job fairs. The reason for this in-house function is to save on the costs of using an external outplacement firm and to build the morale of those employees who remain with the organization and are likely to be affected by their friends' loss of jobs.

Community Agencies

Some agencies in local communities may also provide outplacement assistance for the unemployed who cannot afford outplacement services. The applicants who use these services may also be listed with a state employment service as well. Community agencies may also offer counseling and training.

Job Fairs

Professional associations, schools, employers, the military, and other interested organizations hold career or job fairs to attract job applicants. Typically, the sponsors of a job fair will meet in a central location with a large facility in order to provide information, collect résumés, and screen applicants. Often, there is a fee for employers to participate. Job fairs may provide both short- and long-term gains. In the short run, the organization may identify qualified applicants. In the long run, it may be able to enhance its visibility in the community, which, in turn, may improve its image and ability to attract applicants for jobs.

For a job fair to yield a large number of applicants, it must be advertised well in advance. Moreover, advertisements may need to be placed in specialized publications likely to attract minorities and women. In order for an organization to attract quality candidates from all of those in attendance, the organization must be able to differentiate itself from all the other organizations competing for applicants at the job fair. To do so, giveaway items such as mugs and key chains with company logos can be distributed to remind the applicants of employment opportunities at a particular organization. An even better promotion may be to provide attendees at the fair with assistance in developing their résumés and cover letters.

One strength of job fairs is also a weakness—although a job fair enables the organization to reach many people, the typical job fair has around 1,600 applicants vying for the attention of about 65 employers. Given the ratio of 25 applicants for every employer, the typical contact with an applicant is probably shallow. In response, some employers instead (or also) devote their resources to information sessions geared toward a smaller group of specially qualified candidates. During these sessions, the company presents information about itself, including its culture, working environment, and career opportunities. Small gifts and brochures are also typically given out. One recent research study showed that applicants who were favorably impressed by an organization's information session were significantly more likely to pursue employment with the organization. Thus, both applicants and employers find information sessions a valuable alternative, or complement, to job fairs.[24]

Increasingly, job fairs are being held online. Most online job fairs have pre-established time parameters. One online recruiting site held a job fair that included 240 participating companies. In these virtual job fairs, recruiters link up with candidates through chat rooms.

Co-ops and Internships

Students currently attending school are sometimes available for part-time work. Two part-time working arrangements are co-ops and internships. Under a co-op arrangement, the student works with one employer on an alternating quarter basis. In one quarter the student works full-time, and the next quarter, attends school full-time. Under an internship arrangement, the student has a continuous period of employment with an employer for a specified period of time. These approaches allow an organization to obtain services from a part-time employee for a short period of time, but they also allow the organization the opportunity to assess the person for a full-time position after graduation. One manager experienced in working with interns commented, "Working with them is one of the best talent-search opportunities available to managers."[25] In turn, interns have better employment opportunities as a result of their experiences.

Not only can the co-ops and interns themselves be a good source of candidates for full-time jobs but they can also be a good referral source. Those with a favorable experience with an employer are more likely to refer others from their schools for jobs. In order for this to occur, the students' experiences must be favorable. To ensure this happens, students should not be treated as cheap commodities. Care must be taken to provide them with meaningful job experiences and with the training necessary to do a good job. Increasingly, employers are doing this as they realize that providing students with rewarding and challenging internships gives them a leg up in recruiting these students for full-time employment. Some companies even offer jobs immediately after a summer internship.

Internships and co-op assignments can take a variety of different forms. One type of assignment is to have the student perform a part of the business that occurs on a periodic basis. For example, some amusement parks that operate only in the summer in northern climates may have a large number of employees who need to be hired and trained in the spring. A student with a background in HR could perform these hiring and training duties. Another type of assignment is to have students apply their knowledge of current advancements in their field by critiquing existing programs and developing new programs based on the latest advancements. Students can also conduct research for the organization by conducting literature reviews or benchmarking current employer practices. Occasionally, experience shows that some internships and co-op assignments do not provide these meaningful experiences that build on the qualifications of the student. Research shows that school-to-work programs often do not provide high utility to organizations in terms of benefit–cost ratios. Thus, organizations need to evaluate co-ops and internships not only in terms of the quality for the student but from a cost–benefit economic perspective as well.[26]

Meaningful experiences benefit both the organization and the student. The organization gains from the influence of new ideas the student has been exposed to in his or her curriculum, and the student gains from having the experience of having to apply concepts while facing the realities of organizational constraints. For both parties to gain, it is important that a learning contract be developed and signed by the student, the student's advisor, and the corporate sponsor. The learning contract becomes, in essence, a job description to guide the student's activities. Also, it establishes the criteria by which the student's performance is assessed for purposes of grading by the academic advisor and for purposes of successful completion of the project for the organization. In the absence of a learning contract, internships can result in unrealistic expectations by the corporate sponsor, which, in turn, can result in disappointment when these unspoken expectations are not met.

To secure the services of students, organizations can contact the placement offices of high schools, colleges, universities, and vocational technology schools. Also, teachers, professors, and student chapters of professional associations can be contacted to obtain student assistance. Placement officials can provide the hiring organization with the policies that need to be followed for placements, while teachers and professors can give guidance on the types of skills students could bring to the organization and the organizational experiences the students would benefit from the most.

Innovative Sources

Several innovative sources might also be experimented with, particularly for purposes of widening the search.

Alumni Associations   Another source for experienced personnel is alumni associations at schools. Some schools, such as the Georgia Institute of Technology, offer placement services for past as well as current students.[27] A small fee is assessed for the service. Placement opportunities are made known, and training and career counseling are offered.

Unemployed Youth Services   Youth unemployment is very high relative to that of other demographic groups in the United States. To reach this group for entry-level positions, employers can use unemployed youth services, which provide placement opportunities for youths as well as counseling and training in some local communities.

Religious Organizations   These organizations (e.g., churches) provide another source of labor that is often overlooked. Such institutions typically have many senior and teenage human resources. Organizations can attract members by sponsoring events such as socials and by making donations to charitable causes endorsed by them.

Interest Groups   There are many associations that help facilitate the interests of their members. Two such groups are the American Association for Retired Persons (AARP) and the National Association for the Advancement of Colored People (NAACP). An example of how these groups provide for the employment interests of their members is the NAACP job fair conducted by BPI Tech Fair in Minneapolis.[28]

Realtors   Some realtors now offer employment services for trailing partners. When one person in a relationship must relocate to further a career, the realtor may also help the trailing partner to find a new job.

Senior Networks   Many networks have been formed to advance the employment interests of older workers. These networks include Senior Community Service Employment Programs, the Job Training Partnership Act, Forty Plus, Operation ABLE, the National Clearinghouse on State and Local Older Workers Programs, the National Caucus for Black Aged, the National Association of Spanish-Speaking Elderly, and the Older Women's League. These organizations provide many employment services, such as the training, counseling, and placement of older workers along with programs for employers on how to best utilize the talents of older workers.[29]

Direct Mail Solicitations   Drawing on marketing tactics in business, some organizations now recruit by direct mail solicitations. Likely segments of the labor market are targeted and sent direct mail to inform them of employment opportunities. In addition to mailing letters, employers also communicate with potential applicants via door hangers, bargain shoppers, welcome wagons, point-of-sale messages, and talent scout cards.[30]

Choice of Sources

There is no single best source for recruitment; each source has its strengths and weaknesses. The following criteria can be used to select which sources are most appropriate for each search:

1. *Quantity of labor.* Some sources, such as advertisements, produce a large number of applicants. Such a source is appropriate when the organization needs a large head count. When number of hours of work is the quantity indicator, temporary employee sources may be most beneficial.

2. *Quality of labor.* If a premium is to be paid for high-quality candidates in the recruitment process, then some sources are better than others. If a very

high level of KSAOs is required, an executive search firm is helpful. If certain skills are needed, schools that emphasize these skills may be better sources of employees than others.

3. *Availability of sources.* Not all of the possible sources are available to a given organization. For example, one is unlikely to find temporary agencies in rural areas. Similarly, some jobs do not have members who belong to professional associations.

4. *Past or promised experiences.* Many organizations have a past track record with various sources. Organizations who have not used a certain source in the past can look to the past experiences of other organizations, or the promises made by the source, for validation of its effectiveness. Issues to consider in evaluating experiences with the source include its process and outcomes. Process issues to consider include the types of services provided, the quality of services, and the timing and dependability of services offered. Outcomes of concern include not only the number of candidates but also the quality of candidates.

5. *Budget constraints.* Some organizations have large enough budgets that they can perform many of the services offered by institutions who act as intermediaries in the labor market, such as employment agencies. Other organizations, due to a lack of resources, small size, or infrequency of search, cannot replicate these services in-house.

6. *Contractual obligations.* In organizations where all or part of the workforce is organized by a union, the labor agreement may spell out the conditions under which external and internal sources can be used. Even in nonunion organizations, there may be an agreement between the employment function, where external recruitment is housed, and placement, where internal recruitment is housed, concerning when and which sources can be used to recruit externally.

A considerable amount of research has been conducted on the effectiveness of various recruitment sources and can be used as a starting point as to which sources are likely to be effective.[31] Research has defined effectiveness as the impact of recruitment sources on increased employee satisfaction, performance, and retention. The research suggests that, overall, referrals, job postings, and rehiring of former employees are the most effective sources, whereas newspaper ads and employment agencies are the least effective. Unfortunately, this research has focused on the effectiveness of only a few different sources; newer methods such as the Internet are virtually unstudied. Furthermore, as was noted earlier, effectiveness is likely to vary depending on the organization and context. Hence, organizations need to systematically collect their own data to gauge effectiveness and to guide their choice of recruitment sources. For example, organizations may need to code sources to ascertain which ones produce the greatest yield of qualified applicants.

When to Look

Two factors that drive the decision of when to look for job applicants are lead time concerns and time sequence concerns.

Lead Time Concerns

Although managers would like to have each position filled immediately on approval of requisitions, this goal is not possible, as recruiters handle an average of 17 vacancies at any one time.[32] It is possible, however, to minimize the delay in filling vacancies by planning for openings well in advance of their actual occurrence. Effective planning requires that top management prioritize job openings so that they can be filled in the order that best meets the needs of the business. It also requires that recruiters be fully prepared to conduct the search. To do so, recruiters must be knowledgeable about print deadlines for the placement of ads in appropriate periodicals. Also, recruiters should be knowledgeable about the availability of labor in the market place. For example, the availability of college graduates is determined by graduation dates, which vary from school to school.

Time Sequence Concerns

In a successful recruitment program, the steps involved in the process are clearly defined and sequenced in a logical order. A staffing flowchart should be used to organize all components of the recruitment process. The sequence of recruitment activities has a large bearing on the time that will be required to fill job vacancies.

A very useful set of indicators for time sequence concerns is known as time-lapse statistics. These statistics provide data on the average length of time that expires between various phases in the recruitment process. Organizations should routinely collect these data in order to assist managers in planning when vacancies are to be filled.

SEARCHING

Once the recruitment planning and strategy development phases are completed, it is time to actively conduct the search. Searching for candidates first requires the development of a message and then the selection of a medium to communicate that message. Each of these phases is considered in turn.

Communication Message

Job Requirements and Rewards Matrices

Information presented by the organization to the job applicant is essential to the decision to accept or reject a job offer. The starting point for all information presented by the organization should be the job requirements and job rewards matrices (or their equivalent). These matrices may be used in all forms of communications with job applicants, including advertisements, recruitment brochures, and face-to-face discussions. The job requirements matrix communicates to the applicant what is needed to perform the job. The job rewards matrix describes what rewards are offered to the applicant for performing the job. Both pieces of information are essential to the applicant in formulating a decision whether to become an applicant, to remain an applicant, and ultimately to join an organization.

Types of Messages

Traditional Messages   Information about the organization, also known as the message, varies by the amount of information presented and by the accuracy of that information. With traditional recruitment procedures, the job applicant may be given relatively little concrete or accurate information. For example, it is common to see the phrase "unlimited growth opportunities" in job recruitment advertisements in the paper. This phrase may sound promising, but it is very vague and possibly misleading. Such information may cause applicants to shun the advertised position. It may also create retention problems for misled applicants who joined the organization.

Fortunately, some organizations are now presenting messages that are more specific and accurate than the traditional message. As a result, job applicants are able to make better-informed decisions about their employment with an organization, and organizations gain more credibility in the eyes of the applicants.

Realistic Recruitment Message   A realistic recruitment message portrays the organization and job as it really is, rather than describing what the organization thinks job applicants want to hear. Organizations continue to describe their organizations in overly positive terms, overstating desired values to applicants such as risk-taking, while understating undesirable values such as rules orientation. Some would argue this is not the best message to send applicants on either moral or practical grounds.

A very well-researched recruitment message is known as a realistic job preview or RJP.[33] According to this practice, job applicants are given a "vaccination" by being told verbally, in writing, or on videotape what the actual job is like.[34] An example of the attributes that might be contained in an RJP is shown in Exhibit 5.5. It shows numerous attributes for the job of elementary school teacher. Note that the attributes are quite specific and that they are both positive and negative. Information like this "tells it like it is" to job applicants.

After receiving the vaccination, job applicants can decide whether they want to work for the organization. The hope with the RJP is that job applicants will self-select into and out of the organization. By selecting into the organization, the applicant may be more committed to working there than they might otherwise have been. By selecting out, the organization does not face the costs associated

EXHIBIT 5.5   Example of Job Attributes in an RJP for Elementary School Teachers

Positive Job Attributes

Dental insurance is provided
Innovative teaching strategies are encouraged
University nearby for taking classes
Large support staff for teachers

Negative Job Attributes

Salary growth has averaged only 2% in past three years
Class sizes are large
The length of the school day is long
Interactions with community have not been favorable

with recruiting, selecting, training, and compensating employees, only to then have them leave because the job did not meet their expectations.

Increasingly, the Internet is an important source of organizational information that can provide a "realistic culture preview." For example, whereas Coca-Cola's Web site contains basic job and organizational information, PepsiCo's Web site contains information about Pepsi's heritage, its culture, diversity, and benefits, as well as more specific job information (see *www.cocacola.com* and *www. pepsijobs.com*).

A great deal of research has been conducted on the effectiveness of RJPs, which appear to lead to somewhat higher job satisfaction and lower turnover. This appears to be true because providing applicants with realistic expectations about future job candidates helps them better cope with job demands once they are hired. RJPs also appear to foster the belief in employees that their employer is concerned about them and honest with them, which leads to higher levels of organizational commitment.

RJPs may lead applicants to withdraw from the recruitment process, although a recent review suggests that they have little effect on attrition from the recruitment process. This may appear to be great news to employers interested in using RJPs—providing applicants with realistic information provides employers with more satisfied and committed employees while still maintaining applicant interest in the position. Where the situation may become problematic is when one considers the type of applicant "scared away" by the realistic message. It appears plausible that the applicants most likely to be repelled by the realistic message are high-quality applicants, because they have more options. In fact, research suggests that the negative effects of RJPs on applicant attraction are particularly strong for high-quality applicants (those whose general qualifications are especially strong) and those with direct experience or familiarity with the job.

Although RJPs appear to have both weakly positive (slightly higher job satisfaction and lower turnover among new hires) and negative (slightly reduced ability to hire high-quality applicants) consequences, these outcomes have been found to be affected by a number of factors. A recent review of 40 studies on the effectiveness of RJPs suggested that RJPs had weak effects, but to some extent these effects were affected by a number of factors. The following recommendations can be gleaned from these findings:

- RJPs presented very early in the recruitment process are less effective in reducing posthire turnover than those presented just before or just after hiring.
- Posthire RJPs lead to higher posthire levels of job performance than do RJPs presented before hiring.
- Verbal RJPs tend to reduce turnover more than written or videotaped RJPs.
- RJPs are less likely to lead to turnover when the organization "restricts" turnover for a period of time after the RJP (with contracts, above market salaries, etc.).

In general, these findings suggest that RJPs should be given verbally (rather than in writing or by showing a videotape) and that it is probably best to reserve their use for later in the recruiting process (RJPs should not be part of the initial exposure of the organization to applicants).[35]

Attractive Messages An attractive message portrays the organization in a manner such that applicants are induced to interview, join, or stay with the organization before they actually become employees. For example, most employers pay travel expenses for the applicant to interview. Some organizations go even further. For example, General Mills has wined and dined MBA students from Northwestern University aboard a yacht in hopes of getting them to sign up for an interview.[36] Upon completion of the trip, General Mills also sent each prospective interviewee a Wheaties box with his or her picture and name on it.

Once interviews have been conducted, other attractive messages are used to induce the applicant to accept a job offer. Traditionally, this has meant paying for moving expenses. Some organizations go beyond moving expenses to help the person locate and pay for a new house, sell an old home, or assist a partner in finding a new job.

Organizations also try to induce job applicants to make a long-term commitment to the organization. To do so, organizations have traditionally offered basic benefits such as health care and the possibility of salary increase through merit pay. Borrowing the idea from marketing, more and more organizations are interested in employment branding. In short, employment branding is placing the image of being a "great place to work" or "the employer of choice" in the minds of job candidates. Under a branding strategy, the U.S. Marine Corps emphasized the marines as an elite group of warriors rather than focusing on the financial advantages of enlistment, which had been done in the past. Ideally, a brand communicates the company's culture and values. Southwest Airlines, for example, is an employer of choice (it receives 80 applications for every opening) not because of its food, technology, or even pay but because it has established a brand as a fun, exciting place to work.[37]

Targeted Messages One way to improve upon matching people with jobs is to target the recruitment message to a particular audience. Different audiences may be looking for different rewards from an employer. This would appear to be especially true of special applicant populations, such as teenagers, older workers, welfare recipients, people with disabilities, homeless individuals, veterans, and displaced homemakers, who may have special needs. Older workers, for example, may be looking for employers who can meet their financial needs (e.g., supplement Social Security), security needs (e.g., retraining), and social needs (e.g., place to interact with people). College students appear to be attracted to organizations that provide rewards and promotions on the basis of individual rather than group performance. Also, college students prefer to receive pay in the form of a salary rather than in the form of incentives.[38]

Choice of Messages

The four different types of messages—traditional, realistic, attractive, and targeted—are not likely to be equally effective under the same conditions. Which message to convey depends on the labor market, vacancy characteristics, and applicant characteristics.

If the labor market is tight and applicants are difficult to come by, then realism may not be an effective message, because to the extent that applicants self-select out of the applicant pool, fewer are left for an employer to choose from during an already tight labor market. Hence, if the employment objective is simply to fill job slots in the short run and worry about turnover later, a realistic message will have counterproductive effects. Obviously then, when applicants are in abundance and turnover is an immediate problem, a realistic message is appropriate.

During a tight labor market, attractive and targeted messages are likely to be more effective in attracting job applicants. Attraction is strengthened as there are inducements in applying for a job. In addition, individual needs are more likely to be perceived as met by a prospective employer. Hence, the applicant is more motivated to apply for organizations with an attractive or targeted message than those without. During loose economic times when applicants are plentiful, the attractive or targeted approaches may be more costly than necessary to attract an adequate supply of labor. Also, they may set up false expectations concerning what life will be like on the job, and thus lead to turnover.

Job applicants have better knowledge about the actual characteristics of some jobs than others. For example, service sector jobs, such as that of cashier, are highly visible to people. For these jobs, it may be redundant to give a realistic message. Other jobs, such as an outside sales position, are far less visible to people. They may seem very glamorous (e.g., sales commissions) to prospective applicants who fail to see the less glamorous aspects of the job (e.g., a lot of travel and paperwork).

Some jobs seem to be better suited to special applicant groups, and hence, a targeted approach may work well. For example, older employees may have social needs that can be met well by a job that requires a lot of public contact. Organizations, then, can take advantage of the special characteristics of jobs to attract applicants.

The value of the job to the organization also has a bearing on the selection of an appropriate recruitment message. Inducements for jobs of higher value or worth to the organization are easier to justify in a budgetary sense than jobs of lower worth. The job may be of such importance to the organization that it is willing to pay a premium through inducements to attract well-qualified candidates.

Some applicants are less likely than others to be influenced in their attitudes and behaviors by the recruitment message. In a recent study, for example, it was shown that a realistic message is less effective for those with considerable previous job experience.[39] A targeted message does not work very well if the source is seen as being not credible.[40] Inducements may not be particularly effective with applicants who do not have a family or have considerable wealth.

Communication Medium

Not only is the message itself an important part of the recruitment process, so, too, is the selection of a medium to communicate the message. The most common recruitment mediums are recruitment brochures, videos and video/conferencing, advertisements, voice messages, and online services.

Recruitment Brochures

A recruitment brochure is usually sent or given directly to job applicants. Information in the brochure may be very detailed, and hence, the brochure may be lengthy. A brochure not only covers information about the job but also communicates information about the organization and its location. It may include pictures in addition to written narrative in order to illustrate various aspects of the job, such as the city in which the organization is located and actual coworkers.

The advantage of a brochure is that the organization controls who receives a copy. Also, it can be more lengthy than an advertisement. A disadvantage is that it can be quite costly to develop this medium.

Developing a brochure can be done inside the organization or by outside media professionals. By developing a brochure in-house, the organization may be able to keep the cost down. However, in-house capabilities may not be very technically advanced, so that outside sources may be needed if technical advances are required.

A successful brochure possesses (1) a unique theme or point of view relative to other organizations in same industry and (2) a visual distinctiveness in terms of design and photographs. A good format for the brochure is to begin with a general description of the organization, including its history and its culture (values, goals, "brand"), then include a description of the hiring process, then a characterization of pay/benefits and performance reviews, and concluding with contact information.

Videos and Videoconferencing

A video can be used along with the brochure but should not simply replicate the brochure. The brochure should be used to communicate basic facts and information. The video should be used to communicate the culture and climate of the organization. Professional Marketing Services, Inc., in Milwaukee, helps organizations develop a "profile" of themselves. As part of the profile they can highlight characteristics of the city that the organization resides in such as the climate, housing market, school systems, churches, performing arts, spectator sports, nightlife, and festivals. This profile can be communicated to job seekers via videocassette, diskette, CD-ROM, CD-I, and the Internet.[41] Video diskettes can also be made interactive so that the job seeker can submit an application electronically, request additional information, or even arrange an interview.

A new form of communicating with job applicants is known as videoconferencing.[42] Rather than meeting in person with applicants, organizational representatives meet with applicants in separate locations, face to face on a television monitor. The actual image of the person in action appears on the screen, although the transmission appears to be in slow motion. The technology needed for videoconferencing is expensive, but the costs have decreased in recent years. Moreover, this technology makes it possible for the organization to screen applicants at multiple or remote locations without actually having to travel to these locations. Many college placement offices now have the equipment for videoconferencing. The equipment is also available at some Kinko's copy centers for applicants who do not have access to a college placement office.

Advertisements

Given the expense of advertising in business publications, ads are much shorter and to the point than are recruitment brochures. As a general rule, the greater the circulation of the publication, the greater the cost of advertising in it.

Ads appear in a variety of places other than business publications. Ads can be found in local, regional, and national newspapers; on television and radio; and in bargain shoppers, door hangers, direct mail, and welcome wagons. Advertisements can thus be used to reach a broad market segment. Although they are brief, there are many different types of ads:[43]

1. *Classified advertisements.* These ads appear in alphabetical order in the "Help Wanted" section of the newspaper. Typically, they allow for very limited type and style selection and are usually only one newspaper column in width. These ads are used most often for the purpose of quick résumé solicitation for low-level jobs at a low cost. Most large- and medium-sized newspapers now place their classified ads online, potentially reaching many more prospective job candidates.

2. *Classified display ads.* A classified display ad allows more discretion in the type that is used, and its location in the paper. A classified display ad does not have to appear in alphabetical order and can appear in any section of the newspaper. The cost of these ads is moderate; they are often used as a way to announce openings for professional and managerial jobs. An example of a classified display ad is shown in Exhibit 5.6.

3. *Display ads.* These ads allow for freedom of design and placement in a publication. As such, they are very expensive and begin to resemble recruitment brochures. These ads are typically used when an employer is searching for a large number of applicants to fill multiple openings.

EXHIBIT 5.6   Classified Display Ad for Human Resource Generalist

HUMAN RESOURCE GENERALIST

ABC Health, a leader in the health care industry, currently has a position available for an experienced **Human Resource Generalist.**

This position will serve on the human resources team, which serves as a business partner with our operational departments. Our team prides itself on developing and maintaining progressive and impactful human resources policies and programs.

Qualified candidates for this position will possess a bachelor's degree in business with an emphasis on human resource management, or a degree in a related field, such as industrial psychology. In addition, a minimum of three years of experience as a human resource generalist is required. This experience should include exposure to at least four of the following functional areas: compensation, employment, benefits, training, employee relations, and performance management.

In return for your contributions, we offer a competitive salary as well as comprehensive, flexible employee benefits. If you meet the qualifications and our opportunity is attractive to you, please forward your résumé and salary expectations to:

Human Resource Department
ABC Health
P.O. Box 123
Pensacola, FL 12345

An Equal Opportunity/Affirmative Action Employer

4. *Online ads.* More and more employers are choosing to place ads on the Internet. These ads can take several forms. One form is a clickable banner ad that appears on Web sites visited by likely prospects. Another form of advertising of sorts was reviewed earlier—posting positions using online Web sites such as *Monster.com.*

Telephone Messages

Though the telephone is hardly new, in times of tight labor markets, many employers resort to phoning prospective job candidates. These can be "cold calls" where the potential recruit's name was gleaned from a list (such as those "peeled" from an organization's Web site) or "warm calls" where the prospective candidate was referred to the recruiter, formally or informally.

As a result of the latest advances in the telecommunications industry, a recent development in advertising is voice messages. With this approach, the applicant hears information over the phone about job openings. Callers have access to each of the items on the menu by pressing keys on a touch-tone phone. If what they hear is of interest to them, they can leave a message in a voicemail box. All applicants receive a return call; if they seem to be qualified for a vacant position, they are invited for an interview.

Organizational Web Sites

The Web is somewhat unique in that it can function as both a recruitment source and a recruitment medium. When a Web page only serves to communicate information about the job or organization to potential applicants, it serves as a recruitment medium. However, when a Web page attracts actual applicants, particularly when applicants are allowed to apply online, it also functions as a recruitment source. Many company home pages now allow applicants to apply online. When doing so, these Web sites not only are a powerful means of communicating information about job requirements and rewards but they can also reach applicants who otherwise would not bother (or know how or where) to apply.

Care must be taken to ensure that the organizational Web site is engaging to potential job candidates. Some may believe that to be captivating Web sites must be visually sophisticated, employing flashy colors, movements, sounds, and so on. This would be a mistake. Complexity in Web sites is a disadvantage, not an advantage. Surveys reveal that many Web sites fail to achieve their purpose (generate an application from a qualified applicant); one of the main causes of failure is that a surfer quits the Web site because it was slow in loading or confusing in content. Exhibit 5.7 presents recommendations for the effective design of an organizational Web site. Many organizations have added sophisticated features to their sites— such as pull-down menus that list positions by job type or location, a "shopping cart" that prospective candidates can fill with job openings that interest them. Sophistication is fine—as long as it is clear, accessible, and easy to use on the part of the prospective applicant. Some organizations maintain a "two-click" rule, where sought-after information can be obtained after two clicks.[44]

EXHIBIT 5.7   Factors to Keep in Mind in Designing Organizational Web Sites

1. *Keep it simple*—surveys reveal that potential job candidates are overwhelmed by complex, difficult-to-navigate Web sites; never sacrifice clarity for "jazziness"—remember, a good applicant is there for content of the Web site, not for the bells and whistles.

2. *Make access easy; Web page and links should be easy to download*—studies reveal that individuals will not wait more than eight seconds for a page to download, so that four-color page that looks great will backfire if it takes the user, working from a modem, time to download the page (also make sure that the link to the recruiting site on the home page is prominently displayed).

3. *Provide online application form*—increasingly, potential candidates expect to be able to submit an application online; online forms are not only desired by candidates, organizations can load them directly into searchable databases.

4. *Provide information about company culture*—allow applicants to self-select out if their values clearly do not match those of your organization—you wouldn't want them anyway.

5. *Include selected links to relevant Web sites*—the words "selected" and "relevant" are key here; things to include might be a cost-of-living calculator, a career advice area.

6. *Make sure necessary information is conveyed to avoid confusion*—clearly specify job title, location, etc., so applicants know the job for which they are applying and, if there are several jobs, they don't apply for the wrong job.

7. *Keep information current*—make sure position information is updated regularly (e.g., weekly).

8. *Evaluate and track the results*—periodically evaluate the performance of the Web site based on various criteria (number of hits, number of applications, application/hits ratio, quality of hires, cost of maintenance, user satisfaction, time to hire, etc.).

Radio

Another recruitment medium is radio. Companies that advertise on the radio purchase a 30- or 60-second time slot to advertise openings in specific job categories. Choice of radio stations often implicitly targets specific markets. For example, a classical music station is likely to reach a different audience than an alternative rock station. Organizations must take these market differences into account when choosing a statement. Radio stations generally have detailed demographic information available to potential advertisers. The advantage of radio ads is their reach; more people listen to radio than read newspapers. In fact, estimates are that 95% of Americans listen to the radio daily; the average person listens for four hours. Radio ads often are less costly than one might think. One company, for the cost of one ad in a Sunday newspaper, was able to run a 60-second commercial 73 times over three days. To some extent, the relative advantage of radio over newspapers depends on the job market. Help-wanted ads are generally read by individuals who are less than perfectly happy with their present positions, or who are unemployed. Thus, in tight labor markets, radio ads are more likely to be heard by people with jobs, which is the likely source of applicants in a tight labor market. One limitation with radio ads is that organizations cannot always buy ads when they want to run them if the time spots are already sold (whereas a help wanted section can simply add another page). Another drawback is that they are limited to a local market; thus, they are limited to jobs where the recruitment is confined to local labor markets.[45]

E-Mail

It is tempting for organizations to initiate contact with prospective job candidates via e-mail. There is no direct cost, and support staff could send hundreds or even thousands of e-mail messages to prospective job candidates. In the age of spamming, however, it is important to remember that most individuals will regard mass e-mailings with even less enthusiasm than junk mail. To make the most out of e-mail recruitment, it is important to make the messages highly personal, reflecting some understanding of the candidate's unique qualifications.

One form of e-mail recruitment medium is an e-mail autoresponder. E-mail autoresponders are clickable e-mail addresses where prospective job candidates receive (usually within a few seconds) a text description of the position, organization, and so forth. The advantage of this hybrid of Web and e-mail communication is that applicants do not need to wait for the information to (oftentimes slowly) load on their computer, and they can save the information for later reference. Furthermore, autoresponders can be used to send subsequent e-mails to the individuals who originally requested information, such as when related positions become available.

Finally, some states are considering legislation that would curtail the sending of e-mail messages for commercial (including recruitment) purposes. Thus, organizations need to make sure that their e-mail messages do not run afoul of state regulations.[46]

APPLICANT REACTIONS

An important source of information in designing and implementing an effective recruitment system is applicant reactions to the system. Both attitudinal and behavioral reactions to components of the recruitment system are important. Components of this system that have been studied include the recruiter and the recruitment process.

Reactions to Recruiters

Considerable research has been conducted and carefully reviewed on the reactions of job applicants to the behavior and characteristics of recruiters.[47] The data that have been collected have been somewhat limited by the fact that they focus primarily on reactions to college rather than noncollege recruiters. Despite this limitation, several key themes emerge in the literature.

First, though the recruiter does indeed influence job applicant reactions, he or she does not have as much influence on them as do actual characteristics of the job. This indicates that the recruiter cannot be viewed as a substitute for a well-defined and communicated recruitment message showing the actual characteristics of the job. It is not enough just to have good recruiters to attract applicants to the organization.

Second, the influence of the recruiter is more likely to be felt on the attitudes rather than the behaviors of the job applicant. That is, an applicant who has been exposed to a talented recruiter is more likely to walk away with a favorable impression of the recruiter than to accept a job on the basis of the interaction with a recruiter. This attitudinal effect is important, however, as it may lead to good publicity for the organization. In turn, good publicity may lead to a larger applicant pool to draw from in the future.

Third, demographic characteristics of the recruiter do not have much impact on applicant reactions, with one exception. Recruiters who are HR specialists do not fare as well in terms of applicant reactions as do line managers. Hence, the common practice of using line managers to recruit and HR people to coordinate recruitment activities appears to be appropriate.

Fourth, two behaviors of the recruiter seem to have the largest influence on applicant reactions. The first is the level of warmth that the recruiter shows toward the job applicant. Warmth can be expressed by being enthusiastic, personable, empathetic, and helpful in dealings with the candidate. The second behavior is being knowledgeable about the job. This can be conveyed by being well versed with the job requirements matrix and the job rewards matrix.

Reactions to the Recruitment Process

Only some administrative components of the recruitment process have been shown to have an impact on applicant reactions.[48] First, job applicants are more likely to have favorable reactions to the recruitment process when the screening devices that are used to narrow the applicant pool are seen as job-related. That is, the process that is used should be closely related to the content of the job as spelled out in the job requirements matrix.

Second, delay times in the recruitment process do indeed have a negative effect on applicants' reactions. In particular, when long delays occur between the applicant's expression of interest and the organization's response, negative reactions are formed by the applicant. The negative impression formed is about the organization, rather than the applicant him- or herself. For example, with a long delay between an on-site visit and a job offer, an applicant is more likely to believe that something is wrong with the organization rather than with his or her personal qualifications. This is especially true of the better-quality candidate, who is also likely to act on these feelings by accepting another job offer.

Third, simply throwing money at the recruitment process is unlikely to result in any return. There is no evidence that increased expenditures on the recruitment process result in more favorable attitudes or behaviors by job applicants. For expenditures to pay dividends, they need to be specifically targeted to effective recruitment practices, rather than indiscriminately directed to all practices.

Fourth, the influence of the recruiter on the applicant is more likely to occur in the initial rather than the latter stages of the recruitment process. In the latter stages, actual characteristics of the job carry more weight in the applicant's decision. At the initial screening interview, the recruiter may be the applicant's only contact with the organization. Later in the process, the applicant is more likely to have additional information about the job and company. Hence, the credibility of the recruiter is most critical on initial contact with applicants.

Finally, though little research is available, the increasing use of the Internet in recruitment, and that it is often the applicant's first exposure to an organization, suggests that applicants' reactions to an organization's Web site will increasingly drive their reactions to the organization's recruitment process. A survey revealed that 79% of college students and recent graduates indicated that the quality of a prospective employer's Web site was somewhat important (35%) or very important (44%) in their decision of whether or not to apply for a job. At the same time, most evidence indicates that recruiters are much more satisfied with the Internet as a recruitment device than are applicants. This suggests that organizations concerned with applicant reactions should ensure that their Web site is applicant-friendly (see Exhibit 5.7).[49]

TRANSITION TO SELECTION

Once a job seeker has been identified and attracted to the organization, the organization needs to prepare the person for the selection process. In preparation, applicants need to be made aware of the next steps in the hiring process and what will be required of them. If this transition step is overlooked by the recruiting organization, it may lose qualified applicants who mistakenly think that delays between steps in the hiring process indicate that the organization is no longer interested in them or are fearful that they "didn't have what it takes" to successfully compete during the next steps.

The city of Columbus, Ohio, has done an excellent job of preparing job seekers from external recruitment sources to become applicants for the position of firefighter. To become a firefighter, applicants must pass a series of physical ability exams, which require them to go through an obstacle course, carry heavy equipment up stairs, and complete a number of other timed physical exercises. Many applicants have never encountered these types of tests before and are fearful that they don't have the physical ability to successfully complete the tests.

To prepare job seekers and applicants for these tests, videotapes have been developed showing instructions on how to take the tests and a firefighter actually taking the tests. These tests are shown not only to those who have applied for the position but also on public access television for those job seekers who are thinking about applying for the job. The city of Columbus also provides upper body strength training, as this is a stumbling point for some job applicants in the selection process.

This example from the city of Columbus indicates that in order to successfully prepare people for the transition to selection, organizations should consider reviewing the selection method instructions with the applicants, showing them actual samples of the selection method, and providing them with practice or training if necessary. These steps should be followed not just for physical ability tests but for all selection methods in the hiring process likely to be unfamiliar or uncomfortable to applicants.

LEGAL ISSUES

External recruitment practices are subject to considerable legal scrutiny and influence. Through external recruitment job applicants first establish contact with the organization and then become more knowledgeable about job requirements and rewards. During this process, there is ample room for the organization to exclude certain applicant groups (e.g., minorities, women, and people with disabilities), as well as deceive in its dealings with applicants. Various laws and regulations seek to place limits on these exclusionary and deceptive practices.

Legal issues regarding several of the practices are discussed in this section. These include definition of job applicants and disclaimers, affirmative action programs, electronic recruitment, job advertisements, and fraud and misrepresentation.

Definition of Job Applicant

Exactly what and who is a job applicant? Addressing this question is important because of the need, under federal regulations, to keep applicant records for computing adverse impact statistics, such as applicant flow and differential selection rates. The EEOC and OFCCP consider an applicant a person seeking employment who submits an application, notice, résumé, or expression of interest in a position; this holds true for both hard copy and electronic submissions. In the absence of specific organizational application policies and procedures, these agencies may count any contact by a person as an application for enforcement purposes. Hence, it is advisable for the organization to formulate and strictly adhere to written application policies and procedures that are communicated to organizational representatives and to all persons acting as if they are job applicants. Several suggestions for doing this follow.

First, require a written application from all who seek to be considered, and communicate this policy to all potential applicants. Inform people who apply by other means that they must submit a written application in order to be considered. If this policy is not defined, virtually anyone who contacts the organization or expresses interest by any means could be considered an applicant. Second, require that the applicant indicate the precise position applied for, and establish written minimum qualifications for each position. In this way, the organization can legitimatcly refuse to consider as applicants those who do not meet these requirements. Third, establish a definite period for which the position will remain open, communicate this clearly to applicants, and do not consider those who apply after the deadline. Also, do not keep applications on hold or on file for future consideration. Fourth, return unsolicited applications through the mail. Finally, keep track of applicants who drop out of the process due to lack of interest or acceptance of another job. Such suggestions will help the organization limit the number of "truc" applicants and reduce record keeping while also fostering legal compliance.[50]

Affirmative Action Programs

The Affirmative Action Programs regulations from the OFCCP require the organization to establish placement (hiring and promotion) goals for job groups in which there are disparities between the percentages of women and minorities actually employed and those available for employment. These placement goals are staffing objectives that should be incorporated into the organization's overall staffing planning. The regulations also require that the organization identify problem areas impeding equal employment opportunity and undertake action-oriented programs to correct these problem areas and achieve the placement goals. While recruitment is mentioned as one of those potential problem areas, the regulations say little else specifically about recruitment activities. Based on former (now expired) regulations, however, the OFCCP offered considerable guidance to the organization for its recruitment actions. Suggested actions include:

- Update job descriptions and ensure their accuracy.
- Widely circulate approved job descriptions to hiring managers and recruitment sources.
- Carefully select and train all personnel included in staffing.
- Reach out to organizations prepared to refer women and minority applicants, such as the Urban League, state employment (job) service, National Organization for Women, sectarian women's groups, etc.

- Conduct formal briefings, preferably on company premises, for representatives from recruiting sources.
- Encourage woman and minority employees to refer job applicants.
- Include women and minorities on the HR department staff.
- Actively participate in job fairs.
- Recruit actively at secondary schools and community colleges with predominantly minority and women enrollment.
- Use special employment programs, such as internships, work/study, and summer jobs.
- Include minorities and women in recruitment brochures.
- Expand help-wanted advertising to include women and minority news media.

Many of the above suggestions focus on developing very specific, targeting external recruitment programs. Examples of targeted recruitment occur within the context of larger EEO/AA programs at employers such as McDonald's, Kentucky Fried Chicken (KFC), the California Department of Corrections, and the U.S. Postal Service.[51] McDonald's started its McJobs program for hiring people with disabilities in 1981; it has hired more than 9,000 mentally and physically challenged people since then. The program is a partnership between vocational rehabilitation (VR) agencies, local school systems and workshops, and family members. Individuals are recruited from these sources and then assigned a specific VR counselor to serve as a liaison between them and the company. Recruits then embark on a six- to eight-week training program to learn job skills, both in the classroom and on the job at a McDonald's restaurant.

KFC's targeted recruitment program, called the Designates Program, is intended to identify and attract female and minority executives from other companies. It seeks to place or promote these recruits through the managerial ranks into senior-level management positions. To do this, it uses executive search firms owned by minority group members and women, as well as white men. In a given recruiting initiative, recruiters from these three differently owned search firms (all using the same KSAO job requirements) are asked to produce three different slates of candidates—all white men, all black men, and all women (minority and white). One person is then hired from all three slates.

The California Department of Corrections hires about 2,000 correctional officers each year. It tracks the ethnic composition of its workforce to identify emergent underutilization (recently, Hispanics, Asians, Filipinos, Pacific Islanders, Native Americans, and women). Its multiracial recruitment staff then implements a variety of recruitment initiatives. These include newspaper ads, TV and radio commercials, posters and billboards, mass mailings, job information workshops, and high school and college campus visits.

The U.S. Postal Service (USPS) is undertaking substantial recruitment for Hispanic employees, who comprise 6.4% of the USPS workforce. Recruitment barriers include lack of awareness of job opportunities, misperceptions of kinds of jobs and hours of work, and lack of English language skills. Strategies for recruitment include using Hispanic employees as recruiters; bilingual recruitment advertising in postal lobbies, schools, and neighborhoods; and conducting workshops on the required entrance exams.

Electronic Recruitment

Usage of electronic recruitment technologies has the possibility of creating artificial barriers to employment opportunities in two ways. First, online recruitment and application procedures assume that potential applicants have access to computers and the skills necessary to make online applications. Research suggests these may be poor assumptions, especially for some racial minorities and the economically disadvantaged. Whether such implicit denial of access to job application opportunities is illegal is an open question due to the newness of the issue. To guard against legal challenge and to ensure accessibility, there are several things the organization might do. One action is to supplement online recruitment with recruitment via other widely used sources, such as newspaper advertisements or other sources that organizational experience indicates are frequently used by women and minorities. Alternately, online recruitment and application could be restricted to certain jobs that have strong computer-related KSAO requirements, such as word processing, programming, spreadsheets, and Internet searches. Many managerial, professional, and technical jobs are likely to have such requirements; applicants in all likelihood will have easy access to computers and online recruitment, as well as the skills necessary to successfully navigate and complete the application. Another possibility would be to use the Internet simply as a recruitment tool, providing thorough, realistic information about available jobs and their associated KSAO requirements and rewards offered. Applicants could also be informed of the organization's application procedures, including the need to apply in writing, a requirement that dovetails nicely with our previous discussion of the definition of a job applicant.

A second potential legal issue is the use of recruitment software that conducts résumé searches within an applicant database using keyword search criteria. Organizational representatives, such as staffing specialists or hiring managers, often specify the search criteria to use, and they could select non-job-related criteria that cause adverse impact against women, minorities, or people with disabilities. Examples of such criteria include preferences for graduation from elite colleges or universities, age, and physical requirements. To guard against such a possibility, the organization should be certain that a job analysis has been done to ensure that every job vacancy lists current KSAO requirements, restrict the type of search criteria that may be used by organizational representatives, and train those representatives in the appropriate specification and usage of search criteria.[52]

Job Advertisements

Some of the earliest (and most blatant) examples of discrimination come from job advertisements. Newspaper employment ads were once listed under separate "Help Wanted—Male" and "Help Wanted—Female" sections, and the content of the ads contained statements like "Applicant must be young and energetic." Such types of ads obviously discouraged certain potential applicants from applying because of their gender or age.

The EEOC has issued policy statements regarding age- and sex-referent language in advertising.[53] It bans the use of explicit age- or sex-based preferences. It also addresses more subtle situations in which ads contain implicit age- or sex-based preferences, such as "junior executive," "recent college graduate," "meter maid," and "patrolman." These are referred to in the policy statements as trigger words, and their use may deter certain individuals from becoming applicants. The statements make clear that trigger words, in and of themselves in an advertisement, are not illegal. However, the total context of the ad in which trigger words appear must not be discriminatory, or the trigger words will be a violation of the law.

The EEOC provides the following as an example of an advertisement with a trigger word: "Wanted: Individuals of all ages. Day and evening hours available. Full- and part-time positions. All inquiries welcomed. Excellent source of secondary income for retirees."

Use of the trigger word "retiree" in this ad is considered permissible because the context of the ad makes it clear that applicants of all ages are welcome to apply.

Fraud and Misrepresentation

Puffery, promises, half-truths, and even outright lies are all encountered in recruitment under the guise of selling the applicant on the job and the organization. Too much of this type of selling can be legally dangerous. When it occurs, under workplace tort law, applicants may file suit claiming fraud or misrepresentation.[54] Claims may cite false statements of existing facts (e.g., the nature and profitability of the employer's business) or false promises of future events (e.g., promises about terms and conditions of employment, regarding pay, promotion opportunities, and geographic location). It does not matter if the false statements were made intentionally (fraud) or negligently (misrepresentation). Both types of statements are a reasonable basis for a claim by an applicant or newly hired employee.

To be successful in such a suit, the plaintiff must demonstrate that

1. a misrepresentation occurred;
2. the employer knew, or should have known, about the misrepresentation;
3. the plaintiff relied on the information to make a decision or take action; and

4. the plaintiff was injured because of reliance placed on the statements made by the employer.[55]

Though these four requirements may appear to be a stiff set of hurdles for the plaintiff, they are by no means insurmountable, as many successful plaintiffs can attest.

Avoidance of fraud and misrepresentation claims in recruitment requires straight-forward action by the organization and its recruiters. First, provide applicants with copies of the job requirements matrix and the job rewards matrix. They contain a wealth of specific, truthful information about the job. Second, be truthful about the nature of the business and its profitability. Third, avoid specific promises about future events, regarding terms and conditions of employment or business plans and profitability. Finally, make sure that all recruiters follow these suggestions when they recruit job applicants.

SUMMARY

The objective of the external recruitment process is to identify and attract qualified applicants. To meet this objective the organization must conduct recruitment planning. At this stage, attention must be given to both organizational issues (e.g., centralized versus decentralized recruitment function) and administrative issues (e.g., size of the budget). Particular care needs to be taken in the selection, training, and rewards of recruiters.

The next stage in external recruitment is the development of a strategy. The strategy should consider open versus targeted recruitment, recruitment sources and the choice of sources, and when to look. In general, an organization should consider looking at a wide range of applicant groups to attract a well-qualified applicant pool. Consideration should be given to those with special availabilities, and the search should be guided by the job requirements matrix. Multiple sources should be used to identify specific applicant populations. There are trade-offs involved in using any source to identify applicants, which should be carefully reviewed prior to using it. When to look for applicants depends on the lead time required to fill a vacancy and the time it took to fill previous vacancies.

The next stage is to develop a message to give to the job applicants and to select a medium to convey that message. The message may be traditional, realistic, attractive, or targeted. There is no one best message; it depends on the characteristics of the labor market, the job, and the applicants. The message should, however, be based on the job requirements matrix and the job rewards matrix. The message can be communicated through brochures, videos, advertisements, voice messages, videoconferencing, or online services, each of which has different strengths and weaknesses.

Applicants are definitely influenced by characteristics of recruiters and the recruitment process. Through proper attention to these characteristics, the organization can help provide applicants with a favorable recruitment experience. That experience can be continued by carefully preparing applicants for the selection process.

Recruitment activities are highly visible and sensitive for employees. They raise a host of legal issues regarding potential exclusion of minority and female applicants and truthful communication with job applicants. The organization should carefully define what it considers to be job applicants. For enhanced representation of minorities and women in the applicant pool, targeted recruitment and possible changes in use of conventional recruitment sources should be undertaken. Consistent with this, job advertisements should not openly or implicitly express preferences for or against protected demographic characteristics of applicants. Finally, the organization should be truthful with applicants about the terms and conditions of employment, as well as the overall nature of the business, in order to avoid allegations of fraud and misrepresentation in recruitment.

DISCUSSION QUESTIONS

1. List and briefly describe each of the administrative issues that needs to be addressed in the planning stage of external recruiting.
2. List 10 sources of applicants that organizations turn to when recruiting. For each source, identify needs specific to the source, as well as pros and cons of using the source for recruitment.
3. In designing the communication message to be used in external recruiting, what kinds of information should be included?
4. What are the advantages of conveying a realistic recruitment message as opposed to portraying the job in a way that the organization thinks that job applicants want to hear?
5. What nontraditional inducements are some organizations offering so that they are seen as family-friendly organizations? What result does the organization hope to realize as a result of providing these inducements?

APPLICATIONS

Improving a College Recruitment Program

The White Feather Corporation (WFC) is a rapidly growing consumer products company that specializes in the production and sales of specialty household items such as lawn furniture cleaners, spa (hot tub) accessories, mosquito and tick repellents, and stain-resistant garage floor paints. The company currently employs

400 exempt and 3,000 nonexempt employees, almost all of whom are full-time. In addition to its corporate office in Clucksville, Arkansas, the company has five plants and two distribution centers at various rural locations throughout the state.

Two years ago WFC created a corporate HR department to provide centralized direction and control for its key HR functions—planning, compensation, training, and staffing. In turn, the staffing function is headed by the senior manager of staffing, who receives direct reports from three managers: the manager of nonexempt employment, the manager of exempt employment, and the manager of EEO/AA. The manager of exempt employment is Marianne Collins, who has been with WFC for 10 years and has grown with the company through a series of sales and sales management positions. She was chosen for her current position as a result of the WFC's commitment to promotion from within, as well as her broad familiarity with the company's products and customers. When appointed, Marianne's key area of accountability was defined as college recruitment, with 50% of her time to be devoted to it.

In her first year, Marianne developed and implemented WFC's first ever formal college recruitment program. Working with the HR planning person, they decided there was a need for 40 college graduate new hires by the end of the year. They were to be placed in the production, distribution, and marketing functions; specific job titles and descriptions were to be developed during the year. Armed with this forecast, Marianne began the process of recruitment planning and strategy development. The result was the following recruitment process.

Recruitment was to be conducted at 12 public and private schools throughout the state. Marianne contacted the placement office(s) at each school and set up a one-day recruitment visit for each school. All visits were scheduled during the first week in May. The placement office at each school set up 30-minute interviews (16 at each school) and made sure that applicants completed and had on file a standard application form. To visit the schools and conduct the interviews, Marianne selected three young, up-and-coming managers (one each from production, distribution, and marketing) to be the recruiters. Each manager was assigned to four of the schools. Since none of the managers had any experience as a recruiter, Marianne conducted a recruitment briefing for them. During that briefing she reviewed the overall recruitment (hiring) goal, provided a brief rundown on each of the schools, and then explained the specific tasks the recruiters were to perform. Those tasks were to pick up the application materials of the interviewees at the placement office prior to the interviews, review the materials, conduct the interviews in a timely manner (they were told they could ask any questions they wanted to that pertained to qualifications for the job), and at the end of the day complete an evaluation form on each applicant. The form asked for a 1–7 rating of overall qualifications for the job, written comments about strengths and weaknesses, and a recommendation of whether or not to invite the person for a second interview in Clucksville. These forms were to be returned to Marianne, who would review them and decide which people to invite for a second interview.

After the campus interviews were conducted by the managers, problems began to surface. Placement officials at some of the schools contacted Marianne and lodged several complaints. Among those complaints were that (a) one of the managers failed to pick up the application materials of the interviewees; (b) none of the managers were able to provide much information about the nature of the jobs they were recruiting for, especially jobs outside of their own functional area; (c) the interviewers got off schedule early on, so that applicants were kept waiting and others had shortened interviews as the managers tried to make up time; (d) none of the managers had any written information describing the company and its locations; (e) one of the managers asked female applicants very personal questions about marriage plans, use of drugs and alcohol, and willingness to travel with male coworkers; (f) one of the managers talked incessantly during the interviews, so that the interviewees had little opportunity to present themselves and their qualifications to the manager; and (g) all of the managers told interviewees they did not know when they would be contacted about decisions on invitations for second interviews. In addition to these complaints, Marianne had difficulty getting the managers to complete and turn in their evaluation forms (they claimed they were too busy, especially after being away from the job for a week). Based on the reports she did receive, Marianne extended invitations to 55 of the applicants for second interviews. Of these, 30 accepted the invitation. Ultimately, 25 of these were given job offers, and 15 of them accepted the offers.

To put it mildly, the first ever college recruitment program was a disaster for WFC and Marianne. In addition to her embarrassment, Marianne was asked to meet with her boss and the president of WFC to explain what went wrong and to receive "guidance" from them as to their expectations for the next year's recruitment program. Marianne subsequently learned that she would receive no merit pay increase for the year and that the three managers all received above average merit increases.

To turn things around for the second year of college recruitment, Marianne realized that she needed to engage in a thorough process of recruitment planning and strategy development. As she began this undertaking, her analysis of past events led her to the conclusion that one of her key mistakes was to naively assume that the three managers would actually know how to be good recruiters and were motivated to do the job effectively. Marianne first decides to use 12 managers as recruiters, assigning one to each of the 12 campuses. She also decides that she cannot send them off to the campuses with just a recruitment "briefing." She determines that an intensive, one-day training program must be developed and given to the managers prior to the beginning of the recruitment "season."

You are a professional acquaintance of Marianne's, and you work in HR at another company in Clucksville. Knowing that you have had some experience in both college recruiting and training, Marianne calls you for some advice. She asks you if you would be willing to meet and discuss the following questions:

1. What topics should be covered in the training program?
2. What materials and training aids will be needed for the program?
3. What skills should the trainees actually practice during the training?
4. Who should conduct the training?
5. What other changes might have to be made to ensure that the training has a strong impact on the managers and that during the recruitment process they are motivated to use what they learned in training?

Internet Recruiting

Selma Williams is a recruiter for Mervin/McCall-Hall (MMH), a large publisher of textbooks for education (K–12 and college). Fresh out of college, Selma's first big assignment at MMH is a tough one—to develop an Internet recruitment strategy for the entire company. Previously, MMH had relied on the traditional recruitment methods—college recruiting, word-of-mouth, newspaper advertisements, and search firms. As more and more of MMH's textbook business is connected to the Web, however, it became clear to Selma's boss, Jon Beerfly, that MMH needed to consider upgrading its recruitment process. Accordingly, after Selma had acclimated herself to MMH and worked on a few smaller recruitment projects (including doing a fair amount of recruiting at college campuses in the past three months), Jon described Selma's assignment to her, concluding, "Selma, I really don't know much about this. I'm going to leave it to you to come up with a set of recommendations about what we oughtta be doing. We just had a new intern come into the office for a stint in HR, and I'm going to assign this person to you to help on this assignment." Assume that you are the intern.

At your first meeting, you and Selma discuss many different issues and agree that regardless of what else is done, MMH must have a recruitment area on the MMH corporate Web site. After further discussion, Selma has given you several assignments toward this objective:

1. Look at three to five corporate Web sites that have a recruitment area and note their major features, strengths, and weaknesses. (see Exhibit 5.7)
2. Interview three to five students who have used the recruitment area on a corporate Web site and ask them what they most liked and disliked about the recruitment areas.
3. Prepare a brief report that (a) summarizes your findings from assignments #1 and #2 and (b) recommends the design features that you and Selma will develop for inclusion in the MMH Web site.

ENDNOTES

1. A. S. Wellner, "Focus on Recruitment and Hiring," *HR Magazine,* Jan. 2001, pp. 87–96; J. S. Arthur, "Chamber Aid," *Human Resource Executive,* pp. 124–128; E. B. Coleman, "Fight or

Fix? The Competition for Teachers," *The School Administrator,* Jan. 2001, pp. 28–32; C. Joinson, "Reeling in the Talent," *HR Magazine,* July 1999, pp. 46–52.

2. M. H. Ports, "Trends in Job Search Methods, 1970–1992," *Monthly Labor Review,* 1993, Oct., pp. 63–67; A. E. Barber, C. L. Daily, G. M. Giannantonio, and J. Phillips, "Job Search Activities: An Examination of Changes over Time," *Personnel Psychology,* 1994, 47, pp. 739–765.

3. J. D. Olian and S. L. Rynes, "Organizational Staffing: Integrating Practice with Strategy," *Industrial Relations,* 1984, 23(2), pp. 170–183; "Ten Ways HR Can Take the Lead in Breaking Down Barriers to Employment" (Special Report), *Personnel Journal,* March 1993, pp. 47–99.

4. "Personnel Shop Talk," *BNA Bulletin to Management,* May 23, 1991, p. 154.

5. I. J. Shaver, "Innovative Techniques Lure Quality Workers to NASA," *Personnel Journal,* Aug. 1990, pp. 100–106.

6. R. D. Gatewood, M. A. Gowen, and G. Lautenschlager, "Corporate Image, Recruitment Image, and Initial Job Choice Decisions," *Academy of Management Journal,* 1993, 36(2), pp. 414–427.

7. Coopers and Lybrand, *Employment Policies, Turnover, and Cost-Per-Hire* (New York: Coopers and Lybrand Compensation Resources, 1992).

8. J. A. Breaugh, *Recruitment: Science and Practice* (Boston: PWS-Kent, 1992); R. E. Thaler-Carter, "In-House Recruiters Fill a Specialized Niche," *HR Magazine,* April 1998, pp. 72–78.

9. S. L. Rynes and J. W. Boudreau, "College Recruiting Practices in Large Organizations: Practice, Evaluation, and Research Implications," *Personnel Psychology,* 1986, 39(3), pp. 286–310.

10. E. R. Silverman, "Raiding Talent via the Web," *Wall Street Journal,* Oct. 3, 2000, pp. B1, B18; T. Claybrooke, "Recruiters Are the Marketers," *Employment Management Today,* Winter 2000, pp. 49–52; J. S. Arthur, "Guiding Lights," *Human Resource Executive,* June 18, 1999, pp. 85–87; C. Patton, "Recruiter Attack," *Human Resource Executive,* Nov. 2000, pp. 106–109; E. Zimmerman, "Fight Dirty Hiring Tactics," *Workforce,* May 2001, pp. 30–34.

11. B. J. Asch, "Do Incentives Matter? The Case of Navy Recruiters," *Industrial and Labor Relations Review,* 43 (Special Issue), pp. 89–106.

12. J. Putzier, "Cultivating Strategies to Get Your Best People Back," *Employment Management Today,* Summer 1999, pp. 28–30; C. Vinzant, "They Want You Back," *Fortune,* Oct. 2, 2000, pp. 271–272; P. Brotherton, "Staying in Touch with Past Employees," *Employment Management Today,* Spring 1999, pp. 44–48.

13. C. Scottpyle, "I Want You After the U.S. Army," *HR Magazine,* April 2001, pp. 54–58; B. Gaul, "Reporting for Duty," *Employment Management Today,* Spring 2001, pp. 30–34.

14. Employment Management Association, "Alternative Recruitment Centers Take Center Stage at Fall Conference," *EMA Report,* 1992, 18(1), pp. 3–5.

15. E. Trice, "High-Tech Recruiting," *IPMA News,* Feb. 1998, p. 8; J. Wentworth, "Jumping Through Hoops," *EMA Today,* Spring 1997, pp. 14–17.

16. D. Graham, *Online Recruiting* (Palo Alto, CA: Davis-Black Publishing, 2000); "On-Line Recruiting," *IPMA News,* March 2001, pp. 12, 14; "Online Recruiting On-the-Rise," *Weddle's,* April 15, 2000, p. 1; T. Starner, "Getting It Right," *Human Resource Executive,* July 2001, p. 114.

17. Rynes and Boudreau, "College Recruiting in Large Organizations: Practice, Evaluation, and Research Implications"; G. H. Varma and J. W. Smither, "Selecting Colleges and Universities for On-Campus Recruiting," *Journal of Career Planning and Employment,* Spring 1990, pp. 34–40; P. F. Wernimont, "Recruitment Policies and Practices," in D. Yoder and H. G. Heneman

Jr. (eds.), *ASPA Handbook of Personnel and Industrial Relations* (Washington, DC: Bureau of National Affairs, 1979), pp. 4-85 to 4-115.

18. A. Sanders, "We Luv Booz," *Forbes,* Jan. 24, 2000, p. 64; M. Schneider, "GE Capital's E-Biz Farm Team," *Business Week,* Nov. 27, 2000, pp. 110–111.

19. R. Buckman, "What Price a BMW? At Stanford, It May Only Cost a Resume," *Wall Street Journal,* Aug. 19, 2000, p. A1; S. Grabczynski, "Nab New Grads by Building Relationships with Colleges," *Workforce,* May 2000, pp. 98–103.

20. Deutsch, Shea, and Evans, *Human Resources Manual* (New York: author, 1992–1993).

21. A. Bargerstock, "Low-Cost Recruiting for Quality," *HR Magazine,* 1990, 35(9), pp. 68–70.

22. U.S. Department of Labor, "National Job Bank System Launched in Time for Veterans' Day Celebration," *News,* Nov. 10, 1993.

23. L. Q. Doherty and E. N. Sims, "Quick, Easy Recruitment Help—From a State?" *Workforce,* May 1998, pp. 35–42.

24. D. Aberman, "Smaller, Specialized Recruiting Events Pay Off in Big Ways," *EMA Today,* Winter 1996, pp. 8–10; T. A. Judge and D. M. Cable, "Role of Organizational Information Sessions in Applicant Job Search Decisions," Working paper, Department of Management and Organizations, University of Iowa.

25. C. Hymowitz, "Make a Careful Search to Fill Internships: They May Land a Star," *Wall Street Journal,* May 23, 2000, p. B1; "In a Tight Job Market, College Interns Wooed," *IPMA News,* Nov. 2000, p. 22; S. Armour, "Employers Court High School Teens," *Arizona Republic,* Dec. 28, 1999, p. E5.

26. L. J. Bassi and J. Ludwig, "School-to-Work Programs in the United States: A Multi-Firm Case Study of Training, Benefits, and Costs," *Industrial and Labor Relations Review,* 2000, 53, pp. 219–239.

27. T. Lee, "Alumni Go Back to School to Hunt Jobs," *Wall Street Journal,* June 11, 1991, p. B1.

28. Deutsch, Shea, and Evans, *Human Resources Manual,* p. 24.

29. American Association of Retired Persons, "How to Recruit Older Workers" (Washington, DC: author, 1993).

30. C. D. Fyock, "Ways to Recruit Top Talent," *HR Magazine,* 1991, 36(7), pp. 33–35.

31. "Search Tactics Poll," *Society for Human Resource Management,* April 2001; M. A. Zottoli and J. P. Wanous, "Recruitment Source Research: Current Status and Future Directions," *Human Resource Management Review,* 2000, 10, pp. 353–382.

32. G. A. Cluff, *1990 National Cost-Per-Hire Survey* (Raleigh, NC: Employment Management Association, 1990).

33. S. L. Premack and J. P. Wanous, "A Meta-Analysis of Realistic Job Preview Experiments," *Journal of Applied Psychology,* 1985, 70, pp. 706–719.

34. J. P. Wanous, *Recruitment, Selection, Orientation, and Socialization of Newcomers,* second ed. (Reading, MA: Addison-Wesley, 1992).

35. R. D. Bretz Jr. and T. A. Judge, "Realistic Job Previews: A Test of the Adverse Self-Selection Hypothesis," *Journal of Applied Psychology,* 1998, 83, pp. 330–337; P. W. Hom, R. W. Griffeth, L. E. Palich, and J. S. Bracker, "An Exploratory Investigation into Theoretical Mechanisms Underlying Realistic Job Previews," *Personnel Psychology,* 51, 1998, pp. 421–451; J. M. Phillips, "Effects of Realistic Job Previews on Multiple Organizational Outcomes: A Meta-Analysis," *Academy of Management Journal,* 1998, 41, pp. 673–690; D. M. Cable, L. Aiman-Smith, P. W. Molvey, and J. R. Edwards, "The Sources and Accuracy of Job Applicants' Beliefs about Orga-

nizational Culture," *Academy of Management Journal,* in press; B. M. Meglino, E. C. Ravlin, and A. S. DeNisi, "A Meta-Analytic Examination of Realistic Job Preview Effectiveness: A Test of Three Counter-Intuitive Propositions," *Human Resource Management Review,* 2000, 10, pp. 407–434; "The Fit Factor of Online Recruiting," *Weddle's,* July 2001, pp. 3–4.

36. J. S. Hirsch, "Companies Try Bolder Tactics to Win MBAs," *Wall Street Journal,* Nov. 29, 1989, pp. B1.

37. G. Jaffe, "Uncle Sam Wants Who? New Report Calls Military Ads Off Target," *Wall Street Journal,* July 6, 2000, p. B1; S. Marks, "Recruiting Marketing and Employment Branding," *SHRMessenger,* 2000, p. 6; E. Raimy, "Leading Brands," *Human Resource Executive,* Nov. 1999, pp. 26–30; J. Sullivan, "Employment Branding," *IPMA News,* May 2000, p. 11.

38. R. H. Bretz and T. A. Judge "The Role of Human Resource Systems in Job Applicant Decision Processes," *Journal of Management,* 1994, 20, pp. 531–551; D. Cable and T. Judge, "Pay Preferences and Job Search Decisions: A Person-Organization Fit Perspective," *Personnel Psychology,* 47, pp. 648–657; T. J. Thorsteinson, M. A. Billings, and M. C. Joyce, "Matching Recruitment Messages to Applicant Preferences," Poster presented at 16th annual conference of Society for Industrial and Organizational Psychology, San Diego, 2001.

39. R. J. Vandenberg and V. Scarpello, "The Matching Model: An Examination of the Processes Underlying Realistic Job Previews," *Journal of Applied Psychology,* 1990, 75(1), pp. 60–67.

40. D. R. Ilgen, C. D. Fisher, and M. S. Taylor, "Consequences of Individual Feedback on Behavior in Organizations," *Journal of Applied Psychology,* 1979, 64, pp. 349–371.

41. College Placement Council, *College Relations and Recruitment Sourcebook*; College Placement Council, "Technology," *Spotlight on Career Planning, Placement, and Recruitment,* 1995, 18(1), p. 2.

42. K. O. Magnusen and K. G. Kroeck, "Videoconferencing Maximizes Recruiting," *HR Magazine,* August 1995, pp. 70–72; B. Kelley, "High-Tech Hits Recruiting," *Human Resource Executive,* April 1994, pp. 43–45; College Placement Council, "Technology."

43. Wernimont, "Recruitment Policies and Practices."

44. R. T. Cober, D. J. Brown, A. J. Blumenthal, D. Doverspike, and P. Levy, "The Quest for the Qualified Job Surfer," *Public Personnel Management,* 2000, 29, pp. 479–496; M. N. Martinez, "Driving Candidates to Your Corporate Website," *Employment Management Today,* Spring 2000, pp. 27–31; S. Pollack, "Spinning the Web," *Human Resource Executive,* March 1, 2001, pp. 100–103.

45. C. Johnson, "Turn Up the Radio Recruiting," *HR Magazine,* Sept. 1998, pp. 64–70.

46. J. Dysart, "HR Recruiters Build Interactivity into Web Sites," *HR Magazine,* March 1999, pp. 106–110; "E-Mail Candidates Carefully," *Weddle's,* May 1, 1999, pp. 4–6.

47. S. L. Rynes, "Recruitment, Job Choice, and Post-Hire Decisions," pp. 399–444; J. P. Wanous, *Organizational Entry,* second ed. (Reading, MA: Addison-Wesley, 1992); J. L. Scott, "Total Quality College Relations and Recruitment Programs: Students Benchmark Best Practices," *EMA Journal,* 1995 Winter, pp. 2–5.

48. S. L. Rynes, "Who's Selecting Whom? Effects of Selection Practices in Applicant Attitudes and Behaviors," in N. Schmitt, W. Borman, and Associates (eds.), *Personnel Selection in Organizations* (San Francisco: Jossey-Bass, 1993), pp. 240–276; S. L. Rynes, "Recruitment, Job Choice, and Post-Hire Decisions"; S. L. Rynes, R. D. Bretz, and B. Gerhart, "The Importance of Recruitment and Job Choice: A Different Way of Looking," *Personnel Psychology,* 1991, 44, pp. 487–521; M. S. Taylor and T. J. Bergmann, "Organizational Recruitment Activities and Applicant Reactions to Different Stages of the Recruiting Process," *Personnel Psychology,* 1988,

40, pp. 261–285; A. M. Ryan, J. M. Sacco, L. A. McFarland, and S. D. Kriska, "Applicant Self-Selection: Correlates of Withdrawal from a Multiple Hurdle Process," *Journal of Applied Psychology,* 2000, 85, pp. 163–179.

49. "Latest Survey Finds Important Shifts in Job Seeker Web Views," *Weddle's,* Feb. 1, 2000, p. 1; "Most College Students Consider Employer's Web Site Deciding Factor," *IPMA News,* Aug. 2000, p. 3.

50. G. P. Panaro, *Employment Law Manual,* second ed. (Boston: Warren Gorham Lamont, 1993), pp. I-51 to I-57; R. H. Glover and R. A. Schwinger, "Defining an Applicant: Maintaining Records in the Electronic Age," *Legal Report,* Society for Human Resource Management, Summer 1996, pp. 6–8.

51. J. L. Laabs, "Affirmative Outreach," *Personnel Journal,* 1991, 70, pp. 86–93; J. L. Laabs, "The Golden Arches Provide Golden Opportunities," *Personnel Journal,* 1991, 70, pp. 52–57; J. E. Rigdon, "PepsiCo's KFC Scouts for Blacks and Women for Its Top Echelons," *Wall Street Journal,* Nov. 19, 1991, p. A1; Bureau of National Affairs, "Postal Service Developing Steps to Increase Recruitment of Hispanics," *Daily Labor Report,* May 11, 1994, pp. A-17 to A-18.

52. J. Click, "Blend Established Practices with New Technologies," *HR Magazine,* Nov. 1997, pp. 59–64; R. L. Hogler, C. Henle, and C. Bemus, "Internet Recruiting and Employment Discrimination: A Legal Perspective," *Human Resource Management Review,* 1998, 8, pp. 149–164; J. M. Stanton, "Validity and Related Issues in Web-Based Hiring," *The Industrial-Organizational Psychologist,* 1999, 36, pp. 69–77; Bureau of National Affairs, "Resume Scanning, Tracking Software Raises New Discrimination Issues," *Daily Labor Report,* March 17, 1998, pp. C1–C2.

53. Bureau of National Affairs, *Fair Employment Practices* (Washington, DC: author, periodically updated), pp. 405:4027–4033; 405:6847–6848.

54. R. M. Green and R. J. Reibstein, *Employer's Guide to Workplace Torts* (Washington, DC: Bureau of National Affairs, 1992), pp. 40–61, 200, 254–255.

55. A. G. Feliu, *Primer on Individual Employee Rights* (Washington, DC: Bureau of National Affairs, 1992), p. 270.

CHAPTER SIX

Internal Recruitment

Recruitment Planning
  Organizational Issues
  Administrative Issues

Strategy Development
  Closed, Open, and Targeted Recruitment
  Recruitment Sources
  Choice of Sources
  When to Look

Searching
  Communication Message
  Communication Medium

Applicant Reactions

Transition to Selection

Legal Issues
  Affirmative Action Programs Regulations
  Bona Fide Seniority Systems
  The Glass Ceiling

Summary

Discussion Questions

Applications

The objective of the internal recruitment process is to identify and attract applicants from among individuals already holding jobs with the organization. The first step in this process is recruitment planning, which addresses both organizational and administrative issues. Organizational issues include mobility paths and mobility path policies. Administrative issues include requisitions, number and types of contacts, budgets, and the recruitment guide.

The second step in the internal recruitment process is strategy development. Attention is directed to where, when, and how to look for qualified internal applicants. Knowing where to look requires an understanding of open, closed, and targeted internal recruitment systems. Knowing how to look requires an understanding of job postings, skills inventories, nominations, employee referrals, and in-house temporary pools. Knowing when to look requires an understanding of lead time and time sequence concerns.

The third step in the process is searching for internal candidates. This step consists of the communication message and medium for notification of the job vacancy. The message can be realistic, attractive, or targeted. The medium for delivery can be a job posting, other written documents, and potential supervisors and peers.

The fourth step in the process is developing a system to make the transition to selection for job applicants. Making a transition requires a well-developed job posting system and providing applicants with an understanding of the selection process and how to best prepare for it.

The fifth step in the process is the consideration of legal issues. Specific issues to be addressed include Affirmative Action Programs regulations, bona fide seniority systems, and the glass ceiling. All three of these issues deal with mechanisms for enhancing the identification and attraction of minorities and women for higher-level jobs within the organization.

RECRUITMENT PLANNING

Prior to identifying and attracting internal applicants to vacant jobs, attention must be directed to organizational and administrative issues that facilitate the effective matching of internal applicants with vacant jobs.

Organizational Issues

Just as the external labor market can be divided into segments or strata of workers believed to be desirable job applicants, so, too, can the internal labor market of an organization. This division is often done inside organizations on an informal basis. For example, managers might talk about the talented pool of managerial trainees this year and refer to some of them as "high-potential employees." As another example, people in the organization talk about their "techies," an internal collection of employees with the technical skills needed to run the business.

At a more formal level, organizations must create a structured set of jobs for their employees and paths of mobility for them to follow as they advance in their careers. To do this, organizations create internal labor markets. Each internal labor market has two components: mobility paths and mobility policies. Mobility paths depict the paths of mobility between jobs. Mobility policies cover the operational requirements needed to move people between jobs.

Mobility Paths

A mobility path consists of possible employee movements within the internal labor market structure. Mobility paths are determined by many factors, including workforce, organization, labor union, and labor market characteristics. Mobility paths are of two types: traditional and innovative. Both types of mobility paths determine who is eligible for a new job in the organization.

Traditional Mobility Paths Examples of traditional mobility paths are shown in Exhibit 6.1. As shown, the emphasis is primarily on upward mobility in the organization. Due to the upward nature of traditional mobility paths, they are often labeled promotion ladders. This label implies that each job is a step toward the top of the organization. Upward promotions in an organization are often seen by employees as prizes because of the promotions' desirable characteristics. Em-

EXHIBIT 6.1   Traditional Mobility Paths

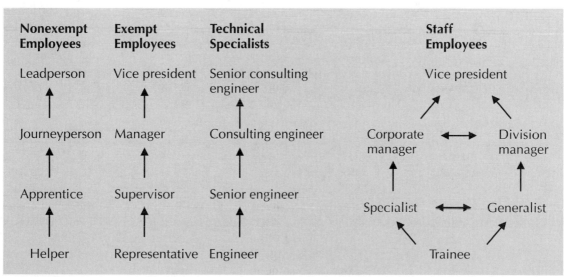

ployees receive these prizes as they compete against one another for available vacancies. For example, a promotion might lead to a higher rate of pay, and a transfer may result in a move to a better work location. Research has shown that these competitions may be contested, as opportunities for upward advancement are limited in most organizations.[1]

An exception to the primarily upward mobility in the promotion ladders in Exhibit 6.1 shows the lateral moves that sometimes occur for the staff member who has both generalist and specialist experiences as well as corporate and division experience. This staff member is considered more well-rounded and better able to work within the total organization. Experience as a specialist helps the person be familiar with technical issues that arise. Experience as a generalist gives the employee a breadth of knowledge about many matters in the staff function. Corporate experience provides a policy and planning perspective, whereas division experience provides greater insight on day-to-day operational matters.

Traditional mobility paths make it very easy, from an administrative vantage point, to identify where to look for applicants in the organization. For promotion, one looks at the next level down in the organizational hierarchy, and over, for transfer. Although such a system is straightforward to administer, it is not very flexible and may inhibit the matching of the best person for the job. For example, the best person for the job may be at two job levels down and in another division from the vacant job. It is very difficult to locate such a person under a traditional mobility path.

Innovative Mobility Paths   Examples of innovative mobility paths are shown in Exhibit 6.2. The emphasis here is no longer simply on upward mobility. Instead, movement in the organization may be in any direction, including up, down, and from side to side. Employee movement is emphasized to ensure continuous learning by employees such that each can make the greatest contribution to the organization. This is in direct contrast to the traditional promotion ladder, where the goal is for each person to achieve a position with ever-higher status. Many organizations have shifted to innovative mobility paths for two reasons: (a) There is the need to be flexible given global and technological changes, and (b) slower organizational growth has made it necessary to find alternative ways to utilize employees' talents.

Parallel tracks allow for employees to specialize in technical work or management work and advance within either. Historically, technical specialists had to shift away from technical to managerial work if they wanted to receive higher-status job titles and pay. In other words, being a technical specialist was a dead-end job. Under a parallel track system, both job titles and salaries of technical specialists are elevated to be commensurate with their managerial counterparts.

With a lateral track system, there may be no upward mobility at all. The individual's greatest contribution to the organization may be to stay at a certain level

EXHIBIT 6.2   Innovative Mobility Paths

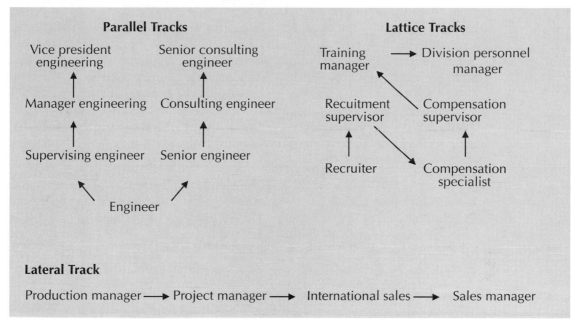

of the organization for an extended period of time while serving in a variety of capacities, as shown in Exhibit 6.2.

A lattice mobility path has upward, lateral, and even downward movement. For example, a recruiter may be promoted to a recruitment supervisor position, but to continue to contribute to the organization, the person may need to take a lateral step to become knowledgeable about all the technical details in compensation. After mastering these details, the person may then become a supervisor again, this time in the compensation area rather than recruitment. From a previous company, the person may have experience in training and be ready to take the next move to training manager without training experience internal to the organization. Finally, the person may take a lateral move to manage all the HR functions (recruitment, compensation, training) in a division as a division personnel manager.

Increasingly, some organizations have abandoned career structures altogether. In these team-based kinds of jobs, employees do not occupy traditional jobs but are "bonded" together with other employees, depending on the project. In this structure, employees are essentially entrepreneurial consultants, and the organization facilitates their activities. One example of such a cellular organization is TCG, based in Sydney, Australia. TCG partners with other organizations to provide computer assistance. TCG employees work on particular projects, depending on their expertise, and are rewarded based on the success of the project. These rewards may involve assignment to larger projects in the future, which is a form of promotion.[2]

The downside to innovative mobility paths, such as those discussed, is that they are very difficult to administer. Neat categories of where to look do not exist to the same degree as with traditional mobility paths. On the positive side, however, talented inside candidates who may not have been identified within a traditional system are identified because the system is flexible enough to do so.

When upward mobility is limited in an organization, as with many organizations using innovative mobility paths, special steps need to be taken to ensure that work remains meaningful to employees. If steps are not taken, the organization with limited promotional opportunities risks turnover of good employees. Examples of steps to make work more meaningful include the following:

1. *Alternative reward systems.* Rather than basing pay increases on promotions, pay increases can be based on knowledge and skill acquisition and contribution to the organization as a team member and individual. An example of a career system focused on skill development was recently established by Sony Technology Center in Pittsburgh. Called the Skill-Based Career Development system, when employees start their careers at the technology center, their first three years are devoted to learning core skills, such as technical and team skills. During this time, their pay is based on acquisition of these core skills. After three years, employees can choose from several options: (a) continue to develop technical skills on an individual basis, (b) continue to develop team skills, or (c) bid for an opportunity in another Sony business unit. With the first two options, pay continues to be based on skill acquisition but is more individually tailored than during the first three years. This program has been so successful that Sony is using it in other divisions within the company.[3]

2. *Team building.* Greater challenge and autonomy in the workplace can be created by having employees work in teams where they are responsible for all aspects of work involved in providing a service or product, including self-management.

3. *Counseling.* Workshops, self-directed workbooks, and individual advising can be used by organizations to ensure that employees have a well-reasoned plan for movement in the organization.

4. *Alternative employment.* Arrangements can be made for employee leaves of absence, sabbaticals, and consulting assignments to ensure that workers remain challenged and acquire new knowledge and skills.

Mobility Policies

Mobility paths show the relationship among jobs, but they do not show the rules by which people move between jobs. These rules are specified in written policies, which must be developed and should specify eligibility criteria.

Development   A well-defined mobility path policy statement is needed for both traditional and innovative mobility paths and has the following characteristics:

1. The intent of the policy is clearly communicated.
2. The policy is consistent with the philosophy and values of top management.
3. The scope of the policy, such as coverage by geographic region, employee groups, and so forth, is clearly articulated.
4. Employees' responsibilities and opportunities for development are clearly defined.
5. Supervisors' responsibilities for employee development are clearly stated.
6. Procedures are clearly described, such as how employees will be notified of openings, time deadlines and data to be supplied by the employee, how requirements and qualifications will be communicated, how the selection process will work, and how job offers will be made.
7. Rules regarding compensation and advancement are included.
8. Rules regarding benefits and benefit changes as they relate to advancement are included.

A well-articulated and well-executed mobility path policy is likely to be seen by employees as being fair. A poorly developed or nonexistent policy is likely to lead to employee claims of favoritism and discrimination.

Eligibility Criteria   An important component of an effective mobility policy is a listing of the criteria by which the organization will decide who is eligible to be considered for an open vacancy in a mobility path. In essence, these criteria restrict eligibility for recruitment to certain individuals. Usually these criteria are based on the amount of seniority, level of experience, KSAOs, or job duties required for the job. For example, to be considered for an international assignment, the applicant may be required to have been with the organization a certain length of time, have experience in a functional area in which there is a vacancy, be proficient in a foreign language, and be interested in performing new duties. These criteria need to be made very clear in the policy, otherwise unqualified people will apply and be disappointed when they are not considered. Also, the organization may be flooded with the paperwork and processing of applicants who are not eligible.

Administrative Issues

Mobility paths and mobility policies must be established as part of the planning process, and so, too, must administrative matters. Those administrative matters include requisitions, coordination, the budget, and the recruitment guide.

Requisitions

A requisition or authorization to fill a position by higher-level management is essential to the internal recruitment process. Without a formal requisition, it is far too easy for managers to make promises or "cut deals" with employees, contrary to organizational objectives. For example, managers may promote their employees into new job titles that have not been authorized by top management. In doing so, they may create perceptions of unfairness among those with similar backgrounds who were not promoted. This action thus runs contrary to the organizational goal of fair HR systems. Thus, formal requisitions should always be used in internal recruitment, just as they are in external recruitment.

Coordination

Internal and external recruitment efforts need to be coordinated and synchronized via the organization's staffing philosophy. If this coordination is not done, disastrous results can occur. For example, if independent searches are conducted internally and externally, then two people may be hired for one open vacancy. If only an external recruitment search is conducted, the morale of existing employees may be reduced when they feel that they have been passed over for a promotion. If only an internal recruitment search is conducted, the person hired may not be as qualified as someone from the external market. Because of these possibilities, internal *and* external professionals must work together with the line manager to coordinate efforts before the search for candidates begins.

To coordinate activities, two steps should be taken. First, internal staffing specialist positions should be designated to ensure that internal candidates are considered in the recruitment process. External staffing specialists are called recruiters; internal staffing specialists are often known as placement or classification professionals, to acknowledge the fact that they are responsible for placing or classifying existing employees rather than bringing in or recruiting employees from outside the organization.

Second, policies need to be created that specify the number and types of candidates sought internally and the number and types of candidates sought externally. For example, at Honeywell's Systems and Research Center in Bloomington, Minnesota, a management team meets regularly as part of the planning and development process to make these determinations.[4]

Budget

An organization's internal recruitment budgeting process should also closely mirror the budgeting process that occurs with external recruitment. The cost per hire may, however, differ between internal and external recruitment. The fact that internal recruitment targets candidates already working for the organization does not mean that the cost per hire is necessarily less than external recruitment.

Sometimes internal recruitment can be more costly than external recruitment because some of the methods involved in internal recruitment can be quite expensive. For example, when internal candidates are considered for the job but not hired, they need to be counseled on what to do to further develop their careers to become competitive for the position the next time it is vacant. When a candidate is rejected with external recruiting, a simple and less costly rejection letter usually suffices.

Recruitment Guide

As with external recruitment, internal recruitment activities involve the development of a recruitment guide, a formal document that details the process to be followed to attract applicants to a vacant job. Included in the plan are details such as the time, money, and staff activities required to fill the job, as well as the steps to be taken to fill the vacancy. An example of an internal recruitment guide is shown in Exhibit 6.3.

STRATEGY DEVELOPMENT

After organizational and administrative issues have been covered in the planning phase of internal recruitment, an organization must develop a strategy to locate viable internal job applicants. It must consider where to look, how to look, and when to look.

Closed, Open, and Targeted Recruitment

The strategy for where to look must be conducted within the constraints of the general eligibility criteria for mobility. Within these constraints it requires a knowledge of closed, open, and targeted systems.

Closed Internal Recruitment System

Under a closed internal recruitment system, employees are not made aware of job vacancies. The only people made aware of promotion or transfer opportunities are those who oversee placement in the HR department, line managers with vacancies, and contacted employees. The way a vacancy is typically filled under a closed system is shown in Exhibit 6.4.

A closed system is very efficient. There are only a few steps to follow, and the time and cost involved are minimal. However, a closed system is only as good as the files showing candidates' KSAOs. If inaccurate or out-of-date files are kept, qualified candidates may be overlooked.

EXHIBIT 6.3　Internal Recruitment Guide

Position Reassignments into New Claims Processing Center

Goal:　Transfer all qualified medical claims processors and examiners from one company subsidiary to the newly developed claims processing center. Terminate those who are not well qualified for the new positions and whose existing positions are being eliminated.

Assumptions:　That all employees have been notified that their existing positions in company subsidiary ABC are being eliminated and they will be eligible to apply for positions in the new claims processing center.

Hiring responsibility:　Manager of Claims Processing and Manager of Claims Examining.

Other resources:　Entire human resource department staff.

Time frames:

Positions posted internally on April 2, 2002
Employees may apply until April 16, 2002
Interviews will be scheduled/coordinated during week of April 19, 2002
Interviews will occur during the week of April 26, 2002
Selections made and communicated by last week in May
Total number of available positions: 60

Positions available and corresponding qualification summaries:

6 claims supervisors—4-year degree with 3 years of claims experience, including 1 year of supervisory experience.

14 claims data entry operators—6 months of data entry experience. Knowledge of medical terminology helpful.

8 hospital claims examiners—12 months of claims data entry/processing experience. Knowledge of medical terminology necessary.

8 physician claims examiners—12 months of claims data entry/processing experience. Knowledge of medical terminology necessary.

8 dental claims examiners—12 months of claims data entry/processing experience and 6 months of dental claims examining experience. Knowledge of dental terminology necessary.

8 mental health claims examiners—12 months of claims data entry/processing experience and 6 months of mental health claims experience. Knowledge of medical and mental health terminology necessary.

8 substance abuse claims examiners—12 months of claims data entry/processing experience and 6 months of substance abuse experience. Knowledge of medical terminology necessary.

(continued)

EXHIBIT 6.3   Continued

Transfer request guidelines: Internal candidates must submit internal transfer requests and an accompanying cover page listing all positions for which they are applying, in order of preference.

Internal candidates may apply for no more than five positions.

Transfer requests must be complete and be signed by the employee and the employee's supervisor.

Candidate qualification review process: Transfer requests from internal candidates will be reviewed on a daily basis. Those not qualified for any positions for which they applied will be notified by phone that day, due to the large volume of requests.

All-transfer requests and accompanying cover pages will be filed by the position to which they refer. If internal candidates applied for more than one position, their transfer packet will be copied so that one copy is in each position folder.

Once all candidate qualifications have been received and reviewed, each candidate's transfer packet will be copied and transmitted to the managers for review and interview selection. Due to the large number of candidates, managers will be required to interview only those candidates with the best qualifications for the available positions. Managers will notify human resources with the candidates with whom they would like interviews scheduled. Whenever possible, the manager will interview the candidate during one meeting for all of the positions applied and qualified for.

Selection guidelines: Whenever possible, the best-qualified candidates shall be selected for the available positions.

The corporation has committed to attempting to place all employees whose positions are being eliminated.

Managers reserve the right to not select employees currently on disciplinary probationary periods.

Employees should be slotted in a position with a salary grade comparable to their current salary grade. Employees' salaries shall not be reduced due to the involuntary nature of the job reassignment.

Notification of nonselection: Candidates not selected for a particular position will be notified by electronic message.

Selection notifications: Candidates selected for a position will be notified in person by the human resource staff and will be given a confirmation letter specifying starting date, position, reporting relationship, and salary.

EXHIBIT 6.4 **Closed Internal Recruitment System**

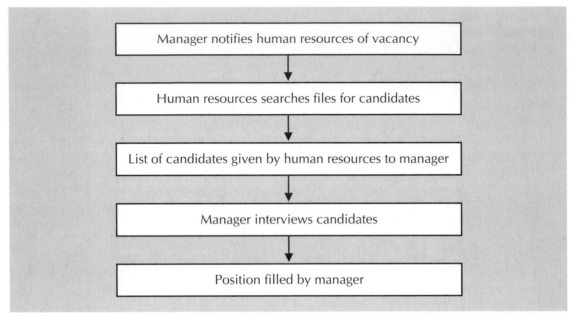

Manager notifies human resources of vacancy

Human resources searches files for candidates

List of candidates given by human resources to manager

Manager interviews candidates

Position filled by manager

Open Internal Recruitment System

Under an open internal recruitment system, employees are made aware of job vacancies. Usually this is accomplished by a job posting and bidding system. The typical steps followed in filling a vacancy under an open internal recruitment system are shown in Exhibit 6.5.

An open system gives employees a chance to measure their qualifications against those required for advancement. It helps minimize the possibility of supervisors selecting only favorite employees for promotion or transfer. Hidden talent is often uncovered.

An open system may, however, create unwanted competition among employees for limited advancement opportunities. It is a very lengthy and time-consuming process to screen all candidates and provide them with feedback. Employee morale may be decreased among those who are not advanced.

Targeted System of Internal Recruitment

Under a targeted system, both open and closed steps are followed at the same time. Jobs are posted, and the HR department conducts a search outside the job posting system. Both systems are used to cast as wide a net as possible. The large applicant pool is then narrowed down by KSAOs, seniority eligibility, demographics, and availability of applicants.

A targeted system is used by Englehard Corporation. At Englehard, an HR

EXHIBIT 6.5   Open Internal Recruitment System

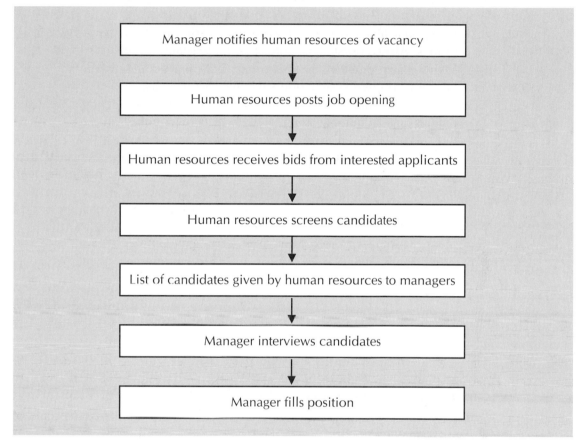

council meets each month to discuss open positions and possible internal candidates. The council includes the CEO and directors of Englehard's business units to ensure that viable candidates are identified and yet the moves make sense for the organization. At the same time, jobs are posted internally so interested (and perhaps overlooked) employees can apply.[5]

A targeted system has three advantages: a thorough search is conducted, people have equal opportunity to apply for postings, and hidden talent is uncovered. The major disadvantage with a targeted system is that it entails a very time-consuming and costly process.

Criteria for Choice of System

In an ideal world, with unlimited resources, one would choose a targeted system of internal recruitment. Resource constraints often make this choice impossible, so organizations must choose between open and closed systems. There are several criteria that need to be considered thoroughly before selecting an internal recruitment system:

1. A closed system is the least expensive in terms of search costs. However, it may lead to high legal costs if minorities and women do not have equal access to jobs. An open system is more costly; a targeted system costs the most.
2. Many managers want a person to start work immediately when they have a vacancy; a closed system offers the quickest response.
3. An open system is more likely than a closed system to identify more candidates, and hidden talent is less likely to be overlooked.
4. Some openings may require a very narrow and specialized KSAO set. A closed system may be able to identify these people quickly. An open system may be very cumbersome when only a select few meet the minimum qualifications needed to perform the job.
5. An open system may motivate migration of labor from jobs that are critical and difficult to fill. If so, then employees may create vacancies in critical areas, which in turn may create new recruitment problems.
6. A labor agreement or contract is a legally binding agreement. Whatever system is specified within must be followed.
7. An open system, where rules and regulations are known, enhances perception of fairness.

Recruitment Sources

Once it has been specified where and how in the organization individuals are likely to be found, there are several major methods that can be used to decide how to look for them: job postings, skills inventory, nominations, employee referral, and in-house temporary pool.

Job Posting

A job posting is very similar to the advertisement used in external recruitment. It spells out the duties and requirements of the job and shows how applicants can apply. Its content should be based on the job requirements matrix. A job posting begins when a job vacancy occurs. A position announcement is then posted. This posting may be through a bulletin board, newsletter, e-mail, or intranet (see subsequent section). At this step, organizations must decide whether to first limit the posting or advertise it throughout the organization. If the first posting is limited to a department, location, or work area and if the job is not filled, then it should be posted more broadly. Applicants respond to job postings using a bid sheet like the one shown in Exhibit 6.6.

At Home Depot, computer kiosks located in break rooms are used to list job openings. Employees can view these job postings during breaks or before or after shifts. If there is a job that appeals to an employee, he or she can take a computerized

EXHIBIT 6.6   Example of Bidding Form

INTERNAL APPLICATION FORM COVER SHEET

To apply for a posted position, interested employees should:

1. Look at the job posting notebook(s) or postings posted on the bulletin boards and choose the job or jobs that you are qualified for and interested in applying for. (Check the Qualifications section of the posting.) Make note of the deadline for applying for this position, which is indicated on the posting.

2. Complete one Internal Application Form to apply for a position or positions. This form acts as a résumé/application form. Obtain your direct supervisor's signature before turning the form into human resources.

3. Indicate below the priority of the jobs for which you would like to be given consideration.

   (Priority: 1 = first choice, 2 = second choice, 3 = third choice)

Priority	Job Title
_____	_____
_____	_____
_____	_____
_____	_____
_____	_____

4. Attach this cover sheet to the UHC Internal Application Form and turn both in to Karen in human resources by the application deadline appearing on the job posting.

5. Sign and date below:

_____   _____
Employee Signature   Date

Source: Reprinted with permission from United HealthCare Corporation and Physicians Health Plan of Ohio, Inc., Columbus, Ohio.

test for an opening at the kiosk. If the employee makes the cut, their application is forwarded. If they fail, supervisors are notified and employees may be offered training so they can compete successfully for the position in the future.[6]

Even advanced job posting systems may have some problems in administration. Examples of such difficulties include situations where employees believe that someone has been selected before the job was posted (a "bagged" job), cumbersome systems where managers and HR personnel are overwhelmed with résumés of unqualified candidates, and criticisms that the HR department is not doing an effective job of screening candidates for positions.

Some of these problems again point to the critical importance of the job requirements matrix. A good job posting system will clearly define the requisite KSAOs needed to perform the job. By having a job requirements matrix, employees, HR staff, and managers can do a more effective and efficient job of screening.

Another important issue with posting systems is feedback. Not only do employees need to know whether they receive the job or not, but those who do not receive the job need to be made aware of *why* they did not. Providing this feedback serves two purposes. First, it makes job posting part of the career development system of the organization. Second, it invites future bidding on postings by candidates. If employees are not given feedback, they may be less likely to bid for another job because they feel that their attempts to do so are futile.

An empirical study shows the characteristics of job posting systems that lead to high satisfaction by users.[7] Key characteristics include the adequacy of job descriptions, the adequacy of job notification procedures, the treatment received during the interview, the helpfulness of counseling, and the fairness of the job posting system. These characteristics should be treated as requirements of a good job posting policy.

As indicated, job posting can be done traditionally by physically posting job openings in a convenient location. Such an approach, however, can be very slow, inefficient, and create a large amount of paperwork. A faster and more efficient way to post jobs is to put them on personal computers, which also gives employees 24-hour-a-day access to job postings.

Skills Inventory

KSAOs that are used in making advancement decisions are stored in a skills inventory. The inventory consists of manual files or computer files for each employee. Examples of computer file screens for employees are shown in Exhibit 6.7. Unfortunately, many skills inventories are plagued by problems that make their usefulness suspect. One such problem is the very careful and tedious record keeping required to keep them up to date and useful. Maintenance of these files is critical. Qualified candidates may be bypassed if current files are not maintained. Another problem is that too much information is sometimes recorded. Variables having little relevance to advancement decisions are included, making them redundant with other files (e.g., payroll). Managers are often overwhelmed by the sheer volume in files and, as a result, may be resistant to using a skills inventory.

A final problem that must be confronted in maintaining a skills inventory is that files must be user-friendly. Files must be understood and accepted by system users. Doing so requires the participation of users in deciding which variables are to be retained. A user-friendly database should also have the following attributes:

EXHIBIT 6.7   Sample Elements in Skills Inventory

Screen 1:   Current employee data

Name:
SS #:
Department:
Position:
Supervisor:
Date in position:
Date of hire:

Screen 2:   Education data

	School Attended	Degree	Major	GPA	Year(s)
High school:					
Undergrad:					
Graduate:					
Doctorate:					

Additional course work:
Certifications/licenses:
Additional training:
Company training:

Additional training recommended:

Screen 3:   Company employment data

	Title	Date in Job	Performance Ratings/Dates
Present position:			
Previous positions:			

Positions in company qualified for:

Screen 4:   Previous employment data

	Company	Title	From	To	Reference Quality
Prev. empl.					
Prev. empl.					
Prev. empl.					
Prev. empl.					

Screen 5:   Express interests/goals

Areas of company:
Positions:
Additional training/education:

- simplicity of format for data collection
- easy method for updating basic information on a scheduled basis
- reasonable and efficient techniques for extracting information from the database
- provisions for varied formats for output
- capability for statistical analysis using relational databases
- confidentiality of information
- representativeness of data provided
- accuracy of data by audit and verification procedures
- simplicity in querying data bank
- inclusive but not unwieldy detail
- integration with other HR files

Nominations

Nominations for internal candidates to apply for open positions can be solicited from potential supervisors and peers. They may be an excellent source of names of internal candidates, as they have a great deal of familiarity with what is required to be successful in the position. They can help establish the criteria for eligibility and then, through their contacts in the organization, search for eligible candidates. Self-nominations are also very useful in that they ensure that qualified candidates are not inadvertently overlooked using other applicant searching methods. Self-nomination is an especially important consideration in the internal recruitment of minorities and women.

Employee Referral

Using employees to refer potential hires to the organization is a common method of looking for candidates in external recruitment. Though it has not been used much in internal recruitment, more companies are using employees' referrals to staff positions internally. One system that helps companies do this is JobTAG of Norristown, Pennsylvania. JobTAG uses Web-based software that rewards employees who refer other employees within the company for open positions. Employees log onto their company's JobTAG site, make referrals, and if a referral is hired, the employee is rewarded (rewards differ from company to company). There are other providers of internal referral systems.[8] Regardless of what system is used, as with external recruitment, employee referral programs used internally may need to rely on formal programs with recognition for participation to get employees actively participating in making referrals. Moreover, they need to be educated on eligibility requirements to ensure that qualified personnel are referred.

In-House Temporary Pools

In-house temporary pools are not only important to the temporary staffing of organizations as the temporary need for personnel arises periodically but they are also an excellent source of permanent internal employment. From the perspective of the organization, they are a known commodity and require less orientation to the organization than would external hires. From the perspective of the applicant, in-house temporary employees are more likely to have realistic expectations regarding the organization and the job than external candidates. Policies must be clearly established in the organization to govern the movement of in-house temporary employees into more permanent positions. For example, accommodations must be made to replace the in-house temporary who has accepted a permanent assignment in a timely manner. Otherwise, the organization may face a shortage of temporaries to fill temporary assignments.

Succession Plans

A critical source of internal recruitment is provided by succession planning. Most succession plans include replacement charts (see Chapter 3), which indicate middle- and upper-level positions and who is scheduled to fill those slots. Replacement charts usually also indicate the time until the individual is ready for the assignment, and identify the KSAOs still in need of development. Unlike a skills inventory, which is organized by employee and lists the employee's current skill set, replacement charts are organized by position and lists the skills needed for the prospective position (i.e., "for the employee to be ready for promotion into this position from her current position, these are the skills she needs to process or develop"). Dow Chemical's succession plan, for example, includes a list of "now ready" candidates; where there are jobs with similar competencies, it clusters roles and lists candidates for these roles as well. Dow has formal succession plans for 50–60 jobs that it has identified as critical corporate roles and also has plans for another 200–300 jobs that are identified as needing continuity.

It is critical that succession planning be future-oriented, lest the organization plan be based on historical competencies that fail to meet new challenges.[9] Software exists to assist companies with succession planning. Succession Plus is a succession planning package that interfaces with a company's HR information system to provide replacement charts and "competency libraries" that allow an organization to identify developmental activities and assignments for individuals in the replacement charts. Many Fortune 500 companies use Succession Plus.

CEO succession has always been an important issue for organizations, but never more so than today. Executive turnover is reported to be at an all-time high, and boards of directors have struggled to find adequate successors in a timely manner. In several companies, such as AT&T and Apple Computers, boards have appointed a CEO only to replace him within a matter of months. Other companies, such as Upjohn Pharmaceuticals, are caught off guard by a resignation and do not know where to turn. The key to avoid such fiascoes is to have a succession plan for CEOs. However, a poll of 518 companies indicated that only 42% had such a formal succession plan in place. According to a study by the National Association of Corporate Directors, a succession plan should begin with a thorough job analysis and with a listing of the characteristics and behaviors of a successful CEO. The company should not leave it to the CEO to identify a successor. CEOs are typically not trained or experienced in staffing, and they may have selfish motives to appoint a hand-picked successor. Or, they may avoid appointing a successor altogether, thus keeping themselves in the job. Thus, the board must be deeply involved in the selection process. Boards also need to realize that the succession process should begin well before the CEO departs; in fact, it should be a continuous process. It is more important than ever that succession plans be flexible when the positions of today may not exist tomorrow. Additionally, many companies are streamlining the formal, lengthy succession plans.[10]

Intranet and Intraplacement

With the growing sophistication of company-wide computer networks, a recent source of internal applicants are internal Web sites known as intranets. An intranet is similar to the Internet, except that it is confined to the organization. This makes it ideal for internal recruitment because jobs can be quickly posted for all employees to see. Some companies have expanded their intranet to include an online career center, where employees not only view job postings but also gain access to information about KSAOs needed for positions that might interest them; it may even include modules that will assist employees in acquiring these KSAOs.[11] The job posting system used by Home Depot (see Job Posting section under Recruitment Sources) is a good example of an intranet system.

Whereas intranets rely on employees to search for positions, so-called intraplacement systems use internal recruiters to recruit and place internal candidates. Why are internal recruiters needed? The combination of slow organizational growth and low unemployment leaves many employees with clear hiring options, but not within the company. Thus, organizations in such circumstances need to be proactive in recruiting strong applicants for positions within the organization. In many ways, successful intraplacement relies on a succession planning system to identify which applicants need to be recruited. Once these internal candidates are identified, internal recruiters are designated to act as internal executive recruiters.[12] Some companies have even launched internal search firms, such as First Union Corporation.

Choice of Sources

As is the case with external recruitment, there is no single best source for internal recruitment. There are a number of factors organizations should consider in deciding which internal sources to use. Not surprisingly, many of these are the same as external recruitment. The criteria organizations should use are provided below.

1. *Quantity of labor.* Although precious little data are available on the subject, it seems likely that some methods, such as job postings and use of an intranet, will produce more internal applicants than other methods, such as nominations and referrals. Other methods, such as skills inventories and succession plans, only identify viable candidates. Thus, when these methods are used, they must be combined with other methods to generate actual interest on the part of internal applicants.

2. *Quality of labor.* Any of the methods of internal recruitment are capable of producing high-quality candidates. However, the quality of "open" sources, such as open job postings, nominations, and referrals, where literally anyone can apply, would seem to produce candidates of variable quality. When it is essential to fill a position with a high-quality employee, the organization should rely on other methods, such as succession plans and intraplacement, which allow the organization to target high-potential employees for recruitment.

3. *Budget constraints.* Internal recruitment methods differ widely in their costs. Some methods, such as nominations and referrals, are virtually cost-free. Other methods, such as using an intranet and succession plans, take a substantial commitment of resources to set up and maintain.

4. *Contractual or legal obligations.* Many unionized environments and government agencies require that jobs be formally posted. Union contracts may also restrict the use of in-house temporary employees to fill positions in the presence of a labor dispute.

When to Look

A final strategic consideration an organization must make is when to look for internal candidates. As with external recruitment, consideration involves calculation of lead time and time sequence concerns.

Lead Time Concerns

A major difference between internal and external recruitment is that internal recruitment not only fills vacancies but also creates them. Each time a vacancy is filled with an internal candidate, a new vacancy is created in the spot vacated by the internal candidate.

As a result of this difference, it is incumbent on the organization to do HR planning along with internal recruitment. This planning involves elements of succession planning (see Chapter 3). Such planning is essential for effective internal recruitment.

Time Sequence Concerns

As previously noted, it is essential that internal and external recruitment activities be coordinated properly. This proper coordination is especially true with the timing and sequencing of events that must be laid out carefully for both recruitment and placement personnel. Many organizations start with internal recruitment followed by external recruitment to fill a vacancy. Issues that need to be addressed include how long the internal search will take place, whether external recruitment can be done concurrently with internal recruitment, and who will be selected if both an internal and external candidate are identified with relatively equal KSAOs.

SEARCHING

Once the planning and strategy development phases are conducted, it is time to conduct the search. As with external recruitment, the search for internal recruits is activated with a requisition. Once the requisition has been approved, the message and medium must be developed to communicate the vacancy to applicants.

Communication Message

As with external recruitment, the message to be communicated can be traditional, realistic, targeted, or attractive. A traditional message provides the applicant with little concrete or accurate information. A realistic message portrays the job as it really is, including positive and negative aspects. A targeted message is one that points out how the job matches the needs of the applicant. An attractive message provides the applicant with monetary and nonmonetary inducements for accepting the invitation to interview and eventually accept a job.

Realistic messages can be communicated using a technique like a realistic job preview (RJP). This technique needs to be applied carefully for internal recruitment because as a result of their already being a member of the organization, applicants may have an accurate picture of the job. Hence, an RJP may not be needed. It should not, however, be automatically assumed that all internal candidates have accurate information about the job and organization. Hence, RJPs are appropriate for internal applicants when they move to an unknown job, a newly created job, or a new geographic area, including an international assignment.

Targeted messages along with inducements are likely to attract experienced internal employees. Targeted messages about the desirability of a position and the actual rewards should come directly from the job rewards matrix. Clearly, the information in the job rewards matrix needs to be communicated by the hiring manager who hopes to catch an experienced employee, rather than offers of elaborate promises that the manager may not be able to keep.

Communication Medium

The actual method or medium used to communicate job openings internally may be a job posting, other written documents, potential supervisors and peers, and informal systems. In a job posting, the duties and requirements of the job should be clearly defined as should the eligibility requirements. To ensure consistency and fair treatment, job postings are usually coordinated by the HR department.

Other written documents used to communicate a vacancy may include a description of the organization and location as well as a description of the job. A brochure, videocassette, or diskette can be created to actually show and describe what the organization and the location of the organization is really like. This message may be of critical importance to the applicant who may, for example, be asked to relocate to a new geographic area or to accept an international assignment.

Potential supervisors and peers can be used to describe to the internal applicant how the position they are considering fits into the larger organizational picture. Supervisors will have knowledge about how the position fits with the strategic direction of the organization. Hence, they can communicate information regarding the expansion or contraction of the business unit within which the organization resides. Moreover, supervisors can convey the mobility paths and requirements for future movement by the applicants within the business unit, should they be hired. Peers can be used to supplement these supervisory observations to give candidates a realistic look at what actually happens by way of career development.

Informal systems exist in organizations where organizational members communicate with one another about job vacancies to be filled internally in the absence of verifiable information. The problem with "word of mouth," the "grapevine," and "hall talk" is that it can be a highly selective, inaccurate, and haphazard method of communicating information. It is selective because, by accident or design, not all employees hear about vacant jobs. Talented personnel, including minorities and women, may thus be overlooked. It is inaccurate because it relies on second- or thirdhand information; important details, such as actual job requirements and rewards, are omitted or distorted as they are passed from person to person. Informal methods are also haphazard in that there is no regular communication channel specifying set times for communicating job information. As a result of these problems, informal systems are not to be encouraged.

APPLICANT REACTIONS

A glaring omission in the research literature is a lack of attention paid to studying the reactions of applicants to the internal recruitment process. This lapse stands in stark contrast to the quantity of research conducted on reactions to the external recruitment process. One notable exception in the internal recruitment process is the study of perceived fairness. Given limited opportunities for promotion and transfer, issues of fairness often arise over mobility decisions within an organization. Issues of fairness can be broken down into the categories of distributive and procedural justice. Distributive justice refers to how fair the employee perceives the actual decision to be (e.g., promote or not promote). This particular aspect of fairness is very salient today because there are a large number of baby boomers competing for the few positions at the top of organizational hierarchies. At the same time, many organizations are eliminating middle management positions. Procedural justice refers to how fair the employee perceives the process (e.g., policies and procedures) that leads to the promotion or transfer decision to be. Reviews of the evidence suggest that procedures may be nearly as great a source of dissatisfaction to employees as decisions.[13] In some organizations, dissatisfaction arises as a result of the fact that there is no formal policy regarding promotion and transfer opportunities. In other organizations, there may be a formal policy, but it may not be closely followed. In yet other organizations, it may be who you know, rather than what you know, that serves as the criterion that determines advancement. Finally, in some organizations there is outright discrimination against women and minorities. All of these examples are violations of procedural justice and likely to be perceived as unfair.

The concepts of procedural and distributive justice indicate that organizations should routinely survey the reactions of organizational members to determine the effectiveness of the internal recruitment process. An example of such a study examining applicants' reactions to job posting is shown in Exhibit 6.8. The first step in this study was to generate a list of questionnaire items showing characteristics of a job posting system. As can be seen, these items closely mirror the concepts of procedural and distributive justice. Next, the questionnaire items were passed out to employees to gather their reactions. These reactions were tallied and summarized, as shown in Exhibit 6.8, according to the percentage of employees who had "favorable," "neutral," or "unfavorable" reactions to each of the characteristics of the job posting system. It can be seen that applicants had diverse reactions to the system. Though not shown, applicants' reactions to characteristics of the job posting system were also correlated with overall satisfaction with the system. The three largest correlations with satisfaction involved the fairness of the job posting system, effect on job mobility, and treatment during the interview.

This exhibit is a good illustration of how applicant reactions to job posting can be measured. The same steps can be followed to evaluate applicant reactions to other steps in the internal recruitment process.

TRANSITION TO SELECTION

As with external recruitment, once a job seeker has been identified and attracted to a new job, the organization needs to prepare the person for the selection process.

It should not be assumed that just because job seekers come from inside the organization they will automatically know and understand the selection procedures. With the rapid advances being made in selection methods, the applicant may be unaware of new methods being used that are different from those used previously to hire the applicant to a previous job. Even if the same selection methods are being used, the applicant may need to be "refreshed" on the process, as a considerable period of time may have transpired between the current and previous selection decisions.

An example of an organization that has done an excellent job of preparing internal job seekers to become applicants is the Public Works Agency for the county of Sacramento, California.[14] The county uses a panel of interviewers together, rather than a series of individual interviews, to make selection decisions.

EXHIBIT 6.8   Evaluation of a Job Posting System

Item	Applicants' Response (Percent)			
	N	Favorable	Neutral	Unfavorable
Adequacy of job description	382	39.7	35.9	24.3
Adequacy of job notification procedures	390	42.0	36.9	21.0
Difficulty of completing application	197	87.3	9.1	3.5
Quality of handbook	155	76.8	18.7	4.5
Treatment during interview	152	61.8	18.4	19.7
How well reasons for nonacceptance were explained	87	23.0	17.2	59.8
How well job requirements match those in job description	79	60.8	24.1	15.2
How well worker met job demands	76	94.8	3.9	1.3
Helpfulness of counseling	52	28.8	26.9	44.2
Effect on job mobility	362	65.2	24.9	9.9
Fairness of job posting system	367	35.8	28.0	34.6
Satisfaction with job posting system	378	28.8	26.9	36.2
Was handbook read?	403	38.6	—	61.4
Did applicant receive a job offer?	173	44.5	—	55.5
Was counseling sought?	403	12.5	—	87.5
Was applicant considered for position?	183	82.5	—	17.5
Average number of times interviewed	153 Mean = 1.83			

Source: L. W. Kleinman and K. J. Clark, "Users' Satisfaction with Job Posting," *HR Magazine*, 1984, 29(9) pp. 104–110. Reprinted with the permission of *HR Magazine* (formerly *Personnel Administrator*) published by the Society for Human Resource Management, Alexandria, VA.

For many lower-level employees in the maintenance department this approach was a first-time experience. Consequently, they were apprehensive about this process because they had no previous experience with the internal selection process. In response to this situation, the HR group initially conducted training classes to describe the process to applicants. However, this was a very time-consuming process for the staff, so they replaced the classroom training with videos. One major component of the video was the preparation required prior to the panel interview. Instructions here included appropriate dress and materials to review. Another major component of the video depicted what happens to the applicant during the panel interview. This component included instructions on types of questions to be asked, the process to be followed, and do's and don't's in answering the panel interview questions. A final component of the video was testimonials from previous exam takers who have become managers. They explain from an organizational perspective what the organization is looking for, as well as study tips and strategies.

LEGAL ISSUES

The mobility of people within the organization, particularly upward, has long been a matter of EEO/AA concern. The workings of the internal labor market rely heavily on internal recruitment activities. As with external recruitment, internal recruitment activities can operate in exclusionary ways, resulting in unequal promotion opportunities, rates, and results for certain groups of employees, particularly women and minorities. The Affirmative Action Programs regulations specifically address internal recruitment as a part of the federal contractor's AAP. Seniority systems are likewise subject to legal scrutiny, particularly regarding the determination of what constitutes a bona fide system under the law. More recently, promotion systems have been studied as they relate to the "glass ceiling" effect and the kinds of barriers that have been found to stifle the rise of minorities and women upward in organizations.

Affirmative Action Programs Regulations

Regulations on Affirmative Action Programs from the OFCCP require promotion placement goals where there are discrepancies between percentages of minority and women employed and available internally in job groups. Accompanying these goals must be an identification of problem areas and action-oriented programs to correct the problem areas. As in the case of external recruitment, the regulations are virtually silent on indications of specific steps the organization might take to correct promotion system problems. Previous (now expired) regulations provide many useful ideas.

Suggestions include:

- Post or otherwise announce promotion opportunities
- Make an inventory of current minority and female employees to determine academic, skill, and experience levels of individual employees
- Initiate necessary remedial job training and work-study programs
- Develop and implement formal employee evaluation programs
- Make certain "worker specifications" have been validated on job performance–related criteria (neither minority nor female employees should be required to possess higher qualifications than those of the lowest qualified incumbent)
- When apparently qualified minority or female employees are passed over for upgrading, require supervisory personnel to submit written justification
- Establish formal career counseling programs to include attitude development, education aid, job rotation, buddy systems, and similar programs
- Review seniority practices and seniority clauses in union contracts to ensure such practices or clauses are nondiscriminatory and do not have a discriminatory effect

As can be seen, the previous regulations contained a broad range of suggestions for reviewing and improving promotion systems. In terms of recruitment itself, the previous regulations appeared to favor developing KSAO-based information about employees as well as an open promotion system characterized by job posting and cautious use of seniority as a basis for governing upward mobility.

Bona Fide Seniority Systems

Title VII (see Chapter 2) explicitly permits the use of bona fide seniority systems as long as they are not the result of an intention to discriminate. This position presents the organization with a serious dilemma. Past discrimination in external staffing may have resulted in a predominantly white male workforce. A change to a nondiscriminatory external staffing system may increase the presence of women and minorities within an organization, but they will still have less seniority there than the white males. If eligibility for promotion is based on seniority and/or if seniority is an actual factor considered in promotion decisions, then those with less seniority will have a lower incidence of promotion. Thus, the seniority system will have an adverse impact on women and minorities, even though there is no current intention to discriminate. Is such a seniority system bona fide?

Two points are relevant here. First, the law never defines the term "seniority system." Generally, however, any practice that uses length of employment as a basis for making decisions (such as promotion decisions) is interpreted as a seniority system. Thus, seniority systems can and do occur outside the context of a collective bargaining agreement.[15]

Second, current interpretation is that, in the absence of a discriminatory intent, virtually any seniority system is likely to be bona fide, even if it causes adverse impact.[16] This interpretation creates an incentive for the organization not to change its current seniority-based practices or systems. Other pressures, such as the Affirmative Action Program regulations or a voluntary AAP, create an incentive to change in order to eliminate the occurrence of adverse impact in promotion. The organization thus must carefully consider exactly what its posture will be toward seniority practices and systems within the context of its overall AAP.

Under the ADA there is potential conflict between needing to provide reasonable accommodation to an employee (such as job reassignment) and provisions of the organization's seniority system (such as bidding for jobs on the basis of seniority). According to the Supreme Court, it will ordinarily be unreasonable (undue hardship) for a reassignment request to prevail over the seniority system unless the employee can show some special circumstances that warrant an exception.

The Glass Ceiling

The "glass ceiling" is a term used to characterize strong but invisible barriers for women and minorities to promotion in the organization, particularly to the highest levels. Evidence demonstrating the existence of a glass ceiling is substantial. The composition of the U.S. labor force is approximately 54.5% male and 45.5% female, and 79% white and 21% minority. In the Fortune 2,000 industrial and service companies, however, only 5% of the senior-level managers are women, and of that 5% virtually all are white. In the Fortune 500 companies, 97% of senior managers are white, and 95% are male.

As one goes down the hierarchy or looks across specific industries, however, a more mixed pattern of evidence is found. Across all executive, administrative, and managerial occupations, 52% are held by males (40% white and 12% minority), and 48% are held by females (36% white and 12% minority); in these occupations the percentage of white males ranges from 75% in construction to 42% in retail to 16% in health services and social services.[17] Thus, the closer to the top of the hierarchy, the thicker the glass in the ceiling. At lower levels, the glass becomes much thinner. There are substantial variations in this pattern, though, across industries.

Where glass ceilings exist, there are two important questions to ask. What are the reasons for a lack of upward mobility and representation for minorities and women at higher levels of the organization? What changes need to be made, especially staffing-related ones, to help shatter the glass ceiling?

Barriers to Mobility

The Federal Glass Ceiling Commission conducted a four-year study of glass ceiling issues, including barriers to mobility. It identified three sets of barriers:[18]

1. Societal—access to educational opportunities; stereotyping, prejudice, and bias related to race, gender, and ethnicity

2. Governmental—weakness in collection and dissemination of glass ceiling information; lack of vigorous and consistent monitoring and law enforcement

3. Internal—lack of outreach recruitment practices, management training, mentoring, tailor training and job assignments in revenue-producing areas, access to critical developmental assignments on committees and task forces; initial selection and placement on jobs in staff and professional jobs outside the upward pipeline to top jobs; biased rating and testing systems; little access to informal networks of communication; counterproductive behavior and harassment by colleagues

An instructive illustration of these barriers, particularly the internal ones, comes from a 21-company study of men and women in sales careers.[19] The study found that 41% of women and 45% of men were eager to move into management, but the women were much less optimistic of their chances of getting promoted. Whereas the sales forces studied were 26% female, only 14% of sales managers were female. The study portrayed "a survivalist culture where career paths are more like obscure jungle trails and where most women say they experience sexual harassment." The study also found "recruiters' use of potentially discriminatory screening tests, managers' negative stereotypes about women, women's lack of access to career-boosting mentors and networks, and difficulty entertaining customers in traditional ways such as fishing and golf outings." Saleswomen were also highly dependent on their mostly male managers for job and territory assignments, which were often based on stereotypes about willingness to travel, relocate, and work long hours.

Overcoming Barriers

The Federal Glass Ceiling Commission also studied in-depth the practices found in many organizations that were successfully changing to overcome barriers to upward advancement for women and minorities. They concluded that such glass ceiling initiatives had the following characteristics in common:[20]

- They have CEO support.
- They are part of the strategic business plan.
- They are specific to the organization.
- They are inclusive; for instance, they do not exclude white non-Hispanic men.

- They address preconceptions and stereotypes.
- They emphasize and require accountability for promoting women and minorities.
- They track progress.
- They are comprehensive.

Based on their findings and deliberations, the commission issued a set of 12 recommendations for eliminating the glass ceiling. A summary of those recommendations is provided in Exhibit 6.9.

In terms of specific staffing practices that are desirable for eliminating the glass ceiling, we offer the following suggestions. Barriers to upward mobility can be addressed and removed, at least in part, through internal recruitment activities. Internal recruitment planning needs to involve the design and operation of internal labor markets that facilitate the identification and flows of people to jobs throughout the organization. This may very well conflict with seniority-based practices or seniority systems, both of which are likely to be well entrenched. Organizations simply have to make hard and clear choices about the role(s) that seniority will play in promotion systems.

EXHIBIT 6.9   Summary of the Federal Glass Ceiling Commission Recommendations

For Business

- Demonstrate CEO commitment
- Include diversity in all strategic business plans; hold line managers accountable for results
- Select and promote qualified individuals; expand recruitment pools; seek candidates from noncustomary sources, backgrounds, and experiences
- Use Affirmative Action
- Prepare minorities and women for senior positions; enhance developmental experiences; provide mentoring
- Provide training throughout the organization to improve sensitivity to gender, racial, and ethnic differences
- Adopt policies that accommodate the balance between work and family responsibilities
- Adopt workplace practices that emphasize high performance

For Government

- Be a leader in eliminating own glass ceilings
- Strengthen enforcement of antidiscrimination laws
- Improve data collection about women and minorities in the workforce and organizations
- Provide for public disclosure of diversity data, especially for senior positions

Source: Federal Glass Ceiling Commission, Washington, DC, 1995.

In terms of recruitment strategy, where to look for employees looms as a major factor in potential change. The organization must increase its scanning capabilities and horizons to identify candidates to promote throughout the organization. In particular, this requires looking across functions for candidates, rather than merely promoting within an area (from sales to sales manager to district manager, for example). Candidates should thus be recruited through both traditional and innovative career paths.

Recruitment sources have to be more open and accessible to far-ranging sets of candidates. Informal, word-of-mouth, and "good old boy" sources do not suffice. Job posting and other recruitment strategies that encourage openness of vacancy notification and candidate application will become necessary.

Recruitment changes must be accompanied by many other changes.[21] Top male managers need to fully understand that women executives differ from them in what they perceive to be the major barriers to advancement. Research suggests that women executives are more likely to see an exclusionary climate (male stereotyping and preconceptions of women, exclusion from informal networks, and inhospitable corporate culture) as a critical barrier, whereas top male managers are more likely to point to experience deficiencies (lack of significant general management and line experience, not being in the pipeline long enough) as the culprit. Hence, top management must take steps to not only create better experience-generating opportunities for women but also to develop and foster a more inclusive climate for women, such as through mentoring and providing access to informal networks. To encourage such changes and improve advancement results for women and minorities, managers must be held formally accountable for their occurrence. For example, Motorola tracks the progress of women and minorities within each senior manager's area of responsibility and formally evaluates managers twice a year on this progress. To lead by example, the CEO has diversity, EEO, and AA goals in his bonus goals; these elements are also part of the bonus calculation for other senior managers. Since 1989, Motorola has gone from 2 to 43 women vice presidents and from 6 to 41 minority vice presidents.

Additional research has shown that HR professionals think both women and minority employees could benefit from a set of changes that would help eliminate career-advancing barriers. The top five changes are (1) CEO support of women and minorities and professional and senior roles, (2) dedicated effort to recruit and retain senior women and minority managers, (3) placement of women and minorities on boards of directors, (4) mentoring programs targeted to women and minorities, and (5) career development programs targeted toward women and minorities.[22]

In summary, solutions to the glass ceiling problem require myriad points of attack. First, women and minorities must have visibility and support at top levels—from the board of directors, the CEO, and senior management. That support must include actions to eliminate prejudice and stereotypes. Second, women and minorities must be provided the job opportunities and assignments that will allow them to develop the depth and breadth of KSAOs needed for ascension to, and success in, top management positions. These developmental experiences include assignments in multiple functions, management of diverse businesses, line management experience with direct profit-loss and bottom-line accountability, diverse geographic assignments, and international experience. Naturally, the relative importance of these experiences will vary according to type and size of the organization. Third, the organization must provide continual support for women and minorities to help ensure positive person/job matches. Included here are mentoring, training, and flexible work hours systems. Fourth, the organization must gear up its internal recruitment to aggressively and openly track and recruit women and minority candidates for advancement. Finally, the organization must develop and use valid methods of assessing the qualifications of women and minority candidates (see Chapters 8 and 9).[23]

SUMMARY

The steps involved in the internal recruitment process closely parallel those in the external recruitment process. These steps include planning, strategy development, and communication. With internal recruitment, the search is conducted inside rather than outside the organization. Where both internal and external searches are conducted, they need to be coordinated with one another.

The planning stage requires that the applicant population be identified. Doing so requires an understanding of mobility paths in the organization and mobility path policies. To get access to the internal applicant population, attention must be devoted in advance of the search to requisitions, number and type of contacts, the budget, and development of a recruitment guide.

In terms of strategy development, a closed, open, or targeted system can be used to decide where to look. How to look requires a knowledge of recruitment sources, such as job postings, skills inventories, nominations, employee referrals, in-house temporary pools, succession plans, and intranet and intraplacement. Just as with external recruitment, there are multiple criteria to be considered in choosing internal sources.

When searching for candidates, the message to be communicated can be traditional, realistic, targeted, or attractive. Which approach is best to use depends on the applicants, job, and organization. The message is usually communicated with a job posting. It should, however, be supplemented with other media including other written documents and potential peers' and supervisors' input. Informal communication methods with information that cannot be verified or with incomplete information are to be discouraged.

The organization needs to provide the applicant with assistance for the transition to selection. This assistance requires that the applicant be made fully aware of the selection process and how to best prepare for it. Taking this step, along with providing well-developed job postings and clearly articulated mobility paths and policies in the organization, should help applicants see the internal recruitment system as fair.

Internal recruitment activities have long been the object of close legal scrutiny. Past and current regulations make several suggestions regarding desirable promotion system features. The relevant laws permit bona fide seniority systems, as long as they are not intentionally used to discriminate. Seniority systems may have the effect of impeding promotions for women and minorities because these groups have not had the opportunity to accumulate an equivalent amount of seniority to that of white males. The glass ceiling refers to invisible barriers to upward advancement, especially to the top levels, for minorities and women. Studies of promotion systems indicate that internal recruitment practices contribute to this barrier. As a portion of an overall strategy to shatter the glass ceiling, changes are now being experimented with for opening up internal recruitment. These include actions to eliminate stereotypes and prejudices, training, and developmental experiences, mentoring, aggresive recruitment, and use of valid selection techniques.

DISCUSSION QUESTIONS

1. Traditional career paths emphasize strict upward mobility within an organization. How does mobility differ in organizations with innovative career paths? List three innovative career paths discussed in this chapter, describing how mobility occurs in each.
2. A sound policy regarding promotion is important. List the characteristics necessary for an effective promotion policy.
3. Compare and contrast a closed internal recruitment system with an open internal recruitment system.
4. What information should be included in the targeted internal communication message?
5. Applicant reactions and perceptions of the fairness of the internal recruitment process are an important consideration when evaluating the effectiveness of the process. Describe the two categories of fairness discussed in this chapter.
6. For each of the recommendations from the Federal Glass Ceiling Commission (Exhibit 6.9), what are specific examples of how organizations could change in order to remove barriers to mobility?

APPLICATIONS

Recruitment in a Changing Internal Labor Market

Mitchell Shipping Lines is a distributor of goods on the Great Lakes in the United States. Not only does it distribute goods but it also manufactures shipping containers used to store the goods while in transit. The name of the subsidiary that manufactures those containers is Mitchell-Cole Manufacturing, and the president and CEO is Zoe Brausch.

Brausch is in the middle of converting the manufacturing system from an assembly line to autonomous work teams. Each team will be responsible for producing a separate type of container, and each team will have different tools, machinery, and manufacturing routines for its particular type of container. Members of each team will have the job title "assembler," and each team will be headed by a permanent "leader." Brausch would like all leaders to come from the ranks of current employees, both in terms of the initial set of leaders and leaders in the future as vacancies arise. In addition, she wants employee movement across teams to be discouraged in order to build team identity and cohesion. The current internal labor market, however, presents a formidable potential obstacle to her internal staffing goals.

Based on a long history in the container manufacturing facility, employees are treated like union employees even though the facility is nonunion. Such treatment was desired many years ago as a strategy to remain nonunion. It was management's belief that if employees were treated like union employees, there should be no need for employees to vote for a union. A cornerstone of the strategy is use of what everyone in the facility calls the "blue book." The blue book looks like a typical labor contract, and it spells out all terms and conditions of employment. Many of those terms apply to internal staffing, and are very typical of traditional mobility systems found in unionized work settings. Specifically, internal transfer and promotions are governed by a facility-wide job posting system. A vacancy is posted throughout the facility and remains open for 30 days; an exception to this is identified entry-level jobs that are filled only externally. Any employee with two or more years of seniority is eligible to "bid" for any posted vacancy; employees with less seniority may also bid, but they are considered for positions only if no two-year-plus employees apply or are chosen. Internal applicants are assessed by the hiring manager and a representative from the HR department. They review applicants' seniority, relevant experience, past performance appraisals, and other special KSAOs. The blue book requires that the most senior employee who meets the desired qualifications should receive the transfer or promotion. Thus, seniority is weighted heavily in the decision.

Brausch is worried about this current internal labor market, especially for recruiting and choosing team leaders. These leaders will likely be required to have many KSAOs that are more important than seniority, and KSAOs likely to not even be positively related to seniority. For example, team leaders will need to have advanced computer, communication, and interpersonal skills. Brausch thinks these skills will be critical for team leaders to have, and that they will more likely be found among junior rather than senior employees. Brausch is in a quandary. She asks for your responses to the following questions:

1. Should seniority be eliminated as an eligibility standard for bidding on jobs—meaning no longer giving the two-year-plus employees priority?
2. Should the job posting system simply be eliminated? If so, what should it be replaced with?
3. Should a strict promotion-from-within policy be maintained? Why or why not?
4. How could career mobility paths be developed that would allow across-team movement without threatening team identity and cohesion?
5. If a new internal labor market system is to be put in place, how should it be communicated to employees?

Succession Planning for a CEO

Lone Star Bank, based in Amarillo, is the fourth largest bank in Texas. The president and CEO of Lone Star, Harry "Tex" Ritter, has been with the company for 30 years, the last 12 in his current position as president and CEO. The last three years have been difficult for Lone Star, as earnings have been below average for the industry, and shareholders have grown increasingly impatient. Last month's quarterly earnings report was the proverbial last straw for the board. Particularly troublesome was Ritter's failure to invest enough of Lone Star's assets in higher-yielding investments. Though banks are carefully regulated in terms of their investment strategies, Ritter's investment strategy was conservative even for a bank.

In a meeting last week, the board decided to allow Ritter to serve out the last year of his contract and then replace him. An attractive severance package was hastily put together; when it was presented to Ritter, he agreed to its terms and conditions. Although the board feels it has made a positive step, it is unsure how to identify a successor. When they met with Ritter, he indicated that he thought the bank's senior vice president of operations, Bob Bowers, would be an able successor. Some members of the board think they should follow Ritter's suggestion because he knows the inner workings of the bank better than anyone on the board. Others are not sure what to do.

1. How should Lone Star go about finding a successor to Ritter? Should Bowers be recruited to be the next CEO?
2. How should other internal candidates be identified and recruited?
3. Does Lone Star need a succession plan for the CEO position? If so, how would you advise the board in setting up such a plan?
4. Should Lone Star have a succession plan in place for other individuals at the bank? If so, why and for whom?

ENDNOTES

1. W. T. Markham, S. L. Harlan, and E. J. Hackett, "Promotion Opportunity in Organizations: Causes and Consequences," in K. M. Rowland and G. R. Ferris (eds.), *Research in Personnel and Human Resources Management,* 1987, 5, pp. 223–287.

2. B. R. Allred, C. C. Snow, and R. E. Miles, "Characteristics of Managerial Careers in the 21st Century," *Academy of Management Executive,* 1998, 10, pp. 17–27.

3. A. Healey, "Implementing a Skill-Based Career Development Program," *ACA News,* May 1998, pp. 15–20.

4. National Foreman's Institute, "The Need for Hiring: A Second Look," *Employee Relations and Human Resources Bulletin* (Waterford, CT: author), Feb. 21, 1993, Report No. 1778, Section 1, p. 7.

5. J. Cook, "Crossover Success," *Human Resource Executive,* September 2000, pp. 117–122.

6. E. R. Silverman, "Break Requests," *Wall Street Journal,* August 1, 2000, p. B1.

7. L. W. Kleinman and K. J. Clark, "Users' Satisfaction with Job Posting," *Personnel Administrator,* 1984, 29(9), pp. 104–110.

8. B. Calandra, "Reeling Them In," *Human Resource Executive,* May 16, 2000, pp. 58–62; "You've Got Friends," *HR Magazine,* August 2001, pp. 49–55.

9. C. Joinson, "Developing a Strong Bench," *HR Magazine,* Jan. 1998, pp. 92–96.

10. J. Beeson, "Succesion Planning," *Across the Board,* February 2000, pp. 38–41; W. C. Byham, "Bench Strength," *Across the Board,* February 2000, pp. 35–38; E. Silverman, "Gone Awry," *Human Resource Executive,* Feb. 1998, pp. 42–45; "Wanted: A Few Good CEOs," *Business Week,* Aug. 11, 1997, pp. 64–70.

11. M. Smith, "Are Intranets the Solution?," *IPMA News,* June 1998, pp. 22–23.

12. J. Sullivan, "Internal Recruiting Takes a New Twist," *EMT,* Winter 1998, pp. 26–29; J. S. Arthur, "The Search Within," *Human Resource Executive,* February 2001, pp. 75–77.

13. F. K. Foulkes, *Personnel Policies in Large Nonunion Companies* (Englewood Cliffs, NJ: Prentice-Hall, 1980); M. London and S. A. Stumpf, *Managing Careers* (Reading, MA: Addison Wesley, 1982); Markham, Harlan, and Hackett, "Promotion Opportunity in Organizations: Causes and Consequences"; S. A. Stumpf and M. London, "Management Promotions: Individual and Organizational Factors Influencing the Decision Process," *Academy of Management Review,* 1981, 6(4), pp. 539–549.

14. "Panic or Pass—Preparing for Your Oral Board Review," *IPMA News,* July 1995, p. 2.

15. Bureau of National Affairs, *Fair Employment Practices* (Washington, DC: author, periodically updated), pp. 421:161–166.

16. Bureau of National Affairs, *Fair Employment Practices,* pp. 421:161–166.

17. Federal Glass Ceiling Commission, "Good for Business: Making Full Use of the Nation's Human Capital—Fact-Finding Report of the Federal Glass Ceiling Commission," *Daily Labor Report,* Bureau of National Affairs, March 17, 1995, Special Supplement.

18. Federal Glass Ceiling Commission, "Good for Business: Making Full Use of the Nation's Human Capital," p. S6.

19. S. Shellenberger, "Sales Offers Women Fairer Pay, but Bias Lingers," *Wall Street Journal,* Jan. 24, 1995, p. B1.

20. Federal Glass Ceiling Commission, "Good for Business: Making Full Use of the Nation's Human Capital," p. S19.

21. P. Digh, "The Next Challenge: Holding People Accountable," *HR Magazine,* Oct. 1998, pp. 63–69; B. R. Rugins, B. Townsend, and M. Mattis, "Gender Gap in the Executive Suite: CEOs and Female Executives Report on Breaking the Glass Ceiling," *Academy of Management Executive,* 1998, 12, pp. 28–42.

22. Society for Human Resource Management, *Barriers to Advancement Survey* (Alexandria, VA: author, 2000).

23. K. L. Lyness and D. E. Thompson, "Climbing the Corporate Ladder: Do Male and Female Executives Follow the Same Route?," *Journal of Applied Psychology,* 2000, 85, pp. 86–101; S. J. Wells, "Smoothing the Way," *HR Magazine,* June 2001, pp. 52–58; S. J. Wells, "A Female Executive Is Hard to Find," *HR Magazine,* June 2001, pp. 40–49.

The Staffing Organization's Model

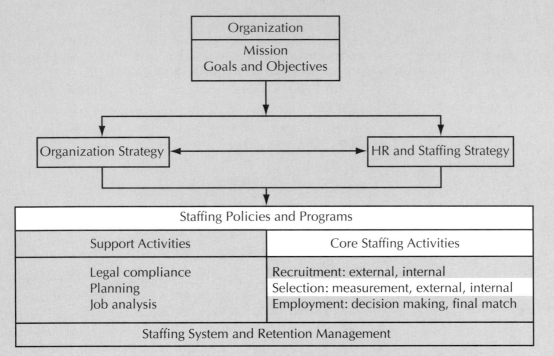

PART FOUR

Staffing Activities: Selection

CHAPTER SEVEN

Measurement

Importance and Use of Measures

Key Concepts
   Measurement
   Scores
   Correlation Between Scores

Quality of Measures
   Reliability of Measures
   Validity of Measures
   Validation of Measures in Staffing
   Validity Generalization

Collection of Assessment Data
   Testing Procedures
   Applicant Reactions
   Acquisition of Tests and Test Manuals
   Professional Standards

Legal Issues
   Disparate Impact Statistics
   Standardization and Validation

Summary

Discussion Questions

Applications

In staffing, measurement is a process used to gather and express information about persons and jobs in numerical form. A common example in which management employs measurement is to administer a test to job applicants and evaluate their responses to determine a test score for each of them. The first part of this chapter presents a view of the process of measurement in staffing decisions.

After showing the vital importance and uses of measurement in staffing activities, three key concepts are then discussed. The first concept is that of measurement itself, along with the issues raised by it—standardization of measurement, levels of measurement, and the difference between objective and subjective measures. The second concept is that of scoring and how to express scores in ways that help in their interpretation. The final concept is that of correlations between scores, particularly as expressed by the correlation coefficient and its significance. Calculating correlations between scores is a very useful way to learn even more about the meaning of scores.

What is the quality of the measures used in staffing? How sound an indicator of the attributes measured are they? Answers to these questions lie in the reliability and validity of the measures and the scores they yield. There are multiple ways of doing reliability and validity analysis; these are discussed in conjunction with numerous examples drawn from staffing situations. As these examples show, the quality of staffing decisions (e.g., who to hire or reject) depends heavily on the quality of measures and scores used as inputs to these decisions.

An important practical concern involved in the process of measurement is the collection of assessment data. There are various decisions about testing procedures (who is qualified to test applicants, what information should be disclosed to applicants, how to assess applicants with standardized procedures) that need to be made. Collection of assessment data also may include data on applicant reactions. The collection of assessment data also includes the acquisition of tests and test manuals. The collection of assessment data and the acquisition of tests and test manuals will vary depending on whether paper-and-pencil or computerized selection measures are utilized. Finally, in the collection of assessment data, organizations need to attend to professional standards that govern their proper use.

Measurement concepts and procedures are directly involved in legal issues, particularly EEO/AA ones. This requires collection and analysis of applicant flow and stock statistics. Requirements for doing these analyses, as expressed in the Uniform Guidelines on Employee Selection Procedures (UGESP) and Affirmative Action Programs regulations, are reviewed. Also reviewed are implications of the results of disparate impact analysis for standardization and validation of measures, particularly as required by the UGESP.

IMPORTANCE AND USE OF MEASURES

Measurement is one of the key ingredients for, and tools of, staffing organizations. Staffing organizations is highly dependent on the availability and use of measures.

Indeed, it is virtually impossible to have any type of systematic staffing process that does not use measures and an accompanying measurement process.

Measures are methods or techniques for describing and assessing attributes of objects that are of concern to us. Examples include tests of applicant KSAOs, evaluations of employees' job performance, and applicants' ratings of their preferences for various types of job rewards. These assessments of attributes are gathered through the measurement process. That process consists of (a) choosing an attribute of concern, (b) developing an operational definition of the attribute, (c) constructing a measure of the attribute (if no suitable measure is available) as it is operationally defined, and (d) using the measure to actually gauge the attribute.

Results of the measurement process are expressed as numbers or scores—for example, applicants' scores on an ability test, employees' performance evaluation rating scores, or applicants' ratings of rewards in terms of their importance. These scores become the indicators of the attribute. Through the measurement process, the initial attribute and its operational definition have been transformed into a numerical expression of the attribute.

KEY CONCEPTS

This section covers a series of key concepts in three major areas: measurement, scores, and correlation between scores.

Measurement

In the preceding discussion, the essence of measurement and its importance and use in staffing were described. It is now important to define the term "measurement" more formally and explore implications of that definition.

Definition

Measurement may be defined as the process of assigning numbers to objects to represent quantities of an attribute of the objects.[1] Exhibit 7.1 contains a depiction of the general process of the use of measures in staffing, along with an example for the job of maintenance mechanic. Following from the definition of measurement provided above, the first step in measurement is to choose and define an attribute (sometimes also called a construct) to be measured. In the example, this is knowledge of mechanical principles. Then, a measure must be developed for the attribute, and at that point the attribute can physically be measured. In the example, a paper-and-pencil test may be developed to measure mechanical knowledge, and this test is then administered to applicants. Once the attribute is physically measured, numbers or scores are determined (e.g., in the example, the mechanical test is scored). At that point, scores are available on the applicants, so an evaluation can be made of the scores (which scores meet the job requirements) and a selection decision can be made (e.g., hire a maintenance mechanic).

EXHIBIT 7.1   Use of Measures in Staffing

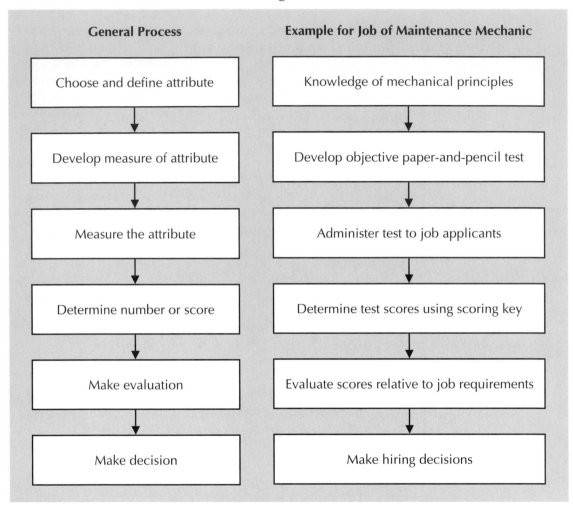

General Process	Example for Job of Maintenance Mechanic
Choose and define attribute	Knowledge of mechanical principles
Develop measure of attribute	Develop objective paper-and-pencil test
Measure the attribute	Administer test to job applicants
Determine number or score	Determine test scores using scoring key
Make evaluation	Evaluate scores relative to job requirements
Make decision	Make hiring decisions

Of course, in practice, this textbook process is often not followed explicitly. When this happens, selection errors are more likely. For example, if the methods used to determine scores on an attribute are not explicitly determined and evaluated, the scores themselves may be incorrectly determined. Similarly, if the evaluation of the scores is not systematic, each selection decision maker may put his or her own "spin" on the scores, thereby defeating the purpose of careful measurement. The best way to avoid these problems is for all of those involved in selection decisions to go through each step of the measurement process depicted in Exhibit 7.1, apply it to the job(s) in question, and reach agreement at each step of the way.

Standardization

The hallmark of sound measurement practice is standardization.[2] Standardization is a means of controlling the influence of outside or extraneous factors on the scores generated by the measure and ensuring that, as much as possible, the scores obtained are a reflection of the attribute measured.

A standardized measure has three basic properties:

1. The content is identical for all objects measured (e.g., all job applicants take the same test).
2. The administration of the measure is identical for all objects (e.g., all job applicants have the same time limit on a test).
3. The rules for assigning numbers are clearly specified and agreed on in advance (e.g., a scoring key for the test is developed before it is administered).

These seemingly simple and straightforward characteristics of standardization of measures have substantial implications for the conduct of many staffing activities. These implications will become apparent throughout the remainder of this text. For example, assessment devices, such as the employment interview and letters of reference, often fail to meet the requirements for standardization, and organizations must undertake steps to make them more standardized.

Levels of Measurement

There are varying degrees of precision in measuring attributes and in representing differences among objects in terms of attributes. Accordingly, there are different levels or scales of measurement.[3] It is common to classify any particular measure as falling into one of four levels of measurement: nominal, ordinal, interval, or ratio.

Nominal   With nominal scales, a given attribute is categorized, and numbers are assigned to the categories. With or without numbers, however, there is no order or level implied among the categories. The categories are merely different, and none is higher or lower than the other. For example, each job title could represent a different category, with a different number assigned to it: managers $= 1$, clericals $= 2$, sales $= 3$, and so forth. Clearly, the numbers do not imply any ordering among the categories.

Ordinal   With ordinal scales, objects are rank-ordered according to how much of the attribute they possess. Thus, objects may be ranked from "best" to "worst," or from "highest" to "lowest." For example, five job candidates, each of whom has been evaluated in terms of overall qualification for the job, might be rank-ordered from 1 to 5, or highest to lowest, according to their job qualifications.

Rank orderings only represent relative differences among objects, and they do not indicate the absolute levels of the attribute. Thus, the rank ordering of the five job candidates does not indicate exactly how qualified each of them is for the job, nor are the differences in their ranks necessarily equal to the differences in their qualifications. The difference in qualifications between applicants ranked 1 and 2 may not be the same as the difference between those ranked 4 and 5.

Interval   Like ordinal scales, interval scales allow us to rank order objects. However, the differences between adjacent points on the measurement scale are now equal in terms of the attribute. If an interval scale is used to rank order of the five job candidates, the differences in qualifications between those ranked 1 and 2 are equal to the differences between those ranked 4 and 5.

It should be pointed out that there are many instances in which the level of measurement falls somewhere between an ordinal and interval scale. That is, objects can be clearly rank-ordered, but the differences between the ranks are not necessarily equal throughout the measurement scale. In the example of the five job candidates, the difference in qualifications between those ranked 1 and 2 might be slight compared with the distance between those ranked 4 and 5.

Unfortunately, this in-between level of measurement is characteristic of many of the measures used in staffing. Though it is not a major problem, it does signal caution in interpreting the meaning of differences in scores among people.

Ratio   Ratio scales are like interval scales in that there are equal differences between scale points for the attribute being measured. In addition, however, ratio scales have a logical or absolute true zero point. Because of this, how much of the attribute each object possesses can be stated in absolute terms.

Normally, ratio scales are involved in counting or weighing things. There are many such examples of ratio scales in staffing. Assessing how much weight a candidate can carry over some distance for physically demanding jobs such as fire fighting or general construction is an example of this. Perhaps the most common example is counting how much previous job experience (general or specific) job candidates have had.

Objective and Subjective Measures

Frequently, staffing measures are described as being either "objective" or "subjective." Often, the term subjective is used in disparaging ways ("I can't believe how subjective that interview was; there's no way they can rate me fairly on the basis of it"). Exactly what is the difference between so-called objective and subjective measures?

The difference, in large part, pertains to the rules used to assign numbers to the attribute being assessed. With objective measures, the rules are predetermined and usually communicated and applied through some sort of scoring key or system. Most paper-and-pencil tests are considered objective. The scoring systems in subjective measures are more elusive and often involve a rater or judge who assigns the numbers. Many employment interviewers fall in this category, especially those with an idiosyncratic way of evaluating people's responses, one that is not known or shared by other interviewers.

In principle, any attribute can be measured objectively, subjectively, or both. Research shows that when an attribute is measured by both objective and subjective means, there is often relatively low agreement between scores from the two types of measures. A case in point pertains to the attribute of "job performance." It may be measured objectively through quantity of output, and it may be measured subjectively through performance appraisal ratings. A review of the research shows that there is very low correlation between scores from the objective and subjective performance measures.[4] Undoubtedly, the raters' lack of sound scoring systems for rating job performance was a major contributor to the lack of obtained agreement.

It thus appears that whatever type of measure is being used to assess attributes in staffing, serious attention should be paid to the scoring system or key that is used. This requires nothing more, in a sense, than having a firm knowledge of exactly what the organization is trying to measure in the first place. This is true for both paper-and-pencil (objective) measures and judgmental (subjective) measures, such as the employment interview. It is simply another way of emphasizing the importance of standardization in measurement.

Scores

Measures yield numbers or scores to represent the amount of the attribute being assessed. Scores thus are the numerical indicator of the attribute. Once scores have been derived, they can be manipulated in various ways to give them even greater meaning, and to help better describe characteristics of the objects being scored.[5]

Central Tendency and Variability

Assume that a group of job applicants was administered a test of the knowledge of mechanical principles. The test is scored using a scoring key, and each applicant receives a score on the test, known as a raw score. Their scores are shown in Exhibit 7.2.

Some features of this set of scores may be summarized through the calculation of summary statistics. These pertain to central tendency and variability in the scores and are also shown in Exhibit 7.2.

The indicators of central tendency are the mean, median, and mode. Since it was assumed that the data were interval-level data, it is permissible to compute all three indicators of central tendency. Had the data been ordinal, the mean should not be computed. For nominal data, only the mode would be appropriate.

EXHIBIT 7.2   **Central Tendency and Variability: Summary Statistics**

Data		Summary Statistics
Applicant	**Test Score (x)**	
A	10	A. Central tendency
B	12	Mean $(\bar{\chi})$ = 338/20 = 16.9
C	14	Median = middle score = 17
D	14	Mode = most frequent score = 15
E	15	
F	15	B. Variability
G	15	Range = 10 to 24
H	15	Standard deviation (SD) =
I	15	
J	17	$\sqrt{\dfrac{\Sigma\ (\chi-\bar{\chi})^2}{N}}$ = 3.52
K	17	
L	17	
M	18	
N	18	
O	19	
P	19	
Q	19	
R	22	
S	23	
T	24	
Total (Σ) = 338		
N = 20		

The variability indicators are the range and the standard deviation. The range shows lowest to highest actual score for the job applicants. The standard deviation shows, in essence, the average amount of deviation of individual scores from the average score. It summarizes the amount of "spread" in the scores. The larger the standard deviation, the greater the variability, or spread, in the data.

Percentiles

A percentile score for an individual is the percentage of people scoring below the individual in a distribution of scores. Refer again to Exhibit 7.2, and consider applicant C. That applicant's percentile score is the 10th percentile (2/20 × 100). Applicant S is in the 90th percentile (18/20 × 100).

Standard Scores

When interpreting scores, it is natural to compare individuals' raw scores to the mean, that is, to ask whether scores are above, at, or below the mean. But a true understanding of how well an individual did relative to the mean takes into account the amount of variability in scores around the mean (the standard deviation). That is, the calculation must be "corrected" or controlled for the amount of variability in a score distribution to accurately present how well a person scored relative to the mean.

Calculation of the standard score for an individual is the way to accomplish this correction. The formula for calculation of the standard score, or Z, is as follows:

$$Z = \frac{X - \overline{X}}{SD}$$

Applicant S in Exhibit 7.2 had a raw score of 23 on the test; the mean was 16.9 and the standard deviation was 3.52. Substituting into the above formula, applicant S has a Z score of 1.7. Thus, applicant S scored about 1.7 standard deviations above the mean.

Standard scores are also useful for determining how a person performed, in a relative sense, on two or more tests. For example, assume the following data for a particular applicant:

	Test 1	Test 2
Raw score	50	48
Mean	48	46
SD	2.5	.80

On which test did the applicant do better? To answer that, simply calculate the applicant's standard scores on the two tests. The Z score on test 1 is .80, and the Z score on test 2 is 2.5. Thus, while the applicant got a higher raw score on test 1 than on test 2, the applicant got a higher Z score on test 2 than on test 1. Viewed in this way, it is apparent that the applicant did better on the second of the two tests.

Correlation Between Scores

Frequently, in staffing there are scores on two or more measures for a group of individuals. One common occurrence is to have scores on two (or often, more than two) KSAO measures. For example, there could be a score on the test of knowledge of mechanical principles and also an overall rating of the applicant's probable job success based on the employment interview. In such instances, it is logical to ask whether there is some relation between the two sets of scores. Is there a tendency for an increase in knowledge test scores to be accompanied by an increase in interview ratings?

As another example, an organization may have scores on a particular KSAO measure (e.g., the knowledge test) and a measure of job performance (e.g., per-

formance appraisal ratings) for a group of individuals. Is there a correlation between these two sets of scores? If there is, then this would provide some evidence
about the probable validity of the knowledge test as a predictor of job performance.
This evidence would help the organization decide whether to incorporate the use
of the test into the selection process for job applicants.

Investigation of the relationship between two sets of scores proceeds through
the plotting of scatter diagrams and through calculation of the correlation coefficient.

Scatter Diagrams

Assume two sets of scores for a group of people, scores on a test and scores on a
measure of job performance. A scatter diagram is simply the plot of the joint distribution of the two sets of scores. Inspection of the plot provides a visual representation of the type of relationship that exists between the two sets of scores. Exhibit
7.3 provides three different scatter diagrams for the two sets of scores. Each X represents a test score and job performance score combination for an individual.

Example A in Exhibit 7.3 suggests very little relationship between the two sets
of scores. Example B shows a modest relationship between the scores, and example C shows a somewhat strong relationship between the two sets of scores.

Correlation Coefficient

The relationship between two sets of scores may also be investigated through
calculation of the correlation coefficient. The symbol for the correlation coefficient
is r. Numerically, r values can range from $r = -1.0$ to $r = 1.0$. The larger the
absolute value of r, the stronger the relationship. When an r value is shown without
the plus or minus sign, the value is assumed to be positive.

Naturally, the value of r bears a close resemblance to the scatter diagram. As a
demonstration of this, Exhibit 7.3 also shows the approximate r value for each of
the three scatter diagrams. In example A, a low r is indicated ($r = .10$). The r in
example B is moderate ($r = .25$), and the r in example C is high ($r = .60$).

Actual calculation of the correlation coefficient is straightforward. An example of this calculation, and the formula for r, are shown in Exhibit 7.4. In the
exhibit, there are two sets of scores for 20 people. The first set of scores is the
set of test scores for the 20 individuals in Exhibit 7.2. The second set of scores
is an overall job performance rating (on a 1–5 rating scale) for these people. As
can be seen from the calculation, there is a correlation of $r = .58$ between the
two sets of scores.

The calculation of the correlation coefficient is straightforward. The resultant
value of r is a value that succinctly summarizes both the strength of the relationship
between two sets of scores and the direction of the relationship. Despite the simplicity of its calculation, there are several notes of caution to sound regarding the
correlation.

EXHIBIT 7.3 **Scatter Diagrams and Corresponding Correlations**

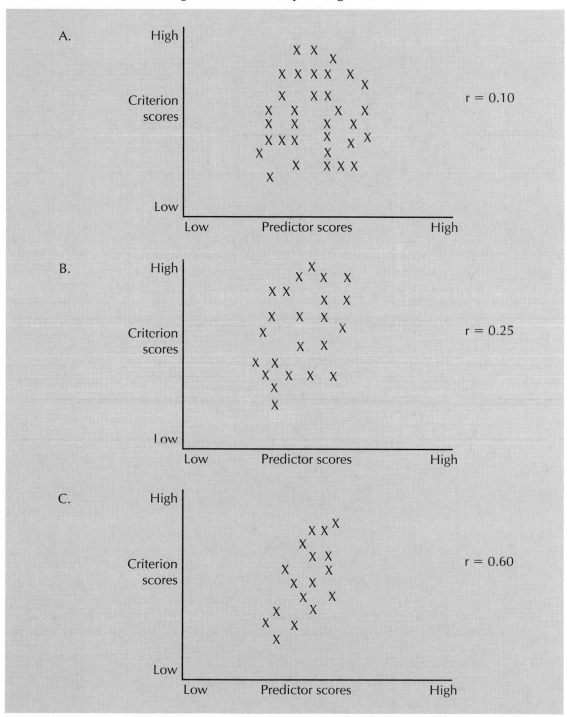

EXHIBIT 7.4   Calculation of Product-Moment Correlation Coefficient

Person	Test Score (X)	Performance Rating (Y)	(X²)	(Y²)	(XY)
A	10	2	100	4	20
B	12	1	144	1	12
C	14	2	196	4	28
D	14	1	196	1	14
E	15	3	225	9	45
F	15	4	225	16	60
G	15	3	225	9	45
H	15	4	225	16	60
I	15	4	225	16	60
J	17	3	289	9	51
K	17	4	289	16	68
L	17	3	289	9	51
M	18	2	324	4	36
N	18	4	324	16	72
O	19	3	361	9	57
P	19	3	361	9	57
Q	19	5	361	25	95
R	22	3	484	9	66
S	23	4	529	16	92
T	24	5	576	25	120
	$\Sigma X = 338$	$\Sigma Y = 63$	$\Sigma X^2 = 5948$	$\Sigma Y^2 = 223$	$\Sigma XY = 1109$

$$r = \frac{N\Sigma XY - (\Sigma X)(\Sigma Y)}{\sqrt{[N\Sigma X^2 - (\Sigma X)^2][N\Sigma Y^2 - (\Sigma Y)^2]}} = \frac{20(1109) - (338)(63)}{\sqrt{[20(5948) - (338)^2][20(223) - (63)^2]}} = .58$$

First, the correlation does not connote a proportion or percentage. An r = .50 between variables X and Y does not mean that X is 50% of Y or that Y can be predicted from X with 50% accuracy. The appropriate interpretation is to square the value of r, for r², and then say that the two variables share that percentage of common variation in their scores. Thus, the proper interpretation of r = .50 is that the two variables share 25% (.5² × 100) common variation in their scores.

Second, the value of r is affected by how much variation there actually is in each set of scores. Other things being equal, the less variation there is in either or both sets of scores, the smaller the calculated value of r will be. At the extreme, if there is no variation in one of the sets of scores, the correlation will be r = .00. That is, for there to be a correlation there must be variation in both sets of scores. The lack of variation in scores is called the problem of restriction of range.

Third, the formula used to calculate the correlation in Exhibit 7.4 is based on the assumption that there is a linear relationship between the two sets of scores.

This may not always be a good assumption; something other than a straight line may best capture the true nature of the relationship between scores. To the extent that two sets of scores are not related in a linear fashion, use of the formula for calculation of the correlation will yield a value of r that understates the actual strength of the relationship.

Finally, the correlation between two variables does not imply causation between them. A correlation simply says how two variables co-vary or co-relate; it says nothing about one variable necessarily causing the other one.

Significance of the Correlation Coefficient

Once the correlation coefficient is calculated, questions frequently arise as to the significance of the correlation. These questions may be addressed through consideration of a correlation's practical and statistical significance.

Practical Significance   The practical significance of the correlation refers to its size, regardless of its sign. The larger the r, the greater its practical significance.

This interpretation is very appealing. Recall that the correlation is really the amount of common or shared variation between two variables. The greater the degree of that covariation, the more we can use one variable to help us understand or predict another variable.

Consider again the correlation between the knowledge of mechanical principles test and the job performance ratings. The greater the r between those two variables, the greater the certainty that knowledge of mechanical principles is a key underlying KSAO of job performance, and that scores on this test are useful in predicting the likely performance of individuals at the time they are job applicants. Indeed, prediction such as this is a major purpose of staffing systems. Calculation and use of correlations is thus an extremely important tool for staffing activities.

Statistical Significance   When a correlation is computed for a particular group of individuals, it describes the relationship between two variables for that group only. However, to the extent that the group is drawn from, or representative of, some larger population, there may also exist a correlation in that population. For example, if there were a correlation between test scores and subsequent job performance ratings for a sample of current job applicants, it is possible to infer that there is a correlation in the population of future job applicants as well. Having made this inference, the organization could use the test to help select future applicants from that population.

The statistical significance of a correlation refers to the likelihood that a correlation exists in a population, based on knowledge of the actual value of r in a sample from that population. Concluding that a correlation is indeed statistically significant means that there is most likely a correlation in the population.

More formally, r is calculated in an initial group, called a sample. From this piece of information, the question arises whether to infer that there is also a correlation in the *population*. To do this, compute the t value of our correlation using the following formula,

$$t = \frac{r}{\sqrt{(1 - r^2)/n - 2}}$$

where r is the value of the correlation, and n is the size of the sample.

A t distribution table in any elementary statistics book shows the significance level of r.[6] The significance level is expressed as p < some value, for example, p < .05. This p level tells the probability of concluding that there is a correlation in the population when, in fact, there is not a relationship. Thus, a correlation with p < .05 means there are fewer than 5 chances in 100 of concluding that there is a relationship in the population when, in fact, there is not. This is a relatively small probability, and usually leads to the conclusion that a correlation is indeed statistically significant.

It is important to avoid concluding that there is a relationship in the population when in fact there is not. Because of this, one usually chooses a fairly conservative or stringent level of significance that the correlation must attain before concluding that it is "significant." Typically, a standard of p < .05 or less (another common standard is p < .01) is chosen. The actual significance level (based on the t value for the correlation) is then compared to the desired significance level, and a decision is reached whether the correlation is statistically significant or not. Here are some examples:

Desired Level	Actual Level	Conclusion About Correlation
p < .05	p < .23	Not significant
p < .05	p < .02	Significant
p < .01	p < .07	Not significant
p < .01	p < .009	Significant

Both the practical and statistical significance of the correlation are of concern in interpreting its significance. For example, if r = .25 and p < .05, the following kind of interpretation is made about significance. The correlation has moderate practical significance (r^2 = .06), and it meets a normal threshold for statistical significance. There is thus likely a relationship between the two variables in the population, based on what was found to be the relationship in this particular sample.

QUALITY OF MEASURES

Measures are developed and used to gauge attributes of objects. Results of measures are expressed in the form of scores, and various manipulations may be done to them. Such manipulations lead to better understanding and interpretation of the scores, and thus the attribute represented by the scores.

For practical reasons, in staffing the scores of individuals are treated as if they were, in fact, the attribute itself, rather than merely indicators of the attribute. For example, scores on a mental ability test are interpreted as being synonymous with how intelligent individuals are. Or, individuals' job performance ratings from their supervisors are viewed as indicators of their true performance.

Treated in this way, scores become a major input to decision making about individuals. For example, scores on the mental ability test are used and weighted heavily to decide which job applicants will receive a job offer. Or performance ratings may serve as a key factor in deciding which individuals will be eligible for an internal staffing move, such as a promotion. In these and numerous other ways, management acts on the basis of scores to guide the conduct of staffing activities in the organization. This is illustrated through such phrases as "let the numbers do the talking," "we manage by the numbers," and "never measured, never managed."

The quality of the decisions and actions taken are unlikely to be any better than the quality of the measures on which they are based. Thus, there is a lot at stake in the quality of the measures used in staffing. Such concerns with the quality of measures are best viewed in terms of reliability and validity of measures.[7]

Reliability of Measures

Reliability of measurement refers to the consistency of measurement of an attribute.[8] A measure is reliable to the extent that it provides a consistent set of scores to represent an attribute. Rarely is perfect reliability achieved because of the occurrence of measurement error. Reliability is thus a matter of degree.

Reliability of measurement is of concern both within a single time period in which the attribute is being measured and between time periods. Moreover, reliability is of concern for both objective and subjective measures. These two concerns help create a general framework for better understanding reliability.

The key concepts for the framework are shown in Exhibit 7.5. In the exhibit, a single attribute, "A" (e.g., knowledge of mechanical principles), is being measured. Scores are available for 15 individuals, and scores range from 1 to 5. A is being measured in time period 1 (T_1) and time period 2 (T_2). In each time period, A may be measured objectively, with two test items, or subjectively, with two raters. The same two items or raters are used in each time period. (In reality, more than two items or raters would probably be used to measure A, but for simplicity, only two are used here.) Each test item or rater in each time period is a submeasure of A. There are thus four submeasures of A—designated X_1, X_2, Y_1, and Y_2—and four sets of scores. In terms of reliability of measurement, the concern is with the consistency or similarity in the sets of scores. This requires various comparisons of the scores.

Comparisons Within T_1 or T_2

Consider the four sets of scores as coming from the objective measure, which used test items. Comparing sets of scores from these items in either T_1 or T_2 is

---

EXHIBIT 7.5 **Framework for Reliability of Measures**

	Scores on Attribute A							
	Objective (Test Items)				Subjective (Raters)			
	Time 1		Time 2		Time 1		Time 2	
Person	X_1	Y_1	X_2	Y_2	X_1	Y_1	X_2	Y_2
A	5	5	4	5	5	5	4	5
B	5	4	4	3	5	4	4	3
C	5	5	5	4	5	5	5	4
D	5	4	5	5	5	4	5	5
E	4	5	3	4	4	5	3	4
F	4	4	4	3	4	4	4	3
G	4	4	3	4	4	4	3	4
H	4	3	4	3	4	3	4	3
I	3	4	3	4	3	4	3	4
J	3	3	5	3	3	3	5	3
K	3	3	2	3	3	3	2	3
L	3	2	4	2	3	2	4	2
M	2	3	4	3	2	3	4	3
N	2	2	1	2	2	2	1	2
O	1	2	3	2	1	2	3	2

Note: X_1 and X_2 are the **same** test item or rater; Y_1 and Y_2 are the same test item or rater. The subscript "1" refers to T_1, and the subscript "2" refers to T_2.

called internal consistency reliability. The relevant comparisons are X_1 and Y_1, and X_2 and Y_2. It is hoped that the comparisons will show high similarity, because both the items are intended to measure A within the same time period.

Now treat the four sets of scores as coming from the subjective measure, which relied on raters. Comparisons of these scores involve what is called interrater reliability. The relevant comparisons are the same as with the objective measure scores, namely X_1 and Y_1, and X_2 and Y_2. Again, it is hoped that there will be high agreement between the raters because they are focusing on a single attribute at a single moment in time.

Comparisons Between T_1 and T_2

Comparisons of scores between time periods involve assessment of measurement stability. When scores from an objective measure are used, this is referred to as test-retest reliability. The relevant comparisons are X_1 and X_2, and Y_1 and Y_2. To the extent that A is not expected to change between T_1 and T_2, there should be high test-retest reliability.

When subjective scores are compared between T_1 and T_2, the concern is with intrarater reliability. Here, the same rater evaluates individuals in terms of A in two different time periods. To the extent that A is not expected to change, there should be high intrarater reliability.

In summary, reliability is concerned with consistency of measurement. There are multiple ways of treating reliability, depending on whether scores from a measure are being compared for consistency within or between time periods and depending on whether the scores are from objective or subjective measures. These points are summarized in Exhibit 7.6. Ways of actually computing agreement between scores will be covered shortly, after the concept of measurement error is explored.

Measurement Error

Rarely will any of the comparisons among scores discussed previously yield perfect similarity or reliability. Indeed, none of the comparisons in Exhibit 7.6 visually shows complete agreement among the scores. The lack of agreement among the scores may be due to the occurrence of measurement error. This type of error represents "noise" in the measure and measurement process. Its occurrence means that the measure did not yield perfectly consistent scores, or so-called true scores, for the attribute.

The scores actually obtained from the measure thus have two components to them, a true score and measurement error. That is,

$$\text{actual score} = \text{true score} + \text{error}$$

EXHIBIT 7.6 Summary of Types of Reliability

	Compare scores within T_1 or T_2	Compare scores between T_1 and T_2
Objective measure (test items)	Internal consistency	Test–retest
Subjective measure (raters)	Interrater	Intrarater

The error component of any actual score, or set of scores, represents unreliability of measurement. Unfortunately, unreliability is a fact of life for the types of measures used in staffing. To help understand why this is the case, the various types or sources of error that can occur in a staffing context must be explored. These errors may be grouped under the categories of deficiency and contamination error.[9]

Deficiency Error   Deficiency error occurs when there is failure to measure some portion or aspect of the attribute assessed. For example, if knowledge of mechanical principles involves gear ratios, among other things, and our test does not have any items (or an insufficient number of items) covering this aspect, then the test is deficient. As another example, if an attribute of job performance is "planning and setting work priorities," and the raters fail to rate people on that dimension during their performance appraisal, then the performance measure is deficient.

Deficiency error can occur in several related ways. First, there can be an inadequate definition of the attribute in the first place. Thus, the test of knowledge of mechanical principles may fail to get at familiarity with gear ratios because it was never included in the initial definition of mechanical principles. Or, the performance measure may fail to require raters to rate their employees on "planning and setting work priorities" because this attribute was never considered an important dimension of their work.

A second way that deficiency error occurs is in the construction of measures used to assess the attribute. Here, the attribute may be well defined and understood, but there is a failure to construct a measure that adequately gets at the totality of the attribute. This is akin to poor measurement by oversight, which happens when measures are constructed in a hurried, ad hoc fashion.

Deficiency error also occurs when the organization opts to use whatever measures are available because of ease, cost considerations, sales pitches and promotional claims, and so forth. The measures so chosen may turn out to be deficient.

Contamination Error   Contamination error represents the occurrence of unwanted or undesirable influence on the measure and on individuals for whom the measure is being used. These influences muddy the scores and make them difficult to interpret.

Sources of contamination abound, as do examples of them. Several of these sources and examples are shown in Exhibit 7.7, along with some suggestions for how they might be controlled. These examples show that contamination error is multifaceted, making it difficult to minimize and control.

Calculation of Reliability Estimates

There are numerous procedures available for calculating actual estimates of the degree of reliability of measurement.[10] The first two of these (coefficient alpha, interrater agreement) assess reliability within a single time period. The other two procedures (test-retest, intrarater agreement) assess reliability between time periods.

Coefficient Alpha   Coefficient alpha may be calculated in instances in which there are two or more items (or raters) for a particular attribute. Its formula is

$$\alpha = \frac{n\,(\bar{r})}{1 + \bar{r}\,(n-1)}$$

where $\bar{r}$ is the average intercorrelation among the items (raters) and n is the number of items (raters). For example, if there are five items (n = 5), and the average correlation among those five items is $\bar{r}$ = .80, then coefficient alpha is .94.

It can be seen from the formula and example that coefficient alpha depends on just two things—the number of items and the amount of correlation between them. This suggests two basic strategies for increasing the internal consistency reliability of a measure—increase the number of items and increase the amount of agreement between the items (raters). It is generally recommended that coefficient alpha be at least .80 for a measure to have an acceptable degree of reliability.

Interrater Agreement   When raters serve as the measure, it is often convenient to talk about interrater agreement, or the amount of agreement among them. For example, if members of a group or panel interview independently rate a set of job applicants on a 1–5 scale, it is logical to ask how much they agreed with each other.

A simple way to determine this is to calculate the percentage of agreement among the raters. An example of this is shown in Exhibit 7.8.

There is no commonly accepted minimum level of interrater agreement that must be met in order to consider the raters sufficiently reliable. Normally, a fairly high level should be set—75% or higher. The more important the end use of the

EXHIBIT 7.7   Sources of Contamination Error and Suggestions for Control

Source of Contamination	Example	Suggestion for Control
Content domain	Irrelevant material on test	Define domain of test material to be covered
Standardization	Different time limits for same test	Have same time limits for everyone
Chance response tendencies	Guessing by test taker	Impossible to control in advance
Rater	Rater gives inflated ratings to people	Train rater in rating accuracy
Rating situation	Interviewees are asked different questions	Ask all interviewees same questions

---

EXHIBIT 7.8   **Calculation of Percentage Agreement Among Raters**

Person (ratee)	Rater 1	Rater 2	Rater 3
A	5	5	2
B	3	3	5
C	5	4	4
D	1	1	5
E	2	2	4

$$\% \text{ Agreement} = \frac{\text{\# agreements}}{\text{\# agreements} + \text{\# disagreements}} \times 100$$

% Agreement
  Rater 1 and Rater 2 = 4/5 = 80%
  Rater 1 and Rater 3 = 0/5 = 0%
  Rater 2 and Rater 3 = 1/5 = 20%

ratings, the greater the agreement required should be. Critical uses, such as hiring decisions, demand very high levels of reliability, well in excess of 75% agreement.

Test-Retest Reliability   To assess test-retest reliability, the test scores from two different time periods are correlated through calculation of the correlation coefficient. The r may be calculated on total test scores, or a separate r may be calculated for scores on each item. The resultant r provides an indication of the stability of measurement; the higher the r, the more stable the measure.

Interpretation of the r value is made difficult by the fact that the scores are gathered at two different points in time. Between those two time points, the attribute being measured has an opportunity to change. Interpretation of test-retest reliability thus requires some sense of how much the attribute may be expected to change, and what the appropriate time interval between tests is. Usually, for very short time intervals (hours or days), most attributes are quite stable, and a large test-retest r ($r = .90$ or higher) should be expected. Over longer time intervals, it is usual to expect much lower r's, depending on the attribute being measured. For example, over six months or a year, individuals' knowledge of mechanical principles might change. If so, there will be lower test-retest reliabilities (e.g., $r = .50$).

Intrarater Agreement   To calculate intrarater agreement, scores assigned the same people by a rater in two different time periods are compared. The calculation could involve computing the correlation between the two sets of scores, or it could involve using the same formula as for interrater agreement (see Exhibit 7.8).

Interpretation of intrarater agreement is made difficult by the time factor. For short time intervals between measures, a fairly high relationship is expected (e.g., $r = .80$, or percentage agreement $= 90\%$). For longer time intervals, the level of reliability may reasonably be expected to be lower.

Implications of Reliability

The degree of reliability of a measure has two implications. The first of these pertains to interpreting individuals' scores on the measure and the standard error of measurement. The second implication pertains to the effect that reliability has on the measure's validity.

Standard Error of Measurement   Measures yield scores, which, in turn, are used as critical inputs for decision making in staffing activities. For example, in Exhibit 7.1 a test of knowledge of mechanical principles was developed and administered to job applicants. The applicants' scores then were used as a basis for making hiring decisions.

The discussion of reliability suggests that measures and scores will usually have some amount of error in them. Hence, scores on the test of knowledge of mechanical principles most likely reflect both true knowledge and error. Since only a single score is obtained from each applicant, the critical issue is how accurate that particular score is as an indication of each applicant's true level of knowledge of mechanical principles alone.

The standard error of measurement addresses this issue. It provides a way to state, within limits, a person's likely score on a measure. The formula for the standard error of measurement (SEM) is

$$SEM = SD_x \sqrt{1 - r_{xx}}$$

where SD_x is the standard deviation of scores on the measure and r_{xx} is an estimate of the measure's reliability. For example, if $SD_x = 10$, and $r_{xx} = .75$ (based on coefficient alpha), then $SEM = 5$.

With the SEM known, the range within which any individual's true score is likely to fall can be estimated. That range is known as a confidence interval or limit. There is a 95% chance that a person's true score lies within ± 2 SEM of his or her actual score. Thus, if an applicant received a score of 22 on the test of knowledge of mechanical principles, the applicant's true score is most likely to be within the range of $22 \pm 2(5)$, or 12–32.

Recognition and use of the SEM allows for care in interpreting people's scores, as well as differences between them in terms of their scores. For example, using the preceding data, if the test score for applicant 1 $= 22$ and the score for applicant 2 $= 19$, what should be made of the difference between the two applicants? Is applicant 1 truly more knowledgeable of mechanical principles than applicant 2? The answer is probably not. This is because of the standard error of measurement and the large amount of overlap between the two applicants' intervals (12–32 for applicant 1, and 9–29 for applicant 2).

In short, there is not a one-to-one correspondence between actual scores and true scores. Most measures used in staffing are sufficiently unreliable that small differences in scores are probably due to error of measurement and should be ignored.

Relationship to Validity   The validity of a measure is defined as the degree to which it measures the attribute it is supposed to be measuring. For example, the validity of the test of knowledge of mechanical principles is the degree to which it measures that knowledge. There are specific ways to investigate validity; these are discussed in the next section. Here, it simply needs to be recognized that the reliability with which an attribute is measured has direct implications for the validity of the measure.

The relationship between the reliability and validity of a measure is

$$r_{xy} \leq \sqrt{r_{xx}}$$

where r_{xy} is the validity of a measure and r_{xx} is the reliability of the measure. For example, it had been assumed previously that the reliability of the test of knowledge of mechanical principles was $r = .75$. The validity of that test thus cannot exceed $\sqrt{.75} = .86$.

Thus, the reliability of a measure places an upper limit on the possible validity of a measure. It should be emphasized that this is only an upper limit. A highly reliable measure is not necessarily valid. Reliability does not guarantee validity; it only makes validity possible.

Validity of Measures

The validity of a measure is defined as the degree to which it measures the attribute it is intended to measure.[11] Refer back to Exhibit 7.1, which involved the development of a test of knowledge of mechanical principles that was then to be used for purposes of selecting job applicants. The validity of that test is the degree to which it truly measures the attribute or construct "knowledge of mechanical principles."

Judgments about the validity of a measure occur through the process of gathering data and evidence about the measure to assess how it was developed and whether accurate inferences can be made from scores on the measure. This process can be illustrated in terms of concepts pertaining to accuracy of measurement and accuracy of prediction. These concepts may then be used to demonstrate how validation of measures occurs in staffing.

Accuracy of Measurement

How accurate is the test of knowledge of mechanical principles? This question asks for evidence about the accuracy with which the test portrays individuals' true levels of that knowledge. This is akin to asking about the degree of overlap between the attribute being measured and the actual measure of the attribute.

Refer to Exhibit 7.9. It shows the concept of accuracy of measurement in Venn diagram form. The circle on the left represents the construct "knowledge of mechanical principles," and the circle on the right represents the actual test of knowledge of mechanical principles. The overlap between the two circles represents the degree of accuracy of measurement for the test. The greater the overlap, the greater the accuracy of measurement.

Notice that perfect overlap is not shown in Exhibit 7.9. This signifies the occurrence of measurement error with the use of the test. These errors, as indicated in the exhibit, are the errors of deficiency and contamination previously discussed.

So how does accuracy of measurement differ from reliability of measurement, since both are concerned with deficiency and contamination? There is disagreement among people on this question. Generally, the difference may be thought of as follows. Reliability refers to consistency among the scores on the test, as determined by comparing scores as previously described. Accuracy of measurement goes beyond this to assess the extent to which the scores truly reflect the attribute

EXHIBIT 7.9   Accuracy of Measurement

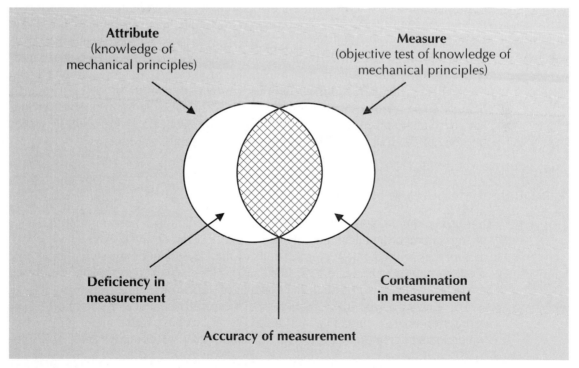

being measured—the overlap shown in Exhibit 7.9. Accuracy requires reliability, but it also requires more by way of evidence. For example, accuracy requires knowing something about how the test was developed. Accuracy also requires some evidence concerning how test scores are influenced by other factors—for example, how do test scores change as a result of employees attending a training program devoted to providing instruction in mechanical principles? Accuracy thus demands greater evidence than reliability.

Accuracy of Prediction

Measures are often developed because they provide information about people that can be used to make predictions about those people. In Exhibit 7.1, the knowledge test was to be used to help make hiring decisions, which are actually predictions about which people will be successful at a job. Knowing something about the accuracy with which a test predicts future job success requires examining the relationship between scores on the test and scores on some measure of job success for a group of people.

Accuracy of prediction is illustrated in the top half of Exhibit 7.10. Where there is an actual job success outcome (criterion) to predict, the test (predictor) will be used to predict the criterion. Each person is classified as high or low on the predictor and high or low on the criterion, based on predictor and criterion scores. Individuals falling into cells A and C represent correct predictions, and individuals falling into cells B and D represent errors in prediction. Accuracy of prediction is the percentage of total correct predictions. Accuracy can thus range from 0% to 100%.

The bottom of Exhibit 7.10 shows an example of the determination of accuracy of prediction using a selection example. The predictor is the test of knowledge of mechanical principles, and the criterion is an overall measure of job performance. Scores on the predictor and criterion measures are gathered for 100 job applicants and are dichotomized into high or low scores on each. Each individual is placed into one of the four cells. The accuracy of prediction for the test is 70%.

Validation of Measures in Staffing

In staffing, there is concern with the validity of predictors in terms of both accuracy of measurement and accuracy of prediction. It is important to have and use predictors that are accurate representations of the KSAOs to be measured, and those predictors need to be accurate in their predictions of job success. The validity of predictors is explored through the conduct of validation studies.

There are two types of validation studies typically conducted. The first of these is criterion-related validation, and the second is content validation. A third type of validation study, known as construct validation, involves components of reliability,

EXHIBIT 7.10   Accuracy of Prediction

A. General Illustration

		D	A
Actual criterion	High	Errors in predictions	Correct predictions
	Low	C Correct predictions	B Errors in predictions
		Low	High

Predicted criterion

$$\text{Accuracy} = \frac{A+C}{A+B+C+D} \times 100$$

B. Selection Example (n=100 job applicants)

Actual performance	High	20	45
	Low	25	10
		Low	High

Predicted performance
(based on test scores)

$$\text{Accuracy} = \frac{45+25}{45+10+25+20} \times 100 = 70\%$$

criterion-related validation, and content validation. Each component is discussed separately in this book, and thus no further reference is made to construct validation.

Criterion-Related Validation

Exhibit 7.11 shows the components of criterion-related validation and their usual sequencing.[12] The process begins with job analysis. Results of job analysis are

EXHIBIT 7.11 Criterion-Related Validation

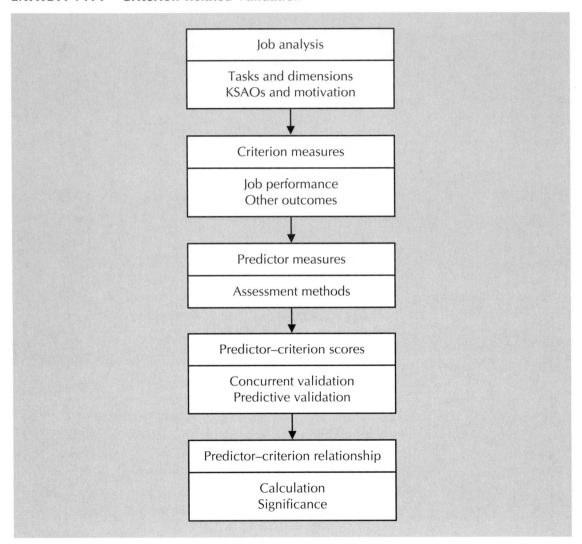

then fed into criterion and predictor measures. Scores on the predictor and criterion are obtained for a sample of individuals; the relationship between the scores is then examined to make a judgment about the predictor's validity.

Job Analysis Job analysis is undertaken to identify and define important tasks (and broader task dimensions) of the job. The KSAOs and motivation thought to be necessary for performance of these tasks are then inferred. Results of the process of identifying tasks and underlying KSAOs are expressed in the form of the job requirements matrix. The matrix is a task × KSAO matrix; it shows the tasks required, combined with the relevant KSAOs for each task.

Criterion Measures   Measures of performance on tasks and task dimensions are needed. These may already be available as part of an ongoing performance appraisal system, or they may have to be developed. However gathered, the critical requirement is that the measures be as free from measurement error as possible.

Criterion measures need not be restricted to performance measures. Others may be used, such as measures of attendance, retention, safety, and customer service. As with performance-based criterion measures, these alternative criterion measures should also be as error-free as possible.

Predictor Measure   The predictor measure is the measure whose criterion-related validity is being investigated. Ideally, it taps into one or more of the KSAOs identified in job analysis. Also, it should be the type of measure most suitable to assess the KSAOs. Knowledge of mechanical principles, for example, is probably best assessed with some form of written, objective test.

Predictor-Criterion Scores   Predictor and criterion scores must be gathered from a sample of current employees or job applicants. If current employees are used, this involves use of a concurrent validation design. Alternately, if job applicants are used, a predictive validation design is used. The nature of these two designs is shown in Exhibit 7.12.

Concurrent validation definitely has some appeal. Administratively, it is convenient and can often be done quickly. Moreover, results of the validation study will be available soon after the predictor and criterion scores have been gathered.

Unfortunately, some serious problems can arise with use of a concurrent validation design. One problem is that if the predictor is a test, current employees may not be motivated in the same way that job applicants would be in terms of desire to perform well. Yet, it is future applicants for whom the test is intended to be used.

In a related vein, current employees may not be similar to, or representative of, future job applicants. Current employees may differ in terms of demographics such as age, race, sex, disability status, education level, and previous job experience. Hence, it is by no means certain that the results of the study will generalize to future job applicants. Also, some unsatisfactory employees will have been terminated, and some high performers may have been promoted. This leads to restriction of range on the criterion scores, which in turn will lower the correlation between the predictor and criterion scores.

Finally, current employees' predictor scores may be influenced by the amount of experience and/or success they have had on their current job. For example, scores on the test of knowledge of mechanical principles may reflect not only that

EXHIBIT 7.12 **Concurrent and Predictive Validation Designs**

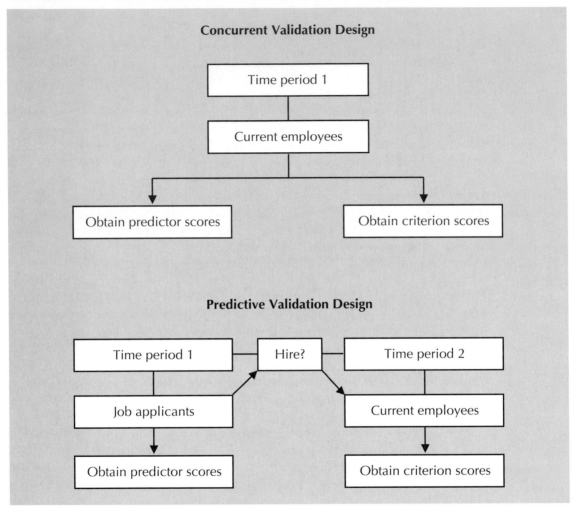

Concurrent Validation Design

Time period 1

Current employees

Obtain predictor scores   Obtain criterion scores

Predictive Validation Design

Time period 1 — Hire? — Time period 2

Job applicants   Current employees

Obtain predictor scores   Obtain criterion scores

knowledge but also how long people have been on the job and how well they have performed it. This is undesirable because one wants predictor scores to be predictive of the criterion, rather than a result of it.

Predictive validation overcomes the potential limitations of concurrent validation, since the predictor scores are obtained from job applicants. Applicants will be motivated to do well on the predictor, and they are more likely to be representative of future job applicants. And applicants' scores on the predictor cannot be influenced by success and/or experience on the job, because the scores were gathered prior to their being on the job.

Predictive validation is not without potential limitations, however. It is neither administratively easy nor quick. Moreover, results will not be available immediately, as some time must lapse before criterion scores can be obtained. Despite these limitations, predictive validation is considered the more sound of the two designs.

Predictor-Criterion Relationship Once predictor and criterion scores have been obtained, the correlation r, or some variation of it, must be calculated. The value of the r is then referred to as the validity of the scores on the predictor. For example, if an r = .35 was found, the predictor would be referred to as having a validity of .35. Then, the practical and statistical significance of the r should be determined. Only if the r meets desired levels of practical and statistical significance should the predictor be consider "valid" and thus potentially usable in the selection system.

Illustrative Study This study sought to identify predictors of job performance for clerical employees in a state university civil service system covering 20 different institutions. The clerical job existed within different schools (e.g., engineering, humanities) and nonacademic departments (e.g., payroll, data processing). The goal was to have a valid clerical test in two parallel forms that could be administered to job applicants in one hour.

The starting point was to conduct a job analysis, the results of which would be used as the basis for constructing the clerical tests (predictors) and the job performance ratings (criteria). Based on observation of the job and previous job descriptions, a task-based questionnaire was constructed by SMEs and administered to clerical incumbents and their supervisors throughout the system. Task statements were rated in terms of importance, frequency, and essentialness (if it was essential for a newly hired employee to know how to do this task). Based on statistical analysis of the ratings' means and standard deviations, 25 of the 188 task statements were retained as critical task statements. These critical task statements were the key input to the identification of key KSAOs and the dimension of job performance.

Analysis of the 25 critical task statements indicated there were five KSAO components of the job: knowledge of computer hardware and software, ability to follow instructions and prioritize tasks, knowledge and skill in responding to telephone and reception scenarios, knowledge of English language, and ability to file items in alphabetical order. A test was constructed to measure these KSAOs as follows:

- Computer hardware and software—17 questions
- Prioritizing tasks—18 questions

- Route and transfer calls—14 questions
- Record messages—20 questions
- Give information on the phone—20 questions
- Correct sentences with errors—22 questions
- Identify errors in sentences—71 questions
- Filing—44 questions
- Typing—number of questions not reported

To develop the job performance (criterion) measure, a behavioral performance rating scale (1–7 rating) was constructed for each of the nine areas, ensuring a high content correspondence between the tests and the performance criteria they sought to predict. Scores on these nine scales were summed to yield an overall performance score.

The nine tests were administered to 108 current clerical employees to obtain predictor scores. A separate score on each of the nine tests was computed, along with a total test score for all tests. In addition, total scores on two short (50-question) forms of the total test were created (Form A and Form B).

Performance ratings of these 108 employees were obtained from their supervisors, who were unaware of their employees' test scores. The performance ratings were summed to form an overall performance rating. Scores on each of the nine tests, on the total test, and on Forms A and B of the test, were correlated with the overall performance ratings.

Results of the concurrent validation study are shown in Exhibit 7.13. It can be seen that seven of the nine specific tests had statistically significant correlations with overall performance (filing and typing did not). Total test scores were significantly correlated with overall performance, as were scores on the two short forms of the total test. The sizes of the statistically significant correlations suggest favorable practical significance of the correlations as well.

Content Validation

Content validation differs from criterion-related validity in one important respect: there is no criterion measure used in content validation. Thus, predictor scores cannot be correlated with criterion scores as a way of gathering evidence about a predictor's validity. Rather, a judgment is made about the probable correlation, had there been a criterion measure. For this reason, content validation is frequently referred to as judgmental validation.[13]

Content validation is most appropriate, and most likely to be found, in two circumstances: when there are too few people to form a sample for purposes of criterion-related validation, and when criterion measures are not available, or they are available but are of highly questionable quality. At an absolute minimum, an n = 30 is necessary for criterion-related validation.

EXHIBIT 7.13   Clerical Test Concurrent Validation Results

Test	Correlation with Overall Performance
Computer software and hardware	.37**
Prioritize tasks	.29*
Route and transfer calls	.19*
Record messages	.31**
Give information on phone	.35**
Correct sentences with errors	.32**
Identify errors in sentences	.44**
Filing	.22
Typing	.10
Total test	.45**
Form A	.55**
Form B	.49**

NOTE: *p < .05, **p < .01

Source: Adapted from J. E. Pynes, E. J. Harrick, and D. Schaefer, "A Concurrent Validation Study Applied to a Secretarial Position in a State University Civil Service System," *Journal of Business and Psychology*, 1997, 12, pp. 3–18.

Exhibit 7.14 shows the three basic steps in content validation—conducting a job analysis, constructing a job requirements matrix, and choosing or developing a predictor. These steps are commented on next. Comparing the steps in content validation with those in criterion-related validation (see Exhibit 7.11) shows that the steps in content validation are a part of criterion-related validation. Because of this, the two types of validation should be thought of as complementary, with content validation being a subset of criterion-related validation.

Job Analysis   As with criterion-related validation, content validation begins with job analysis, which, in both cases, is undertaken to identify and define tasks and task dimensions and to infer the necessary KSAOs and motivation for those tasks. Results are expressed in the job requirements matrix.

Predictor Measures   Sometimes the predictor will be one that has already been developed and is in use. An example here is a commercially available test, interviewing process, or biographical information questionnaire. Other times, there will not be such a measure available. This occurs frequently in the case of job knowledge, which is usually very specific to the particular job involved in the validation.

Lacking a readily available or modifiable predictor means that the organization will have to construct its own predictors. At this point, the organization has built

EXHIBIT 7.14 Content Validation

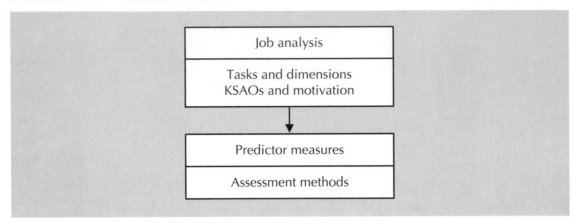

predictor construction into the predictor validation process. Now, content validation and the predictor development processes occur simultaneously. The organization becomes engaged in test construction, a topic beyond the scope of this
book.[14]

It should be emphasized that content validation procedures can be applied to
any type of predictor or combination of predictors, as illustrated in a content
validation study involving police emergency telephone operators.[15] A job analysis
identified six critical KSAO requirements for the job (communication skills, emotional control, judgment, cooperativeness, memory, and clerical/technical skills).
The predictors included

1. a spelling test in which applicants received 10 tape-recorded telephone calls
   and had to accurately record the pertinent information from each call on a
   form
2. a test in which applicants had to accurately record information received from
   monitoring police units
3. a typing test measuring both speed and accuracy
4. a situational interview in which applicants were asked how they would behave in a series of job-related situations
5. a role-playing exercise in which applicants assumed the role of police and
   telephone operators taking calls from complainants

This example makes clear that content validation is a flexible process for establishing task–KSAO–predictor linkages. At the same time that these linkages
are being established administratively, validation evidence is emerging from a
built-in process of content validation.

A final note about content validation emphasizes the importance of continually paying attention to the need for reliability of measurement and standardization of the measurement process. Though these are always matters of concern in any type of validation effort, they are of paramount importance in content validation. The reason for this is that without an empirical correlation between the predictor and criterion, only the likely r can be judged. It is important, in forming that judgment, to pay considerable attention to reliability and standardization.

Illustrative Study   The Maryland Department of Transportation sought to develop a series of assessment methods for identifying supervisory potential among candidates for promotion to a first-level supervising position anywhere within the department. The content validation process and outputs are shown in Exhibit 7.15. As shown in the exhibit, job analysis was first conducted to identify and define a set of performance dimensions and then infer the KSAOs necessary for successful

EXHIBIT 7.15   Content Validation Study

Job Analysis: First-Level Supervisor—Maryland Department of Transportation

Seven performance dimensions and task statements:
    Organizing work; assigning work; monitoring work; managing consequences; counseling, efficiency reviews, and discipline; setting an example; employee development

Fourteen KSAOs and definitions:
    Organizing; analysis and decision making; planning; communication (oral and written); delegation; work habits; carefulness; interpersonal skill; job knowledge; organizational knowledge; toughness; integrity; development of others; listening

Predictor Measures: Five Assessment Methods

- Multiple-choice in-basket exercise
  (assume role of new supervisor and work through in-basket on desk)
- Structured panel interview
  (predetermined questions about past experiences relevant to the KSAOs)
- Presentation exercise
  (make presentation to a simulated work group about change in their work hours)
- Writing sample
  (prepare a written reprimand for a ficticious employee)
- Training and experience evaluation exercise
  (give examples of training and work achievements relevant to certain KSAOs)

Source: Adapted from M. A. Cooper, G. Kaufman, and W. Hughes, " Measuring Supervisory Potential," *IPMA News,* December, 1996, pp. 8–18. Reprinted with permission of *IPMA News,* published by the International Personnel Management Association (IPMA), 703-549-7100, *www.ipma-hr.org.*

performance in those dimensions. Several SMEs met to develop a tentative set of task dimensions and underlying KSAOs. The underlying KSAOs were in essence general competencies required of all first-level supervisors, regardless of work unit within the department. Their results were sent to a panel of experienced HR managers within the department for revision and finalization. Three assessment method specialists then set about developing a set of assessments that would (a) be efficiently administered at locations throughout the state, (b) be reliably scored by people at those locations, and (c) emphasize the interpersonal skills important for this job. As shown in Exhibit 7.15, five assessment methods were developed: multiple-choice in-basket exercise, structured interview panel, presentation exercise, writing sample, and training and experience evaluation exercise.

Candidates' performance on the exercises was to be evaluated by specially chosen assessors at the location in which the exercises were administered. To ensure that candidates' performance was skillfully observed and reliably evaluated by the assessors, an intensive training program was developed. The program provided both a written user's manual and specific skill training.

Validity Generalization

In the preceding discussions of validity and validation, an implicit premise is being made that validity is situation-specific, and therefore validation of predictors must occur in each specific situation. All of the examples involve specific types of measures, jobs, individuals, and so forth. Nothing is said about generalizing validity across those jobs and individuals. For example, if a predictor is valid for a particular job in organization A, would it be valid for the same type of job in organization B? Or is validity specific to the particular job and organization?

The situation-specific premise is based on the following scenario, which, in turn, has its origins in findings from decades of previous research. Assume a large number of criterion-related validation studies have been conducted. Each study involves various predictor measures of a common KSAO attribute (e.g., general mental ability) and various criterion measures of a common outcome attribute (e.g., job performance). The predictor will be designated "X," and the criterion will be designated "Y." The studies are conducted in many different situations (types of jobs, types of organizations), and they involve many different samples (sample sizes, types of employees). In each study, r_{xy} is calculated. The results from all the studies reveal a wide range of r_{xy} values, though the average is $\bar{r}_{xy} = .25$. These results suggest that while on average there seems to be some validity to X, the validity varies substantially from situation to situation. Based on these findings, the best conclusion is that validity most likely is situation-specific and thus cannot be generalized across the situations.

The concept of validity generalization questions this premise.[16] It says that much of the variation in the r_{xy} values is due to the occurrence of a number of methodological and statistical differences across the studies. If these differences were controlled for statistically, the variation in values would shrink and converge toward an estimate of the true validity of X. If that true r is significant (practically and statistically), one can indeed generalize validity of X across situations. Validity thus is not viewed as situation-specific. The logic of this validity generalization premise is shown in Exhibit 7.16.

The distinction between situation-specific validity and validity generalization is important for two related reasons. First, from a scientific viewpoint, it is important to identify and make statements about X and Y relationships in general, without always having to say that everything depends on the sample, criterion measure, and so on. In this regard, validity generalization clearly allows greater latitude than does situation specificity. Second, from a practical standpoint, it would be convenient and less costly not to have to conduct a separate validation study for predictor X in every situation in which its use was a possibility. Validity generalization allows that to happen, whereas situation specificity does not.

Evidence is beginning to surface that is supportive of the validity generalization premise. For example, evidence suggests that tests of general mental ability have meaningful, practical validity for predicting job performance across a wide variety of types of employees and jobs. Until more is known about validity generalization, however, caution is called for in its use in either scientific or practical terms. In this light, the following recommendations are offered as guides to staffing practice:

1. At a minimum, all predictors should routinely be subject to content validation.

2. When feasible, criterion-related validation studies should be conducted unless there is sufficient validity generalization evidence available to support use of a predictor without prior validation.

3. Any claims of validity or validity generalization that are based on no criterion-related validity studies, or only a small number of them, should be suspect.

4. A predictor's validity is specific to the criterion against which it was validated (e.g., performance on a specific job), and the predictor's validity

---

EXHIBIT 7.16   The Logic of Validity Generalization

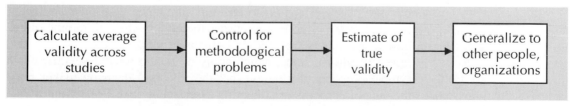

Calculate average validity across studies → Control for methodological problems → Estimate of true validity → Generalize to other people, organizations

should not be extended to other criteria (e.g., performance on a different job, attendance) without validation evidence for those criteria.

5. Organizations should become involved in various cooperative arrangements devoted to validation research in order to explore the extent to which validity may be generalized.

A particular form of validity generalization that has proved useful is called meta-analysis. In meta-analysis the focus is on determining the average correlation between X and Y (i.e., $\bar{r}_{xy}$) noted above, such as between a particular selection technique (X) and job performance (Y) after controlling for methodological problems in the validation studies. For example, the average validity of general cognitive ability tests for predicting job performance is $\bar{r}_{xy} = .50$ (see Chapter 9). This represents our best statement of the average degree of validity found for mental ability tests to date, as well as an expectation of the validity we would likely find for general mental ability tests in future validation studies. We can also compare this $\bar{r}_{xy}$ to the $\bar{r}_{xy}$ of another selection technique, such as the unstructured interview, as a way of indicating the relative validity of the two techniques. Meta-analysis results and comparisons for numerous selection techniques are presented in Chapters 8 and 9.

COLLECTION OF ASSESSMENT DATA

In staffing decisions, the process of measurement is put into practice by collecting assessment data on external or internal applicants. To this point in this chapter, we have discussed how selection measures can be evaluated. To be sure, thorough evaluation of selection measures is important. Selection decision makers must be knowledgeable about how to use the assessment data that have been collected; otherwise the potential value of the data will lay dormant. On the other hand, to put these somewhat theoretical concepts to use in practice, selection decision makers must know how to collect the assessment data. Otherwise, the decision maker may find himself in the unenviable "Big Hat, No Cattle" situation—knowing how to analyze and evaluate assessment data, but not knowing where to find the data in the first place. Thus, knowing how to evaluate selection measures goes hand-in-hand with knowing where to find good assessment data in the first place.

In collecting assessment data, if a predictor is purchased, support services are needed. Consulting firms and test publishers can provide support for scoring of tests. Also necessary is legal support to ensure compliance with laws and regulations. Validity studies are important to ensure the effectiveness of the measures. Training on how to administer the predictor also is needed.

Beyond these general principles, which apply no matter what assessment data are collected, there is other information that the selection decision maker must know about the tangible process of collecting assessment data. Collection of data with respect to testing procedures, applicant reactions, tests and test manuals, and professional standards are discussed.

Testing Procedures

In the past, most data concerning selecting testing procedures was in reference to paper-and-pencil tests. With the growth of computerization and the Internet, however, more and more selection measures are available on the personal computer (PC) and Web. Accordingly, in the sections that follow, we separate our discussion of the collection of testing procedures data into paper-and-pencil measures and PC- or Web-based procedures.

Paper and Pencil

Predictors cannot always be purchased by any firm that wants to use them; many test publishers require the purchaser to have certain expertise to properly use the test. For example, they may want the user to hold a Ph.D. in a field of study related to the test and its use. For smaller organizations, this means that they need to hire the consulting services of a specialist to use a particular test.

Care must be taken to ensure that correct answers for predictors are not shared with job applicants in advance of administration of the predictor. Any person who has access to the predictor answers should be fully trained and sign a predictor security agreement. Also, a regular inventory procedure needs to be established to ensure that predictor materials are not inappropriately dispersed. Should a breach of security take place, use of the predictor should be abandoned and a new one should be used.

The predictor itself should be kept secure, but so should the results of the predictor in order to ensure the privacy of the individual. The results of the predictor should be used only for the intended purposes and by persons qualified to interpret them. Though feedback can be given to the candidate concerning the results, the individual should not be given a copy of the predictor or the scoring key.

Finally, it is imperative that all applicants be assessed with standardized procedures. This means that not only should the same or a psychometrically equivalent predictor be used, but individuals should take the test under the same circumstances. The purpose of the predictor should be explained to applicants, and they should be put at ease, held to the same time requirements to complete the predictor, and take the predictor in the same location.

PC- and Web-Based

Many tests can now be administered on the PC. Many of the test publishers mentioned above offer selection decision makers the choice of paper-and-pencil or PC-based tests. For example, the *Wonderlic Personnel Test* has a version of the test that is administered and scored using a PC. It includes testing and scoring software and user's manual. Typically, the cost of purchasing such tests is no more than the paper-and-pencil version of the tests.

Some test publishers now offer online assessment where applicants take tests online; organizations (as well as applicants) can then receive their results immediately. e-Selex.com offers Web-based screening programs where applicants may apply and be tested online, and selection decision makers can refer to the Web site to monitor applicant information. Other companies, such as ePredix (*www.epredix.com*), offer an online interview builder, and other companies provide reference checking, in addition to testing. Other organizations offer video screening services where applicants tape presentations and companies can then view the presentations online. Some companies, such as Capital One and the state of California, have even devised their own online selection systems.

Although collecting assessment data in such a manner has the benefit of immediacy of results, organizations that choose to outsource pre-employment screening on the Web need to ensure that the data are legally compliant, valid, and secure. Additionally, applicants may be concerned over privacy issues or may lack familiarity or be uncomfortable with tests administered via the Web. Finally, there is a concern about faking, such as the case when an individual other than the applicant takes the test. If organizations are concerned about individuals other than the applicant taking the test, verification procedures can be implemented, including mandating that the applicant take the test at a site that allows verification of their identification.[17]

If selection measures are administered on the PC or Web, some of the issues associated with paper-and-pencil selection measures are relevant, and others are not. It is possible that less expertise is required since the tests may be administered on the PC or via the Web. On the other hand, some expertise is required to interpret the information and validate the tests. Selection decision makers must ensure that the test publisher or consulting firm has procedures to maintain the security and confidentiality of the data. With PC- or Web-based measures, ensuring that applicants take the test under the same circumstances is more difficult, unless applicants take the test at a set location.

Applicant Reactions

Standardization is important when collecting information about applicant reactions to the assessment process. Many selection decision makers might feel they have a good sense of how applicants react to the selection process, but to move beyond subjective "hunches" to objective data, it is important that standardized procedures are followed when collecting information on applicant reactions.

Beyond formally collecting data from applicants regarding their reactions to the selection process, organizations can foster positive applicant reactions by maintaining good records and providing information, where appropriate, to applicants. The Arizona Department of Corrections keeps records on applicant scores on selection measures so that applicants can ask to review why they were denied a position. The department has found that providing applicants with feedback on the questions that they missed on a test, or how they scored on the interview, can encourage overall acceptance of the selection program. When applicants are given this sort of feedback, their greater acceptance of the results might lead them to recommend the organization to others, to refrain from filing a lawsuit or lodging a complaint, or perhaps to reapply for a position later when their scores might improve.[18]

Acquisition of Tests and Test Manuals

The process of acquiring tests and test manuals requires some start-up costs in terms of the time and effort required to contact test publishers. Once one is on a mailing list, however, brochures from the publishers keep the selection decision maker updated on the latest developments and ordering information. In making decisions about which tests to acquire, a decision must be made not only about the particular type of test, but also the manner in which it will be administered and scored—paper and pencil versus PC-based.

Paper and Pencil

Most paper-and-pencil tests are acquired by contacting the publisher of the tests. Some publishers of paper-and-pencil tests used in selection decisions are Wonderlic (*www.wonderlic.com*), Consulting Psychologists Press (*www.cpp-db.com*), Institute for Personality and Ability Testing (*www.ipat.com*), Psychological Assessment Resources (*www.parinc.com*), NCS Assessments (*www.ncs.com*), Hogan Assessment Systems (*www.hoganassessments.com*), and Psychological Services, Inc. (*www.psionline.com*). All of these organizations have brochures that describe the products available for purchase. Most organizations will provide sample copies of the tests and a user's manual that selection decision makers may consult before purchasing the test. Cost of paper-and-pencil tests vary widely depending on the test and the number of copies ordered. One test that can be scored by the selection decision maker, for example, cost $100 for testing 25 applicants and $200 for testing 100 applicants. Another test that comes with a scoring system and interpretive report cost from $25 each for testing 5 applicants to $17 each for testing 100 applicants. Presumably, greater discounts are available for testing larger numbers of applicants.

Any test worth using will have a professional user's manual that accompanies it. This manual should describe the development and validation of the test, including validity evidence in selection contexts. A test manual also should include administration instructions, scoring instructions or information (many test marketers will score tests for organizations [for an additional fee]), interpretation information, and normative data. All of this information is crucial to make sure the test is an appropriate one and that it is used in an appropriate (valid, legal) manner. Avoid using a test that has no professional manual as it is unlikely to have been validated. Using a test without a proven track record is akin to hiring an applicant sight unseen. The *Wonderlic Personnel Test User's Manual* is an excellent example of a professional user's manual. It contains information about various forms of the *Wonderlic Personnel Test* (see Chapter 9), how to administer the test and interpret and use the scores, various norms by age, race, gender, and so on, and validity and fairness of the test.

PC- or Web-Based

When selection measures are administered on the PC or Web, acquisition is simple since copies of the measures are contained in the software. Thus, once an organization decides to administer selection measures in this manner, the consulting firm or test publisher arranges for access to the tests. Generally, organizations are given special user names that applicants use to complete the measures (along with their own identifying information). In some cases, the user's manuals for PC- or Web-based tests are provided on the computer. In other cases, only hard copies of the manuals are available. Irrespective of how the tests were acquired or administered, organizations must make sure they validate the tests. Selection decision makers should not accept vague claims regarding the accuracy of selection measures, no matter how the tests were acquired and administered.

Professional Standards

Developed jointly by the American Educational Research Association, the American Psychological Association (APA), and the National Council on Measurement in Education, the 1999 *Standards for Educational and Psychological Testing* is a guidebook that provides testing standards for use in education, psychology, and employment. The *Standards* covers test construction, evaluation, and documentation (i.e., reliability, validity, test development, test administration) and fairness in testing (rights and responsibilities of test takers and test users, testing individuals of diverse linguistic backgrounds, testing individuals with disabilities), among other topics. The *Standards* resulted from a panel of experts in testing and assessment, and this latest version reflects nearly 8,000 pages of comments from over 200 organizations and individuals. Although some of the material in the standards covers testing and assessment for uses other than employment (e.g., educational testing), most of the material is applicable to employment contexts, and much of the material directly deals with employment testing. Thus, selection decision makers using tests would be well advised to consult this important document, which is written in practical, nontechnical language.

The *Standards* can be ordered for a fee by visiting either of the following web sites:

Society of Industrial and Organizational Psychology:
www.siop.org/Bookorder.htm
American Psychological Association (APA):
www.apa.org/science/standards.html

A related set of standards has been promulgated by the APA. Formulated by the Joint Committee on Testing Practices, *The Rights and Responsibilities of Test Takers: Guidelines and Expectations* enumerates 10 rights and 10 responsibilities of test takers. One of the rights is for the applicant to be treated with courtesy, respect, and impartiality. Another right is to receive prior explanation for the purpose(s) of the testing. One responsibility is to follow the test instructions as given. In addition to enumerating test-taker rights and responsibilities, the document also provides guidelines for organizations administering the tests. For example, the standards stipulate that organizations should inform test takers about the purpose of the test. This document is available online at *www.apa.org/science/ttrr.html*. Organizations testing applicants should consult these guidelines to ensure, wherever possible, these rights are provided.

LEGAL ISSUES

Staffing laws and regulations, particularly EEO/AA laws and regulations, place great reliance on the use of measurement concepts and processes. Here, measurement is an integral part of (a) judging an organization's compliance through the conduct of disparate impact analysis, and (b) requiring standardization and validation of measures.

Disparate Impact Statistics

In Chapter 2, disparate (adverse) impact was introduced as a way of determining whether staffing practices were having potentially illegal impacts on individuals because of race, sex, and so forth. Such a determination requires the compilation and analysis of statistical evidence, primarily applicant flow and applicant stock statistics.

Applicant Flow Statistics

Applicant flow statistical analysis requires the calculation of selection rates (proportions or percentages of applicants hired) for groups, and the subsequent comparison of those rates to determine if they are significantly different from one another. This may be illustrated by taking the example from Exhibit 2.3:

	Applicants	Hires	Selection Rate
Men	50	25	.50 or 50%
Women	45	5	.11 or 11%

It may be seen in this example that there is a sizable difference in selection rates between men and women (.50 as opposed to .11). Does this difference indicate adverse impact?

The Uniform Guidelines on Employee Selection Procedures (UGESP) speak directly to this question. Several points need to be made regarding the determination of disparate impact analysis.

First, the UGESP requires the organization to keep records that will permit calculation of such selection rates, also referred to as applicant flow statistics. These statistics are a primary vehicle by which compliance with the law (Civil Rights Act) is judged.

Second, the UGESP requires calculation of selection rates (a) for each job category, (b) for both external and internal selection decisions, (c) for each step in the selection process, and (d) by race and sex of applicants. To meet this requirement, the organization must keep detailed records of its staffing activities and decisions. Such record keeping should be built directly into the organization's staffing system routines.

Third, comparisons of selection rates among groups in a job category for purposes of compliance determination should be based on the 80% rule in the UGESP, which states that "a selection rate for any race, sex or ethnic group which is less than four-fifths (4/5) (or eighty percent) of the rate for the group with the highest rate will generally be regarded by federal enforcement agencies as evidence of adverse impact, while a greater than four-fifths rate will generally not be regarded by federal enforcement agencies as evidence of adverse impact."

If this rule is applied to the previous example, the group with the highest selection rate is men (.50). The rate for women should be within 80% of this rate, or .40 (.50 × .80 = .40). Since the actual rate for women is .11, this suggests the occurrence of adverse impact.

Fourth, the 80% rule is truly only a guideline. Note the use of the word "generally" in the rule with regard to differences in selection rates. Also, the 80% rule goes on to provide for other exceptions, based on sample size considerations and issues surrounding statistical and practical significance of difference in selection rates. These exceptions represent recognition of the fact that adverse impact statistics may be unstable sample estimates of the amount of true adverse impact occurring. More precise methods of assessing adverse impact are needed.[19] Despite these exceptions, organizations are encouraged to use the 80% rule with stringency for purposes of self-analysis. Deviations from the rule should be treated as red flags that trigger an examination into possible reasons for their occurrence.

Applicant Stock Statistics

Applicant stock statistics require the calculation of the percentages of women and minorities (a) employed and (b) available for employment in the population. These percentages are compared to search for disparities in the percentages. This is referred to as utilization analysis.

To illustrate, the example from Exhibit 2.3 is shown here:

	Employed	Availability
Nonminority	90%	70%
Minority	10%	30%

It can be seen that 10% of employees are minorities, whereas their availability in the population is 30%. A comparison of these two percentages suggests an underutilization of minorities.

Utilization analysis of this sort is an integral part of not only compliance assessment but also affirmative action plans (AAPs). Indeed, utilization analysis is the starting point for the development of AAPs. This may be illustrated by reference to the Affirmative Action Programs regulations.

The regulations require the organization to conduct a formal utilization analysis of its workforce. That analysis must be (a) conducted by job group, and (b) done separately for women and minorities. Though calculation of the numbers and percentages of persons employed is relatively straightforward, determination of their availability in the population is not. The regulations require that the availabilities take into account at least the following factors: (1) the percentage of women or minorities with requisite skills in the recruitment area and (2) the percentage of women or minorities among those promotable, transferable, and trainable within the organization. Accurate measurement and/or estimation of availabilities that take into account these factors is difficult.

Despite these measurement problems, the regulations require comparison of the percentage of women and minorities employed with their availability. When the percentage of minorities or women in a job group is less than would reasonably be expected given their availability, underutilization exists and placement (hiring and promotion) goals must be set. Thus, the organization must exercise considerable discretion in the determination of adverse impact through the use of applicant stock statistics. It would be wise to seek technical and/or legal assistance for conducting utilization analysis.

Standardization and Validation

When it has been determined that an organization is in noncompliance with the law, such as through adverse impact statistics, it must take certain steps to move toward compliance. While the specific steps will obviously depend on the situation, measurement activities invariably will be actively involved in them. These activities will revolve around standardization and validation of measures.

Standardization

A lack of consistency in treatment of applicants is one of the major factors contributing to the occurrence of discrimination in staffing. This is partly due to a lack of standardization in measurement, in terms of both what is measured and how it is evaluated or scored.

An example of inconsistency in what is measured is that the types of background information required of minority applicants may differ from that required of nonminority applicants. Minority applicants may be asked about credit ratings and criminal conviction records, while nonminority applicants are not. Or, the type of interview questions asked male applicants may be different from those asked female applicants.

Even if information is consistently gathered from all applicants, it may not be evaluated the same for all applicants. A male applicant who has a history of holding several different jobs may be viewed as a "career builder," while a female with the same history may be evaluated as an unstable "job hopper." In essence, different scoring keys are being used for men and women applicants.

Reducing, and hopefully eliminating, such inconsistency requires a straightforward application of the three properties of standardized measures discussed previously. Through standardization of measurement comes consistent treatment of applicants, and with it, the possibility of lessened adverse impact.

Validation

Even with standardized measurement, adverse impact may occur. Under these circumstances, the question is whether adverse impact is still justified. The UGESP addresses this issue directly. When there is adverse impact, the organization must either eliminate it or justify it through presentation of validity evidence regarding the measure(s) causing the adverse impact.

The types of validity evidence required under the UGESP are precisely those presented in this chapter. There are also detailed technical standards governing the conduct of these validation studies in the UGESP. The purpose of these requirements is to ensure that, if an organization's staffing system is causing adverse impact, it is for job-related reasons. Evidence of job relatedness thus becomes the employer's rebuttal to the plaintiff's charges of discrimination. In the absence of such validation evidence, the employer must take steps to eliminate the adverse impact. These steps will involve various recruitment, selection, and employment activities that will be discussed throughout the remainder of the book. A detailed review of the UGESP is provided in Chapter 9.

SUMMARY

Measurement, defined as the process of using rules to assign numbers to objects to represent quantities of an attribute of the objects, is an integral part of the foundation of staffing activities. Standardization of the measurement process is sought. This applies to each of the four levels of measurement: nominal, ordinal, interval, and ratio. Standardization is also sought for both objective and subjective measures.

Measures yield scores that represent the amount of the attribute being measured. Scores are manipulated in various ways to aid in their interpretation. Typical manipulations involve central tendency and variability, percentiles, and standard scores. Scores are also correlated to learn about the strength and direction of the relationship between two attributes. The significance of the resultant correlation coefficient is then judged in statistical and practical terms.

The quality of measures involves issues of reliability and validity. Reliability refers to consistency of measurement, both at a moment in time and between time periods. Various procedures are used to estimate reliability, including coefficient alpha, interrater and intrarater agreement, and test-retest. Reliability places an upper limit on the validity of a measure.

Validity refers to accuracy of measurement and accuracy of prediction, as reflected by the scores obtained from a measure. Criterion-related and content validation studies are conducted to help learn about the validity of a measure. In criterion-related validation, scores on a predictor (KSAO) measure are correlated with scores on a criterion (HR outcome) measure. In content validation, there is no criterion measure, so judgments are made about the content of a predictor relative to the HR outcome it is seeking to predict. Traditionally, results of validation studies were treated as situation-specific, meaning that the organization ideally should conduct a new and separate validation study for any predictor in any situation in which the predictor is to be used. Recently, however, results from validity generalization studies have suggested that the validity of predictors may generalize across situations, meaning that the requirement of conducting costly and time-consuming validation studies in each specific situation could be relaxed.

Various practical aspects of the collection of assessment data were described. Decisions about testing procedures, collection of data on application reactions, and the acquisition of tests and test manuals require the attention of organizational decision makers. The collection of assessment data and the acquisition of tests and test manuals vary depending on whether paper-and-pencil or computerized selection measures are utilized. Finally, organizations need to attend to professional standards that govern the proper use of the collection of assessment data.

Measurement is also said to be an integral part of an organization's EEO/AA compliance activities, as the Uniform Guidelines on Employee Selection Procedures (UGESP) and Affirmative Action Programs regulations make clear. Statistics are used to help determine if and where the organization's staffing activities are causing disparate (adverse) impact. When adverse impact is found, changes in measurement practices may be legally necessary. As specified in the UGESP and Affirmative Action Programs regulations, these changes will involve movement toward standardization of measurement and the conduct of validation studies.

DISCUSSION QUESTIONS

1. Imagine and describe a staffing system for a job in which there are no measures used.
2. Describe how you might go about determining scores for applicants' responses to (a) interview questions, (b) letters of recommendation, and (c) questions about previous work experience.
3. Describe examples of when you would want the following for a written job knowledge test: (a) a low coefficient alpha (e.g., $\alpha = .35$), and (b) a low test-retest reliability.
4. Assume you gave a general ability test, measuring both verbal and computational skills, to a group of applicants for a specific job. Also assume that because of severe hiring pressures, you hired all of the applicants, regardless of their test scores. How would you investigate the criterion-related validity of the test?
5. Using the same example as in question four, how would you go about investigating the content validity of the test?
6. What information does a selection decision maker need to collect in making staffing decisions? What are the ways in which this information can be collected?

APPLICATIONS

Evaluation of Two New Assessment Methods for Selecting Telephone Customer Service Representatives

The Phonemin Company is a distributor of men's and women's casual clothing. It sells exclusively through its merchandise catalog, which is published four times per year to coincide with seasonal changes in customers' apparel tastes. Customers may order merchandise from the catalog via mail or over the phone. Currently, 70% of orders are phone orders, and the company expects this to increase to 85% within the next few years.

The success of the company is obviously very dependent on the success of the telephone ordering system and the customer service representatives (CSRs) who staff the system. There are currently 185 CSR employees; that number should increase to about 225 CSRs to handle the anticipated growth in phone order sales. Though the CSRs are trained to use standardized methods and procedures for handling phone orders, there are still seemingly large differences among them in their job performance. The CSRs' performance is routinely measured in terms of error rate, speed of order taking, and customer complaints. The top 25% and lowest 25% of performers on each of these measures differ by a factor of at least 3 (e.g., the error rate of the lowest group is three times as high as that of the top group). Strategically, the company knows that it could enhance CSR performance (and ultimately sales) substantially if it could improve its staffing "batting average" by more accurately identifying and hiring new CSRs who are likely to be top performers.

The current staffing system for CSRs is straightforward. Applicants are recruited through a combination of employee referrals and newspaper ads. Because turnover among CSRs is so high (50% annually), recruitment is a continuous process at the company. Applicants complete a standard application blank, which asks for information about education and previous work experience. The information is reviewed by the staffing specialist in the HR department. Only obvious misfits are rejected at this point; the others (95%) are asked to have an interview with the specialist. The interview lasts 20–30 minutes, and at the conclusion the applicant is either rejected or offered a job. Due to the tightness of the labor market and the constant presence of vacancies to be filled, 90% of the interviewees receive job offers. Most of those offers are accepted (95%), and the new hires then attend a one-week training program before being placed on the job.

The company has decided to investigate fully the possibilities of increasing CSR effectiveness through sounder staffing practices. In particular, it is not pleased with its current methods of assessing job applicants; it feels that neither the interview nor the application blank provides the accurate and in-depth assessments of the KSAOs truly needed to be an effective CSR. Consequently, it has engaged the services of a consulting firm that offers various methods of KSAO assessment, along with validation and installation services. In cooperation with the HR staffing specialist, the consulting firm conducted the following study for the company.

A special job analysis led to the identification of several specific KSAOs likely to be necessary for successful performance as a CSR. Three of these (clerical speed, clerical accuracy, interpersonal skills) were singled out for further consideration because of their seemingly high impact on job performance. Two new methods of assessment, provided by the consulting firm, were chosen for experimentation. The first was a paper-and-pencil clerical test assessing clerical speed and accuracy. It is a 50-item test with a 30-minute time limit. The second was a brief work sample that could be administered as part of the interview process. In the work sample the applicant must respond to four different phone calls: from a customer irate about an out-of-stock item, from a customer wanting more product information about an item than was provided in the catalog, from a customer who wants to change an order placed yesterday, and from a customer with a routine order to place. The applicant is rated by the interviewer (using a 1–5 rating scale) in terms of tactfulness (T) and in terms of concern for customers (C). The interviewer is provided with a rating manual containing examples of exceptional (5), average (3), and unacceptable (1) responses by the applicant.

A random sample of 50 current CSRs were chosen to participate in the study. At Time 1 they were administered the clerical test and the work sample; performance data were also gathered from company records for error rate (number of errors per 100 orders), speed (number of orders filled per hour), and customer complaints (number of complaints per week). At Time 2, one week later, the clerical test and the work sample were readministered to the CSRs. A member of the consulting firm sat in on all the interviews and served as a second rater of applicants' performance on the work sample at Time 1 and Time 2. It was expected that the clerical test and work sample would have positive correlations with speed and negative correlations with error rate and customer complaints.

Results for Clerical Test

	Time 1	Time 2
Mean score	31.61	31.22
Standard deviation	4.70	5.11
Coefficient alpha	.85	.86
Test-retest r		.92**
r with error rate	−.31**	−.37**
r with speed	.41**	.39**
r with complaints	−.11	−.08
r with work sample (T)	.21	.17
r with work sample (C)	.07	.15

Results for Work Sample (T)

	Time 1	Time 2
Mean score	3.15	3.11
Standard deviation	.93	1.01
% agreement (raters)	88%	79%
r with work sample (C)	.81**	.77**
r with error rate	−.13	−.12
r with speed	.11	.15
r with complaints	−.37**	−.35**

Results for Work Sample (C)

	Time 1	Time 2
Mean score	2.91	3.07
Standard deviation	.99	1.10
% agreement (raters)	80%	82%
r with work sample (T)	.81**	.77**
r with error rate	−.04	−.11
r with speed	.15	.14
r with complaints	−.40**	−.31**

(Note: ** means that r was significant at $p < .05$)

Based on the description of the study and results above:

1. How do you interpret the reliability results for the clerical test and work sample? Are they favorable enough for the company to consider using them "for keeps" in selecting new job applicants?

2. How do you interpret the validity results for the clerical test and work sample? Are they favorable enough for the company to consider using them "for keeps" in selecting new job applicants?

3. What limitations in the above study should be kept in mind when interpreting the results and deciding whether or not to use the clerical test and work sample?

Conducting Empirical Validation and Adverse Impact Analysis

Yellow Blaze Candle Shops provide a full line of various types of candles and accessories such as candle holders. There are 150 shops located in shopping malls and strip malls throughout the country. There are over 600 salespeople staffing these stores, each of which has a full-time manager. Staffing the manager's position, by policy, must occur by promotion from within the sales ranks. The company is interested in trying to improve its identification of salespeople most likely to be successful store managers. It has developed a special technique for assessing and rating the suitability of salespeople for the manager's job.

To experiment with this technique, the regional HR department representative met with the store managers in the region to review and rate the promotion suitability of each manager's salespeople. They reviewed sales results, customer service orientation, and knowledge of store operations for each salesperson, and then assigned a 1–3 promotion suitability rating (1 = not suitable, 2 = maybe suitable, 3 = definitely suitable) on each of these three factors. A total promotion suitability (PS) score, ranging from 3 to 9, was then computed for each salesperson.

The PS scores were gathered, but not formally used in promotion decisions, for all salespeople. Over the past year 30 salespeople have been promoted to store manager. Now it is time for the company to preliminarily investigate the validity of the PS scores and to see if their use might lead to the occurrence of adverse impact against women or minorities. Each store manager's annual overall performance appraisal rating, ranging from 1 (low performance) to 5 (high performance), was used as the criterion measure in the validation study. The following data were available for analysis:

Employee ID	PS Score	Performance	Sex M/F	Minority Status (M = Minority NM = Nonminority)
11	9	5	M	NM
12	9	5	F	NM
13	9	1	F	NM
14	9	5	M	M
15	8	4	F	M
16	8	5	F	M
17	8	4	M	NM
18	8	5	M	NM
19	8	3	F	NM
20	8	4	M	NM
21	7	5	F	M
22	7	3	M	M
23	7	4	M	NM
24	7	3	F	NM
25	7	3	F	NM
26	7	4	M	NM
27	7	5	M	M
28	6	4	F	NM
29	6	4	M	NM
30	6	2	F	M
31	6	3	F	NM
32	6	3	M	NM
33	6	5	M	NM
34	6	5	F	NM
35	5	3	M	NM
36	5	3	F	M
37	5	2	M	M
38	4	2	F	NM
39	4	1	M	NM
40	3	4	F	NM

Based on the above data calculate:

1. Average PS scores for the whole sample, males, females, nonminority, minority.

2. The correlation between PS scores and Performance ratings, and its statistical significance (an $r = .37$ or higher is needed for significance at $p < .05$).

3. Adverse impact (selection rate) statistics for males and females, and nonminorities and minorities. Use a PS score of 7 or higher as a hypothetical

passing score (the score that might be used to determine who will or will not be promoted).

Using the data, results, and description of the study, answer the following questions:

1. Is the PS assessment a valid predictor of performance as a store manager? Would you recommend the PS be used in the future to select salespeople for promotion to store manager?
2. With a cut score of 7 on the PS, would its use lead to adverse impact against women? minorities? If there is adverse impact, does the validity evidence justify use of the PS anyway?
3. What are limitations of this study?
4. Would you recommend Yellow Blaze now actually use the PS for making promotion decisions? Why or why not?

ENDNOTES

1. E. F. Stone, *Research Methods in Organizational Behavior* (Santa Monica, CA: Goodyear, 1978), pp. 35–36.
2. F. G. Brown, *Principles of Educational and Psychological Testing* (Hinsdale, IL: Dryden, 1970), pp. 38–45.
3. E. F. Stone, *Research Methods in Organizational Behavior*, pp. 36–40.
4. R. L. Heneman, "The Relationship Between Supervisory Ratings and Results-Oriented Measures of Performance: A Meta-Analysis," *Personnel Psychology*, 1986, 39, pp. 811–826; W. H. Bommer, J. L. Johnson, G. A. Rich, P. M. Podsakoff, and S. B. McKenzie, "On the Interchangeability of Objective and Subjective Measures of Employee Performance: A Meta-Analysis," *Personnel Psychology*, 1995, 48, pp. 587–606.
5. This section draws on F. G. Brown, *Principles of Educational and Psychological Testing*, pp. 158–197; L. J. Cronbach, *Essentials of Psychological Testing*, fourth ed. (New York: Harper and Row, 1984), pp. 81–120; N. W. Schmitt and R. J. Klimoski, *Research Methods in Human Resources Management* (Cincinnati: Southwestern, 1991), pp. 41–87.
6. J. T. McClave and P. G. Benson, *Statistics for Business and Economics*, third ed. (San Francisco: Dellan, 1985).
7. For an excellent review, see N. W. Schmitt and R. J. Klimoski, *Research Methods in Human Resources Management*, pp. 88–114.
8. This section draws on E. G. Carmines and R. A. Zeller, *Reliability and Validity Assessment* (Beverly Hills, CA: Sage, 1979).
9. D. P. Schwab, "Construct Validity in Organization Behavior," in B. Staw and L. L. Cummings (eds.), *Research in Organizational Behavior* (Greenwich, CT: JAI Press, 1980), pp. 3–43.
10. E. G. Carmines and R. A. Zeller, *Reliability and Validity Assessment;* J. M. Cortina, "What Is Coefficient Alpha? An Examination of Theory and Application," *Journal of Applied Psychology*, 1993, 78, pp. 98–104; N. W. Schmitt and R. J. Klimoski, *Research Methods in Human Resources Management*, pp. 89–100.

11. This section draws on R. D. Arvey, "Constructs and Construct Validation," *Human Performance,* 1992, 5, pp. 59–69; W. F. Cascio, *Applied Psychology in Personnel Management,* fourth ed. (Englewood Cliffs, NJ: Prentice-Hall, 1991), pp. 149–170; H. G. Heneman III, D. P. Schwab, J. A. Fossum, and L. Dyer, *Personnel/Human Resource Management,* fourth ed. (Homewood, IL: Irwin, 1989), pp. 300–329; N. Schmitt and F. J. Landy, "The Concept of Validity," in N. Schmitt, W. C. Borman, and Associates, *Personnel Selection in Organizations* (San Francisco: Jossey-Bass, 1993), pp. 275–309; D. P. Schwab, "Construct Validity in Organization Behavior"; S. Messick, "Validity of Psychological Assessment," *American Psychologist,* Sept. 1995, pp. 741–749.

12. H. G. Heneman III, D. P. Schwab, J. A. Fossum, and L. Dyer, *Personnel/Human Resource Management,* pp. 300–310.

13. I. L. Goldstein, S. Zedeck, and B. Schneider, "An Exploration of the Job Analysis-Content Validity Process," in N. Schmitt, W. C. Borman, and Associates, *Personnel Selection in Organizations,* pp. 3–34; H. G. Heneman III, D. P. Schwab, J. A. Fossum, and L. Dyer, *Personnel/ Human Resource Management,* pp. 311–315; P. R. Sackett and R. D. Arvey, "Selection in Small N Settings," in N. Schmitt, W. C. Borman, and Associates, *Personnel Selection in Organizations,* pp. 418–447; D. A. Joiner, *Content Valid Testing for Supervisory and Management Jobs: A Practical/Common Sense Approach* (Alexandria, VA: International Personnel Management Association, 1987).

14. R. S. Barrett, "Content Validation Form," *Public Personnel Management,* 1992, 21, pp. 41–52; E. E. Ghiselli, J. P. Campbell, and S. Zedeck, *Measurement Theory for the Behavioral Sciences* (San Francisco: W. H. Freeman, 1981).

15. N. Schmitt and C. Ostroff, "Operationalizing the Behavioral Consistency Approach: Selection Test Development Based on a Content-Oriented Strategy," *Personnel Psychology,* 1986, 39, pp. 91–108.

16. R. M. Guion, "Personnel Assessment, Selection and Placement," in M. D. Dunnette and L. M. Hough (eds.), *Handbook of Industrial and Organizational Psychology,* Vol. 2, pp. 360–365; F. L. Schmidt and J. E. Hunter, "Development of a General Solution to the Problem of Validity Generalization," *Journal of Applied Psychology,* 1977, 62, pp. 529–540; N. Schmitt, W. C. Borman, and Associates, *Personnel Selection in Organizations,* pp. 295–296.

17. B. Calandra, "Skill Assessors," *Human Resource Executive,* March 4, 1999; K. Coffee, J. Pearce, and R. Nishimura, "State of California: Civil Service Testing Moves into Cyberspace," *Public Personnel Management,* 1999, 28, pp. 283–300; D. Cook, "Screening the Screeners," *Human Resource Executive,* May 16, 2000, p. 57. S. J. Marks, "Passing the Test," *Human Resource Executive,* pp. 59–61; M. N. Martinez, "Online Skills Tests Assist in Selecting Better Qualified Job Candidates," *Employment Management Today,* Winter 2001, pp. 28–30; G. Nicholson, "Automated Assessments for Better Hires," *Workforce,* Dec. 2000, pp. 102–107; D. Shair, "WinASAP Provides Speedy, Accurate Reference Checking," *HR Magazine,* April 1999, pp. 118–122; D. Stafford, "Job Recruiters Like Electronic Screening," *Wisconsin State Journal,* Aug. 27, 2000.

18. J. A. Talcott, "If You Use Employment Tests, Feedback Can Be Important," *IPMA News,* March 2000, p. 28.

19. S. B. Morrise and R.E. Lobsenz, "Significance Tests and Confidence Intervals for the Adverse Impact Ratio," *Personnel Psychology,* 2000, 53, pp. 89–111.

CHAPTER EIGHT

External Selection I

Preliminary Issues
The Logic of Prediction
The Nature of Predictors
Development of the Selection Plan
Selection Sequence

Initial Assessment Methods
Résumés and Cover Letters
Application Blanks
Biographical Information
Reference Reports
Handwriting Analysis
Literacy Testing
Genetic Screening
Initial Interview
Choice of Initial Assessment Methods

Legal Issues
Disclaimers
Reference Checks
Preemployment Inquiries
Bona Fide Occupational Qualifications

Summary

Discussion Questions

Applications

External selection refers to the assessment and evaluation of external job applicants. A variety of different assessment methods are used. Preliminary issues that guide the use of these assessment methods will be discussed. These issues include the logic of prediction, the nature of predictors, development of the selection plan, and the selection sequence.

Initial assessment methods are used to select candidates from among the initial job applicants. The initial assessment methods that will be reviewed are résumés and cover letters, application blanks, biographical information, reference reports (which include letters of recommendation, reference checks, and background testing), handwriting analysis, literacy testing, genetic screening, and initial interviews. The factors that should guide the choice of initial assessment methods will be reviewed. These factors are frequency of use, cost, reliability, validity, utility, applicant reactions, and adverse impact.

The use of assessment methods also requires a firm understanding of legal issues. One method of preventing legal difficulties—the use of disclaimers as a means of protecting employer rights—is described. Due to myriad legal issues surrounding their use, reference reports and preemployment inquires require special attention to numerous details in using these methods of initial assessment. The most important of these details will be reviewed. Finally, bona fide occupational qualifications have particular relevance to initial assessment because such qualifications are usually assessed during the initial stages of selection. The legal issues involved in establishing such qualifications will be reviewed.

PRELIMINARY ISSUES

Many times, selection is equated with one event, namely, the interview. Nothing could be further from the truth if the best possible person/job match is to be made. For the best possible match to be achieved, a series of well-thought-out activities need to take place. Hence, selection is a process rather than an event. It is guided by a logic that determines the steps that need to be taken. The logic applies to all predictors that might be used, even though they differ in terms of several characteristics. Actual implementation of the logic of prediction requires that predictors be chosen through development of a selection plan. Implementation also requires creation of a selection sequence, which is an orderly flow of people through the stages of applicant, candidate, finalist, and offer receiver.

The Logic of Prediction

In Chapter 1, the selection component of staffing was defined as the process of assessing and evaluating people for purposes of determining the likely fit between the person and the job. This process is based on the logic of prediction, which holds that indicators of a person's degree of success in past situations should be predictive of how successful he or she will likely be in new situations. Application of this logic to selection is illustrated in Exhibit 8.1.

A person's KSAOs and motivation are the product of experiences of past job, current job, and nonjob situations. During selection, samples of these KSAOs and motivation are identified, assessed, and evaluated by the organization. The results constitute the person's overall qualifications for the new situation or job. These qualifications are then used to predict how successful the person is likely to be in that new situation or job regarding the HR outcomes. The logic of prediction works in practice if the organization accurately identifies and measures qualifications relative to job requirements, and if those qualifications remain stable over time so that they are carried over to the new job and used on it.

An example of how this logic can be followed in practice comes from a national communications organization with sales volume in the billions of dollars.[1] They were very interested in improving on the prediction of job success (sales volume) for their salespeople, whose sales figures had stagnated. To do so, they constructed what they labeled a "sales competency blueprint," or selection plan, to guide development of a new selection process. The blueprint depicted the KSAOs that needed to be sampled from previous jobs in order to predict sales success in a telemarketing sales job. The blueprint was established on the basis of a thorough job analysis in which subject matter experts identified the KSAOs thought necessary to be a successful telemarketer (e.g., knowledge of the product, how it was developed, and how it compared to the competitors' products). Then a structured interview was developed to sample the extent to which applicants for sales jobs in telemarketing had acquired the necessary KSAOs. In turn, the interview was used in selection to predict the likely success of applicants for the job.

The logic of prediction shown in Exhibit 8.1 demonstrates how critical it is to carefully scrutinize the applicant's past situation when making selection decisions.

EXHIBIT 8.1   The Logic of Prediction

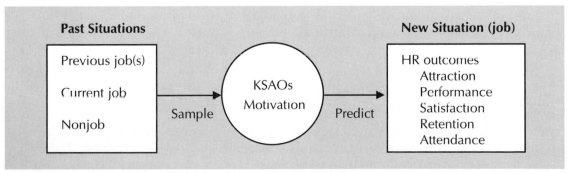

Past Situations

New Situation (job)

Previous job(s)

Current job

Nonjob

Sample

KSAOs
Motivation

Predict

HR outcomes
Attraction
Performance
Satisfaction
Retention
Attendance

For example, in selecting someone for a police officer position, the successfulness of the applicant in a previous security guard position might be considered a relevant predictor of the likelihood that the applicant will succeed in the new police officer position. Alternatively, the fact that the person was previously successful as a homemaker might be viewed as totally irrelevant to the job of police officer. Surprisingly, considering the homemaker role to be irrelevant might well be an incorrect assessment. Research shows that there is a close correspondence between the homemaker and the police officer position. Specifically, thorough job analysis showed that both jobs rely heavily on troubleshooting and emergency handling skills. Hence, in the absence of a sound job analysis, many qualified applicants may inadvertently be overlooked even though they have some of the characteristics needed to perform the job. Nonjob experience in the home, in the community, and in other institutions may be as valuable or more valuable than previous employment experiences.

Job titles, such as homemaker, are not nearly specific enough for making selection decisions. Similarly, the fact that someone has a certain number of years of experience usually does not provide sufficient detail to make selection decisions. What counts, and what is revealed through job analysis, is the specific types of experiences required and the level of successfulness at each. Similarly, the fact that someone was paid or not paid for employment is not relevant. What counts is the quality of the experience as it relates to success on the new job. Thus, for example, someone who volunteered to serve as an arbitrator of disputes in the community may have more relevant experience for the position of labor relations representative than someone who was paid as a bookkeeper. In short, the logic of prediction indicates that a point-to-point comparison needs to be made between requirements of the job to be filled and the qualifications that applicants have acquired from a variety of past situations.

Not only is the logic of prediction important to selection, but it is important to recruitment as well. A recent study shows that applicant reactions to selection procedures are determined in part by the job-relatedness of the selection procedure. If applicants see the selection process as job-related, which should occur if the logic of prediction is used, then they are more likely to view the selection process as being fair.[2] It would be expected that applicants who view the selection procedure as fair are more likely to accept a job offer and/or encourage others to apply for a job in the organization.

The Nature of Predictors

As will be seen shortly, there is a wide variety of different types of predictors used in external selection, ranging from interviews to genetic screening. These types can be differentiated from one another in terms of content and form.

Content

The substance or content of what is being assessed with a predictor varies considerably and may range from a sign to a sample to a criterion.[3] A sign is a predisposition of the person that is thought to relate to performance on the job. Personality as a predictor is a good example here. If personality is used as a predictor, the prediction is that someone with a certain personality (e.g., "abrasive") will demonstrate certain behaviors (e.g., "rude to customers") leading to certain results on the job (e.g., "failure to make a sale"). As can be seen, a sign is very distant from actual on-the-job results. A sample is closer than a sign to actual on-the-job results. Observing a set of interactions between a sales applicant and customer to see if sales are made provides an example of a sample. The criterion is very close to the actual job performance, such as sales during a probationary period for a new employee.

Form

The form or design of the predictor may vary along several different lines.

Speed versus Power A person's score on some predictors is based on the number of responses completed within a certain time frame. One event in a physical abilities test may, for example, be the number of bench presses completed in a given period of time. This is known as a speed test. A power test, on the other hand, presents individuals with items of increasing difficulty. For example, a power test of numerical ability may begin with addition and subtraction, move on to multiplication and division, and conclude with complex problem-solving questions. A speed test is used when speed of work is an important part of the job, and a power test is used when the correctness of the response is essential to the job. Of course, some tests (see the *Wonderlic Personnel Test* in Chapter 9) can be both speed and power tests, in which case few individuals would finish.

Paper and Pencil versus Performance Many predictors are of the paper-and-pencil variety; applicants are required to fill out a form, write an answer, or complete multiple choice items. Other predictors are performance tests, where the applicant is asked to manipulate an object or equipment. Testing running backs for the NFL on their time in the 40-yard dash is a performance test. Paper-and-pencil tests are frequently used when psychological abilities are required to perform the job; performance tests are used when physical and social skills are required to perform the job.

Objective versus Essay An objective paper-and-pencil predictor is one in which multiple choice questions or true/false questions are used. These tests should be used to measure specific knowledge in specific areas. Another form of a predictor is an essay, where a written answer is required of the respondent. Essays are best used to assess written communication, problem-solving, and analytical skills.[4]

Oral versus Written versus Computer Responses to predictor questions can be spoken, written, or entered into the computer. For example, when conducting interviews, some organizations listen to oral responses, read written responses, or read computer printouts of typed-in responses to assess applicants. As with all predictors, the appropriate form depends on the nature of the job. If the job requires a high level of verbal skill, then oral responses should be solicited. If the job requires a large amount of writing, then written responses should be required. If the job requires constant interaction with the computer, then applicants should enter their responses into the computer.[5]

Development of the Selection Plan

To translate the results of a job analysis into the actual predictors to be used for selection, a selection plan must be developed. A selection plan describes which predictor(s) will be used to assess the KSAOs required to perform the job. The recommended format for a selection plan, and an example of such a plan for the job of secretary, is shown in Exhibit 8.2. In order to establish a selection plan, three steps are followed. First, a listing of KSAOs is written in the left-hand column. This list comes directly from the job requirements matrix. Second, for each KSAO, a "yes" or "no" is written to show whether this KSAO needs to be assessed in the selection process. Sometimes the answer is no because it is a KSAO the applicant will acquire once on the job (e.g., knowledge of company policies and procedures). Third, possible methods of assessment are listed for the required KSAOs, and the specific method to be used for each of these KSAOs is then indicated.

Although costly and time-consuming to develop, organizations are increasingly finding that the benefits of developing a selection plan outweigh the costs. As a result, it is and should be a required step in the selection process. For example, a selection plan or "niche testing" was used to select tellers and customer service representatives by Barnett Bank in Jacksonville, Florida.[6] They found that an essential KSAO for both positions is the ability to make judgments when interacting with the public. For this KSAO, a niche test was developed in which applicants watch actual dealings with the public on video and then decide on the appropriate course of action. Their responses are graded and used to predict their likelihood of success in either position.

Selection Sequence

Usually, a series of decisions is made about job applicants before they are selected. These decisions are depicted in Exhibit 8.3. The first decision that is reached is whether initial applicants who have applied for the job become candidates or are rejected. A candidate is someone who has not yet received an offer, but who

EXHIBIT 8.2 Selection Plan Format and Example for Secretarial Position

Major KSAO Category	Necessary for Selection? (Y/N)	WP	CT	DB	LTR	TEF	ML	EM	TM	Inter-view
1. Ability to follow oral directions/listening skills	Y							X	X	
2. Ability to read and understand manuals/guidelines	Y	X	X	X	X	X	X	X		
3. Ability to perform basic arithmetic operations	Y			X		X				
4. Ability to organize	Y					X	X	X		
5. Judgments/priority setting/decision-making ability	Y			X						
6. Oral communication skills	Y				X					X
7. Written communication skills	Y		X					X	X	
8. Interpersonal skills	Y									X
9. Typing skills	Y	X	X	X	X					
10. Knowledge of word processing, graphics, database, and spreadsheet software	Y	X	X	X	X	X				
11. Knowledge of company policies and procedures	N									
12. Knowledge of basic personal computer operations	Y	X	X	X	X	X		X		
13. Knowledge of how to use basic office machines	N									
14. Flexibility in dealing with changing job demands	Y						X	X	X	
15. Knowledge of computer software	Y	X	X	X	X	X		X		
16. Ability to attend to detail and accuracy	Y	X	X	X	X	X	X	X	X	

WP = Word processing test, CT = Correction test, DB = Database exam, LTR = Letter, TEF = Travel expense form, ML = Mail log, EM = Electronic mail messages, and TM = Telephone messages.

Source: Adapted from N. Schmitt, S. Gilliland, R. S. Landis, and D. Devine, "Computer-Based Testing Applied to Selection of Secretarial Positions," *Personnel Psychology*, 1993, 46, pp. 149–165.

EXHIBIT 8.3   Assessment Methods by Applicant Flow Stage

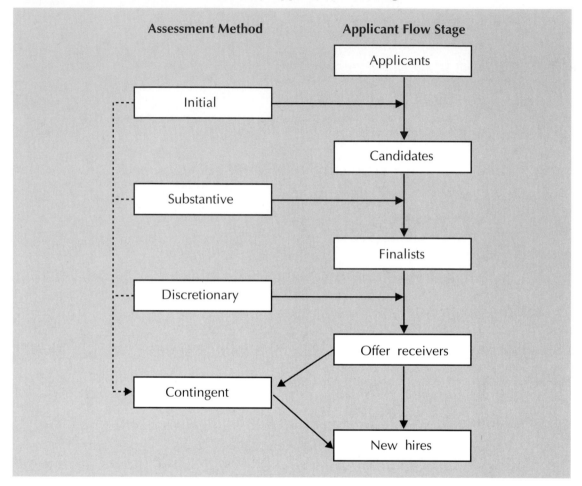

possesses the minimum qualifications to be considered for further assessment. Initial assessment methods are used to choose candidates (these will be discussed later in this chapter). The second decision made is which candidates become finalists. A finalist is someone who meets all the minimum qualifications and whom the organization considers fully qualified for the job. Substantive assessment methods are used to select finalists. These methods will be discussed in the next chapter. The third decision made is which finalist receives the actual job offer. Offer receivers are those finalists to whom the organization extends an offer of employment. Discretionary methods are used to select finalists and also will be described in the next chapter. Contingent methods are sometimes used, meaning the job offer is subject to certain qualifications, such as passing a medical exam or drug test, before the offer receiver can become a new hire. Use of contingent methods, in particular drug testing and medical exams, will be reviewed in the next chapter. Finally, some offer receivers become new hires when they decide to join the organization.

INITIAL ASSESSMENT METHODS

In this section, initial assessment methods are covered. These methods are also referred to as preemployment inquiries and are used to minimize the costs associated with substantive assessment methods by reducing the number of people assessed. Predictors typically used to screen candidates from applicants include application blanks, biographical information, reference reports, handwriting analysis, literacy testing, genetic screening, and initial interviews. Each of these initial assessment methods will be described in turn. Using meta-analysis results, the average validity (i.e., $\bar{r}$) of each method is also provided if possible. Then, a general evaluation will be presented to help guide decisions about which initial assessment methods to use.

Résumés and Cover Letters

The first introduction of the applicant to the organization is often a cover letter and résumé. This introduction is controlled by the applicant as to the amount, type, and accuracy of information provided. As a result, résumés and cover letters always need to be verified with other predictors, such as application blanks, to ensure that there is accurate and complete data across all job applicants with which to make informed selection decisions.

One major issue with résumés as a selection tool is the volume of them that organizations must process. It is very difficult for many organizations to store résumés for any extended period of time and read them accurately. Fortunately, the computer has resolved this issue. For example, résumés from previous searches can be stored on disk so that when a new vacancy arises, a new recruitment search does not have to take place. Also, optical scanners now make it possible to machine read résumés. Some résumé-tracking services even score applicant résumés and place a percentage next to an applicant's name reflecting the number of criteria each résumé meets. Hundreds of large companies currently use résumé-tracking software. Though such methods have powerful time- and cost-saving advantages, there are disadvantages, such as rejection of résumés that the software has trouble reading (e.g., those on colored paper or with special formatting like bullets) and applicants who try to beat the system by loading their résumé with every conceivable skill or skills that appear in the advertisement. Despite these drawbacks, the efficiencies of such services make them particularly attractive for organizations facing large volumes of résumés.

The near universal use of e-mail in organizations has complicated the receipt and use of résumés. Examples include the following:

1. Most résumés are received via surface mail, but surveys reveal that most employers prefer to receive them via e-mail.
2. When many companies receive résumés, they are never read but instead submitted to résumé scanning software as described above.
3. Some consultants offer new formats for applicants to grab the attention of recruiters. These formats may include multimedia packages that include sound bites, photographs, and supporting documents. Some applicants even send employers CD-ROM résumés with sounds, photos, and animated graphics.
4. More and more résumés are submitted using online forms on the organization's Web site. Some online forms are very basic—asking the applicant to fill in standard information, whereas others are online résumé builders.

Because of these changes, some have argued that the age of the traditional résumé is dead. The conclusion seems premature. Many recruiters still prefer the conventional résumés because they are short and easy to read. Other recruiters may be turned off by too many "bells and whistles." The solution for applicants and for recruiters is to tailor the presentation of one's credentials to the situation. Applicants need to have multiple methods of presenting credentials at their disposal, including the traditional résumé. And they need to decide which presentation is best for each position or employer. Applicants would be well advised to follow the following pieces of advice in submitting their credentials to employers:

1. Applicants need to make sure their résumés are electronically scan-ready. This means applicants should avoid unusual fonts and formatting. With today's résumés, form definitely should follow function.
2. When submitting a résumé by e-mail, applicants should consider including it in the e-mail message itself rather attaching it as some have trouble reading attachments.
3. As opposed to the traditional emphasis on action verbs ("managed," "guided," etc.), applicants should use nouns to describe noteworthy aspects of their background ("non-profit," "3.75 GPA," "environmental science experience") as nouns are more likely to be identified as keywords in scanning software. If the applicant believes his or her résumé is likely to be scanned, then the résumé needs to be built around such keywords that will be the focus of the scan.[7]

A well-documented problem with résumés and cover letters is fraud.[8] Consider the extreme case of Eugene Roscoe.[9] Not only did Eugene lie about his degree and experiences but he also lied in his cover letter about interviews. He made over $100,000 in reimbursements for expenses incurred during interviews that he never made. In December 2001, Notre Dame was forced to ask for the resignation of

George O'Leary when it came to light that O'Leary had lied about his past football playing experience (he claimed to have lettered for three years when in fact he never played) and falsely claimed to have earned a master's degree. Although most cases are not nearly this extreme or public, a recent study indicated that 95% of recent college graduates are willing to tell at least one false statement to get a job, and 41% have already done so. The areas most frequently exaggerated are involvement in school activities, future goals, title in previous positions, and computer experience.[10] A survey of executive résumés found that 23% contained inaccuracies. The most common inaccuracies were number of years in a job, accomplishments, size of organization managed, and partial degree indicated as full degree.[11]

A computer does not guard against the falsification of credentials. Résumés need to be verified by other predictors and carefully reviewed. Warnings that should throw up a red flag include gaps in employment dates, a lack of any employment history, a preponderance of former employers listed who are out of business, and a lack of location for previous employers.[12] Vague expressions that sound impressive may not be. Phrases to be on guard for include "was thoroughly involved in," "steered the company through," "worked closely with," "had deep involvement in," "was active in the planning and implementation of," and "quickly responded to."[13] Obviously, these types of statements are not fraudulent per se, but they are so vague and general that they should be judged with caution.

Almost no research exists on résumés and cover letters. We do not know their validity or reliability. Nor is there information on their costs or adverse impact. This situation is unfortunate given their pervasive use in certain types of jobs, especially entry-level management, professional, and technical positions. Thus, organizations using résumés and cover letters in selection should carefully evaluate their effectiveness.

Application Blanks

Most application blanks request in written form the applicant's background in regard to educational experiences, training, and job experiences. This information is often on the résumé as well and may seem unnecessarily duplicated. This is not the case. An application can be used to verify the data presented on the résumé and also can be used to obtain data omitted on the résumé, such as employment dates. The major advantage of application blanks over résumés is that the organization, rather than the applicant, dictates what information is presented. As a result, information critical to success on the job is less likely to be omitted by the applicant or overlooked by the reviewer of the résumé. The major issue with application blanks is to make sure that information requested is critical to job success, following the logic of prediction discussed earlier.

A sample application blank is provided in Exhibit 8.4. As with most application blanks, the major sections of the application are personal information, employment desired, educational background, special interests and abilities, work experience,

EXHIBIT 8.4   Application for Employment

PERSONAL INFORMATION

DATE _____

NAME _____

SOCIAL SECURITY
NUMBER _____

LAST   FIRST   MIDDLE

PRESENT ADDRESS _____

STREET   CITY   STATE   ZIP

PERMANENT ADDRESS _____

STREET   CITY   STATE   ZIP

PHONE NO. _____   ARE YOU 18 YEARS OR OLDER?   Yes ☐   No ☐

ARE YOU PREVENTED FROM LAWFULLY BECOMING EMPLOYED
IN THIS COUNTRY BECAUSE OF VISA OR IMMIGRATION STATUS?   Yes ☐   No ☐

EMPLOYMENT DESIRED

POSITION _____

DATE YOU
CAN START _____

SALARY
DESIRED _____

ARE YOU EMPLOYED NOW? _____

IF SO MAY WE INQUIRE
OF YOUR PRESENT EMPLOYER? _____

APPLIED TO THIS COMPANY BEFORE? _____   WHERE? _____   WHEN? _____

REFERRED BY _____

EDUCATION

	NAME AND LOCATION	NO. OF YEARS ATTENDED	DID YOU GRADUATE?	SUBJECTS STUDIED
GRAMMAR SCHOOL				
HIGH SCHOOL (GED)				
COLLEGE				
OTHER				

(continued)

EXHIBIT 8.4 **Continued**

GENERAL

SUBJECTS OF SPECIAL STUDY

SPECIAL SKILLS

ACTIVITIES: (CIVIC, ATHLETIC, ETC.)

U.S. MILITARY OR NAVAL SERVICE	RANK	PRESENT MEMBERSHIP IN NATIONAL GUARD OR RESERVES

FORMER EMPLOYERS (LIST BELOW LAST 3 EMPLOYERS, STARTING WITH THE LAST ONE FIRST)

	DATE	NAME & ADDRESS	SALARY	POSITION	REASON FOR LEAVING
FROM					
TO					
FROM					
TO					
FROM					
TO					

REFERENCES (GIVE THE NAMES OF 3 PERSONS NOT RELATED TO YOU)

	NAME	ADDRESS	BUSINESS	YEARS ACQUAINTED
1				
2				
3				

"I certify that all the information submitted by me on this application is true and complete, and I understand that if any false information, omissions, or misrepresentations are discovered, my application may be rejected and, if I am employed, my employment may be terminated at any time. In consideration of my employment, I agree to conform to the company's rules and regulations, and I agree that my employment and compensation can be terminated, with or without cause, and with or without notice, at any time, at either my or the company's option. I also understand and agree that the terms and conditions of my employment may be changed, with or without cause, and with or without notice, at any time by the company. I understand that no company representative, other than its president, and only when in writing and signed by the president, has any authority to enter into any agreement for employment for any specific period of time, or to make any agreement contrary to the foregoing."

DATE   SIGNATURE

and suggested references. The only information sought from the application blank should be KSAOs that can be demonstrated as relevant to the job. This not only avoids wasting the organization's and the applicant's time but also protects the employer from charges of unfair discrimination (see Legal Issues at the end of this chapter). It is important to take note of the statement at the bottom of the application blank, known as a disclaimer statement. It provides certain legal protections to the organization, discussed under the Legal Issues section at the end of this chapter. Asking applicants to sign a disclaimer also may decrease the incentive to distort or falsify information.

Educational Requirements

Special care needs to be taken in wording items on an application blank when soliciting information about educational experiences and performance.[14] Following are discussed several particularly important areas pertaining to educational requirement information on application blanks.

Level of Education   Level of education or degree is one element of educational performance used to predict job performance. Often, level of education is measured by the attainment of a degree. The degree should be assessed in conjunction with other educational requirements. A high-level degree from a nonaccredited school may be an indication of a lesser accomplishment than a lower-level degree from an accredited school. Research indicates that level of education is weakly related to job performance ($\bar{r} = .13$).[15]

Furthermore, a recent report indicates that the high school degree may no longer be as good a predictor as it once was because the attainment of a GED (high school equivalency) is often used as a substitute for a diploma on an application form and does not predict as well.[16] Hence, in designing the application form, an item separate from high school degree should be used for high school equivalency.

Even the meaning of a college degree is changing. Currently, the number of students in online degree programs is in the millions and will only grow in the future. There are thousands of courses available online, and most four-year colleges are or will be offering online courses in the next few years. The quality of instruction and the amount of learning in these courses is mixed, and employers are often skeptical.[17]

Grade Point Average   Classroom grades are measured using a grade point average (GPA). Care should be exercised in the interpretation of GPA information. For example, a GPA in one's major in college may be different (usually higher) than one's GPA for all classes. Grades also vary widely by field (e.g., grades in engineering tend to be lower than in other fields). Further, a GPA of 3.5 may be good at one school, but not at another. For example, GPAs are calculated on a 4-point scale at some schools, while they are calculated on a 5-point scale at other schools. Some schools do not report GPAs at all. Some schools (especially colleges) have grade inflation (e.g., at Princeton University 80% of undergraduates receive As and Bs).[18] Graduate students receive higher grades on average than do undergraduates. In short, GPA may be influenced by many factors in addition to the applicant's KSAOs and motivation. Research suggests that the validity of GPA in predicting job performance may be as high as the mid .30s. College grades are no more valid than high school grades, and grades are most valid in predicting early job performance.[19] GPAs do tend to have adverse impact against minorities, and, as with all selection measures with adverse impact, the validity evidence must be balanced against adverse impact implications.

Quality of School   In recent times, much has been said and written about the quality of various educational programs. For example, *U.S. News and World Report* annually publishes the results of a survey showing ratings of school quality. A more comprehensive source on school quality is the *Gourman Report.*[20] The *Gourman Report* assigns numerical scores (ranging from 1.00 = unacceptable to 5.00 = perfect) to virtually every degree-granting university in the United States on the basis of 18 criteria (e.g., faculty qualifications, admission standards, curriculum, quality of instruction). The *Gourman Report* includes ratings for undergraduate and graduate programs in many fields. Although educational quality has not been related to job performance, a recent study indicated that managers whose highest degree was from a school rated as "1" on the *Gourman Report* earned $16,070 less per year than managers whose schools were rated as "4" or "5."[21] (Results suggested that prestige was even more important than quality, though. Graduates of Ivy League schools enjoyed a $32,000 pay advantage, even taking school quality into account.) Though this evidence suggests that quality of school matters (at least to the labor market), care should be taken to critically examine on what basis school quality ratings are made and their relevance to the job for which selection is to occur.

Major Field of Study   The more specialized the knowledge requirements of a particular position, the more important an applicant's major field of study is likely to be as a predictor. An English major may do very well as an editor but may be unsuccessful as a physician. It should also be noted that choice of a major does not guarantee that a certain number or type of classes have been taken. The number and type of classes needed for a major or minor varies from school to school and needs to be carefully scrutinized to ensure comparability across majors. The relationship between field of study and job performance is very difficult to assess; therefore, no conclusive validity evidence is available.[22]

Extracurricular Activities   The usefulness of extracurricular activities as a predictor depends on the job. Being a field hockey player may have little relevance to being a successful manager. However, being elected captain of a hockey team may indeed be a sign of leadership qualities needed to be a successful manager.

Information about extracurricular activities taken from an application blank must be relevant to the job in question. As with field of study, there is insufficient basis to draw any conclusions about the relationship between extracurricular activities and job performance.

Training and Experience Requirements

Many past experiences predictive of future performance do not take place in a classroom. Instead, these experiences come from life experiences in other institutions, which, fortunately, can also be captured on an application blank. A great deal of weight is often put on training and experience requirements on the theory that actions speak louder than words. The drawback of putting too much emphasis on previous work experience, however, is that the amount of experience and training an applicant has may be overstated. Also, applicants with high potential may be overlooked because they have not had the opportunity to gain the training or experience needed.

Various methods can be used to measure training and experience. Since training and experience information is not directly equivalent across applicants, all methods require the judgment of selection decision makers. These decision makers render judgments about how to classify and weight different levels of experience. An approach termed the "behavioral consistency method" has shown the highest degree of validity because it focuses on determining the quality of an applicant's previous training and experience. One of the means by which the behavioral consistency method determines quality is by asking applicants to complete a supplemental application wherein they describe their most significant accomplishments relative to a list of key job behaviors. Due to their involved nature, however, behavioral consistency ratings are time consuming and expensive to administer, and they require the applicant to possess some degree of analytical ability and writing skills. Thus, the choice of weighting methods rests on a trade-off between accuracy and ease and cost of administration.[23]

Licensing, Certification, and Job Knowledge

Many professions and occupations require or encourage people to demonstrate mastery of a certain body of knowledge. A license is required of people by law to perform an activity, whereas a certification is voluntarily acquired. The purpose of a license is to protect the public interest, whereas the purpose of a certification is to identify those people who have met a minimum standard of proficiency. Licensing exams and certification exams are usually developed by subject matter experts in conjunction with testing specialists.

Approximately 800 occupations in the United States are regulated by state government boards. Many others are monitored by professional associations. For example, in human resources, there are seven certifications offered by five certifying agencies. Certifications offered are the Professional in Human Resources, Senior Professional in Human Resources, Certified Compensation Professional, Certified

Employee Benefit Specialist, Associate Safety Professional, Certified Safety Professional, and Occupational Health and Safety Technologist.[24]

Certification helps guard against the misuse of job titles in HR selection. For example, anyone could adopt the title of safety consultant, but a certification from the Board of Certified Safety Professionals and/or American Board of Industrial Hygiene guarantees that the person has mastered a certain amount of technical knowledge in the safety area.

As mentioned earlier, licensing and certification requirements can be used either as an initial or as a contingent assessment method. When used as an initial method, licensing and certification requirements are used to eliminate applicants who fail to possess these credentials. For example, a car repair shop electing to hire only certified mechanics might initially screen out individuals who fail to have the proper certification. When used as a contingent method, the selection process proceeds on the assumption that the applicant has the requisite credential (or will have it by the time of hire). This is then verified after an initial offer decision is made. For example, rather than verifying that each applicant for a nursing position possesses a valid state license, a hospital may assess applicants based on the assumption they have a valid license and then verify this assumption after a tentative hiring decision has been made. Thus, the difference between using licensing and certification requirements as initial or contingent assessment methods depends on when the information is considered in the selection process.

Increasingly, organizations are using voluntary professional certifications as a method of verifying competence in various occupations. There are more than 1,000 professional certifications. Most of these voluntary certifications do so on the basis of experience and education. The vast majority of certifications require examinations. Over time, certifications may expand to most areas of management.[25]

While licensure and certification demonstrate mastery of a general body of knowledge applicable to many organizations, job knowledge tests assess a specific body of knowledge within a particular organization. Job knowledge tests are usually used in the public sector as an initial screening device. In the private sector, they are used primarily for promotion purposes. Although mentioned here, job knowledge tests will be covered in detail in Chapter 9.

Weighted Application Blanks

Not all of the information contained on an application blank is of equal value to the organization in making selection decisions. Depending on the organization and job, some information predicts success on the job better than other information. Procedures have been developed that help weight application blank information by the degree to which the information differentiates between high- and low-performing individuals.[26] This scoring methodology is referred to as a weighted application blank and is useful not only in making selection decisions but also in developing application blanks as well. The statistical procedures involved help the organization discern which items should be retained for use in the application blank and which should be excluded, on the basis of how well they predict performance.

Evaluation of Application Blanks

Evidence suggests that scored evaluations of the unweighted application blank are not particularly valid predictors of job performance (average validity ranges from $\bar{r} = .10$ to $\bar{r} = .20$).[27] This is not surprising given the rudimentary information that is collected in application blanks. Another factor that may undermine the validity of application blanks is distortion. A study of the National Credential Verification Service found that about one-third of the investigations into the background of applicants suggested that misrepresentation occurred on the application blank. Subsequent studies have suggested that the most common questions that are misrepresented include previous salary, education, tenure on previous job, and reasons for leaving previous job. Some individuals even go beyond misrepresentation to outright invention. One study revealed that 15% of supposedly previous employers of applicants indicated that the individual never worked for them.[28] Thus, application information that is given heavy weight in selection decisions should be verified.

The validity evidence for weighted application blanks is much more positive.[29] In a sense, this would almost have to be true since items in the weighted application blank are scored and weighted based on their ability to predict job performance. Thus, as long as *some* of the items are predictive, the scoring and weighting schemes embedded in the weighted application blank will ensure that the overall score is predictive. Because the process used to develop the weighted application blank is time consuming and expensive, more cost-benefit studies need to be conducted on the weighted application blank. Is the validity worth the cost? Unfortunately, there is little recent research on the weighted application blank, so answers to this question are difficult to attain.

The relatively poor validity of unweighted application blanks also should not be taken as indication that they are useless in selection decisions. Unweighted application blanks are a very inexpensive means of collecting basic information on job applicants. Most organizations use unweighted application blanks only for initial screening decisions (to rule out applicants who are obviously unqualified for the job). Thus, it is not necessarily appropriate to condemn unweighted application blanks based on a criterion for which they are rarely used (i.e., used by themselves to make substantive selection decisions about applicants). As long as application blanks are used in this context (and not relied on to a significant degree in making substantive hiring decisions), they can be a useful method of making initial decisions about applicants.

Biographical Information

Biographical information, often called biodata, is personal history information on an applicant's background and interests. Basically, results from a biodata survey formulate a general description of a person's life history. The principal assumption behind the use of biodata is the axiom "The best predictor of future behavior is past behavior." These past behaviors may reflect ability or motivation. Biodata inventories are thought to measure applicant motivation that can be inferred from past choices. However, research also suggests that many ability items are included in biodata inventories.[30]

Like application blanks, biographical information blanks ask applicants to report on their background. Responses to both of these questionnaires can provide useful information in making initial selection decisions about applicants. Unlike application blanks, however, biographical information can also be fruitfully used for substantive selection decisions. In fact, if scores on a biodata inventory are predictive of subsequent job performance (which, as we will see, is often the case), it may be somewhat limiting to use biodata scores only for initial assessment decisions. Thus, although biographical information is as much a substantive as an initial assessment method because it shares many similarities with application blanks, we have included it in this section. Nevertheless, it should also be considered in deliberations about which substantive assessment methods are to be used.

Biographical information also has similarities and differences with background tests (see the section on reference reports). Biodata and background tests are similar in that both look into an applicant's past. However, the two types of selection methods differ in a number of important ways:[31] (1) background checks are used primarily when screening applicants for positions in which integrity and emotional adjustment are necessary (e.g., law enforcement, private security, etc.), whereas biodata inventories are used to screen applicants in many jobs; (2) background information is obtained through interviews and conversations with references, while biodata information is usually collected by survey; (3) the criterion by which background information is validated is typically behavioral reliability (attendance, integrity, etc.), while performance is the principal criterion against which biodata scores are validated. Thus, biodata inventories and background checks are distinct methods of selection that require that they be considered separately.

The type of biographical information collected varies a great deal from inventory to inventory and often depends on the job. For example, a biographical survey for executives might focus on career aspirations, accomplishments, and disappointments. A survey for blue-collar workers might focus on training and work experience. A biodata inventory for federal government workers might focus on school and educational experiences, work history, skills, and interpersonal relations. As can be seen from these examples, most biodata surveys consider individual accomplishments, group accomplishments, disappointing experiences, and stressful situations.[32] The domains in which these attributes are studied often vary from job to job, but can range from childhood experiences to educational or early work experiences to current hobbies or family relations.

Measures

Typically, biographical information is collected in a questionnaire that applicants complete. Exhibit 8.5 provides example biodata items. As can been seen, the items are quite diverse. It has been suggested that each biodata item can be classified according to 10 criteria: *history* (does the item describe an event that has occurred in the past, or a future or hypothetical event?), *externality* (does the item address an observable event or an internal event such as values or judgments?), *objectivity* (does the item focus on reporting factual information or subjective interpretations?), *firsthandedness* (does the item seek information that is directly available to the applicant rather than an evaluation of the applicant's behavior by others?), *discreteness* (does the item pertain to a single, unique behavior or a simple count of events as opposed to summary responses?), *verifiability* (can the accuracy of the response to the item be confirmed?), *controllability* (does the item address an event that was under the control of the applicant?), *equal accessibility* (are the events or experiences expressed in the item equally accessible to all applicants?), *job relevance* (does the item solicit information closely tied to the job?), and *invasiveness* (is the item sensitive to the applicant's right to privacy?).[33] Exhibit 8.6 provides example items that fall into each of these categories. This categorization has important implications for deciding how to construct biodata inventories, as will be discussed shortly.

Most selection tests simply score items in a predetermined manner and add the scores to arrive at a total score. These total scores then form the basis of selection decisions made about the applicants. With most biodata inventories, the process of making decisions on the basis of responses to items is considerably more complex. The traditional recommended approach to the development of a biodata survey is as follows:[34]

Choosing or Developing the Criterion   Generally, the criterion is job performance. Because the items included in the biodata inventory may depend on the nature of the job, great care must be taken to ensure that the measure of job performance reflects the most important job behaviors. Obviously, this is the goal of job analysis. Other criteria beyond job performance may be valued, including length of service, attendance, and advancement.

Identifying Criterion Groups   Empirical keys for biodata generally are developed on the basis of how well they separate different criterion groups (e.g., high versus low performers, low-absenteeism versus high-absenteeism employees, stayers versus leavers, etc.). With criterion measures such as performance ratings, one method that has been developed to accomplish this is to take the upper 27% and lower 27% of performers (e.g., in a sample of 500 this would translate into the 135 highest performers and 135 lowest performers).[35] The 27% figure achieves a compromise between maximizing the difference between the criterion groups and maintaining a reasonably large sample size for each criterion group.

EXHIBIT 8.5   Examples of Biodata Items

1. In college, my grade point average was:
   a. I did not go to college or completed less than two years
   b. Less than 2.50
   c. 2.50 to 3.00
   d. 3.00 to 3.50
   e. 3.50 to 4.00

2. In the past five years, the number of different jobs I have held is:
   a. More than five
   b. Three–five
   c. Two
   d. One
   e. None

3. The kind of supervision I like best is:
   a. Very close supervision
   b. Fairly close supervision
   c. Moderate supervision
   d. Minimal supervision
   e. No supervision

4. When you are angry, which of the following behaviors most often describes your reaction:
   a. Reflect on the situation for a bit
   b. Talk to a friend or spouse
   c. Exercise or take a walk
   d. Physically release the anger on something
   e. Just try to forget about it

5. Over the past three years, how much have you enjoyed each of the following (use the scale at right below):
   a. ____ Reading   1 = Very much
   b. ____ Watching TV   2 = Some
   c. ____ Home improvements   3 = Very little
   d. ____ Music   4 = Not at all
   e. ____ Outdoor recreation

6. In most ways is your life close to ideal?
   a. Agree
   b. Disagree
   c. Undecided or neutral

EXHIBIT 8.6 A Taxonomy of Biodata Items

Historical
How old were you when you got your first paying job?

External
Did you ever get fired from a job?

Objective
How many hours did you study for your real-estate exam?

Firsthand
How punctual are you about coming to work?

Discrete
At what age did you get your driver's license?

Verifiable
What was your grade point average in college?

Controllable
How many tries did it take you to pass the CPA exam?

Equal access
Were you ever class president?

Job relevant
How many units of cereal did you sell during the last calendar year?

Noninvasive
Were you on the tennis team in high school?

Future or hypothetical
What position do you think you will be holding in 10 years?

Internal
What is your attitude toward friends who smoke marijuana?

Subjective
Would you describe yourself as shy?

Secondhand
How would your teachers describe your punctuality?

Summative
How many hours do you study during an average week?

Nonverifiable
How many fresh vegetables do you eat every day?

Noncontrollable
How many brothers and sisters do you have?

Nonequal access
Were you captain of the football team?

Not job relevant
Are you proficient at crossword puzzles?

Invasive
How many young children do you have at home?

Source: F. A. Mael, "A Conceptual Rationale for the Domain and Attributes of Biodata Items," *Personnel Psychology*, 1991, 44, pp. 763–792. Used with permission.

Selecting Items to Be Analyzed Generally, a large number of items (perhaps as many as 200) are administered to current employees. The items can be obtained from consulting firms or from compendiums of biodata items. In deciding which items to include, it is helpful to return to the earlier classification of biodata items into 10 categories (Exhibit 8.6). When using biodata inventories in selection, they are likely to be more useful when the items are characterized by the left-hand side attributes in Exhibit 8.6. Otherwise, the items are likely to be transparent, unverifiable, or may add little validity over other selection measures such as personality tests. In many cases, items are selected based on their ability to separate the criterion groups (e.g., how well they predict job performance). Often, the items that are selected are the ones that display strong differences between high and low performers (thus suggesting that this item will do a good job of forecasting job performance). Naturally, the ability of a particular item to separate criterion groups may vary from job to job. For example, the question, "Have you ever built a model airplane that flew?" is probably invalid for most jobs, but may be predictive in selecting airline pilots, mechanics, or engineers. Thus, although the initial set of items in the biodata inventory may be quite large, many of these items usually end up being excluded because they are not a valid means of separating high and low performers in a particular job. In addition to selecting biodata items based on their ability to separate high and low performers (i.e., validity), items also may be chosen based on adverse impact. A recent study revealed that more than one in four biodata items generated significantly different responses for black and white applicants, particularly items pertaining to views of basic human nature (black applicants were more likely to express cynical views of human nature).[36] Thus, organizations are well advised to consider adverse impact when selecting biodata items.

Specifying Item Response Alternatives As can be seen from Exhibit 8.5, most biodata items are in a multiple-choice format. In many cases, there is not a clearly correct response, which helps ensure that responses are not socially desirable. Often, response options are determined to be those that do the best job of separating high and low performers. For example, rather than asking applicants for an international assignment if they have ever traveled outside of the country and posing a yes/no response alternative (most have), the item might do a better job if individuals were allowed to respond by indicating how many international trips they have taken. As another example, it might be found that response option *(d)* to question 3 in Exhibit 8.5 displays more difference between high and low performers than response option *(e)*. In such a case, option *(e)* could be eliminated or given less weight in scoring the question.

Weighting Items Unlike most selection tests, biodata items generally are not given an equal weight in computing the total score. The traditional approach to weighting responses to biodata inventories is to use the "empirical key" approach. This approach weights items according to their ability to separate criterion groups. Those items that do the best job of separating high and low performers, for example, are given the highest weight. It is important to note that in order for these weighting schemes to be stable (i.e., generalize from one group of applicants to the next), a large sample is required. Generally, the sample should consist of at least 5 to 10 persons for each item or response option.

Cross-Validating   Cross-validation (or validating the initial items and weights with another sample) is especially important in developing empirically keyed biodata items because the process of scoring weights based on a sample will, to some degree, capitalize on sample-specific factors. For example, a question that does a good job of separating good and poor *employees* may not be as effective in separating good and poor *applicants*. If this holds true across many items, the weighting scheme based on current employees will have no validity. The degree to which this process is a problem can be investigated only through the process of cross-validation.

Developing Cutoff Scores   The last step in using biodata for selection is to establish a minimum score that maximizes the number of persons correctly classified on the criterion. For example, if the criterion is job performance, a cutoff score may be set at the point at which the best separation occurs between high and low performers. As is the case with all selection methods, there are numerous specific means of setting cut scores (also see Chapter 11).

The preceding discussion assumes that the process of developing biodata items is completely based on empirical-keying responses to maximize prediction. This empirical-key approach has been criticized, however, because it limits generalizability of biodata inventories and detracts from understanding the validity of the biodata construct. As a result, some have argued for a "rational" approach to developing and validating biodata inventories. Rational approaches involve generating biodata items based on logical hypotheses (often based on job analysis results) about how a particular item should be related to the criterion (usually job performance) as judged by subject matter experts. Thus, in the rational-key approach, both item selection and item weighting are based on theory or expert judgment, as opposed to the empirical-key approach of using the data to reveal how well each item or weight separates high and low performers. While rational-keying approaches do permit greater understanding of the nature of the biodata construct, empirical- and rational-key approaches have been found to have similar levels of predictive validity.[37] In practice, each method has advantages, so compromise methods between the two have been developed.[38]

Accomplishment Records

A selection method that can be considered a form of a biographical information survey is the accomplishment record, sometimes termed an achievement history questionnaire or retrospective life essay.[39] Accomplishment records survey the past accomplishments of job candidates as they relate to dimensions of work that are part of performing effectively at a particular job. Information that is solicited from each candidate includes a written statement of the accomplishment, when it took place, any recognition for the accomplishment, and verification of the accomplishment. The emphasis is on achievements rather than just activities, and in this regard accomplishment records differ from application blanks that solicit data on activities.

An example of an accomplishment record scoring key, developed to select attorneys, is shown in Exhibit 8.7. Specifically, it is used to evaluate the candidate's research and investigation skills. The scale is used to score the accomplishment record submitted by the candidate. Similar scales are used to score other aspects of the candidate's skills. The scale is anchored with behavioral benchmarks. These benchmarks are illustrative of what candidates would have to present in their essay to earn a certain score, which can range from 1 to 6. Research has suggested impressive validity for accomplishment records, although further study is needed.

EXHIBIT 8.7   Scoring Key Excerpt for an Accomplishment Record

Dimensions: Researching/Investigating

General Definition: Obtaining all information, facts, and materials that are important, relevant, or necessary for a case, project, or assignment; gathering accurate information from all possible sources (i.e., persons both within and outside, interviews, journals, publications, company records, etc.); being thorough and overcoming all obstacles in gathering the required information.

Guidelines for Ratings: In RESEARCHING/INVESTIGATING, accomplishments at the lower levels are characterized by projects which require a minimal amount of research or research that is mundane in nature, e.g., routine interviews or journal reviews. At progressively higher levels, the accomplishments describe information gathered from multiple sources or information that would require considerable expertise to collect. The research projects may be part of a case or procedure which is novel or of substantial import. The projects generally demand increasingly complex interpretation of the information gathered. At the highest levels of achievement, awards or commendations are likely.

Scale:

6 =   I assumed major responsibility for conducting an industry-wide investigation of the industry and for preparation of a memorandum in support of complaints against the three largest members of the industry. A complaint was issued unanimously by the commission and a consent settlement was obtained subsequently from all three respondents. I obtained statistical data from every large and medium industry in the United States and from a selection of small ones. I obtained and negotiated subpoenas with, and obtained statistical information from numerous other members of the industry. I deposed *many* employees of manufacturers and renters. I received a Meritorious Service award.

(continued)

EXHIBIT 8.7 **Continued**

5 = I obtained crucial evidence in Docket, which was used as the basis for obtaining consent orders against more than 25 companies. I personally conducted more than 30 investigational hearings by subpoena. I did much outside research and reading to become familiar with technology. I handled all investigational and research work in the Northeastern United States. I obtained documentary material from many sources and obtained the files upon which the matter was finally based.

4 = As a lead attorney in a major investigation at the _____ , I performed all of the tasks described in this category. I supervised the investigation and brought it to its ultimate conclusion, which was to recommend that the matter be closed with no official action. I interviewed witnesses, including interviews on official record, subpoenaed documents from target sources, and spoke with numerous experts about scientific and technical information related to the case.

3 = In the investigation, I helped develop and gather the evidence necessary to pursue litigation. I prepared several complex subpoenas and negotiated them with industry counsel from three major corporations. The subpoenas requested detailed information on activities of major _____ .

2 = I interviewed potential witnesses and compiled evidence that was relevant to the case against Corporation. I analyzed documents submitted pursuant to subpoenas, interviewed witnesses, and wrote admission of fact.

1 = My research involved checking reference books, LEXIS, and telephone interviews with various people—individuals, state officials, etc.

Source: L. M. Hough, M. A. Keyes, and M. D. Dunnette, "An Evaluation of Three 'Alternative' Selection Procedures," *Personnel Psychology*, 1983, 36, p. 265. Used with permission.

Evaluation of Biodata

Research that has been conducted on the reliability and validity of biodata is quite positive.[40] Responses tend to be reliable (test-retest coefficients range from .77 to .90). More important, past research suggests that biodata inventories are some of the most valid predictors of job performance. A number of meta-analyses have been conducted, and the average validity has ranged from $\bar{r} = .32$ to $\bar{r} = .37$.[41]

Because biodata inventories are developed and scored on the basis of a particular job and sample, it has commonly been argued that the validity of a particular inventory in one organization is unlikely to generalize to another organization. However, one study demonstrated that biodata inventories can be constructed in a way that will lead to generalizability across organizations.[42] In this study, items to be included in the biodata inventory were selected based on two criteria: (1) their job relevance (based on job analysis data), and (2) their ability to generalize across organizations (whether the item was a valid predictor of job performance in at least four of the six organizations studied). Scores were computed for the retained items and then tested on a sample of other organizations. The cross-validation effort resulted in a validity coefficient of .33. These results were confirmed by the results from another study. Thus, this research suggests that biodata inventories can generalize across organizations when constructed in an appropriate manner.

Though biographical inventories do have predictive validity, it is not clear exactly what these inventories assess. Some have argued that biographical information represents personality, and, in fact, many biographical items are indistinguishable from personality items. For example, questions about academic interest may reflect openness to experience, questions about past accomplishments may reflect conscientiousness, and so on. Indeed, research suggests that biodata scales do map onto personality traits (e.g., conscientious applicants score higher on a work habits biodata scale).[43] If biodata inventories are, in part, measures of personality, it is important to show that they demonstrate incremental validity over personality measures because they are much more costly to develop. One recent study showed that biodata did provide incremental validity over personality and cognitive ability.[44]

One of the more important issues in evaluating the usefulness of biodata is the issue of falsification. Because responses to most biodata items are difficult if not impossible to verify (e.g., "Did you collect coins or stamps as a child?"), it is conceivable applicants distort their responses to tell prospective employers what they want to hear. In fact, research clearly shows that such faking does occur. Research also suggests, though, that faking can be reduced in a number of ways:

1. *Use less "fakeable" items.* Using the typology of biodata items in Exhibit 8.6, one study found that the least-fakeable items were more historical, objective, discrete, verifiable, external, and *less* job relevant.[45]

2. *Warn applicants against faking.* One study found that warning applicants that faking could be detected and would reduce their score (even if faking could not actually be detected) reduced the faking of transparent items, that is, where the desirable response was clear (e.g., "I hate to see people suffer.").[46]

3. *Use option-keyed scoring.* Option-keyed items refer to analyzing each response separately and scoring only those responses that separate criterion groups or correlate with the criterion. Assume, for example, that of the five responses to item 3 in Exhibit 8.5, only responses *(b)* and *(e)* help separate high and low performers. Using option-keyed scoring, only those two responses would be scored. Option-keyed items are a contrast to those that are item-keyed, where each response is scored in a predetermined manner. For example, an item-keyed scoring strategy for item 3 might entail assigning 0 points to response *(a)*, 1 point to response *(b)*, 2 points to response *(c)*, and so on. Option-keyed formats are hard to fake because the "right" answer is difficult to guess. For example, responses that are circled by

nearly everyone (suggesting some degree of faking) will not do a good job of discriminating between high and low performers and therefore will not be scored. In fact, one study suggests that option-keyed formats are less susceptible to faking.[47]

4. *Validate responses using applicant samples.* One study found that it may not be a good idea to key items based on concurrent validity designs (i.e., using employees) because the cross-validity in predicting performance based on a concurrent design was .08 for item-keyed responses and .09 for option-keyed responses. One of the suggested reasons for this lack of convergence was social desirability.[48]

Though the steps outlined above may reduce the degree of faking present in biodata inventories, it is important to keep in mind that the substantial validities of biodata were found in past research without systematic attempts to control faking. Thus, although the above steps may make biodata inventories even more valid, faking apparently has not undermined the validity of biodata information.[49]

Finally, only a few studies have looked at applicant reactions to biodata inventories. In general, research suggests that biodata inventories are not viewed favorably by applicants. One study found that biodata inventories were viewed as the least valid of 14 specific selection measures examined; another study found that biodata was seen as the least valid of five selection measures studied (the other four were interviews, personality tests, cognitive ability tests, and drug tests).[50] Thus, applicants do not seem to react well to biodata inventories. The likely reason for this is because they believe that items contained in most biographical inventories bear little similarity to job content (see items in Exhibit 8.5). In this regard, accomplishment records may do better. For example, one study found that accomplishment records were viewed as among the *most* job-related selection methods (only interviews and work samples were viewed as more job-related).[51] With respect to biodata, a survey of over 200 professionals revealed that items were seen as verifiable, transparent in purpose, and impersonal were viewed as less invasive.[52] Thus, organizations concerned with applicant reactions should either use an accomplishment record or consider using items that are seen as less invasive by applicants.

Reference Reports

Background information about job applicants can come not only from the applicant but also from people familiar with the applicant in previous situations (e.g., employers, creditors, neighbors).[53] Organizations often solicit this information on their own or use the services of agencies that specialize in investigating applicants. Background information solicited from others is called a reference report and consists of letters of recommendation, reference checks, and background testing. Reference reports can be used to verify information presented by the applicant on the résumé, application form, and biographical information survey.

Letters of Recommendation

A very common selection procedure in some settings (e.g., academic institutions) is to ask applicants to have letters of recommendation written for them. There are two major problems with this approach. First, these letters may do little to help the organization discern more-qualified from less-qualified applicants. The reason for this is that only very poor applicants are unable to arrange for positive letters about their accomplishments. Second, most letters are not structured or standardized. What this means is that the organization receives data from letter writers that are not consistent across organizations. For example, a letter about one applicant may concern the applicant's educational qualifications, whereas a letter about another applicant may focus on work experience. Comparing the qualifications of applicants A and B under these circumstances is like comparing apples and oranges.

The problem with letters of recommendation is demonstrated dramatically in one study that showed there was a stronger correlation between two letters written by one person for two different applicants than between two different people writing letters for the same person.[54] This finding indicates that letters of recommendation have more to do with the letter writer than the person being written about. In fact, a recent study revealed that letter writers who had a dispositional tendency to be positive wrote consistently more favorable letters than letter writers with a tendency to be critical or negative.[55]

Such problems indicate that organizations should downplay the weight given to letters unless a great deal of credibility and accountability can be attached to the letter writer's comments. Also, a structured form should be provided so that each writer provides the same information about each applicant.

Another way to improve on letters of recommendation is to use a standardized scoring key. An example of one is shown in Exhibit 8.8. Using this method, categories of KSAOs are established and become the scoring key (shown at the bottom of the exhibit). Then the adjectives in the actual letter are underlined and classified into the appropriate category. The number of adjectives used in each category constitute the applicant's score.

Reference Checks

With this form of reference report, a check is made on the applicant's background. Usually the person contacted is the immediate supervisor of the applicant or is in the HR department of current or previous organizations with which the applicant has had contact. Surveys reveal that roughly 8 out of 10 organizations conduct reference checks. A roughly equal number conduct the checks in-house (by human resources) versus a third-party vendor. The most common information sought is employment history, criminal records, professional references, and education.[56] Exhibit 8.9 provides a sample reference request. Although this reference request was developed for checking references by mail, the questions contained in the request could easily be adapted for use in checking references via the telephone.

EXHIBIT 8.8   Scoring Letters of Recommendation

Dear Personnel Director:

Mr. John Anderson asked that I write this letter in support of his application as assistant manager and I am pleased to do so. I have known John for six years as he was my assistant in the accounting department.

John always had his work completed <u>accurately</u> and <u>promptly</u>. In his years here, he <u>never missed a deadline</u>. He is very <u>detail</u> oriented, <u>alert</u> in finding errors, and <u>methodical</u> in his problem-solving approach. Interpersonally, John is a very <u>friendly</u> and <u>helpful</u> person.

I have great confidence in John's ability. If you desire more information, please let me know.

MA   0   CC   2   DR   6   U   0   V   0

Dear Personnel Director:

Mr. John Anderson asked that I write this letter in support of his application as assistant manager and I am pleased to do so. I have known John for six years as he was my assistant in the accounting department.

John was one of the most <u>popular</u> employees in our agency as he is a <u>friendly,</u> <u>outgoing, sociable</u> individual. He has a great sense of <u>humor</u>, is <u>poised</u>, and is very <u>helpful</u>. In completing his work, he is <u>independent, energetic,</u> and <u>industrious</u>.

I have great confidence in John's ability. If you desire more information, please let me know.

MA   0   CC   2   DR   0   U   5   V   3

Key   MA = mental ability
CC = consideration-cooperation
DR = dependability-reliability
U = urbanity
V = vigor

Source: M. G. Aumodt, D. A. Bryan, and A. J. Whitcomb, "Predicting Performance with Letters of Recommendation," *Public Personnel Management,* 1993, 22, pp. 81–90. Reprinted with permission of *Public Personnel Management*, published by the International Personnel Management Association.

Both of the problems that occur with letters of recommendation take place with reference checks as well. An even more significant concern, however, is the reluctance of organizations to give out the requested information because they fear a lawsuit due to invasion of privacy or defamation of character.[57] Recall the survey results reported above indicating that 80% of employers always check references. The same survey indicated that 63% of employers *refuse* to provide reference information for fear of being sued. As one executive stated, "There's

EXHIBIT 8.9   **Sample Reference Request**

TO BE COMPLETED BY APPLICANT

NAME (PRINT):   SOCIAL SEC. NUMBER:

I have made application for employment at this company. I request and authorize you to release all information requested below concerning my employment record, reason for leaving your employ, or my education. I hereby release my personal references, my former employers and schools, and all individuals connected therewith, from all liability for any damage whatsoever for furnishing this information.

SIGNATURE _____ DATE _____

SCHOOL REFERENCE

DATES ATTENDED

FROM: TO: GRADUATED?   YES ☐   NO ☐

DEGREE AWARDED:

EMPLOYMENT REFERENCE

POSITION HELD: EMPLOYMENT DATES:

IMMEDIATE SUPERVISOR'S NAME

REASON FOR LEAVING   DISCHARGED ☐   RESIGNED ☐   LAID OFF ☐

FORMER EMPLOYER OR SCHOOL—Please complete the following. Thank you.

IS THE ABOVE INFORMATION CORRECT?   YES ☐   NO ☐

If not, give correct information: _____

_____

PLEASE CHECK

	EXCEL.	GOOD	FAIR	POOR	COMMENTS:
ATTITUDE	____	____	____	____	
QUALITY OF WORK	____	____	____	____	
COOPERATION	____	____	____	____	
ATTENDANCE	____	____	____	____	

WOULD YOU RECOMMEND FOR EMPLOYMENT?   YES ☐   NO ☐

ADDITIONAL COMMENTS

_____

_____

_____   _____

SIGNATURE OF EMPLOYER OR SCHOOL REPRESENTATIVE   TITLE

a dire need for better reference information but fear of litigation keeps employers from providing much more than name, rank, and serial number."[58] As a result of the reluctance to provide reference information, reference checkers claim to receive inadequate information roughly half of the time. To a large degree, this concern over providing even rudimentary reference information is excessive (see Legal Issues at the end of this chapter). It is important to remember that if every organization refuses to provide useful reference information, a potentially important source of applicant information would lose any of its potential value.

Background Testing

How would you feel if you found out that the organization you had hoped to join was having your court record and moral character investigated? How would you feel if an organization did *not* investigate the court record and moral character of guards to be selected for the gun storage depot of the U.S. military base near your home?

Although it may seem to be a very invasive procedure, background investigations are routinely conducted on matters such as these and are sometimes needed to protect the public's interests. Indeed, background testing became an issue in the aftermath of the September 11, 2001, terrorist attacks after it came to light that most airlines did not conduct background testing of security personnel. Many organizations responded to the attacks by instituting background testing programs.[59] Some organizations do background testing on their own, while others employ agencies to do so. As with any predictor, the reasonableness of this procedure depends on how related the factors being investigated are to the requirements of the job.

At a general level, background testing is concerned with the reliability of applicants' behavior, integrity, and personal adjustment. These factors are often used as requirements for the selection of people in occupations such as law enforcement, private security, and nuclear power and in positions requiring government-issued security clearances. Of course, background testing can be important for any position of importance. One executive was CEO of two Fortune 500 companies; only after he was fired from the second Fortune 500 company for financial mismanagement did it come to light that he lied about his former employment history. And this was after the two companies had paid professional executive search firms to hire the CEO (the search firms did not verify the CEO's self-reported employment history).

One practical problem in background testing is that different information is contained in different databases. Criminal records are kept at the county or federal level, depending on the nature of the crime. Credit histories and educational data also must be searched separately. Various firms provide comprehensive background testing services, with fees depending on what databases are checked. The following information can be checked through various services: county criminal court records, social security numbers (identity verifications), address histories, credit information, property ownership, federal court criminal histories, employment verifications, educational histories, license verifications, military service, workers' compensation claims, and driver license histories (including citations, accidents, and DUIs). Extreme care needs to be taken in the use of such measures because of the limited validity reports available to date, as well as legal constraints on preemployment inquiries (see Legal Issues at the end of this chapter).

Evaluation of Reference Reports

The empirical data that does exist on the validity of reference checks is not all that positive. A meta-analysis of a number of studies revealed that the validity coefficients of reference data ranged from $\bar{r} = .16$ to $\bar{r} = .26$. To some degree, the validity depends on who is providing the information. If it is the personnel officer, coworker, or relative, the information is not very valid. On the other hand, reference reports from supervisors and acquaintances are somewhat more valid. The validity of personnel officers may be less valid because they are less knowledgeable about the applicant (their past employee); the reports of coworkers and relatives probably are less valid because these individuals are positively biased toward the applicant.

Although references do not have high validity, we need to take a cost-benefit approach. In general the quality of the information may be low, but in the few cases where reference information changes a decision, the payoff can be significant. An executive with the U.S. Postal Service once told one of the authors that many of the acts of violence by Postal Service employees would have been avoided if a thorough background check had been conducted. Thus, since references are a relatively cheap method of collecting information on applicants, screening out the occasional unstable applicant or in a few cases learning something new and important about an applicant may make reference checks a good investment. As with unweighted application blanks, though, using reference checks requires employers to turn elsewhere to obtain suitable information for making final decisions about applicants.

Handwriting Analysis

An extremely distant sign of job performance is handwriting analysis or graphology. Some employers use this type of analysis to predict job performance. In fact, graphology is widely used in western Europe (particularly France and Switzerland) and Israel as a selection method.[60] While the process of obtaining handwriting samples from applicants is virtually costless, the process of analyzing the samples is not. Estimates are that handwriting assessments cost about $75 per applicant.[61]

The theory behind graphology as a selection device is that handwriting is a measure of personality. So, for example, the height of the bar used to cross one's t's is a measure of one's approach to achievement. The higher the bar used to cross lowercase t's, the stronger the willpower. Individuals who write a sentence on a blank piece of paper that slants upward are thought to be optimists, whereas those whose sentences slant downward are thought to be pessimists. In turn, these signs of personality are believed to have an impact on job performance.

One of the very few advantages of this predictor over other predictors measuring personality is that it is difficult to fake. The problem with this approach is that the link between handwriting, personality, and HR outcomes is tenuous at best. One would expect to find virtually no relationship between handwriting analysis and a distant outcome such as job performance and, in fact, that is exactly what has been found. A well-conducted study of real estate brokers found no relationship between graphologist ratings of handwriting and any measure of job performance (sales volume, supervisor ratings of job performance, or self-ratings of performance).[62] Another well-controlled study reported similarly weak findings.[63] Organizational managers who use graphology seem to be unaware of the unimpressive scientific validity evidence, instead claiming success rates of 70–80% in their use of graphology. We doubt these claims would be supported by sound validity evidence. Thus, although little research has been conducted on the validity of graphology, the evidence that is available suggests that organizations would be best advised to avoid this selection method.

Literacy Testing

Most jobs require that employees possess reading and writing skills. In some jobs, the need for these skills is obvious. In others, though the need is not obvious, these skills are nevertheless critical to successful on-the-job performance. A good example is the position of custodian. Reading skills at first do not seem important for this position. However, reading skills may be very important for custodians, as witnessed by the authors of this book in a small school district in Ohio, where an illiterate night custodian mistakenly used what he thought was a cleaning compound for toilets. The substance turned out to have a large amount of an acid compound, as shown on the label. He then used it to clean the toilet seats. Fortunately, no one was hurt in this incident. This incident emphasizes the importance of carefully identifying all relevant KSAOs when developing the job requirements matrix and selection plan.

Illiteracy is a big problem in the United States. It is estimated that over 30 million Americans are functionally illiterate. Historically, this was not a selection issue in industries where people's physical skills were much more important than their mental skills. Today, all that has changed. Ford, Chrysler, and GM claim to have invested almost $100 million dollars in literacy programs.[64] These dollars have gone toward providing training for presently employed workers who cannot read or write up to the standards required by new jobs in the auto industry.

Another way for employers to address the issue of illiteracy is to select in advance those people who already have the required reading and writing skills. A great deal of theory and research has gone into developing standardized reading tests.[65] In addition, companies are developing their own tests. For example, Southern California Gas Company developed a writing test for its sales position that assesses writing mechanics, written content, and ability to follow exercise directions.[66] It has been well received by the company and by the union as well because of the detailed feedback it gives to applicants.

Genetic Screening

Due to advances in medical technology, it is now possible for employers to screen people on the basis of their genetic code. The testing is done to screen out people who are susceptible to certain diseases (e.g., sickle cell anemia) due to exposure to toxic substances at work.[67] Screening out susceptible people is one way to ensure that workers do not become ill. Another way to do so is to eliminate the toxic substances. Although the use of genetic screening is not widespread, companies such as Du Pont and Dow Chemical experimented with it to protect their employees.[68] Organizations also experimented with genetic screening because of the huge costs associated with work-related diseases and illnesses. However, a recent court decision has ruled that genetic screening is prohibited under the Americans With Disabilities Act.[69] Further, a California court of appeals ruled that genetic testing is permissible only when consent has been granted by the applicant or when test results directly bear on an applicant's ability to perform the job.[70] Federal legislation under consideration would limit employers' ability to conduct genetic testing, so employers should exercise considerable caution in using genetic screening.

Initial Interview

The initial interview occurs very early in the initial assessment process and is often the applicant's first personal contact with the organization and its staffing system. At this point, applicants are relatively undifferentiated to the organization in terms of KSAOs. The initial interview will begin the process of necessary differentiation, a sort of "rough cut."

The purpose of the initial interview is, and should be, to screen out the most obvious cases of person/job mismatches. To do this, the interview should focus on an assessment of KSAOs that are absolute requirements for the applicant. Examples of such minimum levels of qualifications for the job include certification and licensure requirements and necessary (not just preferred) training and experience requirements.

These assessments may be made on the basis of information gathered from written means (e.g., application blank or résumé), as well as the interview per se.

Care should be taken to ensure that the interviewer focuses only on this information as a basis for decision making. Evaluations of personal characteristics of the applicant (e.g., race, sex), as well as judgments about an applicant's personality (e.g., she seems so outgoing and just "right" for this job), are to be avoided. Indeed, to ensure that this focus happens, some organizations (e.g., civil service agencies) have basically eliminated the initial interview altogether and make the initial assessment only on the basis of written information provided by the applicant.

One of the limitations with the initial interview is that it is perhaps the most expensive method of initial assessment. One way to reduce costs is to use companies, such as Gallup, who conduct an initial screening interview via the telephone (applicants dial a toll-free number and answer a series of questions); the company then reports results back to the employer. Some consulting firms use interactive voice technology so that interviews are computerized. Nike recently opened a store in Las Vegas and used the technology to screen 6,000 applicants for 250 positions.[71] Given that the validity evidence for such types of interview is not particularly impressive, such cost-saving methods appear worthwhile.

Video and Computer Interviews

One means of reducing the costs of initial interviews is to use video interviews. Video interviews can take at least one of two forms. One form of the video interview is to link the applicant and recruiter via remote video access. This sort of video conferencing allows the applicant and recruiter to see each other on a monitor and, in some cases, even exchange documents. Viewnet of Madison, Wisconsin, has sold their video interview technology to more than 70 colleges to use as an alternative selection device. A variant of this type of video interview is to hire a consulting firm to conduct the video interviews for the organization. Under this approach, the organization identifies the candidates (perhaps after screening their applications or résumés) and submits their names to the consulting firm. The firm then videotapes the interviews and submits the tapes to the organization. In general, one of the advantages of video-based interviews is that they can dramatically lower the cost of initial interviews. This is particularly true for employers who may wish to interview only a few applicants at a given location. Another advantage of these interviews is that they can be arranged on short notice (no travel and no schedule rearrangements). Of course, a disadvantage of these interviews is that they do not permit face-to-face contact. The effect of this limitation on validity and applicant reactions is unknown.

Another form of video interviews takes the process a step further. Computer-based interviews utilize software that asks applicants questions (e.g., "Have you ever been terminated for stealing?") or presents realistic scenarios (e.g., presents an irate customer on the screen) while recording applicants' responses. These responses are then forwarded to selection decision makers for use in initial screening. The software can also be configured to inform applicants about job duties and requirements. It can even track how long it takes an applicant to answer each question. Retailers are beginning to use computerized interviews on-site, where applicants walk into a store, enter a kiosk, and submit information about their work habits and experiences. As with video interviews, computer-based interviews can offer dramatic costs savings (although start-up costs to customize such programs can be high). As before, though, the accuracy of these high-tech interviews as compared to the old standby, the person-to-person variety, is unclear. The same holds true for how applicants will react to these relatively impersonal methods.

Evaluation of Initial Interview

Whether high-tech or traditional, the interview has benefits and limitations. Nearly all of the research evaluating the interview in selection has considered it a substantive method (see the Structured Interview section in Chapter 9). Thus, there is little evidence about the usefulness of the initial interview. However, organizations using the initial interview in selection are likely to find it more useful by following a few guidelines such as the following:

1. Ask questions that assess the most basic KSAOs identified by job analysis. This requires separating what is required from what is preferred.
2. Stick to basic, qualifying questions suitable for making rough cuts (e.g., "Have you completed the minimum certification requirements to qualify for this job?") rather than subtle, subjective questions more suitable for substantive decisions (e.g., "How would this job fit within your overall career goals?"). Remember, the purpose of the initial interview is closer to cutting with a saw than operating with a scalpel. Ask only the most fundamental questions now, and leave the fine-tuning for later.
3. Keep interviews brief. Most interviewers make up their minds quickly and, given the limited usefulness and the type of information collected, a long interview (e.g., 45–60 minutes) is unlikely to add much over a shorter one (15–30 minutes).
4. As with all interviews, the same questions should be asked of all applicants, and EEO compliance must be monitored.

Choice of Initial Assessment Methods

As described, there is a wide range of initial assessment methods available to organizations to help reduce the applicant pool to bona fide candidates. A range of formats is available as well. Fortunately, with so many choices available to organizations, research results are available to help guide choices of methods to use. This research has been reviewed many times and is summarized in Exhibit 8.10. In Exhibit 8.10, each initial assessment method is rated according to several criteria. Each of these criteria will be discussed in turn.

EXHIBIT 8.10 Evaluation of Initial Assessment Methods

Predictors	Use	Cost	Reliability	Validity	Utility	Reactions	Adverse Impact
Level of education	High	Low	Moderate	Low	Low	?	Moderate
Grade point average	Moderate	Low	Moderate	Moderate	?	?	?
Quality of school	?	Low	Moderate	Low	?	?	Moderate
Major field of study	?	Low	Moderate	Moderate	?	?	?
Extracurricular activity	?	Low	Moderate	Moderate	?	?	?
Training and experience	High	Low	High	Moderate	Moderate	?	Moderate
Licensing and certification	Moderate	Low	?	?	?	?	?
Weighted application blanks	Low	Moderate	Moderate	Moderate	Moderate	?	?
Biographical data	Low	High	High	High	High	Negative	Moderate
Letters of recommendation	Moderate	Low	?	Low	?	?	?
Reference checks	High	Moderate	Low	Low	Moderate	Mixed	Low
Background testing	Low	High	?	?	?	Mixed	Moderate
Résumés and cover letters	Moderate	Low	Moderate	?	?	Moderate	?
Initial interview	High	Moderate	Low	Low	?	Positive	Moderate
Handwriting analysis	Low	Moderate	Low	Low	?	Negative	?
Genetic screening	Low	High	Moderate	?	?	?	High
Literacy testing	Low	Moderate	?	Low	?	?	?

Use

Use refers to how frequently surveyed organizations use each predictor. Use is probably an "overused" criterion in deciding which selection measures to adopt. Benchmarking—basing HR decisions on what other companies are doing—is a predominant method of decision making in all areas of HR, including staffing. However, is this a good basis on which to make decisions about selection methods? Although it is always comforting to do what other organizations are doing, relying on information from other organizations assumes that they know what they are doing. Just because many organizations use a selection measure does not necessarily make it a good idea for a particular organization. Circumstances differ from organization to organization. Perhaps more important, many organizational decision makers (and HR consultants) either lack knowledge about the latest findings in HR research or have decided that such findings are not applicable to their organization. It also is difficult to determine whether a successful organization that uses a particular selection method is successful because it uses this method or if it will be as successful in the future. Thus, from a research standpoint, there may be real strategic advantage in relying on "effectiveness" criteria (e.g., validity, utility, adverse impact) rather than worrying about the practices of other organizations.

Another reason to have a healthy degree of skepticism about the use criterion is that there is a severe lack of broad (i.e., coverage of many industries and regions in the United States) and timely surveys of selection practices. The Bureau of National Affairs (BNA) has conducted broad surveys of selection practices, but the most recent was in 1988. Other surveys of selection practices are available, but they generally cover only a single selection practice (e.g., drug testing) or lack adequate scope or breadth. In providing conclusions about use of various selection methods in organizations, we are forced to make judgment calls concerning which survey to rely on. In the case of some selection measures (e.g., application blanks), there is little reason to believe the BNA figures have changed much. With other predictors, the use figures have shown a fair degree of volatility and change from year to year. Thus, in classifying the use of assessment methods, we rely on the most recent surveys that achieve some degree of breadth. For purposes of classifying the predictors, high use refers to use by more than two-thirds of organizations, moderate is use by one-third to two-thirds of organizations, and low use refers to use by less than one-third of organizations.

Having issued these caveats about the use criterion, Exhibit 8.10 reveals clear differences in the use of different methods of initial assessment. The most frequently used methods of initial assessment are education level, training and experience, reference checks, and initial interview. These methods are considered, to some degree, in selection decisions for most types of positions. Licensing and certification requirements, letters of recommendation, and résumés and cover letters have moderate levels of use. All three of these methods are widely used in filling some types of positions, but infrequently used in filling many others. The least widely used initial assessment methods are weighted application blanks, biographical information, background testing, handwriting analysis, genetic screening, and literacy testing. It is relatively unusual for organizations to use these methods for initial screening decisions. There are no reliable figures on the use of quality of school, major field of study, and extracurricular activity in initial selection decisions; thus, their use could not be estimated.

Cost

Cost refers to expenses incurred in using the predictor. Although most of the initial assessment methods may seem relatively cost-free since the applicant provides the information on his or her own time, this is not entirely accurate. For most initial assessment methods, the major cost associated with each selection measure is administration. Consider an application blank. It is true that applicants complete application blanks on their own time, but someone must be present to hand out applications, answer inquiries in person and over the phone about possible openings, and collect, sort, and forward applications to the appropriate person. Then the selection decision maker must read each application, perhaps make notes and weed out the clearly unacceptable applicants, and then make decisions about candidates. Thus, even for the least expensive methods of initial assessment, costs associated with their use are far from trivial.

On the other hand, utility research has suggested that costs do not play a large part in evaluating the financial benefit of using particular selection methods. This becomes readily apparent when one considers the costs of hiring a poor performer. For example, a secretary who performs one standard deviation below average (16th percentile, if performance is normally distributed) may cost the organization $8,000 in lost productivity per year. This person is likely to remain on the job for more than one year, multiplying the costs. Considered in this light, spending an extra few hundred dollars to accurately identify good secretaries is an excellent investment. Thus, although costs need to be considered in evaluating assessment methods, more consideration should be given to the fact that valid selection measures pay off handsomely and will return many times their cost.

As can be seen in Exhibit 8.10, the least costly initial assessment methods include information that can obtained from application blanks (level of education, grade point average, quality of school, major field of study, extracurricular activity, training and experience, licensing and certification) and other applicant-provided information (letters of recommendation, résumés, and cover letters). Initial assessment methods of moderate cost include weighted application blanks, reference checks, initial interviews, handwriting analysis, and literacy testing. Biographical information, background testing, and genetic screening are relatively expensive assessment methods.

Reliability

Reliability refers to consistency of measurement. As was noted in Chapter 7, reliability is a bound for validity, so it would be very difficult for a predictor with low reliability to have high validity. By the same token, it is unlikely that a valid predictor would have low reliability. Unfortunately, the reliability information on many initial assessment methods is lacking in the literature. Some researchers have investigated distortion of applicant-reported information (application blanks and résumés). One study found that nearly half of the items on application blanks were distorted by 20% of the applicants. Other studies have suggested that one-third of application blanks contain some inaccuracies.[72] Thus, it is probably reasonable to infer that applicant-supplied information in application blanks and résumés is of moderate reliability. The reliability of reference checks appears to be relatively low. In terms of training and experience evaluations, while distortion can occur if the applicant supplies training and experience information, interrater agreement in evaluating this information is quite high.[73] Biographical information also generally has high reliability. The initial interview, like most unstructured interviews, probably has a relatively low level of reliability. Handwriting analysis has a low degree of reliability.

Validity

Validity refers to the strength of the relationship between the predictor and job performance. Low validity refers to validity in the range of about .00 to .15. Moderate validity corresponds to validity in the range of about .16 to .30, and high validity is .31 and above. As might be expected, most initial assessment methods have moderate to low validity because they are used only for making "rough cuts" among applicants rather than for final decisions. Perhaps the two most valid initial assessment methods are biodata and training and experience requirements; their validity can range from moderate to high. Among the least valid initial methods are the initial interview and handwriting analysis.

Utility

Utility refers to the monetary return associated with using the predictor, relative to its cost. According to researchers and decision makers, when comparing the utility of selection methods, validity appears to be the most important consideration.[74] In short, it would be very unusual for a valid selection method to have low utility. Thus, as can be seen in Exhibit 8.10, high, moderate, and low validities tend to directly correspond to high, moderate, and low utility values, respectively. Question marks predominate this column in the exhibit because relatively few studies have directly investigated the utility of these methods. However, based on the argument that validity should be directly related to utility, it is likely that high validity methods also will realize large financial benefits to organizations that choose to use them. Research does indicate that training and experience requirements have moderate (or even high) levels of utility, and reference checks have moderate levels of utility.

Applicant Reactions

Reactions refers to the favorability of applicants' reactions to the predictor. Applicant reactions are an important evaluative criterion because research has indicated that applicants who feel positively about selection methods and the selection process report higher levels of satisfaction with the organization, are more likely to accept a position with the organization, and are more likely to recommend the organization to others.[75]

Research suggests that selection measures that are perceived as job related, present applicants with an opportunity to perform, are administered consistently, and provide applicants with feedback about their performance are likely to generate favorable applicant reactions.[76] Although research on applicants' reactions to specific selection procedures is lacking, evidence has been accumulating and suggests that applicants react more positively to some initial assessment methods, such as interviews, résumés, and references, than to others, such as handwriting analysis.[77]

Adverse Impact

Adverse impact refers to the possibility that a disproportionate number of protected class members may be rejected using this predictor. Several initial assessment methods have moderate degrees of adverse impact against women and/or minorities, including level of education, quality of school, training and experience, biographical information, and the initial interview. Genetic screening may have a high degree of adverse impact while reference checks appear to have little adverse impact.

LEGAL ISSUES

Initial assessment methods are subject to numerous laws, regulations, and other legal considerations. Four major matters of concern pertain to using disclaimers, conducting reference checks, making preemployment inquiries, and making bona fide occupational qualifications claims.

Disclaimers

During the initial stages of contact with job applicants, it is important for the organization to protect itself legally by clearly identifying rights it wants to maintain for itself. This involves the use of disclaimers. Disclaimers are statements (usually written) that provide or confer explicit rights to the employer as part of the employment contract and that are shown to job applicants. The organization needs to decide (or reevaluate) which rights it wants to retain and how these will be communicated to job applicants.

Three areas of rights are usually suggested for possible inclusion in a disclaimer policy. These are (a) employment-at-will (right to terminate the employment relationship at any time, for any reason); (b) verification consent (right to verify information provided by the applicant); and (c) false statement warning (right to not hire, terminate, or discipline prospective employee for providing false information to the employer). Examples of disclaimer statements in these three areas are shown in Exhibit 8.4. Usually, it is recommended that the organization have all three of these disclaimers as part of its planned policy toward job applicants.[78]

To communicate disclaimers, it is advisable that they be shown in writing to job applicants (often on the application blank), reviewed with the applicant if possible, and then signed by the applicant. It should be remembered that signed disclaimer statements will become part of the employment contract for those applicants who accept a job offer. Care should thus be exercised in the development and communication of disclaimers.

Reference Checks

Reference checking creates a legal quagmire for organizations. Current or former employers of the job applicant may be reluctant to provide a reference (especially one with negative information about the applicant) because they fear the applicant may file a defamation suit against them. Hence, the organization may view requesting references to be somewhat fruitless. On the other hand, failure to conduct a reference check opens up the organization to the possibility of a negligent hiring suit, in which it is claimed that the organization hired a person it should have known would cause harm to other employees or customers. To deal with such problems and obtain thorough, accurate information, the following suggestions are offered.

First, gather as much information as possible directly from the applicant, along with a verification consent. In this way, use of reference providers and information demands on them are minimized.

Second, be sure to obtain written authorization from the applicant to check references. To do so, the applicant should sign a blanket consent form. Also, the organization could prepare a request-for-reference form that the applicant would give to the person(s) being asked to provide a reference. That form would authorize the person(s) to provide requested information, release the person from any liability for providing the information, and be signed by the applicant (see Exhibit 8.9).

Third, specify the type of information being requested and obtain the information in writing. That information should be specific, factual, and job-related in content; do not seek health or disability information. Fourth, limit access to reference information to those making selection decisions.

Finally, check relevant state laws about permissible and impermissible reference check practices. Also, determine if your organization is covered by state reference immunity laws—these provide some degree of immunity from civil liability to organizations that in good faith provide information about the job performance and professional conduct of former or current employees. Organizations in these states (currently 32) may be more willing to request and provide reference information.[79]

Preemployment Inquiries

The term "preemployment inquiry" (PI), as used here, pertains to both content and method of assessment. Regarding content, PI refers to applicants' personal and background data. These data cover such areas as demographics (race, color, religion, sex, national origin, age), physical characteristics (disability, height, weight), family and associates, residence, economic status, and education. The information could be gathered by any method; most frequently, it will be gathered with an initial assessment method, particularly the application blank, biodata questionnaire, or preliminary interview. At times, PIs may also occur as part of an unstructured interview.

PIs have been singled out for particular legal (EEO/AA) attention at both the federal and state levels. The reason for this is that PIs have great potential for use in a discriminatory manner early on in the selection process.[80] Moreover, research continually finds that organizations make inappropriate and illegal PIs. One study, for example, found that out of 46 categories of application blank items, there was an average of 7.4 inadvisable items used by employers on their application blanks.[81] It is thus critical to understand the laws and regulations surrounding the use of PIs.

Federal Laws and Regulations

The laws and their interpretation indicate that it is illegal to use PI information that has a disparate impact based on a protected characteristic (race, color, etc.), unless such disparate impact can be shown to be job related and consistent with business necessity. The emphasis here is on the potentially illegal use of the information, rather than its collection per se.

The EEOC makes the following points generally about PIs:[82]

1. It is reasonable to assume that all information on an application form or in a preemployment interview are for some purpose and that selection or hiring decisions are being made on the basis of the answers given. In an investigation of charges of discrimination, the burden of proof is on the employer to show that answers to all questions on application forms or in oral interviews are not used in making hiring and placement decisions in a discriminatory manner prohibited by law.

2. To seek information other than that which is essential to effectively evaluate a person's qualifications for employment is to make oneself vulnerable to charges of discrimination and consequent legal proceedings.

3. It is, therefore, in an employer's own self-interest to carefully review all procedures used in screening applicants for employment, eliminating or altering any not justified by business necessity.

These principles are reflected in two sets of regulations and guidelines.

EEOC Guide to Preemployment Inquiries   This guide provides the principles just given above. It then provides specific guidance (dos and don'ts) on PIs regarding the following: race, color, religion, sex, national origin, age, height and weight, marital status, number of children, provisions for child care, English language skill, educational requirements, friends or relatives working for the employer, arrest records, conviction records, discharge from military service, citizenship, economic status, and availability for work on weekends or holidays.[83]

ADA Regulations   There appears to be a fine line between permissible and impermissible information that may be gathered, and between appropriate and inappropriate methods for gathering it, under the ADA. To help employers, the EEOC has developed specific enforcement guidance on these matters.[84]

The general thrust of the guidance is that the organization may not ask disability-related questions and may not conduct medical examinations until after it makes a conditional job offer to a person. Once that offer is made, however, the organization may ask disability-related questions and conduct medical examinations, so long as this is done for all entering employees in the job category. When such questions or exams screen out a person with a disability, the reason for rejection must be job-related and consistent with business necessity. A person may be rejected for safety reasons if the person provides a direct threat of substantial harm to him- or herself or others. We will have more to say about the legality of medical examinations in the next chapter.

More specific guidance is provided for the preoffer stage as follows. Disability-related questions cannot be asked, meaning questions (a) whether a person has a disability, (b) that are likely to elicit information about a disability, or (c) that are closely related to disability. Along with these general prohibitions, it is impermissible to ask applicants whether they will need reasonable accommodation to perform the functions of the job or can perform major life activities (e.g., lifting, walking), to ask about lawful use of drugs, to ask about workers' compensation history, or to ask third parties (e.g., former employers, references) questions that cannot be asked of the applicant.

Alternatively, preoffer it is permissible to ask:

- if the applicant can perform the job, with or without reasonable accommodation
- the applicant to describe or demonstrate how they would perform the job (including any needed reasonable accommodation)
- if the applicant will need reasonable accommodation for the hiring process (unless there is an obvious disability or the applicant discloses a disability)
- the applicant to provide documentation of a disability if requesting reasonable accommodation for the hiring process
- if the applicant can meet the organization's attendance requirement

- the applicant for certifications and licenses
- about the applicant's current illegal use of drugs (but not past addiction)
- about the applicant's drinking habits (but not alcoholism)

State Laws and Regulations

There is a vast cache of state laws and regulations pertaining to PIs.[85] These requirements vary substantially among the states. They are often more stringent and inclusive than federal laws and regulations. The organization thus must become familiar with and adhere to the laws for each state in which it is located.

An example of Ohio state law regarding PIs is shown in Exhibit 8.11. Notice how the format of the example points out both lawful and unlawful ways of gathering PI information.

Bona Fide Occupational Qualifications

Title VII of the Civil Rights Act explicitly permits discrimination on the basis of sex, religion, or national origin (but not race or color) if it can be shown to be a bona fide occupational qualification (BFOQ) "reasonably necessary to the normal operation" of the business. The ADEA contains a similar provision regarding age. These provisions thus permit outright rejection of applicants because of their sex, religion, national origin, or age, as long as the rejection can be justified under the "reasonably necessary" standard. Exactly how have BFOQ claims by employers fared? When are BFOQ claims upheld as legitimate? Several points are relevant to understanding the BFOQ issue.

The burden of proof is on the employer to justify any BFOQ claim, and it is clear that the BFOQ exception is to be construed narrowly. Thus, it does not apply to the following:[86]

- refusing to hire women because of a presumed difference in comparative HR outcomes (e.g., women are lower performers, have higher turnover rates)
- refusing to hire women because of personal characteristic stereotypes (e.g., women are less aggressive than men)
- refusing to hire women because of the preferences of others (customers or fellow workers)

To amplify on the above points, an analysis of BFOQ claims involving sex reveals four types of justifications usually presented by the employer. These involve inability to perform the work, personal contact with others requires the same sex, customers have a preference for dealing with one sex, and pregnancy or fertility protection concerns.[87]

EXHIBIT 8.11   Ohio Preemployment Inquiry Guide

INQUIRIES BEFORE HIRING	LAWFUL	UNLAWFUL*
1. NAME	Name.	Inquiry into any title which indicates race, color, religion, sex, national origin, handicap, age, or ancestry.
2. ADDRESS	Inquiry into place and length at current address.	Inquiry into any foreign addresses which would indicate national origin.
3. AGE	Any inquiry limited to establishing that applicant meets any minimum age requirement that may be established by law.	A. Requiring birth certificate or baptismal record before hiring. B. Any inquiry which may reveal the date of high school graduation. C. Any other inquiry which may reveal whether applicant is at least 40 and less than 70 years of age.
4. BIRTHPLACE, NATIONAL ORIGIN, OR ANCESTRY		A. Any inquiry into place of birth. B. Any inquiry into place of birth of parents, grandparents, or spouse. C. Any other inquiry into national origin or ancestry.
5. RACE OR COLOR		Any inquiry which would indicate race or color.
6. SEX		A. Any inquiry which would indicate sex. B. Any inquiry made of members of one sex, but not the other.

(continued)

EXHIBIT 8.11   Continued

INQUIRIES BEFORE HIRING	LAWFUL	UNLAWFUL*
7. HEIGHT AND WEIGHT	Inquiries as to ability to perform actual job requirements.	Being a certain height or weight will not be considered to be a job requirement unless the employer can show that no employee with the ineligible height or weight could do the work.
8. RELIGION— CREED		A. Any inquiry which would indicate or identify religious denomination or custom. B. Applicant may not be told any religious identity or preference of the employer. C. Request pastor's recommendation or reference.
9. HANDICAP	Inquiries necessary to determine applicant's ability to substantially perform specific job without significant hazard.	A. Any inquiry into past or current medical conditions not related to position applied for. B. Any inquiry into worker's compensation or similar claims.
10. CITIZENSHIP	A. Whether a U.S. citizen. B. If not, whether applicant intends to become one. C. If U.S. residence is legal. D. If spouse is citizen. E. Require proof of citizenship after being hired. F. Any other requirement mandated by the Immigration Reform and Control Act of 1986, as amended.	A. If native-born or naturalized. B. Proof of citizenship before hiring. C. Whether parents or spouse are native-born or naturalized.
11. PHOTOGRAPHS	May be required after hiring for identification.	Require photograph before hiring.

(continued)

EXHIBIT 8.11   Continued

INQUIRIES BEFORE HIRING	LAWFUL	UNLAWFUL*
12. ARREST AND CONVICTIONS	Inquiries into *conviction* of specific crimes related to qualifications for the job applied for.	Any inquiry which would reveal arrests without convictions.
13. EDUCATION	A. Inquiry into nature and extent of academic, professional, or vocational training. B. Inquiry into language skills such as reading and writing of foreign languages, if job-related.	A. Any inquiry which would reveal the nationality or religious affiliation of a school. B. Inquiry as to what mother tongue is or how foreign language ability was acquired.
14. RELATIVES	Inquiry into name, relationship, and address of person to be notified in case of emergency.	Any inquiry about a relative which would be unlawful if made about the applicant.
15. ORGANIZATIONS	Inquiry into membership in professional organizations and offices held, excluding any organization, the name or character of which indicates the race, color, religion, sex, national origin, handicap, age, or ancestry of its members.	Inquiry into every club and organization where membership is held.
16. MILITARY SERVICE	A. Inquiry into service in U.S. Armed Forces when such service is a qualification for the job. B. Require military discharge certificate after being hired.	A. Inquiry into military service in armed service of any country but U.S. B. Request military service records. C. Inquiry into type of discharge.
17. WORK SCHEDULE	Inquiry into willingness or ability to work required work schedule.	Any inquiry into willingness or ability to work any particular religious holidays.

(continued)

EXHIBIT 8.11   Continued

INQUIRIES BEFORE HIRING	LAWFUL	UNLAWFUL*
18. MISCELLANEOUS	Any question required to reveal qualifications for the job applied for.	Any non–job-related inquiry which may elicit or attempt to elicit any information concerning race, color, religion, sex, national origin, handicap, age, or ancestry of an applicant for employment or membership.
19. REFERENCES	General personal and work references which do not reveal the race, color, religion, sex, national origin, handicap, age, or ancestry of the applicant.	Request references specifically from clergy or any other persons who might reflect race, color, religion, sex, national origin, handicap, age, or ancestry of applicant.

I. Employers acting under bona fide Affirmative Action Programs or acting under orders of Equal Employment law enforcement agencies of federal, state, or local governments may make some of the prohibited inquiries listed above to the extent that these inquiries are required by such programs or orders.

II. Employers having federal defense contracts are exempt to the extent that otherwise prohibited inquiries are required by federal law for security purposes.

III. Any inquiry is prohibited although not specifically listed above, which elicits information as to, or which is not job-related and may be used to discriminate on the basis of race, color, religion, sex, national origin, handicap, age, or ancestry in violation of law.

*Unless bona fide occupational qualification is certified in advance by the Ohio Civil Rights Commission.

Source: Ohio Civil Rights Commission, 1989.

Inability to Perform

The general employer claim here is that one gender (usually women) is unable to perform the job due to job requirements such as lifting heavy weights, being of a minimum height, or long hours of work. The employer must be able to show that the inability holds for most, if not all, members of the gender. Moreover, if it is possible to test the required abilities for each person, then that must be done rather than having a blanket exclusion from the job based on gender.

Same-Sex Personal Contact
Due to a job requirement of close personal contact with other people, the employer may claim that employees must be the same sex as those people with whom they have contact. This claim has often been made, but not always successfully defended, for the job of prison guard. Much will depend on an analysis of just how inhospitable and dangerous the work environment is (e.g., minimum security versus maximum security prisons). Same-sex personal conflict claims have been made successfully for situations involving personal hygiene, health care, and rape victims. In short, the permissibility of these claims depends on a very specific analysis of the job requirements matrix (including the job context portion).

Customer Preference
Organizations may argue that customers prefer members of one sex, and this preference must be honored in order to serve and maintain the continued patronage of the customer. This claim might occur, for example, for the job of salesperson in women's sportswear. Usually, customer preference claims cannot be successfully defended by the employer.

Pregnancy or Fertility
Nonpregnancy could be a valid BFOQ claim, particularly in jobs where the risk of sudden incapacitation due to pregnancy poses threats to public safety (e.g., airline attendant). Threats to fertility of either sex generally cannot be used as a basis for sustaining a BFOQ claim. For example, an employer's fetal protection policy that excluded women from jobs involving exposure to lead in the manufacture of batteries was held to not be a permissible BFOQ.[88]

The discussion and examples here should make clear that BFOQ claims involve complex situations and considerations. The organization should remember that the burden of proof is on it to defend BFOQ claims. BFOQ provisions in the law are and continue to be construed very narrowly. The employer thus must have an overwhelming preponderance of argument and evidence on its side in order to make and successfully defend a BFOQ claim.

SUMMARY

This chapter reviews the processes involved in external selection and focuses specifically on methods of initial assessment. Before candidates are assessed, it is important to base assessment methods on the logic of prediction and to use selection plans. The logic of prediction focuses on the requisite correspondence between elements in applicants' past situations and KSAOs critical to success on the job applied for. The selection plan involves the process of detailing the required

KSAOs and indicating which selection methods will be used to assess each KSAO. The selection sequence is the means by which the selection process is used to narrow down the size of the initial applicant pool to candidates, then finalists, and, eventually, job offer receivers.

Initial assessment methods are used during the early stages of the selection sequence to reduce the applicant pool to candidates for further assessment. The methods of initial assessment were reviewed in some detail. The methods include résumés and cover letters, application blanks, biographical data, reference reports, handwriting analysis, literacy testing, genetic screening, and initial interviews. Initial assessment methods differ widely in their usefulness. The means by which these methods can be evaluated for potential use include frequency of use, cost, reliability, validity, utility, applicant reactions, and adverse impact.

Legal issues need to be considered in making initial assessments about applicants. The use of disclaimers as a protective mechanism is critical. Also, three areas of initial assessment that require special attention are reference checking, preemployment inquiries, and bona fide occupational qualifications.

DISCUSSION QUESTIONS

1. A selection plan describes which predictor(s) will be used to assess the KSAOs required to perform the job. What are the three steps to follow in establishing a selection plan?

2. In what ways are the following three initial assessment methods similar and in what ways are they different: application blanks, biographical information, and reference reports?

3. Describe the criteria by which initial assessment methods are evaluated. Are some of these criteria more important than others?

4. Some methods of initial assessment appear to be more useful than others. If you were starting your own business, which initial assessment methods would you use and why?

5. How can organizations avoid legal difficulties in the use of preemployment inquiries in initial selection decisions?

APPLICATIONS

Reference Reports and Initial Assessment in a Start-Up Company

Stanley Jausneister owns a small high-tech start-up company, called BioSever-Systems (BSS). Stanley's company specializes in selling Web server space to clients. The server space that Stanley markets runs from a network of personal computers. This networked configuration allows BSS to more efficiently manage its server space and provides greater flexibility to its customers, who often want weekly or even daily updates of their Web sites. The other innovation Stanley brought to BSS is special security encryption software protocols, which make the BSS server space nearly impossible for hackers to access. This flexibility is particularly attractive to organizations that need to manage large, security-protected databases with multiple points of access. Stanley even has been contacted by the government, which is interested in using BSS's systems for some of its classified intelligence.

Due to its niche, BSS has experienced rapid growth. In the past year, BSS has hired 12 programmers and 2 marketers, as well as a general manager, a human resource manager, and other support personnel. Before starting BSS, Stanley was a manager with a large pharmaceutical firm. Because of his industry connections, most of BSS's business has been with drug and chemical companies.

Yesterday, Stanley received a phone call from Lee Rogers, head of Biotechnology for Mercelle-Poulet, one of BSS's largest customers. Lee is an old friend, and he was one of BSS's first customers. Yesterday when Lee called, he expressed concerned about BSS's security. One area of Mercelle-Poulet's Biotech division is responsible for research and development on vaccines for various bioterrorist weapons such as anthrax and the plague. Because the research and development on these vaccines require the company to develop cultures of the biotech weapons themselves, Lee has used BSS to house information for this area. A great deal of sensitive information is housed on BSS's servers, including in some cases the formulas that are used in developing the cultures.

Despite the sensitivity of the information on BSS's servers, given BSS's advanced software, Stanley was very surprised to hear Lee's concern about security. "It's not your software that worries me," Lee commented, "It's the people running it." Lee explained that last week a Mercelle-Poulet researcher was arrested for attempting to sell certain cultures to an overseas client. It turns out that this individual had been dismissed from a previous pharmaceutical company for unethical behavior, but this information did not surface during the individual's background check. This incident not only caused Lee to re-examine Mercelle-Poulet's background checks, but it also made him think of BSS, as certain BSS employees have access to Mercelle-Poulet's information.

Instantly after hearing Lee's concern, Stanley realized he had a problem. Like many small employers, BSS did not do thorough background checks on its employees. They assumed that the information provided on the application was accurate and generally only called the applicant's previous employer (often with ineffective results). Stanley realized he needed to do more, not only to keep Lee's business but to protect his company and customers.

1. What sort of background testing should BSS conduct on its applicants?
2. Is there any information BSS should avoid obtaining for legal or EEO reasons?

3. How can BSS know that its background testing programs are effective?

4. In the past, BSS has used the following initial assessment methods: application blank, interviews with Stanley and other BSS managers, and a follow-up with the applicant's former employer. Beyond changes to its background testing program, would you suggest any other alterations to BSS's initial assessment process?

Developing a Lawful Application Blank

The Consolidated Trucking Corporation, Inc. (CTCI) is a rapidly growing short-haul (local) firm within the greater Columbus, Ohio, area. It has grown primarily through the acquisitions of numerous small, family-owned trucking companies. As of now it has a fleet of 150 trucks and over 250 full-time drivers. Most of the drivers were hired initially by the firms that CTCI acquired, and they accepted generous offers from CTCI to become members of the CTCI team. CTCI's expansion plans are very ambitious, but they will be fulfilled primarily from internal growth rather than additional acquisitions. Consequently, CTCI is now faced with the need to develop an external staffing system that will be geared up to hire 75 new truckers within the next two years.

Terry Tailgater is a former truck driver for CTCI who was promoted to truck maintenance supervisor, a position he has held for the past five years. Once CTCI's internal expansion plans become finalized, the firm's HR director (and sole member of the HR department) Harold Hornblower decided he needed a new person to handle staffing and employment law duties. Terry Tailgater was promoted by Harold to the job of staffing manager. One of Terry's major assignments was to develop a new staffing system for truck drivers.

One of the first projects Terry undertook was to develop a new, standardized application blank for the job of truck driver. To do this, Terry looked at the many different application blanks the current drivers had completed for their former companies. (These records were given to CTCI at the time of acquisition.) The application blanks showed that a large amount of information was requested, and that the specific information sought varied among the application forms. Terry scanned the various forms and made a list of all the "questions" the forms contained. He then decided to evaluate each question in terms of its probable lawfulness under federal and state (Ohio) law. Terry wanted to identify and use only lawful questions on the new form he is developing.

Shown below is the list of the "questions" Terry developed, along with columns labeled "probably lawful" and "probably unlawful." Assume that you are Terry and are deciding on the lawfulness of each question. Place a check mark in the appropriate column for each question. For each question, prepare a justification for its mark as "probably lawful" or "probably unlawful."

Questions Terry Is Considering Including on Application Blank

Question About	Probably Lawful	Probably Unlawful
Birthplace	_____	_____
Previous arrests	_____	_____
Previous felony convictions	_____	_____
Distance between work and residence	_____	_____
Domestic responsibilities	_____	_____
Height	_____	_____
Weight	_____	_____
Previous work experience	_____	_____
Educational attainment	_____	_____
High school favorite subjects	_____	_____
Grade point average	_____	_____
Received workers' compensation in past	_____	_____
Currently receiving workers' compensation	_____	_____
Child care arrangements	_____	_____
Length of time on previous job	_____	_____
Reason for leaving previous job	_____	_____
Age	_____	_____
Sex	_____	_____
Home ownership	_____	_____
Any current medical problems	_____	_____
History of mental illness	_____	_____
OK to seek references from previous employer?	_____	_____
Have you provided complete/truthful information?	_____	_____
Native language	_____	_____
Willing to work on Easter and Christmas	_____	_____
Get recommendation from pastor/priest	_____	_____

ENDNOTES

1. G. J. Myszkowski and S. Sloan, "Hiring by Blueprint," *HR Magazine,* May 1991, pp. 55–58.

2. J. W. Smither, R. R. Reilly, R. E. Millsap, K. Pearlman, and R. Stoffey, "Applicant Reactions to Selection Procedures," *Personnel Psychology,* 1993, 46, pp. 49–76.

3. P. F. Wernimont and J. P. Campbell, "Signs, Samples, and Criteria," *Journal of Applied Psychology,* 1968, 52, pp. 372–376.

4. State of Wisconsin, Chapter 134, *Evaluating Job Content for Selection,* Undated.

5. State of Wisconsin, *Evaluating Job Content for Selection.*

6. B. Kelley, "The Right Niche," *Human Resource Executive,* Jan. 1993, pp. 32–34.

7. *Cover Letters and Resume Survey,* Society for Human Resource Management, May 2000; S. Greengard, "Don't Forget to Look Down Both Ends of the Résumé Pipe," *Workforce,* July 2000, pp. 78–79; E. R. Silverman, "Resumes Become Multimedia Productions," *Wall Street Journal,* Feb. 1, 2000, p. B16; L. Stern, "Changing the Results of Résumé Writing," *Kaplan/ Newsweek,* July 2000, pp. 22–23; K. B. Wheeler, "The End of the Resume," *Employment Management Today,* Fall 1999, pp. 7–8.

8. J. E. Rigdon, "Deceptive Resumes Can Be Door-Openers, but Can Become an Employee's Undoing," *Wall Street Journal,* July 17, 1992, pp. B1, B11; A. A. Sloane, "Countering Resume Fraud Within and Beyond Banking: No Excuse for Not Doing More," *Labor Law Journal,* May 1991, pp. 303–310; W. Yu, "Firms Tighten Resume Checks of Applicants," *Wall Street Journal,* Aug. 20, 1985, p. 27.

9. C. Harlan, "He Apparently Succeeded Better Than Most of Us at Avoiding Work," *Wall Street Journal.*

10. "Beware of College Grads Willing to Lie for a Job," *HR Magazine,* Aug. 1997, pp. 22, 24.

11. "Curriculum Vitae Caveats," *Wall Street Journal,* Oct. 2, 2001, p. B8.

12. M. Brown, "Checking the Facts on a Resume," *Human Resource Measurements* (Supplement to the January 1993 *Personnel Journal*), pp. 6–7.

13. K. W. Moore, "The Most Important Things to Know About an Applicant," *Recruiting and Hiring Handbook* (Waterford, CT: Prentice Hall, 1989), pp. 4-1 to 4-8.

14. A. Howard, "College Experiences and Managerial Performance," *Journal of Applied Psychology,* 1986, 71, pp. 530–552; R. Merritt-Halston and K. Wexley, "Educational Requirements: Legality and Validity," *Personnel Psychology,* 1983, 36, pp. 743–753.

15. R. T. Schneider, *The Rating of Experience and Training: A Review of the Literature and Recommendations on the Use of Alternative E & T Procedures* (Alexandria, VA: International Personnel Management Association, 1994); J. Sullivan, "Experience—It Ain't What It Used to Be," *Public Personnel Management,* 2000, 29, pp. 511–516.

16. Wonderlic Personnel Testing, Inc., "New Employment Standards Needed as Meaning of Diploma Changes," *Human Resource Measurements,* Fall 1992, pp. 1–2.

17. S. Caudron, "Evaluating E-Degrees," *Workforce,* February 2001, pp. 61–67; R. E. Silverman, "A Hire Degree?," *Wall Street Journal,* Oct. 17, 2000, p. B16.

18. S. Alexander, "Trophy Transcript Hunters Are Finding Professors Have Become an Easy Mark," *Wall Street Journal,* Apr. 27, 1993, pp. B1, B10.

19. P. L. Roth, C. A. BeVier, F. S. Switzer, and J. S. Schippmann, "Meta-Analyzing the Relationship Between Grades and Job Performance," *Journal of Applied Psychology,* 1996, 81, pp. 548–556; P. L. Roth and P. Bobko, "College Grade Point Average as a Personnel Selection Devise: Ethnic Group Differences and Potential Adverse Impact," *Journal of Applied Psychology,* 2000, 85, pp. 399–406.

20. J. Gourman, *The Gourman Report* (Los Angeles: National Education Standards, 1994).

21. T. A. Judge, D. M. Cable, J. W. Boudreau, and R. D. Bretz, "An Empirical Investigation of the Predictors of Executive Career Success," *Personnel Psychology,* 1995, 48, pp. 485–519.

22. R. T. Schneider, *The Rating of Experience and Training: A Review of the Literature and Recommendations on the Use of Alternative E & T Procedures.*

23. R. A. Ash, "A Comparative Study of Behavioral Consistency and Holistic Judgment Methods of Job Applicant Training and Work Experience Evaluation," *Public Personnel Management,* 1984, 13, pp. 157–172; M. A. McDaniel, F. L. Schmidt, and J. E. Hunter, "A Meta-Analysis of the Validity of Methods for Rating Training and Experience in Personnel Selection," *Personnel Psychology,* 1988, 41, pp. 283–314; R. T. Schneider, *The Rating of Experience and Training: A Review of the Literature and Recommendations on the Use of Alternative E & T Procedures.*

24. C. Wiley, "The Certified HR Professional," *HR Magazine,* Aug. 1992, pp. 77–84.

25. J. McKillip and J. Owens, "Voluntary Professional Certifications: Requirements and Validation Activities," *The Industrial Organizational Psychologist,* July 2000, pp. 50–57; M. Schrage, "You're Nuts If You're Not Certified," *Fortune,* June 26, 2000, p. 338.

26. G. W. England, *Development and Use of Weighted Application Blanks* (Dubuque, IA: W. M. C. Brown, 1961).

27. J. E. Hunter and R. F. Hunter, "Validity and Utility of Alternative Predictors of Job Performance," *Psychological Bulletin,* 1984, 96, pp. 72–98.

28. I. L. Goldstein, "The Application Blank: How Honest Are the Responses?," *Journal of Applied Psychology,* 1974, 59, pp. 491–494.

29. G. W. England, *Development and Use of Weighted Application Blanks,* revised ed. (Minneapolis: University of Minnesota Industrial Relations Center, 1971).

30. B. K. Brown and M. A. Campion, "Biodata Phenomenology: Recruiters' Perceptions and Use of Biographical Information in Resume Screening," *Journal of Applied Psychology,* 1994, 79, pp. 897–908.

31. M. A. McDaniel, "Biographical Constructs for Predicting Employee Suitability," *Journal of Applied Psychology,* 1989, 74, pp. 964–970.

32. C. J. Russell, J. Mattson, S. E. Devlin, and D. Atwater, "Predictive Validity of Biodata Items Generated from Retrospective Life Experience Essays," *Journal of Applied Psychology,* 1990, 75, pp. 569–580.

33. F. A. Mael, "A Conceptual Rationale for the Domain and Attributes of Biodata Items," *Personnel Psychology,* 1991, 44, pp. 763–792.

34. J. B. Hogan, "Empirical Keying of Background Data Measures," in G. S. Stokes, M. D. Mumford, and W. A. Owens (eds.), *Biodata Handbook* (Palo Alto, CA: CPP Books, 1994), pp. 69–107.

35. E. E. Ghiselli, J. P. Campbell, and S. Zedeck, *Measurement Theory for the Behavioral Sciences* (San Francisco: W. H. Freeman, 1981).

36. D. J. Whitney and N. Schmitt, "Relationship Between Culture and Responses to Biodata Employment Items," *Journal of Applied Psychology,* 1998, 83, pp. 113–129.

37. M. D. Mumford, "Construct Validity and Background Data: Issues, Abuses, and Future Directions," *Human Resource Management Review,* 1999, 9, pp. 117–145; L. F. Schoenfeldt, "From Dust Bowl Empiricism to Rational Constructs in Biographical Data," *Human Resource Management Review,* 1999, 9, pp. 147–167; N. Schmitt, D. Jennings, and R. Toney, "Can We Develop Measures of Hypothetical Constructs," *Human Resource Management Review,* 1999, 9, pp. 169–183; G. S. Stokes, C. S. Toth, C. A. Searcy, J. P. Stroupe, and G. W. Carter, "Construct/Rational Biodata Dimensions to Predict Salesperson Performance: Report on the U.S. Department of Labor Sales Study," *Human Resource Management Review,* 1999, 9, pp. 185–218.

38. F. A. Mael and A. C. Hirsch, "Rainforest Empiricism and Quasi-Rationality: Two Approaches to Objective Data," *Personnel Psychology,* 1993, 46, pp. 719–738.

39. L. M. Hough, M. A. Keyes, and M. D. Dunnette, "An Evaluation of Three 'Alternative' Selection Procedures," *Personnel Psychology,* 1983, 36, pp. 261–276; S. Landers, "PACE to be Replaced with Biographical Test," *The APA Monitor,* 1989, 20(4), p. 14; C. J. Russell, J. Matt-

son, S. E. Devlin, and D. Atwater, "Predictive Validity of Biodata Items Generated from Retrospective Life Experience Essays."

40. See M. D. Mumford and G. S. Stokes, "Developmental Determinants of Individual Action: Theory and Practice in Applying Background Measures," in M. D. Dunnette and L. M. Hough (eds.), *Handbook of Industrial and Organizational Psychology,* second ed., vol. 3 (Palo Alto, CA: Consulting Psychologists Press, 1993), pp. 61–138.

41. J. E. Hunter and R. F. Hunter, "Validity and Utility of Alternative Predictors of Job Performance"; R. R. Reilly and G. T. Chao, "Validity and Fairness of Some Alternative Selection Procedures," *Personnel Psychology,* 1982, 35, pp. 1–62.

42. H. R. Rothstein, F. L. Schmidt, F. W. Erwin, W. A. Owens, and C. P. Sparks, "Biographical Data in Employment Selection: Can Validities Be Made Generalizable?," *Journal of Applied Psychology,* 1990, 75, pp. 175–184; K. D. Carlson, S. Sculten, F. L. Schmidt, H. Rothstein, and F. Erwin, "Generalizable Biographical Data Validity Can Be Achieved Without Multi-Organizational Development and Keying," *Personnel Psychology,* 1999, 52, pp. 731–755.

43. F. A. Mael, "A Conceptual Rationale for the Domain and Attributes of Biodata Items"; M. L. Tenopyr, "Big Five, Structural Modeling, and Item Response Theory," in G. S. Stokes, M. D. Mumford, and W. A. Owens (eds.), *Biodata Handbook* (Palo Alto, CA: CPP Books, 1994), pp. 519–533; M. K. Mount, L. A. Witt, and M. R. Barrick, "Incremental Validity of Empirically Keyed Biodata Scales over GMA and the Five Factor Personality Constructs," *Personnel Psychology,* 2000, 53, pp. 299–323.

44. M. K. Mount, L. A. Witt, and M. R. Barrick, "Incremental Validity of Empirically Keyed Biodata Scales over GMA and the Five Factor Personality Constructs."

45. T. E. Becker and A. L. Colquitt, "Potential versus Actual Faking of a Biodata Form: An Analysis Along Several Dimensions of Item Type," *Personnel Psychology,* 1992, 45, pp. 389–406.

46. A. N. Kluger and A. Colella, "Beyond the Mean Bias: The Effect of Warning Against Faking on Biodata Item Variances," *Personnel Psychology,* 1993, 46, pp. 763–780.

47. A. N. Kluger, R. R. Reilly, and C. J. Russell, "Faking Biodata Tests: Are Option-Keyed Instruments More Resistant?" *Journal of Applied Psychology,* 1991, 76, pp. 689–696.

48. G. S. Stokes, J. B. Hogan, and A. F. Snell, "Comparability of Incumbent and Applicant Samples for the Development of Biodata Keys: The Influence of Social Desirability," *Personnel Psychology,* 1993, 46, pp. 739–762.

49. G. S. Stokes, J. B. Hogan, and A. F. Snell, "Comparability of Incumbent and Applicant Samples for the Development of Biodata Keys: The Influence of Social Desirability."

50. T. A. Judge, D. Blancero, D. M. Cable, and D. E. Johnson, "Effects of Selection Systems on Job Search Decisions," Paper presented at the Tenth Annual Conference of the Society for Industrial and Organizational Psychology, 1995, Orlando, FL; J. W. Smither, R. R. Reilly, R. E. Millsap, K. Pearlman, and R. Stoffey, "Applicant Reactions to Selection Procedures."

51. D. A. Kravitz, V. Stinson, and T. L. Chavez, "Evaluations of Tests Used for Making Selection and Promotion Decisions," *International Journal of Selection and Assessment,* 1996, 4, pp. 24–34.

52. F. A. Mael, M. Connerley, and R. A. Morath, "None of Your Business: Parameters of Biodata Invasiveness," *Personnel Psychology,* 1996, pp. 613–650.

53. P. M. Muchinsky, "The Use of Reference Reports in Personnel Selection: A Review and Evaluation," *Journal of Occupational Psychology,* 1979, 52, pp. 287–297.

54. J. C. Baxter, B. Brock, P. C. Hill, and R. M. Rozelle, "Letters of Recommendation: A Question of Value," *Journal of Applied Psychology,* 1981, 66, pp. 296–301.

55. T. A. Judge and C. A. Higgins, "Affective Disposition and the Letter of Reference," *Organizational Behavior and Human Decision Processes,* 1998, 75, pp. 207–221.

56. M. D. Liberatore, "Most Organizations Use Background Checks as Prescreening Tools," *Human Resource Executive,* May 2, 2000, p. 37.

57. C. S. White and L. S. Kleiman, "The Cost of Candid Comments," *HR Magazine,* Aug. 1991, pp. 54–56.

58. J. Click, "SHRM Survey Highlights Dilemmas of Reference Checks," *HR News,* July 1995, p. 13.

59. E. Tahmincioglu, "Terse Employers Step Up Background Checks," *New York Times,* October 3, 2001, p. B3.

60. R. Cohen, "In France, It's How You Cross the t's," *New York Times,* Oct. 19, 1993, pp. D1–D2; B. Leonard, "Reading Employees," *HR Magazine,* April 1999, pp. 67–73.

61. "Hiring: Voodoo Job Screening," *Inc.,* 1994, 16, pp. 133.

62. A. Rafaeli and R. Klimoski, "Predicting Sales Success Through Handwriting Analysis: An Evaluation on the Effects of Training and Handwriting Sample Content," *Journal of Applied Psychology,* 1983, 68, pp. 212–217.

63. G. Ben-Shakhar, M. Bar-Hillel, Y. Bilu, E. Ben-Abba, and A. Flug, "Can Graphology Predict Occupational Success? Two Empirical Studies and Some Methodological Ruminations," *Journal of Applied Psychology,* 1986, 71, pp. 645–653.

64. K. Miller, "At GM, the Three R's Are the Big Three," *Wall Street Journal,* July 3, 1992, p. D1.

65. S. Schwartz (ed.), *Measuring Reading Competence: A Theoretical Prescriptive Approach* (New York: Praeger, 1985).

66. "Assessing Writing Skills," *The Industrial/Organizational Psychologist,* 1992, 30, pp. 27–28.

67. Office of Technology Assessment, *Genetic Monitoring and Screening in the Workplace* (Washington, DC: U.S. Congress, 1990).

68. S. Dentzer, B. Cohn, G. Raine, G. Carroll, and V. Quade, "Can You Pass This Job Test?" *Newsweek,* May 5, 1986, pp. 46–53.

69. V. Kiernan, "US Bans Gene Prejudice at Work," *New Scientist,* 1995, 146, p. 4.

70. M. Minehan, "The Growing Debate over Genetic Testing," *HR Magazine,* April 1998, p. 208.

71. L. Thornburg, "Computer-Assisted Interviewing Shortens Hiring Cycle," *HR Magazine,* Feb. 1998, pp. 73–79.

72. I. L. Goldstein, "The Application Blank: How Honest Are the Responses?"; W. Keichel, "Lies on the Resume," *Fortune,* Aug. 23, 1982, pp. 221–222, 224; J. N. Mosel and L. W. Cozan, "The Accuracy of Application Blank Work Histories," *Journal of Applied Psychology,* 1952, 36, pp. 365–369.

73. R. A. Ash and E. L. Levine, "Job Applicant Training and Work Experience Evaluation: An Empirical Comparison of Four Methods," *Journal of Applied Psychology,* 1985, 70, pp. 572–576.

74. G. P. Latham and G. Whyte, "The Futility of Utility Analysis," *Personnel Psychology,* 1994, 47, pp. 31–46.

75. J. W. Smither, R. R. Reilly, R. E. Millsap, K. Pearlman, and R. Stoffey, "Applicant Reactions to Selection Procedures."

76. S. W. Gilliland, "Fairness from the Applicant's Perspective: Reactions to Employee Selection Procedures," *International Journal of Selection and Assessment,* 1995, 3, pp. 11–19.

77. D. A. Kravitz, V. Stinson, and T. L. Chavez, "Evaluations of Tests Used for Making Selection and Promotion Decisions"; D. D. Steiner and S. W. Gilliland, "Fairness Reactions to Personnel Selection Techniques in France and the United States," *Journal of Applied Psychology,* 1996, 81, pp. 134–141.

78. G. P. Panaro, *Employment Law Manual,* second ed. (Boston: Warren Gorham Lamont, 1993), pp. 1-29 to 1-42.

79. G. P. Panaro, *Employment Law Manual,* 1993, pp. 2-101 to 2-106; J. E. Bahls, "Available upon Request," *HR Magazine Focus,* Jan. 1999, p. 206; W. M. Mercer, Inc., "Hazards of Giving Employee Health References," *The Mercer Report,* July 22, 1998, p. 8.

80. R. D. Arvey and R. H. Faley, *Fairness in Selecting Employees,* second ed. (Reading, MA: Addison-Wesley, 1998), pp. 251–310.

81. S. J. Vodanovich and R. H. Lowe, "They Ought to Know Better: The Incidence and Correlates of Inappropriate Application Blank Inquiries," *Public Personnel Management,* 1992, 21, pp. 363–370.

82. Bureau of National Affairs, "EEOC Guide to Pre-Employment Inquiries," *Fair Employment Practices* (Washington, DC: author, periodically updated), pp. 443:65–80.

83. Bureau of National Affairs, "EEOC Guide to Pre-Employment Inquiries," pp. 443:65–80.

84. Equal Employment Opportunity Commission, *ADA Enforcement Guidance: Pre-Employment Disability Related Questions and Medical Examinations* (Washington, DC: author, 1995).

85. Bureau of National Affairs, *Fair Employment Practices* (Washington, DC: author, periodically updated), 454: whole section.

86. Bureau of National Affairs, *Fair Employment Practices,* pp. 421:352–356.

87. N. J. Sedmak and M. D. Levin-Epstein, *Primer on Equal Employment Opportunity* (Washington, DC: Bureau of National Affairs, 1991), pp. 36–40.

88. Bureau of National Affairs, *Fair Employment Practices,* pp. 405:6941–6943.

CHAPTER NINE

External Selection II

Substantive Assessment Methods
Personality Tests
Ability Tests
Job Knowledge Tests
Performance Tests and Work Samples
Integrity Tests
Interest, Values, and Preference Inventories
Structured Interview
Constructing a Structured Interview
Assessment for Team and Quality Environments
Clinical Assessments
Choice of Substantive Assessment Methods

Discretionary Assessment Methods

Contingent Assessment Methods
Drug Testing
Medical Exams

Legal Issues
Uniform Guidelines on Employee Selection Procedures
Selection Under the Americans With Disabilities Act (ADA)
Drug Testing

Summary

Discussion Questions

Applications

The previous chapter reviewed preliminary issues surrounding external staffing decisions made in organizations, including the use of initial assessment methods. This chapter continues the discussion of external selection by discussing in some detail substantive assessment methods. The use of discretionary and contingent assessment methods, collection of assessment data, and legal issues will also be considered.

Whereas initial assessment methods are used to reduce the applicant pool to candidates, substantive assessment methods are used to reduce the candidate pool to finalists for the job. Thus, the use of substantive methods is often more involved than using initial methods. Numerous substantive assessment methods will be discussed in depth, including various tests (personality, ability, job knowledge, performance/work samples, integrity); interest, values, and preference inventories; structured interviews; assessment for team and quality environments; and clinical assessments. The average validity (i.e., $\bar{r}$) of each method and the criteria used to choose among methods will be reviewed.

Discretionary assessment methods are used in some circumstances to separate those who receive job offers from the list of finalists. The applicant characteristics that are assessed when using discretionary methods are sometimes very subjective. Several of the characteristics most commonly assessed by discretionary methods will be reviewed.

Contingent assessment methods are used to make sure that tentative offer recipients meet certain qualifications for the job. Although any assessment method can be used as a contingent method (e.g., licensing/certification requirements, background checks), perhaps the two most common contingent methods are drug tests and medical exams. These procedures will be reviewed.

All forms of assessment decisions require the collection of assessment data. The procedures used to make sure this process is properly conducted will be reviewed. In particular, several issues will be discussed, including support services, training requirements in using various predictors, maintaining security and confidentiality, and the importance of standardized procedures.

Finally, many important legal issues surround the use of substantive, discretionary, and contingent methods of selection. The most important of these issues will be reviewed. Particular attention will be given to the Uniform Guidelines on Employee Selection Procedures and staffing requirements under the Americans With Disabilities Act.

SUBSTANTIVE ASSESSMENT METHODS

Organizations use initial assessment methods to make "rough cuts" among applicants—weeding out the obviously unqualified. Conversely, substantive assessment methods are used to make more precise decisions about applicants—among those who meet minimum qualifications for the job, which are the most likely to be high performers if hired? Because substantive methods are used to make fine distinctions among applicants, the nature of their use is somewhat more involved than initial assessment methods. As with initial assessment methods, however, substantive assessment methods are developed using the logic of prediction outlined in Exhibit 8.1 and the selection plan shown in Exhibit 8.2. Predictors typically used to select finalists from the candidate pool include personality tests, ability tests, job knowledge tests, performance tests and work samples, interest, values, and preference inventories, structured interviews, team/quality assessments, and clinical assessments. Each of these predictors is described next in some detail.

Personality Tests

Until recently, personality tests were not perceived as a valid selection method. Historically, most studies estimated the validity of personality tests to be between .10 and .15, which would rank them among the poorest predictors of job performance—only marginally better than a coin toss.[1] Starting with the publication of an influential review in the 1960s, personality tests were not viewed favorably, nor were they widely used.[2]

There are several reasons why personality tests had such a dismal record of success. Perhaps the most important factor was that there was no accepted taxonomy of personality for use in selection. Thus, some studies related personality measures to job performance when there was no reason to believe the measure was appropriate to predict job performance. Perhaps the best example of this is the *Minnesota Multiphasic Personality Inventory* (MMPI), which until relatively recently was the most common personality test used for selection decisions. The use of the MMPI to predict job performance always was (and still is) an inappropriate application for nearly all jobs. The MMPI was never intended to be used as a selection tool. Rather, it was developed and validated as an instrument to diagnose severe psychological disorders (e.g., schizophrenia), as the items readily illustrate ("I often feel as if one of my limbs will fall off," "There are persons who try to steal my thoughts and ideas"). In short, the MMPI does a good job of measuring mental imbalance, but screening out the few (if any) individuals in the applicant pool who suffer from, say, psychopathic deviance, is unlikely to be a useful method of making selection decisions. Thus, when inappropriate measures are used to assess traits generally unrelated to job performance, the results are (predictably) very poor.

Recent advances, however, have suggested much more positive conclusions about the role of personality tests in predicting job performance. Mainly, this is due to the widespread acceptance of a major taxonomy of personality, often called the Big Five. The Big Five is used to describe behavioral (as opposed to emotional or cognitive) traits that may capture up to 75% of an individual's personality. The Big Five factors are *emotional stability* (disposition to be calm, optimistic, and well adjusted), *extraversion* (tendency to be sociable, assertive, active, upbeat, and talkative), *openness to experience* (tendency to be imaginative, attentive to inner feelings, have intellectual curiosity and independence of judgment), *agreeableness* (tendency to be altruistic, trusting, sympathetic, and cooperative), and *conscientiousness* (tendency to be purposeful, determined, dependable, and attentive to detail). The Big Five are a reduced set of many more specific traits. The Big Five are very stable over time, and there is even research to suggest a strong genetic basis of the Big Five traits (roughly 50% of the variance in the Big Five traits appears to be inherited).[3] Because job performance is a broad concept that comprises many specific behaviors, it will be best predicted by broad dispositions such as the Big Five. In fact, some research evidence supports this proposition.[4]

Measures of Personality

Measures of personality traits can be surveys, projective techniques, or interviews. Most personality measures used in personnel selection are surveys. There are several survey measures of the Big Five traits that are used in selection. The *Personal Characteristics Inventory* (PCI) is a self-report measure of the Big Five that asks applicants to report their agreement or disagreement (using a "strongly disagree" to "strongly agree" scale) with 150 sentences.[5] The measure takes about 30 minutes to complete and has a 5th- to 6th-grade reading level. Exhibit 9.1 provides sample items from the PCI. Another commonly used measure of the Big Five is the *NEO Personality Inventory* (NEO), of which there are several versions that have been translated into numerous languages.[6] A third alternative is the *Hogan Personality Inventory* (HPI), which also is based on the Big Five typology. Responses to the HPI can be scored to yield measures of employee reliability and service orientation.[7] All three of these measures have shown validity in predicting job performance in various occupations.

Although surveys are the most common means of assessing personality, other methods have been used, such as projective tests and interviews. However, with few exceptions (e.g., the *Miner Sentence Completion Scale* has shown validity in predicting managerial performance[8]), the reliability and validity of projective tests and interviews as methods of personality assessment are questionable at best. Thus, survey measures in general, and the Big Five measures in particular, are the most reliable and valid means of personality testing for selection decisions.

Evaluation of Personality Tests

Many comprehensive reviews of the validity of personality tests have been published. Nearly all of the recent reviews focus on the validity of the Big Five. Although there has been a debate over inconsistencies in these studies, the largest-scale study revealed the following:

EXHIBIT 9.1   Sample Items for Personal Characteristics Inventory

Conscientiousness
I can always be counted on to get the job done.
I am a very persistent worker.
I almost always plan things in advance of work.

Extraversion
Meeting new people is enjoyable to me.
I like to stir up excitement if things get boring.
I am a "take charge" type of person.

Agreeableness
I like to help others who are down on their luck.
I usually see the good side of people.
I forgive others easily.

Emotional Stability
I can become annoyed at people quite easily (reverse-scored).
At times I don't care about much of anything (reverse-scored).
My feelings tend to be easily hurt (reverse-scored).

Openness to Experience
I like to work with difficult concepts and ideas.
I enjoy trying new and different things.
I tend to enjoy art, music, or literature.

Source: M. K. Mount and M. R. Barrick, *Manual for the Personal Characteristics Inventory* (December, 1995). Reprinted with permission of the Wonderlic Personnel Test, Inc.

1. Conscientiousness predicts performance across all occupational groupings.[9]
2. Emotional stability predicts performance in most occupations, especially sales, management, and teaching.[10]
3. Extraversion predicts performance of salespeople.[11]
4. In a meta-analysis of studies in Europe, conscientiousness and emotional stability emerged as significant predictors of performance.[12]

More recent evidence further supports the validity of conscientiousness in predicting job performance. A recent update to the original findings suggested that the validity of conscientiousness in predicting overall job performance is $\bar{r} = .31$, and it seems to predict many specific facets of performance (training proficiency, reliability, quality of work, administration).[13] The conclusion that conscientiousness is a valid predictor of job performance across all types of jobs and organizations studied is significant. Previously, researchers believed that personality was valid only for *some* jobs in *some* situations. These results suggest that conscientiousness is important to job performance whether the job is working on an assembly line or selling automotive parts or driving trucks.

Why is conscientiousness predictive of performance? Exhibit 9.2 provides some possible answers.[14] When employees have autonomy, research shows that conscientious employees set higher work goals for themselves and are more committed to achieving the goals they set. Also, conscientiousness is an integral part of integrity, and two of the key components of conscientiousness, achievement and dependability, are related to reduced levels of irresponsible job behaviors (e.g., absenteeism, insubordination, use of drugs on job). Conscientiousness also predicts work effort and is associated with ambition. Further, conscientious individuals are more technically proficient in their jobs and more organized and thorough.

EXHIBIT 9.2   Possible Factors Explaining the Importance of Conscientiousness in Predicting Job Performance

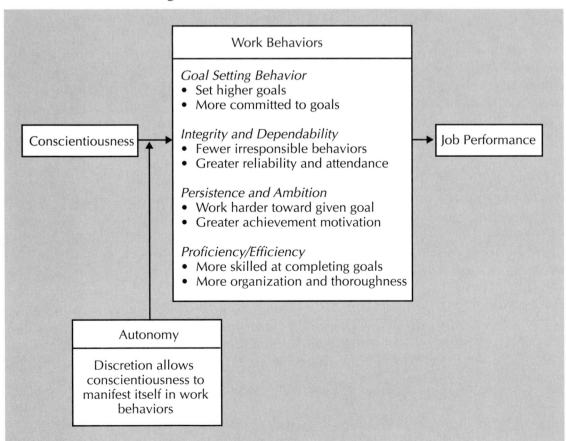

Thus, conscientiousness predicts job performance well because it is associated with a range of attitudes and behaviors that are important to job success.

Beyond conscientiousness, is there a role for the other Big Five traits in selection? Except for emotional stability, the other traits do not predict job performance. In considering the validity of other elements of the Big Five, it is possible that they are too broad and that to predict specific work behaviors, more fine-grained traits are necessary.[15] When predicting criteria more specific than overall job performance, this is undoubtedly true. For example, measures of compliance, trust, and dutifulness (all are subfacets of the NEO) might do a better job of predicting attendance than any of the five general traits. Similarly, the tendency to fantasize or be original or be creative may better predict creative work behaviors than the general openness to experience factor. Furthermore, even among the Big Five, each of the traits is probably predictive of performance in certain types of jobs. For example, agreeableness may be an important trait in predicting the performance of customer service representatives, but the same level of agreeableness might actually be a liability for a bill collector! Openness to experience might be important for artists, inventors, or those in advertising, while it has been argued that conscientiousness is a liability for jobs requiring creativity.[16] Thus, the key is to match traits, both in terms of type and level of generality, to the criteria that are being predicted. Research indicates that such strategies make personality tests valid methods of selection.[17]

Increasingly, consulting firms are marketing personality tests that assess applicants' personalities with respect to particular criteria. For example, several tests assess applicants in terms of service orientation (helpful disposition, cooperative tendencies, nonconfrontational disposition). Other criterion-related personality tests include employee reliability, sales potential, and motivation. Some are so specific as to be tailored to service orientation in particular industries (health care, telemarketing, customer service). Another, related approach is to tailor items with work "tags." For example, the item "I am always on time" might be adapted as "I am always on time at work." Another refinement that has been proposed is the use of job analysis information to match the Big Five traits to relevant dimensions of job performance. Although these approaches to further adding to the validity of personality tests have not been studied extensively, initial evidence on each approach—assessing personality with respect to specific work behaviors or criteria (e.g., service orientation), adding work "tags" to personality test items, and matching Big Five traits to dimensions of job performance shows increased validity.[18]

With respect to emotional stability, evidence indicates that this trait is a much more valid predictor of job performance when it is assessed broadly. Most measures of emotional stability substantially assess anxiety, stress-proneness, and susceptibility to psychological disorders. Such items may be appropriate screens for certain situations, such as public-safety or security-sensitive positions. However, for many occupations, the aspect of emotional stability that may be more relevant to job performance is positive self-concept, or the degree to which individuals feel positively about themselves and their capabilities. Indeed, research suggests that traits that reflect positive self-concept, such as self-esteem, are better predictors of job performance than typical measures of emotional stability.

Researchers have argued that for measures of emotional stability to be as useful as they might, emotional stability needs to be assessed broadly, and specifically needs to include assessment of individuals' beliefs in their worthiness, capabilities, and competence. One measure that assesses these characteristics is the Core Self-Evaluations Scale. This measure is shown in Exhibit 9.3. Research indicates that core self-evaluations is predictive of job performance, and the Core Self-Evaluations Scale appears to have validity equivalent to that of conscientiousness. Thus, organizations that wish to use personality testing should consider supplementing their measures of emotional stability with the Core Self-Evaluations Scale. A further advantage of this measure is that it is nonproprietary (free).[19]

EXHIBIT 9.3   The Core Self-Evaluations Scale

Instructions: Below are several statements about you with which you may agree or disagree. Using the response scale below, indicate your agreement or disagreement with each item by placing the appropriate number on the line preceding that item.

1	2	3	4	5
Strongly Disagree	Disagree	Neutral	Agree	Strongly Agree

1. ____ I am confident I get the success I deserve in life.
2. ____ Sometimes I feel depressed. (r)
3. ____ When I try, I generally succeed.
4. ____ Sometimes when I fail, I feel worthless. (r)
5. ____ I complete tasks successfully.
6. ____ Sometimes I do not feel in control of my work. (r)
7. ____ Overall, I am satisfied with myself.
8. ____ I am filled with doubts about my compentence. (r)
9. ____ I determine what will happen in my life.
10. ____ I do not feel in control of my success in my career. (r)
11. ____ I am capable of coping with most of my problems.
12. ____ There are times when things look pretty bleak and hopeless to me. (r)

Note: r = reverse-scored (for these items, 5 is scored 1, 4 is scored 2, 2 is scored 4, and 1 is scored 5).

Source: T. A. Judge, A. Erez, J. E. Bono, and C. J. Thoresen, "The Core Self-Evaluations Scale: Development of a Measure," Working paper, University of Florida, 2001.

Though personality testing is in much better standing in selection research, some limitations need to be kept in mind. First, there is some concern that applicants may distort their responses. This concern is apparent when one considers the items (see Exhibit 9.1) and the nature of the traits. Few individuals would want to describe themselves as disagreeable, neurotic, closed to new experiences, and unconscientious. Furthermore, since answers to these questions are nearly impossible to verify (e.g., imagine trying to verify whether an applicant really prefers reading a book to watching television), the possibility of "faking good" is quite real. In fact, research suggests that applicants can enhance or even fake their responses if they are motivated to do so. Given that a job is on the line when applicants complete a personality test, the tendency to enhance is undeniable. Although applicants do try to look good by enhancing their responses to personality tests, it seems clear that such enhancement does not significantly detract from the validity of the tests. Furthermore, it does not appear that correcting scores based on applicant scores on social desirability is effective.[20] On the other hand, one study indicated that if hiring was limited to the top 5% of applicants on the NEO measure of conscientiousness, seven of eight people hired would have extreme scores on a measure of response distortion.[21] Thus, it is possible that many top-scoring applicants have distorted their responses to personality tests, but such applicants may be high performers despite (or even because of) their tendencies to distort. More research is needed on this issue.

Finally, it is important to evaluate personality tests not only in terms of their validity but also from the applicant's perspective. From an applicant's standpoint, the subjective and personal nature of the questions asked in these tests may cause questions about their validity and concerns about invasiveness. In fact, the available evidence concerning applicants' perceptions of personality tests suggests that they are viewed negatively. One study reported that 46% of applicants had no idea how a personality test could be interpreted by organizations, and 31% could not imagine how qualifications could be assessed with a personality inventory.[22] Similarly, another study found that newly hired managers perceived personality tests as the 13th least-valid predictor of job performance of 14 selection tools.[23] Other studies suggest that applicants believe personality tests are invasive and unnecessary for companies to make accurate selection decisions.[24] Thus, while personality tests—when used properly—do have validity, this validity does not seem to translate into favorable applicant perceptions. More research is needed into the ways that these tests could be made more acceptable to applicants.

Ability Tests

Ability tests are measures that assess an individual's capacity to function in a certain way. There are two major types of ability tests: aptitude and achievement. Aptitude tests look at a person's innate capacity to function, whereas achievement tests assess a person's learned capacity to function. In practice, these types of abilities are often difficult to separate. Thus, it is not clear this is a productive, practical distinction for ability tests used in selection.

Surveys reveal that between 15% and 20% of organizations use some sort of ability test in selection decisions.[25] Organizations that use ability tests do so because they assume the tests assess a key determinant of employee performance. Without a certain level of ability, innate or learned, performance is unlikely to be acceptable, regardless of motivation. Someone may try extremely hard to do well in a very difficult class (e.g., calculus), but will not succeed unless they have the ability to do so (e.g., mathematical aptitude).

There are four major classes of ability tests: cognitive, psychomotor, physical, and sensory/perceptual.[26] As these ability tests are quite distinct, each will be considered separately below. Because most of the research attention—and public controversy—has focused on cognitive ability tests, they are discussed below in considerable detail.

Cognitive Ability Tests

Cognitive ability tests refer to measures that assess abilities involved in thinking, including perception, memory, reasoning, verbal and mathematical abilities, and the expression of ideas. Is cognitive ability a general construct or does it have a number of specific aspects? Research shows that measures of specific cognitive abilities, such as verbal, quantitative, reasoning, and so on, appear to reflect general intelligence (sometimes referred to as IQ or "g").[27] One of the facts that best illustrates this finding is the relatively high correlations between scores on measures of specific facets of intelligence. Someone who scores well on a measure of one specific ability is more likely to score well on measures of other specific abilities. In other words, general intelligence causes individuals to have similar scores on measures of specific abilities.

Measures of Cognitive Ability   There are many cognitive ability tests that measure both specific cognitive abilities and general mental ability. Many test publishers offer an array of tests. For example, The Psychological Corporation sells the *Employee Aptitude Survey*, a test of 10 specific cognitive abilities (e.g., verbal comprehension, numerical ability, numerical and verbal reasoning, word fluency, etc.). Each of these specific tests is sold separately and each takes no more than five minutes to administer to applicants. Each of the 10 specific tests is sold in packages of 25 for about $44 per package. The Psychological Corporation also sells the *Wonderlic Personnel Test*, perhaps the most widely used test of general mental ability for selection decisions. The Wonderlic is a 12-minute, 50-item test. Items range in type from spatial relations to numerical problems to analogies. Exhibit 9.4 provides examples of items from one of the forms of the Wonderlic. In addition to being a speed (timed) test, the Wonderlic is also a power test—the items get harder as the test progresses (very few individuals complete all 50 items). The Wonderlic has been administered to more than 2.5 million

EXHIBIT 9.4   Sample Cognitive Ability Test Items

Look at the row of numbers below. What number should come next?

8   4   2   1   1/2   1/4   ?

Assume the first 2 statements are true. Is the final one: (1) true, (2) false, (3) not certain?

The boy plays baseball. All baseball players wear hats. The boy wears a hat.

One of the numbered figures in the following drawing is most different from the others. What is the number in that drawing?

A train travels 20 feet in 1/5 second. At this same speed, how many feet will it travel in three seconds?

How many of the six pairs of items listed below are exact duplicates?

3421	1243
21212	21212
558956	558956
10120210	10120210
612986896	612986896
356471201	356571201

The hours of daylight and darkness in SEPTEMBER are nearest equal to the hours of daylight and darkness in

(1) June   (2) March   (3) May   (4) November

Source: Reprinted with permission from C. F. Wonderlic Personnel Test, Inc., *1992 Catalog: Employment Tests, Forms, and Procedures* (Libertyville, IL: author—Charles F. Wonderlic, 1992).

applicants and normative data are available from a database of more than 450,000 individuals. Cost of the Wonderlic ranges from approximately $1.50 to $3.50 per applicant, depending on whether the organization scores the test itself. Costs of other cognitive ability tests are similar. Although cognitive ability tests are not entirely costless, they are among the least expensive of any substantive assessment method.

There are many other tests and test publishers in addition to those reviewed above. Before deciding which test to use, organizations should seek out a reputable testing firm. An association of test publishers has been formed with bylaws to help ensure this process.[28] It is also advisable to seek out the advice of researchers or testing specialists. Many of these individuals are members of the American Psychological Association or the American Psychological Society. Guidelines are available that can serve as a guide in deciding which test to use.[29]

Evaluation of Cognitive Ability Tests

The findings regarding general intelligence have had profound implications for personnel selection. A number of meta-analyses have been conducted on the validity of cognitive ability tests. Although the validities found in these studies have fluctuated to some extent, the most comprehensive reviews have estimated the "true" validity of measures of general cognitive ability to be roughly $\bar{r} = .50$.[30] The conclusions from these meta-analyses are dramatic:

1. Cognitive ability tests are among the most valid, if not *the* most valid, methods of selection.
2. Cognitive ability tests appear to generalize across all organizations, all job types, and all types of applicants; thus, they are likely to be valid in virtually any selection context.
3. Organizations using cognitive ability tests in selection enjoy large economic gains compared to organizations that do not use them.

These conclusions are not simply esoteric speculations from the ivory tower. They are based on hundreds of studies of hundreds of organizations employing hundreds of thousands of workers. Thus, whether an organization is selecting engineers, customer service representatives, or meat cutters, general mental ability is likely the single most valid method of selecting among applicants. A large-scale quantitative review of the literature suggested relatively high average validities for many occupational groups:[31]

- manager, $\bar{r} = .53$
- clerk, $\bar{r} = .54$
- salesperson, $\bar{r} = .61$
- protective professional, $\bar{r} = .42$
- service worker, $\bar{r} = .48$
- trades and crafts, $\bar{r} = .46$
- elementary industrial worker, $\bar{r} = .37$
- vehicle operator, $\bar{r} = .28$
- sales clerk, $\bar{r} = .27$

These results show that cognitive ability tests have some degree of validity for all types of jobs. The validity is particularly high for complex jobs (i.e., manager, engineer), but even for simple jobs the validity is positive. The same review also revealed that cognitive ability tests have very high degrees of validity in predicting training success ($\bar{r} = .37$ for vehicle operators to $\bar{r} = .87$ for protective professionals). This is due to the substantial learning component of training and the obvious fact that smart people learn more.[32]

Whereas cognitive ability tests are more valid for jobs of medium (e.g., police officers, salespersons) and high (e.g., computer programmers, pilots) complexity, they are valid even for jobs of relatively low complexity (e.g., bus driver, factory worker). Why are cognitive ability tests predictive even for relatively simple jobs where intelligence would not appear to be an important attribute? The fact is that some degree of intelligence is important for *any* type of job. The validity of cognitive ability tests even seems to generalize to performance on and of athletic teams (see Exhibit 9.5). In addition to performance as a professional football player, one study also found that college basketball teams high in cognitive ability performed better than teams low in cognitive ability.[33] Thus, cognitive ability may be unimportant to performance in some jobs, but, if this is true, we have yet to find them.

Take the example of the job of garbage collector in Tallahassee, Florida. In Tallahassee, the city supplies each household with a large garbage can, which residents normally place in their backyard. Rather than asking residents to place this garbage can curbside prior to collection, garbage collectors are required to locate each garbage can, haul it to the truck, and replace it when finished. This practice continued until one day a new employee figured out that the workload

---

EXHIBIT 9.5 Cognitive Ability Testing in the National Football League

Lest you think cognitive ability testing is used only to select applicants for unimportant jobs such as rocket scientists or nuclear engineers, completing the *Wonderlic Personnel Test* is an important part of the selection process in the National Football League (NFL). In fact, use of the Wonderlic in the NFL has been likened to use of the SAT or ACT among universities. The NFL uses the Wonderlic as one component in its physical and mental screening of potential draft picks. Most teams rely on Wonderlic scores, to varying degrees, in making draft decisions. The major justification for use of these tests is a belief that players need intelligence to understand the increasingly complex NFL playbooks. NFL officials believe this to be particularly true for positions that rely heavily on the playbook, namely, quarterback and offensive lineman.

The average NFL draftee score is 20 compared to 21 for the population as a whole. Quarterbacks and centers score the highest of players in all positions. Offensive players tend to do better than defensive players. Some teams even have cutoff scores for different positions. For example, one team used to require quarterbacks to score 25 on the Wonderlic compared to a cutoff of only 12 for wide receivers. Cutoffs seem to be highest for quarterbacks and offensive linemen.

Of course, like all selection methods, cognitive ability tests have their limits. George Young, General Manager of the New York Giants, was the individual responsible for convincing the NFL to use the Wonderlic. He recalls a game where a defensive lineman with an IQ of 90 went up against an offensive lineman with a 150 IQ. According to Young, "The defensive lineman told the offensive lineman, 'Don't worry. After I hit you a few times, you'll be just as dumb as I am.'"

Source: Adapted from R. Hofer, "Get Smart," *Sports Illustrated*, Sept. 5, 1994; B. Plaschke and E. Almond, "Has NFL Draft Become Thinking Man's Game?" *Los Angeles Times*, April 21, 1995.

could be cut nearly in half by hauling the last household's emptied garbage can into the next household's backyard, replacing this household's full garbage can with the last household's empty one, and continuing this procedure for each household.[34] The economic benefit to the city of Tallahassee of this action is undoubtedly substantial. It is likely that this intelligent action was the product of an intelligent person. This example illustrates how intelligence can be a critical performance factor in even the most seemingly cognitively simple jobs. Exhibit 9.6 provides another example of common misconceptions about cognitive ability.

Why do cognitive ability tests work so well in predicting job performance? Research has shown that most of the effect of cognitive ability tests is due to the fact that intelligent employees have greater job knowledge.[35] Another important issue in understanding the validity of cognitive ability tests is the nature of specific versus general abilities. As was noted earlier, measures of specific abilities are

---

EXHIBIT 9.6   Can You Be Too Smart for a Job?

Can one be *too* smart? Robert Jordan applied to join the New London, Connecticut, police force, and he was administered the *Wonderlic Personnel Test*. When he called back to see how he did, he was told he scored very high (33 out of 50, which would be in the top 1% of scorers), in fact, too high. Jordan was disqualified on the basis of his "higher than recommended" score on the cognitive ability test. Bruce Rinehart, New London's chief of police, defended the decision. "Police work, believe it or not, is a boring job," Rinehart commented, , "What happens if you get certain people who can't accept being involved in that sort of occupation is that it becomes very frustrating. Either the day they come in they want to be chief of police, or they become very frustrated and they leave."

What may surprise the reader is that the decision of the New London Police Department was upheld by U.S. District Court Judge Peter Dorsey and supported by Harvard Law School Professor Elizabeth Bartholet. Bartholet commented to the effect that employers are concerned that very smart people will be unhappy and bored, and that they will leave their job quickly.

Yet, when one examines the scientific evidence, there is little justification for the claims of the New London Police Department or Professor Bartholet. First, there is no evidence that the effect of cognitive ability on job performance is nonlinear. In short, there is no evidence that within a job type, the positive effects of intelligence on job performance become negative when intelligence is very high. Second, research indicates that intelligence and job satisfaction are unrelated—smart people do not appear to susceptible to disenchantment with their jobs. Third, there does not appear to be evidence suggesting that smart workers are more likely to quit jobs.

So, can you be too smart for a job? No, but convincing certain employers (or courts or Ivy League professors) of this fact is a different matter.

Sources: E. Barry, "Smarter Than Average Cop Force's Rejection of High-IQ Applicant Upheld," *Boston Globe*, Sept. 10, 1999, p. B1 permission obtained from *Boston Globe* via Copyright Clearance Center (*www.copyright.com*). Y. Ganzach, "Intelligence and Job Satisfaction," *Academy of Management Journal*, 1998, 41, pp. 526–539.

available and continue to be used in selection. These specific measures will likely have some validity in predicting job performance, but this is simply because these tests measure general mental ability. Research has suggested rather conclusively that specific abilities do not explain additional variance in job performance over and above that explained by measures of general cognitive ability.[36] One recent study found that the average validity of general mental abilities tests, for various types of jobs, was r̄ = .46. The average incremental validity of a composite of specific abilities (i.e., controlling for general mental ability) was only .02.[37] In fact, in many cases, the validity of a combination of specific cognitive abilities is lower than that for general ability.[38] Thus, in most cases, organizations would be better served by using a measure of general cognitive ability than measures of specific abilities.

Some researchers have argued that cognitive ability tests measure only academic knowledge and that although such tests may be somewhat predictive of job performance, other types of intellectual abilities may be relevant as well. In particular, it has been argued that common sense (termed tacit knowledge or practical intelligence) can be an important predictor of job performance because practical knowledge is important to the performance of any job.[39] It is argued, for example, that a carpenter or nurse or lawyer can have all the intelligence in the world, but without common sense, these people will not be able to adequately perform their jobs. Accordingly, measures of tacit knowledge have been developed. An example is provided in Exhibit 9.7 for a sales manager. In this example, examinees rate the quality of each piece of advice on a 1 (low) to 9 (high) scale. Research suggests that the correlation between scores on a tacit knowledge measure and job performance ranges from .3 to .4. Such measures have modest relations with intelligence, but it has been argued that such measures simply reflect job knowledge.[40] If this is true, the importance of distinguishing common sense from general intelligence is called into question. (We will have more to say about the utility of job knowledge tests in the next section.) In short, arguing that practical intelligence is anything other than job knowledge, without further data, could be likened to "putting old wine in a new bottle."[41]

Potential Limitations

If cognitive ability tests are so valid and cheap, one might be wondering why more organizations aren't using them. One of the main reasons is concern over the adverse impact and fairness of these tests. In terms of adverse impact, regardless of the type of measure used, cognitive ability tests have severe adverse impact against minorities. Specifically, blacks on average score 1 standard deviation below whites, and Hispanics on average score .72 standard deviations below whites. This means that only 10% of blacks score above the average score for whites.[42] Historically, this led to close scrutiny—and sometimes rejection—of cognitive ability tests by the courts. The issue of fairness of cognitive ability tests has been hotly debated and heavily researched. One way to think of fairness

EXHIBIT 9.7   Sample Measure of Tacit Knowledge

You have just learned that detailed weekly reports of sales-related activities will be required of employees in your department. You have not received a rationale for the reports. The new reporting procedure appears cumbersome and it will probably be resisted strongly by your group. Neither you nor your employees had input into the decision to require the report, nor in decisions about its format. You are planning a meeting of your employees to introduce them to the new reporting procedures. Rate the quality of the following things you might do:

- Emphasize that you had nothing to do with the new procedure.
- Have a group discussion about the value of the new procedure and then put its adoption to a vote.
- Promise to make your group's concerns known to the supervisors, but only after the group has made a good faith effort by trying the new procedure for six weeks.
- Since the new procedure will probably get an unpleasant response anyway, use the meeting for something else and inform them about it in a memo.
- Postpone the meeting until you find out the rationale for the new procedure.

Source: R. J. Sternberg, "Tacit Knowledge and Job Success," in N. Anderson and P. Herriot (eds.), *Assessment and Selection in Organizations* (Chichester, England: Wiley, 1994), pp. 27–39. © 1994 John Wiley & Sons. Reprinted with permission of John Wiley & Sons, Limited.

is in terms of accuracy of prediction of a test. If a test predicts job performance with equal accuracy for two groups, such as whites and blacks, then most people would say the test is "fair." The problem is that even though the test is equally accurate for both groups, the average test score may be different between the two groups. When this happens, use of the test will cause some degree of adverse impact. This causes a dilemma: Should the organization use the test because it is an accurate and unbiased predictor, or should it not be used because it would cause adverse impact?

Research shows that cognitive ability tests are equally accurate predictors of job performance for various racial and ethnic groups.[43] But research also shows that blacks and Hispanics score lower on such tests than whites. Thus, the dilemma noted above is a real one for the organization. It must decide whether to (a) use cognitive ability tests, and experience the positive benefits of using an accurate predictor; (b) not use the cognitive ability test to avoid adverse impact, and substitute a different measure that has less adverse impact; or (c) use the cognitive ability test in conjunction with other predictors that do not have adverse impact, thus lessening adverse impact overall. Unfortunately, current research does not offer clear guidance on which approach is best. Research suggests that while using other selection measures in conjunction with cognitive ability tests reduces the adverse impact of cognitive ability tests, it by no means eliminates adverse impact.[44] At this point, the best advice is that organizations should strongly consider using cognitive ability tests due to their validity, but monitor adverse impact closely.

Another aspect of using cognitive ability tests in selection is concern over applicant reactions. Research on how applicants react to cognitive ability tests is scant and somewhat mixed. One study suggested that 88% of applicants for managerial positions perceived the Wonderlic as job-related.[45] Another study, however, demonstrated that applicants thought companies had little need for information obtained from a cognitive ability test.[46] Perhaps one explanation for these conflicting findings is the nature of the test. One study characterized eight cognitive ability tests as either concrete (vocabulary, mathematical word problems) or abstract (letter sets, quantitative comparisons) and found that concrete cognitive ability test items were viewed as job-related while abstract test items were not.[47] Thus, while applicants may have mixed reactions to cognitive ability tests, concrete items are less likely to be objectionable.

Other Types of Ability Tests

In the following section we consider tests that measure other types of abilities. Following the earlier classification of abilities into cognitive, psychomotor, physical, and sensory/perceptual, and having just reviewed cognitive ability tests, we now consider the other types of ability tests: psychomotor, physical, and sensory/perceptual.

Psychomotor Ability Tests   Psychomotor ability tests measure the correlation of thought with bodily movement. Involved here are processes such as reaction time, arm-hand steadiness, control precision, and manual and digit dexterity. An example of testing for psychomotor abilities is a test used by the city of Columbus, Ohio, to select firefighters. The test mimics coupling a hose to a fire hydrant, and it requires a certain level of processing with psychomotor abilities to achieve a passing score. Some tests of mechanical ability are psychomotor tests. For example, the *MacQuarrie Test for Mechanical Ability* is a 30-minute test that measures manual dexterity. Seven subtests require tracing, tapping, dotting, copying, and so on.

Physical Abilities Tests   Physical abilities tests measure muscular strength, cardiovascular endurance, and movement quality.[48] An example of a test that requires all three again comes from the city of Columbus. The test mimics carrying firefighting equipment (e.g., hose, fan, oxygen tanks) up flights of stairs in a building. Equipment must be brought up and down the stairs as quickly as possible in the test. The equipment is heavy, so muscular strength is required. The climb is taxing under limited breathing, so cardiovascular endurance is necessary. The trips up and around the flights of stairs, in full gear, require high degrees of flexibility and balance.

Physical abilities tests are becoming increasingly common to screen out individuals susceptible to repetitive stress injuries, such as carpal tunnel syndrome. One company, Devilbiss Air Power, found that complaints of repetitive stress injuries dropped from 23 to 3 after it began screening applicants for repetitive strain.[49] Physical abilities tests also may be necessary for EEO reasons.[50] Although female applicants typically score 1.5 standard deviations lower than male applicants on a physical abilities test, the distributions of scores for male and female applicants overlap considerably. Therefore, all applicants must be given a chance to pass requirements and not be judged as a class. Another reason to use physical abilities tests for appropriate jobs is to avoid injuries on the job. Well-designed tests will screen out applicants who have applied for positions that are poorly suited to their physical abilities. Thus, fewer injuries should result. In fact, one study found, using a concurrent validation approach on a sample of railroad workers, that 57% of all injury costs were due to the 26% of current employees who failed the physical abilities test.[51]

When carefully conducted for appropriate jobs, physical abilities tests can be highly valid. One comprehensive study reported average validities of $\bar{r} = .39$ for warehouse workers to $\bar{r} = .87$ for enlisted army men.[52] Applicant reactions to these sorts of tests are unknown.

Sensory/Perceptual Abilities Tests   Sensory/perceptual abilities tests assess the ability to detect and recognize environmental stimuli. An example of a sensory/perceptual ability test is a flight simulator used as part of the assessment process for airline pilots. Some tests of mechanical and clerical ability can be considered measures of sensory/perceptual ability, although they take on characteristics of cognitive ability tests. For example, the most commonly used mechanical ability test is the *Bennett Mechanical Comprehension Test*, which contains 68 items that measure an applicant's knowledge of the relationship between physical forces and mechanical objects (e.g., how a pulley operates, how gears function, etc.). In terms of clerical tests, the most widely known is the *Minnesota Clerical Test*. This timed test consists of 200 items in which the applicant is asked to compare names or numbers to identify matching elements. For example, an applicant might be asked (needing to work under time constraints) to check the pair of number series that is the same:

109485 _____ 104985
456836 _____ 456836
356823 _____ 536823
890940 _____ 890904
205837 _____ 205834

These tests of mechanical and clerical ability and others like them have reliability and validity data available that suggests they are valid predictors of performance within their specific area.[53] The degree to which these tests add validity over general intelligence, however, is not known.

Computer Testing

The development of computer technology and its widespread application to the workplace have resulted in an increasing number of ability tests being administered via computer. Allstate Insurance administers a battery of computerized ability tests for certain positions at all 230 of its learning centers nationwide. For example, for the job of claims representative, applicants complete a test on customer service skills and verbal and mathematical abilities.[54] Computerized tests have the advantage of being easy to administer (automatic timing of speed tests, computer self-scores the tests). An example of a company providing computerized testing services is QWIZ (*www.qwiz.com*). Computer testing is available for measuring core skills required for secretarial and clerical positions, such as speed typing, data entry, spelling, and math; other tests assess accounting and information technology skills.[55] Other computerized tests include direct measures of cognitive ability, clerical ability, spatial ability, and so on.[56]

Research on computerized testing is rapidly accumulating.[57] A recent meta-analysis suggests that computerized and paper-and-pencil ability tests have similar levels of validity when they are power tests, but speed versions of these tests are not always the same.[58] In any event, given the proliferation of computers in life and at work, the use of computers in selection, both to assess computer skills and as a medium to assess other abilities, is likely to increase.

Job Knowledge Tests

Job knowledge tests attempt to directly assess an applicant's comprehension of job requirements. Job knowledge tests can be one of two kinds. One type asks questions that directly assess knowledge of the duties involved in a particular job. For example, an item from a job knowledge test for an oncology nurse might be, "Describe the five oncological emergencies in cancer patients." The other type of job knowledge test focuses on the level of experience with, and corresponding knowledge about, critical job tasks and tools/processes necessary to perform the job. For example, the state of Wisconsin uses an *Objective Inventory Questionnaire* (OIQ) to evaluate applicants on the basis of their experience with tasks, duties, tools, technologies, and equipment that are relevant to a particular job.[59] OIQs ask applicants to evaluate their knowledge about and experience using skills, tasks, tools, and so forth by means of a checklist of specific job statements. Applicants can rate their level of knowledge on a scale ranging from "have never performed the task" to "have trained others and evaluated their performance on the task." An example of an OIQ is provided in Exhibit 9.8. An advantage of OIQs is that they are fast and easy to process and can provide broad content coverage. A

EXHIBIT 9.8   An Example of an Objective Inventory Questionnaire

For each of the following tasks, indicate your level of proficiency using the following codes. Use the one code that best describes your proficiency.

A = I have not performed the task or activity.
B = I have not performed the task independently, but have assisted others in performing it.
C = I have performed the task independently, without assistance, and am fully proficient.
D = I have led or trained others in performing this task.

_____ compiled Database (DB2) tables in production
_____ rebuilt a master catalog
_____ installed a tape input system

Source: *Developing Wisconsin State Civil Service Examinations and Assessment Procedures* (Madison, WI: Wisconsin Department of Employment Relations, 1994).

disadvantage of an OIQ is that applicants can easily falsify information. Thus, if job knowledge is an important prerequisite for a position, it is necessary to verify this information independently.

Evaluation

There has been less research on the validity of job knowledge tests than most other selection measures. A recent study, however, provided relatively strong support for the validity of job knowledge tests. A meta-analytic review of 502 studies indicated that the "true" validity of job knowledge tests in predicting job performance is .45. These validities were found to be higher for complex jobs and when job and test content was similar.[60]

As was discussed when reviewing the literature on cognitive ability tests, scores on cognitive ability tests are highly correlated with measures of job knowledge. Typically, this relationship has been interpreted as evidence that intelligence allows employees to process job information more quickly so that they learn more about their job.[61] A question that becomes relevant, however, is the following: "Given the high correlation between scores on a test of general mental ability and a measure of job knowledge, do job knowledge tests explain any additional level of job performance beyond cognitive ability tests?" Numerous studies have found that measures of job knowledge add little to the prediction of job performance over the prediction due to cognitive ability. In fact, most studies have been quite consistent in finding that job knowledge or specific ability measures add an average increase in predictiveness of only .02.[62] These results suggest that although job knowledge plays an important role in understanding how cognitive ability is predictive of job performance, using job knowledge tests in selection will contribute very little to the prediction of job performance beyond that provided by cognitive ability tests. As one research team wrote, "This suggests that given competition for resources, testing of *g* may yield greater gains and should take precedence over testing for prior job knowledge."[63]

Performance Tests and Work Samples

These tests are mechanisms to assess actual performance rather than underlying capacity or disposition. As such, they are more akin to samples rather than signs of work performance. For example, at Domino's Pizza Distribution, job candidates for the positions of dough maker, truck driver, and warehouse worker are given performance tests to ensure that they can safely perform the job.[64] This sample is taken rather than using drug testing as a sign, because candidates may not be able to safely perform the job for a variety of reasons in addition to drug and alcohol abuse. Exhibit 9.9 provides examples of performance tests and work samples for a variety of jobs. As can be seen in the exhibit, the potential uses of these selection measures is quite broad in terms of job content and skill level.

Types of Tests

Performance Test versus Work Sample A performance test measures what the person actually does on the job. The best examples of performance tests are internships, job tryouts, and probationary periods. Although probationary periods have their uses when one cannot be completely confident in an applicant's ability to perform a job, they are no substitute for a valid prehire selection process. Discharging and finding a replacement for a probationary employee is expensive and has numerous legal issues.[65] A work sample is designed to capture parts of the job, for example, a drill press test for machine operators and a programming test for computer programmers.[66] A performance test is more costly to develop than a work sample, but it is usually a better predictor of job performance.

Motor versus Verbal Work Samples A motor work sample test involves the physical manipulation of things. Examples include a driving test and a clothes-making test. A verbal work sample test involves a problem situation requiring language skills and interaction with people. Examples include role-playing tests that simulate contacts with customers, and an English test for foreign teaching assistants.

High- versus Low-Fidelity Tests A high-fidelity test uses very realistic equipment and scenarios to simulate the actual tasks of the job. As such, they elicit actual responses encountered in performing the task.[67] A good example of a high-fidelity test is one being developed to select truck drivers in the petroleum industry. The test is on the computer and mimics all the steps taken to load and unload fuel from a tanker to a fuel reservoir at a service station.[68] It is not a test of perfect

---

EXHIBIT 9.9   Examples of Performance Tests and Work Samples

Professor
Teaching a class while on a campus interview
Reading samples of applicant's research
Mechanic
Repairing a particular problem on a car
Reading a blueprint
Clerical
Typing test
Proofreading
Cashier
Operating cash register
Counting money and totaling balance sheet
Manager
Performing a group problem-solving exercise
Reacting to memos and letters
Airline Pilot
Pilot simulator
Rudder control test
Taxi Cab Driver
Driving test
Street knowledge test
TV Repair Person
Repairing broken television
Finger and tweezer dexterity test
Police Officer
Check police reports for errors
Shooting accuracy test
Computer Programmer
Programming and debugging test
Hardware replacement test

high fidelity, because fuel is not actually unloaded. It is, however, a much safer test because the dangerous process of fuel transfer is simulated rather than performed. Most of Station Casino's applicants (more than 800 per week) are customers, so the casino starts off with a very short high-fidelity test (five minutes behind a bank-type counter); applicants pass through successive simulations, such as assembling a jigsaw puzzle in a group to assess teamwork skills.[69]

A low-fidelity test is one that simulates the task in a written or verbal description and elicits a written or verbal response rather than an actual response. An example of a low-fidelity test is describing a work situation to job applicants and asking them what they would do in that particular situation. This was done in writing in a study by seven companies in the telecommunications industry for the position of manager.[70] Low-fidelity work samples bear many similarities to some types of structured interviews, and in some cases they may be indistinguishable (see Structured Interview section).

Computer Interaction Performance Tests versus Paper-and-Pencil Tests As with ability testing, the computer has made it possible to measure aspects of work not possible to measure with a paper-and-pencil test. The computer can capture the complex and dynamic nature of work. This is especially true in work where perceptual and motor performance is required.

An example of how the computer can be used to capture the dynamic nature of service work comes from Connecticut General Life Insurance Company. Fact-based scenarios, such as processing claims, are presented to candidates on the computer. The candidates' reactions to the scenarios, both mental (e.g., comprehension, coding, calculation) and motor (e.g., typing speed and accuracy), are assessed.[71]

The computer can also be used to capture the complex and dynamic nature of management work. On videotape, AccuVision shows the candidate actual job situations likely to be encountered on the job. In turn, the candidate selects a behavioral option in response in each situation. The response is entered in the computer and scored according to what it demonstrates of the skills needed to successfully perform as a manager.[72]

Situational Judgment Tests A hybrid selection procedure that takes on some of the characteristics of job knowledge tests as well as some of the types of work samples reviewed above is a situational judgment test. Situational judgment tests are tests that place applicants in hypothetical, job-related situations. Applicants are then asked to choose a course of action among several alternatives. For example, 911 operators may listen to a series of phone calls and be asked to choose the best response from a series of multiple-choice alternatives. Or, an applicant for retail sales position may see a clip showing an angry customer and then is asked to choose various questions about how he or she would respond to the situation.

As one can see, there are similarities between situational judgment tests and job knowledge tests and work samples. A job knowledge test more explicitly taps the content of the job (areas that applicants are expected to know immediately upon hire), whereas situational judgment tests are more likely to deal with future hypothetical job situations. Furthermore, job knowledge tests are less "holistic" than situational judgment tests in that the latter are more likely to include video clips and other more realistic material. Situational judgment tests differ from work samples in that the former present applicants with multiple-choice responses to the scenarios, whereas in the latter applicants actually engage in behavior that is observed by others. Despite our distinctions here, the differences among these procedures are subtle, and it is possible what one may term a situational judgment test by one individual may be labeled a job knowledge test or work sample by another.

A recent meta-analysis of the validity of situational judgment tests indicated that such tests were reasonably valid predictors of job performance ($\bar{r} = .34$). Such tests were significantly correlated with cognitive ability ($\bar{r} = .46$). Research does suggest that situational judgment tests have less (but not zero) adverse impact against minorities. Furthermore, video-based situational judgment tests appear to generate positive applicant reactions. Given these advantages, and the correlation between situational judgment and cognitive ability tests, one might be tempted to use situational judgment tests in place of cognitive ability tests. Indeed, it does appear that situational judgment tests add validity controlling for cognitive ability test scores. On the other hand, just because situational judgment tests add beyond cognitive ability tests does not mean that cognitive ability tests do not also add beyond situational judgment tests.[73]

Evaluation

Research indicates that performance or work sample tests have a high degree of validity in predicting job performance. One meta-analysis of a large number of studies suggested that the average validity was $\bar{r} = .54$ in predicting job performance.[74] Because performance tests measure the entire job and work samples measure a part of the job, they also have a high degree of content validity. Thus, when one considers the high degree of empirical and content validity, work samples are perhaps the most valid method of selection for many types of jobs.

Performance tests and work samples have other advantages as well. Research indicates that these measures are widely accepted by applicants as being job related. One study found that no applicants complained about performance tests when 10% to 20% complained about other selection procedures.[75] Another study of American workers in a Japanese automotive plant concluded that work sample tests are best able to accommodate cross-cultural values and therefore are well-suited for selecting applicants in international joint ventures.[76] Another important advantage of performance tests and work samples is that they have low degrees of adverse impact.

Work samples do have several limitations. The costs of the realism embedded in work samples are high. The closer a predictor comes to simulating actual job performance, the more expensive it becomes to use it. Actually having people perform the job, as with an internship, may require paying a wage. Using videotapes and computers adds cost as well. As a result, performance tests and work samples are among the most expensive means of selecting workers. The costs of performance tests and work samples are amplified when one considers the lack of generalizability of such measures. Probably more than any other selection method, performance tests and work samples are tied to the specific job at hand. This means that a different test, based on a thorough analysis of the job, will need to be developed for each job. While their validity may well be worth the cost, in some circumstances the costs of work samples may be prohibitive. One means of mitigating the administrative expense associated with performance tests or work samples is to use a two-stage selection process whereby the full set of applicants is reduced using relatively inexpensive tests. Once the initial cut is made, then performance tests or work samples can be administered to the smaller group of applicants who demonstrated minimum competency levels on the first-round tests.[77]

The importance of safety must also be considered as more realism is used in the selection procedure. If actual work is performed, care must be taken so that the candidate's and employer's safety are ensured. When working with dangerous objects or procedures, the candidate must have the knowledge to follow the proper procedures. For example, in selecting nurse's aides for a long-term health care facility, it would not be wise to have candidates actually move residents in and out of their beds. Both the untrained candidate and resident may suffer physical harm if proper procedures are not followed.

Finally, most performance tests and work samples assume that the applicant already possesses the KSAOs necessary to do the job. If substantial training is involved, applicants will not be able to perform the work sample effectively, even though they could be high performers with adequate training. Thus, if substantial on-the-job training is involved and some or many of the applicants would require this training, work samples simply will not be feasible.

Integrity Tests

Integrity tests attempt to assess an applicant's honesty and moral character. There are two major types of integrity tests: clear purpose (sometimes called overt) and general purpose (sometimes called veiled purpose). Exhibit 9.10 provides examples of items from both types of measures. Clear purpose tests directly assess employee attitudes toward theft. Such tests often consist of two sections: (1) questions of anti-theft attitudes (see items 1–5 in Exhibit 9.10), and (2) questions about the frequency and degree of involvement in theft or other counterproductive activities (see items 6–10 in Exhibit 9.10).[78] General or veiled purpose integrity tests assess employee personality with the idea that personality influences dishonest behavior (see items 11–20 in Exhibit 9.10). Many integrity tests are commercially available. A report issued by the American Psychological Association (APA) has issued guidelines for using integrity tests.[79] Organizations considering adopting such tests must consider the validity evidence offered for the measure. The APA report identified 46 publishers of integrity tests, only 30 of which complied with the task force's request.[80] Thus, it cannot be assumed that all tests being marketed are in good scientific standing.

The use of integrity tests in selection decisions has grown dramatically in the past decade. Estimates are that several million integrity tests are administered to

---

EXHIBIT 9.10 **Sample Integrity Test Questions**

Clear Purpose or Overt Test Questions

1. Do you think most people would cheat if they thought they could get away with it?
2. Do you believe a person has a right to steal from an employer if he or she is unfairly treated?
3. What percentage of people take more than $5 per week (in cash or supplies) from their employer?
4. Do you think most people think much about stealing?
5. Are most people too honest to steal?
6. Do you ever gamble?
7. Did you ever write a check knowing there was not enough money in the bank?
8. Did you make a false insurance claim for personal gain?
9. Have you ever been in serious indebtedness?
10. Have you ever stolen anything?

Veiled Purpose or Personality-Based Test Questions

11. Would you rather go to a party than read a newspaper?
12. How often do you blush?
13. Do you almost always make your bed?
14. Do you like to create excitement?
15. Do you like to take chances?
16. Do you work hard and steady at everything you do?
17. Do you ever talk to authority figures?
18. Are you more sensible than adventurous?
19. Do you think taking chances makes life more interesting?
20. Would you rather "go with the flow" than "rock the boat"?

applicants each year.[81] There are numerous reasons why employers are interested in testing applicants for integrity, but perhaps the biggest factor is the high cost of employee theft in organizations. Although such estimates vary widely, most place the cost of employee theft to the U.S. economy at from $15 to $50 billion per year.[82] One-third of all employees have admitted to stealing something from their employers.[83] Thus, the major justification for integrity tests is to select employees who are less likely to steal or engage in other undesirable behaviors at work. Integrity tests are most often used for clerks, tellers, cashiers, security guards, police officers, and high-security jobs.

The construct of integrity is still not well understood. Presumably, the traits that these tests attempt to assess include reliability, conscientiousness, adjustment, and sociability. In fact, some recent evidence indicates that several of the Big Five personality traits are related to integrity test scores, particularly conscientiousness.[84] One study found that conscientiousness correlated significantly with scores on two integrity tests.[85] It appears that applicants who score high on integrity tests also tend to score high on conscientiousness, low on neuroticism, and high on agreeableness.[86] It has been suggested that integrity tests might measure a construct even more broad than those represented by the Big Five traits.[87] More work on this important issue is needed, particularly the degree to which integrity is related to, but distinct from, more established measures of personality.

Measures

The most common method of measuring employee integrity is paper-and-pencil measures. Some employers had previously used polygraph (lie detector) tests, but for most employers these tests are now prohibited by law. Another approach has been to try to detect dishonesty in the interview. However, research tends to suggest that the interview is a very poor means of detecting lying. In fact, in a study of interviewers who should be experts at detecting lying (members of the Secret Service, CIA, FBI, National Security Agency, Drug Enforcement Agency, California police detectives, and psychiatrists), only the Secret Service performed significantly better than chance.[88] Thus, paper-and-pencil measures are the most feasible for assessing integrity for selection decisions.

Evaluation

Until recently, the validity of integrity tests was poorly studied. However, a recent meta-analysis of more than 500,000 people and more than 650 individual studies was recently published.[89] The principal findings from this study are the following:

1. Both clear and general purpose integrity tests are valid predictors of counterproductive behaviors (actual and admitted theft, dismissals for theft, illegal activities, absenteeism, tardiness, workplace violence). The average validity for clear purpose measures ($\bar{r} = .55$) was higher than for general purpose ($\bar{r} = .32$).

2. Both clear and general purpose tests were valid predictors of job performance ($\bar{r} = .33$ and $\bar{r} = .35$, respectively).

3. Limiting the analysis to estimates using a predictive validation design and actual detection of theft lowers the validity to $\bar{r} = .13$.

4. Integrity test scores are related to several Big Five measures, especially conscientiousness, agreeableness, and emotional stability.[90]

5. Integrity tests have no adverse impact against women or minorities and are relatively uncorrelated with intelligence. Thus, integrity tests demonstrate incremental validity over cognitive ability tests and reduce the adverse impact of cognitive ability tests.

Results from this comprehensive study suggest that organizations would benefit from using integrity tests for a wide array of jobs. Since most of the individual studies included in the meta-analysis were conducted by test publishers (who have an interest in finding good results), however, organizations using integrity tests should consider conducting their own validation studies.

One of the most significant concerns with the use of integrity tests is obviously the possibility that applicants might fake their responses. Consider answering the questions in Exhibit 9.10. Now consider answering these questions in the context of applying for a job that you desire. It seems more than plausible that applicants might distort their responses in such a context (particularly given that most of the answers would be impossible to verify). This possibility becomes a real concern when one considers the prospect that the individuals most likely to "fake good" (people behaving dishonestly) are exactly the type of applicants organizations would want to weed out.

Only recently has the issue of faking been investigated in research literature. One study found that subjects who were asked to respond as if they were applying for a job had 8% more favorable scores than those who were instructed to respond truthfully. Subjects who were specifically instructed to "fake good" had 24% more favorable scores than those who were told to respond truthfully.[91] A more recent study found some enhancement in completing an integrity test, but the degree of distortion was relatively small and did not undermine the validity of the test.[92] These results are consistent with the meta-analysis results reported earlier in the sense that if faking were pervasive, integrity test scores would either have no validity in predicting performance from applicant scores, or the validity would be *negative* (honest applicants reporting worse scores than dishonest applicants). The fact that validity was positive for applicant samples suggests that if faking does occur, it does not severely impair the predictive validity of integrity tests. It has been suggested that dishonest applicants do not fake more than honest applicants because they believe that everyone is dishonest and therefore they are reporting only what everyone else already does.

Objections to Integrity Tests and Applicant Reactions

Integrity tests have proven controversial. There are many reasons for this. Perhaps the most fundamental concern is misclassification of truly honest applicants as being dishonest. For example, the results of one study that was influential in a government report on integrity testing is presented in Exhibit 9.11. In this study, it has been claimed that 93.3% of individuals who failed the test were misclassified because no thefts were detected among 222 of the 238 individuals who failed the test. However, this ignores the strong possibility that some of the 222 individuals who failed the test and for whom no theft was detected may have stolen without being caught. In fact, the misclassification rate is unknown and, most likely, un-knowable. (After all, if all thefts were detected there would be no demand for integrity tests!) Also, all selection procedures involve misclassification of individ-

EXHIBIT 9.11   Integrity Test Results and Theft Detections

Theft Category	Failed Test	Passed Test	Total
No theft detected	222	240	462
Theft detected	16	1	17
Total	238	241	479

Source: U.S. Congress, Office of Technology Assessment, *The Use of Integrity Tests for Preemployment Screening*, OTA-SET-442 (Washington, DC: U.S. Government Printing Office, 1990).

uals because all selection methods are imperfect (have validities less than 1.0). Perhaps a more valid concern is the stigmatization of applicants who are thought to be dishonest based on their test scores,[93] but these problems can be avoided with proper procedures for maintaining the confidentiality of test scores.

There has been little research on how applicants react to integrity tests. Research suggests that applicants view integrity tests less favorably than most selection practices; they also perceive them as more invasive.[94] Thus, although the evidence is scant, it appears that applicants do not view integrity tests favorably. Whether these negative views affect their willingness to join an organization, however, is unknown.

Interest, Values, and Preference Inventories

Interest, values, and preference inventories attempt to assess the activities individuals prefer to do both on and off the job. This is in comparison with predictors that measure whether the person can do the job. However, just because a person can do a job does not guarantee success on the job. If the person does not want to do the job, that individual will fail regardless of ability. Although interests seem important, they have not been used very much in HR selection.

Standardized tests of interests, values, and preferences are available. Many of these measure vocational interests (e.g., the type of career that would motivate and satisfy someone) rather than organizational interests (e.g., the type of job or organization that would motivate and satisfy someone). The two most widely used interest inventories are the *Strong Vocational Interest Blank* (SVIB) and the *Myers-Briggs Type Inventory* (MBTI). Rather than classify individuals along continuous dimensions (e.g., someone is more or less conscientious than another), both the SVIB and MBTI classify individuals into distinct categories based on their responses to the survey. With the MBTI, individuals are classified in 16 types that have been found to be related to the Big Five personality characteristics discussed earlier.[95] Example interest inventory items are provided in Exhibit 9.12. The SVIB classifies individuals into six categories (realistic, investigative, artistic, social,

---

EXHIBIT 9.12   Sample Items from Interest Inventory

1. Are you usually:
   (a) A person who loves parties
   (b) A person who prefers to curl up with a good book?
2. Would you prefer to:
   (a) Run for president
   (b) Fix a car?
3. Is it a higher compliment to be called:
   (a) A compassionate person
   (b) A responsible person?
4. Would you rather be considered:
   (a) Someone with much intuition
   (b) Someone guided by logic and reason?
5. Do you more often:
   (a) Do things on the "spur of the moment"
   (b) Plan out all activities carefully in advance?
6. Do you usually get along better with:
   (a) Artistic people
   (b) Realistic people?
7. With which statement do you most agree?
   (a) Learn what you are, and be such.
   (b) Ah, but a man's reach should exceed his grasp, or what's a heaven for?
8. At parties and social gatherings, do you more often:
   (a) Introduce others
   (b) Get introduced?

enterprising, and clerical) that match jobs that are characterized in a corresponding manner. Both of these inventories are used extensively in career counseling in high school, college, and trade schools.

Past research has suggested that interest inventories are not valid predictors of job performance. The average validity of interest inventories in predicting job performance appears to be roughly $\bar{r} = .10$.[96] This does not mean that interest inventories are invalid for all purposes. Research clearly suggests that when individuals' interests match those of their occupation, they are happier with their jobs and are more likely to remain in their chosen occupation.[97] Thus, although interest inventories fail to predict job performance, they do predict occupational choices and job satisfaction levels. Undoubtedly, one of the reasons why vocational interests are poorly related to job performance is because the interests are tied to the occupation rather than the organization or the job.

Research suggests that while interest inventories play an important role in vocational choice, their role in organizational selection decisions is limited. However, a more promising way of considering the role of interests and values in the staffing process is to focus on person–organization fit.[98] As was discussed in Chapter 1, person–organization fit argues that it is not the applicants' characteristics alone that influence performance but rather the interaction between the applicants' characteristics and those of the organization. For example, an individual with a strong interest in social relations at work may perform well in an organization that emphasizes cooperation and teamwork, but the same individual might do poorly in an organization whose culture is characterized by independence or rugged individualism. Thus, interest and value inventories may be more valid when they consider the match between applicant values and organizational values (person–organization fit).[99] Research has shown that congruence between applicant values and those emphasized within the organization predicts applicant job choice decisions and organizational selection decisions. Employee–organizational value congruence is predictive of employee satisfaction, commitment, and turnover decisions. Although not often studied, values congruence also may predict job performance.[100] Thus, in considering the relationship of interests, values, and preferences with job performance, it seems necessary to also consider how well those characteristics match the culture of the organization.

Structured Interview

The structured interview is a very standardized, job-related method of assessment. It requires careful and thorough construction, as described in the sections that follow. It is instructive to compare the structured job interview with an unstructured or psychological interview. This comparison will serve to highlight the difference between the two.

A typical unstructured interview has the following sorts of characteristics:

- It is relatively unplanned (e.g., just sit down and "wing it" with the candidate) and often "quick and dirty" (e.g., 10–15 minutes).

- Rather than being based on the requirements of the job, questions are based on interviewer "hunches" or "pet questions" in order to psychologically diagnose applicant suitability.

- It consists of casual, open-ended, or subjective questioning (e.g., "Tell me a little bit about yourself").

- It has obtuse questions (e.g., "What type of animal would you most like to be, and why?").

- It has highly speculative questions (e.g., "Where do you see yourself 10 years from now?").

- The interviewer is unprepared (e.g., forgot to review job description and specification before the interview).

- The interviewer makes a quick, and final, evaluation of the candidate (e.g., often in the first couple of minutes).

Interviews are the most commonly used selection practice, and the unstructured interview is the most common form of interview in actual interview practice.[101] Research shows that organizations clearly pay a price for the use of the unstructured interview, namely, lower reliability and validity.[102] Interviewers using the unstructured interview (a) are unable to agree among themselves in their evaluation of job candidates, and (b) cannot predict the job success of candidates with any degree of consistent accuracy.

Fortunately, research has begun to unravel the reasons why the unstructured interview works so poorly and what factors need to be changed to improve reliability and validity. Sources of error or bias in the unstructured interview include the following:

1. Reliability of the unstructured interview is relatively low. Interviewers base their evaluations on different factors, have different hiring standards, and differ in the degree to which their actual selection criteria match their intended criteria.[103]

2. Applicant appearance, including facial attractiveness, cosmetics, and attire, has consistently been shown to predict interviewer evaluations. A recent experiment found that moderately obese applicants (especially female applicants) were much less likely to be recommended for employment, even controlling for job qualifications.[104]

3. Nonverbal cues (eye contact, smiling, etc.) have been found to be related to interview ratings.[105]

4. Negative information receives more weight than positive in the interview. Research suggests it takes more than twice as much positive as negative information to change an interviewer's initial impression of an applicant. As a result, the unstructured interview has been labeled a "search for negative evidence."[106]

5. There are primacy effects, where information obtained prior to the interview or during its early stages, dominates interviewer judgments. An early study suggested that on average, interviewers reached final decisions about applicants after only *four* minutes of a half-hour interview. These first impressions are particularly influential because interviewers engage in hypothesis confirmation strategies that are designed to confirm their initial impressions. Interviewers with positive first impressions sell the applicants more on the company, do more recruiting, and tell them more about the company.[107]

6. Similarity effects, where applicants who are similar to the interviewer with respect to race, gender, or other characteristics receive higher ratings, also seem to exist.[108]

7. Poor recall by interviewers often plagues unstructured interviews. One study demonstrated this by giving managers an exam based on factual information after watching a 20-minute videotaped interview. Some managers got all 20 questions correct, but the average manager only got half right.[109]

Thus, the unstructured interview is not very valid, and research has identified the reasons why this is so. The structured interview is an attempt to eliminate the biases inherent in unstructured formats by standardizing the process.

Characteristics of Structured Interviews

There are numerous hallmarks of structured interviews. Some of the more prominent characteristics are: (a) questions are based on job analysis; (b) the same questions are asked of each candidate; (c) the response to each question is numerically evaluated; (d) detailed anchored rating scales are used to score each response; (e) detailed notes are taken, particularly focusing on interviewees' behaviors.[110]

There are two principal types of structured interviews: situational and experience-based. Situational interviews assess an applicant's ability to project what his or her behavior would be in future, hypothetical situations.[111] The assumption behind the use of the situational interview is that the goals or intentions individuals set for themselves are good predictors of what they will do in the future.

Experienced-based or job-related interviews assess past behaviors that are linked to the prospective job. The assumption behind the use of experienced-based interviews is the same as that for the use of biodata—past behavior is a good predictor of future behavior. It is assumed that applicants who are likely to succeed have demonstrated success with past job experiences similar to the experiences they would encounter in the prospective job. An example of an experienced-based interview is the *Patterned Behavior Description Interview*, which collects four types of experiential information during the interview: (1) *credentials* (objective verifiable information about past experiences and accomplishments); (2) *experience descriptions* (descriptions of applicants' normal job duties, capabilities, and responsibilities); (3) *opinions* (applicants' thoughts about their strengths, weaknesses, and self-perceptions); (4) *behavior descriptions* (detailed accounts of actual events from the applicants' job and life experiences).[112]

Situational and experienced-based interviews have many similarities. Generally, both are based on the critical incidents approach to job analysis where job behaviors especially important to (as opposed to typically descriptive of) job performance are considered. Also, both approaches attempt to assess applicant *behaviors* rather than feelings, motives, values, or other psychological states. Finally, both methods have substantial reliability and validity evidence in their favor.

On the other hand, situational and experienced-based interviews have important differences. The most obvious difference is that situational interviews are future oriented ("what *would* you do if?"), whereas experienced-based interviews are past oriented ("what *did* you do when?"). Also, situational interviews are more standardized in that they ask the same questions of all applicants, while many experienced-based interviews place an emphasis on discretionary probing based on responses to particular questions. Presently, there is little basis to guide decisions about which of these two types of structured interviews should be adopted. However, one factor to consider is that experienced-based interviews may only be relevant for individuals who have had significant job experience. It does not make much sense to ask applicants what they did in a particular situation if they have never been in that situation. Some interview formats strike a balance between past- and future-oriented questions.

Evaluation

Traditionally, the employment interview was thought to have a low degree of validity. Recently, however, evidence for the validity of structured (and even unstructured) interviews has been much more positive. A recent meta-analysis suggested the following conclusions:[113]

1. The average validity of interviews was found to be $\bar{r} = .26$. This figure increased to $\bar{r} = .37$ when estimates were corrected for range restriction, which is not without controversy.[114] To be conservative, the estimates reported here are those uncorrected for range restriction.
2. Structured interviews were more valid ($\bar{r} = .31$) than unstructured interviews ($\bar{r} = .23$).
3. Situational interviews were more valid ($\bar{r} = .35$) than experienced-based interviews ($\bar{r} = .28$).
4. Panel interviews were *less* valid ($\bar{r} = .22$) than individual interviews ($\bar{r} = .31$).

It is safe to say that these values are higher than researchers had previously thought. Even unstructured interviews were found to have moderate degrees of validity. One of the reasons the validity may have been higher than previously thought is because in order to validate unstructured interviews, each interview must be given a numerical score. Assigning numerical scores to an interview imposes some degree of structure (interviewees are rated using the same scale), so it might be best to think of the unstructured interviews included in this analysis as semistructured rather than purely unstructured. Therefore, the estimated validity for "unstructured" interviews included in the meta-analysis is probably higher than that of the typical unstructured interview.

Future Uses of the Structured Interview

Although the meta-analysis reviewed above has offered a comprehensive summary of the literature on the validity of the interview, some of the most important questions in evaluating the usefulness of the interview have not been answered by past research. One potentially important use of the interview involves consideration of the issue of employee value. Without a doubt, performance or productivity is the central aspect of employee value to the organization. But it certainly is not the only criterion. Other important criteria that should be used to evaluate the selection process include applicant reactions, employee attendance and retention, "citizenship" behaviors, and fit within the organization. Thus, a valuable employee is not only a good performer but also is helpful to others, reliable, pleasant to be around, thinks in ways compatible with others, and otherwise contributes to the interpersonal climate of the organization. Clearly there is value in this. Whether one considers sports teams or business enterprises, organizations filled with individual contributors working in a hostile organizational climate are unlikely to succeed in the long run. Thus, the interpersonal orientation of the employee is important beyond its ability to contribute to productivity, and some selection measures, like the interview, are valuable for their ability to predict "nonperformance" aspects of employee value.

Consider the concept of person/organization match (see Chapter 1). Researchers have distinguished between person/*job* match, matching the KSAOs of the applicant to the technical requirements of the job, and person/*organization* match, matching the goals, values, and interpersonal skills of the applicant to the culture of the organization.[115] Thus, if selecting applicants who fit the organization's culture requires assessment of their goals, values, and interpersonal skills, the interview would seem better suited than other selection measures to assess these subjective elements. In fact, interviewers distinguish between interpersonal skills and objective qualifications, and interviews predict subjective performance better than objective measures of productivity.[116]

What implications do these arguments have for the interview? An "alternative" model of selection decisions is presented in Exhibit 9.13. As the model shows, hiring decisions are based not only on the match between applicant KSAOs and job requirements but also on the basis of how the applicant will fit with the goals, values, and culture of the organization. Though some selection methods are suitable for judging technical qualifications (e.g., ability and personality tests, work samples, biodata, and so on), the interview may be ideally suited to assess applicant goals, values, and interpersonal skills. For example, Southwest Airlines interviews applicants for interpersonal fit—to determine whether applicants have the personal qualities necessary to fit into the company's unique culture.[117]

This model is untested, and therefore it can only be offered tentatively. However, it does suggest dramatic changes to the use of the interview in selection decisions. The typical approach to the structured interview is to make it a close approximation of the skill and ability requirements of the job. However, a consequence of structured interviews is that they are highly correlated with cognitive ability tests. In fact, scores on the structured interview correlate $\bar{r} = .40$ with scores on cognitive ability tests.[118] Some research suggests that structured interviews add

EXHIBIT 9.13 **An Alternative Model of the Use of the Interview in Selection Decisions**

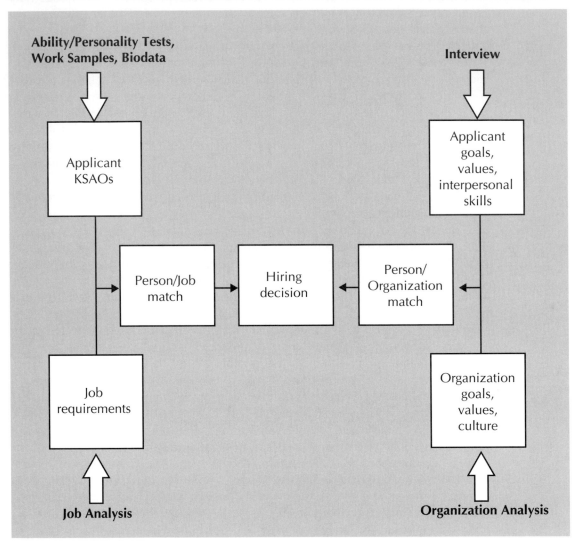

incremental validity beyond cognitive ability, though other studies have found that structured interviews do not add validity in predicting job performance beyond cognitive ability tests. Research even suggests that automated, telephone-based structured interviews achieve the same level of validity as face-to-face structured interviews, perhaps because these structured interviews do a good job of measuring intelligence and conscientiousness.[119] In fact, the meta-analysis of interviews reviewed earlier found that when cognitive ability test scores were available to interviewers prior to the interview, the validity of structured interviews dropped to $\bar{r} = .16$ (this incremental validity was even lower than for unstructured interviews). As a result of the strong linkage between structured interview performance and cognitive ability, some have termed structured interviews as nothing more than "verbal cognitive ability tests." Thus, structuring interviews around KSAOs may cause them to lose their unique contribution to selection decisions—the ability to assess applicant goals, values, and interpersonal skills. If we are correct in our reasoning, the proper use of the interview is not to return to unstructured interviewing. Rather, the key question becomes: Structure the interview around *what*? Under our reasoning, the interview would become structured around those elements of employee value that it is uniquely suited to predict, namely person/organization match.

Another important factor to consider in evaluating the employment interview is that it serves other goals besides identifying the best candidates for the job. One of the most important uses of the interview is recruitment. The interview is the central means through which applicants learn about important aspects of the job and the organization. This information can be very useful to applicants for making decisions about organizations. A recent study suggested that the goals of recruitment and selection in the interview are not complementary. Interviews that are focused solely on recruitment lead applicants to learn more about the job and the organization than interviews that are dual purpose (recruitment and selection).[120] The more information applicants acquire during an interview, the more likely they are to think highly of an organization and thus accept an offer from them.

In fact, applicants tend to react very favorably to the interview. Research suggests that most applicants believe the interview is an essential component of the selection process, and most view the interview as the most suitable measure of relevant abilities.[121] As a result, the interview has been rated by applicants as more job-related than any other selection procedure.[122] Why do applicants react so favorably to the interview? One model of applicant reactions to selection procedures suggested that selection methods that are perceived as controllable by the candidate, obvious in purpose, providing task-relevant information, and offering a means of feedback are considered the most socially valid or acceptable.[123] The interview would appear to offer all of these components. As a result, applicants may perceive the interview as a mutual exchange of relevant information predictive of future performance and therefore job-related. Thus, the interview generates very positive applicant reactions and can serve an important role in recruitment.

Regardless of what information the interview is structured around, the process of structuring an interview requires that organizations follow a systematic and standardized process. Next, the process of constructing a structured interview is described. For purposes of illustration, we describe development of a situational interview.

Constructing a Structured Interview

The structured interview, by design and conduct, standardizes and controls for sources of influence on the interview process and the interviewer. The goal is to improve interview reliability and validity beyond that of the unstructured interview. Research shows that this goal can be achieved. Doing so requires following each of these steps: consult the job requirements matrix, develop the selection plan, develop the structured interview plan, select and train interviewers, and evaluate effectiveness. Each of these steps is elaborated on next.

The Job Requirements Matrix

The starting point for the structured interview is the job requirements matrix. It identifies the tasks and KSAOs that define the job requirements around which the structured interview is constructed and conducted.

The Selection Plan

As previously described, the selection plan flows from the KSAOs identified in the job requirements matrix. The selection plan addresses which KSAOs it is necessary to assess during selection, and whether the structured interview is the preferred method of assessing them.

Is the KSAO Necessary? Some KSAOs must be brought to the job by the candidate, and others can be acquired on the job (through training and/or job experience). The bring-it/acquire-it decision must be made for each KSAO. This decision should be guided by the importance indicator(s) for the KSAOs in the job requirements matrix.

Is the Structured Interview the Preferred Method? It must be decided if the structured interview is the preferred method of assessing each KSAO necessary for selection. Several factors should be considered when making this decision. First, job knowledges are usually best assessed through other methods, such as a written ability or job knowledge test or specific training and experience requirements. The structured interview thus should focus more on skills and abilities. Second, many alternative methods are available for assessing these skills and abilities, as discussed throughout this chapter. Third, the structured interview is probably best suited for assessing only some of these skills and abilities, such as verbal, interpersonal, adaptability, and flexibility skills and abilities.

An example of a selection plan for the job of sales associate in a retail clothing store is shown in Exhibit 9.14. While there were five task dimensions for the job in the job requirements matrix (customer service, use of machines, use of customer service outlets, sales and departmental procedures, cleaning and maintenance), the selection plan is shown only for the dimension customer service.

EXHIBIT 9.14   Partial Selection Plan for Job of Retail Store Sales Associate

Task Dimension: Customer Service

KSAO	Necessary for Selection?	Method of Assessment
1. Ability to make customer feel welcome	Yes	Interview
2. Knowledge of merchandise to be sold	Yes	Written test
3. Knowledge of location of merchandise in store......	No	– – – –
4. Skill in being cordial with customers	Yes	Interview
5. Ability to create and convey ideas to customers	Yes	Interview

Note in the exhibit that the customer service dimension has several required KSAOs. However, only some of these will be assessed during selection, and only some of those will be assessed by the structured interview. The method of assessment is thus carefully targeted to the KSAO to be assessed.

The Structured Interview Plan
Development of the structured interview plan proceeds along three sequential steps: construction of interview questions, construction of benchmark responses for the questions, and weighting of the importance of the questions. The output of this process for the sales associate job is shown in Exhibit 9.15 and is referred to in the discussion that follows.

Constructing Questions   One or more questions must be constructed for each KSAO targeted for assessment by the structured interview. Many different types of questions have been experimented with and researched, including situational interviewing, behavior description interviewing, job content interviewing, and structured behavioral interviewing. Despite differences, there is a major underlying characteristic common to all.

That characteristic is sampling of the candidate's behavior, as revealed by past situations and what the candidate reports would be his or her behavior in future situations. The questions ask in essence, "What have you done in this situation?" and "What would you do if you were in this situation?"

The key to constructing both types of questions is to create a scenario relevant to the KSAO in question and to ask the candidate to respond to it by way of answering a question. Situations may be drawn from past job experiences as well as nonjob experiences. Inclusion of nonjob experiences is important for applicants who have not had similar previous job experience or have not had any previous job experience at all.

The "what would you do if" questions should be constructed around important scenarios or events that the person is likely to encounter on the job. The candidate may draw on both previous job and nonjob situations, as well as more general behavioral intentions, in fashioning a response.

Exhibit 9.15 shows three questions for the KSAOs to be assessed by the interview, as determined by the initial selection plan for the job of sales associate in a retail store. As can be seen, all three questions present very specific situations that a sales associate is likely to encounter. The content of all three questions is clearly job relevant, a logical outgrowth of the process that began with the development of the job requirements matrix.

Benchmark Responses and Rating Scales   The interviewer must somehow evaluate or judge the quality of the candidates' response to the interview questions. Prior development of benchmark responses and corresponding rating scales is the method for providing firm guidance to the interviewer in doing this task. Benchmark responses represent qualitative examples of the types of candidate response that the interviewer may encounter. They are located on a rating scale (usually 1–5 or 1–7 rating scale points) to represent the level or "goodness" of the response.

Exhibit 9.15 contains benchmark responses, positioned on 1–5 rating scales, for each of the three interview questions. Note that all the responses are quite specific, and they clearly suggest that some answers are better than others. These responses represent judgments on the part of the organization as to the desirability of behaviors its employees could engage in.

Weighting Responses   Each candidate will receive a total score for the structured interview. It thus must be decided whether each question is of equal importance in contributing to the total score. If so, the candidate's total interview score is simply the sum of the scores on the individual rating scales.

If some questions are more important than others in assessing candidates, then those questions receive greater weight. The more important the question, the greater its weight relative to the other questions.

Exhibit 9.15 shows the weighting decided on for the three interview questions. As can be seen, the first two questions receive a weight of 1, and the third question receives a weight of 2. The candidate's assigned ratings are multiplied by their weights and then summed to determine a total score for this particular task dimension. In the exhibit, the candidate receives a score of 18 $(5+3+10=18)$ for customer service. The candidate's total interview score would be the sum of the scores on all the dimensions.

Selection and Training of Interviewers

Some interviewers are more accurate in their judgments than others. In fact, several studies have found significant differences in interviewer validity.[124] Thus, rather than asking, "How valid is the interview?" it might be more appropriate to

EXHIBIT 9.15 Structured Interview Questions, Benchmark Responses, Rating Scale, and Question Weights

Job: Sales Associate
Task Dimension: Customer Service

	Rating Scale					Rating	X	Weight	=	Score
	1	2	3	4	5					
Question No. One (KSAO 1) A customer walks into the store. No other salespeople are around to help the person, and you are busy arranging merchandise. What would you do if you were in this situation?		Keep on arranging merchandise	Keep working, but greet the customer		Stop working, greet customer, and offer to provide assistance	5		1		5
Question No. Two (KSAO 4) A customer is in the fitting room and asks you to bring her some shirts to try on. You do so, but by accident bring the wrong size. The customer becomes irate and starts shouting at you. What would you do if you were in this situation?		Tell customer to "keep her cool"	Go get correct size		Apologize, go get correct size	3		1		3
Question No. Three (KSAO 5) A customer is shopping for the "right" shirt for her 17-year-old granddaughter. She asks you to show her shirts that you think would be "right" for her. You do this, but the customer doesn't like any of them. What would you do if you were in this situation?		Tell customer to go look elsewhere	Explain why you think your choices are good ones		Explain your choices, suggest gift certificate as alternative	5		2		10
										18

ask, "Who is a valid interviewer?" Answering this question requires selecting interviewers based on characteristics that will enable them to make accurate decisions about applicants. Little research is available regarding the factors that should guide selection of interviewers. Perhaps not surprisingly, cognitive ability has been linked to accuracy in evaluating others. It also would be possible to design an interview simulation where prospective interviewers are asked to analyze jobs to determine applicant KSAOs, preview applications, conduct hypothetical interviews, and evaluate the applicants. Thus, selecting interviewers who are intelligent and who demonstrate effective interviewing skills in interview simulations likely will improve the validity of the interviewing process.

Training interviewers is another means of increasing the validity of structured interviews. Interviewers will probably need training in the structured interview process. The process is probably quite different from what they have encountered and/or used, and training becomes a way of introducing them to the process. Logical program content areas to be covered as part of the training are:

- problems with the unstructured interview
- advantages of the structured interview
- development of the structured interview
- use of probe questions and note taking
- elimination of rating errors
- actual practice in conducting the structured interview

Though research suggests that interviewers are generally receptive to training attempts, it is not clear that such efforts are successful. As one review concluded, the evidence regarding the ability of training programs to reduce rating errors showed that these programs "have achieved at best mixed results."[125] This makes it even more important to accurately select effective interviewers as a means of making the interview process more accurate.

Finally, whether used for initial or substantive assessment, applicants need to realize that first impressions are lasting ones in the interview. Exhibit 9.16 provides some insights into the factors that create first impressions in the interview.

Evaluating Effectiveness

As with any assessment device, there is a constant need to learn more about the reliability, validity, and utility of the structured interview. This is particularly so because of the complexity of the interview process. Thus, evaluation of the structured interview's effectiveness should be built directly into the process itself.[126]

Assessment for Team and Quality Environments

To be responsive to a rapidly changing business environment, some organizations are decentralizing decision making and putting increased emphasis on quality. In

---

EXHIBIT 9.16   The Importance of First Impressions in the Interview

A firm handshake is one of the common recommendations in the employment interview to create a positive first impression on interviewers. However, there has been no empirical data to verify whether this is good advice for job seekers. Empirical research has revealed insights into both who gives good handshakes and how handshakes are perceived by others. In collecting the data, the researchers analyzed the handshakes of 112 individuals by having each individual shake the hand of four testers. Handshakes were coded along eight characteristics such as strength, vigor, dryness, completeness of grip, and duration. The study found that individuals who scored high on extraversion and emotional stability gave firmer handshakes. Additionally, men had firmer handshakes than did women. Consistent with that hoary advice, firm handshakes did generate more positive impressions on the part of the testers.

What are the implications of this study? First, a dry, firm, vigorous handshake does create a positive first impression on the part of interviewers. And we know from previous interview research that first impressions are lasting ones in the interview. Second, certain individuals who are predisposed to give less than exemplary handshakes need to work on their technique. Specifically, job seekers who are introverted and lack confidence, as well as female interviewees, need to ensure that their handshakes are firm, dry (dry those sweaty palms!), and vigorous and strong.

Additionally, a recent survey of employers revealed that they place heavy weight on candidate grooming in forming first impressions of interviewees. Handshakes also were important to their initial evaluations of interviewees. Though not as important as a handshake in this survey, other aspects of candidate appearance did receive at least some weight from employers, including non-traditional hair color, obvious tattoos, and body piercing.

Source: W. F. Chaplin, J. B. Phillips, J. D. Brown, N. R. Clanton, and J. L. Stein, "Handshaking, Gender, Personality and First Impressions," *Journal of Personality, and Social Psychology,* 2000, 79, pp. 110–117; "Employers Frown on Poor Appearance, Wacky Interview Attire, and Limp Handshakes," *IPMA News,* June 2001, p. 3.

many cases, these business strategies have resulted in total quality management (TQM) programs and the development of team-based jobs. The process of selection in quality and team environments may be different than in the more traditional context. This necessitates consideration of how these new work arrangements may affect staffing processes and decisions. Accordingly, assessment in quality and team environments is considered in turn.

Selection in Quality Environments

Interestingly, organizations with TQM missions often seem to ignore selection systems. One study of Malcolm Baldrige Award winners found that only one had fundamentally altered its selection processes to make them more compatible with a TQM strategy, and it has been noted that the Baldrige Award criteria barely mention selection.[127] In an effort to bring selection activities into closer alignment with quality objectives, it has been suggested that organizations with a strategy of quality enhancement or TQM may need to revise their selection policies in a number of important ways.[128]

1. The types of skills assessed in quality organizations may be different. Quality organizations require that employees demonstrate customer-service skills, self-direction and self-development, and team-development skills. As a result, three of the Big Five personality characteristics—conscientiousness, openness to experience, and agreeableness—may be particularly important to performance in quality organizations. Conscientious individuals are dependable, organized, and persistent. Therefore, they may perform better in quality environments due to the emphasis on control, reliability, and decreased errors. Open individuals are flexible, creative, and autonomous. Openness may be an important characteristic in quality organizations given that TQM requires autonomy, willingness to experiment, taking risks, and continuous learning. Finally, agreeableness may be important because quality organizations emphasize customer relations, cooperation, and collaboration.

2. Specificity of skills assessed may be different in a quality environment. Quality organizations embrace change and emphasize flexibility in production processes and environmental response. Since this requires that employees be flexible and competent in numerous work roles, emphasis on job-spanning KSAOs as opposed to narrow, job-specific skills may be warranted. General mental ability is perhaps the most generalized skill an employee can have; thus, it may be particularly important in adapting to the rapid changes and flexible processes of quality environments.

3. The processes by which selection decisions are made may need to be different. Quality organizations rely more heavily on employee discretion and autonomy to make decisions about work processes, and more work is team-based in quality organizations. Therefore, it would be appropriate for selection in quality organizations to be based on peer (as opposed to manager) decisions.

There is virtually no research on staffing in quality environments. Therefore, it is even more important than in traditional cases that quality organizations validate their selection processes prior to full implementation.

Selection in Team Environments

As with selection for quality environments, the first step in understanding the proper steps for selection in team-based environments is to understand the requirements of the job. A recent analysis of the KSAOs for teamwork is presented in Exhibit 9.17. Identified in the exhibit are 2 major categories of KSAs for teamwork, 5 subcategories, and 14 specific KSAs (the "other" category was not considered in the study). Thus, in order to be effective in a teamwork assignment, an employee needs to demonstrate *interpersonal KSAs* (consisting of conflict resolution, collaborative problem solving, and communication KSAs) and *self-management KSAs* (consisting of goal setting and performance management KSAs

---

EXHIBIT 9.17 Knowledge, Skill, and Ability (KSA) Requirements for Teamwork

I. INTERPERSONAL KSAs

A. Conflict-Resolution KSAs

1. The KSA to recognize and encourage desirable, but discourage undesirable, team conflict.
2. The KSA to recognize the type and source of conflict confronting the team and to implement an appropriate conflict-resolution strategy.
3. The KSA to employ an integrative (win-win) negotiation strategy rather than the traditional distributive (win-lose) strategy.

B. Collaborative Problem-Solving KSAs

4. The KSA to identify situations requiring participative group problem solving and to utilize the proper degree and type of participation.
5. The KSA to recognize the obstacles to collaborative group problem solving and implement appropriate corrective actions.

C. Communication KSAs

6. The KSA to understand communication networks and to utilize decentralized networks to enhance communication where possible.
7. The KSA to communicate openly and supportively, that is, to send messages which are: (1) behavior- or event-oriented, (2) congruent, (3) validating, (4) conjunctive, and (5) owned.
8. The KSA to listen nonevaluatively and to appropriately use active listening techniques.
9. The KSA to maximize consonance between nonverbal and verbal messages and to recognize and interpret the nonverbal messages of others.
10. The KSA to engage in ritual greetings and small talk and a recognition of their importance.

II. SELF-MANAGEMENT KSAs

D. Goal-Setting and Performance-Management KSAs

11. The KSA to help establish specific, challenging, and accepted team goals.
12. The KSA to monitor, evaluate, and provide feedback on both overall team performance and individual team member performance.

E. Planning and Task-Coordination KSAs

13. The KSA to coordinate and synchronize activities, information, and task interdependencies between team members.
14. The KSA to help establish task and role expectations of individual team members and to ensure proper balancing of workload in the team.

Source: M. J. Stevens and M. A. Campion, "The Knowledge, Skill, and Ability Requirements for Teamwork: Implications for Human Resource Management," *Journal of Management*, 1994, 20, pp. 503–530. With permission from Elsevier Science.

and planning and task coordination KSAs). The implication of this framework for selection is that existing selection processes and methods may need to be revamped to incorporate these KSAs.

One means of incorporating team-based KSAs into the existing selection process has been developed.[129] Exhibit 9.18 provides some sample items from the 35-item test. This test has been validated against three criteria (teamwork performance, technical performance, and overall performance) in two studies.[130] The teamwork test showed substantial validity in predicting teamwork and overall performance in one of the studies, but no validity in predicting any of the criteria in the other study. (It is not clear why the teamwork test worked well in one study and not in the other.) It should be noted that tests are not the only method of measuring teamwork KSAs. Other methods of assessment that some leading companies have used in selecting team members include structured interviews, as-

---

EXHIBIT 9.18   Example Items Assessing Teamwork KSAs

1. Suppose that you find yourself in an argument with several coworkers about who should do a very disagreeable but routine task. Which of the following would likely be the most effective way to resolve this situation?
   A. Have your supervisor decide, because this would avoid any personal bias.
   B. Arrange for a rotating schedule so everyone shares the chore.
   C. Let the workers who show up earliest choose on a first-come, first-served basis.
   D. Randomly assign a person to do the task and don't change it.

2. Your team wants to improve the quality and flow of the conversations among its members. Your team should:
   A. Use comments that build on and connect to what others have said.
   B. Set up a specific order for everyone to speak and then follow it.
   C. Let team members with more to say determine the direction and topic of conversation.
   D. Do all of the above.

3. Suppose you are presented with the following types of goals. You are asked to pick one for your team to work on. Which would you choose?
   A. An easy goal to ensure the team reaches it, thus creating a feeling of success.
   B. A goal of average difficulty so the team will be somewhat challenged, but successful without too much effort.
   C. A difficult and challenging goal that will stretch the team to perform at a high level, but attainable so that effort will not be seen as futile.
   D. A very difficult, or even impossible goal so that even if the team falls short, it will at least have a very high target to aim for.

Source: M. J. Stevens and M. A. Campion, "The Knowledge, Skill, and Ability Requirements for Teamwork: Implications for Human Resource Management," *Journal of Management*, 1994, 20, pp. 503–530. With permission from Elsevier Science.

sessment centers, personality tests, and biographical inventories.[131] For example, the PCI personality test described earlier has a special scale that is designed to predict team performance. Furthermore, a study of 51 manufacturing teams revealed that teams comprised of members who, on average, scored high on agreeableness, conscientiousness, and emotional stability outperformed other teams.[132] Thus, personality testing may be a useful means of staffing team positions.

Another important decision in team member selection is who should make the hiring decisions. In many cases, team assessments are made by members of the self-directed work team in deciding who becomes a member of the group. An example of an organization following this procedure is South Bend, Indiana–based I/N Tek, a billion-dollar steel-finishing mill established in a joint venture between the United States' Inland Steel and Japan's Nippon Steel. Employees in self-directed work teams, along with managers and HR professionals, interview candidates as a final step in the selection process. This approach is felt to lead to greater satisfaction with the results of the hiring process because employees have a say in which person is selected to be part of the team.[133]

Thus, staffing processes and methods in team and quality environments require modifications from the traditional approaches to selection. Before organizations go to the trouble and expense of modifying these procedures, however, it would be wise to examine whether the team and quality initiatives are likely to be successful. Many teams fail because they are implemented as an isolated practice, and many quality initiatives also do not succeed.[134] Thus, before overhauling selection practices in an effort to build teams and implement quality initiatives, care must be taken to ensure the proper context for these environments in the first place.

Clinical Assessments

A clinical assessment is a mechanism whereby a trained psychologist makes a judgment about the suitability of a candidate for a job. Typically, such assessments are used for selecting people for middle- and upper-level management positions. A typical assessment takes about half a day. Judgments are formed on the basis of an interview, personal history form, ability tests, and personality tests. Feedback to the organization usually includes a narrative description of the candidate, with or without a stated recommendation.[135]

Scott Paper Company has taken this approach in an effort to improve its selection for 50 management positions in the manufacturing operations of the company. In particular, Scott was very interested in shifting the orientation of its management staff away from an autocratic, hierarchical system of decision making to one in which the participation and the development of subordinates was emphasized. To do so, selection of individuals with this management style was emphasized as opposed to the training of managers to acquire this style. Clinical assessments were made to ensure that this selection procedure worked.[136] This example nicely demonstrates the role that clinical assessments can play in the selection process.

They can be useful when making decisions about criteria in the job requirements matrix that are difficult to quantify. In the case of many companies, as with Scott, management style is one such KSAO. Clinical assessments have the limitation of being unstandardized, however, and very little validity evidence is available.

Choice of Substantive Assessment Methods

As with the choice of initial assessment methods, there has been a large amount of research conducted on substantive assessment methods that can help guide organizations on the appropriate methods to use. Reviews of this research, using the same criteria that were used to evaluate initial assessment methods, are shown in Exhibit 9.19. Specifically, the criteria are use, cost, reliability, validity, utility, applicant reactions, and adverse impact.

Use

As can be seen in Exhibit 9.19, there are no widely used (at least two-thirds of all organizations) substantive assessment methods. Job knowledge tests, structured interviews, and performance tests and work samples have moderate degrees of use. The other substantive methods are only occasionally or infrequently used by organizations.

Cost

The cost of substantive assessment methods vary widely. Some methods can be purchased from vendors quite inexpensively (personality tests, ability tests, interest, value, and preference inventories, integrity tests)—often for less than $2 per applicant. (Of course, the costs of administering and scoring the tests must be factored in.) Some methods, such as job knowledge tests or team/quality assessments, can vary in price depending on whether the organization develops the measure itself or purchases it from a vendor. Other methods, such as structured interviews, performance tests and work samples, and clinical assessments, generally require extensive time and resources to develop; thus, these measures are the most expensive substantive assessment methods.

Reliability

The reliability of all of the substantive assessment methods is moderate or high. Generally, this is true because many of these methods have undergone extensive development efforts by vendors. However, whether an organization purchases an assessment tool from a vendor or develops it independently, the reliability of the method must be investigated. Just because a vendor claims a method is reliable does not necessarily mean it will be so within a particular organization.

Validity

Like cost, the validity of substantive assessment methods varies a great deal. Some methods, such as interest, value, and preference inventories and clinical assessments,

EXHIBIT 9.19 **Evaluation of Substantive Assessment Methods**

Predictors	Use	Cost	Reliability	Validity	Utility	Reactions	Adverse Impact
Personality tests	Low	Low	High	Moderate	?	Negative	Low
Ability tests	Low	Low	High	High	High	Negative	High
Performance tests and work samples	Moderate	High	High	High	High	Positive	Low
Interest, value, and preference inventories	Low	Low	High	Low	?	?	Low
Structured interviews	Moderate	High	Moderate	High	?	Positive	Mixed
Clinical assessments	Low	High	Moderate	Low	?	?	?
Team/quality assessments	Low	Moderate	?	?	?	Positive	?
Job knowledge tests	Moderate	Moderate	High	High	?	Neutral	?
Integrity tests	Low	Low	High	High	High	Negative	Low

have demonstrated little validity in past research. As was noted when reviewing these measures, however, steps can be taken to increase their validity. Some methods, such as personality tests and structured interviews, have at least moderate levels of validity. Some structured interviews have high levels of validity, but the degree to which they add validity beyond cognitive ability tests remains in question. Finally, ability tests, performance tests and work samples, job knowledge tests, and integrity tests have high levels of validity. As with many structured interviews, while the validity of job knowledge tests is high, the degree to which job knowledge is important in predicting job performance beyond cognitive ability is suspect. Integrity tests are moderate to high predictors of job performance; their validity in predicting other important job behaviors (counterproductive work behaviors) appears to be quite high.

Utility

As with initial assessment methods, the utility of most substantive assessment methods is unknown. A great deal of research has shown that the utility of ability tests (in particular, cognitive ability tests) is quite high. Performance tests and work samples and integrity tests also appear to have high levels of utility.

Applicant Reactions

Research is just beginning to emerge concerning applicant reactions to substantive assessment methods. From the limited research that has been conducted, however, applicants' reactions to substantive assessment methods appear to depend on the particular method. Relatively abstract methods that require an applicant to answer questions not directly tied to the job (i.e., questions on personality tests, most ability tests, and integrity tests) seem to generate negative reactions from applicants. Thus, research tends to suggest that personality, ability, and integrity tests are viewed unfavorably by applicants. Methods that are manifestly related to the job for which applicants are applying appear to generate positive reactions. Thus, research suggests that applicants view performance tests and work samples and structured interviews favorably. Job knowledge tests, perhaps because they are neither wholly abstract nor totally experiential, appear to generate neutral reactions.

Adverse Impact

A considerable amount of research has been conducted on adverse impact of some substantive assessment methods. In particular, research suggests that personality tests, performance tests and work samples, and integrity tests have little adverse impact against women or minorities. In the past, interest, value, and preference inventories had substantial adverse impact against women, but this problem has been corrected. Conversely, ability tests have a high degree of adverse impact. In particular, cognitive ability tests have substantial adverse impact against minorities, while physical ability tests have significant adverse impact on women. The adverse impact of structured interviews was denoted as mixed. While evidence suggests that many structured interviews have little adverse impact against women or minorities, other evidence suggests some adverse impact. Furthermore, since even structured interviews have an element of subjectivity to them, the potential always exists for interviewer bias to enter into the process. There is too little data to draw conclusions about the adverse impact of clinical assessments and job knowledge tests.

A comparison of Exhibits 8.10 and 9.19 is instructive. In general, both the validity and the cost of substantive assessment procedures are higher than those of initial assessment procedures. As with the initial assessment procedures, the economic and social impact of substantive assessment procedures is not well understood. Many initial assessment methods are widely used, whereas most substantive assessment methods have moderate or low degrees of use. Thus, many organizations rely on initial assessment methods to make substantive assessment decisions. This is unfortunate because, with the exception of biographical data, the validity of substantive assessment methods is higher. This is especially true of the initial interview relative to the structured interview. At a minimum, organizations need to supplement the initial interview with structured interviews. Better yet, organizations should strongly consider using ability, performance, personality, and work sample tests along with either interview.

DISCRETIONARY ASSESSMENT METHODS

Discretionary assessment methods are used to separate those who receive job offers from the list of finalists. Sometimes discretionary methods are not used because all finalists may receive job offers. When used, discretionary assessment methods are typically very subjective and rely heavily on the intuition of the decision maker. Thus, factors other than KSAOs may be assessed. Organizations intent on maintaining strong cultures may wish to consider assessing the person/ organization match at this stage of the selection process.

Another interesting method of discretionary assessment that focuses on person/ organization match is the selection of people on the basis of likely organizational citizenship behavior.[137] With this approach, finalists not only must fulfill all of the requirements of the job but also are expected to fulfill some roles outside the requirements of the job, called organizational citizenship behaviors. These behaviors include things like doing extra work, helping others at work, covering for a sick coworker, and being courteous.

Discretionary assessments should involve use of the organization's staffing philosophy regarding EEO/AA commitments. Here, the commitment may be to enhance the representation of minorities and women in the organization's workforce, either voluntarily or as part of an organization's AAP. At this point in the selection process, the demographic characteristics of the finalists may be given weight in the decision about to whom the job offer will be extended. Regardless of how the organization chooses to make its discretionary assessments, they should never be used without being preceded by initial and substantive methods.

CONTINGENT ASSESSMENT METHODS

As was shown in Exhibit 8.3, contingent methods are not always used, depending on the nature of the job and legal mandates. Virtually any selection method can be used as a contingent method. For example, a health clinic may verify that an applicant for a nursing position possesses a valid license after a tentative offer has been made. Similarly, a defense contractor may perform a security clearance check on applicants once initial, substantive, and discretionary methods have been exhausted. While these methods may be used as initial or contingent methods, depending on the preferences of the organization, two selection methods, drug testing and medical exams, should be used exclusively as contingent assessment methods for legal compliance. When drug testing and medical exams are used, considerable care must be taken in their administration and evaluation.

Drug Testing

The cost of alcohol and drug abuse in our country is estimated to be $60 billion per year.[138] Additionally, substance abuse leads to higher utilization of benefits, such as sick time and health care. One comprehensive study found that from 1975 to 1986, approximately 50 train accidents were attributed to workers under the influence of drugs or alcohol. These accidents resulted in 37 people being killed, 80 injured, and the destruction of property valued at $34 million.[139] A National Transportation Safety Board study found that 31% of all fatal truck accidents were due to alcohol or drugs.[140] A study of drug abuse at work found that the average drug user was 3.6 times more likely to be involved in an accident, received 3 times the average level of sick benefits, was 5 times more likely to file a workers' compensation claim, and missed 10 times as many work days as nonusers.[141] Substance abuse is also associated with psychological (e.g., daydreaming, spending work time on personal matters) and physical (e.g., falling asleep at work, extra long lunch and rest breaks, theft) withdrawal behaviors while employees are at work.[142] As a result of the manifold problems caused by drug use, drug testing is used by 87% of major U.S. corporations, according to a study of nearly 800 HR managers.[143] Drug testing has increased dramatically in the last decade. Drug testing among the Fortune 500 has grown from one in 20 companies in 1983 to nearly 18 of 20 today.

Drug testing is a procedure used by organizations to assess those who abuse alcohol and drugs. By identifying abusers, employers can potentially select them out of the organization before they engage in negative work behaviors and jeopardize the safety of others or, worse yet, cost the organization large sums of money.

Typical substances that are screened for by employers include alcohol, cocaine, amphetamines, marijuana, heroin, and PCP. Screening usually takes place at a laboratory away from the company premises. Estimates are that roughly 5% of individuals test positive for drugs, with marijuana accounting for a majority of the positive results.[144]

As drug testing has become more widespread, more is being learned about the process under which it is used, as well as its effectiveness. Several surveys have revealed the following:[145]

- Alcohol testing is less common among companies employing more than 50 workers (22%) than drug testing (53%).
- Corporations are less likely to make exclusionary decisions following positive tests for alcohol than for drugs.
- Industries where exposure/risk was apparent (industrial manufacturing, transportation, construction) were more likely to test for drugs and alcohol.
- Lower-level employees are more likely to be tested than upper-level employees.
- Drug and alcohol testing is *more* prominent in unionized industries.
- Large organizations are more likely to test for drugs than small organizations.

Types of Tests

There are a variety of tests to ascertain substance abuse. The major categories of tests are:[146]

1. *Body fluids.* Both urine and blood tests can be used. Urine tests are by far the most frequently used method of detecting substance abuse. There are different types of measures for each test. For example, urine samples can be measured using the enzyme-multiplied immunoassay technique or the gas chromatography/spectrometry technique. The latest innovation in drug testing allows companies to test applicants and receive results on the spot, using a strip that is dipped into a urine sample, similar to a home pregnancy test.
2. *Hair analysis.* Samples of hair are analyzed using the same techniques as are used to measure urine samples. Chemicals remain in the hair as it grows, so it can provide a longer record of drug use.
3. *Pupillary reaction test.* The reaction of the pupil to light is assessed. Applicants' pupils will react differently when under the influence of drugs than when drug free.
4. *Performance tests.* Hand-eye coordination is assessed to see if there is impairment compared with the standard drug-free reactions. One of the limitations of performance tests in a selection context is that there may be no feasible means of establishing a baseline against which performance is compared. Thus, performance tests are usually more suitable for testing employees than applicants.

5. *Integrity test.* Many integrity tests contain a section that asks applicants about drug use. The section on substance abuse often includes 20 or so items that inquire about past and present drug use ("I only drink at work when things get real stressful") as well as attitudes toward drug use (e.g., "How often do you think the average employee smokes marijuana on the job?").[147]

Administration

For the results of drug tests to be accurate, precautions must be taken in their administration. When collecting samples to be tested, care must be exercised to ensure that the sample is authentic and not contaminated. To do so, the U.S. Department of Health and Human Services has established specific guidelines to be followed.[148]

The testing itself must be carefully administered as well. Labs may process up to 3,000 samples per day. Hence, human error can occur in the detection process. Also, false-positive results can be generated due to cross-reactions. What this means is that a common compound (e.g., poppy seeds) may interact with the antibodies and mistakenly identify a person as a substance abuser. Prescription medications may also affect drug test results. One new complicating factor in evaluating drug test results is the use of adulterants that mask the detection of certain drugs in the system. Although most adulterants can be tested, not all are easily detected, and many firms are unaware they can ask drug companies to test for adulterants.

In order for the testing to be carefully administered, two steps need to be taken. First, care must be taken in the selection of a reputable drug testing firm. Various certification programs, such as the College of American Pathologists and the National Institute for Drug Abuse (NIDA), exist to ensure that accurate procedures are followed. More than 50 drug testing laboratories have been certified by NIDA. Second, positive drug tests should always be verified by a second test to ensure reliability.

What would a well-conducted drug testing program look like? Samples are first submitted to screening tests, which are relatively inexpensive ($10 to $20 per applicant), but yield many false positives (test indicates drug use when none occurred) due to the cross-reactions described above. Confirmatory tests are then used, which are extremely accurate, but are more expensive ($60 per applicant). The average total cost per applicant has been estimated to be $41. Error rates for confirmatory tests with reputable labs are very low. It should be noted that to avoid false positives, most companies have nonzero cutoff levels for most drugs. Thus, if a mistake does occur, it is much more likely to be a false negative (testing negative when in fact drug use did occur) than a false positive.[149] Thus, some applicants who occasionally use drugs may pass a test, but it is very rare for an individual who has never used the drug to fail the test—assuming the two-step process described above is followed. Exhibit 9.20 outlines the steps involved in a well-designed drug testing program. In this example:

EXHIBIT 9.20   Example of an Organizational Drug Testing Program

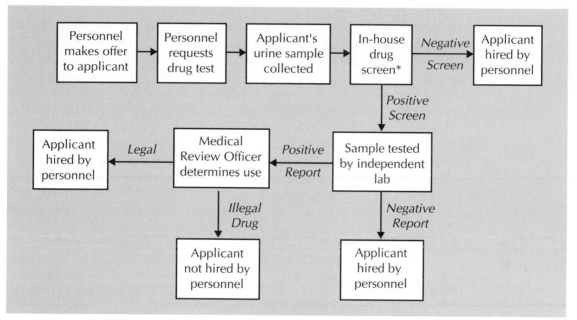

* Most organizations screen for five drugs: amphetamines, cocaine, cannabinoids (e.g., marijuana, hashish), opiates (morphine, heroin), phencyclidine (PCP).

- Applicants are advised in advance of testing.
- All applicants are screened by urine testing.
- Prescreening is done in-house; positives are referred to independent lab.
- A strict chain of custody is followed.
- Verified positive applicants are disqualified.
- Disqualified applicants cannot reapply for two years.

Smoking

Some employers are beginning to ban smokers from hiring consideration. A recent study estimated that about 6% of employers will not hire smokers (urinalysis also picks up nicotine). Such policies are usually aimed at cutting insurance costs (smoking costs employers $27 billion annually), absence rates (smokers' absence rates are 50% higher than those of nonsmokers), and potential liability due to the dangers of secondary smoke. However, about half the states have passed laws prohibiting discrimination against off-the-job smoking. Thus, while some employers may wish to screen out smokers to lower health care costs, the myriad legal and ethical issues make it a risky selection practice.

Evaluation

It is commonly believed that drug testing results in a large number of false positives. In fact, if the proper procedures are followed (as already outlined), drug test results are extremely accurate, and error rates are very low. Accuracy of the test, however, is not the same as its validity in predicting important job criteria. The most accurate drug test in the world will be a poor investment if it cannot be established that substance abuse is related to employee behaviors such as accidents, absenteeism, tardiness, impaired job performance, and so on. One of the factors that may bear on the utility of the drug testing program is the number of individuals detected. A 1991 study of 38 federal agencies put the positive rate at only 0.5%, which translated into a testing cost of $77,000 for each positive.[150]

Although more research on the validity of drug testing programs is needed, some organizations are conducting research on the deleterious effects of substance abuse. The U.S. Postal Service conducted an evaluation of their drug testing program using applicants who applied for positions in 21 sites over a six-month period.[151] A quality-control process revealed that the drug testing program was 100% accurate (zero false positives and false negatives). Ten percent of applicants tested positive for drug use (for the purposes of the study, applicants were hired without regard to their test scores). Of those positive tests, 65% were for marijuana, 24% for cocaine, and 11% were for other drugs. They found higher absenteeism for drug users and higher dismissal rates for cocaine users. Drug use was not related to accidents or injuries. A cost-benefit analysis suggested that full implementation of the program would save the Postal Service several million dollars per year in lower absenteeism and turnover rates.

The validity of performance and psychological drug tests is not well established. London House completed a study on applicants for conductor and ticket agent positions at the Chicago Transit Authority (CTA) and found that 77% of those not recommended for employment based on their psychological test scores were disciplined for excessive absenteeism, whereas the discipline rate for other applicants was 41% (obviously the CTA has an absenteeism problem). Another London House study found that psychological and medical drug tests had the same results for 84% of applicants.[152] As with integrity tests, a major concern is faking, but an advantage of psychological drug tests is that they are likely to be perceived as less intrusive by applicants. However, a 1993 survey suggested that relatively few organizations rely on physical (2%) or psychological (9%) drug tests.[153]

In considering the validity of drug tests, one should not assume that the logical criterion against which the tests are validated is job performance. Typically, the criterion of job performance is central to evaluating the validity of most selection measures, yet drug tests have not been validated against job performance. Thus, it is far from clear that drug tests do a good job of discerning good from poor performers. Drug tests do appear to predict other work behaviors, however, including absenteeism, accidents, and other counterproductive behavior. For the purposes for which they are suited, then, validity of drug tests can be concluded to be high.

Finally, as with other assessment methods, two other criteria against which drug testing should be evaluated are adverse impact and applicant reactions. The adverse impact of drug testing is not universally accepted, but the Postal Service study indicated that drug testing programs did have a moderate to high degree of adverse impact against black and Hispanic applicants. Research on applicant reactions to drug tests has revealed inconsistent results.[154] Research does tend to show that if applicants perceive a need for drug testing, they are more likely to find such a program acceptable.[155] Thus, organizations that do a good job explaining the reasons for the tests to applicants are more likely to find that applicants react favorably to the program.

Recommendations for Effective Drug Testing Programs

Due to the recent upturn in drug use among individuals entering the workforce, and improved methods of detecting drug use, drug testing is likely to continue as one of the most commonly used selection methods. In an effort to make organizations' drug testing programs as accurate and effective as possible, six recommendations are outlined as follows:

1. Emphasize drug testing in safety-sensitive jobs as well as positions where the link between substance abuse and negative outcomes (e.g., as was the case with the Postal Service study described earlier) has been documented.
2. Use only reputable testing laboratories, and ensure that strict chain of custody is maintained.
3. Ask applicants for their consent and inform them of test results; provide rejected applicants with the opportunity to appeal.
4. Use retesting to validate positive samples from the initial screening test.
5. Ensure that proper procedures are followed to maintain the applicant's right to privacy.
6. Review program and validate the results against relevant criteria (accidents, absenteeism, turnover, job performance); conduct a cost-benefit analysis of the program, as a very small number of detections may cause the program to have low utility.

Medical Exams

Medical exams are often used to identify potential health risks in job candidates. Care must be taken to ensure that medical exams are used only when a compelling reason to use them exists. This is to ensure that individuals with disabilities unrelated to job performance are not screened out. As a result of these sorts of potential abuses, the use of medical exams is strictly regulated by the Americans With Disabilities Act (discussed later in this chapter).

Although many organizations use medical exams, they are not particularly valid because the procedures performed vary from doctor to doctor.[156] Also, medical exams are not always job related.[157] Finally, the emphasis is usually on short-term rather than long-term health. A promising new development has recently taken place in medical exams. This development is known as job-related medical standards.[158] Under this procedure, physical health standards have been developed that are highly job related. Physicians' manuals have been developed that provide information on the specific diseases and health conditions that prohibit adequate functioning on specific jobs or clusters of tasks. This procedure should not only improve content validity (because it is job related) but also improve reliability because it standardizes diagnosis across physicians. Along with the manuals, useful data-gathering instruments have been developed to properly assess applicants' actual medical conditions. Again, this helps standardize assessments by physicians, which should improve reliability.

LEGAL ISSUES

This section discusses three major legal issues. The first of these is the Uniform Guidelines on Employee Selection Procedures (UGESP), a document that addresses the need to determine if a selection procedure is causing adverse impact, and if so, the validation requirements for the procedure. The second issue is selection in conformance with the ADA as pertains to reasonable accommodation to job applicants and the use of medical tests. The final issue is that of drug testing for job applicants.

Uniform Guidelines on Employee Selection Procedures

The UGESP is a comprehensive set of federal regulations specifying requirements for the selection systems of organizations covered under the Civil Rights Acts and under E.O. 11246 (see *www.eeoc.gov/regs* for the full text of the UGESP). There are four major sections to the UGESP, namely, general principles, technical standards, documentation of impact and validity evidence, and definitions of terms. Each of these sections is summarized next. An excellent review of the UGESP in terms of court cases and examples of acceptable and unacceptable practices is available and should be consulted. The organization should also consult research that reviews how the UGESP have been interpreted, criticized, and used since their passage.[159]

General Principles

1. *Summary.* The organization must keep records that allow it to determine if its selection procedures are causing adverse impact in employment decisions. If no adverse impact is found, the remaining provisions of the UGESP generally do not apply. If adverse impact is found, the organization must either validate the selection procedure(s) causing the adverse impact or take steps to eliminate the adverse impact (such as stopping use of the procedure or using an alternate selection procedure that has less adverse impact).

2. *Scope.* The scope of the UGESP is very broad in that the guidelines apply to selection procedures used as the basis for any employment decisions. Employment decisions include hiring, promotion, demotion, and retention. A selection procedure is defined as "any measure, combination of measures, or procedure used as a basis for any employment decision." The procedures include "the full range of assessment techniques from traditional paper and pencil tests, performance tests, training programs, or probationary periods and physical, educational, and work experience requirements through informal or casual interviews and unscored application forms."

3. *Discrimination defined.* In general, any selection procedure that has an adverse impact is discriminatory unless it has been shown to be valid. There is a separate section for procedures that have not been validated.

4. *Suitable alternative selection procedures.* When a selection procedure has adverse impact, consideration should be given to the use of any suitable alternative selection procedures that may have lesser adverse impact.

5. *Information on adverse impact.* The organization must keep impact records by race, sex, and ethnic group for each of the job categories shown on the EEO-1 form (see Chapter 13).

6. *Evaluation of selection rates.* For each job or job category, the organization should evaluate the results, also known as the "bottom line," of the total selection process. The purpose of the evaluation is to determine if there are differences in selection rates that indicate adverse impact. If adverse impact is not found, the organization usually does not have to take additional compliance steps, such as validation of each step in the selection process. If overall adverse impact is found, the individual components of the selection process should be evaluated for adverse impact.

7. *Adverse impact and the four-fifths rule.* To determine if adverse impact is occurring, the organization should compute and compare selection rates for race, sex, and ethnic groups. A selection rate that is less than four-fifths (or 80%) of the rate for the group with the highest rate is generally regarded as evidence of adverse impact. There are exceptions to this general rule,

based on sample size (small sample) considerations, and on the extent to which the organization's recruitment practices have discouraged applicants disproportionately on grounds of race, sex, or ethnic group.

8. *General standards for validity studies.* There are three types of acceptable validity studies: criterion-related, content, and construct. There are numerous provisions pertaining to standards governing these validity studies, as well as the appropriate use of selection procedures.

9. *Procedures that have not been validated.* This section discusses the use of alternative selection procedures to eliminate adverse impact. It also discusses instances in which validation studies cannot or need not be performed.

10. *Affirmative action.* Use of validated selection procedures does not relieve the employer of any affirmative action obligation it may have. The employer is encouraged to adopt and implement voluntary affirmative action plans.

Technical Standards

This section contains a lengthy specification of the minimum technical standards that should be met when conducting a validation study. There are separate standards given for each of the three types of validity (criterion-related, content, construct) studies.

Documentation of Impact and Validity Evidence

For each job or job category, the employer is required to keep detailed records on adverse impact and, where adverse impact is found, evidence of validity. Detailed record-keeping requirements are provided.

There are two important exceptions to these general requirements. First, a small employer (fewer than 100 employees) does not have to keep separate records for each job category, but only for its total selection process across all jobs. Second, records for race or national origin do not have to be kept for groups constituting less than 2% of the labor force in the relevant labor area.

Definitions

This section provides definitions of terms (25 total) used throughout the UGESP.

In totality, the UGESP makes substantial demands of an organization and its staffing systems. Those demands exist to ensure organizational awareness of the possibility of adverse impact in employment decisions. When adverse impact is found, the UGESP provides mechanisms (requirements) for coping with it. The UGESP thus should occupy a place of prominence in any covered organization's EEO/AA policies and practices.

Selection Under the Americans With Disabilities Act (ADA)

The Americans With Disabilities Act (ADA), as interpreted by the EEOC, creates substantial requirements and suggestions for compliance pertaining to external selection.[160] The general nature of these is identified and commented upon next.

General Principles

There are two major, overarching principles pertaining to selection. The first principle is that it is unlawful to screen out individuals with disabilities, unless the selection procedure is job related and consistent with business necessity. The second principle is that a selection procedure must accurately reflect the KSAOs being measured, and not impaired sensory, manual, or speaking skills, unless those impaired skills are the ones being measured by the procedure.

The first principle is obviously very similar to principles governing selection generally under federal laws and regulations. The second principle is important because it cautions the organization to be sure that its selection procedures do not inadvertently and unnecessarily screen out applicants with disabilities.

Access to Job Application Process

The organization's job application process must be accessible to individuals with disabilities. Reasonable accommodation must be provided to enable all persons to apply, and applicants should be provided assistance (if needed) in completing the application process. Applicants should also be told about the nature and content of the selection process. This allows them to request reasonable accommodation to testing, if needed, in advance.

Reasonable Accommodation to Testing

In general, the organization may use any kind of test in assessing job applicants. These tests must be administered consistently to all job applicants for any particular job.

A very important provision of testing pertains to the requirement to provide reasonable accommodation, if requested, by an applicant to take the test. The purpose of this requirement is to ensure that the test accurately reflects the KSAO being measured, rather than an impairment of the applicant. Reasonable accommodation, however, is not required for a person with an impaired skill if the purpose of that test is to measure that skill. For example, the organization does not have to provide reasonable accommodation on a manual dexterity test to a person with arthritis in the fingers and hands, if the purpose of the test is to measure manual dexterity.

There are numerous types of reasonable accommodation that can be made, and there is organizational experience and research in providing reasonable accommodation.[161] Examples of what might be done to provide reasonable accommodation include substituting an oral test for a written one (or vice versa), providing extra time to complete a test, scheduling rest breaks during a test, and administering tests in large print, in Braille, or by reader.

Medical Examinations: Job Applicants

There are substantial regulations surrounding medical exams, both before and after a job offer. Prior to the offer, the organization may not make medical inquiries or require medical exams of an applicant. The job offer, however, may be conditional, pending the results of a medical exam.

Postoffer, the organization may conduct a medical exam. The exam must be given to all applicants for a particular job, not just individuals with a known or suspected disability. Whereas the content of the exam is not restricted to being only job related, the reasons for rejecting an applicant on the basis of the exam must be job related. A person may also be rejected if exam results indicate a direct threat to the health and safety of others. Results of medical exams are to be kept confidential, held separate from the employee's personnel file, and released only under very specific circumstances.

It is difficult to determine whether something is a medical examination, and thus subject to the above requirements surrounding their use. The EEOC defines a medical examination as "a procedure or test that seeks information about an individual's physical or mental impairments or health."[162] The following factors are suggestive of a selection procedure that would be considered a medical examination:

- It is administered by a health care professional and/or someone trained by such a professional.
- It is designed to reveal an impairment of physical or mental health.
- It is invasive (e.g., requires drawing blood, urine, or breath).
- It measures the applicant's physiological responses to performing a task.
- It is normally given in a medical setting, and/or medical equipment is used.
- It tests for alcohol consumption.

Though closely allied with medical examinations, several types of tests fall outside the bounds of medical examinations; these may be used preoffer. These include physical agility tests, physical fitness tests, vision tests, drug tests for current illegal use of controlled substances, and tests that measure honesty, tastes, and habits.

A gray area involves the use of psychological tests, such as personality tests. They are considered medical if they lead to identifying a medically recognized mental disorder or impairment, such as those in the American Psychiatric Association's *Diagnostics and Statistical Manual of Mental Disorders*. Future regulations and court rulings may help clarify which types of psychological tests are medical exams.

Medical Examinations: Current Employees

This enforcement guidance applies to employees generally, not just employees with disabilities.[163] An employee who applied for a new (different) job with the same employer should be treated as an applicant for a new job and thus subject to the provisions for Medical Examinations: Job Applicants. An individual is not an applicant where she or he is entitled to another position with the same employer (e.g., because of seniority or satisfactory performance in her or his current position) or when returning to a regular job after being on temporary assignment in another job. Instead, these individuals are considered employees.

For employees, the employer may make disability-related inquiries and require medical examinations only if they are job-related and consistent with business necessity. Any information obtained, or voluntarily provided by the employee, is a confidential medical record. The record may only be shared in limited circumstances with managers, supervisors, first aid and safety personnel, and government officials investigating ADA compliance. Generally, a disability-related inquiry or medical examination is job related and consistent with business necessity when the employer has a reasonable belief, based on objective evidence, that (1) an employee's ability to perform essential job functions will be impaired by medical condition or (2) an employee will pose a direct threat due to a medical condition.

A medical examination for employees is defined the same way as for job applicants. Examples of disability-related inquires include:

- Asking an employee whether she or he was disabled (or ever had a disability) or how she or her became disabled or asking about the nature or severity of an employee's disability.
- Asking employees to provide medical documentation regarding their disability.
- Asking an employee's coworkers, family members, doctor, or another person about an employee's disability.
- Asking about an employee's genetic information.
- Asking about an employee's prior workers' compensation history.
- Asking if an employee is taking any medication or drugs, or has done so in the past.
- Asking an employee broad information that is likely to elicit information about a disability.

Drug Testing

Drug testing is permitted to detect the use of illegal drugs. The law, however, is neutral as to its encouragement.

UGESP

The UGESP do not apply to the ADA or its regulations. This means that the guidance and requirements for employers' selection systems under the Civil Rights

Act may or may not be the same as those that end up being required for compliance with the ADA.

Drug Testing

Drug testing is surrounded by an amalgam of laws and regulations at the federal and state levels. Special law for the Department of Transportation requires alcohol and drug testing for transportation workers in safety-sensitive jobs.[164] The organization should seek legal and medical advice to determine if it should do drug testing, and if so, what the nature of the drug testing program should be. Beyond that, the organization should require and administer drug tests on a contingency (postoffer) basis only to avoid the possibility of obtaining and using medical information illegally. For example, positive drug test results may occur because of the presence of a legal drug, and using these results preoffer to reject a person would be a violation of the ADA.

SUMMARY

This chapter continues discussion of proper methods and processes to be used in external selection. Specifically, substantive, discretionary, and contingent assessment methods are discussed, as well as collection of assessment data and pertinent legal issues.

Most of the chapter discusses various substantive methods, which are used to separate out finalists from candidates. As with use of initial assessment methods, use of substantive assessment methods should always be based on the logic of prediction and the use of selection plans. The substantive methods that are reviewed include personality tests; ability tests; job knowledge tests; performance tests and work samples; integrity tests; interest, values, and preference inventories; structured interview; assessment for team and quality environments; and clinical assessments. As with initial assessment methods, the criteria used to evaluate the effectiveness of substantive assessment methods are frequency of use, cost, reliability, validity, utility, applicant reactions, and adverse impact. In general, substantive assessment methods show a marked improvement in reliability and validity over initial assessment methods. This is probably due to the stronger relationship between the sampling of the applicant's previous situations with the requirements for success on the job.

Discretionary selection methods are somewhat less formal and more subjective than other selection methods. When discretionary methods are used, two judgments are most important: Will the applicant be a good organization "citizen," and do the values and goals of this applicant match those of the organization?

Though discretionary methods are subjective, contingent assessment methods typically involve decisions about whether applicants meet certain objective requirements for the job. The two most common contingent methods are drug testing and medical exams. Particularly in the case of drug testing, the use of contingent methods is relatively complex from an administrative and legal standpoint.

Regardless of predictor type, attention must be given to the proper collection and use of predictor information. In particular, support services need to be established, administrators with the appropriate credentials need to be hired, data need to be kept private and confidential, and administration procedures must be standardized.

Along with administrative issues, legal issues need to be considered as well. Particular attention must be paid to regulations that govern permissible activities by organizations. Regulations include those in the Uniform Guidelines on Employee Selection Procedures and the Americans With Disabilities Act.

DISCUSSION QUESTIONS

1. Describe the similarities and differences between personality tests and integrity tests. When is each warranted in the selection process?
2. How would you advise an organization considering adopting a cognitive ability test for selection?
3. Describe the structured interview. What are the characteristics of structured interviews that improve on the shortcomings of unstructured interviews?
4. What are the selection implications for an organization that has recently adopted a total quality management program?
5. What are the most common discretionary and contingent assessment methods? What are the similarities and differences between the use of these two methods?
6. How should organizations apply the general principles of the Uniform Guidelines on Employee Selection Procedures to practical selection decisions?

APPLICATIONS

Assessment Methods for the Job of Human Resources Director

Nairduwel, Inoalot, and Imslo (NII) is a law firm specializing in business law. Among other areas, they deal in equal employment opportunity law, business litigation, and workplace torts. The firm has more than 50 partners and approximately 120 employees. They do business in three states and have law offices in two major metropolitan areas. The firm has no federal contracts.

NII has plans to expand into two additional states with two major metropolitan areas. One of the primary challenges accompanying this ambitious expansion plan is how to staff, train, and compensate individuals who will fill the positions in the new offices. Accordingly, the firm wishes to hire an HR director to oversee the recruitment, selection, training, performance appraisal, and compensation activities accompanying the business expansion, as well as supervise the HR activities in the existing NII offices. The newly created job description for the HR director is listed in the accompanying exhibit.

The firm wishes to design and then use a selection system for assessing applicants that will achieve two objectives: (1) create a valid and useful system that will do a good job of matching applicant KSAOs to job requirements, and (2) be in compliance with all relevant federal and state employment law.

The firm is considering numerous selection techniques for possible use. For each method listed below, decide whether you would probably use it or not in the selection process and state why.

1. job knowledge test specifically designed for HR professionals that focuses on an applicant's general knowledge of HR management

2. medical examination and drug test at the beginning of the selection process in order to determine if applicants are able to cope with the high level of stress and frequent travel requirements of the job and are drug free

3. paper-and-pencil integrity test

4. a structured, behavioral interview that will be specially designed for use in filling only this job

5. general cognitive ability test

6. Personal Characteristics Inventory

7. a set of interview questions that the firm typically uses for filling any position:

   (a) Tell me about a problem you solved on a previous job.
   (b) Do you have any physical impairments that would make it difficult for you to travel on business?
   (c) Have you ever been tested for AIDS?
   (d) Are you currently unemployed, and if so, why?
   (e) This position requires fresh ideas and energy. Do you think you have those qualities?
   (f) What is your definition of success?
   (g) What kind of sports do you like?
   (h) How well do you work under pressure? Give me some examples.

Exhibit

Job Description for Human Resources Director

JOB SUMMARY

Performs responsible administrative work managing personnel activities. Work involves responsibility for the planning and administration of HRM programs, including recruitment, selection, evaluation, appointment, promotion, compensation, and recommended change of status of employees, and a system of communication for disseminating information to workers. Works under general supervision, exercising initiative and independent judgment in the performance of assigned tasks.

TASKS

1. Participates in overall planning and policy making to provide effective and uniform personnel services.
2. Communicates policy through organization levels by bulletin, meetings, and personal contact.
3. Supervises recruitment and screening of job applicants to fill vacancies. Supervises interviewing of applicants, evaluation of qualifications, and classification of applications.
4. Supervises administration of tests to applicants.
5. Confers with supervisors on personnel matters, including placement problems, retention or release of probationary employees, transfers, demotions, and dismissals of permanent employees.
6. Initiates personnel training activities and coordinates these activities with work of officials and supervisors.
7. Establishes effective service rating system, trains unit supervisors in making employee evaluations.
8. Supervises maintenance of employee personnel files.
9. Supervises a group of employees directly and through subordinates.
10. Performs related work as assigned.

JOB SPECIFICATIONS

1. *Experience and Training*
   Should have considerable experience in area of HRM administration. Six years minimum.
2. *Education*
   Graduation from a four-year college or university, with major work in human resources, business administration, or industrial psychology. Master's degree in one of these areas is preferable.

3. *Knowledge, Skills, and Abilities*
   Considerable knowledge of principles and practices of HRM, including staffing, compensation, training, and performance evaluation.
4. *Responsibility*
   Supervises the human resource activities of six office managers, one clerk, and one secretary.

Choosing Among Finalists for the Job of Human Resources Director

Assume that Nairduwel, Inoalot, and Imslo (NII), after weighing their options, decided to use the following selection methods to assess applicants for the HR director job: résumé, cognitive ability test, job knowledge test, structured interview, and questions *(f)* and *(g)* from the list of generic interview questions.

NII advertised for the position extensively, and out of a pool of 23 initial applicants, they were able to come up with a list of three finalists. Shown in the accompanying exhibit are the results from the assessment of the three finalists using these selection methods. In addition, information from an earlier résumé screen is included for possible consideration. For each finalist, you are to decide whether or not you would be willing to hire the person and why.

Exhibit

Results of Assessment of Finalists for Human Resource Director Position

	Finalist 1— Lola Vega	Finalist 2— Sam Fein	Finalist 3— Shawanda Jackson
Résumé	GPA 3.9/Cornell University B.S. Human Resource Mgmt. 5 years' experience in HRM • 4 years in recruiting	GPA 2.8/SUNY Binghamton B.B.A. Finance 20 years' experience in HRM • Numerous HR assignments • Certified HR professional	GPA 3.2/Auburn University B.B.A. Business and English 8 years' experience in HRM • 3 years HR generalist • 4 years compensation analyst
	No supervisory experience	15 years' supervisory experience	5 years' supervisory experience
Cognitive ability test	90% correct	78% correct	84% correct

Knowledge test	94% correct	98% correct	91% correct
Structured Int. (out of 100 pts)	85	68	75
Question (f)	Ability to influence others	To do things you want to do	Promotions and earnings
Question (g)	Golf, shuffleboard	Spectator sports	Basketball, tennis

ENDNOTES

1. L. M. Hough, "The 'Big Five' Personality Variables—Construct Confusion: Description versus Prediction," *Human Performance,* 1992, 5, 139–155.

2. R. M. Guion and R. F. Gottier, "Validity of Personality Measures in Personnel Selection," *Personnel Psychology,* 1965, 18, pp. 135–164.

3. P. T. Costa Jr. and R. R. McCrae, "Four Ways Five Factors Are Basic," *Personality and Individual Differences,* 1992, 13, pp. 653–665.

4. D. S. Ones and C. Viswesvaran, "Bandwidth-Fidelity Dilemma in Personality Measurement for Personnel Selection," *Journal of Organizational Behavior,* 1996, 17, pp. 609–626.

5. M. K. Mount and M. R. Barrick, *Manual for the Personal Characteristics Inventory* (Iowa City, IA: author, 1995).

6. P. T. Costa Jr. and R. R. McCrae, *Revised NEO Personality Inventory (NEO-PI-R) and NEO Five-Factor (NEO-FFI) Inventory Professional Manual* (Odessa, FL: Psychological Assessment Resources, 1992).

7. J. Hogan and R. Hogan, "How to Measure Employee Reliability," *Journal of Applied Psychology,* 1989, 74, pp. 273–279.

8. J. B. Miner, "The Miner Sentence Completion Scale: A Reappraisal," *Academy of Management Journal,* 1978, 21, pp. 283–294.

9. M. R. Barrick and M. K. Mount, "The Big Five Personality Dimensions and Job Performance: A Meta-Analysis," *Personnel Psychology,* 1991, 44, pp. 1–26; G. M. Hurtz and J. J. Donovan, "Personality and Job Performance: The Big Five Revisited," *Journal of Applied Psychology,* 2000, 85, pp. 869–879.

10. T. A. Judge and J. E. Bono, "Relationship of Core Self-Evaluations to Job Satisfaction and Job Performance: A Meta-Analysis," 1998, Working paper, University of Iowa.

11. A. J. Vinchur, J. S. Schippmann, F. A. Switzer, and P. L. Roth, "A Meta-Analysis of the Predictors of Job Performance for Salespeople," *Journal of Applied Psychology,* 1998, 83, pp. 586–597.

12. J. F. Salgado, "The Five-Factor Model of Personality and Job Performance in the European Community," *Journal of Applied Psychology,* 1997, 82, pp. 30–43.

13. M. K. Mount and M. R. Barrick, "The Big Five Personality Dimensions: Implications for Research and Practice in Human Resources Management," in G. R. Ferris (ed.), *Research in Personnel and Human Resources Management,* vol. 13 (Greenwich, CT: JAI Press), pp. 153–200.

14. M. R. Barrick and M. K. Mount, "Autonomy as a Moderator of the Relationships Between the Big Five Personality Dimensions and Job Performance," *Journal of Applied Psychology,* 1993, 78, pp. 111–118; M. R. Barrick, M. K. Mount, and J. P. Strauss, "Conscientiousness and Performance of Sales Representatives: Test of the Mediating Effects of Goal Setting," *Journal of Applied Psychology,* 1993, 78, pp. 715–722; I. R. Gellatly, "Conscientiousness and Task Performance: Test of a Cognitive Process Model," *Journal of Applied Psychology,* 1996, 81, pp. 474–482; K. R. Murphy and S. L. Lee, "Personality Variables Related to Integrity Test Scores: The Role of Conscientiousness," *Journal of Business and Psychology,* 1994, 9, pp. 413–424.

15. L. M. Hough, "The 'Big Five' Personality Variables—Construct Confusion: Description Versus Prediction"; R. P. Tett, "Is Conscientiousness ALWAYS Positively Related to Job Performance?" *The Industrial-Organizational Psychologist,* 1998, pp. 24–29.

16. B. Azar, "Which Traits Predict Job Performance?" *APA Monitor,* July 1995, pp. 30–31.

17. I. T. Roberston, "Personality Assessment and Personnel Selection," *European Review of Applied Psychology,* 1993, 43, pp. 187–194; R. P. Tett, D. N. Jackson, and M. Rothstein, "Personality Measures as Predictors of Job Performance: A Meta-Analytic Review," *Personnel Psychology,* 1991, 44, pp. 703–742.

18. M. J. Schmit, J. A. Kilm, and C. Robie, "Development of a Global Measure of Personality," *Personnel Psychology,* 2000, 53, pp. 153–193; M. J. Schmit, A. M. Ryan, S. L. Stierwalt, and A. B. Powell, "Frame-of-Reference Effects on Personality Scale Scores and Criterion-Related Validity," *Journal of Applied Psychology,* 1995, 80, pp. 607–620; P. H. Raymark, M. J. Schmit, and R. M. Guion, "Identifying Potentially Useful Personality Constructs for Employee Selection," *Personnel Psychology,* 1997, 50, pp. 723–736.

19. A. Erez and T. A. Judge, "Relationship of Core Self-Evaluations to Goal Setting, Motivation, and Performance," *Journal of Applied Psychology,* in press; T. A. Judge and J. E. Bono, "Relationship of Core Self-Evaluations Traits—Self-Esteem, Generalized Self-Efficacy, Locus of Control, and Emotional Stability—with Job Satisfaction and Job Performance: A Meta-Analysis," *Journal of Applied Psychology,* 2001, 86, pp. 80–92; T. A. Judge, A. Erez, J. E. Bono, and C. J. Thoresen, "The Core Self-Evaluations Scale: Development of a Measure," Working paper, University of Florida, 2001; T. A. Judge, C. J. Thoresen, V. Pucik, and T. M. Welbourne, "Managerial Coping with Organizational Change: A Dispositional Perspective," *Journal of Applied Psychology,* 1999, 84, pp. 107–122.

20. M. R. Barrick and M. K. Mount, "Effects of Impression Management and Self-Deception on the Predictive Validity of Personality Constructs," *Journal of Applied Psychology,* 1996, 81, pp. 261–272; L. M. Hough, N. E. Eaton, M. D. Dunnette, J. D. Kamp, and R. A. McCloy, "Criterion-Related Validities of Personality Constructs and the Effect of Response Distortion of Those Validities," *Journal of Applied Psychology* (Monograph), 1990, 75, pp. 581–595; D. S. Ones, C. Viswesvaran, and A. D. Reiss, "Role of Social Desirability in Personality Testing for Personnel Selection: The Red Herring," *Journal of Applied Psychology,* 1996, 81, pp. 660–679; J. E. Ellingson, P. R. Sackett, and L. M. Hough, "Social Desirability Corrections in Personality Measurement: Issues of Applicant Comparison and Construct Validity," *Journal of Applied Psychology,* 1999, 84, pp. 155–166.

21. J. G. Rosse, M. D. Stecher, J. L. Miller, and R. A. Levin, "The Impact of Response Distortion on Preemployment Personality Testing and Hiring Decisions," *Journal of Applied Psychology,* 1998, 83, pp. 634–644.

22. H. Schuler, "Social Validity of Selection Situations: A Concept and Some Empirical Results," in H. Schuler, J. L. Farr and M. Smith (eds.), *Personnel Selection and Assessment: Individual and Organizational Perspectives* (Hillsdale, NJ: Erlbaum, 1993), pp. 11–26.

23. J. W. Smither, R. R. Reilly, R. E. Millsap, K. Pearlman, and R. W. Stoffey, "Applicant Reactions to Selection Procedures," *Personnel Psychology,* 1993, 46, pp. 49–76.

24. J. G. Rosse, J. L. Miller, and M. D. Stecher, "A Field Study of Job Applicants' Reactions to Personality and Cognitive Ability Testing," *Journal of Applied Psychology,* 1994, 79, pp. 987–992; S. L. Rynes and M. L. Connerley, "Applicant Reactions to Alternative Selection Procedures," *Journal of Business and Psychology,* 1993, 7, pp. 261–277; D. D. Steiner and S. W. Gilliland, "Fairness Reactions to Personnel Selection Techniques in France and the United States," *Journal of Applied Psychology,* 1996, 81, pp. 134–141.

25. P. M. Rowe, M. C. Williams, and A. L. Day, "Selection Procedures in North America," *International Journal of Selection and Assessment,* 1994, 2, pp. 74–79.

26. E. A. Fleishman and M. E. Reilly, *Handbook of Human Abilities* (Palo Alto, CA: Consulting Psychologists Press, 1992).

27. M. J. Ree and J. A. Earles, "The Stability of Convergent Estimates of g," *Intelligence,* 1991, 15, pp. 271–278.

28. F. Wonderlic Jr., "Test Publishers Form Association," *Human Resource Measurements* (Supplement to the January 1993 *Personnel Journal*), p. 3.

29. B. Azar, "Could 'Policing' Test Use Improve Assessments?," *APA Monitor,* June 1994, p. 16.

30. L. S. Gottfredson, "Societal Consequences of the g Factor in Employment," *Journal of Vocational Behavior,* 1986, 29, pp. 379–410.

31. J. E. Hunter, "Cognitive Ability, Cognitive Aptitudes, Job Knowledge, and Job Performance," *Journal of Vocational Behavior,* 1986, 29, pp. 340–362.

32. M. J. Ree and J. A. Earles, "Predicting Training Success: Not Much More Than g," *Personnel Psychology,* 1991, 44, pp. 321–332.

33. P. M. Wright, G. McMahan, and D. Smart, "Team Cognitive Ability as a Predictor of Performance: An Examination of the Role of SAT Scores in Determining NCAA Basketball Team Performance." Working paper, Department of Management, Texas A&M University.

34. R. J. Sternberg, R. K. Wagner, W. M. Williams, and J. A. Horvath, "Testing Common Sense," *American Psychologist,* 1995, 50, pp. 912–927.

35. J. E. Hunter, "Cognitive Ability, Cognitive Aptitudes, Job Knowledge, and Job Performance"; F. L. Schmidt and J. E. Hunter, "Development of a Causal Model of Processes Determining Job Performance," *Current Directions in Psychological Science,* 1992, 1, pp. 89–92.

36. J. J. McHenry, L. M. Hough, J. L. Toquam, M. A. Hanson, and S. Ashworth, "Project A Validity Results: The Relationship Between Predictor and Criterion Domains," *Personnel Psychology,* 1990, 43, pp. 335–354.

37. M. J. Ree, J. A. Earles, and M. S. Teachout, "Predicting Job Performance: Not Much More than g," *Journal of Applied Psychology,* 1994, 79, pp. 518–524.

38. J. E. Hunter, "Cognitive Ability, Cognitive Aptitudes, Job Knowledge, and Job Performance."

39. R. J. Sternberg, et al., "Testing Common Sense"; R. J. Sternberg, "Tacit Knowledge and Job Success," in N. Anderson and P. Herriot (eds.), *Assessment and Selection in Organizations* (Chichester, England: Wiley, 1994), pp. 27–39.

40. F. L. Schmidt and J. E. Hunter, "Tacit Knowledge, Practical Intelligence, General Mental Ability, and Job Knowledge," *Current Directions in Psychological Science,* 1992, 1, pp. 8–9.

41. F. J. Landy and L. J. Shankster, "Personnel Selection and Placement," *Annual Review of Psychology,* 1994, 45, pp. 261–296.

42. P. R. Sackett and S. L. Wilk, "Within-Group Norming and Other Forms of Score Adjustment in Preemployment Testing," *American Psychologist,* 1994, 49, pp. 929–954; P. L. Roth, C. A.

Bevier, P. Bobko, F. S. Switzer, and P. Tyler, "Ethnic Group Differences in Cognitive Ability in Employment and Educational Settings: A Meta-Analysis," *Personnel Psychology,* 2001, 54, pp. 297–330.

43. R. D. Arvey and P. R. Sackett, "Fairness in Selection: Current Developments and Perspectives," in N. Schmitt, W. C. Borman, and Associates (eds.), *Personnel Selection in Organizations* (San Francisco: Jossey-Bass, 1993), pp. 171–202; R. P. DeShon, M. R. Smith, D. Chan, and N. Schmitt, "Can Racial Differences in Cognitive Test Performance Be Reduced by Presenting Problems in a Social Context?" *Journal of Applied Psychology,* 1998, 83, pp. 438–451; F. L. Schmidt, "The Problem of Group Differences in Ability Test Scores in Employment Selection," *Journal of Vocational Behavior,* 1988, 33, pp. 272–292.

44. D. S. Ones, C. Viswesvaran, and F. L. Schmidt, "Comprehensive Meta-Analysis of Integrity Test Validities: Findings and Implications for Personnel Selection and Theories of Job Performance," *Journal of Applied Psychology* (monograph), 1993, 78, pp. 531–537; A. M. Ryan, R. E. Ployhart, and L. A. Friedel, "Using Personality to Reduce Adverse Impact: A Cautionary Note," *Journal of Applied Psychology,* 1998, 83, pp. 298–307; P. Boko, P. L. Roth, and D. Potosky, "Derivation and Implications of a Meta-Analytic Matrix Incorporating Cognitive Ability, Alternative Predictors, and Job Performance," *Personnel Psychology,* 1999, 52, pp. 561–589.

45. T. A. Judge, D. Blancero, D. M. Cable, and D. E. Johnson, "Effects of Selection Systems on Job Search Decisions." Paper presented at the Tenth Annual Conference of the Society for Industrial and Organizational Psychology, 1995, Orlando, FL.

46. S. L. Rynes and M. L. Connerley, "Applicant Reactions to Alternative Selection Procedures."

47. J. W. Smither, et al., "Applicant Reactions to Selection Procedures."

48. J. Hogan, "Physical Abilities," in M. D. Dunnette and L. M. Hough (eds.), *Handbook of Industrial and Organizational Psychology,* vol. 2 (Palo Alto, CA: Consulting Psychologists Press, 1991), pp. 753–831.

49. R. Britt, "Hands and Wrists Are Thrust into the Hiring Process," *New York Times,* Sept. 21, 1997, p. 11.

50. M. A. Campion, "Personnel Selection for Physically Demanding Jobs: Review and Recommendations," *Personnel Psychology,* 1987, 36, pp. 527–550.

51. T. A. Baker, *The Utility of a Physical Test in Reducing Injury Costs.* Paper presented at the Ninth Annual Meeting of the Society for Industrial and Organizational Psychology, Nashville, TN, 1995.

52. B. R. Blakley, M. A. Quinones, M. S. Crawford, and I. A. Jago, "The Validity of Isometric Strength Tests," *Personnel Psychology,* 1994, 47, pp. 247–274.

53. E. E. Ghiselli, "The Validity of Aptitude Tests in Personnel Selection," *Personnel Psychology,* 1973, 61, pp. 461–467.

54. V. C. Smith, "An Upgrade for Testing," *Human Resource Executive,* 1995, 8, pp. 41–43.

55. QWIZ, Atlanta, Georgia.

56. F. Drasgow, J. B. Olson, P. A. Keenan, P. Moberg, and A. D. Mead, "Computerized Assessment," in G. R. Ferris and K. M. Rowland (eds.), *Research in Personnel and Human Resources Management* (Greenwich, CT: JAI Press, 1993), pp. 163–206.

57. R. C. Overton, L. R. Taylor, M. J. Zickar, and H. J. Harms, "The Pen-Based Computer as an Alternative Platform for Test Administration," *Personnel Psychology,* 1996, 49, pp. 455–464; J. B. Olson-Buchanan, F. Drasgow, D. J. Moberg, A. D. Mead, P. A. Keenan, and M. A. Donovan, "Interactive Video Assessment of Conflict Resolution Skills," *Personnel Psychology,* 1998, 51, pp. 1–24.

58. A. D. Mead and F. Drasgow, "Equivalence of Computerized and Paper-and-Pencil Cognitive Ability Tests: A Meta-Analysis," *Psychological Bulletin*, 1993, 114, pp. 449–458.

59. Wisconsin Department of Employment Relations, *Developing Wisconsin State Civil Service Examinations and Assessment Procedures* (Madison, WI: author, 1994).

60. D. M. Dye, M. Reck, and M. A. McDaniel, "The Validity of Job Knowledge Measures," *International Journal of Selection and Assessment*, 1993, 1, pp. 153–157.

61. J. E. Hunter, "Cognitive Ability, Cognitive Aptitudes, Job Knowledge, and Job Performance."

62. M. J. Ree, J. A. Earles, and M. S. Teachout, "Predicting Job Performance: Not Much More than *g*"; M. M. Olea and M. J. Ree, "Predicting Pilot and Navigator Criteria: Not Much More than *g*," *Journal of Applied Psychology*, 1994, 79, pp. 845–851.

63. M. J. Ree, T. R. Carretta, and M. S. Teachout, "Role of Ability and Prior Job Knowledge in Complex Training Performance," *Journal of Applied Psychology*, 1995, 80, pp. 721–730.

64. L. McGinley, "Fitness Exams Help to Measure Worker Activity," *Wall Street Journal*, Apr. 21, 1992, p. B1.

65. R. Miller, "The Legal Minefield of Employment Probation," *Benefits & Compensation Solutions*, 1998, 21, pp. 40–43.

66. J. J. Asher and J. A. Sciarrino, "Realistic Work Sample Tests: A Review," *Personnel Psychology*, 1974, 27, pp. 519–533.

67. S. J. Motowidlo, M. D. Dunnette, and G. Carter, "An Alternative Selection Procedure: A Low-Fidelity Simulation," *Journal of Applied Psychology*, 1990, 75, pp. 640–647.

68. W. Arthur Jr., G. V. Barrett, and D. Doverspike, "Validation of an Information Processing-Based Test Battery Among Petroleum-Product Transport Drivers," *Journal of Applied Psychology*, 1990, 75, pp. 621–628.

69. J. Cook, "Sure Bet," *Human Resource Executive*, Jan. 1997, pp. 32–34.

70. S. J. Motowidlo, et al., "An Alternative Selection Procedure: A Low-Fidelity Simulation."

71. S. Sillup, "Applicant Screening Cuts Turnover Costs," *Personnel Journal*, May 1992, pp. 115–116.

72. Electronic Selection Systems Corporation, *AccuVision: Assessment Technology for Today, Tomorrow, and Beyond* (Maitland, FL: author, 1992).

73. D. Chan and N. Schmitt, "Video-Based versus Paper-and-Pencil Method of Assessment in Situational Judgment Tests: Subgroup Differences in Test Performance and Face Validity Perceptions," *Journal of Applied Psychology*, 1997, 82, pp. 143–159; J. Clevenger, G. M. Pereira, D. Wiechmann, N. Schmitt, and V. S. Harvey, "Incremental Validity of Situational Judgment Tests," *Journal of Applied Psychology*, 2001, 86, pp. 410–417; M. A. McDaniel, F. P. Morgeson, E. B. Finnegan, M. A. Campion, and E. P. Braverman, "Use of Situational Judgment Tests of Predict Job Performance: A Clarification of the Literature," *Journal of Applied Psychology*, 2001, 86, pp. 730–740; N. Schmitt and A. E. Mills, "Traditional Tests and Job Simulations: Minority and Majority Performance and Test Validities," *Journal of Applied Psychology*, 2001, 86, pp. 451–458; J. A. Weekley and C. Jones, "Further Studies of Situational Tests," *Personnel Psychology*, 1999, 52, pp. 679–700.

74. J. E. Hunter and R. F. Hunter, "Validity and Utility of Alternative Predictors of Job Performance," *Psychological Bulletin*, 1984, 96, pp. 72–98.

75. W. Cascio and W. Phillips, "Performance Testing: A Rose Among Thorns?," *Personnel Psychology*, 1979, 32, pp. 751–766.

76. K. G. Love, R. C. Bishop, D. A. Heinisch, and M. S. Montei, "Selection Across Two Cultures:

Adapting the Selection of American Assemblers to Meet Japanese Job Performance Dimensions,'' *Personnel Psychology,* 1994, 47, pp. 837–846.

77. K. A. Hanisch and C. L. Hulin, ''Two-Stage Sequential Selection Procedures Using Ability and Training Performance: Incremental Validity of Behavioral Consistency Measures,'' *Personnel Psychology,* 1994, 47, pp. 767–785.

78. P. R. Sackett, and J. E. Wanek, ''New Developments in the Use of Measures of Honesty, Integrity, Conscientiousness, Dependability, Trustworthiness, and Reliability for Personnel Selection,'' *Personnel Psychology,* 1996, 49, pp. 787–829.

79. L. R. Goldberg, J. R. Grenier, R. M. Guion, L. B. Sechrest, and H. Wing, *Questionnaires Used in the Prediction of Trustworthiness in Pre-Employment Selection Decisions: An APA Task Force Report* (Washington, DC: American Psychological Association, 1991).

80. W. J. Camera and D. L. Schneider, ''Integrity Tests: Facts and Unresolved Issues,'' *American Psychologist,* 1994, 49, pp. 112–119.

81. P. R. Sackett, ''Integrity Testing for Personnel Selection,'' *Current Directions in Psychological Science,* 1994, 3, pp. 73–76.

82. M. R. Cunningham, D. T. Wong, and A. P. Barbee, ''Self-Presentation Dynamics on Overt Integrity Tests: Experimental Studies of the Reid Report,'' *Journal of Applied Psychology,* 1994, 79, pp. 643–658.

83. R. C. Hollinger and J. P. Clark, *Theft by Employees* (Lexington, MA: Lexington Books, 1983).

84. D. S. Ones, ''The Construct Validity of Integrity Tests.'' Unpublished doctoral dissertation, University of Iowa, Iowa City, Iowa, 1993.

85. K. R. Murphy and S. L. Lee, ''Personality Variables Related to Integrity Test Scores: The Role of Conscientiousness,'' *Journal of Business and Psychology,* 1994, 9, pp. 413–424.

86. D. S. Ones, C. Viswesvaran, F. L. Schmidt, and A. D. Reiss, ''The Validity of Honesty and Violence Scales of Integrity Tests in Predicting Violence at Work.'' Paper presented at the Academy of Management Annual Meeting, Dallas, TX, Aug. 1994.

87. D. S. Ones, F. L. Schmidt, and C. Viswesvaran, ''Do Broader Personality Variables Predict Job Performance with Higher Validity?''; D. S. Ones, C. Viswesvaran, and F. L. Schmidt, ''Integrity Tests: Overlooked Facts, Resolved Issues, and Remaining Questions,'' *American Psychologist,* 1995, 50, pp. 456–460.

88. P. Ekman and M. O'Sullivan, ''Who Can Catch a Liar?'' *American Psychologist,* 1991, 46, pp. 913–920.

89. D. S. Ones, C. Viswesvaran, and F. L. Schmidt, ''Comprehensive Meta-Analysis of Integrity Test Validities: Findings and Implications for Personnel Selection and Theories of Job Performance.''

90. J. Hogan and K. Brinkenmeyer, ''Bridging the Gap Between Overt and Personality-Based Integrity Tests,'' *Personnel Psychology,* 1997, 50, pp. 587–599; D. S. Ones, ''The Construct Validity of Integrity Tests''; D. S. Ones and C. Viswesvaran, ''Gender, Age and Race Differences on Overt Integrity Tests: Results Across Four Large-Scale Job Applicant Data Sets,'' *Journal of Applied Psychology,* 1998, 83, pp. 35–42.

91. A. M. Ryan and P. R. Sackett, ''Preemployment Honesty Testing: Fakability, Reactions of Test Takers, and Company Image,'' *Journal of Business and Psychology,* 1987, 1, pp. 248–256.

92. M. R. Cunningham, D. T. Wong, and A. P. Barbee, ''Self-Presentation Dynamics on Overt Integrity Tests: Experimental Studies of the Reid Report,'' *Journal of Applied Psychology,* 1994, 79, pp. 643–658.

93. S. O. Lilienfeld, G. Alliger, and K. Mitchell, ''Why Integrity Testing Remains Controversial,''

American Psychologist, 1995, 50, pp. 457–458; M. L. Rieke and S. J. Guastello, "Unresolved Issues in Honesty and Integrity Testing," *American Psychologist,* 1995, 50, pp. 458–459.

94. S. W. Gilliland, "Fairness from the Applicant's Perspective: Reactions to Employee Selection Procedures," *International Journal of Selection and Assessment,* 1995, 3, pp. 11–19; D. A. Kravitz, V. Stinson, and T. L. Chavez, "Evaluations of Tests Used for Making Selection and Promotion Decisions," *International Journal of Selection and Assessment,* 1996, 4, pp. 24–34.

95. R. R. McCrae and P. T. Costa Jr., "Reinterpreting the Myers-Briggs Type Indicator from the Perspective of the Five-Factor Model of Personality," *Journal of Personality,* 1989, 57, pp. 17–40.

96. L. M. Hough, "The 'Big Five' Personality Variables—Construct Confusion: Description Versus Prediction."

97. M. Assouline and E. I. Meir, "Meta-Analysis of the Relationship Between Congruence and Well-Being Measures," *Journal of Vocational Behavior,* 1987, 31, pp. 319–332.

98. See B. Schneider, H. W. Goldstein, and D. B. Smith, "The ASA Framework: An Update," *Personnel Psychology,* 1995, 48, pp. 747–773.

99. D. M. Cable, "The Role of Person-Organization Fit in Organizational Entry." Unpublished doctoral dissertation, Cornell University, Ithaca, New York, 1995.

100. D. F. Caldwell and C. A. O'Reilly III, "Measuring Person-Job Fit with a Profile Comparison Process," *Journal of Applied Psychology,* 1990, 75, pp. 648–657; J. A. Chatman, "Matching People to Organizations: Selection and Socialization in Public Accounting Firms," *Administrative Science Quarterly,* 1989, 36, pp. 459–484; C. A. O'Reilly III, J. Chatman, and D. F. Caldwell, "People and Organizational Culture: A Profile Comparison Approach to Assessing Person-Organization Fit," *Academy of Management Journal,* 1991, 34, pp. 487–516.

101. A. M. Ryan and P. R. Sackett, "A Survey of Individual Assessment Practices by I/O Psychologists," *Personnel Psychology,* 1987, 40, pp. 455–488.

102. R. L. Dipboye, *Selection Interviews: Process Perspectives* (Cincinnati, OH: South-Western, 1992), pp. 150–180; R. W. Eder and M. Harris (eds.), *The Employment Interview Handbook* (Thousand Oaks, CA: Sage, 1999).

103. L. M. Graves and R. J. Karren, "The Employee Selection Interview: A Fresh Look at an Old Problem," *Human Resource Management,* 1996, 35, pp. 163–180.

104. R. Pingatore, B. L. Dugoni, R. S. Tindale, and B. Spring, "Bias Against Overweight Job Applicants in a Simulated Employment Interview," *Journal of Applied Psychology,* 1994, 79, pp. 909–917.

105. J. R. Burnett and S. J. Motowidlo, "Relation Between Different Sources of Information in the Structured Selection Interview," *Personnel Psychology,* 1998, 51, pp. 963–980.

106. P. M. Rowe, "Unfavorable Information and Interview Decisions," in R. W. Eder and G. R. Ferris (eds.), *The Employment Interview: Theory, Research, and Practice* (Newbury Park, CA: Sage, 1989), pp. 77–89.

107. T. W. Dougherty, D. B. Turban, and J. C. Callender, "Confirming First Impressions in the Employment Interview: A Field Study of Interviewer Behavior," *Journal of Applied Psychology,* 1994, 79, pp. 659–665.

108. A. J. Prewett-Livingston, H. S. Feild, J. G. Veres, and P. M. Lewis, "Effects of Race on Interview Ratings in a Situational Panel Interview," *Journal of Applied Psychology,* 1996, 81, pp. 178–186.

109. R. E. Carlson, P. W. Thayer, E. C. Mayfield, and D. A. Peterson, "Improvements in the Selection Interview," *Personnel Journal,* 1971, 50, pp. 268–275.

110. J. R. Burnett, C. Fan, S. J. Motowidlo, and T. DeGroot, "Interview Notes and Validity," *Personnel Psychology,* 1998, 51, pp. 375–396; M. A. Campion, D. K. Palmer, and J. E. Campion, "A Review of Structure in the Selection Interview," *Personnel Psychology,* 1997, 50, pp. 655–702.

111. G. P. Latham, L. M. Saari, E. D. Pursell, and M. A. Campion, "The Situational Interview," *Journal of Applied Psychology,* 1980, 65, pp. 422–427; S. D. Maurer, "The Potential of the Situational Interview: Existing Research and Unresolved Issues," *Human Resource Management Review,* 1997, 7, pp. 185–201.

112. T. Janz, "The Patterned Behavior Description Interview: The Best Prophet of the Future Is the Past," in R. W. Eder and G. R. Ferris (eds.), *The Employment Interview: Theory, Research, and Practice* (Newbury Park, CA: Sage, 1989), pp. 158–168.

113. M. A. McDaniel, D. L. Whetzel, F. L. Schmidt, and S. D. Maurer, "The Validity of Employment Interviews: A Comprehensive Review and Meta-Analysis," *Journal of Applied Psychology,* 1994, 79, pp. 599–616.

114. L. R. James, R. G. Demaree, S. A. Mulaik, and R. T. Ladd, "Validity Generalization in the Context of Situational Models, *Journal of Applied Psychology,* 1992, 77, pp. 3–14.

115. T. A. Judge and G. R. Ferris, "The Elusive Criterion of Fit in Human Resources Staffing Decisions," *Human Resource Planning,* 1992, 15, pp. 47–68.

116. J. E. Hunter and R. F. Hunter, "Validity and Utility of Alternative Predictors of Job Performance"; S. Rynes and B. Gerhart, "Interviewer Assessments of Applicant 'Fit': An Exploratory Investigation," *Personnel Psychology,* 1990, 43, pp. 13–22.

117. M. N. Martinez, "Hiring for Attitude Makes Airlines Fly," *Employment Management Today,* Spring 1998, pp. 34–37.

118. M. A. Campion, J. E. Campion, and J. P. Hudson, "Structured Interviewing: A Note on Incremental Validity and Alternative Question Types," *Journal of Applied Psychology,* 1994, 79, pp. 998–1002; A. I. Huffcutt, P. L. Roth, and M. A. McDaniel, "A Meta-Analytic Investigation of Cognitive Ability in Employment Interview Evaluations: Moderating Characteristics and Implications for Incremental Validity," *Journal of Applied Psychology,* 1996, 81, pp. 459–473.

119. M. A. Campion, E. D. Pursell, and B. K. Brown, "Structured Interviewing: Raising the Psychometric Properties of the Employment Interview,"*Personnel Psychology,* 1988, 41, pp. 25–42; L. C. Walters, M. R. Miller, and M. J. Ree, "Structured Interviews for Pilot Selection: No Incremental Validity," *International Journal of Aviation Psychology,* 1993, 3, pp. 25–38; for an exception see E. D. Pulakos and N. Schmitt, "Experience-Based and Situational Interview Questions: Studies of Validity," *Personnel Psychology,* 1995, 48, pp. 289–308; T. A. Judge, C. A. Higgins, and D. M. Cable, "The Employment Interview: A Review of Recent Research and Recommendations for Future Research," *Human Resource Management Review,* 2000, 10, pp. 383–406; J. M. Cortina, N. B. Goldstein, S. C. Payne, H. K. Davison, and S. W. Gilliland, "The Incremental Validity of Interview Scores over and above Cognitive Ability and Conscientiousness Scores," *Personnel Psychology,* 2000, 53, pp. 325–351; F. L. Schmidt and M. Rader, "Exploring the Boundary Conditions for Interview Validity: Meta-Analytic Validity Findings for a New Interview Type," *Personnel Psychology,* 1999, 52, pp. 445–464.

120. A. E. Barber, J. R. Hollenbeck, S. L. Tower, and J. M. Phillips, "The Effects of Interview Focus on Recruitment Effectiveness: A Field Experiment," *Journal of Applied Psychology,* 1994, 79, pp. 886–896.

121. G. N. Powell, "Applicant Reactions to the Initial Employment Interview: Exploring Theoretical and Methodological Issues," *Personnel Psychology,* 1991, 44, pp. 67–83; S. Rynes and

B. Gerhart, "Interviewer Assessments of Applicant 'Fit': An Exploratory Investigation"; H. Schuler, "Social Validity of Selection Situations: A Concept and Some Empirical Results."

122. S. L. Rynes and M. L. Connerley, "Applicant Reactions to Alternative Selection Procedures"; J. W. Smither, et al., "Applicant Reactions to Selection Procedures."

123. H. Schuler, "Social Validity of Selection Situations: A Concept and Some Empirical Results."

124. T. W. Dougherty, D. B. Turban, and J. C. Callender, "Confirming First Impressions in the Employment Interview: A Field Study of Interviewer Behavior"; G. F. Dreher, R. A. Ash, and P. Hancock, "The Role of the Traditional Research Design in Underestimating the Validity of the Employment Interview," *Personnel Psychology,* 1988, 41, pp. 315–327; L. M. Graves and R. J. Karren, "Interviewer Decision Processes and Effectiveness: An Experimental Policy-Capturing Investigation," *Personnel Psychology,* 1992, 45, pp. 313–340; A. J. Kinicki, C. A. Lockwood, P. W. Hom, and R. W. Griffeth, "Interviewer Predictions of Applicant Qualifications and Interviewer Validity: Aggregate and Individual Analyses," *Journal of Applied Psychology,* 1990, 75, pp. 477–486; E. D. Pulakos, N. Schmitt, D. Whitney, and N. Smith, "Individual Differences in Interviewer Ratings: The Impact of Standardization, Consensus Discussion, and Sampling Error on the Validity of a Structured Interview," *Personnel Psychology,* 1996, 49, pp. 85–102.

125. R. L. Dipboye, *Selection Interviews: Process Perspectives;* see also M. Harris, "Reconsidering the Employment Interview: A Review of Recent Literature and Suggestions for Future Research," *Personnel Psychology,* 1989, 42, pp. 691–726.

126. R. L. Dipboye, *Selection Interviews: Process Perspectives,* pp. 150–179.

127. R. Blackburn and B. Rosen, "Total Quality and Human Resources Management: Lessons Learned from Baldrige Award-Winning Companies," *Academy of Management Executive,* 1992, 7, pp. 49–66; S. L. Rynes and C. Q. Trank, "Moving Upstream in the Employment Relationship: Using Recruitment and Selection to Enhance Quality Outcomes," in S. Ghosh and D. Fedor (eds.), *Advances in the Management of Organizational Quality* (Greenwich, CT: JAI Press, 1996).

128. R. Blackburn and B. Rosen, "Total Quality and Human Resources Management: Lessons Learned from Baldrige Award-Winning Companies"; S. L. Rynes and C. Q. Trank, "Moving Upstream in the Employment Relationship: Using Recruitment and Selection to Enhance Quality Outcomes."

129. M. J. Stevens and M. A. Campion, "The Knowledge, Skill, and Ability Requirements for Teamwork: Implications for Human Resource Management," *Journal of Management,* 1994, 20, pp. 503–530.

130. M. J. Stevens, "Staffing Work Teams: Testing for Individual-Level Knowledge, Skill, and Ability Requirements for Teamwork." Unpublished doctoral dissertation, Purdue University, West Lafayette, Indiana, 1993.

131. R. S. Wellens, W. C. Byham, and G. R. Dixon, *Inside Teams* (San Francisco: Jossey-Bass, 1995).

132. M. R. Barrick, G. L. Stewart, M. J. Neubert, and M. K. Mount, "Relating Member Ability and Personality to Work-Team Processes and Team Effectiveness," *Journal of Applied Psychology,* 1998, 83, pp. 377–391.

133. M. Levinson, "When Workers Do the Hiring," *Newsweek,* June 21, 1993, p. 48; S. M. Colarelli and A. L. Boos, "Sociometric and Ability-Based Assignment to Work Groups: Some Implications for Personnel Selection," *Journal of Organizational Behavior Management,* 1992, 13, pp. 187–196.

134. B. Dumaine, "The Trouble with Teams," *Fortune,* Sept. 5, 1994, pp. 86–92.

135. A. M. Ryan and P. R. Sackett, "A Survey of Industrial Assessment Practices by I/O Psychologists."

136. R. J. Stahl, "Succession Planning Drives Plant Turnaround," *Personnel Journal,* Sept. 1992, pp. 67–70.

137. W. C. Borman and S. J. Motowidlo, "Expanding the Criterion Domain to Include Elements of Contextual Performance," in N. Schmitt, W. Borman, and Associates (eds.), *Personnel Selection in Organizations* (San Francisco: Jossey-Bass, 1993), pp. 71–98.

138. S. Dentzer, B. Cohn, G. Raine, G. Carroll, and V. Quade, "Can You Pass This Job Test?," *Newsweek,* May 5, 1986, pp. 46–53.

139. Smithers Institute, "Drug Testing: Cost and Effect," *Cornell/Smithers Report* (Ithaca, NY: Cornell University, 1992), 1, pp. 1–5.

140. Smithers Institute, "Drug Testing: Cost and Effect."

141. Smithers Institute, "Drug Testing: Cost and Effect."

142. W. E. K. Lehman and D. D. Simpson, "Employee Substance Abuse and On-the-Job Behaviors," *Journal of Applied Psychology,* 1992, 77, pp. 309–321.

143. "More Major U.S. Firms Test Workers for Drugs," *Daily Labor Report,* April 8, 1994, p. A-4.

144. "Number of Workers Testing Positive for Drugs Dips to Less Than 5 Percent, Report Says," *Daily Labor Report,* April 8, 1998.

145. J. P. Guthrie and J. D. Olian, "Drug and Alcohol Testing Programs: Do Firms Consider Their Operating Environment?," *Human Resource Planning,* 1992, 14, pp. 221–232; T. D. Hartwell, P. D. Steele, and N. F. Rodman, "Workplace Alcohol Testing Programs: Prevalence and Trends," *Monthly Labor Review,* June 1998, pp. 27–34.

146. J. A. Segal, "To Test or Not to Test," *HR Magazine,* Apr. 1992, pp. 40–43.

147. S. L. Martin and D. J. DeGrange, "How Effective Are Physical and Psychological Drug Tests?," *EMA Journal,* Fall 1993, pp. 18–22.

148. M. D. Urich, "Are You Positive the Test Is Positive?" *HR Magazine,* Apr. 1992, pp. 44–48.

149. S. L. Martin and D. J. DeGrange, "How Effective Are Physical and Psychological Drug Tests?"

150. Smithers Institute, "Drug Testing: Cost and Effect."

151. J. Normand, S. D. Salyards, and J. J. Mahoney, "An Evaluation of Preemployment Drug Testing," *Journal of Applied Psychology,* 1990, 75, pp. 629–639.

152. S. L. Martin and D. J. DeGrange, "How Effective Are Physical and Psychological Drug Tests?"

153. J. Michaelis, "Waging War," *Human Resource Executive,* Oct. 1993, pp. 39–42.

154. T. A. Judge, D. Blancero, D. M. Cable, and D. E. Johnson, "Effects of Selection Systems on Job Search Decisions"; S. L. Rynes and M. L. Connerley, "Applicant Reactions to Alternative Selection Procedures."

155. J. M. Crant and T. S. Bateman, "An Experimental Test of the Impact of Drug-Testing Programs on Potential Job Applicants' Attitudes and Intentions," *Journal of Applied Psychology,* 1990, 75, pp. 127–131; K. R. Murphy, G. C. Thornton III, and D. H. Reynolds, "College Students' Attitudes Toward Employee Drug Testing Programs," *Personnel Psychology,* 1990, 43, pp. 615–631.

156. E. A. Fleishman, "Some New Frontiers in Personnel Selection Research," *Personnel Psychology,* 1988, 41, pp. 679–701.

157. M. A. Campion, "Personnel Selection for Physically Demanding Jobs: Review and Recommendations," *Personnel Psychology,* 1983, 36, pp. 527–550.

158. E. A. Fleishman, "New Research Frontiers in Personnel Selection."

159. G. P. Panero, *Employment Law Manual,* second ed. (Boston: Warren Gorham Lamont, 1993), pp. 3-28 to 3-82; C. Daniel, "Separating Law and Professional Practice from Politics: The Uniform Guidelines Then and Now," *Review of Public Personnel Administration,* 2001, 21, pp. 175–184; A. I. E. Ewoh and J. S. Guseh, "The Status of the Uniform Guidelines on Employee Selection Procedures: Legal Developments and Future Prospects," *Review of Public Personnel Administration,* 2001, 21, pp. 185–199; W. F. Cascio and H. Aquinis, "The Federal Uniform Guidelines on Employee Selection Procedures: An Update on Selected Issues," *Review of Public Personnel Administration,* 2001, 21, pp. 200–218.

160. Equal Employment Opportunity Commission, *Technical Assistance Manual of the Employment Provisions (Title 1) of the Americans With Disabilities Act* (Washington, DC: author, 1992), pp. 51–88; J. G. Frierson, *Employer's Guide to the Americans With Disabilities Act* (Washington, DC: Bureau of National Affairs, 1992); D. L. Stone and K. L. Williams, "The Impact of the ADA on the Selection Process: Applicant and Organizational Issues," *Human Resource Management Review,* 1997, 7, pp. 203–231.

161. L. Daley, M. Dolland, J. Kraft, M. A. Nester, and R. Schneider, *Employment Testing of Persons with Disabling Conditions* (Alexandria, VA: International Personnel Management Association, 1988); L. D. Eyde, M. A. Nester, S. M. Heaton, and A. V. Nelson, *Guide for Administering Written Employment Examinations to Persons with Disabilities* (Washington, DC: U.S. Office of Personnel Management, 1994).

162. Equal Employment Opportunity Commission, *ADA Enforcement Guidance: Preemployment Disability Related Questions and Medical Examinations* (Washington, DC: author, 1995).

163. Equal Employment Opportunity Commission, *Enforcement Guidance on Disability-Related Inquires and Medical Examinations of Employees Under the Americans With Disabilities Act* (Washington, DC: author, 2001).

164. A. G. Feliu, *Primer on Employee Rights* (Washington, DC: Bureau of National Affairs, 1998), pp. 137–166; J. E. Balls, "Dealing with Drugs: Keep It Legal," *HR Magazine,* March 1998, pp. 104–116.

CHAPTER TEN

Internal Selection

Preliminary Issues
The Logic of Prediction
Types of Predictors
Selection Plan

Initial Assessment Methods
Skills Inventory
Peer Assessments
Self-Assessments
Managerial Sponsorship
Informal Discussions and Recommendations
Choice of Initial Assessment Methods

Substantive Assessment Methods
Seniority and Experience
Job Knowledge Tests
Performance Appraisal
Promotability Ratings
Assessment Centers
Interview Simulations
Promotion Panels and Review Boards
Choice of Substantive Assessment Methods

Discretionary Assessment Methods

Applicant Reactions

Legal Issues
Uniform Guidelines on Employee Selection Procedures
The Glass Ceiling

Summary

Discussion Questions

Applications

Internal selection refers to the assessment and evaluation of employees from within the organization as they move from job to job via transfer and promotion systems. Many different assessment methods are used to make internal selection decisions. Preliminary issues we will discuss to guide the use of these assessment methods include the logic of prediction, the nature of predictors, and the development of a selection plan.

Initial assessment methods are used to select internal candidates from among the internal applicants. Initial assessment methods that will be reviewed include skills inventories, peer and self assessments, managerial sponsorship, and informal discussions and recommendations. The criteria that should be used to choose among these methods will be discussed.

Substantive assessment methods are used to select internal finalists from among internal candidates. Various methods will be reviewed, including seniority and experience, job knowledge tests, performance appraisal, promotability ratings, assessment centers, interview simulations, and promotion panels and review boards. The criteria used to choose among the substantive assessment methods will also be discussed.

Discretionary assessment methods are used to select offer recipients from among the finalists. The factors on which these decisions are based, such as EEO/AA concerns, whether the finalist had previously been a finalist, and second opinions about the finalist by others in the organization, will be considered.

All of these assessment methods require the collection of a large amount of data. Accordingly, attention must be given to support services, the required expertise needed to administer and interpret predictors, security, privacy and confidentiality, and the standardization of procedures. Since candidates for internal selection decisions are usually valued employees, employee reactions to the selection process will also be discussed.

The use of internal selection methods requires a clear understanding of legal issues. In particular, the Uniform Guidelines on Employee Selection Procedures and the glass ceiling are reviewed.

PRELIMINARY ISSUES

The Logic of Prediction

The logic of prediction described in Chapter 8 is equally relevant to the case of internal selection. Specifically, indicators of internal applicants' degree of success in past situations should be predictive of their likely success in new situations. Past situations importantly include previous jobs, as well as the current one, held by the applicant with the organization. The new situation is the internal vacancy the applicant is seeking via the organization's transfer or promotion system.

There also may be similarities between internal and external selection in terms of the effectiveness of selection methods. As you may recall from Chapters 8 and 9, three of the most valid external selection measures are biographical data, cognitive ability tests, and work samples. These methods also have validity in internal selection decisions. Biographical information has been found to be a valid predictor in selecting top corporate leaders. Research indicates that cognitive ability is strongly predictive of long-term job performance and advancement. Finally, work samples are valid predictors of advancement.[1] In this chapter we focus on processes and methods of selection that are unique to promotion and transfer decisions. However, in considering these methods and processes, it should be kept in mind that many of the techniques of external selection may be relevant as well.

Although the logic of prediction and the likely effectiveness of selection methods are similar for external and internal selection, in practice there are several potential advantages of internal over external selection. In particular, the data collected on internal applicants in their previous jobs often provide greater depth, relevance, and verifiability than the data collected on external applicants. This is because organizations usually have much more detailed and in-depth information about internal candidates' previous job experiences. In this age of computers, where organizations can store large amounts of data on employees' job experiences, this is especially true. It is far more difficult to access data in a reliable manner when external candidates are used. As indicated in Chapter 8, previous employers are often hesitant to release data on previous employees due to legal concerns, such as potential invasion of privacy. As a result, employers often have to rely on reports by external candidates of their previous experiences, and the candidates may not always present the whole picture or an accurate picture of their past experiences.

In terms of the relevance of past experiences, organizations may also have better data with which to make selection decisions on internal than external candidates. The experiences of insiders may more closely mirror the experiences likely to be encountered on the new job than the experiences of outsiders. For example, organizations often worry about whether some candidate will be willing to live in a certain geographic area. The answer may be obvious with an internal candidate who already lives in that location. As another example, organizations often wonder about the transferability of skills learned in another organization to their own. Hence, when a new CEO is brought to a computer company from a tobacco company, many will comment on whether he or she will do well in this new environment.

Along with depth and relevance, another positive aspect of the nature of predictors for internal selection is verifiability. Rather than simply relying on the opinion of one person as to the suitability of an internal candidate for the job, multiple assessments may be solicited. Opinions about the suitability of the candidate also can be solicited from other supervisors and peers. By pooling opinions, it is possible to get a more complete and accurate picture of a candidate's qualifications.

Types of Predictors

The distinctions made between types of predictors used in external selection are also applicable to types of internal predictors. One important difference to note between internal and external predictors pertains to content. There is usually greater depth and relevance to the data available on internal candidates. As a result, greater emphasis can be placed on samples and criteria rather than signs in selection. This is possible because the data on previous situations are more readily available with internal candidates. That is, the organization can go to their own files or managers to get reports on the applicants' previous experiences.

Selection Plan

Often it seems that internal selection is done on the basis of who you know rather than relevant KSAOs. Managers tend to rely heavily on the subjective opinions of previous managers who supervised the internal candidate. When asked why they rely on these subjective assessments, the answer is often, "Because the candidate has worked here for a long time, and I trust his supervisor's feel for the candidate."

Decision errors often occur when relying on subjective feelings for internal selection decisions. For example, in selecting managers to oversee engineering and scientific personnel in organizations, it is sometimes felt that those internal job candidates with the best technical skills will be the best managers. This is not always the case. Some technical wizards are poor managers and vice versa. Sound internal selection procedures need to be followed to guard against this error. A sound job analysis will show that both technical and managerial skills need to be assessed with well-crafted predictors.

Feel, hunch, gut instinct, intuition, and the like do not substitute for well-developed predictors. Relying solely on others' "feelings" about the job applicant may result in lowering hiring standards for some employees, discrimination against protected class employees, and decisions with low validity. As a result, it is imperative that a selection plan be used for internal as well as external selection. As described in Chapter 8, a selection plan lists the predictors to be used for assessment of each KSAO.

INITIAL ASSESSMENT METHODS

The internal recruitment process may generate a large number of applications for vacant positions. This is especially true when an open rather than closed recruitment system is used—where jobs are posted for employees to apply. Given the time and cost of rigorous selection procedures, organizations use initial assessment methods to screen out applicants who do not meet the minimum qualifications needed to become a candidate. Initial assessment methods for internal recruitment typically include the following predictors: skills inventories, peer evaluations, self-assessments, managerial sponsorship, and informal discussions and recommendations. Each of these predictors will be discussed in turn, followed by a general evaluation of them all.

Skills Inventory

An immediate screening device in applicant assessment is to rely on existing data on employee skills. These data can be found in personnel files, which are usually on the computer in larger organizations and in file drawers in smaller organizations. The level of sophistication of the data kept by organizations varies considerably, depending on the method used. Methods include traditional skills inventories, upgraded skills inventories, and customized skills assessments.

Traditional Skills Inventory

A traditional skills inventory is a listing of the KSAOs held by each employee in the organization. Usually, the system records a small number of skills listed in generic categories, such as education, experience, and supervisory training received. A sound traditional system should be systematically updated on a periodic basis by the HR group. Unfortunately, the maintenance of the database is often a low-priority project; as a result, traditional skills inventories often do not reflect current skills held by employees.

Upgraded Skills Inventory

In an upgraded skills inventory, managers systematically enter the latest skills acquired by employees into the database as soon as they occur. The system may also include a listing of the skill sets held by external job candidates who were not hired. Members of the HR group systematically record and enter the skills of people whose résumés they receive. Thus, even though some individuals were not hired for an initial position, their résumés can be drawn on for future positions where they match the qualifications. In essence, HR is enlarging the existing internal applicant pool with external applicants' files.

Customized Skill Inventory

Both the traditional and upgraded skills inventory rely on broadly defined skill categories. As has been indicated repeatedly throughout this book, the more specific the KSAOs required for the job, the more likely is a good person/job match. A customized skills assessment (CSA) moves in this direction. With a CSA, specific skill sets are recorded for specific jobs. Skills are not included simply because they are relevant to all jobs or because they happen to match a particular computer software package. Instead, subject matter experts (e.g., managers and experienced job incumbents) identify skills that are critical to job success.

An example of a customized skills inventory is shown in Exhibit 10.1. As can be seen, each job requires increasing numbers of KSAOs. The associate position

EXHIBIT 10.1 **Customized Skill Inventory**

Name: _____

	Skills Required for Future Position		
KSAO Dimension	**Associate**	**Team Leader**	**Manager**
Technical knowledge	1. _____ 2. _____ 3. _____	1. _____ 2. _____ 3. _____	1. _____ 2. _____ 3. _____
Coaching, counseling, teamwork		1. _____ 2. _____ 3. _____	1. _____ 2. _____ 3. _____
Strategic management			1. _____ 2. _____ 3. _____

requires technical skills only; the team leader position requires technical skills plus coaching, counseling, and teamwork skills. The manager position requires all of these skills plus strategic management skills. An inventory like this is kept for each employee. As the person gains skills, they are entered into the appropriate boxes. Once a column of boxes is completed, the person then becomes eligible for the appropriate position when a vacancy exists.

Peer Assessments

Assessments by peers or coworkers can be used to evaluate the promotability of an internal applicant. A variety of methods can be used, including peer ratings, peer nominations, and peer rankings.[2] Examples of all three are shown in Exhibit 10.2.

As can be seen in Exhibit 10.2, whereas peers are used to make promotion decisions in all three methods of peer assessments, the format of each is different. With peer ratings, readiness to be promoted is assessed for each peer using a rating scale. The person with the highest ratings is deemed most promotable. On the other hand, peer nominations rely on voting for the most promotable candidates. Peers receiving the greatest number of "votes" are the most promotable. Finally, peer rankings rely on a rank ordering of peers. Those peers with the highest rankings are the most promotable.

Peer assessments have been used extensively in the military over the years and to a lesser degree in industry. A virtue of peer assessments is that they rely on raters who presumably are very knowledgeable of the applicants' KSAOs due to their day-to-day contact with them. A possible downside to peer assessments, however, is that they may encourage friendship bias. Also, they may undermine morale in a work group by fostering a competitive environment.

Another possible problem with peer assessment is that the criteria by which assessments are made are not always made clear. For peer assessments to work, care should be taken in advance to carefully spell out the KSAOs needed for successful performance in the position the peer is being considered for. To do so, a job requirements matrix should be used.

A probable virtue of peer assessments is that peers are more likely to feel that the decisions reached are fair, because they had an input into the decision. The decision is thus not seen as a "behind the backs" maneuver by management. As such, peer assessments are used more often with open rather than closed systems of internal recruitment.

Self-Assessments

Job incumbents can be asked to evaluate their own skills as a basis for determining promotability. This procedure is sometimes used with open recruitment systems. An example of this approach is shown in Exhibit 10.3. Caution must be exercised in using this process for selection, as it may raise the expectations of those rating

EXHIBIT 10.2   **Peer Assessments Methods**

Peer Rating

Please consider each of the following employees and rate them using the following scale for the position of manager described in the job requirements matrix:

	Not Promotable		Promotable in One Year		Promotable Now
	1	**2**	**3**	**4**	**5**
Jean	1	2	3	4	5
John	1	2	3	4	5
Andy	1	2	3	4	5
Herb	1	2	3	4	5

Peer Nominations

Please consider each of the following employees and mark an X for the one employee who is most promotable to the position of manager as described in the job requirements matrix:

Joe   _____
Carolyn   _____
Jeffrey   _____
Shelly   _____
Renee   _____

Peer Ranking

Please rank order the following employees from the most promotable (1) to the least promotable (5) for the position of manager as described in the job requirements matrix:

Ila   _____
Karen   _____
Phillip   _____
Rebecca   _____
Buster   _____

themselves that they will be selected. Also, this approach should be coupled with other internal selection procedures as employees may have a tendency to overrate themselves.

Managerial Sponsorship

Increasingly, organizations are relying on higher-ups in the organization to identify and develop the KSAOs of those at lower levels in the organization. Historically,

EXHIBIT 10.3 **Self-Assessment Form Used for Application in Job Posting System**

SUPPLEMENTAL QUESTIONNAIRE

This supplemental will be the principle basis for determining whether or not you are highly qualified for this position. You may add information not identified in your SF-171 or expand on that which is identified. You should consider appropriate work experience, outside activities, awards, training, and education for each of the items listed below.

1. Knowledge of the Bureau of Indian Affairs' mission, organization, structure, policies, and functions, as they relate to Real Estate.
2. Knowledge of technical administrative requirements to provide technical guidance in administrative areas, such as personnel regulations, travel regulations, time and attendance requirements, budget documents, Privacy Act, and Freedom of Information Act, etc.
3. Ability to work with program directors and administrative staff and ability to apply problem solving techniques and management concepts; ability to analyze facts and problems and develop alternatives.
4. Ability to operate various Computer programs and methodology in the analysis and design of automated methods for meeting the information and reporting requirements for the Division.
5. Knowledge of the Bureau Budget process and statistical Profile of all field operations that impact in the Real Estate Services program.

On a separate sheet of paper, address the above items in narrative form. Identify the vacancy announcement number across the top. Sign and date your Supplemental Questionnaire.

Source: Department of the Interior, Bureau of Indian Affairs. Form BIA-4450 (4/22/92).

the higher-up has been the person's immediate supervisor. Today, however, the higher-up may be a person at a higher level of the organization who does not have direct responsibility for the person being rated. Higher-ups are sometimes labeled coaches, sponsors, or mentors, and their roles are defined in Exhibit 10.4. In some organizations, there are formal mentorship programs where employees are assigned coaches, sponsors, and mentors. In other organizations, these matches may naturally occur, often progressing from coach to sponsor to mentor as the relationship matures. Regardless of the formality of the relationship, these individuals are often given considerable influence in promotion decisions. Their weight is due to their high organizational level and in-depth knowledge of the employee's KSAOs. Not only is the judgment of these advocates important but so, too, are their behaviors. Mentors, for example, are likely to put employees in situations where they receive high visibility. That visibility may increase the applicants' chances of promotion.

EXHIBIT 10.4 **Employee Advocates**

Coach

- Provides day-to-day feedback
- Diagnoses and resolves performance problems
- Creates opportunities for employees using existing training programs and career development programs

Sponsor

- Actively promotes person for advancement opportunities
- Guides person's career rather than simply informing them of opportunities
- Creates opportunities for people in decision-making capacities to see the skills of the employee (e.g., lead a task force)

Mentor

- Becomes personally responsible for the success of the person
- Available to person on and off the job
- Lets person in on "insider" information
- Solicits and values person's input

Source: Reprinted with permission from Dr. Janina Latack, PhD, Nelson O'Connor & Associates/Outplacement International, Phoenix/Tucson.

Informal Discussions and Recommendations

Not all promotion decisions are made on the basis of formal HR policy and procedures. Much of the decision process occurs outside normal channels, through informal discussions and recommendations. These discussions are difficult to characterize because some are simply idle hall talk, while others are directly job related. For example, a lawyer who is expected to be a rainmaker (someone who brings in clients and possible revenue) may be assessed by his contacts in the community. An assessment of the person's qualifications for rainmaking may be done by an informal conversation between a senior partner and a previous client of the supposed rainmaker at a board meeting. Unfortunately, many informal discussions are suspect in terms of their relevance to actual job performance.

Choice of Initial Assessment Methods

As was discussed, there are several formal and informal methods of initial assessment available to screen internal applicants to produce a list of candidates. Research has been conducted on the effectiveness of each method, which will now be presented to help determine which initial assessment methods should be used. The reviews of this research are summarized in Exhibit 10.5.

EXHIBIT 10.5   Evaluation of Initial Assessment Methods

Predictors	Use	Cost	Reliability	Validity	Utility	Reactions	Adverse Impact
Self-nominations	Low	Low	Moderate	Moderate	?	Mixed	?
Skills inventories	High	High	Moderate	Moderate	?	?	?
Peer assessments	Low	Low	High	High	?	Negative	?
Managerial sponsorship	Low	Moderate	?	?	?	Positive	?
Informal methods	High	Low	?	?	?	Mixed	?

In Exhibit 10.5, the same criteria are applied to evaluating the effectiveness of these predictors as were used to evaluate the effectiveness of predictors for external selection. Cost refers to expenses incurred in using the predictor. Reliability refers to the consistency of measurement. Validity refers to the strength of the relationship between the predictor and job performance. Low validity refers to validity in the range of about .00 to .15, moderate validity corresponds to validity in the range of about .16 to .30, and high validity is .31 and above. Utility refers to the monetary return, minus costs, associated with using the predictor. Adverse impact refers to the possibility that a disproportionate number of women and minorities are rejected using this predictor. Finally, reaction refers to the likely impact on applicants.

Two points should be made about the effectiveness of initial internal selection methods. First, skills inventories and informal methods are used extensively. This suggests that many organizations continue to rely on closed rather than open internal recruitment systems. Certainly this is a positive procedure when administrative ease is of importance. However, it must be noted that these approaches may result in overlooking talented applicants. Also, there may be a discriminatory impact on women and minorities.

The second point to be made is that peer assessment methods are very promising in terms of reliability and validity. They are not frequently used, but need to be given more consideration by organizations as a screening device. Perhaps this will take place as organizations continue to decentralize decision making and empower employees to make business decisions historically made only by the supervisor.

SUBSTANTIVE ASSESSMENT METHODS

The internal applicant pool is narrowed down to candidates using the initial assessment methods. A decision as to which internal candidates will become finalists is usually made using the following substantive assessment methods: seniority and experience, job knowledge tests, performance appraisal, promotability ratings, assessment centers, interview simulations, and review boards. After each of these methods is discussed, an evaluation is made.

Seniority and Experience

At first blush the concepts of seniority and experience may seem the same. In reality, they may be quite different. Seniority typically refers to length of service or tenure with the organization, department, or job. For example, company seniority is measured as length of continuous employment in an organization and is operationalized as the difference between the present date of employment and the date of hire. Thus, seniority is a purely quantitative measure that has nothing to do with the type or quality of job experiences.

Conversely, experience generally has a broader meaning. While seniority may be one aspect of experience, experience also reflects *type* of experience. Two employees working in the same company for 20 years may have the same level of seniority, but very different levels of experience if one employee has performed a number of different jobs, worked in different areas of the organization, enrolled in various training programs, and so on. Thus, experience includes not only length of service in the organization or in various positions in the organization but also the kinds of activities employees have undertaken in those positions. Thus, although seniority and experience are often considered synonymous, they are quite different, and—as we will see in the following discussion—these differences have real implications for internal selection decisions.

Use and Evaluation

Seniority and experience are among the most prevalent methods of internal selection. In most unionized companies, heavy reliance is placed on seniority over other KSAOs for advancement.[3] Between two-thirds and four-fifths of union contracts stipulate that seniority be considered in promotion decisions, and about 50% mandate that it be the determining factor. In policy, nonunion organizations claim to place less weight on seniority than other factors in making advancement decisions. In practice, however, at least one study showed that regardless of the wording in policy statements, heavy emphasis is still placed on seniority in nonunion settings.[4] Research has shown that seniority is more likely to be used for promotions in small, unionized, and capital-intensive companies.[5] Although little data are available, there is reason to believe that experience also is frequently considered in internal selection decisions.

There are various reasons why seniority and experience are so widely used as methods of internal selection decisions. First, organizations believe that direct experience in a job content area reflects an accumulated stock of KSAOs necessary to perform the job. In short, experience may be content valid because it reflects on-the-job experience. Second, seniority and experience information is easily and cheaply obtained. Furthermore, unions believe that reliance on objective measures such as seniority and experience protects the employee from capricious treatment and favoritism. Finally, promoting experienced or senior individuals is socially acceptable because it is seen as rewarding loyalty. In fact, it has been found that most decision makers feel that negative repercussions would result if a more junior employee is promoted over a more senior employee.

In evaluating seniority and experience as methods of internal selection, it is important to return to our earlier distinction between the two concepts. Several studies have found that seniority is unrelated to job performance.[6] In fact, one study of unionized plants found that 97% of the promotions went to the most senior employee, yet in nearly half the cases this person was not the highest performer. Thus, seniority does not seem to be a particularly valid method of internal selection. In fact, the "Big Three" automakers cite abandoning seniority for promotions as a reason for their improved performance in the mid-1990s.[7]

As compared to seniority, evidence for the validity of experience is more positive. A large-scale review of the literature has shown that experience is moderately related to job performance.[8] Research suggests that experience is predictive of job performance in the short run, but is followed by a plateau during which experience loses its ability to predict job performance. It appears that most of the effect of experience on performance is due to the fact that experienced employees have greater job knowledge. However, while experience may result in increased performance due to greater job knowledge, it does not remedy performance difficulties due to low ability; initial performance deficits of low-ability employees are not remedied by increased experience over time.[9] Thus, while experience is more likely to be related to job performance than seniority, neither ranks among the most valid predictors for internal selection decisions.

Based on the research evidence, several conclusions about the use of seniority and experience in internal selection decisions seem appropriate:

1. Experience is a more valid method of internal selection than seniority (although unionized employers may have little choice but to use seniority).
2. Experience is better suited to predict short-term rather than long-term potential.
3. Experience is more likely to be content valid if the past or present jobs are similar to the future job.
4. Employees seem to expect that promotions will go to the most senior or experienced employee, so using seniority or experience for promotions may yield positive reactions from employees.
5. Experience is unlikely to remedy initial performance difficulties of low-ability employees.

Job Knowledge Tests

Job knowledge measures one's mastery of the concepts needed to perform certain work. Job knowledge is a complex concept that includes elements of both ability (capacity to learn) and seniority (opportunity to learn). It is usually measured with a paper-and-pencil test. To develop a paper-and-pencil test to assess job knowledge, the content domain from which test questions will be constructed must be clearly identified. For example, a job knowledge test used to select sales managers from among salespeople must identify the specific knowledge necessary for being a successful sales manager.

An innovative video-based job knowledge test to be used as part of the promotion system was developed by Federal Express Corporation.[10] Federal Express developed the interactive video test to assess employees' ability to deal with customers. The test is based on job analysis data derived from the critical tasks necessary to deliver high levels of customer service. The test, termed QUEST (Quality Using Electronic Systems Training), presents employees with a menu of modules on CD-ROM (e.g., delivering packages, defensive driving, etc.). A 90% competency level on the test is established as the expectation for minimum performance—and subsequent promotability. This suggests that such assessments could fruitfully be used in internal selection decisions when promoting employees into customer-sensitive positions. The greater the portfolio of customer skills employees have, the better able they should be to help Federal Express meet its customer service goals.

Although job knowledge is not a well-researched method of either internal or external employee selection, it holds great promise as a predictor of job performance. This is because it reflects an assessment of previous experiences of an applicant and an important KSAO, namely, cognitive ability.[11]

Performance Appraisal

One possible predictor of future job performance is past job performance. This assumes, of course, that elements of the future job are similar to the past job. Data on employees' previous performance are routinely collected as a part of the performance appraisal process and thus available for use in internal selection.

One advantage of performance appraisals over other internal assessment methods is that they are readily available in many organizations. Another desirable feature of performance appraisals is that they probably capture both ability and motivation. Hence, they offer a very complete look at the person's qualifications for the job. Care must still be taken in using performance appraisals because there is not always a direct correspondence between the requirements of the current job and the requirements of the position applied for. Performance appraisals should only be used as predictors when job analysis indicates a close relationship between the current job and the position applied for.

For example, performance in a highly technical position (e.g., scientist, engineer) may require certain skills (e.g., quantitative skills) that are required in both junior- and senior-level positions. As a result, using the results of the performance appraisal of the junior position is appropriate in predicting the performance in the senior position. It is not, however, appropriate to use the results of the performance appraisal for the junior-level technical job to predict performance in a job, such as manager, requiring a different set of skills (e.g., planning, organizing, staffing).

Although there are some advantages to using performance appraisal results for internal selection, they are far from perfect predictors. They are subject to many influences that have nothing to do with the likelihood of success in a future job.[12]

The well-known "Peter Principle"—that individuals rise to their lowest level of incompetence—illustrates another limitation with using performance appraisal as a method of internal staffing decisions.[13] The argument behind the Peter Principle is that if organizations promote individuals on the basis of their past performance, the only time that people stop being promoted is when they are poor performers at the job into which they were last promoted. Thus, over time, organizations will have internally staffed positions with individuals who are incompetent. In fact, the authors have data from a Fortune 100 company showing that less than one-fifth of the variance in an employee's current performance rating can be explained by their previous three year's performance ratings. Thus, although past performance may have some validity in predicting future performance, the relationship may not be overly strong.

This is not to suggest that organizations should abandon using performance ratings as a factor in internal staffing decisions. Rather, the validity of using performance appraisal as an internal selection method may depend on a number of considerations. Exhibit 10.6 provides several questions that should be used in deciding how much weight to place on performance appraisal as a means of making internal selection decisions. Affirmative answers to these questions suggest that past performance may be validly used in making internal selection decisions.

An advance over simple use of performance ratings is to review past performance records more thoroughly, including an evaluation of various dimensions of performance that are particularly relevant to job performance (where the dimensions are based on job analysis results). For example, a study of police promotions used a pool of six supervisors to score officers on four job-relevant police officer performance dimensions—supervisory-related education and experience, disciplined behavior, commendatory behavior, and reliability—with the goal of predicting future performance. Results of the study indicated that ratings of past performance records was an effective method of promoting officers.[14] Such a method might be adapted to other positions and provide a useful means of incorporating past performance data into a more valid prediction of future potential.

Promotability Ratings

In many organizations, an assessment of promotability (assessment of potential for higher-level job) is made at the same time that performance appraisals are conducted. An example of a form to be used is shown in Exhibit 10.7.

EXHIBIT 10.6 **Questions to Ask in Using Performance Appraisal as a Method of Internal Staffing Decisions**

- Is the performance appraisal process reliable and unbiased?
- Is future job content representative of present job content?
- Have the KSAOs required for performance in the future job(s) been acquired and demonstrated in the previous job(s)?
- Is the organizational or job environment stable such that what led to past job success will lead to future job success?

EXHIBIT 10.7 **Promotability Rating Form**

Form BIA-4450 (4/22/92)	DEPARTMENT OF THE INTERIOR BUREAU OF INDIAN AFFAIRS	44 BIAM335 Illustration 4 Page 1 of 2

SUPERVISORY APPRAISAL OF DEMONSTRATED
PERFORMANCE OF POTENTIAL

ANNOUNCEMENT NO. CO-92-125

PLEASE HAVE THIS APPRAISAL COMPLETED BY YOUR
SUPERVISOR AND SUBMIT WITH YOUR APPLICATION.
SF-171 (If the appraisal is submitted directly by the
Supervisor, the Applicant will be permitted to review
and/or obtain a copy of the appraisal upon request.)

Name of Applicant: _____   Position: Program Specialist _____

Basis of Appraisal					Level of Performance			
Check One					Check as appropriate:			
Outside Activities	On-the-job Performance	Formal Training	Unable to Appraise	RANKING FACTORS (Knowledge, Skills, Abilities, and Personal Characteristics)	4 – Exceptional 3 – Above average 2 – Average/Satisfactory 1 – Rarely Satisfactory			
					4	3	2	1
				1. Knowledge of the Bureau of Indian Affairs' mission, organizaton, structure, policies, and functions, as they relate to Real Estate.				
				2. Knowledge of technical administrative requirements to provide technical guidance in administrative areas, such as personnel regulations, travel regulations, time and attendance requirements, budget documents, Privacy Act, and Freedom of Information Act, etc.				
				3. Ability to work with program directors and administrative staff and ability to apply problem solving techniques and management concepts; ability to analyze facts and problems and develop alternatives.				
				4. Ability to operate various Computer programs and methodology in the analysis and design of automated methods for meeting the information and reporting requirements for the Division.				
				5. Knowledge of the Bureau Budget process and statistical Profile of all field operations that impact in the Real Estate Services program.				

44 BIAM, 335, REL. 127, 4/22/92

(continued)

EXHIBIT 10.7   Continued

Form BIA-4450   DEPARTMENT OF THE INTERIOR   44 BIAM 335
(Rev. 4/22/92)   BUREAU OF INDIAN AFFAIRS   Illustration 4
                                                                             Page 2 of 2

SUPERVISORY APPRAISAL OF DEMONSTRATED
PERFORMANCE OF POTENTIAL

ANNOUNCEMENT NO.: <u>CO-92-125</u>

NARRATIVE: BRIEFLY EVALUATE THE CANDIDATE'S OVERALL ABILITY TO PERFORM THE
DUTIES AND RESPONSIBILITIES OF THE POSITION. NARRATIVE COMMENTS ARE REQUIRED
FOR ALL EVALUATIONS.

IN WHAT CAPACITY ARE YOU MAKING THIS APPRAISAL? (Please ✓ as appropriate)

( ) Present Immediate Supervisor   ( ) Present 2nd Level Supervisor   ( ) Other
                                                                        (Specify)
                                    ( ) Former 2nd Level Supervisor
( ) Former Immediate Supervisor

Period during which you supervised the Applicant:
                                     From: To:

Appraiser:

              (Signature)   (Date)   (Phone No.)

Source: Department of the Interior, Bureau of Indian Affairs, Form BIA-4450 (4/22/92).

Promotability ratings are useful not only from a selection perspective but also from a recruitment perspective. By discussing what is needed to be promotable, employee development may be encouraged as well as coupled with organizational sponsorship of the opportunities needed to develop. In turn, the development of new skills in employees increases the internal recruitment pool for promotions.

Caution must be exercised in using promotability ratings as well. If employees receive separate evaluations for purposes of performance appraisal, promotability, and pay, the possibility exists of mixed messages going out to employees that may be difficult for them to interpret. For example, it is difficult to understand why one receives an excellent performance rating and a solid pay raise, but at the same time is rated as not promotable. Care must be taken to show employees the relevant judgments that are being made in each assessment. In the example presented, it must be clearly indicated that promotion is based not only on past performance but also on skill acquisition and opportunities for advancement.

Assessment Centers

An elaborate method of employee selection, primarily used internally, is known as an assessment center. An assessment center is a collection of predictors used to forecast success, primarily in higher-level jobs. It is used for higher-level jobs because of the high costs involved in conducting the center. The assessment center can be used to select employees for lower-level jobs as well, though this is rarely done.

The theory behind assessment centers is relatively straightforward. Concern is with the prediction of an individual's behavior and effectiveness in critical roles, usually managerial. Since these roles require complex behavior, multiple KSAOs will predict those behaviors. Hence, there is a need to carefully identify and assess those KSAOs. This will require multiple methods of assessing the KSAOs, as well as multiple assessors. The result should be higher validity than could be obtained from a single assessment method or assessor.

As with any sound selection procedure, the assessment center predictors are based on job analysis to identify KSAOs and aid in the construction of content valid methods of assessment for those KSAOs. As a result, a selection plan must be developed when using assessment centers. An example of such a selection plan is shown in Exhibit 10.8.

Characteristics of Assessment Centers

Whereas specific characteristics vary from situation to situation, assessment centers generally have some common characteristics. Job candidates usually participate in an assessment center for a period of days rather than hours. Most assess-

EXHIBIT 10.8 **Selection Plan for an Assessment Center**

KSAO	Writing Exercise	Speech Exercise	Analysis Problem	In-Basket		Leadership Group Discussion	
				Tent.	Final	Management Problems	City Council
Oral communications					X	X	X
Oral presentation		X				X	
Written communications	X		X	X	X		
Stress tolerance				X	X	X	X
Leadership					X	X	
Sensitivity			X	X	X	X	X
Tenacity				X	X	X	
Risk taking			X	X	X	X	X
Initiative			X	X	X	X	X
Planning & organization			X	X	X	X	X
Management control			X	X	X		
Delegation				X	X		
Problem analysis			X	X	X	X	X
Decision making			X	X	X	X	X
Decisiveness			X	X	X	X	X
Responsiveness			X	X	X	X	X

Source: Department of Employment Relations, State of Wisconsin.

ment centers last two to three days, but some may be as long as five days. Exhibit 10.9 is an example of a three-day assessment center (exercises are defined below). Participants take part in a series of simulations and work sample tests known as exercises. The participants may also be assessed with other devices, such as interviews, personality and ability tests, and biographical information blanks. As they participate in the exercises, trained assessors evaluate participants' performance. Assessors are usually line managers, but sometimes psychologists are used as well. The average ratio of assessors to assessees ranges from 1:1 to 4:1.

The participants in the center are usually managers who are being assessed for higher-level managerial jobs. Normally, they are chosen to participate by other organizational members, such as their supervisor. Often selection is based on an employee's current level of job performance.

At the conclusion of the assessment center, the participants are evaluated by the assessors. Typically, this involves the assessor examining all of the information gathered about each participant. The information is then translated into a series of ratings on several dimensions of managerial jobs. Typical dimensions assessed include communications (written and oral), leadership and human relations, and planning, problem solving, and decision making. In evaluating these dimensions, assessors are trained to look for critical behaviors that represent highly effective

EXHIBIT 10.9   Assessment Center Program Schedule

Sunday	P.M.	Candidates arrive for social hour, orientation, meeting, and discussion.
Monday	A.M.	Leaderless group discussion. The candidates were divided into two groups of five to discuss a possible business investment. Each group was observed by three assessors who took notes on the total activity and the individual participants.
	P.M.	1. Individual interview with clinical psychologist. 2. Psychological testing with candidates for assessment information and research purposes.
Tuesday	A.M.	Individual exercise (in-basket).
	P.M.	1. Interview regarding in-basket performance. 2. Additional testing. 3. Group exercise.
Wednesday	A.M.	Case analysis.
	P.M.	1. Assessors write two- to three-page narrative reports based on observation of participants. 2. Candidates are notified of their overall assessment.

or ineffective responses to the exercise situations in which participants are placed. There may also be an overall assessment rating that represents the bottom-line evaluation for each participant. Exhibit 10.10 provides a sample rating form.

A variety of different exercises are used at a center, but those most frequently used are the in-basket exercise, leaderless group discussions, and case analysis. Each of these exercises will be briefly described.

In-Basket Exercise An element common to most higher-level positions is an in-basket. The in-basket usually contains memoranda, reports, phone calls, and letters that require a response. In an assessment center, a simulated in-basket is presented to the candidate. The candidate is asked to respond to the paperwork in the in-basket by prioritizing items, drafting memos, scheduling meetings, and so forth. It is a timed exercise, and usually the candidate has two to three hours to respond. Even when used alone, the in-basket exercise seems to forecast ascendancy, one of the key criteria of assessment centers. The in-basket is the most often used exercise; a recent study of assessment centers indicated that the in-basket was used in 82% of assessment centers.[15]

Leaderless Group Discussion In a leaderless group discussion, a small group of candidates is given a problem to work on. The problem is one they would likely encounter in the higher-level position for which they are applying. As a group, they are asked to resolve the problem. As they work on the problem, assessors sit around the perimeter of the group and evaluate how each candidate behaves in an unstructured setting. They look for skills such as leadership and communication. Roughly 60% of assessment centers include a leaderless group discussion.

Case Analysis Cases of actual business situations can also be presented to the candidates. Each candidate is asked to provide a written analysis of the case, describing the nature of the problem, likely causes, and recommended solutions. Not only are the written results evaluated but the candidate's oral report is scored as well. The candidates may be asked to give an oral presentation to a panel of managers and to respond to their questions, comments, and concerns. Case analyses are used in roughly half of all assessment centers.

Validity and Effective Practices
In a study of 50 different assessment centers, their average validity was very favorable ($\bar{r} = .37$). This study showed that the validity of the assessment center was higher when multiple predictors were used, when assessors were psychologists rather than managers, and when peer evaluations as well as assessor evaluations were used. The latter results question the common practice of using only managers as assessors. It suggests that multiple assessors be used, including psychologists and peers as well as managers. Such usage provides a different perspective on participants' performance, one that may be overlooked by managers.[16] Assessment centers have incremental validity in predicting performance and pro-

EXHIBIT 10.10   Sample Assessment Center Rating Form

Participant Name: _____

Personal Qualities:

    1. Energy   _____

    2. Risk taking _____

    3. Tolerance for ambiguity _____

    4. Objectivity _____

    5. Reliability _____

Communication Skills:

    6. Oral _____

    7. Written _____

    8. Persuasion _____

Human Relations:

    9. Teamwork _____

    10. Flexibility _____

    11. Awareness of social environment _____

Leadership Skills:

    12. Impact _____

    13. Autonomy _____

Decision-Making Skills:

    14. Decisiveness _____

    15. Organizing _____

    16. Planning _____

Problem-Solving Skills:

    17. Fact-Finding _____

    18. Interpreting information _____

Overall Assessment Rating:

Indication of potential to perform
effectively at the next level is:

    Excellent

    Good _____

    Moderate

    Low

motability beyond personality traits and cognitive ability tests, though the incremental validity may be relatively small because assessment center scores are substantially correlated with cognitive ability.[17]

There are some problems with past assessment center research.[18] One of the most commonly cited problems is the "crown prince or princess" syndrome. Here, it is alleged, decision makers may know how people did on the assessment center and therefore promote those who did well versus those who did not do well. Thus, assessment centers could be a self-fulfilling prophecy—they are valid only because decision makers think they are. However, research indicates that assessment centers are valid even when the results of the assessment center are "blind" to decision makers. Thus, due to the validity of assessment centers, they should be seriously considered in making promotion decisions—if they can be afforded.

There is little research that has examined participant reactions to assessment centers. However, it is commonly noted that although assessment centers are stressful to participants, they generate positive reactions for assessors and assessees. This probably is partly due to the fact that they are seen as valid by participants. Furthermore, they may result in increased self-confidence for participants, even for those who are not promoted as a result of the assessment center. The positive effects of assessment centers on employee attitudes and self-confidence may be relatively fleeting, however, as one study of British managers found. Thus, it is possible that the positive impact of assessment centers on assessees wanes over time. The International Task Force on Assessment Center Guidelines has published a set of guidelines for the development and use of assessment centers. They are a useful tool for those wishing to ensure that an assessment center is conducted in a valid, fair, and effective manner.[19]

Assessment for Global Assignments

When assessment centers were developed, little thought was given to the prospect of using assessment data to forecast job success in a foreign environment. As globalization continues, however, organizations increasingly are promoting individuals into positions overseas. A survey indicated that 80% of midsize and large companies send professional abroad and many plan on increasing this percentage. Because overseas assignments present additional demands on an employee beyond the typical skills and motivations required to perform a job in the host country, staffing overseas positions presents special challenges for employers. Indeed, one study revealed that cultural factors were much more important to success in an overseas assignment than were technical skills factors. Although many competencies are important to expatriate success, such as family stability/support and language skills, the most important competency is cultural adaptability and flexibility.

One means of predicting success in overseas assignments is a personality test. For example, employees who respond positively to items such as "It is easy for me to strike up conversations with people I do not know" or "I find it easy to put myself in other people's position." Personnel Decisions International has developed a personality test designed to assess whether employees will be successful in overseas assignments. The company reports a positive relationship between scores on the test and success in overseas assignments. Another tool is simulations or interviews designed to simulate conditions overseas or typical challenges that arise.[20] As one can see, bringing these methods together may make the assessment process for global assignments closely resemble an assessment center.

Interview Simulations

An interview simulation simulates the oral communication required on the job. It is sometimes used in an assessment center, but less frequently than in-baskets, leaderless group discussions, and case analysis. It is also used as a predictor separate from the assessment center. There are several different forms of interview simulations.[21]

Role-Play

With a role-play, the job candidate is placed in a simulated situation where he or she must interact with a person at work, such as the boss, a subordinate, or a customer. The interviewer or someone else plays one role, and the job candidate plays the role of the person in the position applied for. So, for example, in selecting someone to be promoted to a supervisory level, the job candidate may be asked to role-play dealing with a difficult employee.

Fact Finding

In a fact-finding interview, the job candidate is presented with a case or problem with incomplete information. It is the job of the candidate to solicit from the interviewer or a resource person the additional facts needed to resolve the case. If one was hiring someone to be an equal employment opportunity manager, one might present him or her with a case where adverse impact is suggested, and then evaluate the candidate according to what data he or she solicits to confirm or disconfirm adverse impact.

Oral Presentations

In many jobs, presentations need to be made to customers, clients, or even boards of directors. To select someone to perform this role, an oral presentation can be required. This approach would be useful, for example, to see what sort of "sales pitch" a consultant might make or to see how an executive would present his or her proposed strategic plan to a board of directors.

Given the importance of interpersonal skills in many jobs, it is unfortunate that not many organizations use interview simulations. This is especially true with internal selection where the organization knows if the person has the right credentials (e.g., company experiences, education, and training), but may not know if the person has the right interpersonal "chemistry" to fit in with the work group. Interview simulations allow for a systematic assessment of this chemistry rather than relying on the instinct of the interviewer. To be effective, these interviews need to be structured and evaluated according to observable behaviors identified in the job analysis as necessary for successful performance.

Promotion Panels and Review Boards

In the public sector, it is a common practice to use a panel or board of people to review the qualifications of candidates. Frequently, a combination of both internal and external candidates are being assessed. Typically, the panel or board consists of job experts, HR professionals, and representatives from constituencies in the community that the board represents. Having a board such as this to hire public servants, such as school superintendents or fire and police officials, offers two advantages. First, as with assessment centers, there are multiple assessors with which to ensure a complete and accurate assessment of the candidate's qualifications. Second, by participating in the selection process, constituents are likely to be more committed to the decision reached. This "buy-in" is particularly important for community representatives with whom the job candidate will interact. It is hoped that by having a say in the process, they will be less likely to voice objections once the candidate is hired.

Choice of Substantive Assessment Methods

Along with research on initial assessment methods, there has also been research conducted on substantive assessment methods. The reviews of this research are summarized in Exhibit 10.11. The same criteria are applied to evaluating the effectiveness of these predictors as were used to evaluate the effectiveness of initial assessment methods.

An examination of Exhibit 10.11 indicates that there is no single best method of narrowing down the candidate list to finalists. What is suggested, however, is that some predictors are more likely to be effective than others. In particular, job knowledge, promotability ratings, and assessment centers have a strong record in terms of reliability and validity in choosing candidates. A very promising development for internal selection is use of job knowledge tests. The validity of these tests appears to be substantial, but, unfortunately, few organizations use them for internal selection purposes.

The effectiveness of several internal selection predictors (case analysis, interview simulations, panels and review boards) is not known at this stage. Interview simulations appear to be a promising technique for jobs requiring public contact skills. All of them need additional research. Other areas in need of additional

EXHIBIT 10.11 Evaluation of Substantive Assessment Methods

Predictors	Use	Cost	Reliability	Validity	Utility	Reactions	Adverse Impact
Seniority	High	Low	High	Low	?	?	High
Experience	High	Low	High	Moderate	High	Positive	Mixed
Job knowledge tests	Low	Moderate	High	High	?	?	?
Performance appraisal	Moderate	Moderate	?	Moderate	?	?	?
Promotability ratings	Low	Low	High	High	?	?	?
Assessment center	Low	High	High	High	High	?	?
In-basket exercise	Low	Moderate	Moderate	Moderate	High	Mixed	Mixed
Leaderless group discussion	Low	Low	Moderate	Moderate	?	?	?
Case analysis	Low	Low	?	Moderate	?	?	?
Global assignments	High	Moderate	?	?	?	?	?
Interview simulations	Low	Low	?	?	?	?	?
Panels and review boards	Low	?	?	?	?	?	?

research are the utility, reactions, and adverse impact associated with all of the substantive assessment methods.

DISCRETIONARY ASSESSMENT METHODS

Discretionary methods are used to narrow down the list of finalists to those who will receive job offers. Sometimes all finalists will receive offers, but at other times, there may not be enough positions to fill for each finalist to receive an offer. As with external selection, discretionary assessments are sometimes made on the basis of organizational citizenship behavior and staffing philosophy regarding EEO/AA.

Two areas of discretionary assessment differ from external selection and need to be considered in deciding job offers. First, previous finalists who do not receive job offers do not simply disappear. They may remain with the organization in hopes of securing an offer the next time the position is open. At the margin, this may be a factor in decision making because being bypassed a second time may create a disgruntled employee. As a result, a previous finalist may be given an offer over a first-time finalist, all other things being equal.

Second, multiple assessors are generally used with internal selection. That is, not only can the hiring manager's opinion be used to select who will receive a job offer but so can the opinions of others (e.g., previous manager, top management) who are knowledgeable about the candidate's profile and the requirements of the current position. As a result, in deciding which candidates will receive job offers, evaluations by people other than the hiring manager may be accorded substantial weight in the decision-making process.

APPLICANT REACTIONS

While applicant reactions to an external staffing process are an important part of its evaluation, such reactions are likely to be even more important for internal candidates. Organizations are likely to be more reticent to use a negatively perceived selection measure for internal than external applicants. Though it may be understandable to leave external *applicants* unhappy with the selection process, the consequences of causing a valued *employee* to be dissatisfied are even more serious. There is little research on applicant reactions to internal selection processes, but one experiment conducted in a large service company in Israel found that nonpromoted candidates reported greater feelings of inequity, lower commitment to the organization, and heightened levels of absenteeism.[22] Thus, organizations must realize that internal promotions may carry negative consequences for the employees who are not selected.

Research also suggests that employees who feel unfairly treated by an organization restore equity ("get even") with a variety of behaviors ranging from reducing work effort to stealing.[23] This suggests that employees who feel unfairly treated in the selection process may behave in ways that are likely to be seen as undesirable by organizations. Any useful selection process will lead to the rejection of some employees, and thus it is impossible to make everyone happy with the results of internal selection decisions. However, research has suggested that beliefs that the process is unfair are more important in influencing subsequent attitudes and behaviors than negative feelings resulting from rejection. Thus, organizations who ensure that the internal process is fair will mitigate many of the negative consequences of rejecting internal applicants.

LEGAL ISSUES

From a legal perspective, methods and processes of internal selection are to be viewed in the same ways as external selection ones. The laws and regulations make no major distinctions between them. Consequently, most of the legal influences on internal selection have already been treated in Chapters 8 and 9. There are, however, some brief comments to be made about internal selection legal influences. Those influences are the Uniform Guidelines on Employee Selection Procedures (UGESP) and the glass ceiling.

Uniform Guidelines on Employee Selection Procedures

It should be remembered that the UGESP defines a "selection procedure" in such a way that virtually any selection method, be it used in an external or internal context, is covered by the requirements of the UGESP. It should also be remembered that the UGESP applies to any "employment decision," which explicitly includes promotion decisions.

When there is adverse impact in promotions, the organization is given the option of justifying it through the conduct of validation studies. These are primarily criterion-related or content validity studies. Ideally, criterion-related studies with predictive validation designs will be used, as has been partially done in the case of assessment centers. Unfortunately, this places substantial administrative and research demands on the organization that are difficult to fulfill most of the time. Consequently, content validation appears to be a better bet for validation purposes.

Many of the methods of assessment used in internal selection attempt to gauge KSAOs and behaviors directly associated with a current job that are felt to be related to success in higher-level jobs. Examples include seniority, performance appraisals, and promotability ratings. These are based on current, as well as past, job content. Validation of these methods, if legally necessary, likely occurs along content validation lines. The organization thus should pay particular and close attention to the validation and documentation requirements for content validation in the UGESP.

The Glass Ceiling

In Chapter 6, the nature of the glass ceiling was discussed, as well as staffing steps to remove it from organizational promotion systems. Most of that discussion centered on internal recruitment and supporting activities that could be undertaken. Surprisingly, selection methods used for promotion assessment are rarely mentioned in literature on the glass ceiling.

This is a major oversight. Whereas the internal recruitment practices recommended may enhance the identification and attraction of minority and women candidates for promotion, effectively matching them to their new jobs requires application of internal selection processes and methods. What might this require of an organization committed to shattering the glass ceiling?

The first possibility is for greater use of selection plans. As discussed in Chapter 8, these plans lay out the KSAOs required for a job, which KSAOs are necessary to bring to the job (as opposed to being acquired on the job), and of those necessary, the most appropriate method of assessment for each. Such a plan forces an organization to conduct job analysis, construct career ladders or KSAO lattices, and consider alternatives to many of the traditional methods of assessment used in promotion systems.

A second suggestion is for the organization to back away from use of these traditional methods of assessment as much as possible, in ways consistent with the selection plan. This means a move away from casual, subjective methods, such as supervisory recommendation, typical promotability ratings, quick reviews of personnel files, and informal recommendations. In their place should come more formal, standardized, and job-related assessment methods. Examples here include assessment centers, promotion review boards or panels, and interview simulations.

A final suggestion is for the organization to pay close attention to the types of KSAOs necessary for advancement, and undertake programs to impart these KSAOs to aspiring employees. These developmental actions might include key job and committee assignments, participation in conferences and other networking opportunities, mentoring and coaching programs, and skill acquisition in formal training programs. Internal selection methods would then be used to assess proficiency on these newly acquired KSAOs, in accordance with the selection plan.

SUMMARY

The selection of internal candidates follows a process very similar to the selection of external candidates. The logic of prediction is applied, and a selection plan is developed and implemented.

One important area where internal and external selection methods differ is in the nature of the predictor. Predictors used for internal selection tend to have greater depth and more relevance and are better suited for verification. As a result, there are often different types of predictors used for internal than for external selection decisions.

Initial assessment methods are used to narrow down the applicant pool to a qualified set of candidates. Approaches used are skills inventories, peer assessments, self-assessments, managerial sponsorship, informal discussions and recommendations, and career concepts. Of these approaches, no single approach is particularly strong in predicting future performance. Hence, consideration should be given to using multiple predictors to verify the accuracy of any one method. These results also point to the need to use substantive as well as initial assessment methods in making internal selection decisions.

Substantive assessment methods are used to select finalists from the list of candidates. Predictors used to make these decisions include seniority and experience, job knowledge tests, performance appraisals, promotability ratings, the assessment center, interview simulations, and panels and review boards. Of this set of predictors, ones that work well are job knowledge tests, promotability ratings, and assessment centers. Organizations need to give greater consideration to the latter three predictors to supplement traditional seniority and experience.

Although very costly, the assessment center seems to be very effective. It is so effective because it is grounded in behavioral science theory and the logic of prediction. In particular, samples of behavior are analyzed, multiple assessors and predictors are used, and predictors are developed on the basis of job analysis.

Internal job applicants have the potential for far greater access to selection data than do external job applicants due to their physical proximity to the data. As a result, procedures must be implemented to ensure that manual and computer files with sensitive data are kept private and confidential.

Two areas of legal concern for internal selection decisions are the Uniform Guidelines on Employee Selection Procedures (UGESP) and the glass ceiling. In terms of the UGESP, particular care must be taken to ensure that internal selection methods are valid if adverse impact is occurring. To minimize glass ceiling effects, organizations should make greater use of selection plans and more objective internal assessment methods, as well as help impart the KSAOs necessary for advancement.

DISCUSSION QUESTIONS

1. Explain how internal selection decisions differ from external selection decisions.
2. What are the differences between peer ratings, peer nominations, and peer rankings?
3. Explain the theory behind assessment centers.
4. Describe the three different types of interview simulations.
5. Evaluate the effectiveness of seniority, assessment centers, and job knowledge as substantive internal selection procedures.

6. What steps should be taken by an organization that is committed to shattering the glass ceiling?

APPLICATIONS

Changing a Promotion System

Bioglass Inc. specializes in sales of a wide array of glass products. One area of the company, the Commercial Sales Division (CSD), specializes in selling high-tech mirrors and microscope and photographic lenses. Sales associates in CSD are responsible for selling the glass products to corporate clients. In CSD there are four levels of sales associates, ranging in pay from $28,000 to $76,000 per year. There are also four levels of managerial positions in CSD; those positions range in pay from $76,000 to $110,000 per year (that's what the division president makes).

Tom Caldwell has been a very effective sales associate. He has consistently demonstrated good sales techniques in his 17 years with Bioglass and has a large and loyal client base. Over the years, Tom has risen from the lowest level of sales associate to the highest. He has proven himself successful at each stage. An entry- (first-) level management position in CSD opened up last year, and Tom was the natural candidate. Although several other candidates were given consideration, Tom was the clear choice for the position.

However, once in the position, Tom had a great deal of difficulty being a manager. He was not accustomed to delegating and rarely provided feedback or guidance to the people he supervised. Although he set goals for himself, he never set performance goals for his workers. Morale in Tom's group was low, and group performance suffered. The company felt that demoting Tom back to sales would be disastrous for him and present the wrong image to other employees; firing such a loyal employee was considered unacceptable. Therefore, Bioglass decided to keep Tom where he was, but never promote him again. They were also considering enrolling Tom in some expensive managerial development programs to enhance his management skills.

Meanwhile, Tom's replacement, although successful at the lower three levels of sales associate positions, was having a great deal of difficulty with the large corporate contracts that the highest-level sales associates must service. Two of Tom's biggest clients had recently left Bioglass for a competitor. CSD was confused about how such a disastrous situation had developed when they seemed to make all the right decisions.

Based on this application and your reading of this chapter, answer the following questions:

1. What is the likely cause of CSD's problems?
2. How might CSD, and Bioglass more generally, make better promotion decisions in the future? Be specific.

3. In general, what role should performance appraisals play in internal selection decisions? Are there some cases in which they are more relevant than others? Explain.

Promotion from Within at Citrus Glen

Mandarine "Mandy" Pamplemousse is vice president of human resources for Citrus Glen, a juicier based in south Florida that supplies orange and grapefruit juice to grocery stores, convenience stores, restaurants, and food processors through the United States. Citrus Glen has been growing rapidly, and a constant feature of Mandy's job for the last few years has been worry about how to hire and promote enough qualified individuals to staff the ever-expanding array of positions within the company.

One of the ways Mandy has been able to staff positions internally is by contracting with Staffing Systems International (SSI), a management consulting firm based in Charlotte, North Carolina. When positions open up at Citrus Glen that are appropriate to staff internally, Mandy has sent a group of candidates for the position up to SSI to participate in their assessment center. The candidates return from SSI three days later, and a few days after that, SSI sends Mandy the results of the assessment with a recommendation. Though Mandy had never formally evaluated the accuracy of the promotions, it was her feeling that the process was pretty accurate. Of course, Mandy thought, for $5,500 per candidate, it should be accurate.

A few days ago, Mandy was hosting Thanksgiving, and her brother-in-law, Vin Pomme, joined them. Vin is a doctoral student in industrial psychology at Ohio International University. After Thanksgiving dinner, while Mandy, Vin, and their family were relaxing on her lanai and enjoying the warm Florida sunshine, Mandy was talking to Vin about her difficulties in promoting from within and the cost of SSI's assessment process. Vin quickly realized that SSI was using an assessment center. He was also aware of research suggesting that once one takes an applicant's personality and cognitive ability into account, assessment center scores may contribute little additional validity. Given the high cost of assessment centers, he reasoned, one must wonder whether this "incremental" validity (the validity that assessment centers contribute beyond the validity provided by personality and cognitive ability tests) would prove cost effective. After Vin conveyed these impressions to Mandy, she felt that after the holidays she was going to re-examine Citrus Glen's internal selection processes.

Questions

1. Drawing from concepts presented in Chapter 7 (Measurement), how could Mandy more formally evaluate SSI's assessment process, as well as the alternative presented to her by Vin?

2. Construct a scenario in which you think Mandy should continue her business relationship with SSI. On the other hand, if Mandy decides on an alternative assessment process, what would that process be? How would she evaluate whether that process was effective?

3. Citrus Hill has considered expanding their operations into the Caribbean and Latin America. One of Mandy's concerns is how to staff such positions. If Citrus Hill does expand its operations to different cultures, how should Mandy go about staffing such positions? Be specific.

ENDNOTES

1. A. Howard and D. W. Bray, "Predictions of Managerial Success over Long Periods of Time: Lessons from the Management Progress Study," in K. E. Clark and M. B. Clark (eds.), *Measures of Leadership* (West Orange, NJ: Leadership Library of America, 1990), pp. 113–130; C. J. Russell, "Selecting Top Corporate Leaders: An Example of Biographical Information," *Journal of Management,* 1990, 16, pp. 73–86; J. S. Schippman and E. P. Prien, "An Assessment of the Contributions of General Mental Ability and Personality Characteristics to Management Success," *Journal of Business and Psychology,* 1989, 3, pp. 423–437.

2. J. J. Kane and E. E. Lawler, "Methods of Peer Assessment," *Psychological Bulletin,* 1978, 85, pp. 555–586.

3. Bureau of National Affairs, *Basic Patterns in Union Contracts* (Washington, DC: author, 1995).

4. F. K. Folkes, *Personnel Policies in Large Non-Union Companies* (Englewood Cliffs, NJ: Prentice-Hall, 1985).

5. C. Ichniowski, J. T. Delaney, and D. Lewin, "The New Resource Management in US Workplaces: Is It Really New and Is It Only Nonunion?" *Industrial Relations,* 1989, 44, pp. 97–119.

6. K. G. Abraham and J. L. Medoff, "Length of Service and Promotions in Union and Nonunion Work Groups," *Industrial and Labor Relations Review,* 1985, 38, pp. 408–420; M. E. Gordon and W. J. Fitzgibbons, "An Empirical Test of the Validity of Seniority as a Factor in Staffing Decisions," *Journal of Applied Psychology,* 1982, 67, pp. 311–319.

7. A. Lienert, "From Rust to Riches," *Management Review,* 1994, 83, pp. 10–14.

8. M. A. Quinones, J. K. Ford, and M. S. Teachout, "The Relationship Between Work Experience and Job Performance: A Conceptual and Meta-Analytic Review," *Personnel Psychology,* 1995, 48, pp. 887–910; P. E. Tesluk and R. R. Jacobs, "Toward an Integrated Model of Work Experience," *Personnel Psychology,* 1998, 51, pp. 321–355.

9. F. L. Schmidt, J. E. Hunter, and A. N. Outerbridge, "Joint Relation of Experience and Ability with Job Performance: Test of Three Hypotheses," *Journal of Applied Psychology,* 1988, 73, pp. 46–57.

10. W. Wilson, "Video Training and Testing Supports Customer Service Goals," *Personnel Journal,* 1994, 73, pp. 47–51.

11. F. L. Schmidt and J. E. Hunter, "Development of a Causal Model of Processes Determining Job Performance," *Current Directions in Psychological Science,* 1992, 1, pp. 89–92.

12. K. R. Murphy and J. M. Cleveland, *Performance Appraisal: An Organizational Perspective* (Boston: Allyn and Bacon, 1991).

13. L. J. Peter and R. Hull, *The Peter Principle* (New York: William Morrow, 1969).

14. G. C. Thornton III and D. M. Morris, "The Application of Assessment Center Technology to the Evaluation of Personnel Records," *Public Personnel Management,* 2001, 30, pp. 55–66.

15. A. C. Spychalski, M. A. Quinones, B. B. Gaugler, and K. Pohley, "A Survey of Assessment Center Practices in Organizations in the United States," *Personnel Psychology,* 1997, 50, pp. 71–90.

16. B. B. Gaugler, D. B. Rosenthal, G. C. Thornton III, and C. Bentson, "Meta-Analysis of Assessment Center Validity," *Journal of Applied Psychology,* 1987, 72, pp. 493–511.

17. R. D. Goffin, M. G. Rothstein, and N. G. Johnson, "Personality Testing and the Assessment Center: Incremental Validity for Managerial Selection," *Journal of Applied Psychology,* 1996, 81, pp. 746–756; H. W. Goldstein, K. P. Yusko, E. P. Brauerman, D. B. Smith, and B. Chung, "The Role of Cognitive Ability in Subgroup Differences and Incremental Validity of Assessment Center Exercises," *Personnel Psychology,* 1998, 51, pp. 357–374; F. L. Schmidt and J. E. Hunter, "The Validity and Utility of Selection Methods in Personnel Psychology: Practical and Theoretical Implications of 85 Years of Research Findings," *Psychological Bulletin,* 1998, 124, pp. 262–274.

18. B. B. Gaugler et al., "Meta-Analysis of Assessment Center Validity"; A. Howard, "An Assessment of Assessment Centers," *Academy of Management Journal,* 1974, 17, pp. 115–134; R. Klimoski and M. Brickner, "Why Do Assessment Centers Work? The Puzzle of Assessment Center Validity," *Personnel Psychology,* 1987, 40, pp. 243–260; P. R. Sackett, "A Critical Look at Some Common Beliefs About Assessment Centers," *Public Personnel Management,* 1988, 11, pp. 140–146.

19. C. Fletcher, "Candidates' Reactions to Assessment Centres and Their Outcomes: A Longitudinal Study," *Journal of Occupational Psychology,* 1991, 64, pp. 117–127; "Guidelines and Ethical Considerations for Assessment Center Operations," *Public Personnel Management,* 2000, 29, pp. 315–331.

20. J. E. Abueva, "Return of the Native Executive," *New York Times,* May 17, 2000, pp. B1, B8; P. Caligiuri and W. F. Cascio, "Sending Women on Global Assignments," *WorldatWork,* Second Quarter 2001, pp. 34–41; J. A. Hauser, "Filling the Candidate Pool: Developing Qualities in Potential International Assignees," *WorldatWork,* Second Quarter 2000, pp. 26–33; M. Mukuda, "Global Leaders Wanted . . . Apply Within," *Workspan,* April 2001, pp. 36–41; C. Patton, "Match Game," *Human Resource Executive,* June 2000, pp. 36–41.

21. G. C. Thornton, *Assessment Centers in Human Resource Management* (Reading, MA: Addison-Wesley, 1992).

22. J. Schwarzwald, M. Kuslowsky, and B. Shalit, "A Field Study of Employees' Attitudes and Behaviors After Promotion Decisions," *Journal of Applied Psychology,* 1992, 77, pp. 511–514.

23. J. Greenberg, "Stealing in the Name of Justice: Informational and Interpersonal Moderators of Theft Reactions to Underpayment Treatment," *Organizational Behavior and Human Decision Processes,* 1993, 54, pp. 81–103.

The Staffing Organizations Model

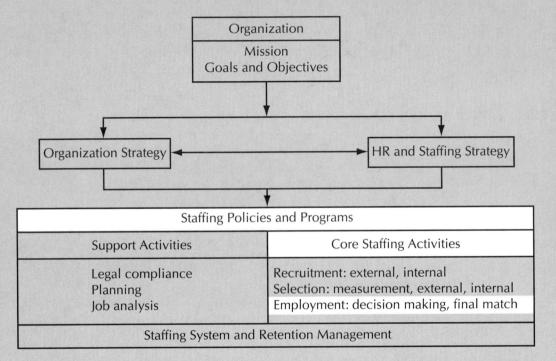

PART FIVE

Staffing Activities: Employment

CHAPTER ELEVEN

Decision Making

Choice of Assessment Method
    Validity Coefficient
    Correlation with Other Predictors
    Adverse Impact
    Utility

Determining Assessment Scores
    Single Predictor
    Multiple Predictors

Hiring Standards and Cut Scores
    Description of the Process
    Consequences of Cut Scores
    Methods to Determine Cut Scores
    Professional Guidelines

Methods of Final Choice
    Random Selection
    Ranking
    Grouping

Decision Makers
    Human Resource Professionals
    Managers
    Employees

Legal Issues
    Uniform Guidelines on Employee Selection Procedures
    Choices Among Finalists

Summary

Discussion Questions

Applications

I ndividuals flow through the staffing process, passing through several stages: applicant, candidate, finalist, offer receiver, and new hire. To implement and manage this flow, key decisions that must be made in several areas will be discussed. First, the factors that determine the choice of assessment methods to be used will be reviewed. Discussion will focus on the important considerations of validity, the correlation of one assessment method with other methods, likely adverse impact, and the utility of the method.

Once assessment data have been collected from applicants, decisions must be made about how to determine assessment scores. The process of translating predictor scores into assessment scores will be discussed for using single predictors and multiple predictors. In the case of multiple predictors, methods to combine predictor scores will be considered. Methods that will be reviewed are a compensatory model, multiple hurdles, and a combined approach. Each has distinct strengths and weaknesses.

Hiring standards and cut scores must be established to determine passing levels for the assessment scores. The process used to determine cut scores will be described, as well as the consequences of cut scores and methods to determine cut scores. Methods that will be covered are minimum competency, top-down, and banding. Professional guidelines for determining cut scores also will be reviewed.

Methods of final choice must be considered to determine who from among the finalists will receive a job offer. Methods of final choice that will be reviewed include random selection, ranking, and grouping. Each method may be advantageous, depending on one's objectives.

For all of the preceding decisions, consideration must be given to who should be involved in the decision process. The role of various potential decision makers will be discussed, including HR professionals, line managers, and employees. In general, decisions about the staffing procedures to be followed are determined by HR professionals. Actual hiring decisions are usually made by managers. Increasingly, employees are being involved in both decisions.

Finally, legal issues should also guide the decision making. Particular consideration will be given to the Uniform Guidelines on Employee Selection Procedures. Of special concern are the use of cutoff scores and choices from among finalists.

CHOICE OF ASSESSMENT METHOD

In our discussions of external and internal selection methods, we listed multiple criteria to consider when deciding which method(s) to use (e.g., validity, utility). Some of these criteria require more amplification, specifically validity, correlation with other predictors (newly discussed here), adverse impact, and utility.

Validity Coefficient

Validity refers to the relationship between predictor and criterion scores. Often this relationship is assessed using a correlation (see Chapter 7). The correlation between predictor and criterion scores is known as a validity coefficient. For example, the validity coefficient for an ability test may be $r = .40$ when scores on the test (predictor) are correlated with performance ratings (criterion). The usefulness of a predictor is determined on the basis of the practical significance and statistical significance of its validity coefficient. As was noted in Chapter 7, reliability is a necessary condition for validity. Selection measures with questionable reliability will have questionable validity. This reinforces the need to use only those selection measures that are standardized and have proven reliability.

Practical Significance

Practical significance refers to the extent to which the predictor adds value to the prediction of job success. It is assessed by examining the sign and the magnitude of the validity coefficient.

Sign The sign of the validity coefficient refers to the direction of the relationship between the predictor and criterion. A useful predictor is one where the sign of the relationship is positive or negative and is consistent with the logic or theory behind the predictor.

A positive or negative sign in and of itself, however, says nothing about the usefulness of a predictor. A positive sign does not mean a good predictor, and a negative sign does not mean a poor predictor. The signs should not be considered independent of the theory because a positive sign may be desirable in one situation, but not another. A useful predictor is one where the sign is consistent with the theory. For example, if an ability test is used to predict job performance, then the test would probably be most useful when there is a positive sign. This is because theory suggests that ability is positively related to how well people perform on the job.

Magnitude The magnitude of the validity coefficient refers to its size. It can range from 0 to 1.00, with a coefficient of 0 being the least desirable and a coefficient of 1.00 being the most desirable. The closer the validity coefficient is to 1.00, the more useful the predictor. Predictors with validity coefficients of 1.00 are not to be expected given the inherent difficulties in predicting human behavior. Instead, as shown in Chapters 8 and 9, validity coefficients for current assessment methods range from 0 to about .60. Any validity coefficient above 0 is better than random selection and may be somewhat useful. Validities above .15 are of moderate usefulness, and validities above .30 are of high usefulness.

Statistical Significance

Statistical significance, as assessed by probability or p values (see Chapter 7), is another factor that should be used to interpret the validity coefficient. If a validity coefficient has a reasonable p value, it indicates that chances are good that, if the same predictor were used with different sets of job applicants, it would yield a similar validity coefficient. That is, a reasonable p value indicates that the method of prediction, rather than chance, produced the observed validity coefficient.

Convention has it that a reasonable level of significance is $p < .05$. This means there are fewer than 5 chances in 100 of concluding there is a relationship in the population of job applicants, when, in fact, there is not. In most cases, this is a reasonable level of certainty, indicating that the validity coefficient is statistically significant. Other times, a smaller p value, such as .001, is chosen for statistical significance. This may be the case, for example, when selecting people for a hazardous occupation, such as firefighting, and using a nonvalid predictor may have many disastrous and expensive consequences.

It should be pointed out that caution must be exercised in using statistical significance as a way to gauge the usefulness of a predictor. Research has clearly shown that nonsignificant validity coefficients may simply be due to the small samples of employees used to calculate the validity coefficient. Rejecting the use of a predictor solely on the basis of a small sample may lead to the rejection of a predictor that would have been quite acceptable had a larger sample of employees been used to test for validity.[1] These concerns over significance testing have led some researchers to recommend the use of "confidence intervals," for example, showing that one can be 90% confident that the true validity is no less than .30 and no greater than .40.[2]

Face Validity

Face validity concerns whether the selection measure appears valid to the applicant. Face validity is potentially important to selection decision making in general, and choice of selection methods in particular, if it affects applicant behavior (willingness to continue in the selection process, performance and turnover once hired). Judgments of face validity are closely associated with applicant reactions, which we discussed in Chapter 7.

Correlation with Other Predictors

If a predictor is to be considered useful, it must add value to the prediction of job success. To add value, it must add to the prediction of success above and beyond the forecasting powers of current predictors. In general, a predictor is more useful the smaller the correlation it has with other predictors and the higher the correlation it has with the criterion.

In order to assess whether the predictor adds anything new to forecasting, a matrix showing all the correlations between the predictors and the criteria should always be generated. If the correlations between the new predictor and existing predictors are higher than the correlations between the new predictor and criterion, then the new predictor is not adding much that is new. There are also relatively straightforward techniques, such as multiple regression, that take the correlation among predictors into account.[3]

Predictors are likely to be highly correlated with one another when their domain of content is similar. For example, both biodata and application blanks may focus on previous training received. Thus, using both biodata and application blanks as predictors may be redundant, and neither one may augment the other much in predicting job success.

Adverse Impact

A predictor discriminates between people in terms of the likelihood of their success on the job. A predictor may also discriminate by screening out a disproportionate number of minorities and women. To the extent that this happens, the predictor has adverse impact, and it may result in legal problems. As a result, when the validity of alternative predictors is the same and one predictor has less adverse impact than the other predictor, then the predictor with less adverse impact should be used.

A very difficult judgment call arises when one predictor has high validity and high adverse impact while another predictor has low validity and low adverse impact. From the perspective of accurately predicting job performance, the former predictor should be used. From an EEO/AA standpoint, the latter predictor is preferable. Balancing the trade-offs is difficult and requires use of the organization's staffing philosophy regarding EEO/AA. One of the suggested solutions to this trade-off is banding, discussed later in this chapter.

Utility

Utility refers to the expected gains to be derived from using a predictor. Expected gains are of two types: hiring success and economic.

Hiring Success Gain
Hiring success refers to the proportion of new hires who turn out to be successful on the job. Hiring success *gain* refers to the increase in the proportion of successful new hires that is expected to occur as a result of adding a new predictor to the selection system. If the current staffing system yields a success rate of 75% for new hires, how much of a gain in this success rate will occur by adding a new predictor to the system? The greater the expected gain, the greater the utility of

the new predictor. This gain is influenced not only by the validity of the new predictor (as already discussed) but also by the selection ratio and base rate.

Selection Ratio The selection ratio is simply the number of people hired divided by the number of applicants (sr = number hired / number of applicants). The lower the selection ratio, the more useful the predictor. When the selection ratio is low, the organization is more likely to be selecting successful employees.

If the selection ratio is low, then the denominator is large or the numerator is small. Both conditions are desirable. A large denominator means that the organization is reviewing a large number of applicants for the job. The chances of identifying a successful candidate are much better in this situation than when an organization hires the first available person or only reviews a few applicants. A small numerator indicates that the organization is being very stringent with its hiring standards. The organization is hiring people likely to be successful rather than hiring anyone who meets the most basic requirements for the job; it is using high standards to ensure that the very best people are selected.

Base Rate The base rate is defined as the proportion of current employees who are successful on some criterion or HR outcome (br = number of successful employees / number of employees). A high base rate is desired for obvious reasons. A high base rate may come about from the organization's staffing system alone or in combination with other HR programs, such as training and compensation.

When considering possible use of a new predictor, one issue is whether the proportion of successful employees (i.e., the base rate) will increase as a result of using the new predictor in the staffing system. This is the matter of hiring success gain. Dealing with it requires simultaneous consideration of the organization's current base rate and selection ratio, as well as the validity of the new predictor.

The Taylor-Russell tables provide the necessary assistance for addressing this issue. An excerpt from the Taylor-Russell tables is shown in Exhibit 11.1.

The Taylor-Russell table shows in each of its cells the percentage of new hires who will turn out to be successful. This is determined by a combination of the validity coefficient for the new predictor, the selection ratio, and the base rate. The top matrix (A) shows the percentage of successful new hires when the base rate is low (.30), the validity coefficient is low (.20) or high (.60), and the selection ratio is low (.10) or high (.70). The bottom matrix (B) shows the percentage of successful new hires when the base rate is high (.80), the validity coefficient is low (.20) or high (.60), and the selection ratio is low (.10) or high (.70). Two illustrations show how these tables may be used.

The first illustration has to do with the decision whether or not to use a new test to select computer programmers. Assume that the current test used to select programmers has a validity coefficient of .20. Also assume that a consulting firm has approached the organization with a new test that has a validity coefficient of .60. Should the organization purchase and use the new test?

EXHIBIT 11.1   Excerpts from the Taylor-Russell Tables

A.

		Base Rate = .30 Selection Ratio	
Validity		**.10**	**.70**
.20		43%	33
.60		77	40

B.

		Base Rate = .80 Selection Ratio	
Validity		**.10**	**.70**
.20		89%	83
.60		99	90

Source: H. C. Taylor and J. T. Russell, "The Relationship of Validity Coefficients to the Practical Effectiveness of Tests in Selection," *Journal of Applied Psychology*, 1939, 23, pp. 565–578.

At first blush, the answer might seem to be affirmative, because the new test has a substantially higher level of validity. This initial reaction, however, must be gauged in the context of the selection ratio and the current base rate. If the current base rate is .80 and the current selection ratio is .70, then, as can be seen in the lower matrix (B) of Exhibit 11.1, the new selection procedure will only result in a hiring success gain from 83% to 90%. The organization may already have a very high base rate due to other facets of HR management it does quite well (e.g., training, rewards). Hence, even though it has validity of .20, the base rate of its current predictor is already .80.

On the other hand, if the existing base rate of the organization is .30 and the existing selection ratio is .10, then it should strongly consider use of the new test. As shown in the top matrix (A) in Exhibit 11.1, the hiring success gain will go from 43% to 77% with the addition of the new test.

A second illustration using the Taylor-Russell tables has to do with recruitment in conjunction with selection. Assume that the validity of the organization's current predictor, a cognitive ability test, is .60. Also assume that a new college recruitment program has been very aggressive. As a result, there is a large swell in the number of applicants, and the selection ratio has decreased from .70 to .10. The decision the organization faces is whether to continue this college recruitment program.

An initial reaction may be that the program should be continued because of the large increase in applicants generated. As shown in the top matrix of Exhibit 11.1, this answer would be correct if the current base rate is .30. By decreasing the selection ratio from .70 to .10, the hiring success gain increases from 40% to 77%. On the other hand, if the current base rate is .80, the correct decision may be to not continue the program. The hiring success increases from only 90% to 99%, which may not justify the very large expense associated with aggressive college recruitment campaigns.

The point of these illustrations is that when confronted with the decision of whether or not to use a new predictor, the decision depends on the validity coefficient, base rate, and selection ratio. They should not be considered independent of one another. HR professionals should carefully record and monitor base rates and selection ratios. Then, when asked by management whether they should be using a new predictor, they can respond appropriately. Fortunately, the Taylor-Russell tables are for any combination of validity coefficient, base rate, and selection ratio values. The values shown in Exhibit 11.1 are excerpts for illustration only. When other values need to be considered, then the original tables should be consulted to provide the appropriate answers.

Economic Gain

Economic gain refers to the bottom line or monetary impact of a predictor on the organization. A predictor is more useful the greater the economic gain it produces. Considerable work has been done over the years on assessing the economic gain associated with predictors. The basic utility formula used to estimate economic gain is shown in Exhibit 11.2.

At a general level, the economic gain formula shown in Exhibit 11.2 works as follows. Economic gains derived from using a valid predictor versus random se-

EXHIBIT 11.2 Economic Gain Formula

$$\Delta U = N_s TrSDy\bar{Z}_s - NC$$

Where:

ΔU = expected dollar value increase to the organization using the predictor versus random selection

T = tenure of selected group

N_s = number of applicants selected

r = correlation between predictor and job performance

SDy = standard deviation of job performance

$\bar{Z}_s$ = average standard predictor score of selected group

N = number of applicants

C = cost per applicant

Source: Wayne F. Cascio, *Applied Psychology in Personnel Management*, 4th edition, © 1991, p. 300. Adapted with permission of Prentice-Hall, Englewood Cliffs, NJ.

lection (the left-hand side of the equation) depend on two factors (the right-hand side of the equation). The first factor (the entry before the subtraction sign) is the revenue generated by hiring productive employees using the new predictor. The second factor (the entry after the subtraction sign) is the costs associated with using the new predictor. Positive economic gains are achieved when revenues are maximized and costs are minimized. Revenues are maximized by using the most valid selection procedures. Costs are minimized by using the predictors with the least costs. To estimate actual economic gain, values are entered into the equation for each of the variables shown. Values are usually generated by experts in HR research relying on the judgments of experienced line managers.

Several variations on the economic gain (utility) formula shown in Exhibit 11.2 have been developed. For the most part, these variations require consideration of additional factors, such as assumptions about tax rates and applicant flows. In all of these models, the most difficult factor to estimate is the standard deviation of job performance (SDy), which represents the difference between productive and nonproductive employees in dollar value terms. A variety of methods have been proposed to measure SDy, ranging from manager estimates of employee value to percentages of compensation (usually 40% of base pay).[4] Despite this difficulty, economic gain formulas represent a significant way of estimating the economic gains that may be anticipated with the use of a new (and valid) predictor.

Limitations with Utility Analysis

Although utility analysis can be a powerful method to communicate the bottom-line implications of using valid selection measures, it is not without its limitations. Perhaps the most fundamental concern among researchers and practitioners is that utility estimates lack realism because:

1. Virtually every organization uses multiple selection measures, yet existing utility models assume that the decision is whether to use a single selection measure rather than selecting applicants by chance alone.[5]

2. There are many important variables missing from the model, such as EEO/AA concerns and applicant reactions.[6]

3. The utility formula is based on many assumptions that are probably overly simplistic, including that validity does not vary over time,[7] that nonperformance criteria such as attendance, trainability, applicant reactions, and fit are irrelevant,[8] and that applicants are selected in a top-down manner and all job offers are accepted.[9]

Perhaps as a result of these limitations, several factors indicate that utility analysis may have a limited effect on managers' decisions about selection measures. For example, a survey of managers who have discontinued use of utility analysis found that 40% did so because they felt that utility analysis was too complicated, whereas 32% discontinued use because they believed that the results were unbelievable.[10] Other studies have found that managers' acceptance of utility analysis is low; one study found that reporting simple validity coefficients was more likely to persuade HR decision makers to adopt a particular selection method than was reporting utility analysis results.[11]

These criticisms should not be taken as arguments that organizations should ignore utility analysis when evaluating selection decisions. However, decision makers are much less likely to become disillusioned with utility analysis if they are informed consumers and realize some of the limitations inherent in such analyses. Researchers have the responsibility of better embedding utility analysis in the strategic context in which staffing decisions are made, while HR decision makers have the responsibility to use the most rigorous methods possible to evaluate their decisions.[12] By being realistic about what utility analysis can and cannot accomplish, the potential to fruitfully inform staffing decisions will increase.

DETERMINING ASSESSMENT SCORES

Single Predictor

Using a single predictor in selection decisions makes the process of determining scores easy. In fact, scores on the single predictor *are* the final assessment scores. Thus, concerns over how to combine assessment scores are not relevant when a single predictor is used in selection decisions. Although using a single predictor has the advantage of simplicity, there are some obvious drawbacks. First, few employers would feel comfortable hiring applicants on the basis of a single attribute. In fact, almost all employers use multiple methods in selection decisions. A second and related reason for using multiple predictors is that utility increases as the number of valid predictors used in selection decisions increases. In most cases, using two valid selection methods will result in more effective selection decisions than using a sole predictor. For these reasons, although basing selection decisions on a single predictor is a simple way to make decisions, it is rarely the best one.

Multiple Predictors

Given the less-than-perfect validities of predictors, most organizations use multiple predictors in making selection decisions. With multiple predictors, decisions must be made about combining the resultant scores. These decisions can be addressed through consideration of compensatory, multiple hurdles, and combined approaches.

Compensatory Model

With a compensatory model, scores on one predictor are simply added to scores on another predictor to yield a total score. What this means is that high scores on one predictor can compensate for low scores on another. For example, if an employer is using an interview and grade point average (GPA) to select a person, an applicant with a low GPA who does well in the interview may still get the job.

The advantage of a compensatory model is that it recognizes that people have multiple talents and that many different constellations of talents may produce success on the job. The disadvantage to a compensatory model is that, at least for some jobs, level of proficiency for specific talents cannot be compensated for by other proficiencies. For example, a firefighter requires a certain level of strength that cannot be compensated for by intelligence.

In terms of making actual decisions using the compensatory model, there are four procedures that may be followed: clinical prediction, unit weighting, rational weighting, and multiple regression. The four methods differ from one another in terms of the manner in which predictor scores (raw or standardized) are weighted before being added together for a total or composite score.

The following example will be used to illustrate these procedures. In all four, raw scores are used to determine a total score. Standard scores (see Chapter 7) may need to be used rather than raw scores if each predictor variable uses a different method of measurement or is measured under different conditions. Differences in weighting methods are shown in Part A of Exhibit 11.3. In Part B of Exhibit 11.3, there is a selection system consisting of interviews, application blanks, and recommendations. For simplicity, assume that scores on each predictor range from 1 to 5. Scores on these three predictors are shown for three applicants.

Clinical Prediction   Returning to Exhibit 11.3, note that with a clinical prediction, managers use their expert judgment to arrive at a total score for each applicant. That final score may or may not be a simple addition of the three predictor scores shown in Exhibit 11.3. Hence, applicant A may be given a higher total score than applicant B even though simple addition shows that applicant B had one point more (4 + 3 + 4 = 11) than applicant A (3 + 5 + 2 = 10).

The advantage to this approach is that it draws on the expertise of managers to weight and combine predictor scores. In turn, managers may be more likely to accept the selection decisions than if a mechanical scoring rule (e.g., add up the points) were used. The problem with this approach is that the reasons for the weightings are known only to the manager. Also, clinical predictions have generally been shown to be less accurate than mechanical decisions.[13]

Unit Weighting   With unit weighting, each predictor is weighted the same at a value of 1.00. What this means is shown in Exhibit 11.3 (Part A): the predictor scores are simply added together to get a total score. So, in Exhibit 11.3 (Part B), the total scores for applicants A, B, and C are 10, 11, and 12, respectively. The advantage to unit weighting is that it is a simple and straightforward process to follow and makes the importance of each predictor explicit to decision makers.

EXHIBIT 11.3 Four Compensatory Model Procedures for Three Predictors

A. Models

Clinical Prediction

$P_1 \rightarrow P_2 \rightarrow P_3 \rightarrow$ Total Score

Unit Weighting

$P_1 + P_2 + P_3 =$ Total Score

Rational Weighting

$w_1 P_1 + w_2 P_2 + w_3 P_3 =$ Total Score

Multiple Regression

$a + b_1 P_1 + b_2 P_2 + b_3 P_3 =$ Total Score

Where: P = predictor score
w = rational weight
a = intercept
b = statistical weight

B. Raw Scores for Applicants on Three Predictors

	Predictors		
Applicant	Interview	Application Blank	Recommendation
A	3	5	2
B	4	3	4
C	5	4	3

The problem with this approach is that it assumes that each predictor contributes equally to the prediction of job success, which often will not be the case.

Rational Weighting   With rational weighting, each predictor receives a differential rather than equal weighting. Managers and other subject matter experts establish the weights for each predictor according to degree to which each is believed to predict job success. These weights (w) are then multiplied times each raw score (P) to yield a total score as shown in Exhibit 11.3 (Part A).

For example, the predictors in Exhibit 11.3 (Part B) may be weighted .5, .3, and .2 for the interview, application blank, and recommendation. Each applicant's raw score in Exhibit 11.3 (Part B) is multiplied times the appropriate weight to yield a total score. For example, the total score for applicant A is $(.5) 3 + (.3) 5 + (.2) 2 = 3.4$.

The advantage to this approach is that it considers the relative importance of each predictor and makes this assessment explicit. The downside, however, is that it is an elaborate procedure that requires managers and subject matter experts to agree on the differential weights to be applied.

Multiple Regression   Multiple regression is similar to rational weighting in that the predictors receive different weights. With multiple regression, however, the weights are established on the basis of statistical procedures rather than on the basis of judgments by managers or other subject matter experts. The statistical weights are developed on the basis of (a) the correlation of each predictor with the criterion, and (b) the correlations among the predictors. As a result, regression weights provide optimal weights in the sense that the weights are those that will yield the highest total validity.

The calculations result in a multiple regression formula like the one shown in Exhibit 11.3 (Part A). A total score for each applicant is obtained by multiplying the statistical weight (b) for each predictor by the predictor (P) score and summing these along with the intercept value (a). As an example, assume the statistical weights are .9, .6, and .2 for the interview, application blank, and recommendation, respectively, and that the intercept is .09. Using these values, the total score for applicant A is $.09 + (.9)3 + (.6)5 + (.2)2 = 6.19$.

Multiple regression offers the possibility of a much higher degree of precision in the prediction of criterion scores than do the other methods of weighting. Unfortunately, this level of precision is realized only under a certain set of circumstances. In particular, for multiple regression to be more precise than unit weighting, there must be a small number of predictors, low correlations between predictor variables, and a large sample.[14] Many selection settings do not meet these criteria, so in these cases consideration should be given to unit or rational weighting instead. In situations where these conditions are met, however, multiple regression weights can produce higher validity and utility than the other weighting schemes.

Choice Among Weighting Schemes   The choice from among different weighting schemes is important because how various predictor combinations are weighted is critical in determining the usefulness of the selection process. To illustrate, Exhibit 11.4 provides the changes in validity and utility that occur when supplementing the most empirically valid method of selection (cognitive ability tests) with another selection method. The first column shows that change in validity by unit weighting scores on the cognitive ability test with the specified selection measure. For example, the validity of a cognitive ability test, when used by itself to predict job performance, has been estimated to be .50. Past research suggests that the validity of an integrity test, when used by itself to predict job performance, is .41. When scores on the cognitive ability and integrity test are combined by weighting them equally, the total validity increases to .65, an increase of 27.6% over the validity of the cognitive ability test alone. When scores are weighted according to multiple regression, however, the increase in validity becomes 28.2%. In fact, the exhibit shows that when supplementing cognitive ability

EXHIBIT 11.4 Effects of Unit Weighting and Multiple Regression Weighting on the Validity and Utility of Cognitive Ability Tests

Additional Selection Method	Unit-Weighted Composite	Regression-Weighted Composite
Integrity Test	27.6%	28.2%
Structured Interview	27.0%	27.1%
Work Sample	23.9%	24.1%
Conscientiousness	13.7%	17.1%
Job Knowledge Test	12.8%	12.9%
Unstructured Interview	10.8%	12.8%
Reference Check	6.8%	12.2%
Assessment Center	−1.5%	2.8%
Biodata	−2.6%	2.4%
Job Experience	−4.3%	6.1%
Interest Inventory	−15.4%	2.0%
Handwriting Analysis	−26.5%	0.0%

Columns show the change in validity and utility by adding specified selection method to cognitive ability tests (general mental ability test) in predicting job performance.

Source: Adapted from D. S. Ones, F. L. Schmidt, and K. Yoon, "Validity of an Equally-Weighted Composite of General Mental Ability and a Second Predictor" and "Predictive Validity of General Mental Ability Combined with a Second Predictor Based on Standardized Multiple Regression." Working papers (University of Iowa, Iowa City, Iowa: author, 1996). Used with permission.

tests with additional selection procedures, using multiple regression to establish weights always yields higher validity than unit weighting. Furthermore, when using selection methods that have moderate or low levels of validity in conjunction with cognitive ability tests, unit weighted combinations often provide lower levels of validity than using only cognitive ability tests.

These results do not prove that multiple regression weighting is a superior method in all circumstances. In fact, limitations of regression-based weighting schemes were noted above. What this example does help illustrate, though, is that the choice of the best weighting scheme is consequential, and likely depends on answers to the most important questions about clinical, unit, rational, and multiple regression schemes (in that order):

- Do selection decision makers have considerable experience and insight into selection decisions, and is managerial acceptance of the selection process important?

- Is there reason to believe that each predictor contributes relatively equally to job success?

- Are there adequate resources to use relatively involved weighting schemes such as rational weights or multiple regression?
- Are the conditions under which multiple regression is superior (relatively small number of predictors, low correlations among predictors, large sample) satisfied?

Answers to these questions—and the importance of the questions themselves—will go a long way toward deciding which weighting scheme to use. We also should note that while statistical weighting is more valid than clinical weighting, the combination of both methods may yield the highest validity. One study indicated that regression-weighted predictors were more valid than clinical judgments, but clinical judgments contributed uniquely to performance controlling for regression-weighted predictors. This suggests that both statistical and clinical weighting might be used. Thus, the weighting schemes are not necessarily mutually exclusive.[15]

Multiple Hurdles Model

With a multiple hurdles approach, an applicant must earn a passing score on each predictor before advancing in the selection process. Such an approach is taken when each requirement measured by a predictor is critical to job success. Passing scores are set using the methods to determine cut scores discussed in the next section. With multiple hurdles, unlike the compensatory model, a high score on one predictor cannot compensate for a low score on another predictor.

Multiple hurdles are used to prevent false positive errors. They are costly and time consuming to set up. As a result, they are used to select people for jobs where the occupational hazards are great (e.g., astronaut) or the consequences of poor performance have a great impact on the public at large (e.g., police officers and firefighters).

Combined Model

For jobs where some but not all requirements are critical to job success, a combined method may be used in which the compensatory and multiple hurdles models are combined together. The process starts with the multiple hurdles and ends with the compensatory method.

An example of the combined approach for the position of recruitment manager is shown in Exhibit 11.5. The selection process for recruitment manager starts with two hurdles that must be passed, in succession, by the applicant. These are the application blank and the job knowledge test. Failure to clear either hurdle results in rejection. Having passed them, applicants take an interview and have their references checked. Information from the interview and the references is combined in a compensatory manner. Those who pass are offered the job, and those who do not pass are rejected.

EXHIBIT 11.5 **Combined Model for Recruitment Manager**

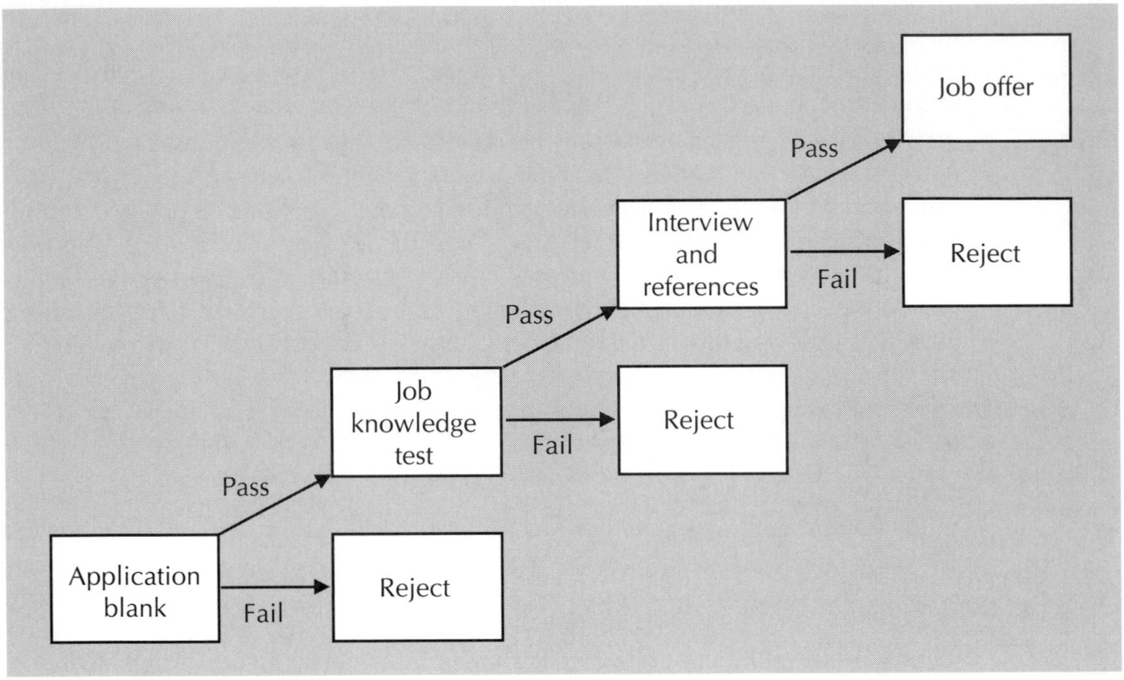

HIRING STANDARDS AND CUT SCORES

Hiring standards or cut scores address the issue of what constitutes a passing score. The score may be a single score from a single predictor, or a total score from multiple predictors. To address this, a description of the process and the consequences of cut scores are presented. Then, methods that may be used to establish the actual cut score are described.

Description of the Process

Once one or more predictors have been chosen for use, a decision must be made as to who advances further in the selection process. This decision requires that one or more cut scores be established. A cut score is the score that separates those who advance further in the process (e.g., applicants who become candidates) from those who are rejected. For example, assume a test is used on which scores may range from 0 to 100 points. A cut score of 70 would mean that those applicants with a 70 or more would advance, while all others would be rejected for employment purposes.

Consequences of Cut Scores

Setting a cut score is a very important process, as it has consequences for the organization and the applicant. The consequences of cut scores can be shown using Exhibit 11.6, which contains a summary of a scatter diagram of predictor and criterion scores. The horizontal line shows the criterion score at which the organization has determined whether an employee is successful or unsuccessful—for example, a 3 on a 5-point performance appraisal scale where 1 is the low performance and 5 is the high performance. The vertical line is the cut score for the predictor—for example, a 3 on a 5-point interview rating scale where 1 reveals no chance of success and 5 a high chance of success.

The consequences of setting the cut score at a particular level are shown in each of the quadrants. Quadrants A and C represent correct decisions, which have positive consequences for the organization. Quadrant A applicants are called true positives because they were assessed as having a high chance of success using the predictor and would have succeeded if hired. Quadrant C applicants are called true negatives because they were assessed as having little chance for success and, indeed, would not be successful if hired.

Quadrants D and B represent incorrect decisions, which have negative consequences to the organization and affected applicants. Quadrant D applicants are called false negatives because they were assessed as not being likely to succeed,

---

EXHIBIT 11.6   Consequences of Cut Scores

Criterion	Predictor Cut Score	
	D	A
Successful	False negative	True positive
	C	B
Unsuccessful	True negative	False positives
	No hire	Hire → Predictor

but had they been hired, they would have been successful. Not only was an incorrect decision reached but a person who would have done well was not hired. Quadrant B applicants are called false positives. They were assessed as being likely to succeed, but would have ended up being unsuccessful performers. Eventually, these people would need to receive remedial training, be transferred to a new job, or even be terminated.

How high or low a cut score is set has a large impact on the consequences shown in Exhibit 11.6, and trade-offs are always involved. Compared with the moderate cut score in Exhibit 11.6, a high cut score results in fewer false positives, but a larger number of false negatives. Is this a good, bad, or inconsequential set of outcomes for the organization? The answer depends on the job open for selection and the costs involved. If the job is an astronaut position for NASA, then it is essential that there be no false positives. The cost of a false positive may be the loss of human life.

Now consider the consequences of a low cut score, relative to the one shown in Exhibit 11.6. There are fewer false negatives and more true positives, but more false positives are hired. In organizations that gain competitive advantage in their industry by hiring the very best, this set of consequences may be unacceptable. Alternatively, for EEO/AA purposes it may be desirable to have a low cut score so that the number of false negative minorities and women are minimized.

In short, when setting a cut score, attention must be given to the consequences. As indicated, these consequences can be very serious. As a result, different methods of setting cut scores have been developed to guide decision makers. These will now be reviewed.[16]

Methods to Determine Cut Scores

There are three different methods that may be used to determine cut scores: minimum competency, top-down, and banding. Each of these is described below along with professional guidelines for setting cutoff scores.

Minimum Competency

Using the minimum competency method, the cut score is set on the basis of the minimum qualifications deemed necessary to perform the job. Subject matter experts are usually used to establish a minimum competency score. This approach is often needed in situations where the first step in the hiring process is the demonstration of minimum skill requirements. Exhibit 11.7 provides an illustration of the use of cut scores in selection. The exhibit lists the scores of 25 applicants on a particular test. Using the minimum competency method, the cut score is set at the level at which applicants who score below the line are deemed unqualified for the job. In this case, a score of 75 was determined to be the minimum competency level necessary. Thus, all applicants who scored below 75 are deemed unqualified

EXHIBIT 11.7   Use of Cut Scores in Selection Decisions

Rank	Test Scores	Minimum Competency		Top Down			Banding*
1.	100	100		100	1st	choice	100
2.	98	98		98	2nd	choice	98
3.	97	97		97	3rd	choice	97
4.	96	96		96	4th	choice	96
T5.	93	93		95	5th	choice	93
T5.	93	93		95	5th	choice	93
7.	91	91		91	"		91
T8.	90	90		90	"		90
T8.	90	90		90	"		90
10.	88	88	Qualified	88	"		88
11.	87	87		87	"		87
T12.	85	85		85	"		85
T12.	85	85		85	"		85
14.	83	83		83	"		83
15.	81	81		81	"		81
16.	79	79		79	"		79
T17.	77	77		77	"		77
T17.	77	77		77	"		77
19.	76	76		76	"		76
20.	75	75	Min. competency	75	"		75
21.	74	74		74	21st	choice	74
22.	71	71		71	22nd	choice	71
23.	70	70	Unqualified	70	23rd	choice	70
24.	69	69		69	24th	choice	69
25.	65	65		65	25th	choice	65

*All scores within brackets treated as equal; choice of applicants within brackets (if necessary) can be made on the basis of other factors, such as EEO/AA considerations.

and rejected, and all applicants who scored 75 or above are deemed at least minimally qualified. Finalists and ultimately offer receivers can then be chosen among these qualified applicants on the basis of other criteria.

Top-Down

Another method of determining at what level the cut score should be set is to simply examine the distribution of predictor scores for applicants and set the cut score at the level that best meets the demands of the organization. Demands of the organization may include the number of vacancies to be filled and EEO/AA requirements. This top-down method of setting cut scores is illustrated in Exhibit

11.7. As the exhibit shows, under top-down hiring, cut scores are established by the number of applicants that need to be hired. Once that number has been determined, applicants are selected from the top based on the order of their scores until the number desired is reached. The advantage of this approach is that it is a system that is easy to administer. It also minimizes judgment required because the cut score is determined on the basis of the demand for labor. The big drawback to this approach is that validity has often not been established prior to the use of the predictor. Also, there may be overreliance on the use of a single predictor and cut score, while other potentially useful predictors are ignored.

A well-known example of a top-down method is the Angoff method.[17] According to this approach, subject matter experts are used to set the minimum cut scores needed to proceed in the selection process. These experts go through the content of the predictor (e.g., test items) and determine which items the minimally qualified person should be able to pass. Usually 7 to 10 subject matter experts (e.g., job incumbents, managers) are used who must agree on the items to be passed. The cutoff score is the sum of the number of items that must be answered correctly.

There are several problems with this particular approach and subsequent modifications to it. First, it is a time-consuming procedure. Second, the results are dependent on the subject matter experts. It is a very difficult matter to get members of the organization to agree on who are "the" subject matter experts. Which set of subject matter experts are selected may have a bearing on the actual cut scores developed. Finally, it is unclear how much agreement there must be among subject matter experts when they evaluate test items. There also may be judgmental errors and biases in how cut scores are set.[18]

Banding

The traditional selection cut score method is the top-down approach. For both external hiring and internal promotions, the top-down method will yield the highest validity and utility. This method has been criticized, however, for ignoring the possibility that small differences between scores are due to measurement error. The top-down method also has been criticized for its ability to yield socially undesirable outcomes. Particularly in the area of cognitive ability testing, top-down decisions are likely to exclude substantial numbers of minorities. As a result, the selection measures are likely to have adverse impact against minorities. The magnitude of the adverse impact is such that, on a standard cognitive ability test, if half the white applicants are hired, only 16% of the black applicants would be expected to be hired.[19]

One suggestion that has been made for reducing the adverse impact of top-down hiring is using different norms for minority and majority groups; thus, hiring decisions are based on normatively defined (rather than absolute) scores. For example, a black employee who achieved a score of 75 on a test where the mean of all black applicants was 50 could be considered to have the same normative score as a white applicant who scored a 90 on a test where the mean for white applicants was 60. However, this "race-norming" of test scores, which was a common practice in the civil service and among some private employers, is expressly forbidden by the Civil Rights Act. As a result, another approach, termed "banding," is being considered.

Banding refers to the procedure whereby applicants who score within a certain score range or band are considered to have scored equivalently. A simple banding procedure is provided in Exhibit 11.7. In this example, using a 100-point test, all applicants who score within the band of 10-point increments are considered to have scored equally. For example, all applicants who score 91 and above could be assigned a score of 9, those who score 81–90 are given a score of 8, and so on. (In essence, this is what is done when letter grades are assigned based on exam scores.) Hiring within bands then could be done at random or, more typically, based on race or sex in conjunction with other factors (e.g., seniority, experience, etc.). Banding might reduce the adverse impact of selection tests because such a procedure tends to reduce differences between higher- and lower-scoring groups (as is the case with whites and minorities on cognitive ability tests). In practice, band widths are usually calculated on the basis of the standard error of measurement.

Research suggests that banding procedures result in substantial decreases in the adverse impact of cognitive ability tests while, under certain conditions, the losses in terms of utility are relatively small.[20] Various methods of banding have been proposed, but the differences between these methods are relatively unimportant.[21]

Although banding does have considerable social appeal in terms of increasing diversity and reducing the adverse impact of selection processes, numerous limitations are evident. One limitation is that decreases in validity and utility resulting from banding become significant when even moderately reliable tests are used. Because the standard error of the difference between test scores is partly a function of the reliability of the test, when test reliability is low, band widths are wider than when the reliability of the test is high. For example, if the reliability of a test is .80, at a reasonable level of confidence, nearly half the scores on a test can be considered equivalent.[22] Obviously, taking scores on a 100-point test and lumping applicants into only two groups wastes a great deal of important information on applicants (it is very unlikely that an applicant who scores a 51 on a valid test will perform the same on the job as an applicant who scores 99). Therefore, if the reliability of a test is even moderately high, the validity and utility decrements that result from banding become quite severe.

Another limitation of banding is that although it will always be expected to yield lower utility, using banding and random selection within bands may not reduce the adverse impact of cognitive ability tests.[23] Given the adverse impact of cognitive ability tests, too few minorities may be placed into the upper bands. Thus, even if selection from the upper bands is done at random, there may not be enough minorities in these bands to prevent adverse impact. As a result, banding may require more drastic modifications to ensure that the desired result (less adverse impact) is achieved. Finally, it appears that when banding is associated with affirmative action goals, applicants react negatively.[24]

The scientific merits of test banding is hotly debated.[25] It is unlikely that we could resolve here the myriad ethical and technical issues underlying their use. Organizations considering the use of banding in personnel selection decisions must weigh the pros and cons carefully. However, it should be noted that, when using cognitive ability tests in selection, the goals of validity and diversity may not be complementary. If organizations decide to use banding as a means of promoting diversity, they do so at some potential cost to the validity and utility of their selection process. Given that banding often can be expected to result in validity and utility losses, perhaps a better solution to the sometimes conflicting goals of utility and diversity is to supplement cognitive ability tests with other valid selection methods that have less (or no) adverse impact. Research suggests that the adverse impact of a selection process that uses cognitive ability tests can be reduced, and overall validity increased, by supplementing ability tests with other selection procedures, such as biodata inventories, personality tests, and structured interviews. On the other hand, it is unlikely that using such tests will eliminate adverse impact altogether. In short, there is a tradeoff between validity and diversity given that the most valid single selection measure (cognitive ability tests) also has the highest adverse impact. Researchers have developed various frameworks that will help organizations better balance the dual goals of validity and diversity.[26]

Unfortunately, as a recent review concluded, though "there is extensive evidence supporting the validity" of cognitive tests, "adverse impact is unlikely to be eliminated as long as one assesses" cognitive abilities in the selection process.[27] There are some methods to reduce adverse impact when cognitive tests are used, such as test-taking coaching programs, use of more generous time limits, and removal of culturally biased items. However, as the review cited above indicates, these programs have a relatively small effect on adverse impact. Some research suggests that increased weighting on noncognitive aspects of performance, such as helping behaviors in the workplace, reduces the adverse impact of cognitive ability tests.[28] Whether increasing the weight placed on noncognitive aspects of performance (e.g., helping or citizenship behaviors), relative to core task performance, is justified from a cost-benefit perspective is open to question.

Professional Guidelines

Much more research is needed on systematic procedures that are effective in setting optimal cut scores. In the meantime, a sound set of professional guidelines for setting cut scores is shown in Exhibit 11.8.

METHODS OF FINAL CHOICE

The discussion thus far has been on decision rules that can be used to narrow down the list of people to successively smaller groups who advance in the selection

---

EXHIBIT 11.8   Professional Guidelines for Setting Cutoff Scores

1. It is unrealistic to expect that there is a single "best" method of setting cutoff scores for all situations.

2. The process of setting a cutoff score (or a critical score) should begin with a job analysis that identifies relative levels of proficiency on critical knowledge, skills, abilities, or other characteristics.

3. The validity and job relatedness of the assessment procedure are crucial considerations.

4. How a test is used (criterion-referenced or norm-referenced) affects the selection and meaning of a cutoff score.

5. When possible, data on the actual relation of test scores to outcome measures of job performance should be considered carefully.

6. Cutoff scores or critical scores should be set high enough to ensure that minimum standards of job performance are met.

7. Cutoff scores should be consistent with normal expectations of acceptable proficiency within the workforce.

Source: W. F. Cascio, R. A. Alexander, and G. V. Barrett, "Setting Cutoff Scores: Legal, Psychometric, and Professional Issues and Guidelines," *Personnel Psychology*, 1988, 41, pp. 21–22. Used with permission.

process from applicant to candidate to finalist. How can the organization now choose from among the finalists to decide which of them will receive job offers? Discretionary assessments about the finalists must be converted into final choice decisions. The methods of final choice are the mechanisms by which discretionary assessments are translated into job offer decisions.

Methods of final choice include random selection, ranking, and grouping. Examples of each of these methods of final choice are shown in Exhibit 11.9 and are discussed here.

Random Selection

With random selection, each finalist has an equal chance of being selected. The only rationale for the selection of a person is the "luck of the draw." For example, the six names from Exhibit 11.9 could be put in a hat and the finalist drawn out. The one drawn out would be the person selected and made a job offer. This approach has the advantage of being quick. Also, with random selection, one cannot be accused of favoritism because everyone has an equal chance of being selected. The disadvantage to this approach is that discretionary assessments are simply ignored.

EXHIBIT 11.9   Methods of Final Choice

Random		Ranking	Grouping	
Casey		1. Goldie	Goldie	⎤
Goldie		2. Roxie	Roxie	⎦ Top choices
Buster	Pick one	3. Buster		
Abby		4. Abby	Buster	⎤
Roxie		5. Casey	Abby	⎦ Acceptable
Harold		6. Harold		
			Casey	⎤
			Harold	⎦ Last resorts

Ranking

With ranking, finalists are ordered from the most desirable to the least desirable based on results of discretionary assessments. As shown in Exhibit 11.9, the person ranked 1 (Goldie) is the most desirable, and the person ranked 6 (Harold) is the least desirable. It is important to note that desirability should be viewed in the context of the entire selection process. When this is done, persons with lower levels of desirability (e.g., ranks of 3, 4, 5) should not be viewed necessarily as failures. Job offers are extended to people on the basis of their rank ordering, with the person ranked 1 receiving the first offer. Should that person turn down the job offer or suddenly withdraw from the selection process, then the finalist ranked 2 receives the offer, and so on.

The advantage to ranking is that it provides an indication of the relative worth of each finalist for the job. It also provides a set of backups should one or more of the finalists withdraw from the process.

It should be remembered that backup finalists may decide to withdraw from the process to take a position elsewhere. Although ranking does give the organization a cushion if the top choices withdraw from the process, it does not mean that the process of job offers can proceed at a leisurely pace. Immediate action needs to be taken with the top choices in case they decide to withdraw and there is a need to go to backups. This is especially true in tight labor markets where there is a strong demand for the services of people on the ranking list.

Grouping

With the grouping method, finalists are banded together into rank-ordered categories. For example, in Exhibit 11.9, the finalists are grouped according to whether they are top choices, acceptable, or last resorts. The advantage of this method is that it permits ties among finalists, thus avoiding the need to assign a different rank to each person. The disadvantage is that choices still have to be made from among the top choices. These might be made on the basis of factors such as probability of each person accepting the offer.

DECISION MAKERS

A final consideration in decision making for selection is who should participate in the decisions. That is, who should determine the process to be followed (e.g., establishing cut scores) and who should determine the outcome (e.g., who gets the job offer)? The answer is that both HR professionals and line managers must play a role. Although the two roles are different, both are critical to the organization. Employees may play certain roles as well.

Human Resource Professionals

As a general rule, HR professionals should have a high level of involvement in the processes used to design and manage the selection system. They should be consulted in matters such as which predictors to use and how to use them best. In particular, they need to orchestrate the development of policies and procedures in the staffing areas covered. These professionals have or know where to find the technical expertise needed to develop sound selection decisions. Also, they have the knowledge to ensure that relevant laws and regulations are being followed. Finally, they can also represent the interests and concerns of employees to management.

Although the primary role to be played by HR professionals is in terms of process, they should also have some involvement in determining who receives job offers. One obvious area where this is true is with staffing the HR function. A less obvious place where HR professionals can play an important secondary role is in terms of providing input into selection decisions made by managers.

HR professionals may be able to provide some insight on applicants that is not always perceived by line managers. For example, they may be able to offer some insight on the applicants' people skills (e.g., communications, teamwork). HR professionals are sensitive to these issues because of their training and experience. They may have data to share on these matters as a result of their screening interviews, knowledge of how to interpret paper-and-pencil instruments (e.g., personality test), and interactions with internal candidates (e.g., serving on task forces with the candidates).

The other area where HR professionals may make a contribution to outcomes is in terms of initial assessment methods. Many times, HR professionals are and should be empowered to make initial selection decisions, such as who gets invited into the organization for administration of the next round of selection. Doing so saves managers time to carry out their other responsibilities. Also, HR professionals can ensure that minorities and women applicants are actively solicited and not excluded from the applicant pool for the wrong reasons.

Managers

As a general rule, a manager's primary involvement in staffing is in determining who is selected for employment. Managers are the subject matter experts of the business, and, thus, they are held accountable for the success of the people hired. They are far less involved in determining the processes followed to staff the organization because they often do not have the time or expertise to do so.

Although they may not play a direct role in establishing process, managers can and should periodically be consulted by HR professionals on process issues. They should be consulted because they are the consumers of HR services. As such, it is important to provide them input into the staffing process to ensure that it is meeting their needs in making the best possible person/job matches.

There is an additional benefit to allowing management a role in process issues. As a result of their involvement, managers may develop a better understanding of why certain practices are prescribed by HR professionals. When they are not invited to be a part of the process to establish staffing policy and procedures, line managers may view HR professionals as an obstacle to hiring the right person for the job.

It should also be noted that the degree of managers' involvement usually depends on the type of assessment decisions made. Decisions made using initial assessment methods are usually delegated to the HR professional, as just discussed. Decisions made using substantive assessment methods usually involve some degree of input from the manager. Decisions made using discretionary methods are usually the direct responsibility of the manager. As a general rule, the extent of managerial involvement in determining outcomes should only be as great as management's knowledge of the job. If managers are involved in hiring decisions for jobs with which they are not familiar, then legal, measurement, and morale problems are likely to be created.

Employees

Traditionally, employees are not considered part of the decision-making process in staffing. Slowly this tradition is changing. For example, in team assessment approaches (see Chapter 8), employees may have a voice in both process and outcomes. That is, they may have ideas about how selection procedures are established and make decisions about or provide input into who gets hired. Employee involvement in the team approach is encouraged because it may give a sense of ownership of the work process and help employees to better identify with organizational goals. Also, it may result in the selection of members who are more compatible with the goals of the work team. In order for employee involvement to be effective, employees need to be provided with staffing training just as managers do (see Chapter 9).

LEGAL ISSUES

The legal issue of major importance in decision making is that of cut scores or hiring standards. These scores or standards regulate the flow of individuals from applicant to candidate to finalist. Throughout this flow, adverse impact may occur. When it does, the Uniform Guidelines on Employee Selection Procedures (UGESP) come into play. At the finalist stage, decisions about to whom to offer the job are made, and the UGESP has less direct relevance.

Uniform Guidelines on Employee Selection Procedures

If there is no adverse impact in decision making, the UGESP are essentially silent on the issue of cutoff scores. The discretion being exercised by the organization as it makes its selection decisions is thus unconstrained legally. If there is adverse impact occurring, however, then the UGESP become directly applicable to decision making.

Recall that under conditions of adverse impact, the UGESP require the organization to either eliminate its occurrence or justify it through the conduct of validity studies. As part of the general standards for such validity studies, the UGESP say the following about cut scores:

> Where cutoff scores are used, they should normally be set as to be reasonable and consistent with normal expectations of acceptable proficiency within the workforce. Where applicants are ranked on the basis of properly validated selection procedures and those applicants scoring below a higher cutoff score than appropriate in light of such expectations have little or no chance of being selected for employment, the higher cutoff score may be appropriate, but the degree of adverse impact should be considered.

This provision suggests that the organization should be cautious in general about setting cut scores that are above those necessary to achieve acceptable proficiency among those hired. In other words, even with a valid predictor, the organization should be cautious that its hiring standards are not so high that they create needless adverse impact. This is particularly true with ranking systems. Use of random, or to a lesser extent grouping, methods would help overcome this particular objection to ranking systems.

Whatever cut score procedure is used, the UGESP also require that the organization be able to document its establishment and operation. Specifically, the UGESP say that "if the selection procedure is used with a cutoff score, the user should describe the way in which normal expectations of proficiency within the workforce were determined and the way in which the cutoff score was determined."

The preceding validation and cut score approach is one option for dealing with problems of adverse impact. The UGESP also suggest two other options, both of which seek to eliminate adverse impact rather than justify it as in the validation and cutoff score approach. The next option is the "alternative procedures" one. Here, the organization must consider using an alternative selection procedure that causes less adverse impact (e.g., work sample instead of a written test), but has roughly the same validity as the procedure it replaces.

The final selection option is that of affirmative action. The UGESP do not relieve the organization of any affirmative action obligations it may have. Also, the UGESP strive to "encourage the adoption and implementation of voluntary affirmative action programs" for organizations that do not have any affirmative action obligations.

Choices Among Finalists

Where there is more than one finalist for a job, a decision must be made as to which will receive the job offer. There is little legal influence on this finalist decision. Presumably, if the steps in the selection process leading up to this point have been within legal bounds, the finalist choice is a legal matter of relative indifference. Despite this, the organization should once again review its EEO/AA commitments, policies, and results to date. Such a review may prove instructive as final choices are made. It represents the organization's "last chance" concerning selection, and the organization should be sure that its decision is consistent with its affirmative action objectives.

SUMMARY

The selection component of a staffing system requires that decisions be made in several areas. The critical concerns are deciding which predictors (assessment methods) to use, determining assessment scores and setting cut scores, making final decisions about applicants, considering who within the organization should help make selection decisions, and complying with legal guidance.

In deciding which assessment methods to use, consideration should be given to the validity coefficient, face validity correlation with other predictors, adverse impact, utility, and applicant reactions. Ideally, a predictor would have a validity coefficient with large magnitude and significance, high face validity low correlations with other predictors, little adverse impact, and high utility. In practice, this ideal situation is hard to achieve, so decisions about trade-offs are necessary.

How assessment scores are determined depends on whether a single predictor or multiple predictors are used. In the case of a single predictor, assessment scores are simply the scores on the predictor. With multiple predictors, a compensatory, multiple hurdles, or combined model must be used. A compensatory model allows a person to compensate for a low score on one predictor with a high score on another predictor. A multiple hurdles model requires that a person achieve a passing score on each predictor. A combined model uses elements of both the compensatory and multiple hurdles models.

In deciding who earns a passing score on a predictor or combination of predictors, cut scores must be set. When doing so the consequences of setting different levels of cut scores should be considered, especially those of assessing some applicants as false positives and false negatives. Approaches to determining cut scores include minimum competency, top-down, and banding methods. Professional guidelines are reviewed on how best to set cut scores.

Methods of final choice involve determining, from among those who have passed the initial hurdles, who will receive job offers. Several methods of making these decisions are reviewed, including random selection, ranking, and grouping. Each has advantages and disadvantages.

Multiple individuals may be involved in selection decision making. HR professionals play a role primarily in determining the selection process to be used and in making selection decisions based on initial assessment results. Managers play a role primarily in deciding whom to select during the final choice stage. Employees are becoming part of the decision-making process, especially in team assessment approaches. A basic legal issue is conformance with the Uniform Guidelines on Employee Selection Procedures. The UGESP provide guidance on how to set cut scores in ways that help minimize adverse impact and allow the organization to fulfill its EEO/AA obligations.

DISCUSSION QUESTIONS

1. Your boss is considering using a new predictor. The base rate is high, the selection ratio is low, and the validity coefficient is high for the current predictor. What would you advise your boss and why?

2. What are the positive consequences associated with a high predictor cutoff score? What are the negative consequences?

3. Under what circumstances should a compensatory model be used? When should a multiple hurdles model be used?

4. What are the advantages of ranking as a method of final choice over random selection?

5. What roles should HR professionals play in staffing decisions? Why?
6. What guidelines do the Uniform Guidelines on Employee Selection Procedures offer to organizations when it comes to setting cut scores?

APPLICATIONS

Utility Concerns in Choosing an Assessment Method

Randy May is a 32-year-old airplane mechanic for a small airline based in Nantucket Island, Massachusetts. Recently, Randy won $2 million in the New England Lottery. Because Randy is relatively young, he decided to invest his winnings in a business to create a future stream of earnings. After weighing many investment decisions, Randy opted to open up a chain of ice cream shops in the Cape Cod area. (As it turns out, Cape Cod and the nearby islands are short of ice cream shops.) Based on his own budgeting, Randy figured he had enough cash to open shops on each of the two islands (Nantucket and Martha's Vineyard) and two shops in small towns on the Cape (Falmouth and Buzzards Bay). Randy contracted with a local builder and the construction/renovation of the four shops is well under way.

The task that is occupying Randy's attention now is how to staff the shops. Two weeks ago, he placed advertisements in three area newspapers. So far, he has received 100 applications. Randy has done some informal HR planning and figures he needs to hire 50 employees to staff the four shops. Being a novice at this, Randy is unsure how to select the 50 people he needs to hire. Randy consulted his friend, Mary, who owns the lunch counter at the airport. Mary advised Randy that she used the interview to get "the most knowledgeable people possible," and recommended it to Randy because her people had "generally worked out well." While Randy greatly respected Mary's advice, on reflection several questions came to mind. Does Mary's use of the interview mean that it meets Randy's requirements? How could Randy determine whether his chosen method of selecting employees was effective or ineffective?

Confused, Randy also sought the advice of Professor Ray Higgins, from whom Randy took an HR management course while getting his business degree. After learning of the situation and offering his consulting services, Professor Higgins suggested that Randy choose between one of two selection methods (after paying Professor Higgins' consulting fees, he cannot afford to use both methods). The two methods Professor Higgins recommended are, like Mary, the interview and also a work sample test that entails scooping ice cream and serving it to the customer. Randy estimates that it would cost $100 to interview an applicant and $150 per applicant to administer the work sample. Professor Higgins has told Randy that the validity of the interview is $r = .30$ while the validity of the work sample is $r = .50$. Professor Higgins also informed Randy that if the selection ratio is .50, the average score on the selection measure of those applicants selected is $z = .80$ (.80

standard deviations above the mean). Randy plans to offer employees a wage of $6.00 per hour. (Over the course of a year, this would amount to a $12,000 salary.)

Based on the information presented above, Randy would really appreciate it if you could help him answer the following questions:

1. How much money would Randy save using each selection method?
2. If Randy can use only one method, which should he use?
3. If the number of applicants increases to 200 (more applications are coming in every day), how would your answers to questions 1 and 2 change?
4. What limitations are inherent in the estimates you have made?

Choosing Entrants into a Management Training Program

Come As You Are, a convenience store chain headquartered in Fayetteville, Arkansas, has developed an assessment program to promote nonexempt employees into its management training program. The minimum entrance requirements into the program are five years of company experience, a college degree from an accredited university, and a minimum acceptable job performance rating (3 or higher on their 1–5 scale). Any interested applicant into the program can enroll in the half-day assessment program, where the following assessments are made:

1. cognitive ability test
2. handwriting test
3. integrity test
4. signed permission for background test
5. brief (30-minute) interview by various members of the management team
6. drug test

At the Hot Springs store, 11 applicants have applied for openings in the management training program. The selection information on the candidates is provided in the following exhibit. (The scoring key is provided at the bottom of the exhibit.) It is estimated that there are three slots in the program available for qualified candidates from the Hot Springs location. Given this information and what you know about external and internal selection, as well as staffing decision making, answer the following questions:

1. How would you go about the process of making decisions about who to select for the openings? In other words, without providing your decisions for the individual candidates, describe how you would weigh the various selection information to reach a decision.
2. Using the decision-making process from the previous question, who would you select into the training program? Explain your decisions.

EXHIBIT

Predictor Scores for Eleven Applicants to Management Training Program

Name	Company Experience	College Degree	Performance Rating	Cognitive Ability Test	Handwriting Test	Integrity Test	Background Test	Interview Rating	Drug Test
Peter	4	Yes	4	9	3	6	OK	6	P
Paul	12	Yes	3	3	9	6	OK	8	P
Mary	9	Yes	4	8	1	5	Arrest '95	4	P
Harry	5	Yes	4	5	4	5	OK	4	P
Sally	14	Yes	5	7	6	8	OK	8	P
Ginger	7	No	3	3	7	4	OK	6	P
Fred	6	Yes	4	7	7	8	OK	2	P
Felix	9	Yes	5	2	10	5	OK	7	P
Oscar	10	Yes	4	10	3	9	OK	3	P
Sonny	18	Yes	3	3	8	7	OK	6	P
Cher	11	Yes	4	7	4	6	OK	5	P
Scale	Years	Yes–No	1–5	1–10	1–10	1–10	OK–Other	1–10	P–F

3. Although the data provided in the exhibit reveals that all selection measures were given to all 11 candidates, would you advise Come As You Are to continue to administer all the predictors at one time during the half-day assessment program? Or, should the predictors be given in a sequence so that a multiple hurdles or combined approach could be used? Explain your recommendation.

ENDNOTES

1. F. L. Schmidt and J. E. Hunter, "Moderator Research and the Law of Small Numbers," *Personnel Psychology,* 1978, 31, pp. 215–232.

2. J. Cohen, "The Earth Is Round ($p < .05$)," *American Psychologist,* 1994, 49, pp. 997–1003; F. L. Schmidt, "Quantitative Methods and Cumulative Knowledge in Psychology: Implications for the Training of Researchers," Paper presented at the meeting of the American Psychological Association, Los Angeles, CA, 1994.

3. L. G. Grimm and P. R. Yarnold, *Reading and Understanding Multivariate Statistics* (Washington, DC: American Psychological Association, 1995).

4. J. W. Boudreau, "Utility Analysis for Decisions in Human Resource Management," in M. D. Dunnette and L. M. Hough (eds.), *Handbook of Industrial and Organizational Psychology,* vol. 2 (Palo Alto, CA: Consulting Psychologists Press), pp. 621–745.

5. M. C. Sturman and T. A. Judge, "Utility Analysis for Multiple Selection Devices and Multiple Outcomes," Working paper, Cornell University, 1994.

6. J. Hersch, "Equal Employment Opportunity Law and Firm Profitability," *Journal of Human Resources,* 1991, 26, pp. 139–153.

7. G. V. Barrett, R. A. Alexander, and D. Doverspike, "The Implications for Personnel Selection of Apparent Declines in Predictive Validities over Time: A Critique of Hulin, Henry, and Noon," *Personnel Psychology,* 1992, 45, pp. 601–617; C. L. Hulin, R. A. Henry, and S. L. Noon, "Adding a Dimension: Time as a Factor in Predictive Relationships," *Psychological Bulletin,* 1990, 107, pp. 328–340; C. T. Keil and J. M. Cortina, "Degradation of Validity over Time: A Test and Extension of Ackerman's Model," *Psychological Bulletin,* 2001, 127, pp. 673–697.

8. J. W. Boudreau, M. C. Sturman, and T. A. Judge, "Utility Analysis: What Are the Black Boxes, and Do They Affect Decisions?," in N. Anderson and P. Herriot (eds.), *Assessment and Selection in Organizations* (Chichester, England: Wiley, 1994), pp. 77–96.

9. K. M. Murphy, "When Your Top Choice Turns You Down," *Psychological Bulletin,* 1986, 99, pp. 133–138; F. L. Schmidt, M. J. Mack, and J. E. Hunter, "Selection Utility in the Occupation of US Park Ranger for Three Modes of Test Use," *Journal of Applied Psychology,* 1984, 69, pp. 490–497.

10. T. H. Macan and S. Highhouse, "Communicating the Utility of Human Resource Activities: A Survey of I/O and HR Professionals," *Journal of Business and Psychology,* 1994, 8, pp. 425–436.

11. G. P. Latham and G. Whyte, "The Futility of Utility Analysis," *Personnel Psychology,* 1994, 47, pp. 31–46; K. C. Carson, J. S. Becker, and J. A. Henderson, "Is Utility Really Futile? A Failure to Replicate and an Extension," *Journal of Applied Psychology,* 1998, 83, pp. 84–96; J. T. Hazer and S. Highhouse, "Factors Influencing Managers' Reactions to Utility Analysis:

Effects of SDy Method, Information Frame, and Focal Intervention," *Journal of Applied Psychology,* 1997, 82, pp. 104–112; G. Whyte and G. Latham, "The Futility of Utility Analysis Revisited: When Even an Expert Fails," *Personnel Psychology,* 1997, 50, pp. 601–610.

12. C. J. Russell, A. Colella, and P. Bobko, "Expanding the Context of Utility: The Strategic Impact of Personnel Selection," *Personnel Psychology,* 1993, 46, pp. 781–801.

13. J. Sawyer, "Measurement and Predictions, Clinical and Statistical," *Psychological Bulletin,* 1966, 66, pp. 178–200.

14. F. L. Schmidt, "The Relative Efficiency of Regression and Sample Unit Predictor Weights in Applied Differential Psychology," *Educational and Psychological Measurement,* 1971, 31, pp. 699–714.

15. Y. Ganzach, A. N. Kluger, and N. Klayman, "Making Decisions from an Interview: Expert Measurement and Mechanical Combination," *Personnel Psychology,* 2000, 53, pp. 1–20.

16. W. F. Cascio, R. A. Alexander, and G. V. Barrett, "Setting Cutoff Scores: Legal, Psychometric, and Professional Issues and Guidelines," *Personnel Psychology,* 1988, 41, pp. 1–24.

17. W. H. Angoff, "Scales, Norms, and Equivalent Scores," in R. L. Thorndike (ed.), *Educational Measurement* (Washington, DC: American Council on Education, 1971), pp. 508–600; R. E. Biddle, "How to Set Cutoff Scores for Knowledge Tests Used in Promotion, Training, Certification, and Licensing," *Public Personnel Management,* 1993, 22, pp. 63–79.

18. J. P. Hudson Jr. and J. E. Campion, "Hindsight Bias in an Application of the Angoff Method for Setting Cutoff Scores," *Journal of Applied Psychology,* 1994, 79, pp. 860–865.

19. P. R. Sackett and S. L. Wilk, "Within-Group Norming and Other Forms of Score Adjustment in Preemployment Testing," *American Psychologist,* 1994, 49, pp. 929–954.

20. W. F. Cascio, J. Outtz, S. Zedeck, and I. L. Goldstein, "Statistical Implications of Six Methods of Test Score Use in Personnel Selection," *Human Performance,* 1991, 4, pp. 233–264; P. R. Sackett and L. Roth, "A Monte Carlo Examination of Banding and Rank Order Selection Methods of Test Score Use in Personnel Selection," *Human Performance,* 1991, 4, pp. 279–296.

21. K. R. Murphy, K. Osten, and B. Myors, "Modeling the Effects of Banding in Personnel Selection," *Personnel Psychology,* 1995, 48, pp. 61–84.

22. K. R. Murphy, "Potential Effects of Banding as a Function of Test Reliability," *Personnel Psychology,* 1994, 47, pp. 477–495.

23. P. R. Sackett and S. L. Wilk, "Within-Group Norming and Other Forms of Score Adjustment in Preemployment Testing."

24. D. M. Truxillo and T. N. Bauer, "Applicant Reactions to Test Score Banding in Entry-Level and Promotional Contexts," *Journal of Applied Psychology,* 1999, 84, pp. 322–339.

25. M. A. Campion, J. L. Duttz, S. Zedeck, F. L. Schmidt, J. F. Kehoe, K. R. Murphy, and R. M. Guion, "The Controversy over Banding in Personnel Selection: Answers to 10 Key Questions," *Personnel Psychology,* 2001, 54, 149–185

26. W. Arthur, D. Doverspike, and G. V. Barrett, "Development of a Job Analysis-Based Procedure for Weighting and Combining Content-Related Tests into a Single Test Battery Score," *Personnel Psychology,* 1996, 49, pp. 971–985; P. R. Sackett and J. E. Ellingson, "The Effects of Forming Multi-Predictor Composites on Group Differences and Adverse Impact," *Personnel Psychology,* 1997, 50, pp. 707–721; P. R. Sackett and L. Roth, "Multi-Stage Selection Strategies: A Monte Carlo Investigation of Effects on Performance and Minority Hiring," *Personnel Psychology,* 1996, 49, pp. 549–572; N. Schmitt, D. Chan, L. Sheppard, and D. Jennings, "Adverse Impact and Predictive Efficiency of Various Predictor Combinations," *Journal of Applied Psychology,* 82, pp. 719–730.

27. P. R. Sackett, N. Schmitt, J. E. Ellingson, and M. B. Kabin, "High-Stakes Testing in Employment, Credentialing, and Higher Education," *American Psychologist,* 2001, 56, pp. 302–318.

28. W. De Corte, "Weighing Job Performance Predictors to Both Maximize the Quality of the Selected Workforce and Control the Level of Adverse Impact," *Journal of Applied Psychology,* 1999, 84, pp. 695–702; K. Hattrup, J. Rock, and C. Scalia, "The Effects of Varying Conceptualizations of Job Performance on Adverse Impact, Minority Hiring, and Predictor Performance," *Journal of Applied Psychology,* 1997, 82, pp. 656–664.

CHAPTER TWELVE

Final Match

Employment Contracts
   Requirements for an Enforceable Contract
   Parties to the Contract
   Form of the Contract
   Disclaimers
   Contingencies
   Reneging
   Other Employment Contract Sources
   Unfulfilled Promises

Job Offers
   Applicant Attraction Strategies
   Job Offer Content

Job Offer Process
   Formulation of the Job Offer
   Presentation of the Job Offer
   Job Offer Acceptance and Rejection
   Reneging

New Employee Orientation and Socialization
   Orientation
   Socialization

Legal Issues
   Authorization to Work
   Negligent Hiring
   Employment-at-Will

Summary

Discussion Questions

Applications

In the previous chapter, the focus was on organizational aspects of decision making regarding the likely match or fit between an individual and an organization. The emphasis was on reducing the initial applicant pool to a smaller set of candidates and identifying one or more job finalists from that candidate set to whom to offer employment.

A final match occurs when the offer receiver and the organization have determined that the probable overlap between the person's KSAOs/motivation and the job's requirements/rewards is sufficient to warrant entering into the employment relationship. Once this decision has been made, the organization and the individual seek to become legally bound to each other through mutual agreement on the terms and conditions of employment. They thus enter into an employment contract, and each expects the other to abide by the terms of the contract. Failure to do so constitutes a breach of contract, which may lead to litigation between the parties as well as potential recovery of damages for the breach.

The formation of, and agreement on, the employment contract occurs in both external and internal staffing. Any time the matching process is set in motion, either through external or internal staffing, the goal is establishment of a new employment relationship.

Knowledge of employment contract concepts and principles is central to understanding the final match. This chapter begins with an overview of such material, emphasizing the essential requirements for establishing a legally binding employment contract, as well as some of the nuances in doing so. Then major components of a job offer, and points to address in it, are suggested. As is apparent, staffing organizations effectively demands great skill and care by the employer as it enters into employment contracts. The employer and offer receiver are accorded great freedom in the establishment of terms and conditions of employment; both parties have much to decide and agree on pertaining to job offer content.

Through the job offer process, these terms and conditions are proposed, discussed, negotiated, modified, and, ultimately, agreed on. The process, therefore, is frequently complex, requiring planning by those responsible for it. Elements and considerations in this process are discussed next.

Once agreement on the terms and conditions of employment has been reached, the final match process is completed, and the formal employment relationship is established. In a sense, staffing activities end at this point. In another sense, however, it is important to phase these activities into initial postemployment activities that help the new employee adapt and adjust to the new job. Employee orientation and socialization activities are discussed as ways to facilitate this.

The chapter concludes with a discussion of specific legal issues that pertain not only to the establishment of the employment contract but also to potential long-term consequences of that contract that must be considered at the time it is established.

EMPLOYMENT CONTRACTS

The establishment and enforcement of employment contracts is a very complex and constantly changing undertaking. Covered next are some very basic, yet subtle, issues associated with this undertaking. It is crucial to understand the elements that comprise a legally enforceable contract and to be able to identify the parties to the contract (employees or independent contractors, third-party representatives), the form of the contract (written, oral), disclaimers, fulfillment of other conditions, reneging on an offer or acceptance, and other sources (e.g., employee handbooks) that may also constitute a portion of the total employment contract.

Requirements for an Enforceable Contract

There are three basic elements required for a contract to be legally binding and enforceable: offer, acceptance, and consideration.[1] If any one of these is missing, there is no binding contract.

Offer

The offer is usually made by the employer. It is composed of the terms and conditions of employment desired and proposed by the employer. The terms must be clear and specific enough to be acted on by the offer receiver. Vague statements and offers are unacceptable (e.g., "Come to work for me right now; we'll work out the details later"). The contents of newspaper ads for the job and general written employer material, such as a brochure describing the organization, probably are also too vague to be considered offers. Both the employer and the offer receiver should have a definite understanding of the specific terms being proposed.

Acceptance

To constitute a contract, the offer must be accepted on the terms as offered. Thus, if the employer offers a salary of $25,000 per year, the offer receiver must either accept or reject that term. Acceptance of an offer on a contingency basis does not constitute an acceptance. If the offer receiver responds to the salary offer of $25,000 by saying, "Pay me $27,500, and I'll come to work for you," this is not an acceptance. Rather, it is a counteroffer, and the employer must now either formally accept or reject it.

The offer receiver must also accept the offer in the manner specified in the offer. If the offer requires acceptance in writing, for example, the offer receiver must accept it in writing. Or, if the offer requires acceptance by a certain date, it must be accepted by that date.

Consideration

Consideration entails the exchange of something of value between the parties to the contract. Usually, it involves an exchange of promises. The employer offers or promises to provide compensation to the offer receiver in exchange for labor, and the offer receiver promises to provide labor to the employer in exchange for compensation. The exchange of promises must be firm and of value, which is usually quite straightforward. Occasionally, consideration can become an issue. For example, if the employer makes an offer to a person that requires a response by a certain date, and then does not hear from the person, there is no contract, even though the employer thought that they "had a deal."

Parties to the Contract

Two issues arise regarding the parties to the contract: whether the employer is entering into a contract with an "employee" or with an "independent contractor,"[2] and whether an outsider or "third party" can execute or otherwise play a role in the employment contract.[3]

Employee or Independent Contractor

Individuals are acquired by the organization as either employees or independent contractors. Both of these terms have definite legal meaning that should be reviewed (see Chapter 2) prior to entering into a contractual relationship. The organization should be clear in its offer whether the relationship being sought is that of employer–employee or employer–independent contractor. Care should be taken to avoid misclassifying the offer receiver as an independent contractor when in fact the receiver will be treated practically as an employee (e.g., subject to specific direction and control by the employer). Such a misclassification can result in substantial tax and other legal liability problems for the organization.

Third Parties

Often, someone other than the employer or offer receiver speaks on their behalf in the establishment or modification of employment contracts. These people serve as agents for the employer and offer receiver. For the employer, this may mean the use of outsiders such as employment agencies, executive recruiters, or search consultants; it also usually means the use of one or more employees, such as the HR department representative, the hiring manager, higher-level managers, and other managers within the organization. For the offer receiver, it may mean the use of a special agent, such as a professional agent for a sports player or executive. These possibilities raise three important questions for the employer.

First, who, if anyone, speaks for the offer receiver? This is usually a matter of checking with the offer receiver as to whether any given person is indeed authorized by the offer receiver to be a spokesperson, and what, if any, limits have been placed on that person regarding terms that may be discussed and agreed on with the employer.

Second, who is the spokesperson for the employer? In the case of its own employees, the employer must recognize that, from a legal standpoint, any of them could be construed as speaking for the employer. Virtually anyone could thus suggest and agree to contract terms, knowingly or unknowingly. This means that the employer should formulate and enforce explicit policies as to who is authorized to speak on its behalf.

Third, exactly what is that person authorized to say? Here, the legal concept of apparent authority is relevant. If the offer receiver believes that a person has the authority to speak for the employer, and there is nothing to indicate otherwise, that person has the apparent authority to speak for the employer. In turn, the employer may be bound by what that person says and agrees to, even if the employer did not grant express authority to do so to this person. It is thus important for the organization to clarify to both the offer receiver and designated spokespersons what the spokesperson is authorized to discuss and agree to without approval from other organizational members.

Form of the Contract

Employment contracts may be written, oral, or even a combination of the two.[4] All may be legally binding and enforceable. Within this broad parameter, however, are numerous caveats and considerations.

Written Contracts

As a general rule, the law favors written contracts over oral ones. This alone should lead an organization to use only written contracts whenever possible.

A written contract may take many forms, and all may be legally enforceable. Examples of a written document that may be construed as a contract include a letter of offer and acceptance (the usual example), a statement on a job application blank (such as an applicant voucher to the truthfulness of information provided), internal job posting notices, and statements in employee handbooks or other personnel manuals. The more specific the information and statements in such documents, the more likely they are to be considered employment contracts.

Unintended problems may arise with these documents. They may become interpreted as enforceable contracts even though that was not their intent (perhaps the intent was merely informational). Or, statements on a given term or condition of employment may contradict each other in various documents.

An excellent illustration of these kinds of problems involves the issue of employment-at-will. Assume an employer wishes to be, as a matter of explicit policy, a strict at-will employer. That desire may be unintentionally undercut by written documents that imply something other than an employment-at-will relationship. For example, correspondence with an applicant may talk of "continued employment after you complete your probationary period." This statement might be legally interpreted as creating something other than a strict at-will employment relationship. To further muddy the waters, the employee handbook may contain an explicit at-will statement, thus contradicting the policy implied in the correspondence with the applicant.

Care must thus be taken to ensure that all written documents accurately convey only the intended meanings regarding terms and conditions of employment. To this end, the following suggestions should be heeded:[5]

- Before putting anything in writing, ask, Does the company mean to be held to this?
- Choose words carefully; where appropriate, avoid using words that imply binding commitment.
- Make sure all related documents are consistent with each other.
- Always have a second person review what another has written.
- Form the habit of looking at the entire hiring procedure and consider any writings within that context.

Oral Contracts

While oral contracts may be every bit as binding as written contracts, there are two notable exceptions that support placing greater importance on written contracts.

The first exception is the one-year rule, which comes about in what is known as the statute of frauds.[6] Under this rule, a contract that cannot be performed or fulfilled within a one-year interval is not enforceable unless it is in writing. Thus, oral agreements for any length greater than one year are not enforceable. Because of this rule, the organization should not make oral contracts that are intended to last more than one year.

The second exception involves the concept of parole evidence, which pertains to oral promises that are made about the employment relationship.[7] Legally, parole evidence (e.g., the offer receiver's claim that "I was promised that I wouldn't have to work on weekends") may not be used to enforce a contract if it is inconsistent with the terms of a written agreement. Thus, if the offer receiver's letter of appointment explicitly stated that weekend work was required, the oral promise of not having to work weekends would not be enforceable.

Note, however, in the absence of written statements to the contrary, oral statements may indeed be enforceable. In the preceding example, if the letter of appointment was silent on the issue of weekend work, then the oral promise of no weekend work might well be enforceable.

More generally, oral statements are more likely to be enforceable as employment contract terms[8]

- when there is no written statement regarding the term (e.g., weekend work) in question;

- when the term is quite certain ("You will not have to work on weekends," as opposed to, "Occasionally, we work weekends around here");
- when the person making the oral statement is in a position of authority to do so (e.g., the hiring manager as opposed to a coworker);
- the more formal the circumstances in which the statement was made (the manager's office as opposed to around the bar or dinner table as part of a recruiting trip); and
- the more specific the promise ("You will work every other Saturday from 8:00 to 5:00," as opposed to, "You may have to work from 8:00 to the middle of the afternoon on the weekends, but we'll try to hold that to a minimum").

As this discussion makes clear, from a legal perspective, oral statements are a potential minefield in establishing employment contracts. They obviously cannot be avoided (employer and applicant have to speak to each other), and they may serve other legitimate and desired outcomes, such as providing realistic recruitment information to job applicants. Nonetheless, the organization should use oral statements with extreme caution and alert all members to its policies regarding their use. As further protection, the organization should include in its written offer that, by accepting the offer, the employee agrees the organization has made no other promises than those contained in the written offer.

Disclaimers

A disclaimer is a statement (oral or written) that explicitly limits an employee right and reserves that right for the employer.[9] Disclaimers are often used in letters of appointment, job application blanks, and employee handbooks.

A common, and increasingly important, employee "right" that is being limited through the use of disclaimer is that of job security. Here, through its policy of employment-at-will, the employer explicitly makes no promise of any job security and reserves the right to terminate the employment relationship at its own will. The following is an example of such a disclaimer that survived legal challenge:

> In consideration of my employment, I agree to conform to the rules and regulations of Sears, Roebuck and Company, and recognize that employment and compensation can be terminated, with or without cause, and with or without notice, at any time, at the option of either the company or myself. I understand that no store manager or representative of Sears, Roebuck and Company, other than the president or vice-president of the company, has any authority to enter into any agreement for employment for any specified period of time, or to make any agreement contrary to the foregoing.[10]

An employment-at-will disclaimer should appear on the application blank, along with two other disclaimers (see Chapter 8). First, there should be a statement of consent by the applicant for the organization to check provided references, along with a waiver of the right to make claims against them for anything they said. Second, there should be a so-called false statement warning, indicating that any false statement, misleading statement, or material omission may be grounds for dismissal.

Disclaimers are generally enforceable. They can thus serve as an important component of employment contracts. Their use should be guided by the following set of recommendations:[11]

1. They should be clearly stated and conspicuously placed in appropriate documents.
2. The employee should acknowledge receipt and review of the document and the disclaimer.
3. The disclaimer should state that it may be modified only in writing and by whom.
4. The terms and conditions of employment, including the disclaimer, as well as limits on their enforceability, should be reviewed with offer receivers and employees.

It would be wise to obtain legal counsel for drafting language for all disclaimers.

Contingencies

Often, the employer may wish to make a job offer that is contingent on certain other conditions being fulfilled by the offer receiver.[12] Examples of such contingencies include (a) passage of a particular test, such as a licensure exam (e.g., CPA or bar exam); (b) passage of a medical exam, including alcohol/drugs/screening tests; (c) satisfactory background and reference checks; and (d) proof of employability under the Immigration Reform and Control Act.

Though contingencies to a contract are generally enforceable, contingencies to an employment contract (especially those involving any of the preceding examples) are exceedingly complex and may be made only within defined limits. For this reason, contingencies should not be used in employment contracts without prior legal counsel.

Reneging

At times, the employer may wish to withdraw an offer that has already been made to an offer receiver. Or, the offer receiver may wish to withdraw from an offer that has already been extended and accepted. These withdrawals are known as reneging. Though reneging is usually an unfortunate event, and one that may invoke ill feelings, it generally may be done without legal recourse or penalty by either party. This is a logical extension of the employment-at-will concept. An important exception to this conclusion regarding reneging involves the doctrine of promissory estoppel discussed below (see Unfulfilled Promises).[13]

Other Employment Contract Sources

As alluded to previously, employment contract terms may be established through multiple sources, not just the letters of job offer and acceptance. Such establishment may be the result of both intentional and unintentional acts by the employer. Moreover, these terms may come about not only when the employment relationship is first established but also during the course of the employment relationship.[14]

The employer thus must constantly be alert to the fact that terms and conditions of employment may come into being and be modified through a variety of employment contract sources. Sources worth reiterating here are employee handbooks (and other written documents) and oral statements made by employer representatives. Job advertisements and job descriptions are generally not considered employment contracts.

In the case of employee handbooks, the employer must consider whether statements in them are legally enforceable or merely informational. While there is legal opinion on both sides of this question, handbooks are being considered increasingly as a legally enforceable part of the employment contract. To avoid this occurrence, the employer may wish to place an explicit disclaimer in the handbook that states the intent to provide only information to employees and that it will not be bound by any of the statements contained in the handbook.

In the case of oral statements, their danger and the need for caution in their use has already been addressed. It should be remembered that oral statements may present legal problems and challenges when made not only at the time of the initial employment contract but also throughout the course of the employment relationship. Of particular concern here are oral promises made to employees regarding future events, such as job security ("Don't worry, you will always have a place with us") or job assignments ("After training, you will be assigned as the assistant manager at our new store"). With oral statements, there is thus a constant need to be careful regarding the messages being delivered to employees, as well as who delivers those messages.

Unfulfilled Promises

Since the staffing process in general, and the job offer process in particular, involve the making of promises to offer receivers about terms and conditions of employment, it is important for the organization to (1) not make promises it is unwilling to keep, and (2) be sure that promises made are actually kept. Unfulfilled promises may spur the disappointed person to pursue a legal action against the organization. Three types of claims might be pursued.[15]

The first claim is that of breach of contract, and it may be pursued for both written and oral promises. The employee will have to show that both parties intended to be legally bound by the promise and that it was specific enough to establish an actual oral agreement. The second claim is that of promissory estoppel. Here, even if there is no enforceable oral contract, employees may claim that they relied on promises made by the organization, to their subsequent detriment, since the actual or presumed job offer was withdrawn. Examples of detrimental effects include resigning from one's current employer, passing up other job opportunities, relocating geographically, and incurring expenses associated with the job offer. When the offer receiver experiences such detrimental reliance, the person may sue the employer for compensatory damages; actual hiring of the person is rarely sought. The final claim is that of fraud, where the employee claims the organization made promises it had no intention of keeping. Employees may legally pursue fraud claims and seek both compensatory and punitive damages.

JOB OFFERS

A job offer is an attempt by the organization to induce the offer receiver into the establishment of an employment relationship. Assuming that the offer is accepted and that consideration is met, the organization and offer receiver will have established their relationship in the form of a legally binding employment contract. That contract is the culmination of the staffing process. The contract also signifies that the person/job match process has concluded and that the person/job match is now about to become a reality. That reality, in turn, becomes the start of, and foundation for, subsequent employee effectiveness on the various HR outcomes. For these reasons, the content and extension of the job offer become critical final parts of the overall staffing process.

This section discusses job offers as part of an overall applicant attraction strategy, and it relates the job rewards matrix to making job offers. Also, the content of job offers is discussed, with a dual emphasis on what is normally required by way of content, and some of the complexities often associated with determining job offer content.

Applicant Attraction Strategies

A basic theme of this book has been that applicants are exposed and subjected to numerous forces throughout the staffing process. These forces include labor markets, laws and regulations, recruitment and selection activities, and knowledge of likely job requirements and rewards. The job offer is the final confluence of these forces and must be crafted and extended within them. It is the organization's attempt to "make it all happen"—to realize the person/job match within this set of forces. Doing this requires thinking of the job offer in strategic terms.

A helpful model for these purposes is the applicant attraction strategy model shown in Exhibit 12.1.[16] This model shows that there are three basic attraction strategy components: recruitment activities, inducements, and applicant pools. The inducements component is of most interest here, for it represents the job rewards (pecuniary or extrinsic, nonpecuniary or intrinsic) that become part and parcel of the job offer. Recruitment activities and applicant pool characteristics are also important components.

The three attraction strategy components combine to influence pre- and postemployment outcomes. The preemployment outcomes are those that occur either before or at the point of job offer acceptance. They include applicant quantity (e.g., number of applicants, percent of vacancies filled), applicant quality (e.g., KSAOs), and spillover effects (e.g., applicants' reports of their recruitment experiences to other people, such as customers or potential future applicants).

Postemployment outcomes represent long-term effects of the attraction strategy, and are also expressed in terms of quantity, quality, and spillover. A quantity indicator might be the one-year retention rate for new hires. For quality, indicators might be such things as KSAOs of new hires, their success in entry-level training programs, their performance ratings, and their promotion rates over time. Spillover effects might include the impact of the new hires on other employees, such as their socialization with other employees and acceptance into work groups.

The model suggests that the three recruitment strategy components have definite links to or impact on the attraction outcomes. These linkages are conditioned, however, by various contingencies, such as labor markets and legal influences. The linkages also depend on the operation and effectiveness of other HR activities, such as training and compensation.

The applicant attraction strategy model thus shows that job offers (inducements) do not occur in a vacuum, but in a much broader strategic context. This means that job offers must be synchronized and meshed with other attraction activities and external forces for purposes of achieving effectiveness on the attraction outcomes. For example, the desirability of job offers from the offer receiver's perspective may depend on the credibility of the organizational representative who delivers it. Or, the content of job offers may have to vary according to characteristics of the recipients. Higher salaries may have to be offered to certain persons, for example, because of their higher levels of qualifications.

Despite these interactions of the job offer content with other forces, it is ultimately the content of the job offer itself that is likely the most important force influencing offer receivers and, thus, determines the effectiveness of the attraction process. It is through the job offer, more than anything else, that the organization seeks to provide the types and amounts of rewards that are sufficient to induce acceptance of the offer by the offer receiver. A "yes" to an offer is explicit rec-

EXHIBIT 12.1 **Model of the Applicant Attraction Process**

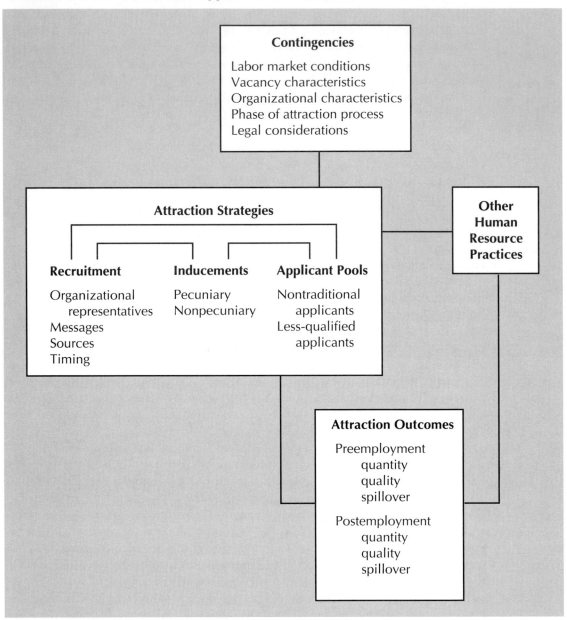

Source: S. L. Rynes and A. E. Barber, "Applicant Attraction Strategies: An Organizational Perspective," *Academy of Management Review*, 1990, 15, pp. 286–310.

ognition by the receiver that the person/job match is sufficiently promising to warrant formally entering into it via an employment contract.

To illustrate applicant attraction strategies and how multifaceted they are, consider what is being done by trucking companies to attract long-distance truck drivers.[17] On a nationwide basis, the companies need to hire 400,000 drivers a year, due to employment growth and to considerable turnover (job-hopping to other trucking companies and leaving truck driving all together). Drivers typically spend 14 or more consecutive days on the road, drive up to 18 hours a day in cramped quarters (one driver said, "it's like being in a kennel"), and receive $34,000 in pay per year based on miles driven. Recruiting into this type of job and work environment is challenging. The major attraction outcomes are mostly quantity ones—both finding sufficient numbers of new applicants and retaining new hires. Recruitment strategies include use of full-time recruiters from the trucker ranks, massive advertising (on billboards, on radio, on Web sites, in newspapers, and in magazines such as *Pro Trucker*), messages emphasizing new inducements, and employee referral systems paying cash awards of up to $1,000 for new hires, as well as prizes like vacations and color televisions. For monetary inducements, higher pay and benefits (especially health insurance and retirement plans), more favorable routes, and less downtime are the lures. For nonmonetary inducements, truck cabs are being equipped with televisions, microwaves, and closets to provide a friendlier work environment. In addition, assignments are changed to provide less time away from home, and listening to drivers' concerns is increasing. Applicant pools include not only poaching drivers from other trucking organizations but also nontraditional applicants recruited from unemployment offices, churches, job fairs, festivals, and even overseas military bases. These efforts attract accountants, cooks, nursing assistants, and construction workers.

Job Offer Content

The organization has considerable latitude in the terms and conditions of employment that it may offer to people. That latitude, of course, should be exercised within the organization's particular applicant attraction strategy, as well as the rewards generally available and shown in the job rewards matrix.

With some degree of latitude in terms and conditions offered for almost any job, it is apparent that job offers should be carefully constructed. There are definite rewards that can, and for the most part should, be addressed in any job offer. Moreover, the precise terms or content of the offer to any given finalist requires careful forethought. What follows is a discussion of the types of rewards to address, as well as some of their subtleties and complexities.

Starting Date

Normally, the organization desires to control when the employment relationship begins. To do so, it must provide a definite starting date in its offer. If it does not, acceptance and consideration of the offer occurs at the time the new hire actually begins work. Normally, the starting date is one that allows the offer receiver at least two weeks to provide notification of resignation to a current employer.

Duration of Contract

As noted in Chapter 2, employment contracts may be of a fixed term (i.e., have a definite ending date) or indeterminate term (i.e., have no definite ending date). The decision about duration is intimately related to the employment-at-will issue.

A fixed-term contract provides certainty to both the new hire and organization regarding the length of the employment relationship. Both parties decide to and must abide by an agreed-on term of employment. The organization can then (according to common law) terminate the contract prior to its expiration date for "just cause" only. Determination and demonstration of just cause can be a complicated legal problem for the organization.

Most organizations are unwilling to provide such employment guarantees. They much prefer an employment-at-will relationship in which either party may terminate the employment relationship at any time without having to demonstrate just cause.[18] Should the organization decide to have indeterminate-term employment contracts, it should carefully state in its written offer that the duration is indeterminate and that it may be terminated by either party at any time, for any reason. Because of the overriding importance of this issue, all wording should be approved at the highest organizational level.

A compromise between a fixed-term and indefinite-term provision is to have a contract provision that states it is for an indefinite term, that the employer may terminate the agreement at any time for good cause, and that either the employer or the employee may terminate the contract on 30 days (or some other time period) written notice. Such a provision provides protection to the employee against arbitrary, immediate termination, and to the employer against a sudden and unanticipated loss of an employee.[19]

Compensation

Compensation is the most important reward that the organization has to offer in its attraction strategy. It is a multifaceted reward that may be presented to the offer receiver in many forms. Sometimes that may consist of a standard pay rate and benefit package, which must be simply accepted or rejected. Other times the offer may be more tailor-made, often negotiated in advance.

It should be remembered that job seekers carry with them a set of pay preferences and expectations that shape how they respond to the compensation components of the job offer. For example, a study of engineering and hotel administration soon-to-graduate job seekers found that they would respond more favorably to a pay package that had (a) a high, fixed rate of pay that was not contingent on the success of the organization; (b) pay pegged to a particular job, rather than the number of skills they possessed; (c) pay raises based on individual, rather than group, performance; and (d) a flexible, as opposed to standard, benefits package.[20]

The compensation portion of the job offer should thus be carefully thought out and planned in advance. This pertains to starting pay, variable pay, and benefits.

Starting Pay: Flat Rate   In flat-rate job offers, all persons are offered an identical rate of pay, and variance from this is not permitted. Starting pay is thus offered on a "take it or leave it" basis.

Use of flat rates is appropriate in many circumstances. Examples of these include:

- jobs for which there is a plentiful supply of job applicants
- where applicants are of quite similar KSAO quality
- where there is a desire to avoid creating potential inequities in starting pay among new employees

It should also be noted that under some circumstances, use of flat rates may be mandatory. Examples here include pay rates under many collective bargaining agreements and for many jobs covered by civil service laws and regulations.

Starting Pay: Differential Rates   Organizations often opt out of flat rates, despite their simplicity, and choose differential starting pay rates. In general, this occurs under two sets of circumstances.

First, there are situations where the organization thinks there are clear qualitative (KSAO) differences among finalists. Some finalists are thus felt to be worth more than others, and starting pay differentials are used in recognizing this. A good example here involves new college graduates. Research clearly shows that differences in major and previous work experience lead to starting pay differentials among them.[21] Another example involves differences in starting pay for MBA graduates that reflect the quality of the MBA program from which they graduated. On the assumption that graduates from the elite programs (top 25 nationally ranked schools) represent better "raw business talent" than the mass of graduates from the other schools, the elite program graduates are receiving starting pay offers about twice the amount of other program graduates ($120,000 versus $60,000). A final example is paying a premium for applicants with bilingual language skills. The city of Los Angeles provides a bilingual pay premium to ensure that city services are accessible to non-English speakers. New hires (and current employees) who are required to speak, write, or interpret a language other than English receive a 5.5% bilingual premium.[22]

The second situation occurs when the organization is concerned about attraction outcomes, almost regardless of applicant KSAO differences. Here, the organization is under intense pressure to acquire new employees and fill vacancies promptly. To accomplish these outcomes, flexibility in starting pay rate offers is used to be responsive to finalists' demands, to sweeten offers, and otherwise impress applicants with an entrepreneurial spirit of wheeling and dealing. Hence, the organization actively seeks to strike a bargain with the offer receiver, and differential starting pay rates are a natural part of the attraction package.

Use of differential starting pay rates requires attention to several potential problems.[23] One problem is that offer receivers, though similarly qualified, may have different pay "mix" preferences. Some offer receivers may place higher (or lower) value on salary than on stock options or benefits than do others, leading them to demand higher (or lower) salaries. The organization must decide how much it is willing to provide offer receivers salary trade-offs for other forms of compensation. A second problem, often heightened by the first one, is that issues of fairness and internal equity among employees may arise when there is too much discretion in the range of starting salaries that exist. Naturally, similarly qualified employees receiving wide differences in starting pay is a guaranteed recipe for perceived pay inequities, and paying new hires starting salaries that exceed those of current "leapfrogged" employees also fuels the perceived inequity flames. Finally, research shows that starting pay expectations are often lower among women than men applicants. For example, a survey of 1,600 undergraduate and graduate students found that the average starting pay expectation for men was $55,950, compared to $49,190 for women. If these expectations shape salary negotiations and acceptances, the average starting pay of women will be lower than men, and "catch up" for women may be difficult since raises are usually a percentage of one's salary. These represent potential salary discrimination issues confronting the organization.

For such reasons, whenever differential rates of starting pay are used, there is the need for the organization to carefully consider what is permissible and within bounds. At times, the organization may choose to provide minimal guidance to managers making the offers. Often, however, there is a need for some constraints on managers. These constraints may specify when differential starting pay offers may be made and where within a pay range starting pay rates must fall. Exhibit 12.2 contains examples of such starting pay policies.

Variable Pay: Short Term   Short-term variable pay may be available on jobs, and, if so, the organization should address this in the job offer.

Prior to the job offer itself, the organization should give serious thought to whether there should be variable pay in the first place. This is a major issue that transcends staffing per se, but it does have important implications for the likely effectiveness of staffing activities.

Consider an organization with sales jobs, a classic example of a situation in which incentive or commission pay systems might be used. The mere presence/ absence of such a pay plan will likely affect the motivation/job rewards part of

---

EXHIBIT 12.2   Example of Starting Pay Policies

The Wright Company

The following policies regarding starting pay must be adhered to:

1. No person is to be offered a salary that is below the minimum, or above the midpoint, of the salary range for the job.
2. Generally, persons with reasonable qualifications should be offered a salary within the first quartile (bottom 25%) of the salary range for the job.
3. Salary offers above the first quartile, but not exceeding the midpoint, may be made for exceptionally well-qualified persons, or when market conditions dictate.
4. Salary offers should be fair in relation to other offers made and to the salaries paid to current employees.
5. Salary offers below the first quartile may be made without approval; offers at or above the first quartile must be approved in advance by the Manager of Compensation.
6. Counteroffers may not be accepted without approval of the Manager of Compensation.

the matching process. Different "breeds of cat" may be attracted to jobs providing incentive plans as opposed to those that do not.

More generally, research shows that the use of short-term incentive pay is quite common, with almost 90% of private sector, 76% of partnerships, and 44% of public sector organizations offering incentive pay plans of various sorts. Of these organizations, 95% provide cash payments via individual incentive pay and bonuses, based on financial, customer service, production, goal attainment, efficiency, and cost reduction measures. Two of the major reasons these organizations provide for such short-term incentive offerings are to compete for qualified employees and to retain employees.[24]

If there are to be short-term variable pay plans, the organization should communicate this in the offer letter. Beyond that, the organization should give careful consideration to how much detail about such plans, including payout formulas and amounts, it wants to include in the job offer. The more specific the information, the less flexibility the organization will have in the operation or modification of the plan.

Variable Pay: Long Term   Long-term variable pay plans provide employees ownership opportunity and the opportunity to increase their income as the value of the organization increases. Applicable only in the private sector, the most commonly used long-term variable pay is stock options—either an incentive stock option or a nonqualified stock option.[25] A stock option is a right to purchase a share of stock for a predetermined price at a later date; there is both a time span during which the right may be exercised (e.g., 10 years) and waiting period before the employee is eligible (vested) to make purchases (e.g., one year). Incentive stock option plans provide special tax treatment for the employee, primarily regarding capital gains when the employee sells the purchased stock (hopefully at a net gain), but these plans place many statutory restrictions on employers. Non-qualified stock options do not have to meet the statutory requirements like those of incentive stock option plans, thus providing the organization greater flexibility in granting options. But the options do not qualify for special tax treatment for the employee, whereas the organization can receive a tax deduction for the corporation expense of the stock options. Many publicly held organizations, especially larger ones, provide stock options, and to most employees at all levels.

Though stock options provide potential incentive value to offer receivers, some may prefer cash in the form of base pay or short-term variable pay incentives. In addition, stock options only have actual value to the recipient if the value of the stock appreciates beyond the purchase price and if the employee remains eligible to participate in the plan—such as through remaining with the organization for a specified time period.

Inclusion of stock options in the job offer requires considerable care and expertise. Experts should draft the actual language in the offer, and the organization should take special steps to ensure that the offer receiver actually understands what is being offered.

Benefits   Normally there is a fixed benefit package for a job, and it is offered as such to all offer receivers. Examples include health insurance and retirement and work/life plans. When a fixed or standard benefits package is offered, the offer letter should not spell out all of the specific benefit provisions. Rather, it should state that the employee will be eligible to participate in the benefit plans maintained by the organization, as provided in written descriptions of these plans. In this way, the job offer letter does not inadvertently make statements or promises that contradict or go beyond the organization's actual benefit plan.

Sometimes the offer may provide not only standard benefits but also additional custom-made benefits or other perquisites, known as "perks." These "deal sweeteners" may be offered to all potential new hires in a job category, or they may be tailor-made to the preferences of the individual offer receiver. In other instances, they may be offered in direct response to requests or demands from the offer receiver. The number and value of perks offered (or demanded) varies with the degree of difficulty in successfully attracting new hires. Perks are most likely provided to top executives, managers, and professionals. The set of perks used by organizations is almost endless. Commonly used ones are shown in Exhibit 12.3. More unique perks used for enticing executive stars to relocate include providing a family clothing allowance, moving pet horses, covering a housekeeper's medical insurance, paying children's tuition at private schools, and reimbursing for financial counseling services and tax preparation.

EXHIBIT 12.3 Examples of Perquisites

- Severance pay packages
- Stock options
- Country club membership
- Automobile
- Car phone
- Tuition reimbursement
- Pay-off of student loans

- Specially equipped computer
- Fax machine at home
- Adoption assistance
- Corporate plane
- Housing supplement
- Interest-free loans
- Selling home

Whether to offer perks, which ones, and to whom are perplexing issues. Although they may have definite applicant enticement appeal, they increase hiring costs, raise numerous tax issues, and may cause feelings of inequity and jealously among other employees.

Hours

Statements regarding hours of work should be carefully thought out and worded. For the organization, such statements will affect staffing flexibility and cost. In terms of flexibility, a statement such as, "Hours of work will be as-needed and scheduled," provides maximum flexibility. Designation of work as part-time, as opposed to full-time, may affect cost because the organization may provide restricted, if any, benefits to part-time employees.

Factors other than just number of hours may also need to be addressed in the job offer. If there are to be any special, tailor-made hours of work arrangements, these need to be clearly spelled out. Examples include "Weekend work will not be required of you," and "Your hours of work will be from 7:30 to 11:30 A.M. and 1:30 to 5:30 P.M." Overtime hours requirements and overtime pay, if applicable, could also be addressed.

Special Hiring Inducements

At times, the organization may want or need to offer special inducements to increase the likelihood that an offer will be accepted. Examples of these inducements are hiring bonuses, relocation assistance, hot skill premiums, and severance packages.

Hiring Bonuses Hiring, signing, or "up-front" bonuses are one-time payments offered and subsequently paid on acceptance of the offer. Typically, the bonus is in the form of an outright cash grant; the bonus may also be in the form of a cash advance against future expected earnings.

One example of hiring bonuses is that employed by brokerage firms, who have long used them as a way of luring applicants away from competitors. Bonuses up to $100,000 are not uncommon. The bonus is usually a combination of cash grant and cash advance against future sales commissions.[26]

Another example is the use of hiring bonuses for new bachelor's and master's degree graduates. A survey of employers found 45% of them were paying hiring bonuses.[27] Usage of hiring bonuses has expanded due to pervasive head count and "hot skill" shortages. Information technology jobs, such as software engineering and development, systems analysis, and database administration, are very likely candidates. Many nondegree jobs now also pay hiring bonuses, including fast food, butchers, bartenders, hairstylists, and pizza cooks. The size of the bonus appears to vary according to job level, severity of employee or skill shortage, and the need to match or "one-up" competitors.[28]

Hiring bonuses not only help snare new hires but they do so without permanent elevation in base pay, thus holding down long-term labor costs. However, hiring bonuses may cause problems. Employees who receive no bonus, or one of a lesser amount than others, may feel inequitably treated or resentful, threatening employee cohesion and commitment to the organization. Also, bonus recipients may be tempted to "take the money and run," and their performance motivation may be lessened because their bonus money is not contingent on their job performance. To address these problems, the organization may place restrictions on the bonus payment, paying half up front and the other half after some designated time period, such as 6 or 12 months; another option is to make payment of a portion or all of the bonus contingent on meeting certain performance goals within a designated time period. Such payment arrangements should help other employees see the hiring bonus as not a total "freebie" and should encourage only serious and committed offer receivers to actually accept the offer.[29]

Relocation Assistance   Acceptance of the offer may require a geographic move and entail relocation costs for the offer receiver. The organization may want to provide assistance to conduct the move, as well as totally or partially defray moving costs. Thus, a relocation package may include assistance with house hunting, guaranteed purchase of the applicant's home, a mortgage subsidy, and actual moving cost reimbursement. To simplify things, a lump-sum relocation allowance may be provided, thus reducing record keeping and other paperwork.[30]

Recently, relocation has become even more difficult in dual-career circumstances.[31] With both people working, it may be necessary to move both the offer receiver and the accompanying partner. Such a move may entail employing both people or providing job search assistance to the accompanying partner. The problem is likely to grow in magnitude.

Hot Skill Premiums   A hot skill premium is a temporary pay premium added to the regular base pay to account for a temporary market escalation in pay for certain skills in extreme shortage. An example where hot skill premiums might be used is many newly created jobs in the information technology arena. The job offer should clearly indicate the amount of base pay that constitutes the premium, the length of time the premium will be in effect, and the mechanism by which the premium will be halted or phased out. Before offering such premiums, it is wise to recognize that there will likely be pressure to maintain rather than discontinue the premium and that careful communication with the offer receiver about the temporary nature of the premium will be necessary.[32]

Severance Packages   Terms and conditions that the organization states the employee is entitled to upon departure from the organization constitute a severance package. Content of the package typically includes one or two weeks of pay for every year of service, earned vacation and holiday pay, extended health insurance coverage and premium payment, and outplacement assistance in finding a new job.[33] What is the organization willing to provide?

Other thorny issues surround these packages. When does an employee become eligible for the package? Will severance be granted for voluntary or involuntary termination, or both? If involuntary, are there exceptions, such as for unacceptable job performance or misconduct? Questions such as those above illustrate the need to very carefully craft the terms that will govern the package and define its contents.

Restrictions on Employees

In some situations, the organization may want to place certain restrictions on employees to protect its own self-interests. These restrictions should be known, and agreed to, by the new employee at the time of hire. As such, they should be incorporated into the job offer and resultant employment contract. Because of the potential complexities in these restrictions and the fact that they are subject to state contract laws, legal counsel should be sought to guide the organization in drafting appropriate contract language. Several types of restrictions are possible.[34]

One form of restriction involves so-called confidentiality clauses that prohibit current or departing employees from the unauthorized use or disclosure of confidential information during or after employment. Confidential information is any information not made public and that gives the organization an advantage over its competitors. Examples of such information include trade secrets, customer lists, secret formulas, manufacturing processes, marketing and pricing plans, and business forecasts. It will be necessary to spell out, in some degree, exactly what information the organization considers confidential, as well as the time period after employment for which confidentiality must be maintained.

Another restriction seeks to keep departed employees from competing against the organization, known as a noncompete agreement. Such agreements cannot keep departed employees from practicing their trade or profession completely or indefinitely, for this would in essence restrict the person from earning a living in a chosen field. Accordingly, the noncompete agreement must be crafted carefully in order to be enforceable. The agreement should probably not be a blanket statement that applies to all employees, but only to employees who truly could turn into competitors, such as high-level managers, scientists, and technical staff. Also, the agreement must be limited in time and geography. The time should be of short duration (less than two years) and limited to the geographic area of the organization's competitive market. For example, the vice president of sales for an insurance agency with locations in two counties of a state might have a noncompete agreement that prohibits working with any other agencies within the two counties, and the solicitation of the agency's policy holders, for one year.

Another form of restriction may involve the matter of stipulating how employment disputes, such as discrimination charges, are to be pursued and resolved. Here, an arbitration agreement will specify that any dispute must be submitted to an arbitrator for resolution, rather than being pursued with an enforcement agency, such as the EEOC, or in court. The agreement may specify specifics of the arbitration process, such as how the arbitrator will be chosen and whether the arbitrator's decision may be appealed.[35] For example, the agreement may indicate that the arbitrator will be chosen by the organization (not the employee) and the arbitrator's decision will be final and binding (not subject to appeal to an agency or the courts). Such arbitration agreements are very controversial, for they involve the employee waiving a legally protected right to pursue complaints through legal channels. For this reason, the EEOC opposes arbitration agreements that shut off all legal recourse for the employee.

A final type of restriction is a "golden handcuff," or payback agreement. The intent of this restriction is to retain new hires for some period of time and to financially discourage them from leaving the organization, particularly soon after they have joined. A typical golden handcuff will require the employee to repay (in full or pro rata) the organization for any upfront payments made at time of hire if the employee departs within the first year of employment. These payments might include hiring bonuses, relocation expenses, tuition reimbursements, or any other financial hiring lures. Executive pay packages might contain even more restrictions, designed to tie the executive to the organization for an extended period of time. Annual bonuses might be deferred for two or three years and be contingent on the executive not leaving during that time, or an executive may forfeit accrued pension benefits if departing before a particular date.

Other Terms and Conditions

Job offers are by no means restricted to the terms and conditions discussed so far. Virtually any terms and conditions may be covered and presented in a job offer, provided they are legally permissible. Hence, the organization should carefully and creatively think of other terms it may wish to offer. None of these other possible terms should be offered, however, unless the organization is truly willing to commit itself to them as part of a legally binding contract.

The organization should also give careful thought to the possible use of contingencies, which, as mentioned previously, are terms and conditions that the applicant must fulfill before the contract becomes binding (e.g., passage of a medical exam). As was noted, inclusion of these contingencies should not be done without prior knowledge and understanding of their potential legal ramifications (e.g., in the case of a medical exam, potential factors to consider under the Americans With Disabilities Act).

Acceptance Terms

The job offer should specify terms of acceptance required of the offer receiver. For reasons previously noted regarding oral contracts, acceptances should normally be required in writing only. The receiver should be required to accept or reject the offer in total, without revision. Any other form of acceptance is not an acceptance, merely a counteroffer. Finally, the offer should specify the date, if any, by which it will lapse. A lapse date is recommended so that certainty and closure are brought to the offer process.

Sample Job Offer Letter

A sample job offer letter is shown in Exhibit 12.4 that summarizes and illustrates the previous discussion and recommendations regarding job offers. This letter should be read and analyzed for purposes of becoming familiar with job offer letters, as well as gaining an appreciation for the many points that need to be addressed in such a letter. Remember that, normally, whatever is put in the job offer letter, once accepted by the receiver, becomes a binding employment contract.

JOB OFFER PROCESS

Besides having a knowledge of the types of issues to address in a job offer, it is equally important to have an understanding of the total job offer process. The content of any specific job offer must be formulated within a broad context of considerations. Once these have been taken into account, the specific offer must be developed and presented to the finalist. Following this, there will be matters to address in terms of either acceptance or rejection of the offer. Finally, there will be an occasional need to deal with the unfortunate issue of reneging, either by the organization or by the offer receiver.

Formulation of the Job Offer

When the organization puts together a job offer, several factors should be explicitly considered. These factors are knowledge of the terms and conditions offered by competitors, applicant truthfulness about KSAO and reward information provided,

EXHIBIT 12.4 **Example of Job Offer Letter**

The Wright Company

Mr. Vern Markowski
152 Legion Lane
Clearwater, Minnesota

Dear Mr. Markowski:

We are pleased to offer you the position of Human Resource Specialist, beginning March 1, 2002. Your office will be located here in our main facility at Silver Creek, Minnesota.

This offer is for full-time employment, meaning you will be expected to work a minimum of 40 hours per week. Weekend work is also expected, especially during peak production periods.

You will receive a signing bonus of $2,500, half payable on March 1, 2002, and the other half on August 1, 2002, if you are still an employee of the company. Your starting pay will be $3,100 per month. Should you complete one year of employment, you will then participate in our managerial performance review and merit pay process. You will be eligible to participate in our benefit plans as provided in our written descriptions of those plans.

Should you choose to relocate to the Silver Creek area, we will reimburse you for one house/apartment hunting trip for up to $1,000. We will also pay reasonable and normal moving expenses up to $7,500, with receipts required.

It should be emphasized that we are an employment-at-will employer. This means that we, or you, may terminate our employment relationship at any time, for any reason. Only the president of the Wright Company is authorized to provide any modification to this arrangement.

This offer is contingent on (a) your receiving certification as a Professional in Human Resources (PHR) from the Human Resource Certification Institute prior to March 1, 2002, and (b) your passing a company-paid and -approved medical exam prior to March 1, 2002.

We must have your response to this offer by February 1, 2002, at which time the offer will lapse. If you wish to accept our offer as specified in this letter, please sign and date at the bottom of the letter and return it to me (a copy is enclosed for you). Should you wish to discuss these or any other terms prior to February 1, 2002, please feel free to contact me.

Sincerely yours,

Mary Kaiser
Senior Vice President, Human Resources

I accept the employment offer, and its terms, contained in this letter. I have received no promises other than those contained in this letter.

_____   _____
Signed   Date

the receiver's likely reaction to the offer, and policies on negotiation of job offer content with the offer receiver.

Knowledge of Competitors

The organization competes for labor within labor markets. The job offer must be sensitive to the labor demand and supply forces operating, for these forces set the overall parameters for job offers to be extended.

On the demand side, this requires becoming knowledgeable about the terms and conditions of job contracts offered and provided by competitors. Here, the organization must confront two issues: Exactly who are the competitors, and exactly what terms and conditions are they offering for the type of job for which the hiring organization is staffing?

Assume the hiring organization is a national discount retailer, and it is hiring recent (or soon-to-be) college graduates for the job of management trainee. It may identify as competitors other retailers at the national level (e.g., Sears), as well as national discount retailers (e.g., Target, Wal-Mart, and Kmart). There may be fairly direct competitors in other industries as well (e.g., banking, insurance) that typically place new college graduates in training programs.

Once such competitors are identified, the organization needs to determine, if possible, what terms and conditions they are offering. This may be done through formal mechanisms such as performing salary surveys, reading competitors' ads, or consulting with trade associations. Information may be gathered informally as well, such as through telephone contacts with competitors, and conversations with actual job applicants who have firsthand knowledge of competitors' terms.

The organization may quickly acquire salary information through use of free online salary sites (e.g., *salary.com, wageweb.com, acinet.com*) or ones that charge fees (e.g., *towers.com, wwdssurveys.com*). Listings of these sites and discussions of their advantages and disadvantages are available.[36] Generally, the user should be cautious in use of these data, being careful to assess salary survey characteristics such as sample nature and size, currency of data, definitions of terms and job descriptions, and data presentation. It should also be remembered that job seekers can and will access these data, making the job seeker a very knowledgeable "shopper" and negotiator.

Through all of the above mechanisms, the organization becomes "marketwise" regarding its competitors. Invariably, however, the organization will discover that, for any given term or condition, there will be a range of values offered. For example, starting pay might range from $30,000 to $40,500 per year, and the length of the training program may vary from three months to two years. The organization will thus need to determine where within these ranges it wishes to position itself in general, as well as for each particular offer receiver.

On the labor supply side, the organization will need to consider its needs concerning both labor quantity and quality (KSAOs and motivation). In general, offers need to be attractive enough that they yield the head count required. Moreover, offers need to take into account the KSAOs each specific receiver possesses, and what these specific KSAOs are worth in terms and conditions offered the person. This calculation is illustrated in Exhibit 12.2, which shows an example of an organization's policies regarding differential starting pay offers among offer receivers. Such differential treatment, and all the issues and questions it raises, applies to virtually any other term or condition as well.

Applicant Truthfulness

Throughout the recruitment and selection process, information about KSAOs and other factors (e.g., current salary) is being provided by the applicant. Initially, this information is gathered as part of the assessment process, whose purpose is to determine which applicants are most likely to provide a good fit with job requirements and rewards. For applicants who pass the hurdles and are to receive job offers, the information that has been gathered may very well be used to decide the specific terms and conditions to include in a job offer. Just how truthful or believable is this information? The content and cost of job offers depends on how the organization answers this question.

There is little solid evidence on the degree of applicant truthfulness. However, there are some anecdotal indications that lack of truthfulness by applicants may be a problem, especially for current salary, salary history, job title, and job duties and accomplishments.

Consider the case of starting pay. Quite naturally, the organization may wish to base its starting pay offer on knowledge of what the offer receiver's pay is currently. Will the person be truthful or deceitful in reporting current salary? Indications are that deceit may be common. People may embellish or enhance not only their reported salaries but also their KSAOs to provide an artificially high base or starting point for the organization as it prepares its job offer. A production analyst earning $55,000 did this and obtained a new job at $150,000, with a company car and a country club membership also included in the package.[37]

To combat such deceit by applicants, organizations are becoming increasingly prone to pursue verification of all applicant information, including salary, and may go to extremes to do so. At the executive level, for example, some organizations now require people to provide copies of their W-2 income forms that are used for reporting to the Internal Revenue Service. The organization should not act on finalist-provided information in the preparation of job offers unless it is willing to assume, or has verified, that the information is accurate.

Likely Reactions of Offer Receivers

Naturally, the terms and conditions to be presented in an offer should be based on some assessment of the receiver's likely reaction to it. Will the receiver jump at it or laugh at it, or something in between?

One way to gauge likely reactions to the offer is to gather information about various preferences from the offer receiver during the recruitment/selection process. Such preliminary discussions and communications will help the organization construct an offer that is likely to be acceptable. At the extreme, the process may lead to almost simultaneous presentation and acceptance of the offer.

Another way to assess likely reactions to offers from offer receivers is to conduct research on why they accept or decline job offers. An example of this is a study of finalists for entry-level jobs in a broad range of occupations (e.g., accounting, mathematics, biology, immigration inspection) in the federal civil service.[38] While all finalists had been certified as qualified and thus eligible to receive a job offer, some accepted the offer and others declined to even receive the offer. Results of the study are shown in Exhibit 12.5.

EXHIBIT 12.5   Comparison of Job Offer Accepters and Decliners in Federal Government

A.   SURVEY METHODOLOGY

We obtained hiring data from the Office of Personnel Management for June through November 1990. This data was the most recent available. During this period, 78 people accepted offers and were hired for entry-level professional and administrative positions from OPM job registers; 132 people declined those same jobs.

Because of the limited hiring and timing period, the conclusions that can be drawn from our survey data are limited. The data represent only the 52 accepters and 94 decliners who responded to our survey questionnaires. Nevertheless, we believe the information is important because it sheds light on some of the reasons for the government's recruiting difficulties.

B.   SURVEY RESULTS

Financial considerations dominated the decliners' reasons for their decisions. Two-thirds or more said low salaries or the high cost of living in the job locations caused them to lose interest in federal employment. A comment one of the decliners wrote on her questionnaire reflected a typical concern: "To the best of my knowledge, this job offered below $20,000 per year. With the cost of living anywhere, much less New York City, I don't know how anyone could make it."

Two-thirds of the 61 decliners who were in permanent jobs or self-employed said they would have suffered pay cuts if they had taken the federal jobs. For 24 decliners (39 percent), the loss would have been more than $6,000 a year.

In contrast, most of the accepters said salaries were not the driving force behind their decisions. Over three-fourths said opportunities for career advancement or a chance to apply their education and skills were of great or very great importance in selecting federal employment. Sixteen accepters (31 percent) said salary was an important factor. The location of the job was influential with about half of the accepters.

(continued)

EXHIBIT 12.5 **Continued**

Unlike the decliners, the majority of the 19 accepters who were self-employed or in permanent jobs said they received pay increases when they joined the government. For five accepters, the increase was more than $6,000.

Another important difference between accepters and decliners related to their employment status. Compared to the decliners, a larger proportion of accepters were unemployed at the time they were offered a federal job. Thus, the need for a better paying job, or a job of any kind, appears to have been a major factor in many of the accepters' decisions.

Fifty-six decliners (65 percent) said the location of the job was a great or very great factor in their decisions to reject federal employment.

The next highest factors related to the decliners' perceptions of the nature and quality of federal work. Thirty-nine decliners (45 percent) thought they would be unable to apply their education and skills, while the same number thought there would be few opportunities for career advancement.

The length of the hiring process was a great or very great consideration to 35 decliners (42 percent). In fact, 47 decliners (56 percent) said they had accepted other jobs while waiting to hear the results of their federal job applications. One candidate wrote the following in her questionnaire:

"... I declined because it was too far to travel for an interview and I had already found a full-time job. However, I have applied for several other federal government jobs and the hiring process is worse than any I have encountered. ... In the length of time it takes to start, I imagine that most of the good candidates have already found other jobs."

Thirty-three decliners (38 percent) said they turned down federal employment because they believed the work would not be challenging.

Source: U.S. Government Accounting Office, "Survey of Applicants Who Accepted or Declined Federal Job Offers" (Washington, DC: author, 1992, B-243207).

The results show that several terms and conditions were responsible for the split between accepters and decliners. The most important were starting pay and cost of living in the relevant location. Also important were other extrinsic and intrinsic rewards, such as opportunities for advancement and quality of work (i.e., utilization of KSAOs). Note also that, rewards aside, the excessive length of the recruitment process itself also played a role in decliners' decisions.

How would such results be used in the formulation of job offers? There seems to be a clear need for higher starting pay to be offered. This may not only address low pay and high cost of living issues but also help compensate for deficiencies in intrinsic rewards. Steps will also have to be taken to shorten the recruitment process. More generally, there is probably a need to examine the total applicant attraction strategy used (i.e., recruitment practices, extrinsic and intrinsic rewards, and applicant pools). Once this examination has been completed, the narrower issue of job offer formulation can be more thoughtfully addressed.

Policies on Negotiations and Initial Offers

Prior to making job offers, the organization should decide whether or not it will negotiate on them. In essence, the organization must decide whether its first offer to a person will also be its final offer.

Several considerations should be kept in mind when formulating strategies and policies for making job offers. First, remember that job offers occur for both external and internal staffing. For external staffing, the job offer is intended to convert the offer receiver into a new hire. For internal staffing, the job offer is being made to induce the employee to accept a new job assignment or to attempt to retain the employee by making a counteroffer to an offer the employee has received from another organization. These separate types of job offers (new hires, new assignment, retention) will likely require separate job offer strategies and policies.

Second, consider fully the costs of not having a job offer be accepted by the offer receiver. Are there other equally qualified individuals available as backup offer receivers? How long can the organization afford to let a position remain vacant? How will current employees feel about job offers being rejected—will they, too, feel rejected, or that something they are unaware of is amiss in the organization? Will those next in line to receive an offer feel like second-class citizens or choices of desperation and last resort? Answers to such questions will often suggest it may be desirable to negotiate (up to a point) with the offer receiver.

Third, recognize that many people to whom you will be making offers may in turn be seeking and receiving counteroffers from their current employer. Anecdotal evidence suggests that counteroffers are being used much more frequently in attempts to retain increasingly less loyal employees. ("People are jumping jobs so frequently these days that U.S. business is beginning to look like a French bedroom farce. The new morality says that you have to be more loyal to your career than to your company, and the new math adds, if you are typical, you'll have about ten employers during your working life. So even if you're not hopping around now, you may soon be."[39]) Shortages of qualified replacements and the high cost of hiring replacements also contribute to the counteroffer wave. Hence, the organization should recognize that any offer it makes may lead to a bidding war of sorts with other organizations.

Fourth, a currently employed offer receiver normally incurs costs for leaving and will expect a "make whole" offer from the organization. Often these costs can amount to 20–30% of the offer receiver's current base pay. In addition to relocation or higher commuting costs, the offer receiver may forfeit employer contribution to a retirement plan, vacation time and holidays, various perks, and so forth. In addition, there may be waiting periods before the offer receiver would be eligible for various benefits, leading to opportunity costs of lost coverage and possibly paying the costs (e.g., health insurance premiums) out of pocket until coverage begins.

Finally, job seekers are often quite sophisticated in formulating and presenting their demands to the organization. They will know what it truly costs them to leave their current job and frame their demands accordingly. They will be aware of the particular KSAOs that they uniquely have to offer, make these acutely known to the organization, and demand a high price for them. The terms demanded (or more politely, "proposed") may focus not only on salary but on myriad other possibilities, including vacation time, a flexible work schedule to help balance work and family pressures, guaranteed expenditures on training and development, higher employer matching to a 401(k) retirement plan, and so on. In short, unless it is illegal, it is negotiable, and the organization must be prepared to handle demands from job seekers on virtually every term and condition of employment.

Presumably, each term or condition contained in an offer is a mini-offer itself. For each term or condition, therefore, the organization must decide

- whether it will negotiate on this term or condition; and
- if it negotiates, what are its lower and (especially) upper bounds.

Once these questions have been answered, the organization may determine its posture regarding the presentation of the initial offer to the receiver. There are three basic strategies to choose from: lowball, competitive, and best shot.

Lowball   This strategy involves offering the lower bounds of terms and conditions to the receiver. Advantages to this strategy include getting acceptances from desperate or unknowledgeable receivers, minimizing initial employment costs, and leaving plenty of room to negotiate upward. Dangers to the lowball strategy are failing to get any acceptances, driving people away from and out of the finalist pool, developing an unsavory reputation among future potential applicants, and creating inequities and hard feelings that the reluctant accepter may carry into the organization, which may then influence postemployment attraction outcomes, such as retention.

Competitive   With a competitive strategy, the organization prepares an offer that it feels is "on the market," neither too high nor too low. The competitive strategy should yield a sufficient number of job offer acceptances overall, though not all of the highest-quality (KSAO) applicants. This strategy leaves room for subsequent negotiation, should that be necessary. Competitive offers are unlikely to either offend or excite the receiver, and they probably will not have negative consequences for postemployment outcomes.

Best Shot   With this strategy, the organization "goes for broke" and gives a high offer, one right at the upper bounds of feasible terms and conditions. Accompanying this offer is usually a statement to the receiver that this is indeed the organization's "best shot," thus leaving little or no room for negotiation. These offers should enhance both preemployment attraction outcomes (e.g., filling vacancies quickly) and postemployment outcomes (e.g., job satisfaction). Best-shot offers obviously increase employment costs. They also leave little or no room for negotiation or for "sweetening" the offer. Finally, they may create feelings of inequity or jealousy among current employees.

None of these initial offer strategies is inherently superior. But the organization does need to make some choices as to which to generally use. It could also choose to tailor a strategy to fit the finalist pursued, as well as other circumstances. For example, the best-shot strategy may be chosen (a) for high-quality finalists, (b) when there are strong competitive hiring pressures from competitors, (c) when the organization feels great pressure to fill vacancies quickly, and (d) as part of an aggressive EEO/AA recruitment program.

Presentation of the Job Offer

Presentation of the offer may proceed along many different paths. The precise path chosen depends on the content of the offer, as well as factors considered in formulating the offer. To illustrate, two extreme approaches to presenting the job offer—the mechanical and the sales approaches—are detailed.

Mechanical Approach

The mechanical approach is a dry, sterile one that relies on simple one-way communication from the organization to the offer receiver. Little more than a standard, or "form," written offer is sent to the person. The organization then awaits a response. Little or no input about the content of the offer is received from the person, and after the offer has been made, there is no further communication with the person. If the person rejects the offer, another form letter acknowledging receipt of the rejection is sent. Meanwhile, the offer process is repeated anew, without modification, for a different receiver.

Sales Approach

The sales approach treats the job offer as a product that must be developed and sold to the customer (i.e., receiver). There is active interaction between the organization and the receiver as the terms and conditions are developed and incorporated into an offer package. There is informal agreement that unfolds between the receiver and organization, and reduction of that agreement into an actual job offer is a mere formality. After the formal offer has been presented, the organization continues to have active communication with the receiver. In this way, the organization can be alert to possible glitches that occur in the offer process, and continue to sell the job to the receiver.

An excellent example of the sales approach is shown in Exhibit 12.6. This example is based on two premises:

EXHIBIT 12.6   Example of a Sales Approach to Job Offers

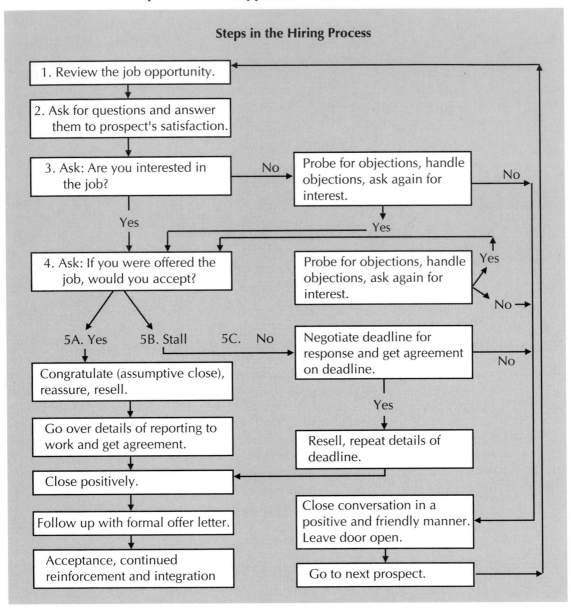

Source: R. Goddard, J. Fox, and W. E. Patton, "The Job-Hire Sale," *Personnel Administrator,* 1989, 34(6), p. 121. Reprinted with the permission of *HR Magazine* (formerly *Personnel Administrator*) published by the Society for Human Resource Management, Alexandria, VA.

1. The offer is not a gift. Instead, it must be sold to the receiver. Extending the job offer is a sales job and should be treated as such.
2. If possible, an offer should not be left open awaiting a response, since this generally precludes making an offer to another person.[40]

As the mechanical and sales approaches to job offer presentation make clear, the organization has considerable discretion in choosing how it delivers the offer. When it develops its job offer presentation process, it should be ever mindful of the applicant attraction strategy (Exhibit 12.1), and its emphasis on both the recruitment process and job offer content, as factors affecting applicant attraction outcomes.

Job Offer Acceptance and Rejection

Ultimately, of course, job offers are accepted and rejected. How this happens and how it is handled are often as important as the outcomes themselves.

Provided next are some general suggestions and recommendations about acceptances and rejections. These are intended to serve as advice about additional practices and issues involved in the job offer process.

Acceptance

When the offer receiver accepts a job offer, the organization should do two important things. First, it should check the receiver's actual acceptance to ensure that it has been accepted as required in the offer. Thus, the acceptance should not come in the form of a counteroffer or with any other contingencies attached to it. Also, the acceptance should occur in the manner required (normally, writing), and it should arrive on or before the date specified.

The second thing the organization must do is maintain contact with the new hire. Initially, this means acknowledging receipt of the acceptance. Additional communication may also be appropriate to further "cement the deal" and build commitment to the new job and organization. Examples of such continued communication include soon-to-be coworkers calling and offering congratulations to the new hire, sending work materials and reports to the new hire to help phase the person into the new job, and inviting the new hire to meetings and other activities prior to that person's starting date.

Rejection

The organization may reject the finalist, and the finalist may reject the organization.

By the Organization Depending on the decision-making process used, the acceptance of an offer by one person means that the organization will now have to reject others. This should be done promptly and courteously. Moreover, the organization should keep records of those it rejects. This is necessary for legal purposes (e.g., applicant flow statistics), and for purposes of building and maintaining a pool of potential applicants that the organization may wish to contact about future vacancies.

The content of the rejection message (usually a letter) is up to the discretion of the organization. Most organizations opt for short and vague content that basically mentions a lack of fit between applicant and job characteristics. Providing more specific reasons for rejection should only be done with caution. The reasons provided should be candid and truthful, and they should match with the reasons recorded and maintained on other documents by the organization.

By the Offer Receiver When the receiver rejects the job offer, the organization must first decide whether it wants to accept the rejection or extend a new offer to the person. If the organization's position on negotiations has already been determined, as ideally it should, then there is little reason to reconsider the position chosen on negotiations.

When the rejection is accepted, it should be done so promptly and courteously. Moreover, records should also be kept of these rejections, for the same reasons they are kept when rejection by the organization occurs.

Reneging

Occasionally, and unfortunately, reneging occurs. Organizations rescind offers extended, and receivers rescind offers accepted. Solid evidence on reneging, and exactly why it occurs, is lacking. Sometimes reneging is unavoidable. The organization may experience a sudden downturn in business conditions, so that planned-on jobs evaporate. Or, the offer receiver may experience sudden changes in circumstances requiring reneging, such as a change in health status.

While some reneging by the organization may be necessary, we believe that the organization can and should take steps to lessen its occurrence. We also believe that there are steps the organization should take to handle reneging if the steps to lessen it are insufficient. Examples of the steps for lessening and handling reneging are shown in Exhibit 12.7. These steps represent attempts to be very fair to the offer receiver while still representing the interests of the organization.

For the offer receiver, high standards of fairness are also required. The receiver should not be frivolous, just going through the application process "for the experience." Nor should the receiver accept an offer as a way of extracting a counteroffer out of his or her current employer. Indeed, organizations should be aware of the fact that some of the people to whom they make job offers will receive such counteroffers, and this should be taken into account during the time the offer is

---

EXHIBIT 12.7   Organization Actions to Deal with Reneging

A. To Lessen the Occurence of Reneging

- Extend offers only for positions known to exist and be vacant
- Require top management approval of all reneging
- Conduct thorough assessments of finalists prior to job offer
- Honor outstanding offers but make no new ones
- Discourage offer receiver from accepting offer
- Defer starting date and provide partial pay in interim
- Keep offer open but renegotiate or reduce salary and other economic items
- Stagger new hire starting dates to smooth out additions to payroll

B. To Handle Reneging

- Communicate honestly and quickly with offer receiver
- Provide consolation or "apology" package (e.g., hiring bonus, three months salary)
- Pay for any disruption costs (e.g., relocation)
- Hire as consultant (independent contractor), convert to employee later
- Guarantee priority over other applicants when future vacancies occur

---

initially formulated and presented. Finally, the receiver should do a careful assessment of probable fit for the person/job match prior to accepting an offer.

NEW EMPLOYEE ORIENTATION AND SOCIALIZATION

Establishment of the employment relationship through final match activities does not end a concern with the person/job match. Rather, that relationship must now be nurtured and maintained over time to ensure that the intended match becomes and remains effective. The new hires become newcomers, and their initial entry into the job and organization should be guided by orientation and socialization activities.[41]

Orientation

Orientation of newcomers should start immediately on the beginning of the employment relationship.[42] The overall focus of the orientation should be on both the person/job and person/organization matches and making them become an effective reality.

It should be remembered that the newcomer is entering a situation of uncertainties and unknowns. Though these may have been lessened through a realistic recruitment program, there will remain much to be communicated and resolved.

Hence, orientation is a natural extension of the organization's searching component (communication medium and message) of its recruitment efforts. Both requirements and rewards must be communicated and understood during orientation.

Orientation requires considerable advanced planning in terms of topics to cover, development of materials for the newcomer, and scheduling of the myriad activities that contribute to an effective orientation program. Often, the HR department is responsible for the design and conduct of the orientation, and it will seek close coordination of actual orientation activities and schedules with the newcomer's supervisor.

The message portion of orientation involves determining and providing key "need-to-know" information to the newcomer. Spacing out of the information is also usually necessary to avoid information overload. As with any realistic recruitment, the information should be accurate and broad in scope; usually, multiple media should be used: written, interpersonal, and audiovisual.

Exhibit 12.8 contains a far-ranging set of suggested topics of information for an orientation program, delivery of which is accomplished via written materials, training programs, meetings with various people, and visual inspection. Note that these activities are spaced out rather than concentrated in just the first day at work for the newcomer. Also, the orientation program begins even before the newcomer starts work, as a way of both getting the newcomer gradually "up to speed" and making the newcomer feel welcome. The newcomer's supervisor is expected to play a critical role in all aspects of orientation, particularly past the starting dates, when orientation becomes appropriately focused on job performance–related issues. In team-based environments, these supervisory actions would be the responsibility of the team leader and team members.

An excellent example of an orientation program is the one provided at the DuPont Merck Pharmaceutical Company. Designed by consultants, the program involves three tiers (stages) of newcomer introduction (called "orienteering") to their work unit, division, and organization. There is an orienteering kit containing posters illustrating the company's mission and vision, a checklist summarizing the many actions and steps (similar to those shown in Exhibit 12.8) to be taken during orientation, and guidelines for putting together and implementing an orienteering team. During the first tier, the newcomer receives work unit orienteering from a team made up of the supervisor, a "sponsor," work unit members, and an administrative coordinator. The team seeks to provide the newcomer a sense of direction, define objectives, identify resources, and assist the newcomer in assimilating company values. During the second tier (30 to 90 days later), a half-day company orienteering program is attended by the newcomer. A welcome from top management, a review of the company's culture and products, and distribution of informational materials by HR managers are elements of this tier. The third tier occurs 30 to 90 days later and focuses on division orienteering. The intent is to bring company goals into focus, explain division objectives, and help align these goals and objectives with those of the newcomer.[43]

EXHIBIT 12.8   New Employee Orientation Program Suggestions

Preemployment

Prepare supervisor and review orientation responsibilities
Send information to new hire about:

- work area or unit, organization, products, and services
- community and surrounding area
- important contact people and phone numbers

Put name on internal mailing lists and begin delivery to new employee
Have supervisor and coworkers contact and welcome new hire

Starting Day(s)

Introduce newcomer to coworkers
Meet with HR department representative
Conduct work-site tour
Have work station or office ready and waiting
Provide information regarding:

- policies and procedures (work rules, personal conduct, payroll, use of equipment and supplies, time sheets and time clocks)
- locations
- communications (phone and voice mail, email, fax, internal mail directory, business cards, cellular phone, pager, network)
- security (identification, keys, off-limit areas, passwords)
- parking and transportation
- safety and medical

Schedule meeting with supervisor
Conduct formal orientation program
Provide employee handbook and obtain acknowledgment of receipt

Subsequent Days

Have supervisor meetings with newcomer to:

- review job requirements matrix and related information
- discuss performance standards and expectations
- discuss performance appraisal/management system
- identify and remove performance obstacles
- identify training and development needs
- discuss adaptation to job, organization, coworkers
- listen to employee questions and concerns
- review job rewards matrix and related information

Conduct additional orientation training covering:

- organization philosophy and values
- products and services
- customers
- general skills (interpersonal, communication, customer service)

Provide sponsor, buddy, or mentor for newcomer
Introduce newcomer to, and meet with, key people

Socialization

Socialization of the newcomer is a natural extension of orientation activities. Like orientation, the goal of socialization is to achieve effective person/job and person/organization matches. Whereas orientation focuses on the initial and immediate aspects of newcomer adaptation, socialization emphasizes helping the newcomer fit into the job and organization over time. The emphasis is on the long haul, seeking to gain newcomers' adaptation in ways that will make them want to be successful, long-term contributors to the organization.[44] There are two key issues to address in developing and conducting an effective socialization process. First, what are the major elements or contents of socialization that should occur? Second, how can the organization best deliver those elements to the newcomer?

Content

While the content of the socialization process should obviously be somewhat job- and organization-specific, there are several components that are likely candidates for inclusion. From the newcomer's perspective these are:[45]

1. People—meeting and learning about coworkers, key contacts, informal groups and gatherings, and networks; becoming accepted and respected by these people as "one of the gang"
2. Performance proficiency—becoming very familiar with job requirements; mastering tasks; having impacts on performance results; and acquiring necessary KSAOs for proficiency in all aspects of the job
3. Organization goals and values—learning of the organization's goals; accepting these goals and incorporating them into my "line of sight" for performance proficiency; learning about values and norms of desirable behavior (e.g., working late and on weekends; making suggestions for improvements)
4. Politics—learning about how things "really work"; becoming familiar with "key players" and their quirks; taking acceptable shortcuts; schmoozing and networking
5. Language—learning special terms, buzzwords, and acronyms; knowing what not to say; learning the jargon of people in my trade or profession
6. History—learning about the origins and growth of the organization; becoming familiar with customs, rituals, and special events; understanding the origins of my work unit and the backgrounds of people in it

Many of the above topics overlap with the possible content of an orientation program, suggesting that orientation and socialization programs be developed in tandem so that they are synchronized and seamless as the newcomer passes from orientation into socialization.

Delivery

Delivery of socialization to the newcomer should be the responsibility of several people. First, it should be the responsibility of the newcomer's supervisor to personally socialize the newcomer, particularly in terms of performance proficiency and organization goals and values. The supervisor is intimately familiar with and the "enforcer" of these key elements of socialization. It is well that the newcomer and supervisor communicate directly, honestly, and formally about these elements.

Peers in the newcomer's work unit or team are promising candidates for assisting in socialization. They can be most helpful in terms of politics, language, and history, drawing on and sharing their own accumulated experiences with the newcomer. They can also make their approachability and availability known to the newcomer when he or she wants to ask questions or raise issues in an informal manner.

To provide a more formal information and support system to the newcomer, but one outside of a chain of command, a mentor or sponsor may be assigned to (or chosen by) the newcomer. The mentor functions as an identifiable "point of contact" for the newcomer, as well as someone who actively interacts with the newcomer to provide the inside knowledge, savvy, and personal contacts that will help the newcomer "settle in" to the current job and prepare for future job assignments. Mentors can also play a vital role in helping shatter the glass ceiling of the organization.

Finally, the HR department can be very useful to the socialization process. Its representatives can help establish formal, organization-wide socialization activities such as mentoring programs, special events, and informational presentations. Also, representatives may undertake development of training programs on socialization topics for supervisors and mentors. Representatives might also work closely, but informally, with supervisors as coaches for them in how to become a successful socializer of their own newcomers.

LEGAL ISSUES

The employment contract establishes the actual employment relationship and the terms and conditions that will govern it. In the process of establishing it, there are certain obligations and responsibilities that the organization must reckon with. These pertain to (a) employing only those people who meet the employment requirements under the Immigration Reform and Control Act (IRCA), (b) avoiding the negligent hiring of individuals, and (c) maintaining the organization's posture toward employment-at-will. Each of these is discussed in turn.

Authorization to Work

Under the IRCA (see Chapter 2), the organization is prohibited from hiring or continuing to employ an alien who is not authorized to work in the United States.

Moreover, the organization must verify such authorization for any person hired (after November 6, 1986, only), and it must not discriminate against individuals on the basis of national origin or citizenship status. There are specific federal regulations detailing the requirements and methods of compliance.[46]

Compliance with these means the following for the organization.[47] First, the organization must verify the employability status of each new employee (not just aliens). This is accomplished through the completion of the I-9 verification form, which in turn requires documents that verify the new employee's identity and eligibility. Both identity and eligibility must be verified. Some documents (e.g., U.S. passport) verify both identity and eligibility; other documents verify only identity (e.g., state-issued driver's license or ID card) or employment eligibility (e.g., original Social Security card or birth certificate).

Second, verification must occur within three days of being hired. Note, therefore, that verification need not have occurred at the time of the extension of the job offer. Offers extended without verification should contain a contingency clause making the offer contingent on satisfactory employment verification.

Finally, to avoid possible national origin or citizenship discrimination, it is best not to ask for proof of employment eligibility prior to making the offer. The reason for this is that many of the identity and eligibility documents contain personal information that pertain to national origin and citizenship status, and such personal information might be used in a discriminatory manner. As a further matter of caution, the organization should not refuse to make a job offer to a person based on that person's foreign accent or appearance.

Negligent Hiring

Negligent hiring is a workplace torts issue (see Chapter 2) involving claims by an injured plaintiff (e.g., customer or employee) that the plaintiff was harmed by an unfit employee who was negligently hired by the organization. The employer is claimed to have violated its common-law duty to protect its employees and customers from injury by hiring an employee it knew (or should have known) posed a threat of risk to them.[48] To have a successful suit, there are several things that the plaintiff must prove:

1. The person was, in fact, an employee of the organization.
2. The employee was, in fact, incompetent, as opposed to being a competent employee who acted in a negligent manner.
3. The employer knew, or should have known, of the employee's incompetence.
4. The employer had a legal duty to select competent employees.
5. The injury or harm was a foreseeable consequence of hiring the unfit employee.
6. The hiring of the unfit employee was the proximate cause of the injury or harm.

Examples of negligent hiring cases abound, particularly extreme ones involving violence, bodily injury, physical damage, and death. As a specific example, negligent hiring of nursing aides in nursing homes appears to be an acute problem, with nursing home patients suffering crimes ranging from death to physical abuse to theft. Some states have even passed legislation requiring background investigations of applicants for nursing home jobs. Illinois mandates background checks for nursing assistants, and the law specifies 74 employment disqualifying crimes, from theft to first-degree murder. Under this law, of 56,008 checks made, 2,670 applicants were found to have a disqualifying background for this job, though 42% of these were allowed to take the job anyway.[49]

What should the organization do to minimize negligent hiring occurrences? There are several straightforward recommendations that can be made.[50] First, staffing any job should be preceded by a thorough job analysis that identifies all the KSAOs required by the job. Failure to identify or otherwise consider KSAOs prior to the final match is not likely to be much of a defense in a negligent hiring lawsuit.

Second, particular attention should be paid to the *O* part of KSAOs, such as licensure requirements, criminal records, references, unexplained gaps in employment history, and alcohol and illegal drug usage. Of course, these should be derived separately for each job, rather than applied identically to all jobs.

Third, methods for assessing these KSAOs that are valid and legal must be used. This is difficult to do in practice because of lack of knowledge about the validity of some predictors, or their relatively low levels of validity. Also, difficulties arise because of legal constraints on the acquisition and use of preemployment inquiries, as explained in Chapter 8.

Fourth, require all applicants to sign disclaimer statements allowing the employer to check references and otherwise conduct background investigations. In addition, have the applicant sign a statement indicating that all provided information is true and that the applicant has not withheld requested information.

Fifth, apply utility analysis to determine whether it is worthwhile to engage in the preceding recommendations to try to avoid the (usually slight) chance of a negligent hiring lawsuit. Such an analysis will undoubtedly indicate great variability among jobs in terms of how many resources the organization wishes to invest in negligent hiring prevention.

Finally, when in doubt about a finalist and whether to extend a job offer, do not extend it until those doubts have been resolved. Acquire more information from the finalist, verify more thoroughly existing information, and seek the opinions of others on whether or not to proceed with the job offer.

Employment-at-Will

As discussed in this chapter and Chapter 2, employment-at-will involves the right of either the employer or employee to unilaterally terminate the employment relationship at any time, for any legal reason. In general, the employment relationship is at-will, and usually the employer wishes it to remain that way. Hence, during the final match (and even before) the employer must take certain steps to ensure that its job offers in fact clearly establish the at-will relationship. These steps are merely a compilation of points already made regarding employment contracts and employment-at-will.

The first thing to be done is ensure that job offers are for an indeterminate time period, meaning that they have no fixed term or specific ending date. Second, include in the job offer a specific disclaimer stating that the employment relationship will be strictly at-will. Third, review all written documents (e.g., employee handbook, application blank) to ensure that they do not contain any language that implies anything but a strictly at-will relationship. Finally, take steps to ensure that organizational members do not make any oral statements or promises that would serve to create something other than a strictly at-will relationship.[51]

SUMMARY

During the final match, the offer receiver and the organization move toward each other through the job offer/acceptance process. They seek to enter into the employment relationship and become legally bound to each other through an employment contract.

Knowledge of employment contract principles is central to understanding the final match. The most important principle pertains to the requirements for a legally enforceable employment contract (offer, acceptance, and consideration). Other important principles focus on the identity of parties to the contract, the form of the contract (written or oral), disclaimers by the employer, contingencies, reneging by the organization or offer receiver, other sources (e.g., employee handbooks) that may also specify terms and conditions of employment, and unfulfilled promises.

Job offers are designed to induce the offer receiver to join the organization. Offers should be viewed and used in the context of an applicant attraction strategy by the organization. In that strategy, job offers, recruitment activities, and applicant characteristics all interact to exert forces on applicants that will have positive impacts on recruitment outcomes (preattraction, postattraction, and spillover). Use of the job rewards matrix may be helpful in preparing and communicating the job offer.

Job offers may contain virtually any legal terms and conditions of employment. Generally, the offer addresses terms pertaining to starting date, duration of contract, compensation, hours, special hiring inducements (if any), other terms (such as contingencies), and acceptance of the offer.

The process of making job offers can be complicated, involving a need to think through multiple issues prior to making formal offers. Offers should take into account the content of competitors' offers, potential problems with applicant truthfulness, likely reactions of the offer receiver, and the organization's policies on negotiating offers. Presentation of the offer can range from a mechanical process all the way to a major sales job. Ultimately, offers are accepted and rejected, and all offer receivers should receive prompt and courteous attention during these events. Steps should be taken to minimize reneging by either the organization or the offer receiver.

Acceptance of the offer marks the beginning of the employment relationship. To help ensure that the initial person/job match starts out and continues to be effective, the organization should undertake both orientation and socialization activities for newcomers.

From a legal perspective, the organization must be sure that the offer receiver is employable according to provisions of the Immigration Reform and Control Act. Both identity and eligibility for employment must be verified. The potential negligent hiring of individuals who, once on the job, cause harm to others (employees or customers) is also of legal concern. Those so injured may bring suit against the organization. There are certain steps the organization can take in an attempt to minimize the occurrence of negligent hiring lawsuits. There are limits on these steps, however, such as other legal constraints on the gathering of background information about applicants. Finally, the organization should have its posture, policies, and practices regarding employment-at-will firmly developed and aligned. There are numerous steps that can be taken to help achieve this.

DISCUSSION QUESTIONS

1. If you were the HR staffing manager for an organization, what guidelines might you recommend regarding oral and written communication with job applicants by members of the organization?

2. Using the applicant attraction strategy model (Exhibit 12.1), what are some examples of how the same job offer has different effects on pre- and post-attraction outcomes?

3. What are the advantages and disadvantages to the sales approach in the presentation of the job offer?

4. What are examples of orientation experiences you have had as a new hire that have been particularly effective (or ineffective) in helping to make the person/job match happen?

5. What are the steps an employer should take to develop and implement its policy regarding employment-at-will?

APPLICATIONS

Making a Job Offer

Clean Car Care (3Cs) is located within a western city of 175,000 people. The company owns and operates four full-service car washes in the city. The owner of 3Cs, Arlan Autospritz, has strategically cornered the car wash market, with his only competition being two coin-operated car washes on the outskirts of the city. The unemployment rate in the city and surrounding area is 3.8%, and it is expected to go somewhat lower.

Arlan has staffed 3Cs by hiring locally and paying wage premiums (above market wages) to induce people to accept job offers and to remain with 3Cs. Hiring occurs at the entry level only, for the job of washer. If they remain with 3Cs, washers have the opportunity to progress upward through the ranks, going from washer to shift lead person to assistant manager to manager of one of the four car wash facilities. Until recently, this staffing system worked well for Arlan. He was able to hire high-quality people, and a combination of continued wage premiums and promotion opportunities meant he had relatively little turnover (under 30% annually). Every manager at 3Cs, past or present, had come up through the ranks. But that is now changing with the sustained low unemployment and new hires who just naturally seem more turnover prone. The internal promotion pipeline is thus drying up, since few new hires are staying with 3Cs long enough to begin climbing the ladder.

Arlan has a vacancy for the job of manager at the north-side facility. Unfortunately, he does not think that any of his assistant managers are qualified for the job, and he reluctantly concluded that he has to fill the job externally.

A vigorous three-county recruitment campaign netted Arlan a total of five applicants. Initial assessments resulted in four of those being candidates, and two candidates became finalists. Jane Roberts is the number one finalist, and the one to whom Arlan has decided to extend the offer. Jane is excited about the job and told Arlan she will accept an offer if the terms are right. Arlan is quite certain Jane will get a counteroffer to his offer from her company. Jane has excellent supervisory experience in fast-food stores and a light manufacturing plant. She is willing to relocate, a move of about 45 miles. She will not be able to start for 45 days, due to preparing for the move and the need to give adequate notice to her present employer. As a single parent, Jane wants to avoid work on either Saturday or Sunday each week. The number two finalist is Betts Cook. Though she lacks the supervisory experience that Jane has, Arlan views her as superior to Jane in customer service skills. Jane has told Arlan she needs to know quickly if she is going to get the offer, since she is in line for a promotion at her current company and she wants to begin at 3Cs before being offered and accepting the promotion.

Arlan is mulling over what kind of an offer to make to Jane. His three managers make between $28,000 and $35,000, with annual raises based on a merit review conducted by Arlan. The managers receive one week's vacation the first year, two weeks of vacation for the next four years, and three weeks of vacation after that. They also receive health insurance (with a 20% employee co-pay on the premium). The managers work five days each week, with work on both Saturday and Sunday frequently occurring during peak times. Jane currently makes $31,500, receives health insurance with no employee co-pay, and one week's vacation (she is due to receive two weeks shortly, after completing her second year with the company). She works Monday through Friday, with occasional work on the weekends. Betts earns $34,500, receives health insurance fully paid by her employer, and has one week of vacation (she is eligible for two weeks in another year). Weekend work, if not constant, is acceptable to her.

Arlan is seeking input from you on how to proceed. Specifically, he wants you to:

1. Recommend whether Jane should receive a best-shot, competitive, or low-ball offer, and why.
2. Recommend other inducements beyond salary, health insurance, vacation, and hours schedule that might be addressed in the job offer, and why.
3. Draft a proposed job offer letter to Jane, incorporating your recommendations in points (1) and (2) above, as well as other desired features that should be part of a job offer letter.

Evaluating a Hiring and Variable Pay Plan

Effective Management Solutions (EMS) is a small, rapidly growing management consulting company. EMS has divided its practice into four areas: management systems, business process improvement, human resources, and quality improvement. Strategically, EMS has embarked on an aggressive revenue growth plan, seeking a 25% revenue increase in each of the next five years for each of the four practice areas. A key component of its plan involves staffing growth, since most of EMSs current entry-level consultants (associates) are at peak client loads and cannot take on additional clients; the associates are also at peak hours load, working an average of 2,500 billable hours per year.

Staffing strategy and planning have resulted in the following information and projections. Each practice area currently has 25 associates, the entry-level position and title. Each year, on average, each practice area has five associates promoted to senior associate within the area (there are no promotions or transfers across areas, due to differing KSAO requirements across the areas), and five associates leave EMS, mostly to go to other consulting firms. Replacement staffing thus averages 10 new associates in each practice area, for a total of 40 per year. To meet the revenue growth goals, each practice area will need to hire 15 new associates each year, or a total of 60. A total of 100 associate new hires will thus be needed each year (40 for replacement and 60 for growth).

Currently, EMS provides each job offer receiver a generous benefits package plus what it deems to be a "competitive" salary that is nonnegotiable. About 50% of such offers are accepted. Most of those who reject the offer are the highest-quality applicants; they take jobs in larger, more established consulting firms that provide somewhat below market salaries but high upside monetary potential through various short-term variable pay programs, plus rapid promotions.

Faced with these realities and projections, EMS recognizes that its current job offer practices need to be revamped. Accordingly, it has asked Manuel Rodriquez, who functions as a one-person HR "department" for EMS, to develop a job offer proposal for the EMS partners to consider at their next meeting. The partners tell Rodriquez they want a plan that will increase the job offer acceptance rate, slow down the outflow of associates to other firms, and not create dissatisfaction problems among the currently employed associates.

In response, Rodriquez developed the proposed Hiring and Variable Pay (HVP) program. It has as its cornerstone varying monetary risk/reward packages through a combination of base and short-term variable (bonus) pay plans. The specifics of the HVP program are as follows:

- The offer receiver must choose one of three plans to be under, prior to receiving a formal job offer. The plans are the high-risk, standard, and low-risk plans.
- The high-risk plan provides a starting salary from 10–30% below the market average and participation in the annual bonus plan with a bonus range from 0–60% of current salary.
- The standard plan provides a starting salary of ±10% of the market average and participation in the annual bonus plan with a bonus range from 0–20% of current salary.
- The low-risk plan provides a starting salary that is 5% above the market average and no participation in the annual bonus plan.
- The average market rate will be determined by salary survey data obtained by HR.
- The individual bonus amount will be determined by individual performance on three indicators: number of billable hours, number of new clients generated, and client satisfaction survey results.
- The hiring manager will negotiate starting salary for those in the high-risk and standard plans, based on likely person/job and person/organization fit and on need to fill the position.
- The hiring manager may also offer a "hot skills" premium of up to 10% of initial starting salary under all three plans—the premium will lapse after two years.
- Switching between the three plans is only permitted once every two years.

- Current associates may remain in their current plan or opt into one of the new plans at their current salary.

Evaluate the HVP program as proposed, answering the following questions:

1. If you were an applicant, would the HVP program be attractive to you? Why or why not? If you were going to be an offer receiver, which of the three plans would you choose and why?
2. Will the HVP program likely increase the job offer acceptance rate? Why or why not?
3. Will the HVP program likely reduce turnover? Why or why not?
4. How will current associates react to the HVP program, and why?
5. What issues and problems will the HVP plan create for HR? For the hiring manager?
6. What changes would you make in the HVP program, and why?

ENDNOTES

1. M. W. Bennett, D. J. Polden, and H. J. Rubin, *Employment Relationships: Law and Practice* (New York: Aspen, 2001), pp. 3-3 to 3-4, A. G. Feliu, *Primer on Individual Employee Rights*, second ed. (Washington, DC: Bureau of National Affairs, 1996), pp. 7–29; G. P. Panaro, *Employment Law Manual* (Boston, MA: Warren, Gorham and Lamont, 1993), pp. 4-2 to 4-4.

2. G. C. Pierson, "Independent Contractor v. Employees: Guess Who's Coming to Work," *SHRM Legal Report,* Summer 1993, pp. 1–4.

3. G. P. Panaro, *Employment Law Manual,* pp. 4-61 to 4-63.

4. G. P. Panaro, *Employment Law Manual,* pp. 4-5 to 4-60; M. W. Bennett, D. J. Polden, and H. J. Rubin, *Employment Relationships: Law and Practice,* pp. 3-22 to 3-23.

5. G. P. Panaro, *Employment Law Manual,* pp. 4-18 to 4-19.

6. C. J. Bakaly Jr. and J. M. Grossman, *The Modern Law of Employment Relationships* (Englewood Cliffs, NJ: Prentice-Hall, 1992), pp. 61–74; A. G. Feliu, *Primer on Individual Employee Rights,* pp. 23–25; G. P. Panaro, *Employment Law Manual,* pp. 4-30 to 4-31.

7. A. G. Feliu, *Primer on Individual Employee Rights,* pp. 26–28.

8. A. G. Feliu, *Primer on Individual Employee Rights,* pp. 48–51.

9. A. G. Feliu, *Primer on Individual Employee Rights,* pp. 22–25; M. W. Bennett, D. J. Polden, and H. J. Rubin, *Employment Relationships: Law and Practice,* pp. 3-30 to 3-32.

10. A. G. Feliu, *Primer on Individual Employee Rights,* p. 24.

11. A. G. Feliu, *Primer on Individual Employee Rights,* p. 26.

12. G. P. Panaro, *Employment Law Manual,* pp. 4-66 to 4-136.

13. A. G. Feliu, *Primer on Individual Employee Rights,* pp. 15–18.

14. A. G. Feliu, *Primer on Individual Employee Rights,* pp. 39–50; M. W. Bennett, D. J. Polden, and H. J. Rubin, *Employment Relationships: Law and Practice,* pp. 3-24 to 3-34.

15. J. A. Segal, "An Offer They Couldn't Refuse," *HR Magazine,* April 2001, pp. 131–144.

16. S. L. Rynes and A. E. Barber, "Applicant Attraction Strategies: An Organizational Perspective," *Academy of Management Review,* 1990, 15, pp. 286–310.

17. A. W. Matthews, "Wanted: 400,000 Long Distance Truck Drivers," *Wall Street Journal,* Sept. 11, 1997, p. B1; R. Romell, "Truckers in the Driver's Seat," *Milwaukee Journal Sentinel,* Nov. 30, 1997, p. 1D.

18. M. W. Bennett, D. J. Polden, and H. J. Rubin, *Employment Relationships: Law and Practice,* pp. 2-1 to 2-49.

19. D. S. Fortney and B. Nuterangelo, "Written Employment Contracts: When?, How?, Why?," *Legal Report,* Society for Human Resource Management, Spring 1998, pp. 5–8.

20. D. M. Cable and T. A. Judge, "Pay Preferences and Job Search Decisions: A Person–Organization Fit Perspective," *Personnel Psychology,* 1994, 47, pp. 317–348.

21. P. D. Gardner, *Recruiting Trends 2000–2001* (East Lansing, MI: Michigan State University Student Services, 2000).

22. S. Nasar, "A Top MBA Is a Hot Ticket as Pay Climbs," *New York Times,* Aug. 2, 1998, p. B1; E. Price, "Paying for Bilingual Skills: Job Requirement or Added Value?" *International Personnel Management Association News,* Feb. 1997, p. 10.

23. Y. J. Dreazen, "When #$% + ! Recruits Earn More," *Wall Street Journal,* July 25, 2000, p. B1; K. J. Dunham, "Back to Reality," *Wall Street Journal,* April 12, 2001, p. R5; E. R. Silverman, "Great Expectations," *Wall Street Journal,* July 25, 2000, p. B10; M. Gasser, N. Flint, and R. Tan, "Reward Expectations: The Influence of Race, Gender, and Type of Job," *Journal of Business and Psychology,* 2000, 15, pp. 321–329.

24. Society for Human Resource Management, *Strategic Compensation Survey* (Alexandria, VA: author, 2000), pp. 35–47.

25. Society for Human Resource Management, *Strategic Compensation Survey,* pp. 48–57; M. A. Jacobs, "The Legal Option," *Wall Street Journal,* April 12, 2001, p. R9.

26. W. Power and M. Siconolfi, "Wall Street Sours on Up-Front Bonuses," *Wall Street Journal,* June 13, 1991, p. C1.

27. P. Gardner, *Recruiting Trends 2000–2001.*

28. J. S. Lublin, "Now Butchers, Engineers Get Signing Bonuses," *Wall Street Journal,* June 2, 1997, p. B1.

29. J. R. Bratkovich and J. Ragusa, "The Perils of the Signing Bonus," *Employment Management Today,* Spring 1998, pp. 22–25.

30. J. S. Lublin, "The Going Rate," *Wall Street Journal,* Jan. 11, 2000, p. B14.

31. J. S. Lublin, "As More Men Become 'Trailing Spouses,' Firms Help Them Cope," *Wall Street Journal,* April 13, 1993, p. A1.

32. L. Rivenbark, "Short Term Pay Hikes Can Last Indefinitely," *HR News,* July 2000, p. 16.

33. J. S. Lublin, "You Should Negotiate a Severance Package—Even Before the Job Starts," *Wall Street Journal,* May 1, 2001, p. B1.

34. T. D. Egler, "A Manager's Guide to Employment Contracts," *HR Magazine,* May 1996, pp. 28–33; J. J. Meyers, D. V. Radack, and P. M. Yenerall, "Making the Most of Employment Contracts," *HR Magazine,* Aug. 1998, pp. 106–109; D. R. Sandler, "Noncompete Agreements," *Employment Management Today,* Fall 1997, pp. 14–19; S. G. Willis, "Protect Your Firm Against Former Employees' Actions," *HR Magazine,* Aug. 1997, pp. 117–122.

35. J. D. Wetchler, "Agreements to Arbitrate," *HR Magazine,* Aug. 2001, pp. 127–134; G. Flynn, "High Court Weighs in on Arbitration," *Workforce,* June 2001, pp. 100–101.

36. S. J. Marks, "Can the Internet Help You Hit the Salary Mark?," *Workforce,* Jan. 2001, pp. 86–93; A. S. Wellner, "Salaries in Site," *HR Magazine,* May 2001, pp. 89–96.

37. J. A. Lopez, "The Big Lie," *Wall Street Journal,* April 21, 1993, pp. R6–R8.

38. U.S. Government Accounting Office, "Survey of Applicants Who Accepted or Declined Federal Job Offers" (Washington, DC: author, 1992, B-243207).

39. M. Loeb, "The Smart Way to Change Jobs," *Fortune,* Sept. 4, 1995, p. 139; G. McWilliams, "To Have and to Hold," *Business Week,* June 19, 1995, p. 43; B. Kelley, "Is Your Counter Productive?," *Human Resource Executive,* April 1995, pp. 57–61.

40. R. Goddard, J. Fox, and W. E. Patton, "The Job-Hire Sale," *The Personnel Administrator,* 1989, 34(6), pp. 119–122.

41. J. P. Wanous, *Organizational Entry,* second ed. (Reading, MA: Addison-Wesley, 1992), pp. 155–234.

42. Bureau of National Affairs, "Induction and Orientation," in *Personnel Management* (Washington, DC: author, periodically updated), pp. 201:401–428.

43. C. S. Klein and J. Taylor, "Employee Orientation Is an Ongoing Process at the DuPont Merck Pharmaceutical Company," *Personnel Journal,* 1994, 73(5), p. 67.

44. C. L. Adkins, "Previous Work Experience and Organizational Socialization: A Longitudinal Examination," *Academy of Management Journal,* 1995, 38, pp. 839–862.

45. G. T. Chao, A. M. O'Leary-Kelly, S. Wolf, H. J. Klein, and P. D. Gardner, "Organizational Socialization: Its Content and Consequences," *Journal of Applied Psychology,* 1994, 79, pp. 730–743.

46. Bureau of National Affairs, *Fair Employment Practices Manual* (Washington, DC: author, periodically updated), pp. 403:5937–5941, 6169–6191.

47. G. P. Panaro, *Employment Law Manual,* pp. 1-48 to 1-54.

48. A. G. Feliu, *Primer on Individual Employee Rights,* pp. 283–285; R. M. Green and R. J. Reibstein, *Employers Guide to Workplace Torts* (Washington, DC: Bureau of National Affairs, 1992), pp. 1–18, 198–200, 245–250; A. M. Ryan and M. Lasek, "Negligent Hiring and Defamation: Areas of Liability Related to Preemployment Inquiries," *Personnel Psychology,* 1991, 44, pp. 293–319; W. J. Woska, "Negligent Employment Practices," *Labor Law Journal,* 1991, pp. 603–610.

49. M. Moss, "Many Elders Receive Care at Criminals' Hands," *Wall Street Journal,* March 18, 1998, p. B1.

50. Bureau of National Affairs, "Recruiting Exposure to Negligent Hiring Suits Requires Preventive Action, Practitioner Says," *Daily Labor Report,* June 18, 1998, p. C1.

51. N. K. Kubasek and M. Neil Browne, "Recruiter Beware: The Oral Promise of Lifetime Employment May Be More Than a Mere Inducement," *Labor Law Journal,* 1991, pp. 273–285; B. B. Dunford and D. J. Devine, "Employment-at-Will and Employee Discharge: A Justice Perspective on Legal Action Following Termination," *Personnel Psychology,* 1998, 51, pp. 903–934.

The Staffing Organizations Model

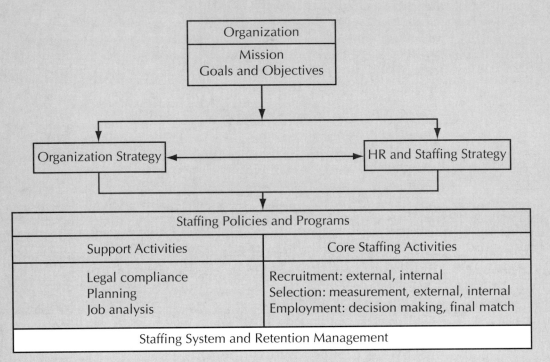

PART SIX

Staffing System and Retention Management

CHAPTER THIRTEEN

Staffing System Management

Administration of Staffing Systems
Organizational Arrangements
Jobs in Staffing
Policies and Procedures
Information Systems
Outsourcing

Evaluation of Staffing Systems
Staffing Validity
Staffing Process Standardization
Staffing Process Results
Staffing Costs
Customer Satisfaction

Legal Issues
Records and Reports
Audits
Managing Legal Compliance

Summary

Discussion Questions

Applications

S taffing systems involve complex processes and decisions that require organizational direction, coordination, and evaluation. Most organizations must create mechanisms for managing their staffing system and its components. Such management of staffing systems requires consideration of both administration and evaluation, as well as legal issues.

Regarding administration, this chapter shows how the staffing (employment) function is one of the key areas within the HR department. It provides illustrations of typical organizational arrangements for the staffing function. Various jobs held by people in the staffing function are also described. The role and nature of staffing policies and procedures in administering the staffing function is explained, as is the use of HR information systems to enhance efficient operation of staffing systems. Finally, outsourcing specific staffing activities to other organizations is described as a way of streamlining the staffing function.

Presented next is a discussion of ways to evaluate the effectiveness of the staffing function. This begins by emphasizing the importance of validity of selection procedures and the need to conduct validation studies of them. Then, evaluation of how standardized the staffing process is and various results of the staffing process are described as additional ways to gauge the effectiveness of staffing systems. Compilation and analysis of staffing system costs are also suggested as an evaluation technique. Last, assessment of customer (hiring managers, applicants) satisfaction is presented as a new, innovative approach to the evaluation of staffing systems.

Legal issues, as always, surround the management of staffing systems. Partly, this involves matters of compiling various records and reports and of conducting legal audits of staffing activities. Increasingly, however, legal issues are raising the need for the development of more formal mechanisms for managing the totality of legal compliance. The chapter concludes with a discussion of all of these issues.

ADMINISTRATION OF STAFFING SYSTEMS

Organizational Arrangements

Staffing activities are usually placed and conducted within a separate unit or functional area of the organization's HR department. An example of this organizational arrangement for a multiplant manufacturing organization is shown in Exhibit 13.1. At the corporate level, the HR department is headed by the vice president (VP) of Human Resources. Reporting to the VP are directors of Employment and EEO/ AA, Compensation and Benefits, Training and Development, Labor Relations, and HR Information Systems. These directors, along with the vice president, formulate and coordinate HR strategy and policy, as well as manage their own functional units.

EXHIBIT 13.1   Example of HR Department and Employment (Staffing) Function

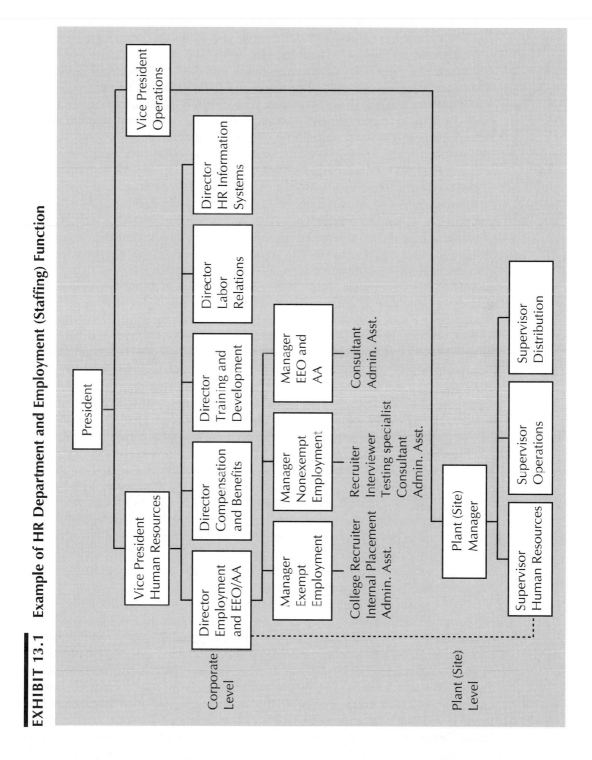

The director of Employment and EEO/AA has three direct reports: the managers of exempt, nonexempt, and EEO/AA employment areas. Each manager, in turn, is responsible for the supervision of specialists and assistants. The manager of exempt employment, for example, handles external and internal staffing for managerial and professional jobs. There are two specialists in this unit, college recruiter and internal placement specialist, plus an administrative assistant. The manager of nonexempt employment is responsible for external and internal staffing for hourly paid employees. Reporting to this manager are four specialists (recruiter, interviewer, testing specialist, and consultant) plus two administrative assistants. The EEO/AA manager has a consultant plus an administrative assistant as direct reports. The consultants are individuals who serve in liaison roles with the line managers of units throughout the organization when hiring is occurring. Functioning as internal customer service representatives to these managers, the consultants help the managers understand corporate employment policies and procedures, determine specific staffing needs, handle special staffing problems and requests, and answer questions.

At the plant level, there is a single HR supervisor, plus an administrative assistant, who perform all HR activities, including staffing. This HR supervisor is a true generalist and works closely with the plant manager on all issues involving people concerns. Regarding staffing, the dotted line shows that the HR supervisor has an indirect reporting relationship to the director of Employment and EEO/AA (as well as the other corporate-level HR directors, not shown). Very important, these directors will work with the HR supervisor to develop policies and programs (including staffing) that are consistent with corporate strategy while also tailor-made to the particular needs and workforce of the plant.

The above example shows staffing to be a critical area within the HR department, and research confirms this importance. For example, a survey of 628 organizations found that "employment and recruitment are considered core HR department functions by most organizations, with virtually all responding companies assigning sole or partial responsibility for these activities to human resources." Moreover, the staffing function typically receives a greater percentage of the total HR department budget than any other function, averaging about 20% of the total budget. Salaries for people in the staffing function are comparable to those in the other HR functions. Increasingly, employees in all HR areas are becoming eligible for short-term incentives and bonuses.[1]

Those employed within the staffing function must work closely with members of all the other functional HR areas. For example, staffing members must coordinate their activities with the compensation and benefits staff in developing policies on the economic components of job offers, such as starting pay, hiring bonuses, and special perks. Staffing activities must also be closely coordinated with the training and development function. This will be needed to identify training needs for external, entry-level new hires, as well as for planning transfer and promotion-enhancing training experiences for current employees. The director of Labor Relations will work with the staffing area to determine labor contract language pertaining to staffing issues (e.g., promotions and transfers) and to help resolve grievances over staffing procedures and decisions. Record keeping, staffing software, and EEO/AA statistics requirements will be worked out with the director of HR Information Systems.

It should also be noted that although staffing activities are concentrated within the HR department, members of any specific organizational unit for which staffing is occurring will (and should) also play a role in the overall staffing process. The unit manager will submit the hiring authorization request, work closely with HR in developing KSAOs required/preferred for the vacant position, and actively participate in making discretionary assessments and job offers. Other members of the unit may provide input to the unit manager on KSAOs sought, formally meet and interact with candidates for recruiting and attracting purposes, and provide inputs to the unit manager on their preferences about who should receive the job offer. In team-based work units, team members may play an even more active role in all phases of the staffing process.[2] Each organization needs to work out for itself the organizational arrangements for staffing that best fit its own staffing strategy and preferences of organizational members.

Jobs in Staffing

Jobs in staffing are quite varied. In the private sector, most are housed within the HR department (corporate and plant or office site level). In the public sector, they are found within the central personnel or HR office, as well as in various specified agencies, such as transportation or human services.

The types and scope of tasks and responsibilities in staffing jobs is also varied. Some jobs are specialist ones, involving a functional specialty such as interviewing, recruiting, or college relations. These are often entry-level jobs as well. Other jobs may have a more generalist flavor to them, particularly in smaller organizations or smaller units (plant or office) of a larger organization. In such units, one person may handle all staffing-related activities. At higher organizational levels, both specialist and generalist jobs are found. Examples of specialist positions include test development and validation, executive assessment, and affirmative action. Generalists usually have broader managerial responsibilities that cut across specialties; the job of staffing manager is one example.

Exhibit 13.2 provides job descriptions for two staffing jobs—Junior Recruiter/ HR Generalist, and Corporate Manager of Staffing (Western Region)—at Science Applications International Corporation (SAIC), taken from the SAIC Website (*www.saic.com*). The first job is an entry-level staffing job and the second is a generalist, corporate-level, staffing job. The SAIC is a Fortune 500, employee-owned research and engineering organization with offices in over 150 cities worldwide.

Entry into staffing jobs normally occurs at the specialist rank in the areas of recruiting and interviewing, in both private and public organizations. Staffing of these jobs may come from the new hire ranks of the organization. It may also come from an internal transfer from a management training program, from a line management job, or from another HR function. In short, there is no fixed point or method of entry into staffing jobs.

Mobility within staffing jobs may involve both traditional and nontraditional career tracks. In a traditional track, the normal progression is from entry-level specialist up through the ranks to staffing manager, with assignments at both the

---

EXHIBIT 13.2   Staffing Jobs at Science Applications International Corporation

A. Junior Recruiter/HR Generalist

Job Description:
Performs technical and administrative recruiting for the Pacific Programs Division. Recruits for several different locations throughout the Pacific to include Hawaii, Alaska, Guam, California, Korea, and Japan. Responsibilities include job requisition tracking, job posting and ad placement, pre-screening candidates, coordinating with hiring manager on scheduling and conducting interviews and conducting reference checks. Secondary responsibility includes performing HR Generalist job duties which may include benefits, compensation and employee relations.

Education:
Bachelor's degree preferred.

Required Skills:
One to three years of recruiting experience. Ability to establish effective working relationships with peers, applicants and hiring managers. Must project a positive professional image through written and verbal communication and must be able to work independently with minimal supervision. Must be proficient in MS Office (Word, Excel, Power Point). Some travel may be required.

Desired Skills:
Recruiting for technical positions to include systems engineers, software engineers and systems administrators. Experience working with Resumix or other automated recruitment and staffing tools.

Job Category:	Human Resources	**Ref. No:**
Location:	Honolulu, Hawaii US	
Contact:		

Part Time or Temporary: Full-time (1st shift)

Must be able to obtain clearance level: Secret

SAIC is an Equal Opportunity/Affirmative Action Employer

Source: Science Applications International Corporation. Used with permission.

EXHIBIT 13.2   Continued

B. Corporate Manager of Staffing—Western Region (San Diego Based)

Job Description:
The incumbent provides strategic staffing support to HR managers, recruiters and general-ists within SAIC Western Region. Analyzes, develops, implements and evaluates the effec-tiveness of employment process addressing the business needs of Sectors and Groups within the Western Region, while meeting legal and corporate compliance requirements. Coordinates College Relations and College Recruitment activities, including advertising strategies, within the Region. Develops and coordinates Regional print and Internet adver-tising strategies, diversity and professional recruiting processes, employee referral programs, student internships and the collection of employment metrics. Develops and implements tools and processes to improve ROI [Return on Investment] by optimizing recruiting strate-gies. Will be required to travel to meet business needs supporting any incumbent captures, acquisitions, outsourcing, and other engagements with critical hiring needs. The incumbent will have a dual reporting relationship to the Corporate Staffing Director and Director of HR, Western Region. Directly supervises regional service center recruiting and administra-tive staff. In addition, responsible for ensuring all recruiters receive timely training and re-fresher courses for Applicant Tracking Information System (e.g., Resumix) operations. Will develop and lead a team of superusers, providing user support and development, upgrade, implementation requirements, and some vendor relations.

Education:
BA/BS in a relevant field plus a minimum of 10 years of experience, with a minimum of 3 years in a supervisory capacity required. Masters degree in HR or a related area is desir-able.

Required Skills:
Must have supervisory experience leading a successful high volume recruiting team in a tight labor market. Experience with electronic applicant tracking systems required, Resumix preferred. Must be well organized with excellent interpersonal skills. Must be a team player with outstanding persuasive, negotiation, and motivational skills. Must possess the ability to manage a team and achieve results through influence, without the benefit of direct man-agement authority. Must possess the proven ability to facilitate the exchange of information through leadership of meetings, and in the development and delivery of effective training and information sessions. Must be knowledgeable of EEO, labor laws and immigration compliance practices.

Desired Skills:
Prefer experience with managing IT industry high volume recruiting programs.

Job Category: Human Resources   **Ref. No:**
Location: San Diego, California US
Contact:

Part Time or Temporary: Full-time (1st shift)

SAIC is an Equal Opportunity/Affirmative Action Employer

Source: Science Applications International Corporation. Used with permission.

corporate and operating unit level. A nontraditional track might involve entry into a staffing specialist job, lateral transfer after a year to another functional HR area, rotation from there into an entry-level supervisory position, advancement within the supervisory ranks, and then promotion to the job of staffing manager. In short, there is often no established upward mobility track. One should expect the un-expected.

If a person advances beyond or outside of the staffing function, this will usually serve the person well for advancement to the highest HR levels (director or vice president). At these levels, job occupants have typically held varied assignments, including working outside HR in managerial or professional capacities. Interest-ingly, though, a majority of high-level HR executives have experience as a spe-cialist, and employment and recruiting is the most frequent specialty experience, followed by compensation and labor relations.[3]

It should be noted that jobs in staffing (and other areas of HR) are becoming increasingly more customer focused and facilitative in nature. As staffing activities become more decentralized and subject to line management control, holders of staffing jobs will exist to provide requested services and act as consultants to the service requesters. This will be a challenge because many of those newly respon-sible for staffing (line managers and team leaders) will be untrained and inexpe-rienced in staffing matters.

Increasing numbers of staffing jobs are found in staffing firms. One such firm is Staffmark, a large, diversified staffing firm with offices nationwide (*www.Staffmark.com*). Services offered by Staffmark include supplemental staffing (short- and long-term), supplemental to direct staffing, direct hire, executive search, on-site managed programs, national multisite workforce management, and training programs. Exhibit 13.3 provides a job description for the entry-level job of Staffing Specialist for Staffmark. More advanced jobs include Senior Staff-ing Specialist, Direct Hire Recruiter, On-Site Staffing Supervisor, and Staffing Manager. Individuals in on-site staffing roles work directly with the client's HR department to conduct all phases of staffing. Use of such specialists occurs when the client lacks staffing expertise or is seeking to hire large numbers of new employees quickly.[4]

Another new type of staffing job is that of Chief Talent Officer or Vice President for Talent Acquisition. Organizations that are critically dependent on talent, such as technology and entertainment ones, and that need to conduct specialized talent searches outside the mainstream of the normal staffing processes, are creating such positions. One organization, America Online, went even further and created a special talent acquisition department with 35 people who conduct both external and internal searches. It is suggested that such individuals have a background in recruiting, understand accountability in organizations, possess some marketing experience to help sell the organization and build relationships, and can draw on an ability to think "out of the box" and devise a strategic vision for recruits and their roles within the organization.[5]

EXHIBIT 13.3 **Staffing Job at Staffwork**

Job Title: Staffing Specialist

Job Summary:

This position is responsible for taking complete and accurate job orders and identifying and placing temporary associates on temporary assignments or direct placement with client companies according to specified job orders and requirements and identifying business development opportunities through penetration of existing accounts.

Essential Duties and Responsibilities:

1. Carries out such functions as identifying qualified applicants, conducting screening interviews, administering tests, checking references, and evaluating applicant qualifications.
2. Hires qualified temporary associates and establishes appropriate pay rates for temporary associates based on skills, abilities, and experience.
3. Makes job offer to associate explaining full job description, term of assignment, pay rate, benefits.
4. Obtains complete and accurate information from clients placing job orders and matches best temporary associate to the client job order. May quote and explain base rates to client.
5. Determines appropriate client placement of qualified associates (may be through skill marketing) and conducts basic associate orientation.
6. Monitors associate activity at client, e.g. track attendance, performance, etc.
7. Maintains current, accurate data in the computer of client activity and associate inventory.
8. Conducts regular service calls (retail accounts <$500,000) to assigned clients to ensure quality service, identify any problems, and obtain feedback.
9. Completes quality control procedures including check-in calls and follow-up calls on completed job orders.
10. Completes accurate payroll processing for temporary associates.
11. Follows and communicates all safety rules and regulations as established by Staffmark to associates.
12. Ensures worker's compensation claims are properly filed.
13. Under the supervison of management, will counsel associates and handle conflict resolution.
14. At the direction of Branch Manager, will record drug testing results and follow drug testing policy.
15. Performs telephone marketing and recruiting in order to identify suitable temporary associates for current and prospective clients.
16. Represents the company in a professional manner at various professional, academic, and/or civic activities as requested.

Other Duties and Responsibilites:

1. Occasionally, may be given responsibility for handling worker's compensation or unemployment compensation hearings.
2. Needs to be available for on-call duty after hours and on weekends.
3. May require shift work.

Note: Additional responsibilities not listed here may be assigned at times.

(continued)

EXHIBIT 13.3   Continued

Supervisory Responsibilities:
Supervises temporary associates including monitoring extension or completion of assignments, addressing problems or concerns of temporary associates, coaching, counseling, and taking corrective action with temporary associates. Terminates temporary associates when appropriate. Does not have responsibility for supervising internal Staffmark employees.

Required Competencies:
Utilizes independent judgment and exhibits sound reasoning.
Has a working knowledge of Staffmark's unemployment compensation and worker's compensation filing process.

Required Qualifications: To perform this job successfully, an individual must be able to perform each essential duty satisfactorily. The requirements listed below are representative of the knowledge, skill, and/or ability required. Reasonable accommodations may be made to enable individuals with disabilities to perform the essential functions.

Education and/or Experience:
High school diploma or general education degree (GED); or one to three months' related experience and/or training; or equivalent combination of education and experience.

Language Skills:
Ability to read and interpret documents such as safety rules, operating and maintenance instructions, and procedure manuals. Ability to write routine reports and correspondence. Ability to speak effectively before groups of customers or employees of organization.

Mathematical Skills:
Ability to add, subtract, multiply, and divide in all units of measure, using whole numbers, common fractions, and decimals. Ability to compute rate, ratio, and percent and to draw and interpret bar graphs.

Reasoning Ability:
Ability to apply common sense understanding to carry out detailed but uninvolved written or oral instructions. Ability to deal with problems involving a few concrete variables in standardized situations.

Computer Skills:
Microsoft Word, Microsoft Outlook, Caldwell, Excel, Powerpoint, and Internet.

Certificates, Licenses, Registrations:
Must have current, valid driver's license. Position requires travel to and from client companies and civic events.

Physical Demands: The physical demands described here are representative of those that must be met by an employee to successfully perform the essential functions of this job. Reasonable accommodations may be made to enable individuals with disabilities to perform the essential functions.

While performing the duties of this job, the employee is regularly required to sit; use hands to finger, handle, or feel; and talk or hear. The employee is frequently required to walk and reach with hands and arms. The employee is occasionally required to stand; climb or balance and stoop, kneel, crouch, or crawl. The employee must frequently lift and/or move up

EXHIBIT 13.3   Continued

to 10 pounds and occasionally lift and/or move up to 25 pounds. Specific vision abilities required by this job include close vision, distance vision, color vision, peripheral vision, depth perception and ability to adjust focus.

Work Environment: The work environment characteristics described here are representative of those an employee encounters while performing the essential functions of this job. Reasonable accommodations may be made to enable individuals with disabilities to perform the essential functions. While performing the duties of this job, the employee is occasionally exposed to wet and/or humid conditions; moving mechanical parts; outside weather conditions; extreme cold and extreme heat. The noise level in the work environment is usually moderate. On occasion, duties may require the wearing of proper safety equipment in areas where such equipment is required

Needs to be available for on-call duty after hours and on weekends. May require shift work.

Source: Staffmark. Used with permission.

Policies and Procedures

It is highly desirable to have written policies and procedures to guide the administration of staffing systems. Understanding the importance of policies and procedures first requires definition of these terms.

A policy is a selected course or guiding principle. It is an objective to be sought through appropriate actions. For example, the organization might have a promotion from-within policy as follows: It is the intent of XXX organization to fill from within all vacancies above the entry level, except in instances of critical, immediate need for a qualified person unavailable internally. This policy makes it clear that promotion from within is the desired objective; the only exception is the absence of an immediately available qualified current employee.

A procedure is a prescribed routine or way of acting in similar situations. It provides the rules that are to govern a particular course of action. To carry out the promotion-from-within policy, for example, the organization may have specific procedures to be followed for listing and communicating the vacancy, identifying eligible applicants, and assessing the qualifications of the applicants.

Policies and procedures thus indicate desirable courses of action and the steps to be taken to carry out the action. Without staffing policies and procedures, staffing becomes an ad hoc, casual, whimsical process. Such a process is fraught with possibilities of hurried and catch-up recruiting, nonstandardized and nonvalid assessments of applicants, decision making based on non–job-related qualification considerations, such as personal or political preferences, and job offers that exceed allowable limits on salary (and other terms) and create internal equity problems between the new hires and job incumbents. Lack of policies and procedures may also lead to practices that may foster negative applicant reactions, as well as run afoul of applicable laws and regulations.

The scope of staffing actions and practices is large, ranging across a broad spectrum of recruitment, selection, and employment issues, both external and internal. Consequently, the organization's staffing policies and procedures also need to be broad in scope. To illustrate this, Exhibit 13.4 provides an overview of the content of CompuServe's staffing policies. The total statement of these policies, and accompanying procedures, consumes more than 20 pages in CompuServe's policies and procedures manual.

EXHIBIT 13.4   Staffing Topics in CompuServe's HR Policy Manual

Affirmative Action
Affirmative Action Plan
Americans With Disabilities Act
Associate Status
    Exempt/Nonexempt
    Full-time/Part-time
    Independent Contractor
    Internship
    Temporary Agencies
Balanced Workforce
Charges of Discrimination
Confidential Information
Diversity
Employment Agencies
Employment-at-Will
Equal Employment and Affirmative
    Action
Essential Functions of the Job
External Recruiting
Flextime
Immigration
Internal Moves
Internal Recruiting
Interviews
Job Descriptions
Job Posting
Letter of Recommendation
Offers of Employment
Outreach Programs: EEO/AA

Performance Reviews
Personnel Records and Files
Procedures
    Internal Moves
    Job Descriptions
    Promotion
    Recruiting and Selecting
    Transfer
Promotion
Reasonable Accommodation
Recruiting and Selecting
    Associate Referrals
    Classified Advertising
    Employment Agencies
    Former Associates
    Interviews
    Relatives
    Screening
    Targeted Selection
    Testing
Reference Checks
Release of Information: Personnel Files
Relocation
Right to Privacy
Secondary Job
Selection of Candidates
Temporary Agencies
Testing
Valuing Diversity
Visa Status

Source: Compliments of CompuServe, Columbus, OH. Used with permission.

Information Systems

Staffing activities generate and use considerable information, often in paper form. Job descriptions, application materials, résumés, correspondence, applicant profiles, applicant flow and tracking, and reports are examples of the types of information that are necessary ingredients for the operation of a staffing system. Naturally, problems regarding what types of information to generate, and how to file, access, and use it, will arise when managing a staffing system. Addressing and solving these problems have important implications for paperwork burdens, administrative processing costs, and speed in filling job vacancies. Thus, management of a staffing system involves management of an information system.

For many organizations, the information system will continue to be a primarily paper-based and manual system. This will most likely occur in smaller organizations, single-site organizations, and organizations where there is a limited amount of staffing activity (few vacancies to fill) in a given time period. For such systems, a careful scrutiny should be done to determine if they are requiring excessive and duplicative paper documents, as well as unnecessary files and logs.

As organizations increase in size, complexity (e.g., multiple sites), and level of staffing activity, the paperwork, paper flows, and manual handling become expensive and burdensome. Moreover, the number of individuals needed to operate the staffing system and its paper become excessive. These problems cause the organization to seek staffing system efficiencies through improvements in its information systems.

The primary improvements come about through a combination of conversion to electronic information and automation of staffing tasks and processes. A central feature is the creation of electronic databases of applicant and employee information. Computer systems (PC and/or mainframe) will also be needed to provide data entry, access, and manipulation. Also, relevant software will need to be developed or purchased commercially through vendors. These information system requirements naturally mean that HR information system specialists will need to work closely with members of the staffing function.

Armed with the above ingredients, a myriad of staffing tasks can be performed. A suggestive listing of these tasks is provided in Exhibit 13.5. As can be seen, the tasks run the full gamut of staffing activities.

Scores of vendors and consultants are available to provide hardware, software, and system design and installation services to the organization. One example is HotJobs.com (*www.hotjobs.com*), which provides a range of products and services pertaining to job posting, candidate databases, interface with staffing firms, online advertising, job fairs, and applicant tracking. A key software product of HotJobs.com is its applicant tracking system (on client-server architecture) known as Resumix. With Resumix software, applicant résumés are received via scanning, e-mail, or fax. Key KSAO information is then extracted from the résumé and used to create a résumé summary database, which may be accessed instantly. The ré-

---

EXHIBIT 13.5   **Computerized Staffing Tasks**

- Forecasting workforce supply and demand
- Employee succession planning
- Applicant/employee KSAO database
- Job requisitions
- Job posting reports
- Applicant logs, status, and tracking reports
- Correspondence with applicants
- New hire reports (numbers, qualifications, assignments)
- Employment activity (vacancies, requisitions, positions filled)
- EEO data analysis and reports (EEO-1 form)
- Person/job matching
- Electronic résumé routing
- Recruitment source effectiveness

sumé summary includes contact information, education data, working history, and up to 80 job skills. A manager with a vacancy to fill can then create an electronic job order that specifies KSAO requirements (both necessary and preferred). The system then automatically conducts searches among the résumé summaries, yielding one or more person/job matches that are rank ordered based on the number of successful matching criteria. Another feature is that a recruiter can look up and identify all currently unfilled job orders, so that a candidate the recruiter is working with can then be matched against all such job orders. Also, as new résumé summaries are entered into the database they are automatically matched against all open job orders and "flagged" for recruiter attention if there is a potential match. Other features of Resumix are generation of standard letters (acknowledgments, interview invitation, etc.), preparation of reports and staffing metrics, shipment of résumés and résumé summaries to interested parties via fax and e-mail, creation of an employment folder that adds documents (e.g., interviewer's notes) to the résumé summary, and operation of a job posting system.

Web-based staffing management systems are also available from application service providers (ASPs). With such systems, the vendor provides both the hardware (e.g., servers, scanners) and the software, as well as day-to-day management of the system. Recruiters and hiring managers access the system through a Web browser. One example of such a system is the Enterprise system from Brass Ring, Inc. (*www.brassring.com*). The system posts job openings to job boards and other Web sites. It accepts all forms of résumés (paper, fax, e-mail, Web-based), scans and codes them, and stores them in a relational database on a secure server. The hiring manager or recruiter can then access the database to submit job requisitions, perform résumé searches based on specified KSAOs, schedule interviews, conduct correspondence with applicants, forward résumés to others, track the search status of current applicants, track current employee KSAOs, and conduct various recruitment reports, such as average cost per hire for each recruitment source used, and EEO compliance. An extension of the Enterprise system is its Talent Gateways software, which focuses on specific applicant sources. These sources include custom career sites, staffing and search firms, campuses, employee referrals, and international candidates. Another popular ASP is Webhire Recruiter (*www.webhire.com*).

Usage of such automated staffing systems is most appropriate for larger organizations, organizations with large applicant pools, and organizations constantly recruiting and filling multiple job openings simultaneously. Also, the organization should be sure it has the internal information system expertise to manage the system and provide training to those who will use it. No specific studies evaluating the effectiveness of these systems have been reported. It is claimed, however, that they reduce paperwork and paper flows, expand the visibility of applicants throughout the organization, streamline the hiring process, and reduce average cost per hire and time to hire.

Outsourcing

Outsourcing refers to contracting out work to a vendor or third-party administrator. Use of staffing firms is a common staffing example of outsourcing. Outsourcing HR functions and services generally is on the rise. A survey of HR departments in 121 organizations of all sizes found that 91% of them outsourced one or more HR functions or tasks, with contracts usually less than $100,000, though some were in excess of $1,000,000.[6] Respondents also indicated they would probably be expanding their use of outsourcing in the future. The following were outsourced, in descending order of frequency: outplacement, training, relocation, salary surveys, preemployment testing, benefits, organizational development, recruitment and staffing, safety and security, and HR information services.

As these data suggest, the HR department and its traditional activities, including staffing, are being selectively parceled out to HR service providers. Why? The above survey found that, in order of decreasing importance, the major reasons were to use the expertise of specialists, save time and money, save administrative costs, and be able to focus more on core HR functions. Thus, the decision to outsource was strategic, driven by not only a search for cost reduction but also flexibility and service quality. Many comments from respondents suggested that HR departments wanted to focus their limited resources on what they do best— their core HR competencies.

Within the staffing domain, another survey has studied the specific staffing tasks that are being outsourced.[7] In addition to seeking temporary employees, other tasks respondents indicated that they outsourced included recruiting for specific vacancies, checking references, relocating new hires, administering skill/aptitude tests, updating affirmative action plans, coordinating job fairs, and maintaining applicant databases.

An emerging type of vendor is the professional employer organization (PEO), formerly referred to as an employee leasing firm. It is similar to a temporary help agency, but differs from it by providing a wider range of HR services and having a long-term commitment to the client. Under a typical arrangement, the client organization enters into a contractual relationship with a PEO to conduct some or all HR activities and functions. The client and the PEO are considered co-employers of record. A PEO is particularly appealing to small employers because it can provide special HR expertise and technical assistance, conduct the administrative activities and transactions of an HR department, provide more affordable employee benefits, meet legal obligations (payroll, withholding, workers compensation, unemployment insurance), and manage legal compliance. PEOs are licensed in many states.[8]

It seems certain that HR outsourcing generally will continue to increase for the strategic and operational reasons noted above—expertise, flexibility, time savings, service quality, reduction of legal liability, and cost reduction. The extent to which staffing outsourcing specifically will likely increase is unknown. One recent study found that the perceived benefits of staffing outsourcing were less than they were for most other HR activities, suggesting that organizations may be reluctant to turn over responsibility for the design and delivery of staffing systems to vendors.[9] Such reluctance is greatest in organizations when the HR function does not have a strong strategic orientation, where there are fairly predictable staffing levels to be managed, and where the HR department provides substantial career advancement opportunities for HR staff members within the department.[10] Moreover, when outsourcing does happen, mistakes and problems can arise. Two common mistakes are losing sight of the desired end result (such as increased hiring speed or lower recruitment costs) for the outsourcing and not preparing for the resistance from HR staff members whose own job requirements and rewards may change as a result of changes in technology and staffing processes that flow from the outsourcing.[11] In short, despite the many appeals of staffing outsourcing, there are limited circumstances in which it should be considered as a viable initiative likely to achieve significant staffing efficiencies and enhanced staffing outcomes.

In making the outsourcing decision, it is critical to become knowledgeable about exactly what services the vendor will provide and the probable quality of those services. As pertains to staffing services, the organization should carefully scrutinize whatever services are being sought within the context of its overall staffing planning process. Beyond that, it will also be necessary to negotiate all details of the contractual agreement, including cost, managing the outsourcing transition, managing the vendor relationship, and monitoring and evaluating vendor performance.[12]

EVALUATION OF STAFFING SYSTEMS

Staffing Validity

The overriding goal of all staffing activities is to achieve effective person/job matches. A major portion of that match is the successful alignment of people's KSAOs with the requirements of the job. Staffing validity is the degree to which selection techniques being used by the organization accurately match people's qualifications to job requirements. Ideally, the organization will conduct validation studies on selection techniques and then use only those techniques with demonstrated validity. Unfortunately, organizational practice falls far short of this ideal.

Research clearly shows that the norm is to not conduct validation studies. For example, in one survey it was found that only 24% of organizations conducted either criterion-related or content validation studies.[13] In another survey it was found that only 10% of organizations conducted validation studies, and only 24% of organizations even thought it was important to do so.[14] Primary reasons given by organizations for not conducting validation studies are lack of familiarity with validation procedures, a belief that validation is not useful, and resource constraints.[15] Regarding usage of valid techniques, research indicates that the most valid techniques are not the most widely used.[16] For example, mental ability tests and biodata are highly valid techniques on average, but their rate of usage is quite low. Alternatively, the typical, unstructured employment interview is of dubious validity but almost universal use. On average, therefore, organizations appear to avoid investigating the validity of selection techniques and to ignore validity evidence when choosing selection techniques for use.

In addition to unawareness of validation concepts and procedures, the presumed excessive cost of validation is also often offered as an explanation for why validation seems to be on a back burner in most organizations. Although sound cost estimates for conducting validation studies are almost nonexistent, their cost may be less than is commonly assumed. One experienced consultant, for example, estimates that the average cost of conducting a job-specific content validation study is $10,000 for a consultant or $2,500 for an internal HR staff member. For a criterion-related validation study, the respective estimates are $20,000 and $5,000. Also, most tests do not need to be revalidated every year since job requirements do not change that much. Test experts indicate that the "shelf life" of a typical validation study is up to five years in length. Thus, the cost of the validation study can be amortized over a number of years, which effectively lowers validation costs.[17]

The tools and techniques for conducting validation studies are well established (Chapter 7), and the costs of doing these studies are usually low enough to be manageable. Any evaluation of a staffing system can and should begin with an assessment of the validity of its selection techniques. Failure to do so means the organization will not know how well it is matching people to jobs, or how it might improve the matching process. Failure to conduct validation also means the organization will lack evidence to support the job relatedness of their staffing systems if those systems' legality are challenged.

Staffing Process Standardization

Standardization refers to the consistency of operation of the organization's staffing system. Use of standardized staffing systems is desirable for several reasons. First, standardization ensures that the same KSAO information is gathered from all job applicants, which, in turn, is a key requirement for reliably and validly measuring these KSAOs. Second, standardization ensures that all applicants receive the same information about job requirements and rewards. Thus, all applicants can make equally informed evaluations of the organization. Third, standardization will enhance applicants' perceptions of the procedural fairness of the staffing system and of the decisions made about them by the organization. Having applicants feel they were treated fairly and got a "fair shake" can reap substantial benefits for the organization. Applicants will speak favorably of their experience and the organization to others, they may seek employment with the organization in the future (even if rejected), they may be more likely to say "yes" to job offers, and they may become organizational newcomers with a very upbeat frame of mind as they begin their new jobs. Finally, standardized staffing systems are less likely to generate legal challenges by job applicants; if they are challenged, they are more likely to successfully withstand the challenge.

Conducting an evaluation of staffing system standardization should proceed along the following lines. First, map out a flowchart of the staffing process used for a particular job or job category (see Chapter 3). Second, develop a list of the set of steps followed and actions taken throughout that process. For example, during recruitment, note such steps and actions as acknowledging receipt of an application, conducting prescreening, providing information to job applicants, and informing applicants of whether they will progress forward in the staffing process. For selection, indicate when the various predictors are used sequentially, what the time limits are for tests or interviews, whether there are scoring keys available for determining applicants' scores on assessment devices, and so forth. For employment activities, take note of how cut scores are set, how accept-reject decisions are made, how job offers and rejections are communicated, and the content of job offers. After these two steps are completed, there will be a detailed specification of the staffing process in flow terms, along with specific actions and events that occur over the course of the process. This represents the staffing process that should be operating for the organization.

Once the staffing process has been mapped out, the next step is to check for deviations from it that have actually occurred. This will require an analysis of some past staffing "transactions" with job applicants, following what was done and what actions were taken as the applicants entered and flowed through the staffing system. All identified deviations should be recorded.

The next step is to analyze all discovered deviations and determine the reason(s) for their occurrence. The final step is to determine and make changes in the staffing system in order to reduce deviations and enhance standardization.

Staffing Process Results

Over the course of the staffing process it is possible to develop quantitative indicators that show how effectively and efficiently the staffing system is operating. For example, how many applicants does a given vacancy attract, on average? Or, what percentage of job offers are accepted? What is the average number of days it takes to fill a vacancy? What percentage of new hires remain with the organization for one year post-hire? Answers to such questions can be determined by a tracking and analysis of applicant flows through the staffing pipeline.

Exhibit 13.6 shows the required layout for this tracking and analysis, as well as some staffing process results that may be easily calculated. In the upper part (A) of the exhibit, the steps in the staffing process start with announcement of a vacancy and run through a sequential flow of selection, job offer, offer acceptance, start as new hire, and retention. Also shown is a timeline, in average number of days, for completion of each step. For illustration purposes, it is assumed there are 25 vacancies that have been filled and that these vacancies attracted 1,000 applicants who then proceeded through the staffing process. Ultimately, all 25 vacancies were filled, and these new hires were then tracked to see how many of them remained with the organization for six months and one year post-hire.

At the bottom (B) of Exhibit 13.6 are staffing process results indicators, also referred to as metrics, along with calculations of them for the example. The first indicator is applicants per vacancy, which averaged 40. This is an indication of the effectiveness of recruitment activities to attract people to the organization. The second indicator is the yield ratio; it indicates the percentage of people who moved on to one or more of the next steps in the staffing process. For example, the percentage of applicants who became candidates is 20%; the percentage of job offers accepted is 83.3%. The third indicator, time lapse (or cycle time), shows the average amount of time lapsed between each step in the staffing process. It can be seen that the average days to fill a vacancy is 44. The final indicator is retention rate; for the new hires it can be seen that the six-month retention rate was 80%, and the one-year rate fell to 52%.

These types of metrics are very useful barometers for gauging the pulse of the staffing flow. They have an objective, "bottom-line" nature that can be readily communicated to managers and others in the organization. These types of data are also very useful for comparative purposes. For example, the relative effectiveness and efficiency of staffing systems in two different units of the organization could be assessed by comparing their respective yield ratios and so forth. Another comparison could be the same staffing system compared to itself over time. Such time-based comparisons are useful for tracking trends in effectiveness and efficiency.

EXHIBIT 13.6 **Evaluation of Staffing Process and Results: Example**

A. Staffing Process Example
No. of vacancies filled = 25

Process step	Vacancy announced (1)	Applicants (2)	Candidates (3)	Finalists (4)	Offer receiver (5)	Offer acceptance (6)	Start as new hire (7)	On the job	
								Six months (8)	One Year (9)
No. of people	0	1,000	200	125	30	25	25	20	13
Process time Avg. no. of days	0	14	21	28	35	42	44		

B. Staffing Process Results

Applicants/Vacancy = 1,000/25 = 40

Yield ratio: candidates/applicant = 20%; new hires/applicant = 2.5%; offers accepted/received = 83.3%

Time Lapse: avg. days to offer = 35; avg. days to start = 44 (cycle time)

Retention rate: $\dfrac{\text{on job six months}}{\text{new hires}}$ = 80% for six months; $\dfrac{\text{on job one year}}{\text{new hires}}$ = 52% for first year

These comparisons are also used to help judge how well changes in staffing practices have actually worked to improve staffing process performance.

For example, Mirage Resorts in Las Vegas was going to conduct a mass, one-time staffing process to hire 9,600 employees for the opening of Bellagio, its new luxury resort. Mirage Resorts' previous mass hire had taken nine months; it sought to design a new staffing process that would shorten that staffing time and cost. A new, computerized staffing process was developed that accomplished the staffing objective within five-and-one-half months, at a cost savings of $600,000. The system operated as follows: Based on a newspaper help-wanted ad, interested applicants called a toll-free number to schedule an appointment to apply in person. Up to 1,200 applicants daily completed an application on a computer screen, then went to an HR checkout desk to make sure they had completed the application appropriately and to have their appearance and behavior noted. Applicants were placed in a database, which was searched by individual hiring departments. Viable candidates were interviewed by one of 180 specially trained interviewers; interview results were fed back into the database. Background checks were then conducted, and those chosen as finalists by hiring managers in the hiring departments took a drug test. Job offers were then extended by departments, though this took up to a few months after the interview. Only 3% of the initial applicants that were favorably evaluated by Mirage withdrew somewhere along the staffing process.[18]

Increasingly, organizations are emphasizing time to fill vacancies as a key indicator of staffing effectiveness based on the reasonable assumption that the shorter the vacancy time, the less the employee contribution foregone. Vacancies in sales jobs, for example, often mean lost sales and revenue generation, so shortening the time to fill means lessening the revenue foregone. Reducing time-to-fill vacancies has led organizations to develop "speed hiring" and continuous hiring programs, which in turn causes them to redesign their staffing systems to eliminate any excessive delays or bottlenecks in the process.[19]

It is possible to compare the organization's own staffing metrics with those of

EXHIBIT 13.7   Staffing Metrics: Average Time and Cost

	Days to Fill	Days to Start	Cost/Hire
A. External Hires			
Exempt	64	83	$8,924
Nonexempt	42	59	$865
B. Internal Hires			
Exempt	43	63	$930
Nonexempt	35	50	$456

Source: Saratoga Institute, *Human Capital Benchmarking Report,* Santa Clara, CA 2001. Used with permission.

other organizations. Results from two staffing metrics surveys might be consulted for this purpose, from Staffing.org (*www.staffing.org.com*) and the Saratoga Institute (*www.saratogainstitute.com*). The Saratoga Institute, for example, annually collects and compiles HR metrics data, including staffing from over 900 organizations. Some examples of the staffing metrics from the Saratoga Institute are shown in Exhibit 13.7. The data are shown separately for external and internal hires, and for exempt and nonexempt employees. It can be seen, for example, that for exempt employees the average time to fill a position was 64 days and the average days to start was 83 days. It should be noted that these results will vary in a given time period by such factors as organization size and industry. They will also vary over time according to tightness of the labor market, with tighter labor markets having larger average times.

Staffing Costs

Though staffing costs are an obviously important concern for evaluating staffing activities, actually deriving the cost estimates is difficult. There is no commonly used way of costing out the staffing process. One suggested way for doing so is provided by the Saratoga Institute; Staffing.org also might be consulted.

The previously mentioned survey by the Saratoga Institute is also used to collect organizations' estimates of staffing costs and then report a cost-per-hire estimate. The staffing cost estimates are composed of (a) advertising, employment agency, and search firm fees; (b) employee referral bonuses; (c) travel costs for recruiter and applicants; (d) relocation costs; (e) recruiter salary and benefit costs; and (f) a 10% add-on to approximate costs of testing, reference checking, bonding, hiring unit staff time, administrative support, and minor expenses. Based on these cost estimates, the average cost per hire is shown in Exhibit 13.7. It can be seen that for external hires, the average cost was $8,924 for exempt employees and $865 for nonexempt employees; costs were less for internal hires. These cost data also vary by organization size, industry, and labor market tightness.

Customer Satisfaction

Staffing systems, by their very nature, influence users of them. Such users can be thought of as customers of the system. Two of the key customers are managers and job applicants. Managers look to the staffing system to provide them the right numbers and types of new hires to meet their own staffing needs. Job applicants expect the staffing system to recruit, select, and make employment decisions about them in ways that are fair and legal. For both sets of customers, therefore, it is important to know how satisfied they are with the staffing systems that serve them. Detection of positive satisfaction can reinforce the usage of current staffing practices. Discovering areas of dissatisfaction, alternately, may serve as a trigger for needed changes in the staffing system and help pinpoint the nature of those changes.

Customer satisfaction with staffing systems is of very recent origin as an organizational concern. Rarely were managers and job applicants even thought of as customers, and rarer yet were systematic attempts made to measure their customer satisfaction as a way of evaluating the effectiveness of staffing systems. Recently, that has begun to change. Described next are two innovative studies that successfully developed measures of customer satisfaction, one for managers and one for job applicants.

Managers

The state of Wisconsin Department of Employment Relations houses the Division of Merit Recruitment and Selection (DMRS), which is the central agency responsible for staffing the state government. Annually, it helps the 40 state agencies to fill about 4,000 vacancies through hiring and promoting. Managers within these agencies, thus, are customers of the DMRS and its staffing systems.

To help identify and guide needed staffing system improvements, the DMRS decided to develop a survey measure of managers' satisfaction with staffing services. Through the use of focus groups, managers' input on the content of the survey were solicited. The final survey had 53 items on it, grouped into five areas: communication, timeliness, candidate quality, test quality, and service focus. Examples of the survey items are shown in Exhibit 13.8.

The survey was administered via internal mail to 645 line and HR managers throughout the agencies. Statistical analyses provided favorable psychometric evidence supporting usage of the survey. Survey results served as a key input to implementation of several initiatives to improve staffing service delivery. These initiatives led to increases in the speed of filling vacancies, elimination of paperwork, higher reported quality of job applicants, and positive applicant reactions to the staffing process.[20]

Job Applicants

Researchers sought to develop the Selection Fairness Survey (SFS) that could be used to assess the satisfaction of job applicants with the staffing process. The SFS contained 40 items, all designed to tap perceptions about the fairness of the selection phases of staffing. The items were grouped into 10 categories. These categories, and sample SFS items, are shown in Exhibit 13.9. The survey was administered to over 300 recent college graduates who had searched for and found a job. Statistical analysis of their responses to the SFS showed it had favorable psychometric properties.[21]

LEGAL ISSUES

Records and Reports

In staffing systems, substantial information is generated, used, recorded, and disclosed. There are numerous legal constraints and requirements surrounding staff-

---

EXHIBIT 13.8 Examples of Survey Items for Assessing Manager's Satisfaction with Staffing Services

Communication: How well are you kept informed on the staffing process?

How satisfied are you with:

1. the clarity of instructions and explanation you receive on the staffing process
2. your overall understanding of the steps involved in filling a vacancy
3. the amount of training you receive in order to effectively participate in the total staffing process

Timeliness: How do you feel about the speed of recruitment, examination, and selection services?

How satisfied are you with the time required to:

1. obtain central administrative approval to begin the hiring process
2. score oral and essay exams, achievement history questionnaires, or other procedures involving scoring by a panel of raters
3. hire someone who has been interviewed and selected

Candidate Quality: How do you feel about the quality (required knowledges and skills) of the job candidates?

How satisfied are you with:

1. the number of people you can interview and select from
2. the quality of candidates on new register
3. your involvement in the recruitment process

Test Quality: How do you feel about the quality of civil service exams (tests, work samples, oral board interviews, etc.)?

How satisfied are you with:

1. your involvement in exam construction
2. the extent to which the exams assess required KSAOs
3. the extent to which the exams test for new technologies used on the job

Service Focus: To what extent do you believe your personnel/staffing representatives are committed to providing high-quality service?

How satisfied are you with:

1. the accessibility of a staffing person
2. the expertise and competence of the staffing representative
3. responses to your particular work unit's needs

Source: H. G. Heneman III, D. L. Huett, R. J. Lavigna, and D. Ogsten, "Assessing Managers' Satisfaction with Staffing Services," *Personnel Psychology*, 1995, 48, pp. 170–173. ©*Personnel Psychology*, 1995. Used with permission.

EXHIBIT 13.9   Selection Fairness Survey: Dimensions and Sample Items for Each Dimension

Job Relatedness
> The types of questions asked during the selection process were directly related to the job.

Opportunity to Perform
> I was given adequate opportunity to demonstrate my skills and abilities.

Feedback
> I received information on the hiring decision in a timely manner.

Selection Information
> I was given a reasonable explanation for why the specific selection procedures were used to hire people.

Honesty
> I was treated honestly and openly during the selection process.

Interpersonal Treatment
> I was treated with warmth, sincerity, and thoughtfulness during the selection process.

Two-Way Communication
> In a way I was able to conduct my own interview, asking questions about the job and company.

Question Propriety
> I was asked questions that I felt were inappropriate or discriminatory.

Consistency Bias
> Personal motives or biases appeared to influence the selection process.

Ease of Faking
> It would be easy for people to be dishonest when answering questions and make themselves look good.

Equity
> Given my past experience looking for a job, I feel I received an appropriate evaluation.

Source: S. W. Gilliland and H. Honig, "Development of the Selection Fairness Survey." Paper presented at the Society for Industrial and Organizational Psychology, Nashville, TN, 1994. Used with permission of the authors.

ing information. These pertain to the creation and maintenance of records, privacy concerns, and preparation of reports.

Creation and Maintenance of Records

A wide range of information is created by the organization during staffing and other HR activities. Examples include personal data (name, address, date of birth, dependents, etc.), KSAO information (application blank, references, test scores, etc.), medical information, performance appraisal and promotability assessments, and changes in employment status (promotion, transfers, etc.). Why should records of such information be created?

Basically, records should be created and maintained for four purposes in staffing. First, they are necessary for legal compliance. Federal, state, and local laws specify what information should be kept, and for how long. Second, the information is often used in staffing decisions, and having it available in centralized records is convenient and efficient. Third, having records allows the organization to provide documentation to justify staffing decisions or to defend these decisions against legal challenge. For example, performance appraisal and promotability assessments might be used to explain to employees why they were or were not promoted. Or, these same records might be used as evidence in a legal proceeding to show that promotion decisions were job related and unbiased. Fourth, records may be used to audit staffing practices and conduct staffing research. Investigating staffing processes and results (Exhibit 13.6) and conducting validation studies are examples of such use.

It is strongly recommended that two sets of records be created. The first set should be the individual employee's personnel file. It should comprise only documents that relate directly to the job and the employee's performance of it. To determine which documents to place in the personnel file, ask if it is a document on which the organization could legally base an employment decision. If the answer is "no," "probably no," or "unsure," the document should not be placed in the employee's personnel file. The second set of records should contain documents that cannot be used in staffing decisions. Examples include documents pertaining to medical information (both physical and mental), equal employment opportunity (e.g., information about protected characteristics such as age, sex, religion, race, color, national origin, and disability), and information about authorization to work (e.g., I-9 forms).[22]

Any document that is to be placed in an employee's personnel file should be reviewed before it becomes part of that record. Examine the document for incomplete, inaccurate, or misleading information, as well as potentially damaging notations or comments about the employee. All such information should be completed, corrected, explained, and, if necessary, eliminated. Remember that any document in the personnel file is a potential court exhibit that may work either for or against the employer's defense of a legal challenge.[23]

Various laws specify record-keeping requirements for the organization. Failure to maintain and have available such records may result in substantial liability. Some of the requirements are specific and absolute, meaning that the record must be created and retained for some time period. An example here is that of I-9 immigration form records for employees. Other requirements are not as specific. They indicate only the general types of records that are to be retained, if they are created by the organization. Information created and contained in personnel files, as described above, falls into this category.

Federal EEO/AA laws contain general record-keeping requirements. Though

EXHIBIT 13.10 Federal Record-Keeping Requirements

Records that should be kept include:

- applications for employment (hire, promote, transfer)
- reasons for refusal to hire, promote, transfer
- tests and test scores, plus other KSAO information
- job orders submitted to labor unions and employment agencies
- medical exam results
- advertisements or other notices to the public or employees about job openings and promotion opportunities
- requests for reasonable accommodation
- impact of staffing decisions on protected groups (adverse impact statistics)
- records related to filing of a discrimination charge

All records should be kept for a minimum of one year.

the laws' requirements vary somewhat from law to law, major subject areas for which records are to be kept (if created) are shown in Exhibit 13.10. Requirements by the OFCCP are broader than those shown, and records must be maintained for at least two years.

The various laws also have requirements about length of retention of records. As a general rule, most records must be kept for a minimum of one year from the date a document is made or a staffing action is taken, whichever is later. Exceptions to the one-year requirements all provide for even longer retention periods. The specific record keeping and retention requirements of each law are readily available and should be consulted for amplification and clarification.[24]

Privacy Concerns

The organization must observe legal requirements governing employees' and others' access to information in personnel files, as well as guard against unwarranted disclosure of the information to third-party requesters (e.g., other employers) of it. Information access and disclosure matters raise privacy concerns under both constitutional and statutory law.[25]

Several (not all) states have laws guaranteeing employees reasonable access to their personnel files. The laws generally allow the employee to review and copy pertinent documents; some documents such as letters of reference or promotion plans for the person may be excluded from access. The employee may also have a right to seek to correct erroneous information in the file. Where there is no state law permitting access, employees are usually allowed access to their personnel file only if the organization has a policy permitting it. Disclosure of information in personnel files to third parties is often regulated, as well, requiring such procedures as employees' written consent for disclosure.

At the federal level, numerous laws and regulations restrict access to and disclosure of employee personnel information. An example here is the ADA and its provisions regarding the confidentiality of medical information. There is, however, no general federal privacy law covering private employees. Public employees' privacy rights are protected by the Privacy Act of 1974.

Reports

Under the Civil Rights Act and Affirmative Action Programs regulations, private employers with more than 100 employees (50 for federal contractors) are required to file an annual report with the EEOC. The basis of that report is completion of the EEO-1 form, shown in Exhibit 13.11. It can be seen that the primary purpose of the report is to provide employment data (see section D) on the composition of the organization's workforce. The data is to be provided for each of nine job categories; it should show the number of permanent full-time and part-time employees according to sex, race, and ethnicity. Such information may be gathered from the organization's records or by visual inspection. A detailed instruction booklet is provided to aid in preparation of the report. Each federal contractor must also prepare a report detailing its affirmative action plan (AAP) according to requirements specified in the Affirmative Action Programs regulations. Federal contractors are also required to prepare and provide additional affirmative action reports if requested by the OFCCP.

Audits

It is highly desirable to periodically conduct audits or reviews of the organization's degree of compliance with laws and regulations pertaining to staffing. The audit forces the organization to study and specify what in fact its staffing practices are and to compare these current practices against legally desirable and required practices. Results can be used to identify potential legal trouble spots and to map out changes in staffing practices that will serve to minimize potential liability and reduce the risk of lawsuits being filed against the organization. Note that development of AAPs and reports includes a large audit and review component. They do not, however, cover the entire legal spectrum of staffing practices, nor do they require sufficient depth of analysis of staffing practices in some areas. For these reasons, AAPs and reports are not sufficient as legal audits, though they are immensely important and useful inputs to a legal audit.

The audit could be conducted by the organization's own legal counsel. Alternately, the HR department might first conduct a self-audit, then review its findings with legal counsel.

An example of such a self-audit is the Employment Labor Law Audit (ELLA).[26] It has sections covering recruitment, selection, and hiring; application forms; ref-

EXHIBIT 13.11   Employer Information Report EEO-1 Form

Joint Reporting Committee

- **Equal Employment Opportunity Commission**
- **Office of Federal Contract Compliance Programs (Labor)**

EQUAL EMPLOYMENT OPPORTUNITY

EMPLOYER INFORMATION REPORT EEO—1

Standard Form 100
(Rev. 4–82)
O.M.B. No. 3046–0007
EXPIRES 12/31/93
100–213

Section A—TYPE OF REPORT
Refer to instructions for number and types of reports to be filed.

1. Indicate by marking in the appropriate box the type of reporting unit for which this copy of the form is submitted (MARK ONLY ONE BOX).

    (1) ☐ Single-establishment Employer Report

    Multi-establishment Employer:
    (2) ☐ Consolidated Report (Required)
    (3) ☐ Headquarters Unit Report (Required)
    (4) ☐ Individual Establishment Report (submit one for each establishment with 50 or more employees)
    (5) ☐ Special Report

2. Total number of reports being filed by this Company (Answer on Consolidated Report only) _____

Section B—COMPANY IDENTIFICATION (To be answered by all employers)

OFFICE USE ONLY

1. Parent Company

    a. Name of parent company (owns or controls establishment in item 2) omit if same as label

a.

Address (Number and street)

b.

City or town	State	ZIP code

c.

2. Establishment for which this report is filed. (Omit if same as label)

    a. Name of establishment

d.

Address (Number and street)	City or Town	County	State	ZIP code

e.

    b. Employer Identification No. (IRS 9-DIGIT TAX NUMBER)

f.

    c. Was an EEO–1 report filed for this establishment last year? ☐ Yes ☐ No

Section C—EMPLOYERS WHO ARE REQUIRED TO FILE (To be answered by all employers)

☐ Yes ☐ No   1. Does the entire company have at least 100 employees in the payroll period for which you are reporting?

☐ Yes ☐ No   2. Is your company affiliated through common ownership and/or centralized management with other entities in an enterprise with a total employment of 100 or more?

☐ Yes ☐ No   3. Does the company or any of its establishments (a) have 50 or more employees AND (b) is not exempt as provided by 41 CFR 60–1.5, AND either (1) is a prime government contractor or first-tier subcontractor, and has a contract, subcontract, or purchase order amounting to $50,000 or more, or (2) serves as a depository of Government funds in any amount or is a financial institution which is an issuing and paying agent for U.S. Savings Bonds and Savings Notes?

    If the response to question C–3 is yes, please enter your Dun and Bradstreet identification number (if you have one):

NOTE: If the answer is yes to questions 1, 2, or 3, complete the entire form, otherwise skip to Section G.

NSN 7540–00–180–6384

(continued)

EXHIBIT 13.11 **Continued**

Section D—EMPLOYMENT DATA

Employment at this establishment—Report all permanent full-time and part-time employees including apprentices and on-the-job trainees unless specifically excluded as set forth in the instructions. Enter the appropriate figures on all lines and in all columns. Blank spaces will be considered as zeros.

JOB CATEGORIES		OVERALL TOTALS (SUM OF COL. B THRU K)	MALE					FEMALE				
			WHITE (NOT OF HISPANIC ORIGIN)	BLACK (NOT OF HISPANIC ORIGIN)	HISPANIC	ASIAN OR PACIFIC ISLANDER	AMERICAN INDIAN OR ALASKAN NATIVE	WHITE (NOT OF HISPANIC ORIGIN)	BLACK (NOT OF HISPANIC ORIGIN)	HISPANIC	ASIAN OR PACIFIC ISLANDER	AMERICAN INDIAN OR ALASKAN NATIVE
		A	B	C	D	E	F	G	H	I	J	K
Officials and Managers	1											
Professionals	2											
Technicians	3											
Sales Workers	4											
Office and Clerical	5											
Craft Workers (Skilled)	6											
Operatives (Semi-Skilled)	7											
Laborers (Unskilled)	8											
Service Workers	9											
TOTAL	10											
Total employment reported in previous EEO–1 report	11											

NOTE: Omit questions 1 and 2 on the Consolidated Report.

1. Date(s) of payroll period used:

2. Does this establishment employ apprentices?
   1 ☐ Yes   2 ☐ No

Section E—ESTABLISHMENT INFORMATION *(Omit on the Consolidated Report)*

1. What is the major activity of this establishment? (Be specific, i.e., manufacturing steel castings, retail grocer, wholesale plumbing supplies, title insurance, etc. Include the specific type of product or type of service provided, as well as the principal business or industrial activity.)

OFFICE USE ONLY

g.

Section F—REMARKS

Use this item to give any identification data appearing on last report which differs from that given above, explain major changes in composition or reporting units and other pertinent information.

Section G—CERTIFICATION *(See Instructions G)*

Check one
1 ☐ All reports are accurate and were prepared in accordance with the instructions (check on consolidated only)
2 ☐ This report is accurate and was prepared in accordance with the instructions.

Name of Certifying Official	Title	Signature	Date

Name of person to contact regarding this report (Type or print)	Address (Number and Street)

Title	City and State	ZIP Code	Telephone Number (Including Area Code)	Extension

All reports and information obtained from individual reports will be kept confidential as required by Section 709(e) of Title VII. WILLFULLY FALSE STATEMENTS ON THIS REPORT ARE PUNISHABLE BY LAW, U.S. CODE, TITLE 18, SECTION 1001.

erence checking and responding; immigration law; the ADA; employee handbooks; antidiscrimination; and the drug-free workplace. For each section, a series of audit questions are asked, and each is answered "yes" or "no." Examples of these questions for the recruitment area are: "Do you accept unsolicited applications and/or résumés?" and "Do you use a centralized personnel department to recruit new hires?" Following the questions, a written analysis is provided explaining what the best answer is to each question, along with suggestions and dos and don'ts for guiding permissible practices.

Not only is it desirable that legal audits be conducted but they should be done on a recurring basis. The appearance of new laws or amendments to them, issuance of new policy guidance and regulations by federal agencies, and changing court interpretations all mean that the line of demarcation between permissible and impermissible staffing practices is fuzzy and in need of periodic reexamination.

Managing Legal Compliance

How should the organization seek to minimize the occurrence of legal problems, and how should the organization handle legal problems that do arise? These are questions of legal prevention and reaction, answers to which form the basis of decisions on how to manage legal compliance. A description of current legal compliance practices is provided first to show the wide range of issues to be addressed and how they are currently handled by organizations. This is followed by some suggested questions to ask for deciding what type of legal compliance system might be best for the organization.

Current Practices

Given the great importance of legal issues to staffing, how do organizations actually manage their legal compliance? Results of a survey provide an interesting description of current practices among the 630 responding organizations.[27] The findings include the following:

- Virtually all organizations sought legal consultation on HR issues.
- Twenty-six percent had an in-house attorney, and 22% of those housed the attorney(s) in the HR department.
- Thirty-seven percent specified circumstances in which an attorney must be consulted.
- Seeking legal guidance was prompted primarily by new laws and regulations, complaints from employees and applicants, and changes in HR policies and procedures.
- Legal guidance was not usually sought on pending hiring or promotion decisions; but guidance was sought at the onset of discrimination and negligent hiring complaints.

- Major staffing matters subject to legal review were employee handbooks, personnel forms, EEO/AA plans, and preemployment tests.
- Planned legal audits of the HR department were rare; however, 25% of organizations conducted legal reviews on a routine, scheduled basis.

Those findings suggest that, on average, legal compliance is managed on a casual, as-needed basis, with an emphasis on reaction to legal issues rather than prevention of legal problems. There is also an emphasis on review of written documents, rather than participating in decisions or otherwise interacting with managers.

Elements of a Legal Compliance System

Provided below are some suggested questions to ask when considering development of a legal compliance system within the organization. They represent key decisions that the organization must address as it seeks to determine the type of system that will be best for it.

First, will the organization have its own in-house attorney(s), or will legal counsel be sought externally as needed? If in-house counsel is desired, will the people be located within the HR department or elsewhere, such as the legal department?[28]

Second, to what extent should the organization seek to establish formal compliance systems and routines, as opposed to handling matters on a more ad-hoc basis? Given the growing complexity of the law and the growing volume of complaints, the organization might well opt for establishment of more formal compliance systems. By doing so, the organization would be able to assume a more preventive (as opposed to reactive) stance. It might also be less costly in the long run to have in place established policies and procedures to handle legal issues, relative to the ad-hoc approach.

A third question is how much will legal compliance become a formal area of responsibility and accountability for individual managers, and how will managers be both helped and motivated to perform these new tasks? The answer to this question involves consideration of several matters. Managers will need to become aware and accepting of this new responsibility. This will require changes in job descriptions and performance appraisals to formalize the new responsibility, and to evaluate and reward managers on how well they perform it. Accompanying this will be a need for management training that covers such topics as requirements of the law, organizational policies and procedures for handling legal issues, examples of permissible and impermissible practices, consequences of mistakes, and the roles of the HR department and legal counsel. The HR department will also need to gear up for, and be prepared to deliver, advice to managers when it is sought. The organization should anticipate a strong advisory role for the HR department, given the complexity of the laws and organizational policies and procedures. Managers should be encouraged to seek advice on legal matters, and they should receive it when it is sought.[29]

Another question is how will the organization conduct investigations of employee complaints? Here, it is useful to differentiate between complaints that are filed within the organization and those filed externally to an enforcement agency such as the EEOC. Separate systems will probably be necessary for these two types of complaints, and complaints filed with an agency should probably be handled with a very formal, step-by-step investigation process.[30]

Finally, should the organization set up a dispute resolution process, and if so, what should be its characteristics? For unionized employees, such a process is available in the form of the grievance procedure. For nonunion employees, however, what is referred to as an alternative dispute resolution (ADR) procedure will be needed. Exhibit 13.12 shows the numerous approaches to ADR that might be used. Research shows that most organizations do in fact use one or more of these procedures, with negotiation and fact finding being the most prevalent by far. Peer review and mediation are used substantially less, and arbitration is the least used.[31]

Organizations are experimenting with more formal ADR systems that combine elements of all the approaches shown in Exhibit 13.12. An example of such an ADR with five sequential steps is shown in Exhibit 13.13. Step 1 corresponds to negotiation, step 2 to fact finding, steps 3 and 4 to peer review and mediation, and step 5 to arbitration. It should be noted that such ADRs are highly experimental; their effectiveness and legality is open to question. Also, many guidelines are being suggested for their establishment and use.[32]

Despite the attraction of ADR as a replacement for more formal enforcement mechanisms, such as filing complaints with enforcement agencies and litigation,

EXHIBIT 13.12 **Alternative Dispute Resolution Approaches**

Approach	Description
Negotiation	Employer and employee discuss complaint with goal of resolving complaint.
Fact finding	A neutral person, from inside or outside the organization, investigates a complaint and develops findings that may be the basis for resolving the complaint.
Peer review	A panel of employees and managers work together to resolve the complaint.
Mediation	A neutral person (mediator) from within or outside the organization helps the parties negotiate a mutually acceptable agreement. Mediator is trained in mediation methods. Settlement is not imposed.
Arbitration	A neutral person (arbitrator) from within or outside the organization conducts formal hearing and issues a decision that is binding on the parties.

EXHIBIT 13.13 **Example of Alternative Dispute Resolution (ADR) Procedure**

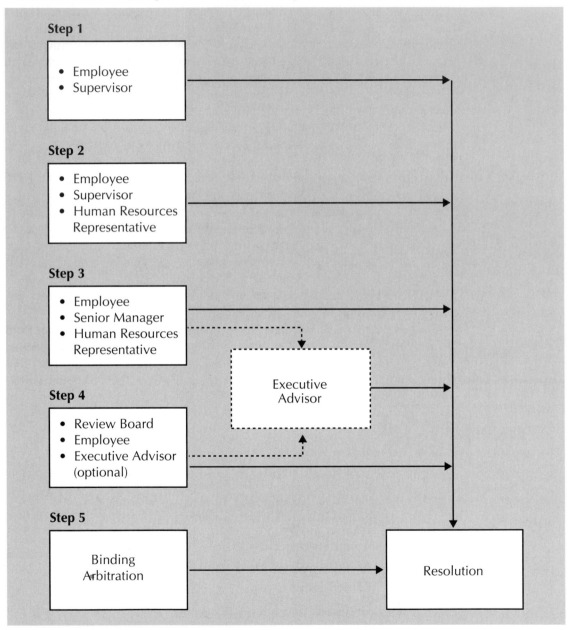

Source: U.S. Government Accounting Office, *Employment Discrimination: Most Private Sector Employers Use Alternative Dispute Resolution,* Report 95–150 (Washington, DC: author, 1995), p. 9.

a major stumbling block to their adoption occurs if individuals are required to use the ADR system and forego the right to use other mechanisms. Such a possibility exists when new hires are required as part of an employment contract to sign a provision waiving their protected rights under civil rights laws to file or participate in a proceeding against the organization and to instead use only a specified ADR system to resolve complaints. The EEOC has issued guidance indicating that such waiver provisions are null and void, and that their existence cannot stop the EEOC from enforcing the law.[33] The Supreme Court has agreed that a binding arbitration agreement does not preclude the EEOC from pursuing its statuatory function or the remedics that are otherwise available. So the EEOC may pursue a discrimination claim even when there is an ADR waiver signed by the employee.

The Special Case of Arbitration

With arbitration as the ADR procedure, the employer and employee (or job applicant) agree in advance to submit their dispute to a neutral third-party arbitrator, who will issue a final and binding decision. Such arbitration agreements usually include statutory discrimination claims, meaning that the employee agrees to not pursue charges of discrimination against the employer by any means (e.g., lawsuit) except arbitration. While such arbitration agreements generally are legally enforceable, as noted above they do not serve as a bar to pursuit by the EEOC of a discrimination claim.

If the organization decides to require mandatory arbitration agreements from job applicants and employees, it should be aware that there are many specific, suggested standards that the arbitration agreement and process must meet in order to be enforceable.[34] For example, the agreement must be "knowing and voluntary," meaning that it is clearly written, obvious as to purpose, and presented to the employee as a separate document for a signature. Examples of other suggested standards include:

- The arbitrator must be a neutral.
- The process should provide for more than minimal discovery (presentation of evidence).
- The same remedies as permitted by the law should be allowed.
- The employee should have the right to hire an attorney and the employer should reimburse the employee a portion of attorney's fees.
- The employee should not have to bear excessive responsibility for the cost of the arbitrator.
- The types of claims (e.g., sex discrimination, retaliation) subject to arbitration should be indicated.
- There should be a written award issued by the arbitrator.

The above points are complex and only illustrative of all of the issues. Because of this, legal counsel should be sought prior to use of arbitration agreements. In addition, it should be noted that arbitration agreements, the arbitration process, and reasons for it must be carefully explained to employees in order to help ensure employee understanding and acceptance.

SUMMARY

The multiple and complex set of activities collectively known as a staffing system must be integrated and coordinated throughout the organization. Such management of the staffing system requires both careful administration and evaluation, as well as compliance with legal mandates.

To manage the staffing system, the usual organizational arrangement in all but very small organizations is to create an identifiable staffing or employment function, and to place it within the HR department. That function then manages the staffing system at the corporate and/or plant and office level. Numerous types of jobs, both specialist and generalist, are found within the staffing function. Entry into these jobs, and movement among them, is very fluid and does not follow any set career mobility path.

The myriad staffing activities require staffing policies to establish general staffing principles and procedures to guide the conduct of those activities. Lack of clear policies and procedures can lead to misguided and inconsistent staffing practices, as well as potentially illegal ones. Information systems can help achieve these consistencies and aid in improving staffing system efficiency. Electronic systems are increasingly being used to conduct a wide range of staffing tasks. Outsourcing of some staffing activities is also being experimented with as a way of improving staffing system efficiency.

Evaluation of the effectiveness of the staffing system should proceed along several fronts. First is investigation of the validity of selection procedures to determine the quality of person/job matches that are occurring. Second is assessment of the staffing system from a process perspective. Here, it is desirable to examine the degree of standardization (consistency) of the process, and the results of the process according to indicators such as yield ratios and time lapse (cycle time). Costs of staffing system operation should also be estimated. Finally, the organization should consider assessing the satisfaction of staffing system users, such as managers and job applicants.

Considerable attention should be devoted to legal issues. Various laws require maintenance of numerous records and compilation of reports, especially as pertains to EEO/AA. Care must be taken to guard privacy rights and access to information maintained in files. It is desirable to periodically conduct an actual legal audit of all the organization's staffing activities. This will help identify potential legal trouble spots that require attention. Finally, consideration should be given to the best mechanism for managing the overall legal compliance of staffing and other HR activities. This will require attention to both the staffing system and to the individual line managers.

DISCUSSION QUESTIONS

1. What are the advantages of having a centralized staffing function, as opposed to letting each manager be totally responsible for all staffing activities in his or her unit?

2. What are examples of staffing tasks and activities that cannot or should not be simply delegated to a staffing information system for their conduct?

3. What arguments would you make in attempting to persuade an organization that it should periodically assess the validity of its selection procedures?

4. In developing a report on the effectiveness of the staffing process being conducted for entry-level jobs, what factors would you address and why?

5. How would you try to get individual managers to be more aware of the legal requirements of staffing systems and to take steps to ensure that they themselves engage in legal staffing actions?

APPLICATIONS

Learning About Jobs in Staffing

The purpose of this application is to have you learn in detail about a particular job in staffing currently being performed by an individual. The individual could be a staffing job holder in the HR department of a company or public agency (state or local government), a nonprofit agency, a staffing firm, an employment agency, a consulting firm, or the state employment (job) service. The individual may perform staffing tasks full-time, such as a recruiter, interviewer, counselor, employment representative, or employment manager. Or, the individual may perform staffing duties as part of the job, such as the HR manager in a small company or an HR generalist in a specific plant or site.

Contact the job holder and arrange for an interview with that person. Explain that the purpose of the interview is for you to learn about the person's job in terms of job requirements (tasks and KSAOs) and job rewards (both extrinsic and intrinsic). To prepare for the interview, review the examples of job descriptions for staffing jobs in Exhibit 13.2 and 13.3, obtain any information you can about the organization, and then develop a set of questions that you will ask the job holder. Either before or at the interview, be sure to obtain a copy of the job holder's job description if one is available. Based on the written and interview information, prepare a report of your investigation. The report should cover:

1. the organization's products and services, size, and staffing (employment) function

2. the job holder's job title, and why you chose that person's job to study

3. a summary of the tasks performed by the job holder and the KSAOs necessary for the job
4. a summary of the extrinsic and intrinsic rewards received by the job holder
5. unique characteristics of the job that you did not expect to be a part of the job

Evaluating Staffing Process Results

The Keepon Trucking Company (KTC) is a manufacturer of custom-built trucks. It does not manufacture any particular truck lines, styles, or models. Rather, it builds trucks to customers' specifications; these trucks are used for specialty purposes, such as snow removal, log hauling, and military cargo hauling. One year ago KTC received a new, large order that would take three years to complete and require the external hiring of 100 new assemblers. To staff this particular job, the HR department manager of nonexempt employment hurriedly developed and implemented a special staffing process for filling these new vacancies. Applicants were recruited from three different sources: newspaper ads, employee referrals, and a local employment agency. All applicants generated by these methods were subjected to a common selection and decision-making process. All offer receivers were given the same terms and conditions in their job offer letters and told there was no room for any negotiation. All vacancies were eventually filled.

After the first year of the contract, the manager of nonexempt employment, Dexter Williams, decided to pull together some data in an attempt to determine how well the staffing process for the assembler jobs had worked. Since he had not originally planned on doing any evaluation, Dexter was able to retrieve only the following data to help him with his evaluation:

Exhibit

Staffing Data for Filling the Job of Assembler

Method	Applicants	Offer receivers	Start as new hires	Remaining at six months
Newspaper ads				
No. apps.	300	70	50	35
Avg. no. days	30	30	10	
Employee referral				
No. apps.	60	30	30	27
Avg. no. days	20	10	10	
Employment agency				
No. apps.	400	20	20	8
Avg. no. days	40	20	10	

1. Determine the yield ratios (offer receivers/applicants, new hires/applicants), time lapse or cycle times (days to offer, days to start), and retention rates associated with each recruitment source.

2. What is the relative effectiveness of the three sources in terms of yield ratios, cycle times, and retention rates?

3. What are possible reasons for the fact that the three sources differ in their relative effectiveness?

4. How do these data compare to national staffing metrics data (Exhibit 13.7)?

5. What would you recommend that Dexter do differently in the future to improve his evaluation of the staffing process?

ENDNOTES

1. Bureau of National Affairs, "The Personnel/Human Resources Function," *Personnel Management* (Washington, DC: author, periodically updated), p. 251:15; J. Fitz-Enz (ed.), *Human Resource Financial Report* (Santa Clara, CA: Saratoga Institute, 1998), pp. 95–98; M. Arvey, "HR Pay Growth Accelerates," *HR Magazine,* Nov. 1998, pp. 122–126; L. Lorber, "Too Many Jobs, Too Few Candidates in HR," *National Business Employment Weekly,* June 14–20, 1998, pp. 12–13.

2. S. Candron, "Team Staffing Requires New HR Role," *Personnel Journal,* May 1994, pp. 88–94.

3. Bureau of National Affairs, "A Profile of Human Resource Executives," *Bulletin to Management,* June 22, 1995.

4. A. Rosenthal, "Hiring Edge," *Human Resource Executive,* April 2000, pp. 96–98.

5. J. S. Arthur, "Title Wave," *Human Resource Executive,* Oct. 2000, pp. 115–118; K. J. Dunham, "Tapping Talent," *Wall Street Journal,* April 10, 2001, p. B14.

6. P. J. Harkins, S. M. Brown, and R. Sullivan, "Shining New Light on a Growing Trend," *HR Magazine,* Dec. 1995, pp. 75–79.

7. W. J. Kucker, "Outsourcing Trends in the Employment Arena," *Employment Management Association Journal,* Spring 1995, pp. 20–25.

8. F. Jossi, "The PEO Panacea," *Human Resource Executive,* Aug. 1997, pp. 32–35; L. Smytko, "Renewed Lease," *Human Resource Executive,* Aug. 1998, pp. 23–25.

9. B. S. Klaus, J. McClendon, and T. W. Gainey, "Human Resource Outsourcing: The Role of Transaction Costs," *Personnel Psychology,* 1999, 52, pp. 113–136.

10. B. S. Klaas, J. A. McClendon, and T. W. Gainey, "Outsourcing HR: The Impact of Organizational Characteristics," *Human Resource Management,* 2001, 40, pp. 125–138.

11. T. Starner, "Biggest Blunders," *Human Resource Executive,* June 2001, pp. 39–44.

12. C. R. Greer, S. A. Youngblood, and P. A. Gray, "Do People Make the Place? The Make or Buy Decision of Human Resources Outsourcing," *Academy of Management Executive,* 1999, 13(3), pp. 85–96; D. P. Lepak and S. A. Snell, "Virtual HR: Strategic Human Resources in the 21st Century," *Human Resource Management Review,* 1999, 3, pp. 215–234.

13. D. E. Terpstra and E. J. Rozell, "The Relationship of Staffing Practices to Organizational Level Measures of Performance," *Personnel Psychology,* 1993, 46, pp. 27–48.

14. C. Ostroff, "Best HR Practices," *1995 SHRM/CCH Survey* (Chicago: Commerce Clearing House, June 21, 1995).

15. D. E. Terpstra and E. J. Rozell, "Why Some Potentially Effective Staffing Practices Are Seldom Used," *Public Personnel Management,* 1997, 26, pp. 483–495.

16. Exhibits 8.10, 9.19, and 10.11 in this book.

17. L. W. Seberhagen, "How Difficult Is It to Conduct a Validation Study?," *The Industrial-Organizational Psychologist,* 1990, 28, pp. 41–46; J. Lefkowitz and M. Gebbia, "The Shelf-Life of a Test Validation Study: A Survey of Expert Opinion," *Journal of Business and Psychology,* 1997, 11, pp. 381–397.

18. E. P. Gunn, "How Mirage Resorts Sifted 75,000 Applicants to Hire 9,600 in 24 weeks," *Fortune,* Oct. 12, 1998, p. 195.

19. L. Micco, "Lockheed Wins the Best Catches," *Employment Management Association Today,* Spring 1997, pp. 18–20; E. R. Silverman, "The Fast Track," *Human Resource Executive,* Oct. 1998, pp. 30–34.

20. H. G. Heneman III, D. L. Huett, R. J. Lavigna, and D. Ogsten, "Assessing Managers' Satisfaction with Staffing Service," *Personnel Psychology,* 1995, 48, pp. 163–172.

21. S. W. Gilliland, "Development of the Selection Fairness Survey." Paper presented at the *Society for Industrial and Organizational Psychology* meeting, Nashville, TN, 1994.

22. H. P. Coxson, "The Double-Edged Sword of Personnel Files and Employee Records," *Legal Report* (Alexandria, VA: Society for Human Resource Management, 1992); Warren Gorham Lamont, *How Long Do We Have to Keep These Records?* (Boston: author, 1993).

23. H. P. Coxson, "The Double-Edged Sword of Personnel Files and Employee Records."

24. Bureau of National Affairs, "Federal Record Keeping Requirements," *Personnel Management* (Washington, DC: author, periodically updated), p. 251:751.

25. Bureau of National Affairs, "Employee Information and Record Keeping," *Personnel Management* (Washington, DC: author, periodically updated), pp. 251:651 to 251:671; International Personnel Management Association, "Employee Privacy and Recordkeeping—I and II," *IPMA News,* Aug. and Sept. 1998, pp. 16–18, 17–18.

26. R. L. Adler and F. T. Coleman, *Employment Labor Law Audit* (Washington, DC: Bureau of National Affairs, 1995).

27. Bureau of National Affairs, "Legal Oversight of the HR Department," *Bulletin to Management* (Washington, DC: author, Feb. 2, 1995).

28. D. M. Pfadenhauer, "Selecting and Using Outside Labor and Employment Counsel," *HR Magazine,* March 1998, pp. 119–126.

29. C. Palmer, "Avoiding the Courtroom," *HR Magazine,* Oct. 1995, pp. 32–37.

30. E. D. Cooke Jr. and J. R. Altes, "Eleven Tips for Effectively Handling and Responding to a Charge of Discrimination," *Legal Report* (Alexandria, VA: Society for Human Resource Management, Summer 1995).

31. U.S. Government Printing Office, *Employment Discrimination: Most Private Sector Employers Use Alternative Dispute Resolution* (Washington, DC: author, 1995).

32. U.S. Government Printing Office, *Employment Discrimination: Most Private Sector Employers Use Alternative Dispute Resolution*; C. Wittenberg, S. MacKenzie, M. Shaw, and D. Ross, "And Justice for All," *HR Magazine,* Sept. 1997, pp. 131–137; L. B. Bingham, "Employment Arbitration and the Courts," *Industrial Relations Research Association Perspectives on Work,* 1998, 2(2), pp. 19–23.

33. Equal Employment Opportunity Commission, *EEOC Enforcement Guidance on Non-Waivable Employee Rights Under EEOC Enforcement Statutes* (Washington, DC: author, 1997).

34. L. P. Postol, "To Arbitrate Employment Disputes or Not, That Is the Question," *Society for Human Resource Management Legal Report,* Sept.–Oct. 2001, pp. 5–8; C. Hirschman, "Order in the Hear," *HR Magazine,* July 2001, pp. 58–64; M. E. Bruno, "The Future of ADR in the Workplace," *Compensation and Benefits Review,* Nov.–Dec. 2001, pp. 46–59.

CHAPTER FOURTEEN

Retention Management

Turnover and Its Causes
Nature of the Problem
Types of Turnover
Causes of Turnover

Analysis of Turnover
Measurement
Reasons for Leaving
Costs and Benefits

Retention Initiatives: Voluntary Turnover
Current Practices and Deciding to Act
Desirability of Leaving
Ease of Leaving
Alternatives

Retention Initiatives: Discharge
Performance Management
Progressive Discipline

Retention Initiatives: Downsizing
Weighing Advantages and Disadvantages
Staffing Levels and Quality
Alternatives to Downsizing
Employees Who Remain

Legal Issues
Separation Laws and Regulations
Performance Appraisal

Summary

Discussion Questions

Applications

R etention of employees is the final component of an overall staffing system. While some loss of employees is both inevitable and desirable, retention management seeks to keep sufficient numbers and types of employees so that organizational effectiveness is not jeopardized.

In this chapter, turnover and its causes are first discussed. Three types of turnover are identified—voluntary, discharge, and downsizing. Each type of turnover has different causes or drivers, and these are identified and discussed. Particular attention is paid to voluntary turnover and its three primary causes, namely, ease of leaving, cost of leaving, and alternatives.

Retention management must be based on a thorough analysis of the organization's turnover. The analyses discussed are measuring turnover, determining employees' reasons for leaving, and assessing the costs and benefits of turnover.

Attention then turns to retention initiatives, with the first discussion focused on ways of enhancing retention by reducing voluntary turnover. Examples of current organization practices and a decision process to follow for deciding whether to move forward with such practices are presented. This is followed by numerous examples of how to increase retention by attacking its underlying causes.

The next retention initiative discussed is that of reducing the occurrence of employee discharges. This is shown to involve use of both performance management and progressive discipline initiatives.

The final retention initiative is the matter of downsizing. Here, the first concern is with keeping a sufficiently high number and quality of employees that the organization does not go overboard, shedding so many employees that the ability to rebound back is threatened. Also, there are many alternatives to downsizing that might be used. How to treat employees who survive a downsizing is also discussed.

The final topic is that of legal issues. The first issue is a complex one, reminding those responsible for staffing of the myriad laws and regulations pertaining to employee separation from the organization. The second issue is that of performance appraisal, a matter of critical importance for organizations seeking to retain their best performers.

TURNOVER AND ITS CAUSES

Nature of the Problem

The focus of this book so far has been on acquiring and deploying people in ways that contribute to organizational effectiveness. Attention now shifts to retaining employees as another part of staffing that can contribute to organizational effectiveness. Despite the desirability of employee retention, however, it is important to recognize at the outset that employee turnover is not only costly but also beneficial to both the organization and the employee. An extremely important part of employee retention strategy and tactics thus must involve careful assessment of both retention costs and benefits and the design of retention initiatives that provide positive benefits at reasonable cost to the organization. Moreover, retention strategies and tactics must focus not only on how many employees are retained but exactly who is retained. Both within and between jobs and organization levels, some employees are "worth" more than others in terms of their contributions to job and organizational effectiveness. Another important matter for the retention agenda is thus making special efforts to retain what we call "high-value" employees, both those who might leave voluntarily and those who might be at risk for involuntary termination via discharge or downsizing.

Retention must be tackled realistically, however, since some amount of employee turnover is simply inevitable.[1] People constantly move out of organizations voluntarily, and organizations shed employees as well. For example, for employees between the ages of 18 and 34, the Department of Labor estimates that (1) the median number of years they have been with their current employer (called tenure) is 3–5 years, and (2) they have held an average of 9.2 jobs. While job-hopping decreases and median tenure increases with age, some amount of turnover persists throughout workers' careers. In some industries, high voluntary turnover is a continual fact of life and cost of doing business. Turnover among sit-down restaurant managers, for example, hovers around 50% annually year after year. It is not clear that even costly retention initiatives, such as substantial pay level increases or converting managers to franchisees, can reduce this turnover. A final example is that in 2000 the Department of Labor estimates there were over 5,500 mass layoffs (those involving 50 or more employees), creating over one million unemployed workers. This was a relatively low number of mass layoffs due to generally favorable economic conditions that year.

When people voluntarily leave the organization, they do so for a variety of reasons, only some of which are potentially avoidable (controllable) by the organization. Sound retention management thus must be based on a gathering and analysis of employees' reasons for leaving. Specific retention initiatives then must be tailor-made to address these reasons and hopefully neutralize them and take them "out of play," but in a cost-effective way. Against this backdrop we now turn to a more detailed discussion of types of turnover and their causes.

Types of Turnover

There are many different types of employee turnover. Exhibit 14.1 provides a basic classification of these types.[2] It can be seen that turnover is either voluntary, being initiated by the employee, or involuntary, being initiated by the organization.

Voluntary
Voluntary turnover, in turn, is broken down into avoidable and unavoidable turnover. Avoidable turnover is that which potentially could have been prevented by

certain organization actions, such as a pay raise or a new job assignment. Unavoidable turnover represents employee quits that the organization probably could not have prevented, such as people who quit and withdraw from the labor force through retirement or returning to school. Other examples of unavoidable turnover are people who quit due to: dual career problems, pursuit of a new and different career, health problems that require taking a different type of job, child care and elder care responsibilities, and leaving the country. The line of demarcation between avoidable and unavoidable is fuzzy and depends on decisions by the organization as to exactly what types of voluntary turnover it thinks it could potentially prevent.

A further line of demarcation involves just avoidable turnover, in which the organization explicitly chooses to either try to prevent or not try to prevent employees from quitting. As shown in Exhibit 14.1, the organization will try to prevent high-value employees from quitting—those employees with high job performance, strong KSAOs, key intellectual capital, high promotion potential, high

EXHIBIT 14.1   Types of Employee Turnover

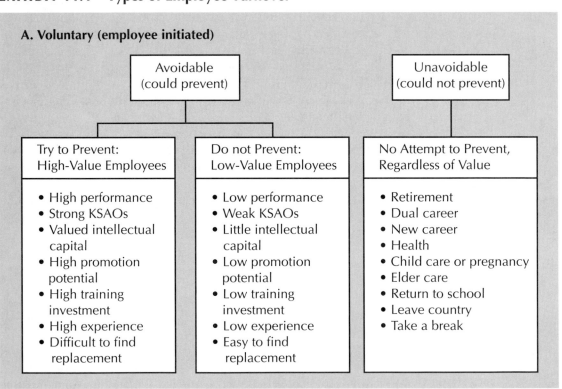

A. Voluntary (employee initiated)

Avoidable (could prevent)		Unavoidable (could not prevent)
Try to Prevent: High-Value Employees	**Do not Prevent:** Low-Value Employees	**No Attempt to Prevent,** Regardless of Value
• High performance • Strong KSAOs • Valued intellectual capital • High promotion potential • High training investment • High experience • Difficult to find replacement	• Low performance • Weak KSAOs • Little intellectual capital • Low promotion potential • Low training investment • Low experience • Easy to find replacement	• Retirement • Dual career • New career • Health • Child care or pregnancy • Elder care • Return to school • Leave country • Take a break

(continued)

EXHIBIT 14.1 Continued

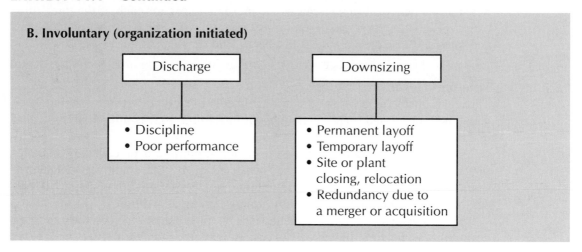

B. Involuntary (organization initiated)

Discharge
- Discipline
- Poor performance

Downsizing
- Permanent layoff
- Temporary layoff
- Site or plant closing, relocation
- Redundancy due to a merger or acquisition

training and development invested in them, high experience, and who are difficult to find replacements for. Retention attempts for low-value employees are less likely to be made—this is a specific decision the organization must make.

Involuntary

Involuntary turnover is split into discharge and downsizing types. Discharge turnover is aimed at the individual employee, due to discipline and/or job performance problems. Downsizing turnover typically targets groups of employees and is also known as reduction in force (RIF). It occurs as part of an organizational restructuring or cost-reduction program to improve organizational effectiveness and increase shareholder value (stock price). RIFs may occur as permanent or temporary layoffs for the entire organization, or as part of a plant or site closing or relocation. RIFs may also occur as the result of a merger or acquisition, in which some employees in the combined workforces are viewed as redundant in the positions they hold. It is important to recognize that even though the organization is considering terminating employees through discharge and downsizing, it can take many steps to lessen or eliminate discharges or downsizing, thereby having positive employee retention impacts.

It is apparent that there are many different types of turnover, and these types have different underlying causes. Because of this, the organization must think very selectively in terms of the different types of retention strategies and tactics it wishes to deploy. It is first necessary to explore the underlying causes of turnover, since knowledge of those causes is necessary for developing and implementing those retention strategies and tactics.

Causes of Turnover

Separate models of turnover causes are presented next for each of the three turnover types that the organization may seek to influence with its retention strategies and tactics. These are voluntary, discharge, and downsizing turnover.

Voluntary Turnover

Through considerable research, various models of voluntary turnover have been developed and tested.[3] The model shown in Exhibit 14.2 is a distillation of that research.

In the model, the actual employee behavior of quitting is preceded by an intention to quit, which may or may not get acted on by the employee. Matters of timing, indecision, fear, cost, and retention attempts by the organization all may act to deter an intention to quit from turning into an actual quit.

The employee's intention to quit depends on three general factors: the perceived desirability of leaving, the perceived ease of leaving, and alternatives available to

EXHIBIT 14.2   Causes (Drivers) of Voluntary Turnover

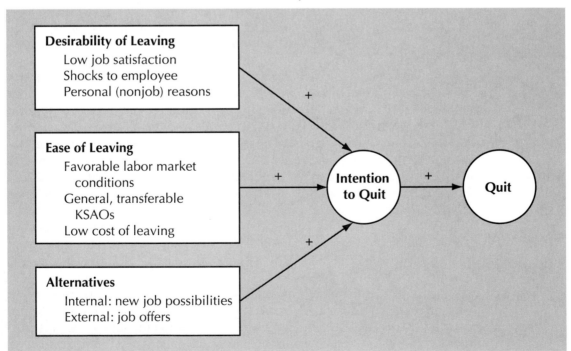

Note: The relative importance of the drivers and how they interact to determine the decision to quit varies across situations.

the employee. The perceived desirability of leaving is often an outgrowth of a poor person/job or person/organization match. One form of the mismatch may be a difference between the rewards provided by the job and rewards desired by the employee, leading to job dissatisfaction. In addition to mismatches, certain shocks may occur to the employee, which trigger a more impulsive intention to quit, such as finding out that the organization is being acquired and one's job might be eliminated. Finally, employees may find it desirable to leave for personal, nonjob reasons that are unavoidable.

The perceived ease of leaving represents a sense of lack of barriers to leaving and of being able to likely find a new job. Labor market conditions, specifically the tightness or looseness of the labor market, are very important types of information for the employee in helping to frame an intention to quit. Tight labor markets fuel the intention-to-quit flames, and loose labor markets douse the flames. The flames may also be doused by the employee knowing that many of his or her KSAOs are specific and only useful to the current employer. Ease of leaving may also be heightened by a low cost of leaving, such as not having to give up valuable benefits because none were provided by the organization. In short, the ease of leaving will be higher when labor market conditions provide plentiful job opportunities with other organizations, when the employee possesses KSAOs that are transferable to other organizations, and when leaving is not a very costly proposition for the employee.

Finally, the intention to quit will depend on other job alternatives available to the employee within and outside the organization. Specifically, availability of promotion, transfer, and relocation alternatives may lessen or eliminate any intentions to quit by the employee, even though the employee is very dissatisfied with the current job. Also, actual or potential receipt of a job offer from another employer represents a clear external alternative for the employee.

The model in Exhibit 14.2 illustrates both avoidable and unavoidable turnover. Retention initiatives must be directed toward the avoidable types of turnover. Using the model, that will be turnover due to job dissatisfaction, employee possession of general, transferable KSAOs, a low cost of leaving, the availability of other job opportunities within the organization, and the employee's receipt of a job offer.

Discharge Turnover

Discharge turnover is due to extremely poor person/job matches, particularly the mismatch between job requirements and KSAOs. One form of the mismatch involves the employee failing to follow rules and procedures. These requirements range from the relatively minor (e.g., dress code violations, horseplay) to the very serious (e.g., bringing a firearm to work). Often it is the cumulative effect of multiple incidents that results in the discharge.

The other form of discharge turnover involves unacceptable job performance. Here, the KSAO–job requirements mismatch is severe. In fact, the employee's performance is so deficient that the organization has decided that it is intolerable and the only solution is termination.

Downsizing Turnover

Downsizing turnover is a reflection of a staffing level mismatch in which the organization actually is, or is projected to be, overstaffed. In other words, the head count available exceeds the head count required. Overstaffing may be due to (1) a lack of forecasting and planning, (2) inaccuracies in forecasting and planning, or (3) unanticipated changes in labor demand and/or labor supply. For example, optimistic forecasts of demand for products and services that do not materialize may lead to overstaffing, as may sudden unanticipated downturns in demand that create sudden excess head count. Or, increasing looseness in the labor market may reduce the ease of movement, causing fewer employees to leave the organization—an unanticipated decrease in the voluntary turnover rate and thus increase in workforce head count available. Quite naturally, these types of demand/supply imbalances create strong downsizing pressure on the organization to which it must respond.

ANALYSIS OF TURNOVER

Analysis of turnover requires that the three types be measured and benchmarked, that specific reasons for employees' leaving be identified, and that costs and benefits of each type of turnover be assessed.

Measurement

Formula

Since turnover involves the discrete action of leaving or staying with the organization, it is expressed as the proportion or percentage of employees who leave the organization in some time period. Thus:

$$\text{turnover rate} = \frac{\text{number of employees leaving}}{\text{average number of employees}} \times 100$$

Use of this formula to calculate turnover rates will require data on, and decisions about, (1) what is the time period of interest (e.g., month, year), (2) what is an employee that "counts" (e.g., full time only? part time? seasonal?), and (3) how to calculate the average number of employees over the time period, such as straight or weighted average.

Breakouts and Benchmarks

Analysis and interpretation of turnover data is aided by making breakouts of the data according to various factors, including (1) type of turnover: voluntary—avoidable and unavoidable; involuntary—discharge; involuntary—downsizing, (2) type of employee (e.g., exempt–nonexempt, demographics, KSAOs, performance level), (3) job category, and (4) geographic location. Such breakouts help in identifying how much variation in turnover there is around the overall average and pockets of the most and least severe turnover. Such data are the foundation for development of strategic retention initiatives.

It is also useful to benchmark turnover data in order to have comparative statistics that will aid in interpretation of the organization's turnover data. One benchmark is an internal one, looking at the trends in the organization's own turnover data over time. Such trend analysis is very useful for identifying where turnover problems are worsening or improving and for evaluating the effectiveness of retention initiatives. Internal benchmarking requires a commitment to a sustained data collection process.

The other form of benchmarking is external, in which the organization compares its own data to that of other organizations, looking both at current turnover rates and turnover trends. Comparative data are available from trade and industry associations and private organizations such as the Saratoga Institute (*www.saratoga-institute.com*). The Saratoga Institute publishes annual turnover data among approximately 900 organizations varying in location, size, and industry. Exhibit 14.3 provides a sample of these data for the year 2000, with breakouts by type of turnover and type of employee. (Breakouts by organization size and industry are also available—they reveal large industry, but not size, differences in turnover.) Rather than "turnover rate," the Saratoga Institute uses the term "separation rate."

It can be seen that the voluntary turnover rate was higher than the involuntary rate and that both rates were higher for nonexempt employees than for exempt employees.

A new external benchmarking source is the Job Openings and Labor Turnover Survey (JOLTS) data, collected and published by the U.S. Department of Labor

EXHIBIT 14.3   Sample Annual Separation (Turnover) Data

	Exempt Employees	Nonexempt Employees
Total Separation Rate	16.6%	25.1%
Voluntary	12.7%	18.5%
Involuntary	3.9%	6.6%

Source: *Human Capital Benchmarking Report,* Saratoga Institute, Santa Clara, CA 2001. Used with permission.

(*www.bls.gov/jlt*). The JOLTS is conducted monthly among 16,000 business establishments. It provides data on total employment, job openings, hires, quits, layoffs and discharges, and other separations. As of this writing, the first JOLTS data had not been published online, though they will be.

Reasons for Leaving

It is important to ascertain, record, and track the various reasons for why employees are leaving the organization. The data are essential for measuring and analyzing turnover. At a minimum, the exit of each employee should be classified as a voluntary, discharge, or downsizing exit, thus permitting the calculation of turnover rates for these three major types of turnover. In order to learn more about the specific reasons underlying exit decisions, however, more in-depth probing of employees is necessary. Three tools for conducting such probing are exit interviews, postexit surveys, and employee satisfaction surveys.[4] All three tools can be used to help gauge whether the decision to leave was voluntary or not, and if voluntary, the specific reasons—thus allowing a determination of avoidable and unavoidable turnover.

Exit Interviews

Exit interviews are formally planned and conducted interviews with departing employees. In addition to help learn about the employee's reasons for leaving, exit interviews are used to explain such things as rehiring rights, benefits, and confidentiality agreements.

The following are suggestions for conducting an appropriate interview that will hopefully elicit truthful information from the interviewee: (1) the interviewer should be a neutral person (normally someone from the HR department or a consultant) who has been trained in how to conduct exit interviews; (2) the training should cover how to put the employee at ease and explain the purposes of the interview, how to follow the structured interview format and avoid excessive probing and follow-up questions, the need for taking notes, and how to end the interview on a positive note; (3) there should be a structured interview format that contains questions about unavoidable and avoidable reasons for leaving, and for the avoidable category, the questions should focus on desirability of leaving, ease of leaving, and job alternatives (Exhibit 14.4 contains an example of structured exit interview questions, with questions focused on desirability of leaving, ease of leaving, and alternatives); (4) the interviewer should prepare for each exit interview by reviewing the interview format and the interviewee's personnel file; (5) the interview should be conducted in a private place, before the employee's last day; and (6) the interviewee should be told that the interview is confidential and that only aggregate results will be used to help the organization better understand why employees leave and to possibly develop new retention initiatives. The organization much decide whether to conduct exit interviews with all departing

EXHIBIT 14.4   Examples of Exit Interview Questions

1. Current job title _____ department/work unit _____
2. Length of time in current job _____ length of time with organization _____
3. Are you leaving for any of the following reasons?
   retirement _____ dual career _____ new career _____ health _____
   child care or pregnancy _____ elder care _____ return to school _____
   leave the country _____ take a break _____
4. Do you have another job lined up _____ new employer _____
5. What aspects of your new job will be better than current job _____
6. Before deciding to leave did you check the possibility of
   job transfer _____ promotion _____ relocation _____
7. Was it easy to find another job _____ why _____
8. Did many of your current skills fit with your new job _____
9. What aspects of your job have been most satisfying _____
   least satisfying _____
10. What could the company have done to improve your job satisfaction _____
11. How satisfactory has your job performance been since your last review _____
12. What are things the company or your manager could have done to help you improve
    your performance _____
13. If you could have had a different manager, would you have been more likely to stay
    with the company _____
14. Are you willing to recommend the company to others as a place to work _____
15. Would you be willing to hire back with the company _____
16. Is there anything else you would like to tell us about your decision to leave the company _____

employees or only those who are leaving voluntarily. The advantages of including all departing employees are that it expands the sample from which information is drawn and even employees leaving involuntarily can provide useful information.

Postexit Surveys

To minimize departing employees' concerns about exit interviews regarding confidentiality and possible employer retaliation, postexit surveys might be used. It is recommended that (1) the surveys should cover the same areas as the exit interview; (2) the survey should be sent shortly after the employee's last day; (3) a cover letter should explain the purpose of the survey, use of only aggregate results, and confidentiality of individual responses; and (4) a stamped, preaddressed envelope be included for return of the survey. It is unknown what types of response rates are typical for postexit surveys.

Employee Satisfaction Surveys

Since employee job dissatisfaction (desirability of leaving) is known to be a potent predictor of voluntary turnover, conduct of job satisfaction surveys is an important way to discover the types of job rewards that are most dissatisfying to employees and might therefore become reasons for leaving. Conducting job satisfaction surveys has the advantage of learning from all employees (at least those who respond to the survey), rather than just those who are leaving. Satisfaction survey results also give the organization information it can use to hopefully pre-empt turnover by making changes that will increase job satisfaction. Designing, conducting, analyzing, and interpreting results from these surveys require substantial organizational resources and should only be undertaken with the guidance of a person explicitly trained in job satisfaction survey techniques. Oftentimes this will be a consultant retained for this purpose.

Costs and Benefits

Costs and benefits may be estimated for each of the three turnover types. These costs are both financial and nonfinancial in nature. Most involve actual costs or benefits, though some are potential, depending on how events transpire. Some of the costs and benefits may be estimated financially, a useful and necessary exercise. Such financial analysis must be supplemented with a careful consideration of the other costs and benefits to arrive at a reasonable estimate of the total costs and benefits of turnover. It may well turn out that the nonfinancial costs and benefits outweigh the financial ones in importance and impact for the development of retention strategies and tactics.

Voluntary Turnover

Exhibit 14.5 shows the major types of costs and benefits that can occur when an employee leaves the organization.[5] These are obviously considerable in nature and scope. An assessment of these costs and benefits could be used in the case of an individual employee who is threatening to leave for avoidable reasons; the assessment will help frame decisions about whether a retention attempt should be made, and if so, how far the organization is willing to go in that attempt. Or at the aggregate level the costs and benefits assessment could be developed for the work or business unit, division, or total organization. Results may then be used to communicate with top management about the nature and severity of employee turnover and to help fashion the development of retention strategies and tactics.

Inspection of Exhibit 14.5 shows that on the cost side there are separation, replacement, and training costs, both financial and nonfinancial. The financial costs mainly involve the cost of people's time, cost of materials and equipment, cash outlays, and productivity losses. The other costs are less discernable and harder to estimate but may entail large negative impacts on organizational effectiveness; such as loss of clients. On the benefits side, a number of positive things may occur,

EXHIBIT 14.5   Voluntary Turnover: Costs and Benefits

I. Separation Costs
  A. Economic Costs
  • HR staff time (e.g., exit interview, payroll, benefits)
  • Manager's time (e.g., retention attempts, exit interview)
  • Accrued paid time off (e.g., vacation, sick pay)
  • Temporary coverage (e.g., temporary employee; overtime for current employees)

  B. Other Costs
  • Production and customer service delays or quality decreases
  • Lost or unacquired clients
  • Leaves—goes to competitor or forms competitive business
  • Contagion—other employees decide to leave
  • Teamwork disruptions
  • Loss of workforce diversity

II. Replacement Costs
  • Staffing costs for new hire (e.g., cost/hire calculations)
  • Hiring inducements (e.g., bonus, relocation, perks)
  • Hiring manager and work-unit employee time
  • Orientation program time and materials
  • HR staff induction costs (e.g., payroll, benefits enrollment)

III. Training Costs
  • Formal training (trainee and instruction time, materials, equipment)
  • On-the-job training (supervisor and employee time)
  • Mentoring (mentor's time)
  • Socialization (time of other employees, travel)
  • Productivity loss (loss of production until full proficient employee)

IV. Benefits
  • Replacement employee better performer and organization citizen than last employee
  • New KSAO and motivation infusion to organization
  • Opportunity to restructure work unit
  • Savings from not replacing employee
  • Vacancy creates transfer or promotion opportunity for others
  • Replacement less expensive in salary and seniority-based benefits

including finding a higher-quality, less-expensive replacement for the departing employee(s).

Accurate cost and benefit calculations require diligence and care in development, particularly those involving people's time. To estimate time costs, it is necessary to know the average amount of time spent by each person in the specific activity, plus each person's compensation (pay rate plus benefits). Consider the case of an exit interview, a separation cost. Assume that (1) the staffing manager spends one hour conducting the interview and writing up a brief summary to add to the voluntary turnover data file, (2) the staffing manager's salary is $46,000 ($23/hour) and the employee's salary is $50,000 ($25/hour), and (3) benefits are 30% of pay ($6.90/hour for the staffing manager and $7.50/hour for the employee). The time cost of the exit interview is $62.40. At the aggregate level, if the staffing manager conducts 100 exit interviews annually, and the average pay rate of those interviewed is $20/hour, the annual time cost of exit interviews is $5,590 (staffing manager pay = $2,300 and benefits = $690; employee's pay = $2,000 and benefits = $600).

Materials and equipment costs are likely to be most prevalent in replacement and training costs. For example, they will be a part of staffing costs in such things as recruitment brochures and testing materials, orientation program materials, and induction materials such as benefits enrollment forms. Formal training may involve the use of both materials and equipment that must be costed. Cash outlays include paying for (1) the departing employee's accrued but unused paid time off, (2) possible temporary coverage for the departed employee, and (3) hiring inducements for the replacement employee.

On the benefits side, the primary immediate benefit is the labor cost savings from not having the departing employee on the payroll until a permanent replacement is hired (if ever), or of hiring a temporary replacement at a lower pay rate until a permanent replacement is acquired. And the hired permanent replacement may be hired at a lower wage or salary than the departing employee, resulting in additional pay and benefit savings. The other benefits shown in Exhibit 14.5 are less tangible but potentially very important in a longer run sense of improved work-unit and organizational effectiveness.

An example of a financial cost estimate for voluntary turnover involving a single employee is shown in Exhibit 14.6. It involves the sales unit of an industrial supplies company that employs 40 salespeople who receive an average compensation of $20/hour ($15 direct pay and $5 benefits; variable pay is ignored for simplicity's sake) and who have average annual sales of $200,000. Total annual sales are $8,000,000. It takes an average of four weeks to find a permanent replacement at a cost-per-hire of $4,500. A permanent new hire receives on average $15/hour (direct pay and benefits), a hiring bonus of $3,000, a laptop computer worth $2,000, and two weeks (80 hours) of formal classroom training conducted by an instructor who devotes 100 hours to the program. A fellow salesperson serves as a mentor for one year, averaging one hour per week. It takes the new permanent replacement six months (24 weeks × 40 hours = 960 hours) to reach the average sales proficiency of $200,000, and $50,000 in lost sales occurs during this learning period. Once average sales proficiency is reached, the new permanent replacement receives an average compensation of $20/hour. To fill in for the departed employee until a permanent replacement is found (4 weeks × 40 hours =

EXHIBIT 14.6   Example of Financial Cost Estimates for One Voluntary Turnover

	Time		Materials and Equipment ($)	Other Costs ($)
	Hours	Cost ($)		
A. Separation Costs				
Staffing manager	1	25		
HR staff	1	15		
Employee's manager	3	120		
Accrued paid time off	160	2,400		
Processing			30	
B. Replacement Costs				
Temporary replacement				
Compensation difference	160	(800)		
Staffing manager	1	25		
Employee's manager	1	40		
Staffing firm fee (markup)				800
Permanent replacement				
Compensation difference	960	(4,800)		
Cost-per-hire				4,500
Hiring bonus				3,000
Laptop computer				2,000
Employee's manager	3	120		
Orientation	8	160		
C. Training Costs				
Training program			1,000	
Trainee	80	1,200		
Instructor	100	1,600		
Mentor	52	1,040		
Productivity/sales loss				
Permanent replacement				50,000
Temporary replacement				2,000
D. Total Costs		1,545	1,030	62,300

160 hours), a temporary employee is obtained from a staffing firm that specializes in sales occupations. The staffing firm charges $15/hour plus a 33.3% markup of $800. On average, the temporary sales person has $2,000 less in sales than a regular employee over the four weeks of the assignment.

Exhibit 14.6 shows the financial cost estimates for this single incident of voluntary turnover. There are three categories of costs (separation, replacement, training), and for each category cost estimates are provided for time, materials and equipment, and "other." Referring to the time estimates, the accrued paid time off and the involvement of numerous people consumes many hours and resultant costs. These costs are partially offset by cost savings that occur from compensation differences due to hiring less-expensive temporary and permanent replacements. For the permanent replacement, however, these cost savings last for only six months since the employee's pay is increased from $15/hour to $20/hour in response to the employee's rising sales. Materials and equipment costs can be seen to be minor. The "other" costs reflect primarily costs of acquiring the permanent replacement and the substantial sales losses from use of the temporary replacement and from the permanent replacement during the first six-month "break-in" period. Across these three categories, total costs for a single turnover are $64,875 ($1,545 + $1,030 + $62,300).

It should be recognized that turnover cost estimates require considerable judgment and "guesstimate." Nonetheless, the example above illustrates that many turnover costs are hidden in (1) the time demands placed on the many employees who must handle the separation, replacement, and training activities, and (2) the sales or productivity losses experienced. Such costs might be offset at least in part, however, through the acquisition of less-expensive temporary and permanent replacement employees, at least for a while. It should also be noted that when turnover costs for a single employee loss are aggregated to an annual level for multiple losses, the costs can be substantial. In the above example, if the sales unit experienced just a 20% annual voluntary turnover rate, it would lose eight employees at a total cost of $519,000, or 6.5% of annual sales.

Discharge

In the case of an employee discharge, some of the costs and benefits are the same as for voluntary turnover. Referring to Exhibit 14.7, it can be seen that separation, replacement, and training costs are still incurred. There may be an additional separation cost for a contract buyout of guarantees (salary, benefits, perks) made in a fixed-term contract. Such buyouts are very common for high-level executives and public sector leaders such as school superintendents. These guarantees are negotiated and used to make the hiring package more attractive and to reduce the financial risk of failure for the new hire. Such guarantees can drive up the costs of discharge substantially and reinforce the need for careful selection decisions followed by support to help the new hire turn out to be a successful performer who will remain with the organization for at least the full term of the contract.

EXHIBIT 14.7   Discharge: Costs and Benefits

I. Separation Costs

  A. Economic Costs
- Same as for voluntary turnover plus
- Contract buyout (salary, benefit, perks)

  B. Other Costs
- Manager and HR staff time handling problem employee
- Grievance, alternative dispute resolution
- Possibility of lawsuit, loss of lawsuit, settlement or remedy
- Damage to harmonious labor–management relations

II. Replacement Costs
- Same as for voluntary turnover

III. Training Costs
- Same as for voluntary turnover

IV. Benefits
- Departure of low-value employee
- High-value employee replacement possibility
- Reduced disruption for manager and work unit
- Improved performance management and disciplinary skills

It is the other costs that are potentially very large. A discharge is usually preceded by the manager and others spending considerable time, often unpleasant and acrimonious, with the employee in seeking to change the person's behavior through progressive discipline or performance management activities. Many times these attempts fail, an actual discharge is threatened or made, and it is decided to submit the issue to an alternative dispute resolution (ADR) forum for handling. The ADR process will often consume considerable time costs and cash outlays. Instead of using ADR, the discharge may be made and followed by a lawsuit, such as a claim that the discharge was tainted by discrimination based on the race or sex of the dischargee. In turn, the time costs for handling the matter, and the potential cash outlays required in a settlement or court-imposed remedy, can be substantial.[6] In short, compared to voluntary turnover, discharge is a more costly, and unpleasant, type of turnover to experience. Moreover, in unionized settings, discharge problems may pose a serious threat to labor–management relations.

Against these often large costs are many potential benefits. First and foremost is that the organization will be rid of a truly low-value employee whose presence has caused considerable disruption, ineffective performance, and possibly declines in organizational effectiveness. A following benefit is the opportunity to replace the discharge with a high-quality new hire that will hopefully turn out to be a high-value employee. A side benefit of a discharge experience is that many members of the organization will gain improved disciplinary and performance management skills, and the HR department's awareness of the need for better discipline and performance management systems may be heightened and lead to these necessary changes.

Downsizing

Downsizing costs are concentrated in separation costs for a permanent RIF since there will presumably be no replacement hiring and training. These costs are shown in Exhibit 14.8, along with potential benefits.[7] For economic costs, the

---

EXHIBIT 14.8   Downsizing: Costs and Benefits

I. Separation Costs
  A. Economic Costs
  - HR staff time in planning and implementing layoff
  - Managers' time in handling layoff
  - Accrued paid time off (e.g., vacation, sick pay)
  - Early retirement package
  - Voluntary severance package (e.g., one week pay/year of service, continued health insurance, outplacement assistance)
  - Involuntary severance package
  - Contract buyouts for fulfillment of guarantees
  - Higher unemployment insurance premiums
  - Change in control (CIC) guarantees for key executives during a merger or acquisition

  B. Other Costs
  - Shareholder value (stock price) may not improve
  - Loss of critical employees and KSAOs
  - Inability to respond quickly to surges in product and service demand; restaffing delays and costs
  - Contagion—other employees leave
  - Threat to harmonious labor–management relations
  - Possibility of lawsuit, loss of lawsuit, costly settlement or remedy
  - Decreased morale, increased feelings of job insecurity
  - Difficulty in attracting new employees

II. Benefits
  - Lower payroll and benefit costs
  - Increased production and staffing flexibility
  - Ability to relocate facilities
  - Improved promotion and transfer opportunities for stayers
  - Focus on core businesses, eliminate peripheral ones
  - Spread risk by outsourcing activities to other organizations
  - Flatten organization hierarchy—especially among managers
  - Increase productivity

major cost areas are time costs, cash outlays for various severance and buyout packages, and increased unemployment compensation insurance premiums. The time costs involve both HR staff and managers' time in planning, implementing, and handling the RIF.

Severance costs may take numerous forms. First, employees can be paid for accrued time off. Second, early retirement packages may be offered to employees as an inducement to leave early. Third, employees ineligible for early retirement may be offered a voluntary severance package as an inducement to leave without being laid off. A typical severance package includes one week's pay for each year of service, continued health insurance coverage and premium payment, and out-placement assistance. More generous terms may be provided to key executives, such as two weeks pay for each year of service and a lump-sum exit bonus. A danger with both early retirement and voluntary severance packages is that their provisions may turn out to be so attractive that more employees take them and leave than had been planned for in the RIF.

If the early retirement and voluntary severance packages do not serve as an adequate inducement to sufficient numbers of employees, the organization may also institute an involuntary RIF with a severance package, oftentimes not as generous as the voluntary package offered. It is customary to inform employees of the content of both the voluntary and involuntary packages at the time the RIF is announced so they may decide which to take. Some employees may decide to take their chances by not accepting the voluntary package and gambling that they won't be laid off (or if they are, being willing to live with the involuntary severance package).

Some employees may receive special severance consideration. For those on a fixed-term contract, a contract buy-out will be necessary. Others, usually key executives, may have change in control (CIC) clauses in their contract that must be fulfilled if there is a merger or acquisition; CICs are also known as "golden parachutes." In addition to the terms in typical severance packages, a CIC may provide for immediate vesting of stock options, a retirement payout sweetener or buyout, bonus payments, continuation of all types of insurance for an extended time period, and maintenance of various perks.

Severance costs can be considerable. The Wall Street securities firm Merrill Lynch and Company reduced its workforce 14% over a two-year period as part of a restructuring effort. About 15,000 employees were cut, at a severance cost of $1.2 billion ($80,000 per employee).[8]

Other costs of downsizing shown in Exhibit 14.8 may also be considerable. Shareholder value (stock price) may not improve, suggesting the stock market views the probable effectiveness of the restructuring as low. There will be a critical talent loss and an inability to respond quickly to need for workforce additions to cover new demand surges. And a reputation for job instability among job seekers will create added difficulties in attracting new employees. Terminated employees may pursue legal avenues, claiming, for example, that decisions about whom to layoff were tainted by age discrimination. Employees who survive the job cuts may have damaged morale and fear even more cuts, which may harm performance and cause them to look for another job with a more secure organization. Finally, as with discharges, downsizing may place great strains on labor–management harmony.

Against this backdrop of heavy costs are many potential benefits. There will in fact be lower payroll and benefits costs. The organization may gain production and staffing flexibility, an ability to outsource parts of the business that are not mission-critical, and opportunities for facilities redesign and relocation. The restructuring may also entail a flattening of the organization hierarchy through elimination of management layers, leading to increased speed in decision making and productivity boosts. Finally, new promotion and transfer opportunities may open up as the restructuring leads to the hoped-for rebound in organizational effectiveness.

Summary

Despite their many potential benefits, voluntary turnover, discharges, and downsizing are typically costly propositions. Time costs, materials costs, performance and revenue losses, severance costs, legal costs, and so forth can create substantial cost challenges and risks for the organization. Potentially even more important are the human costs of frayed relationships, critical talent losses, performance declines, disruptive discipline, the contagion effect of other employees leaving along with the departing employee, and the risk of not being able to locate, attract, and hire high-quality replacements.

The organization must carefully weigh these costs and benefits generally for each type of turnover, as well as specifically for separate employee groups, job categories, and organizational units. Clear cost/benefit differences in turnover will likely emerge from these more fine-grained analyses. Such analyses will help the organization better understand its turnover, where and among whom it is most worrisome, and how to fashion tailor-made retention strategies and tactics.

RETENTION INITIATIVES: VOLUNTARY TURNOVER

For most organizations, of the three types of turnover, voluntary turnover is the most prevalent and the one they choose to focus on in the continual "war for talent." Described first below are examples of retention initiatives undertaken by organizations to increase retention. These are vast in number, but little is known about how organizations actually decide to act on a turnover problem and go forth with one or more retention initiatives. To fill this void, a retention decision process is described that will help the organization more systematically and effectively pursue the right retention initiatives. Based on the causes of turnover model (Exhibit 14.2), ways to influence the three primary turnover drivers—desirability of leaving, ease of leaving, and alternatives—are suggested for retention initiatives.

Current Practices and Deciding to Act

Turnover analysis does not end with the collection and analysis of data. These activities are merely a precursor to the critical decisions of whether or not to act to solve a perceived turnover problem, and if so, how to intervene to attack the problem and ultimately assess how effective the intervention was. Presented first are some examples of organization retention initiatives that illustrate the breadth and depth of attempts to attack retention concerns. Then a systematic decision process for retention initiatives is provided as a framework to help with deciding to act or not act. Such decision guidance is necessary given the complexity of the retention issue and the lack of demonstrated best practices for improving retention.

What Do Organizations Do?

Several descriptive surveys provide glimpses and hints of what actions organizations decide to take to attack retention. These examples come mostly from relatively large organizations, so what happens in small organizations is more of an unknown. Nonetheless, the data provide interesting illustrations of organization tenacity and ingenuity, along with a willingness to commit resources, in their approaches to retention.

SHRM Survey   The Society for Human Resource Management (SHRM) surveyed HR professionals in 473 organizations nationwide.[9] It was found that the annual voluntary turnover rate was 17%. Turnover increased somewhat with organization size, going from 14% to 26% for organizations with an average of 100 and 5,000 employees, respectively. Turnover rates also varied across job categories: office and clerical (19%), unskilled (15%), semiskilled (12%), service (9%), technicians (6%), sales (5%), skilled (4%), and officials and managers (3%).

A multitude of reasons for leaving were given. The top 10 reasons, and percentage of organizations citing it, were as follows: pursuit of career opportunities elsewhere (78%), better pay and benefits package (65%), poor management (21%), relocating spouse/partner (18%), return to school (15%), retire (14%), job security fears (10%), poor relationships with coworkers (10%), child care issues (8%), and perceived discriminatory treatment (5%). Survey respondents stated that the three biggest threats to employee retention were higher salaries obtainable elsewhere, lack of career development opportunities, and the rising acceptability of job hopping.

What do these organizations do about retention problems and threats? Exhibit 14.9 shows the percentage of organizations offering 36 different retention initiatives and the judged effectiveness of each one. It can be seen that base and variable

EXHIBIT 14.9 Retention Initiatives: Usage and Effectiveness

Scale: 1 = very effective; 5 = not effective at all

	Effectiveness Average	Offer the Initiative?		
		Yes	No	Plan To
1. Health care benefits	1.96	94%	3%	—
2. Competitive salaries	2.02	83%	8%	5%
3. Competitive salary increases	2.05	75%	15%	6%
4. Competitive vacation/holiday benef.	2.09	92%	4%	1%
5. Regular salary reviews	2.11	89%	6%	4%
6. Defined contribution retirement	2.21	73%	21%	2%
6. Paid personal time off	2.21	75%	20%	2%
8. Flexible Work Schedules	2.25	60%	32%	4%
9. Training and development opp.	2.26	88%	4%	4%
10. Open door policy	2.32	93%	3%	2%
10. New hire orientation	2.32	92%	2%	3%
10. Defined benefit plan	2.32	52%	41%	2%
13. Child care paid/onsite	2.4	3%	89%	5%
14. Early eligibility for benefits	2.41	40%	54%	2%
14. Workplace location	2.41	59%	23%	—
16. Tuition reimbursement	2.42	77%	17%	3%
17. Retention bonuses	2.43	22%	71%	4%
18. Child care subsidies	2.46	8%	84%	4%
19. Spot cash	2.48	43%	47%	6%
20. Stock options	2.53	27%	66%	3%
21. Succession planning	2.54	32%	46%	16%
22. Non- or low-cash rewards	2.56	63%	25%	8%
23. Casual dress	2.59	76%	18%	1%
24. 360 degree feedback	2.6	31%	51%	14%
25. Onsite parking	2.64	86%	10%	1%
26. Domestic partner benefits	2.66	12%	74%	4%
26. Eldercare subsidies	2.66	4%	89%	2%
28. Attitude surveys/focus groups	2.67	46%	41%	10%
28. Alternative dispute resolution	2.67	31%	60%	5%
30. Transportation subsidies	2.74	16%	75%	4%
31. Fitness facilities	2.75	26%	62%	8%
32. Severance package	2.77	56%	38%	1%
33. Sabbaticals	2.78	12%	82%	2%
34. Telecommuting	2.79	26%	64%	7%
35. Noncompete agreements	2.84	46%	48%	—
36. Concierge services	2.92	5%	87%	4%

Note: Data in a row may not add up to 100% due to missing data.
Source: Society for Human Resource Management, *Retention Practices Survey* (Alexandria, VA: author, 2000), p. 12. Used with permission.

pay, benefits, hours of work, and training and development practices dominated in terms of usage. Also apparent is a fairly less-than-perfect relationship between usage and effectiveness overall, though the top 10 most effective initiatives also had high usage. Missing from Exhibit 14.9 are initiatives associated with providing greater intrinsic rewards, such as job enlargement. Their usage and effectiveness is thus not known.

WorldatWork Survey   The WorldatWork surveyed HR professionals in 2,554 organizations, of which 72% indicated they had concerns about the attraction and retention of talent.[10] Retention problems varied substantially among job categories. In response to retention problems, the organizations had developed numerous attraction and retention initiatives. The top 10 initiatives in percentage usage were: market adjustment/base salary increase (62%); hiring bonus (60%); work environment—including flexible work schedules, compressed work weeks, related dress code, and telecommuting (49%); retention bonus (28%); promotion and career development opportunities (27%); paying above market (24%); special training and education opportunities (22%); individual spot bonuses (22%); stock programs (19%); and project milestone/completion bonuses (15%).

As in the SHRM survey described above, the major retention initiatives reported in this survey center mostly on base and variable pay, hours of work, and training and development. Also, intrinsic reward programs again receive no mention, though such programs may not have been in the list given to respondents.

The Best 100 Companies   Each year *Fortune* magazine reports on "The Best 100 Companies to Work For."[11] Organizations apply for competition to be on the list, and their score is based on randomly chosen employees' responses to the Great Place to Work Trust Index survey and an evaluation of a Culture Audit. Winners are ranked in order according to their final score, and brief descriptions are provided about the number of U.S. employees (including % women and % minorities), job growth, annual number of job applicants and voluntary turnover rate, average number of employee training hours, entry-level salary for production and for professional employees, revenues, and what makes the organization stand out.

Voluntary turnover averaged 15.7% and ranged from 3% to 54% in these 100 organizations. Job growth ranged from –28% to +36%, averaging 5.7%. The number one- and two-rated organizations (Edward Jones and Container Store) had job growth of 15% and 12%, and voluntary turnover rates of 22% and 24%. Their ratings were not one-year flukes either since both finished in the top 10 the year before.

Unfortunately, the study did not provide specific information on patterns of usage and effectiveness of retention initiatives among the 100 organizations. However, comments about "what makes the organization stand out" provide intriguing tidbits as to special practices that might contribute to enhanced retention. Mentioned for Edward Jones were providing brokers their bonuses a week early to help them through trading declines, and widely held employee beliefs in management honesty. For Container Store, mentioned were good pay (average of $36,256 for salespeople), good retirement (a 100% employer match of employee contributions to 401(k), up to 4% of pay), and a widely held belief by employees that they are respected. The reader should consult the 100 Best Companies results each year to gain glimpses such as these about what organizations are doing to make themselves attractive to job applicants and employees, which may aid in retention enhancement.

Decision Process

It is quite clear that organizations (1) on average experience extensive voluntary turnover, (2) vary considerably in how much turnover they have, (3) think their turnover is due to many different causes, (4) commit substantial resources to multiple retention initiatives, and (5) view retention initiatives as varying in effectiveness. Against this backdrop, decisions about whether to try to improve retention and how to do so should not be made lightly. There is much that must be carefully thought through prior to actual action. Provided in Exhibit 14.10 is a suggested decision process to follow.

As shown in Exhibit 14.10, there are five sequential questions to ask and analyze. Listed under each question are several factors to consider when addressing the question.

The first question—do we think turnover is a problem?—requires consideration and analysis of several types of data. First and most important is what percentage of turnover is voluntary and avoidable, followed closely by what are the relevant organization units for looking at the data. A breakout of voluntary avoidable turnover should be available for each unit. Then, it is necessary to judge whether the turnover rate(s) are increasing and/or high relative to internal and external benchmarks such as industry or direct competitor data. If turnover is relatively high or getting higher, this is cause for concern. Now additional digging is necessary, such as whether managers are complaining about retention problems, if mostly high-value employees are leaving, and whether there are demographic disparities among the leavers. If these indicators also show trouble signs, then it is likely that turnover is a problem. The final analysis should involve the type of costs/benefits described earlier. Even though turnover may be high and so forth, in the final analysis it is only a problem if its costs are judged to exceed the benefits it provides at its current rate, or future projected rate.

The second question—how might we attack the problem?—requires consideration of desirability of leaving, ease of leaving, and alternative turnover causes. Also, within each of these areas, which specific factors is it possible to change? Referring to Exhibit 14.10, for desirability of leaving it shows that increasing job satisfaction is possible, while it is likely not possible to change personal shocks or personal reasons for leaving. Likewise, for ease of leaving it is possible to provide organization-specific KSAOs and to increase the cost of leaving for the

EXHIBIT 14.10 **Decision Process for Retention Initiatives**

Do We Think Turnover Is a Problem?	How Might We Attack the Problem?	What Do We Need to Decide?	Should We Proceed?	How Should We Evaluate the Initiatives?
• Proport on of turnover that is available is high • Turnover calculated for separate units • Turnover high or increasing relative to internal and external benchmarks • Managers complain about retention problems • High-va ue employees are leaving • Demographic disparities among leavers • Overall costs exceed benefits of turnover	• Lower desirability of leaving? Increase job satisfaction—yes Decrease shocks—no personal reasons—no • Lower ease of leaving? Change market conditions—no Provide organization-specific KSAOs—yes Make leaving more costly—yes • Change alternatives? Promotion and transfers—yes Respond to job offers—yes	• Turnover goals • Targeted to units and groups • High-value employees • General and targeted retention initiatives • Lead, match, or lag the market • Supplement or supplant • HR and managers' roles	• Feasibility • Probability of success • Timing	• Lower proportion of turnover if avoidable • Turnover low or decreasing compared to benchmarks • Fewer complaints about retention problems • Fewer high-value employees leaving • Reduced demographic disparities • Lower costs relative to benefits

employee; it is not possible to alter labor market conditions. Finally, for alternatives it is possible to increase promotion and transfer opportunities and to respond to job offers. In short, if there are to be retention initiatives designed to solve turnover problems, on the table for consideration should be some combination of increasing job satisfaction, providing more training and development for KSAOs that are specific to the organization, making it more costly for employees to leave, enhancing employees' promotion and transfer options, and providing counteroffers to outside job offers that employees receive. During the deliberations as to possible retention initiatives, it should be remembered that since turnover has many different causes, no single retention initiative itself is likely to have a very big impact on retention.

Question three—what do we need to decide?—crosses the boundary from consideration to possible implementation. First to be decided are specific numerical turnover (retention) goals in the form of desired turnover rates. Retention programs without retention goals are bound to fail. Then it must be decided whether the goals and retention programs will be across the board, targeted to specific organization units and employee groups, or both. Examples of targeted groups include certain job categories in which turnover is particularly troublesome, women and minorities, and first-year employees (newcomers)—a group that traditionally experiences high turnover. Next to be considered is if and how high-value employees will be treated. If the organization has not previously identified high-value employees, then an employee assessment system for guiding such a determination will be the necessary first step. Many organizations develop special retention initiatives for high-value employees, on top of other retention programs, and it will have to be decided whether to follow this path of special treatment for such employees.[12] Having identified organizational units, targeted groups, and high-value employees (and established turnover goals for them), the retention program specifics must be designed. These may be general (across-the-board) initiatives applicable to all employees, or they may be targeted ones. For each such initiative, it must then be decided how to position the organization's initiatives relative to the marketplace. Will it seek to lead, match, or lag the market? For example, will base pay on average be set to be higher than the market average (lead), to be the same as the market average (match), or be lower than the market average (lag)? Likewise, will new variable pay plans try to outdo competitors (e.g., more favorable stock option plan) or simply match them, and so forth. Adding to the complexity of the decision process is the delicate issue of whether new retention initiatives will supplement (add on to) or supplant (replace) existing rewards and programs. If the latter, the organization should be prepared for the possibility of employee backlash against what employees may perceive as "take-backs" of rewards they currently have and must give up. Finally, the respective rules of HR and individual managers will have to be worked out, and this may vary among the retention initiatives. If the initiative involves responding to job offers, for example, line managers may demand a heavy or even exclusive hand in making them. Alternatively, some initiatives may be HR-driven; examples here include hours of work and variable pay plans.

Should we proceed? is question four in the decision process. It will depend on judgments about feasibility, such as ease of implementation. Judgments about probability of success will also enter in, and having specific turnover (retention) goals will be of immense help in making the decision. Finally, matters of timing should enter in. Even if judged to be feasible and a likely success, a retention program may not be launched immediately. Other HR problem areas and initiatives may have emerged and taken on higher priority. Or, turnover problems may have lost urgency because looser labor markets may have intervened to reduce turnover at the very time the retention initiatives were being planned.

The final question—how should we evaluate the initiatives?—may seem quite hypothetical since the decision to proceed with the intervention has not been made or has just been made. It is important, however, to ask the question early on. Answers will provide focus to the design of the intervention and agreed upon criteria on which to later judge intervention effectiveness. Ideally, the same criteria that led to the conclusion that turnover was a problem (question one) will be used to determine if the solution that has been chosen actually works (question five). For this reason, the same criteria as shown under question one are shown under question five.

Desirability of Leaving

Employees' desirability of leaving depends on their job satisfaction, shocks they experience, and personal (nonjob) reasons. Of these, only job satisfaction can usually be meaningfully influenced by the organization. So the first strategy for improving retention is to improve job satisfaction. The myriad examples of retention initiatives used by organizations described above represent mostly attempts to improve job satisfaction through delivery of various rewards to employees. Indeed, refer back to the multitude of job rewards displayed in Exhibits 4.20 and 4.21. These include direct compensation (base and variable pay), indirect compensation (benefits), hours of work, career advancement, job security, and several intrinsic rewards. Providing either greater amounts of these rewards or adding them to the set of rewards already provided to employees represent key strategies for improving job satisfaction and hopefully retention.

It is critical to understand that merely "throwing" more or new rewards at employees is not a sound retention initiative. Which rewards are chosen, and how they are delivered to employees, will determine how effective they are in improving job satisfaction. Accordingly, described below are 10 guidelines for reward choice and delivery.

Guidelines for Increasing Job Satisfaction and Retention

Exhibit 14.11 contains a summary of the 10 guidelines. They are discussed in detail below.

Match Rewards to Employee Preferences The person/job match model emphasizes that it is the match between rewards desired by employees and offered by the job that leads to job satisfaction. Employee reward preferences may be discerned through exit interviews, postexit surveys, and job satisfaction surveys. In addition, job applicants may provide useful information. It should be remembered that there will be differences in preferences among employees that should be taken into account. A predominantly young workforce may show low preferences for retirement benefits, whereas older employees may place retirement-related rewards at the top of their list. Work/life rewards such as flexible work hours and part-time work, and nonwork rewards such as having a loving family and companionship with family and friends, may have higher appeal to Generation X (under 40) women than Baby Boomer women.[13] Preferred rewards have high potential retention impact, while nonpreferred rewards definitely do not.

Make Rewards Unique To have attraction and retention power, rewards must be unique and unlikely to be offered by competitors. The organization must benchmark against its competitors and on that basis provide rewards at levels that exceed competitors or are not offered by competitors. Doing this requires a commitment to being an organization that leads the market, rather than matches or lags the market.

Base pay levels are the most prevalent reward involved in the lead-lag decision.[14] Based on market salary survey data, the organization might choose to exceed market pay averages by 10%. Justifications for this expensive retention initiative are that it will help attract a higher-quality workforce, permit the organization to hire only the

---

EXHIBIT 14.11   Guidelines for Increasing Job Satisfaction and Retention

- Match rewards to employee preferences
- Make rewards unique
- Rewards must be meaningful
- Link rewards to retention behaviors
- Deliver on rewards that are promised
- Reward permanency is important
- Remember intrinsic rewards
- Fairness and justice are key
- Communicate continuously
- The manager matters

very best, provide a workforce that is very satisfied with its pay and unlikely to even look for other jobs, and lock in employees because they will not be able to obtain higher pay elsewhere.

A "lead the market" strategy can be pursued for any reward. It is a costly strategy, however, and one that most likely cannot be carried out for all rewards. So the organization must choose which (if any) rewards it seeks to be a leader on. It may, for example, concede leadership on base pay but assume leadership on variable pay. Or, if the organization is a seasonal employer in, say, the recreation and tourism industry, it may concede pay leadership (as many seem to do) and lead with benefits such as free use of equipment (e.g., boats, bikes), clothing at cost, and free passes for use of facilities.

Rewards Must Be Meaningful It is important to provide rewards large and unique enough to be meaningful to the recipient—a "noticeable difference." Consider base pay and pay raises that will be built into the base. A raise that constitutes a "noticeable difference" must at a minimum be greater than the inflation rate, in after-tax dollars. An employee earning $50,000 who receives a gross 4% raise of $2,000 will only realize a raise of 2.8% if inflation and taxes combined are at 30%. Such a net raise may not be viewed as very meaningful.

Similar logic applies to any reward. Marginal or trivial-size rewards, a characteristic of most perks such as cell phones and free snacks, probably have marginal (if any) retention power.

Link Rewards to Retention Behaviors One retention behavior is simple organization membership—the employees receive the reward as long as they remain members of the organization. Here, being a market leader and providing rewards not even offered by competitors can be a powerful retention tool. For example, providing health care benefits when competitors don't can be a strong force that holds employees to the organization.

Another retention behavior is seniority, in which the amount or choice of the reward increases with employees' length of service. Vacation and hours of work schedules are examples. But seniority can play a role in many other rewards, such as career advancement opportunities and job security in the form of protection from layoffs. In unionized work settings, labor contracts typically spell out numerous rewards that are seniority-based, as well as the specific rules governing allocations of the rewards.[15]

A more subtle way of rewarding seniority is to make the reward contingent on the person's base pay level. Base pay levels typically increase over time through a combination of general base pay and merit pay raise increases that are built into the base, so that higher base pay in a job typically signifies higher seniority. Defined benefit retirement pay plans, for example, typically calculate retirement pay as some percentage (say, 50%) of the average of the person's three highest (or last three) years of pay multiplied by years of service. Seniority thus enters into retirement pay twice—through average highest salaries and through length of service. Another example is overtime pay, which is calculated off the base salary. Some employees place high value on overtime pay, and opportunities to earn it and see it grow in size as seniority increases constitute a strong financial incentive to stay with the organization.

Another increasingly important retention behavior is job performance. Organizations with a strong performance management culture thrive on high performance expectations, coupled with a solid performance review process and large rewards (base pay raises, bonuses, stock options) for high performers. Lesser performers receive substantially less. Through such major performance reward differentiation, the organization signals who are the key performers it would like to keep. Lesser performers may even be counseled to leave the organization.

Finally, a more generic assessment than just a job performance review may be undertaken to identify certain individuals for special retention initiatives. Such individuals are judged to be high-value employees or key contributors that the organization wishes to retain at almost any cost.[16] Accordingly, these employees may participate in special retention programs and receive special retention bonuses, desired new job assignments and promotions, extended numbers of stock options, repricing of current options, additional perks, and so forth in order to entice them to remain with the organization.

Deliver on Rewards That Are Promised   The organization must live up to its promise and deliver on new rewards or current reward "sweeteners." Failure to do so not only violates a firm expectation on the part of the employee but also jeopardizes the potency and believability of future reward initiatives. Sometimes, for example, changing economic conditions dictate sudden reductions or elimination of pay raises or bonuses. Such actions not only undermine the retention potential of the reward, but they may encourage active pursuit of the very thing they were trying to prevent—the employee beginning to look elsewhere for a job.

Reward Permanency Is Important   While no reward plan is or should be etched in stone, a general intent of reward plan permanence is desirable. Changing reward payouts, eliminating or modifying plans, and switching plans send confusing signals as to what is the desired behavior, as well as foster questions of procedural justice. It is wise to not push forth reward plans that are "experimental" or have an uncertain future.

Remember Intrinsic Rewards   The set of intrinsic rewards (Exhibit 4.21) desired by employees should not be overlooked as potentially important determinants of employees' decisions to stay or quit. While debates continually surface about the relative importance of extrinsic versus intrinsic rewards to employees, it is clear that intrinsic rewards are highly valued by many employees, and steps could be taken to increase them as a way of enhancing retention.[17]

These steps involve assignment of employees (or new hires) to jobs, or the redesign of jobs, in ways that better meet their intrinsic reward preferences. For example, employees with high skill variety needs could be assigned to more complex jobs or projects within a work unit. Or, employees with high autonomy needs could be assigned to a job where the manager has a very "hands off" style of leadership. Jobs could also be redesigned in ways that would meet skill variety and autonomy needs. For skill variety, the manager may work with the employee to broaden the scope of tasks and responsibilities assigned to the employee over time, allowing for personal growth in the job. Or through job rotation the employee could literally change jobs as a way of enhancing skill variety. Some organizations combine intrinsic and extrinsic rewards through the development of formal knowledge and skill-based plans, in which specific knowledges or skills are designated as critical and the employee receives a predetermined increase in base pay for demonstrated proficiency or acquisition of the knowledge or skill. Enhancing job autonomy might occur through establishment of formal performance goals for the job and then providing the employee the resources to accomplish the goals in ways determined by the employee, without close supervision or needing to "do it by the book." Similar strategies for improving the other intrinsic rewards—task identity, task significance, feedback from job and agents, and dealing with others—might be conceived and undertaken.

Fairness and Justice Are Key Employees' needs for fair treatment are always present, and justice mechanisms must be in place to ensure that employees indeed continuously experience that the organization's reward systems are fair. Two forms of justice are necessary.[18] The first is known as distributive or outcome justice, and it refers to perceptions by the employee that the amount of the reward (or punishment) received is fair. The second form is referred to as procedural justice, meaning the employee perceives that the process by which the reward (or punishment) was determined is fair. A sense of injustice of either kind can create job dissatisfaction that may end up in turnover (or in court).

Developing positive senses of distributive and procedural justice requires careful reward system design. Distributive justice requires that there be a rational and preferably measurable basis for reward decisions. Seniority-based rewards score high here because of employee beliefs in the legitimacy of seniority and its objective, measurable nature. Performance-based rewards may be a bit more problematic if employees question the legitimacy of performance-driven rewards in principle, such as through a belief that these rewards foster divisiveness among employees and detract from the intrinsically rewarding aspects of the job. Actual procedures for determining rewards, especially the performance measurement system, must also be understood and accepted by employees.

Communicate Continuously If reward systems are going to increase employees' job satisfaction, employees must know why the system was developed, the mechanics of the system, and the payouts to be expected. Such knowledge and understanding require continuous communication with employees. Research shows that a very common form of employee dissatisfaction with reward systems is their failure to understand them or actual misinformation about them.[19] Any retention initiative intended to increase job satisfaction then must have a solid communication component built into it.

The Manager Matters   The employees' manager may make a difference in retention in several ways. First, the manager him- or herself can serve as a source of reward or punishment. It is often said that "employees don't quit their jobs, they quit their bosses." Thus, interpersonal compatibility or "chemistry" between the manager and employee may be a critical part of the employee's decision to stay or leave, particularly when the two are in close proximity and/or have frequent contact with each other.

Second, at the extreme, the manager may engage in abusive or harassing behaviors that are threatening and discomforting to the employee, causing dissatisfaction and a desire to leave. In one study, for example, employees' ratings of their supervisor on a set of "abusive supervision" items were found to be a significant predictor of whether they stayed or left their job. Examples of the items include: "tells me my thoughts and feelings are stupid," "puts me down in front of others," "tells me I'm incompetent," "invades my privacy," "breaks promises he/she makes," "blames me to save himself/herself from embarrassment," and "makes negative comments to me about others."[20] Even more extreme supervisory behaviors, such as sexual harassment, obviously may also have negative impacts on the employee's desire to remain on the job.

Third, managers control many, if not most, of the rewards that employees experience. The manager functions as an intermediary between the employee and the rewards, deciding both the amount of the reward and the process by which the amount will be determined. In short, to the employee, the manager represents a critical source or control of both distributive and procedural justice.

Finally, the manager may function as a key communication conduit regarding reward systems. If the manager does indeed mete out rewards, it is important for the manager to be the communicator and explainer about the reward systems. It is important to communicate about the purpose and mechanics of the program, as well as clarify exactly what the employee needs to do in order to receive the reward. It is through such communication that procedural and distributive justice perceptions of the employee may be positively shaped.

Ease of Leaving

The decision process (Exhibit 14.10) indicates two points of attack on ease of leaving—providing organization-specific training and increasing the cost of leaving. The third possible factor, changing labor market conditions, cannot be influenced and represents a variable that will continuously influence the organization's voluntary turnover.

Organization-Specific Training

Training and development activities provide KSAOs to employees that they did not possess at the time they entered the organization as new hires. Training and development seeks to increase labor quality in ways that will enhance employees' effectiveness. As shown previously, training represents a substantial investment (cost) that evaporates when an employee leaves the organization.

The organization may invest in training to provide KSAOs that vary along a continuum of general to organization specific. The more general the KSAOs, the more transferable they are to other organizations, thus increasing the likelihood they improve the employee's marketability and raise the probability of leaving. Organization-specific KSAOs are not transferable, and possession of them does not improve employee marketability. Hence, it is possible to lower the employee's ease of leaving by providing, as much as possible, only organization-specific training content that has value only as long as the employee remains with the organization.

This strategy needs to be coupled with a selection strategy in which any general KSAOs required for the job are assessed and selected on so that they will not have to be invested in once the employee is on the job. For example, applicants for an entry-level sales job might be assessed and selected for general sales competencies such as written and verbal communication and interpersonal skills. Those hired may then receive more specialized training in such areas as product knowledge, specific software, and knowledge of territories. To the extent such organization-specific KSAOs become an increasingly large proportion of the employee's total KSAO package over time, they help restrict the employee's mobility.

This strategy entails some risk. It assumes the general KSAOs are available and affordable among applicants. It also assumes these applicants will not be turned off by the job if they learn about the organization-specific training and development they will receive.

Increased Cost of Leaving

Driving up the cost of leaving is a way to make it less easy to leave. Providing above-market pay and benefits is one way to do this since employees will find it difficult to find better-paying jobs elsewhere. Any form of deferred compensation, such as deferred bonuses, will also raise the cost of leaving since the compensation will be lost if the employee leaves prior to being eligible to receive it.

Retention bonuses might also be used. Normally, these are keyed to high-value employees whose loss would wreak organizational havoc. Such may be the case during mergers and acquisitions, when retention of key managers is essential to a smooth transition. For example, when TransWorld Airlines (TWA) sold itself to American Airlines, TWA had a plan to pay retention bonuses of 15% to 30% of annual salaries to 100 key managers. The bonuses were paid in three phases over a one-year period. In addition, a separate $500,000 discretionary fund was used to pay other people retention bonuses.[21]

Another long-term way to make leaving costly is to locate the organization's facilities in an area where it is the dominant employer and other amenities (housing, schools, health care) are accessible and affordable. This may entail location in the outer rings of suburban areas or relatively small and rural communities. Once employees move to and settle into these locations, the cost of leaving is high because of the lack of alternative jobs within the area and a need to make a costly geographic shift in order to obtain a new job.

Alternatives

In confronting outside alternatives available to employees, the organization must fashion ways to make even better internal alternatives available and desirable. Two key ways to do this involve internal staffing and responding to outside job offers.

Internal Staffing

The nature and operation of internal staffing systems have been explored already. It is important to reiterate that open systems serve as a safety value, retention-wise, in that employees are encouraged to look internally for new job opportunities and managers benefit by seeking internal candidates rather than going to the outside. The organization should also think of ways outside the realm of its traditional internal staffing systems to provide attractive internal alternatives to its employees.

For example, Mercer Management Consulting has developed a rotational externship program for some of its consultants. These consultants are allowed to take on a full-time operational role for a client for 6 to 24 months, rather than handle multiple clients, allowing the consultant the satisfaction of seeing a project through to completion and to gain valuable operating experience. It is hoped that these consultants will return to Mercer at the end of the project, based on the bird-in-the-hand theory—if you love it, let it go; if it loves you, it will come back. Another example is a temporary internal transfer system used by Interbrand Group, Inc., a unit of Omnicom Group, Inc. Certain high-performance employees are offered short-term transfers to any of its 26 offices worldwide. The lateral moves last from three months to one year. The transfers allow employees to get a change of life without having to quit their jobs.[22]

Response to Job Offers

When employees receive an actual outside job offer, or are on the verge of receiving one, they clearly have a solid job alternative in hand. How should the organization respond, if at all, in order to make itself the preferred alternative?

The organization should confront this dilemma with some carefully thought through policies in advance. This will help prevent some knee-jerk, potentially regrettable actions being taken on the spot when an employee brings forth a job offer and wants to use it for leverage.

First, the organization should decide whether it will or will not be willing to respond to job offers. Some organizations choose not to, thereby avoiding bidding wars and counteroffer games; and even if the organization successfully retained the employee, the employee may now lack commitment to the organization, and other employees may resent the special retention deal that was cut. Other organizations choose to respond to job offers, not wanting to automatically close out an opportunity to at least respond to, and hopefully retain, the employee. Other times, job offers are welcomed because they help the organization sort out who its stars are and what kinds of offer packages it may have to give other recruits in order to lure them into the organization's fold. There is even an example of an organization that pays $1,000 "notification bonuses" to employees who disclose receiving an outside offer so that it can learn its content and have the option of being able to respond to it.[23] The price for such an openness to outside offers is that it may encourage employees to actively solicit them in order to try to squeeze a counteroffer out of the organization, thus improving the "deal."

The second major policy issue is for which employees will the organization respond to outside offers. Will it be all employees, or only select ones, and if so, which select ones? Here, the focus should likely be on high-value employees.

A third set of policy issues pertains to who will put together the counteroffer, and what approval process must be followed. While individual managers will likely want wide latitude over these issues, the HR function will need to be an important player for cost-control purposes, as well as for ensuring procedural and distributive justice overall.

RETENTION INITIATIVES: DISCHARGE

Performance Management

Performance management is used by many organizations to help ensure that the initial person/job match made during staffing yields an effectively performing employee, to facilitate employee performance improvement and competency growth, and to detect and hopefully remedy performance problems. Performance management systems focus most of their attention on planning, enabling, appraising, and rewarding employee performance.[24] Having a performance management system in place, however, also allows the organization to systematically detect and treat performance problems employees exhibit before those problems become so harmful and intractable that discharge is the only recourse. The discharge prevention possibilities of a performance management system make it another important retention initiative to use within an overall retention program. Also, a sound performance management system can be very useful in helping organizations successfully defend itself against legal challenges to discharges that do occur.

Exhibit 14.12 portrays the performance management process. Organization strategy drives work-unit plans, which in turn become operational and doable for employees through a four-stage process. Stage one—performance planning—involves setting performance goals for each employee and identifying specific competencies the employee will be evaluated on. After performance planning, stage two—performance execution—begins. Here the focus is on the employee actually performing the job. Assistance to the employee could or should be made in the form of resources to aid in job performance, coupled with coaching and feedback from the employee's manager, peers, and others. At the end of the performance

EXHIBIT 14.12 **Performance Management Process**

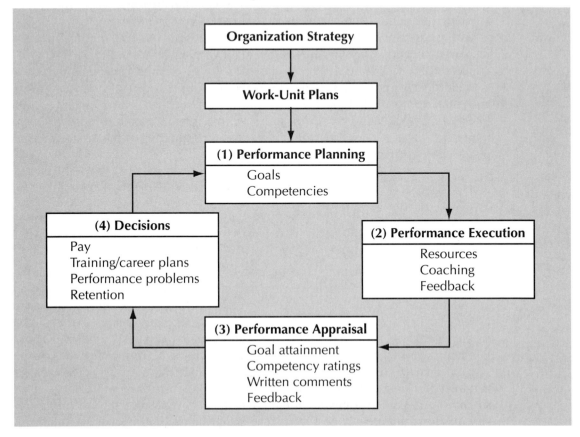

period, such as quarter or year, stage three begins and a formal performance review is conducted, usually by the manager. In this stage, an assessment is made of the employee's success in reaching established goals, ratings of the employee's competencies are made, written comments are developed to explain ratings and provide suggestions for performance improvement, and feedback of the assessment is provided to the employee. Collectively, these actions are known as performance appraisal. In stage four, the information developed during the performance review is used to help make decisions that will affect the employee. Most likely, these decisions pertain to pay raises and to training and career plans. They may also pertain to formal identification of performance problems, where the employee either has shown, or is headed toward, unacceptable performance. Or, an actual decision to retain or terminate an employee is made. After decisions are made, the performance management cycle is complete, and performance planning begins again.

It should be noted that the design, implementation, and operation of a performance management system is a complex undertaking, and the specific ways that the four stages described above are actually carried out vary among organizations.[25] For purposes here, however, the performance management system depicted in Exhibit 14.12 shows how such a system can be a critical retention tool for the organization when it is confronted with employees who are having severe performance problems that place them on the cusp of termination.

Specifically, it may be decided that an employee has severe performance problems (stage four), and this can then set in motion a focused performance improvement process throughout the next performance management cycle. To begin, performance directions and standards are established for the performance problem employee. These are the critical yardsticks that can be used to communicate performance expectations to employees and later laid against the employee's performance to determine actual performance attainments. Employees who are experiencing performance problems will thus have clear indications of performance expectations and needed performance improvements. It is unwise to then simply turn the employee "loose" to perform unaided. There is no reason to recycle and repeat past actions. Instead, assistance in the form of resources to do the job and particularly attentive coaching and feedback from the manager are ingredients for performance improvement by the employee. During performance review, special attention will have to be paid to those areas in which the employee's performance was deemed to be a problem, and a very thorough documentation and review of all the performance data will be necessary. Based on the analysis and evaluation of the data, it will then have to be decided whether sufficient performance improvement has occurred to warrant continued retention of the employee.

Manager Training and Rewards

There are many components required for a successful performance management system. None are probably more critical than training and rewards for the managers who will be users of the performance management system with employees in their work units.[26]

Performance management requires a complex set of knowledges and skills that managers must possess, particularly for the performance execution and performance appraisal stages. Training for managers is essential to provide them these requisites to being effective performance managers. Examples of training content include purposes of performance management, policies and procedures of the performance management system, appraisal forms and how to complete them, keeping records of employee performance incidents, rating accuracy, coaching techniques, finding and providing resources, methods of providing feedback, goal setting, and legal compliance requirements. It is especially important to stress exactly why and how performance management is to be used as a retention initiative that seeks to prevent discharge through intensive performance improvement attempts.

Managers must also be provided incentives for using these new knowledges and skills to effectively conduct performance management. At a minimum it is necessary to formally make performance management a part of the manager's job, during the performance planning stage for the manager, so that the manager will have performance management as an area of responsibility requiring attention and that the manager's own performance appraisal results will depend on how well the manager practices performance management. Of course, reward decisions such as pay raises can then be driven at least in part by this portion of the performance appraisal. One of the manager's most important rewards will be an intrinsic one, namely, the experience of helping a performance problem employee improve sufficiently that the employee is retained by the organization.

Another important part of training should be concerned with employee termination. Here managers must come to understand that a decision to discharge an employee for performance problems falls outside of the normal performance management process (Exhibit 14.12) and is not a decision that can or should be made alone by the individual manager. Terminations require separate procedural and decision-making processes.[27] These could also be covered as part of a regular performance management training program, or a separate program devoted to termination could be conducted.

Progressive Discipline

Employee discipline pertains to problems of behavioral conduct that violate rules, procedures, laws, and professional and moral standards.[28] Discipline may also come into play for performance problem employees. Progressive discipline has a series of penalties for misconduct that increase in severity if the misconduct is repeated, starting with an informal warning and going all the way up to termination. The goal of progressive discipline is retention, except in circumstances of repeated misconduct or extreme misconduct that warrant termination. In progressive discipline, employees are given notice of their misconduct and are provided the opportunity (and often the assistance) to change their behavior; termination is a last resort.

Progressive discipline systems are rooted in major principles of fairness and justice that can be summarized in the following five requirements for a progressive discipline system: (1) give employees notice of the rules of conduct and misconduct, (2) give employees notice of the consequences of violation of the rules, (3) provide equal treatment for all employees, (4) allow for full investigation of the alleged misconduct and defense by the employee, and (5) provide employees the right to appeal a decision.[29] Failure to incorporate these requirements into the organization's discipline process can result in very negative reactions of employees—work-unit disruption, job actions such as work slowdowns, sabotage, and turnover—because employees feel justice is being meted out unfairly.

Actions to Take

To address those fairness requirements, several things should be done. First, establish what constitutes misconduct and the penalties for misconduct. Exhibit 14.13 provides examples of various forms of misconduct, grouped according to severity (minor, moderate, major). Also shown are examples of penalties for each category of severity. The penalties start with an oral warning and progress through a written warning, suspension, and termination. Second, provide training to employees and managers so that they are aware of the types of misconduct, penalties, investigation and documentation requirements, and appeal rights. Third, work with managers to ensure that there is consistency of treatment (no favoritism) of employees, meaning that similar misconduct results in similar penalties for all employees. Finally, establish an appeals procedure in which employees may challenge disciplinary actions if one is not already in place. This could be based on a variety of alternative dispute resolution procedures described in Chapter 13.

Documentation by the manager is critical in all but the least severe instances of misconduct (e.g., first-time minor offense with an oral warning).[30] Thus, the manager must investigate allegations of misconduct, gather evidence, and write down and keep records of what was learned. Allegations of tardiness, for example, might involve inspection of time cards and interviews with other employees. The time cards and interview notes should then be kept as part of the documentation record. Employees should have the right to see all documentation and provide written documentation in self-defense.

Though not shown in Exhibit 14.13, performance problems could be incorporated into, or dovetailed with, the progressive discipline system.[31] Here, it would be wise if possible to first adhere to the normal performance management cycle, so that correction of performance deficiencies is done in a consultative way between the employee and the manager, and the manager assumes major responsibility for providing resources to the employee, as well as for attentive coaching

---

EXHIBIT 14.13 **Progressive Discipline Examples: Misconduct and Penalties**

A. Misconduct

Minor Offense	Moderate Offense	Major Offense
• Punctuality • Horseplay • Cleanliness • Computer—personal use • Smoking • Dress code	• Equipment damage • Misdemeanor (on job) • Harassment • Unsafe behaviors • Hostile work environment • Professional standards breach	• Dishonesty • Felony • Sabotage • Theft • Drug/alcohol on job • Firearms/explosives

B. Penalties

Minor Offense

First Time	Second Time	Third Time	Fourth Time
Oral warning or written reprimand	Written reprimand or suspension	Suspension or discharge	Discharge

Moderate Offense

First Time	Second Time	Third Time	Fourth Time
Written reprimand	Suspension	Longer suspension	Discharge

Major Offense

First Time	Second Time	Third Time	Fourth Time
Suspension or discharge	Discharge	Not applicable	Not applicable

and feedback. If performance improvement is not forthcoming, then shifting to the progressive discipline system will be necessary. For very serious performance problems, it may be necessary for the manager to address them with an expedited performance management cycle, coupled with a clear communication to the employee that failure to correct performance problems could lead immediately to the beginning of formal disciplinary actions.

Employee termination is the final step in progressive discipline, and ideally it would never be necessary. Rarely, if ever, will this be the case. The organization thus must be prepared for the necessity of conducting terminations. Termination processes, guidelines, training for managers, and so forth must be developed and implemented. Considerable guidance is available to help the organization in this regard.[32]

RETENTION INITIATIVES: DOWNSIZING

Downsizing involves reduction in the organization's staffing levels through layoffs (RIFs). Many factors contribute to layoff occurrences: decline in profits, restructuring of the organization, substitution of the core workforce with a flexible workforce, obsolete job or work unit, mergers and acquisitions, loss of contracts and clients, technological advances, productivity improvements, shortened product life cycles, and financial markets that favor downsizing as a positive organizational action.[33] While downsizing obviously involves the elimination of jobs and employees, it also encompasses several retention matters. These involve balancing the advantages and disadvantages of downsizing, staffing levels and quality, alternatives to layoffs, and dealing with employees who remain after downsizing.

Weighing Advantages and Disadvantages

There are multiple advantages (benefits) and disadvantages (costs) of downsizing; refer back to Exhibit 14.8 for a review. A thoughtful consideration of these makes it clear that if downsizing is to be undertaken, it should be done with great caution. It is simply not usually an effective "quick fix" to financial performance problems confronting the organization.

Moreover, research suggests that the presumed and hoped-for benefits of downsizing may not be as great as it might seem.[34] For example, one study looked at how employment level changes affected profitability and stock returns of 537 organizations over a 14-year period. Downsizing did not significantly improve profitability, though it did produce somewhat better stock returns. But organizations that combined downsizing with asset restructuring fared better. Another study looked at the incidence of downsizing across the regional sales offices of a large financial services organization and found layoffs ranged from 0–29% of the workforce, with an average of 7%. It was also found that the amount of downsizing had a significant negative impact on sales offices' profitability, productivity, and customer satisfaction. Additional research has found that downsizing has negative impacts on employee morale and health, workgroup creativity and communication, and workforce quality.[35]

In short, downsizing is not a panacea for poor financial health. It has many negative impacts on employees and should be combined with a well-planned total restructuring if it is to be effective. Such conclusions suggest the organization should carefully ponder if in fact it wants to downsize; if so, by how much, and which employees should it seek to retain.

Staffing Levels and Quality

Reductions in staffing levels should be mindful of retention in at least two ways. First, enthusiasm for a financial quick fix needs to be tempered by a realization that once lost, many downsized employees may be unlikely to return later if economic circumstances improve. It will then have to engage in costly restaffing, as opposed to potentially less costly and quicker retention initiatives. At a minimum, therefore, the organization should consider alternatives to downsizing simultaneous with downsizing planning. Such an exercise may well lead to lesser downsizing and greater retention.

Staffing level reductions should also be thought of in selective or targeted terms, rather than across the board. Such a conclusion is a logical outgrowth of human resource planning, through which it is invariably discovered that the forecasted labor demand and supply figures lead to differing human resource head-count requirements across organizational units and job categories. Indeed, it is possible that some units or job categories may be confronting layoffs while others will actually be hiring. Such an occurrence is increasingly common in organizations.[36]

If cuts are to be made, who should be retained? Staffing quality and employee acceptance concerns combine to produce some alternatives to choose from. The first alternative would be to retain the most senior employees, and cut the least senior employees, in each work unit. Such an approach explicitly rewards the most senior employees, thus likely enhancing long-run retention efforts by signaling job security commitments to long-term employees. Such seniority-based retention also likely meets with strong employee acceptance. On the downside, the most senior employees may not be the best performers, and looking ahead, the most senior employees may not have the necessary qualifications for job requirements changes that will be occurring as part of the restructuring process. In addition, seniority-based layoffs raise important but thorny procedural internal labor market issues, such as how to exactly count seniority and what (if any) "bumping" rights employees targeted for layoff might have. Bumping is a process by which an employee may avoid layoff by taking over the job of another employee, usually one with less seniority, who will be laid off instead. In unionized settings, such issues are typically spelled out at length in the labor contract.[37]

A second alternative would be to make performance-based retention decisions. Employees' current and possibly past performance appraisals' would be consulted in each work unit. The lowest-performing employees would be designated for layoff. This approach seeks to retain the highest-quality employees, those who through their performance are contributing most to organizational effectiveness. It may meet with less employee acceptance than the first alternative among some employees because of perceived injustice in the performance appraisal process. It also assumes that the current crop of best performers will continue to be so in the future, even though job requirements might be changing. And legal challenges may arise, as discussed later.

A third alternative focuses on retaining what were called "high-value employees" and concentrating layoffs on "low-value employees" (Exhibit 14.1). Here, multiple criteria of value are used, rather than a single one such as seniority or performance, though both of these value indicators would likely be included in the value assessments of employees. Recognition of multiple indicators of value is more encompassing in terms of employees' likely future contributions to organizational effectiveness, and because of this it may also meet with high employee acceptance. Use of this approach, however, requires a complex and potentially burdensome process. Indeed, the process is directly akin to an internal selection system in which the value indicators must be identified, assessed, scored, and weighted to come up with a composite value score for each employee that would then be used as the basis for the retention decision. Cut scores are also probably required.

Alternatives to Downsizing

A no-layoffs or a guaranteed employment policy as an organization strategy is the most dramatic alternative to downsizing. Several major organizations pursue this strategy, including S.C. Johnson, Pella, Nucor, Northwestern Mutual, Enterprise Rent-A-Car, Erie Insurance, and Lincoln Electric.[38] At Lincoln Electric, every employee who has three or more years of continuous service is guaranteed a minimum of 75% of a normal workweek. This guarantee is for a job, not a specific position, so cross-training and flexible internal mobility is practical. To create a staffing buffer, during peak times overtime is paid rather than staffing up with new employees; then during downturns, overtime hours, but not employees, are cut. Incentive pay systems are used, along with letting go of people who don't meet performance expectations. Senior executives have a higher percentage of their pay in profit sharing than the rest of the workforce, which functions as an economic buffer during downturns.

No-layoff strategies require considerable organization and HR planning, along with a commitment to a set of programs necessary for successfully implementing the strategy. The strategies also require a gamble and bet that, if lost, could severely damage employee loyalty and trust.

Other organizations are unwilling to make a no-layoff guarantee but pursue layoff minimization through many different programs. Exhibit 14.14 provides an example, based on a survey of 226 organizations. It can be seen that multiple steps were taken prior to layoff, headed by attrition (not replacing employees who leave), employment freezes, and nonrenewal of contract workers. A series of direct and indirect pay changes (e.g., salary reduction, early retirement) also played some role in their layoff minimization. Other actions are also possible, such as temporary layoff with some proportion of pay and benefits continued, substitution of stock options for bonuses, conversion of regular employees to independent contractors, temporary assignments at a reduced time (and pay) commitment, and off-site Internet employees who temporarily convert to work-at-home on a reduced time (and pay) basis.[39]

EXHIBIT 14.14   **Layoff Minimization Examples**

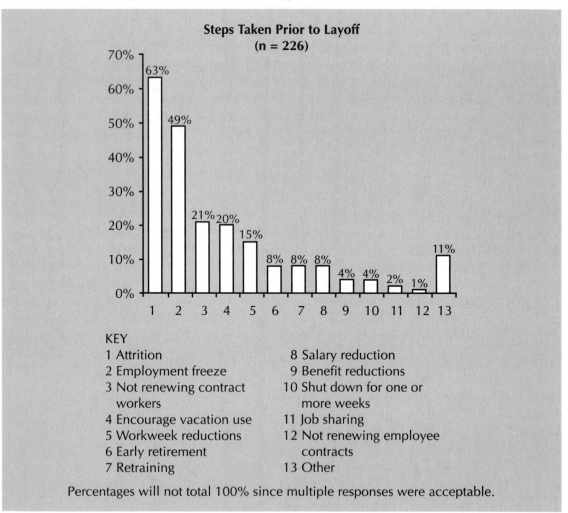

Steps Taken Prior to Layoff
(n = 226)

KEY
1 Attrition
2 Employment freeze
3 Not renewing contract workers
4 Encourage vacation use
5 Workweek reductions
6 Early retirement
7 Retraining
8 Salary reduction
9 Benefit reductions
10 Shut down for one or more weeks
11 Job sharing
12 Not renewing employee contracts
13 Other

Percentages will not total 100% since multiple responses were acceptable.

Source: Society for Human Resource Management, *Layoffs and Job Security Survey* (Alexandria, VA: author, 2001), p. 9. Used with permission.

Employees Who Remain

Employees who remain either in their prelayoff or in a redeployed job after a downsizing must not be ignored. Doing otherwise creates a new retention problem—survivors who are stressed and critical of the downsizing process. One study of survivors found that less than 50% of them rated management's honesty as positive in regard to layoffs, felt support for remaining staff was adequate, and thought their organizations recognized the value of remaining employees. Moreover, almost half of the survivors learned about the downsizing through rumors or word-of-mouth.[40] In terms of stress, it is heightened by loss of coworkers and friends, higher workloads, new locations and work hours, new and/or more responsibilities, and fear of job loss just around the corner.

These many examples of "survivor sickness" suggest a need to anticipate and attack it directly within downsizing planning. One survey reported that organizations sought to meet survivors' needs through enhanced communication programs, morale-boosting events, promotion of the employee assistance program, and stress-related training. Surprisingly, 30% of organizations surveyed reported they took no steps to deal with survivors.[41] Unless steps are taken to help survivors plan for and adjust to the new realities they will confront, heightened job dissatisfaction seems inevitable. In turn, voluntary turnover may spike upward, increasing even more the cost of downsizing.

LEGAL ISSUES

Retention initiatives are closely intertwined with the occurrence of employee separations since the result of an unsuccessful retention initiative is the voluntary or involuntary separation of the employee from the organization. The organization's retention initiatives thus must be guided in part by the laws and regulations governing separations. A brief overview of these is provided. Then a detailed look at the role of performance appraisal in separation is presented since a thrust of this chapter has been performance-based retention.

Separation Laws and Regulations

A desire to provide protection and safeguards to employees leaving the organization, especially for discharge and downsizing, has led to a myriad of laws and regulations governing the separation process.[42] These include:

- Public policy restrictions on employment-at-will
- Employment discrimination laws and regulations
- Affirmative action requirements
- Employment contract principles
- Labor contract provisions

- Civil service laws and regulations
- Negligent supervision and retention
- Advanced warning about plant closings

A basic tenet underlying restrictions on employee separation is the need for fair and consistent treatment of employees. Included here are concerns for ensuring procedural fairness and for basing separations on legitimate bases, such as merit, seniority, or performance. The organization should be thoroughly familiar with these numerous laws and regulations, and their underlying principles, as it designs and administers its retention initiatives.

Performance Appraisal

Organizations often favor retention and separation systems and decisions being driven by employee performance. Laws and regulations generally uphold or even encourage such a role for performance. However, the law as interpreted also insists that the performance appraisals, and the performance appraisal system generally, be fair and equitable in application to employees undergoing separation. Interpretations come about from a combination of court decisions and governmental regulations that have evolved around the issue of performance appraisal in practice.

Based on these decisions and regulations, numerous specific suggestions have been put forth to guide the organization in the design and use of its performance appraisal (or management) system.[43] The recommendations include:

- Appraisal criteria should be job-related, specific, and communicated in advance to the employee.
- The manager (rater) should receive training in the overall performance appraisal process and how to avoid common rating errors.
- The manager should be familiar with employee's job description and actual performance.
- There should be agreement among different raters in their evaluation of the employee's performance.
- Evaluations should be in writing.
- The employee should be able to review the evaluation and comment on it before it becomes final.
- The employee should receive timely feedback about the evaluation and an explanation for any outcome decision (e.g., retention or separation).
- There should be an upward review of the employee's appraisal.
- There should be an appeal system for employees dissatisfied with their evaluation.

Conforming to the above recommendations will help (not guarantee) provide a fair evaluation process and the defensible evaluation decisions pertaining to retention and separation. If the organization wants to manage a performance-driven retention system, it would be wise to ensure the adequacy of its performance appraisal system relative to the above recommendations.

SUMMARY

Retention management seeks to control the numbers and types of employees who leave and who remain with the organization. Employee loss occurs via voluntary turnover or involuntary turnover in the form of discharge or downsizing. Voluntary turnover is caused by a combination of perceived desirability of leaving, ease of leaving, and alternatives to one's current job. Some of these reasons are avoidable, and others are not. Avoidable turnover can also be said to occur among high- and low-value employees. Discharge occurs for performance and discipline-related problems. Downsizing or reduction in force (RIF) comes about because the organization is, or is projected to be, overstaffed in head-count terms.

It is important for the organization to conduct thorough analyses of its turnover. Using a simple formula, turnover rates can be calculated, both overall and broken down by types of turnover, types of employees, job categories, and geographic location. It is also useful to benchmark the organization's turnover rates internally and externally. Another form of analysis is determining reasons that people leave. This can be done via exit interviews, postexit surveys, and employee satisfaction surveys. Analysis of costs and benefits of each of the three types of turnover should also be done. The three major cost categories are separation, replacement, and training. Within each category numerous costs, both financial and nonfinancial, may be estimated. Likewise, each type of turnover has both financial and nonfinancial benefits associated with it that must be weighed against the many costs. A thorough understanding of costs and benefits will help the organization determine where and among whom turnover is the most worrisome, and how to fashion retention strategies and tactics.

To reduce voluntary turnover, organizations engage in numerous retention initiatives centered around direct and variable pay programs, benefits, hours of work schedules, and training and development. Little is known about attempts to increase intrinsic rewards. A decision process may be followed to help decide which, if any, of such retention initiatives to undertake. The process follows five basic questions: Do we think turnover is a problem? How might we attack the problem? What do we need to decide? Should we proceed? How should we evaluate the programs? To influence the desirability of leaving, the organization must raise job satisfaction by providing either more rewards or different rewards than are currently being given to employees. There are 10 guidelines to follow for such attempts. Ease of leaving can possibly be reduced by providing organization-specific training and by increasing the costs of leaving. Finally, retention might be improved by providing more internal job alternatives to employees and by responding forcefully to other job offers they receive.

Discharges might be reduced via formal performance management and progressive discipline systems. The performance management system involves four stages—performance planning, performance execution, performance appraisal, and decisions about the employee. This helps prevent, and correct, performance problems. A progressive discipline system addresses problems of behavioral conduct that violate rules, procedures, laws, and professional and moral standards. It has a series of penalties for misconduct that progress up to termination, which the system seeks to prevent if at all possible. The system should be based on five important principles of fairness and justice.

Downsizing involves layoffs, but also retention issues. While downsizing seems to have some obvious benefits, research indicates that there are many costs as well, so that the organization should carefully consider if it really wants to downsize, or if so and by how much in terms of employee numbers and quality. Staffing levels should be achieved in a targeted way, rather than across the board. From a staffing quality perspective, cuts could be based on seniority, job performance, or a more holistic assessment of who are the high-value employees the organization desires to retain. There are also many alternatives to downsizing that could be pursued. Attention must be paid to employees who survive a downsizing, or they might create a new retention problem for the organization by starting to leave.

Legally, employee separation from the organization, especially on an involuntary basis, is subject to myriad laws and regulations the organization must be aware of and incorporate into its retention strategy and tactics. If the organization wishes to base retention decisions on employees' job performance, it should recognize that laws and regulations require performance management systems to be fair and equitable to employees during separation. Based on regulations and court decisions, there are numerous recommendations to be followed for a performance management system to have a chance at withstanding legal challenges and scrutiny.

DISCUSSION QUESTIONS

1. For the three primary causes of voluntary turnover (desirability of leaving, ease of leaving, alternatives), might their relative importance depend on the type of employee or type of job? Explain.

2. Which of the costs and benefits of voluntary turnover are most likely to vary according to type of job? Give examples.

3. If a person says to you—"It's easy to reduce turnover, just pay people more money"—what is your response?

4. Why should an organization seek to retain employees with performance or discipline problems—why not just fire them?

5. Discuss some potential problems with downsizing as an organization's first response to a need to cut labor costs.

APPLICATIONS

Managerial Turnover: A Problem?

HealthCareLaunderCare (HCLC) is a company that specializes in picking up, cleaning, and delivering all the laundry for health care providers, especially hospitals, nursing homes, and assisted care facilities. Basically, these health care providers have outsourced their laundry operations to HCLC. In this very competitive business, a typical contract between HCLC and a health care provider is only two years, and HCLC experiences a contract nonrenewal rate of 10%. Most nonrenewals occur because of dissatisfaction with service costs and especially quality (e.g., surgical garb that is not completely sterilized).

HCLC has 20 laundry facilities throughout the country, mostly in large metropolitan areas. Each laundry facility is headed by a site manager, and there are unit supervisors for the intake, washing, drying, inspection and repair, and delivery areas. An average of 100 nonexempt employees are employed at each site.

Operation of a facility is technologically sophisticated and very health and safety sensitive. In the intake area, for example, employees wear protective clothing, gloves, and eyewear because of all the blood, gore, and germs on laundry that comes in. The washing area is comprised of huge washers in 35-foot stainless steel tunnels with screws that move the laundry through various wash cycles. Workers in this area are exposed to high temperatures and must be proficient in operation of the computer-control systems. Laundry is lifted out of the tunnels by robots and moved to the drying room area, where laundry is dried, ironed, and folded by machines tended by employees. In the inspection and repair area, quality inspection and assurance occurs. Laundry is inspected for germs and pinholes (in the case of surgical garb—pinholes could allow blood and fluids to come into contact with the surgeon), and other employees complete repairs on torn clothing and sheets. In the delivery area, the laundry is hermetically sealed in packages and placed in delivery vans for transport.

HCLC's vice president of operations, Tyrone Williams, manages the sites, and site and unit managers, with an iron fist. Mr. Williams monitors each site with a weekly report of a set of cost, quality, and safety indicators for each of the five areas. When he spots what he thinks are problems or undesirable trends, he has a conference telephone call with both the site manager and the area supervisor. In the decidedly one-way conversation, marching orders are delivered and are expected to be fulfilled. If a turnaround in the "numbers" doesn't show up in the next weekly report, Mr. Williams gives the manager and supervisor one more week to improve. If sufficient improvement is not forthcoming, various punitive actions are taken, including base pay cuts, demotions, reassignments, and terminations. Mr. Williams feels such quick and harsh justice is necessary to keep HCLC competitive and to continually drive home to all employees the importance of working "by the numbers." Fed up with this management system, many managers have opted to say "bye-bye numbers!" by leaving HCLC.

Recently, the issue of retention of site and unit managers came up on the radar screen of HCLC's president, Roman Dublinski. Mr. Dublinski glanced at a payroll report showing that 30 of the 120 site and unit managers had left HCLC in the past year, though no reasons for leaving were given. In addition, Mr. Dublinski had received a few copies of angry resignation letters written to Mr. Williams. Having never confronted or thought about possible employee retention problems or how to deal with them, Mr. Dublinski calls you (the corporate manager of staffing) to prepare a brief written analysis that will then be used as the basis for a meeting between the two of you and the vice president of HR, Debra Angle (Ms. Angle recommended this). Address the following questions in your report:

1. Is the loss of 30 managers out of 120 in one year cause for concern?
2. What additional data should we try to gather to learn more about our managerial turnover?
3. What are the costs of this turnover; might there be any benefits?
4. Are there any lurking legal problems?
5. If retention is a serious problem for HCLC, what are the main ways we might attack it?

Retention: Deciding to Act

Wally's Wonder Wash (WWW) is a full-service, high tech and high touch, car wash company owned solely by Wally Wheelspoke. Located in a Midwestern city of 200,000 people (with another 100,000 in suburbs and more rural towns throughout the county), WWW currently has four facilities within the city. Wally has plans to add four more facilities within the city in the next two years, plus plans a little farther out to begin placing facilities in suburban locations and the rural towns. Major competitors include two other full-service car washes (different owners), plus three touchless automatic facilities (same owner) in the city.

Wally's critical strategy is to provide the very best to customers who want and relish extremely clean and "spiffy" vehicles and to have customers feel a positive experience each time they come to WWW. To do this, WWW seeks to provide high-quality car washes and car detailing and to generate considerable repeat business through competitive prices combined with attention to customers. To make itself accessible to customers, WWW is open seven days a week, 8:00 A.M. to 8:00 P.M. Peak periods, volumewise, are after 1:00 on weekdays and 10:00 to 5:00 on weekends. In addition, Wally uses his workforce to drive his strategy. Though untrained in HR, Wally knows that he must recruit and retain a stable, high-quality workforce if his current businesses, let alone his ambitious expansion plans, are to succeed.

WWW has a strong preference for full-time employees, who work either 7:30 to 4:00 or 11:00 to 8:00. Part-timers are used occasionally to help fill in during peak demand times and during the summer when full-timers are off on vacation.

There are two major jobs at WWW—attendant (washer) and custom service specialist (detailer). Practicing promotion from within, all specialists are promoted from the attendant ranks. There are currently 70 attendants and 20 customer service specialists at WWW. In addition, each facility has a manager. Wally has filled the manager's job by promotion-from-within (from either attendant or custom service specialist ranks) but is unsure if he will be able to continue doing this as he expands.

The job of attendant is a demanding one. Attendants vacuum vehicles front and rear (and trunk if requested by the customer), wash and dry windows and mirrors, dry vehicles with hand towels, apply special cleaning compounds to tires, wipe down the vehicle's interior, and wash or vacuum floor mats. In addition, attendants wash and fold towels, lift heavy barrels of cleaning compounds and waxes, and perform light maintenance and repair work on the machinery. Finally, and very important, attendants consistently provide customer service by asking customers if they have special requests and by making "small talk" with them. A unique feature of customer service at WWW is that the attendant must ask the customer to personally inspect the vehicle before leaving to ensure that the vehicle is satisfactorily cleaned (attendants also correct any mistakes pointed out by the customer). The attendants work as a team, with each attendant being expected to be able to perform all of the above tasks.

Attendants start at a base pay of $8.00/hour, with automatic $.50 raises at six months and one year. They receive a brief training from the manager before starting work. Custom service specialists start at $9.00/hour, with $.50 raises after six months and one year. Neither attendants nor custom service specialists receive performance reviews. Managers at each facility all receive a salary of $27,000, plus an annual "merit" raise based on a very casual performance review conducted by Wally (whenever he gets around to it). All attendants share equally in a customer tip pool; custom service specialists receive individual tips. The benefits package is comprised of (1) major medical health insurance with a 20% employee copay on the premium, (2) paid holidays for Christmas, Easter, July 4, and Martin Luther King, Jr.'s birthday, and a generous paid sick pay plan of two days per month (in recognition of high illness due to extreme working conditions).

In terms of turnover, Wally has spotty and general data only. WWW experienced an overall turnover rate the past year of 65% for attendants and 20% for custom service specialists; no managers left. Though lacking data further back, Wally thinks the turnover rate for attendants has been increasing. WWW's managers constantly complain to Wally about the high level of turnover among attendants and the problems it creates, especially in fulfilling the strong customer service orientation for WWW. Though the managers have not conducted exit interviews, the major complaints they hear from attendants are (1) pay is not competitive relative to the other full service car washes or many other entry-level jobs in the area, (2) training is hit-and-miss at best, (3) promotion opportunities are limited, (4) managers provide no feedback or coaching, and (5) customer complaints and mistreatment of attendants by customers are on the rise.

Wally is frustrated by attendant turnover and its threat to his customer service and expansion strategies. Assume he calls on you for assistance in figuring what to do about the problem. Use the decision process shown in Exhibit 14.10 to help develop a retention initiative for WWW. Address each of the questions in the process, specifically:

1. Do we think turnover is a problem?
2. How might we attack the problem?
3. What do we need to decide?
4. Should we proceed?
5. How should we evaluate the initiatives?

ENDNOTES

1. U.S. Department of Labor, "Employee Tenure Study," *News,* Aug. 29, 2000; U.S. Department of Labor, "Number of Jobs Held, Labor Market Activity, and Earnings Growth over Two Decades: Results from a Longitudinal Survey Summary," *News,* April 25, 2000; U.S. Department of Labor, "Mass Layoffs in October 2001," *News,* Nov. 30, 2001; B. Wysocki Jr., "When the Job Is from Hell, Recruiting Is Tough," *Wall Street Journal,* July 10, 2001, p. B1.

2. P. W. Hom and R. W. Griffeth, *Employee Turnover* (Cincinnati, OH: South-Western, 1995), pp. 1–12; Saratoga Institute, *Human Capital Benchmarking Report* (Santa Clara, CA: author, 2001).

3. P. W. Hom and R. W. Griffeth, *Employee Turnover,* pp. 51–107; C. O. Trevor, "Interactions Among Actual Ease of Movement Determinants and Job Satisfaction in the Prediction of Voluntary Turnover," *Academy of Management Journal,* 2001, 44, pp. 621–638; T. R. Mitchell, B. C. Holtom, and T. W. Lee, "How to Keep Your Best Employees: Developing an Effective Retention Policy," *Academy of Management Executive,* 2001, 15(4), pp. 96–107; T. W. Lee and T. R. Mitchell, "An Alternative Approach: The Unfolding Model of Employee Turnover," *Academy of Management Review,* 1994, 19, pp. 51–89; J. G. March and H. A. Simon, *Organizations* (New York: Wiley, 1958); R. W. Griffeth, P. W. Hom, and S. Gaertner, "A Meta-Analysis of Antecedents and Correlates of Employee Turnover," *Journal of Management,* 2000, 26, pp. 463–488.

4. R. W. Griffeth and P. W. Hom, *Retaining Value Employees,* pp. 203–222; N. Drake and I. Robb, "Exit Interviews," (www.shrm.org/whitepapers, 2001).

5. R. W. Griffeth and P. W. Hom, *Retaining Valued Employees,* pp. 10–22; P. W. Hom and R. W. Griffeth, *Employee Turnover,* pp. 13–35; W. F. Cascio, *Costing Human Resources,* fourth ed. (Cincinnati, OH: South-Western, 2000), pp. 23–57.

6. W. F. Cascio, *Costing Human Resources,* pp. 83–105; P. C. Gibson and K. S. Piscitelli, *Basic Employment Law Manual for Managers and Supervisors* (Chicago: Commerce Clearing House, 1997); E. E. Schuttauf, *Performance Management Manual for Managers and Supervisors* (Chicago: Commerce Clearing House, 1997).

7. W. F. Cascio, *Costing Human Resources,* pp. 23–57; J. N. Barron and D. M. Kreps, *Strategic Human Resources* (New York: Wiley, 1999), pp. 421–445; J. A. Schmidt (ed.), *Making Mergers Work* (New York: Towers, Perrin, Foster and Crosby, 2001), pp. 257–268.

8. S. Craig and J. Singer, "Merrill Confirms 9,000 Job Cuts, Earnings Charge of 2.2 Billion," *Wall Street Journal,* Jan. 10, 2002, p. C1.

9. Society for Human Resource Management, *Retention Practices Survey* (Alexandria, VA: author, 2000).

10. B. Parus and J. Handel, "Companies Battle Talent Drain," *Workspan,* Sept. 2000, pp. 16–72.

11. L. Muñoz and P. Hjelt, "The 100 Best Companies to Work For," *Fortune,* Feb. 4, 2002, pp. 72–90.

12. H. Axel, "Strategies for Retaining Critical Talent," *The Conference Board,* 1998, 6(2), pp. 4–18; T. Wilson, "Brand Imaging," *ACA News,* May 2000, pp. 44–48; P. Cappelli, "A Market Driven Approach to Retaining Talent," *Harvard Business Review,* Jan.–Feb. 2000, pp. 103–111.

13. T. Gutner, "A Balancing Act for Gen X Women," *Business Week,* Jan. 21, 2002, p. 82.

14. L. Gomez-Mejia and D. Balkin, *Compensation, Organization Strategy, and Firm Performance* (Cincinnati, OH: Southwestern, 1992), pp. 290–307; B. Klaas and J. McClendon, "To Lead, Lag, or Match: Estimating the Financial Impact of Pay Level Policies," *Personnel Psychology,* 1996, 49, pp. 121–140.

15. Bureau of National Affairs, *Basic Patterns in Union Contracts* (Washington, DC: author, 1995).

16. P. Cappelli, "A Market Driven Approach to Retaining Talent."

17. R. W. Griffeth and P. Hom, *Retaining Valued Employees,* pp. 31–45; J. Cohen, "I/Os in the Know Offer Insights on Generation X Workers," *Monitor on Psychology,* Feb. 2002, pp. 66–67.

18. R. Folger and R. Cropanzano, *Organizational Justice and Human Resource Management* (Thousand Oaks, CA: Sage, 1998).

19. K. D. Scott, D. Morajda, and J. W. Bishop, "Increase Company Competitiveness," *WorldatWork Journal,* 2002, 11(1), pp. 35–42; S. Fournier, "Keeping Line Managers in the Know," *ACA News,* 2000, 43(3), pp. 1–3.

20. B. J. Tepper, "Consequences of Abusive Supervision," *Academy of Management Journal,* 2000, 43, pp. 178–190.

21. D. J. Hanford, "Stay. Please." *Wall Street Journal,* April 12, 2001, p. R8.

22. E. R. Silverman, "Mercer Tries to Keep Its Employees Through Its 'Externship' Program," *Wall Street Journal,* Nov. 7, 2000, p. B18.

23. J. S. Lublin, "In Hot Demand, Retention Czars Face Tough Job," *Wall Street Journal,* Sept. 12, 2000, p. B1.

24. D. Grote, *The Complete Guide to Performance Appraisal* (New York: AMACOM, 1996); E. E. Schuttauf, *Performance Management Manual for Managers and Supervisors* (Chicago: Commerce Clearing House, 1997); G. P. Latham and K. N. Wexley, *Increasing Productivity Through Performance Appraisal,* second ed. (Reading, MA: Addison-Wesley, 1994); M. Armstrong, *Performance Management,* second ed. (London: Kogan-Page, 2000).

25. D. Grote, *The Complete Guide to Performance Appraisal;* Society for Human Resource Management, *Performance Management Survey* (Alexandria, VA: author, 2000).

26. G. A. Stoskopf, "Taking Performance Management to the Next Level," *Workspan,* Feb. 2002, pp. 26–33.

27. P. C. Gibson and K. S. Piscitelli, *Basic Employment Law Manual for Managers and Supervisors;* J. G. Frierson, *Preventing Employment Lawsuits* (Washington, DC: Bureau of National Affairs, 1997); F. T. Coleman, *Ending the Employment Relationship Without Ending Up in Court* (Alexandria, VA: Society for Human Resource Management, 2001).

28. P. C. Gibson and K. S. Piscitelli, *Basic Employment Law Manual for Managers and Supervisors,* pp. 51–53.

29. J. G. Frierson, *Preventing Employment Lawsuits,* pp. 140–141.

30. E. E. Schuttauf, *Performance Management Manual for Managers and Supervisors,* pp. 43–45.

31. P. C. Gibson and K. S. Piscitelli, *Basic Employment Law Manual for Managers and Supervisors,* pp. 48–53; J. G. Frierson, *Preventing Employment Lawsuits,* pp. 358–365.

32. F. T. Coleman, *Ending the Employment Relationship Without Ending Up in Court,* pp. 51–84.

33. J. N. Barron and D. M. Kreps, *Strategic Human Resources,* pp. 421–443; Society for Human Resource Management, *Layoffs and Job Security Survey* (Alexandria, VA: author, 2001).

34. W. F. Cascio, L. E. Young, and J. R. Morris, "Financial Consequences of Employment-Change Decisions in Major U.S. Corporations," *Academy of Management Journal,* 1997, 40, pp. 1175–1189; J. C. McElroy, P. C. Morrow, and S. N. Rude, "Turnover and Organizational Performance: A Comparative Analysis of the Effects of Voluntary, Involuntary, and Reduction-in-Force Turnover," *Journal of Applied Psychology,* 2001, 86, pp. 1294–1299.

35. J. N. Barron and D. M. Kreps, *Strategic Human Resources,* pp. 424–430.

36. P. Barta, "In This Expansion, As Business Booms, So Do the Layoffs," *Wall Street Journal,* March 13, 2000, p. A1; L. Uchitelle, "Pink Slip? Now It's All in a Day's Work," *New York Times,* Aug. 5, 2001, p. BU1.

37. J. A. Fossum, *Labor Relations,* eighth ed. (Burr Ridge, IL: McGraw-Hill/Irwin, 2002), pp. 126–127; Bureau of National Affairs, *Basic Patterns in Union Contracts,* pp. 67–88.

38. M. Conlin, "Where Layoffs Are a Last Resort," *Business Week,* Oct. 8, 2001, p. 42; Q. Hardy, "Cease Firing," *Fortune,* Nov. 26, 2001; "How No Layoffs Can Work" (www.businessweek.com/careers, Nov. 6, 2001).

39. F. Crandall and M. J. Wallace Jr., "Down(sized) but Not Out," *Workspan,* Nov. 2001, pp. 31–35.

40. A. Freedman, "Serving the Survivors," *Human Resource Executive,* Dec. 2001, p. 47.

41. A. Freedman, "Serving the Survivors."

42. F. T. Coleman, *Ending the Employment Relationship Without Ending Up in Court;* J. G. Frierson, *Preventing Employment Lawsuits;* D. P. Twomey, *Labor and Employment Law,* eleventh ed. (Cincinnati, OH: West, 2001); S. C. Kahn, B. B. Brown, and M. Lanzarone, *Legal Guide to Human Resources* (Boston: Warren, Gorham and Lamont, 2001), pp. 9-3 to 9-82.

43. J. M. Werner and M. C. Bolino, "Explaining U.S. Courts of Appeals Decisions Involving Performance Appraisals: Accuracy, Fairness, and Validation," *Personnel Psychology,* 1997, 50, pp. 1–24; D. C. Martin, K. M. Bartol, and P. E. Kehoe, "The Legal Ramifications of Performance Appraisal," *Public Personnel Management,* 2000, 29, pp. 379–406; S. C. Kahn, B. B. Brown and M. Lanzarone, *Legal Guide to Human Resources,* pp. 6-2 to 6-58.

NAME INDEX

SUBJECT INDEX